Mother India

OTHER BOOKS BY PRANAY GUPTE

*The Silent Crisis: Hope and Development in
a World Without Borders* (1990)
India: The Challenge of Change (1989)
Vengeance: India After the Assassination of Indira Gandhi (1985)
The Crowded Earth: People and the Politics of Population (1984)

Mother India

A Political Biography of Indira Gandhi

PRANAY GUPTE

A ROBERT STEWART BOOK

CHARLES SCRIBNER'S SONS
New York

MAXWELL MACMILLAN
Canada   Toronto

MAXWELL MACMILLAN INTERNATIONAL
New York   Oxford   Singapore   Sydney

The quotations on pages 258 and 280 are taken from *The Poetry of Robert Frost*, edited by Edward Connery Lathem. Copyright 1923, © 1969 by Holt, Rinehart and Winston. Copyright 1951 by Robert Frost. Reprinted by permission of Henry Holt and Company, Inc.

Charles Scribner's Sons
Macmillan Publishing Company
866 Third Avenue
New York, NY 10022

Maxwell Macmillan Canada, Inc.
1200 Eglinton Avenue East, Suite 200
Don Mills, Ontario M3C 3N1

Macmillan Publishing Company is part of the Maxwell Communication Group of Companies.

Library of Congress Cataloging-in-Publication Data
Gupte, Pranay.
    Mother India: a political biography of Indira Gandhi / Pranay
Gupte.
        p.   cm.
    "A Robert Stewart book."
    Includes bibliographical references and index.
    ISBN 0-684-19296-9
    1. Gandhi, Indira, 1917–1984.   2. India—Politics and
government—1947–   3. Prime ministers—India—Biography.   I. Title.
DS481.G23G86   1992
954.04'5'092—dc20
[B]   91-22174

Macmillan Books are available at special discounts for bulk purchases for sales promotions, premiums, fund-raising, or educational use. For details, contact:

Special Sales Director
Macmillan Publishing Company
866 Third Avenue
New York, NY 10022

10   9   8   7   6   5   4   3   2   1
Printed in the United States of America

This book is dedicated to the memory of my mother, Charusheela Gupte; my father, Balkrishna Gupte; and my maternal uncle, Keshav Ramchandra Pradhan.

I miss them very much.

This book is also dedicated to Professor Ralph Buultjens, friend and teacher,

with my gratitude.

Contents

Contents

Preface

This is an unconventional book about Indira Gandhi—part biography, part personal history of the author, and part political assessment of contemporary India as it lurches into the next century. I have introduced here dozens of Indians whose lives were directly touched by Indira Gandhi, for better or for worse, people in leadership positions as well as from everyday walks of life. Rajiv Gandhi, who succeeded his mother as India's prime minister in 1984 and who was assassinated on May 21, 1991, appears here, too. Although Rajiv was nowhere near the major figure that Indira was, his death removed from the Indian political scene a genuinely national leader who could have sustained the Nehru-Gandhi political dynasty well into the twenty-first century. That dynasty has dominated India's national life—and consciousness—for much of an extraordinary century.

This book is based partly on my reportage for previous works relating to India, where I was born and raised. This latest book owes its provenance to those earlier books, and therefore represents a continuum. Much of the material here, however, draws on fresh reporting and analysis in India, the United States and the West, and the Third World at large. The story of India is one of continuity yet change, and I have tried to record this in my new book. I might add that recent developments in the Subcontinent—such as Rajiv Gandhi's murder—have been so dramatic that any author attempting to keep abreast of these changes is left dazed and even depressed. This book is intended for general readers who wish to learn something about India and its culture, and for students who are beginning to study the Subcontinent. It will be obvious to India specialists that a lot of what I have to say on Indira Gandhi and on India is based on the research of others. I have tried to relay the key facts, and to interpret them—often in the light of what others have written. Indira Gandhi's life covered such a huge span of modern Indian history that any biographer is forced to be highly selective about which events to select.

Beyond the story of Indira Gandhi's life, I have dealt extensively in this book with topics such as population growth and nonalignment, because Mrs. Gandhi took a great deal of interest in them (although her policies were not necessarily successful). And I deal with the political acrobatics of her son and successor, Rajiv. Much popular hope was invested in him following Indira's death, but he botched an unprecedented opportunity to get India moving again by not following through with sufficient vigor on his pledges of rapid economic development and clean government. And now that he is gone, the victim of a bomb blast during an election rally in southern India, we will never know what sort of prime minister Rajiv Gandhi would have made had Indians returned his Congress Party to power again under his stewardship.

A political biography of Indira Gandhi seemed a natural continuation of my book-writing career, although I had never been an ardent admirer of the late prime minister. *Mother India* owes its appearance to Robert Stewart, president and editor-in-chief of Charles Scribner's Sons in New York. Robert suggested this book to my literary agent, Julian Bach. Supportive always, Robert also exhibited awesome patience during the three years that it took to deliver the manuscript. He understood that I did not want to write a hagiography, and agreed with me fully. I have taken the liberty of using the same title as that of a book by Katherine Mayo that appeared in the United States back in the late 1920s. That patronizing and largely inaccurate book portrayed an India that was mostly a figment of the writer's imagination. But its distortions influenced a vast readership for many years. Still, *Mother India* seemed an especially appropriate title for a biography of a woman who was indeed that.

My thanks are also due to Julian Bach, my literary agent, who nursed this project with his usual blend of tact and rectitude. And my thanks to my literary agent in London, Michael Thomas of A. M. Heath, Inc. My warm thanks, too, to Sharmila Tandon in New Delhi, whose research for this book was invaluable. My thanks also to Rahul Singh, Sudheendra Kulkarni, and Bakul Rajni Patel in Bombay for their assistance in research. And a special thanks to Ajai and Indu Lal, in New Delhi, for their continuing hospitality; to Hazel Staloff, who uncomplainingly typed portions of my manuscript and offered wise counsel; to Sherry-Ann Zelt-man, my secretary in New York, who patiently maintained and updated my voluminous files on Indira; and to Ashali Varma, who selected the photographs in India. And, of course, special thanks to Samuel Wein-traub and Jon Quint for their unending supply of wit and wisdom.

My task was made considerably more pleasant by scores of people who assisted enormously during the reporting, writing, and production of this book. Some of them would prefer not to be identified for various reasons. Anonymous or not, their help was critical; the errors in the book are solely mine. Fortunately, there are several people whom I can cite pub-licly as having been indispensable.

To start with, my warm thanks to James W. Michaels, editor of *Forbes* magazine, for his analysis of Indira Gandhi and the Nehru-Gandhi dy-nasty. Few people know India as intimately as Jim Michaels does, and few Westerners understand and love this vast land as he does. Romesh and Raj Thapar of New Delhi, two of the loveliest and warmest people I have had the privilege of knowing, shared with me many perspectives and gave me a lot of their time. They are both gone now, but they live on in the hearts of their vast numbers of friends—and in the work of hundreds of writers and journalists around the world whom they in-spired and assisted.

In Andhra Pradesh, my warm thanks to Anand Mohan Lal, my father-in-law, for his suggestions and his insights into the Indian condition; and to my mother-in-law, Malati Lal, for her encouragement and her extraordinary recollections of the British Raj. Special thanks also to Pramila and Lessel David for their time and their assistance in arranging for visits to the countryside. And thanks also to Ramoji Rao, publisher of *Newstime*; to Potla and Nandita Sen, also of Hyderabad, for their trenchant assessments of the Indian scene; and to Santosh and Asha Reddy.

In Cochin and Madras, my thanks to T. C. and Bhawani Narayan; and N. Ram, of *The Hindu*. In Bombay: Rahul Singh and Niloufer Billimoria were generous with their time, as were Vir and Malavika Sanghvi. My gratitude to Prabhakar Korgaonkar and his sister, Tai. And special thanks to: Russi Mody; Aditya Kashyap; R. V. Pandit, the veteran editor and publisher; Sailesh and Gajra Kottary; Dr. Russi H. Dastur; Shabana Azmi; Dr. Mahendra Jain; Bakul Rajni Patel and her son, Sanjay; Khalid Ansari of *Midday*; Geeta Kanar; the late Dhiren Bhagat; H. P. Roy; Bhaichand Patel; Anil and Jaymala Bhandarkar; Arun and Gayatri Bewoor; Dr. Verghese Kurien; Tina Khote; Dom Moraes and his wife, Leela Naidu; Ramchandra Moray; Murli and Hema Deora; Anil

Dharker of the *Independent*; Hari Jaisingh; M. A. Manuel; Nani A. Palkhivala, one of India's most distinguished lawyers and thinkers, who generously shared with me his thoughts on the Indian scene; Dr. M. R.Srinivasan, the eminent physicist, and his wife, Geeta; and Charles Correa, the noted architect and urban planner.

In the United States: special thanks to Andrew J. Joseph for his warm friendship—and his stern reading of the manuscript. My thanks, too, to Professor Robert S. Hirschfield of the City University of New York for his scrutiny of the manuscript. Thanks also to Tushar Kothari, Mayuri Chawla, Richard Steele, and Homai Saha. And my gratitude to Professor Anand Mohan of Queens College, whose own wonderful biography of Indira Gandhi served as a foundation for my book. I have freely adapted the scholarship of Professor Mohan, and of Inder Malhotra, Trevor Drieberg, Dom Moraes, and the late Krishan Bhatia, whose own biographies of Indira Gandhi were remarkable works and will withstand the test of time and revisionism. All references to their work have been cited in extensive footnotes. I am truly obligated to them.

My warm thanks also to Janki Ganju, a longtime friend of the Nehrus and Gandhis, for sharing his intimate knowledge of an extraordinary dynasty. My thanks also to my colleagues at *Newsweek International* for the opportunity to write essays on topics that constituted the backbone of many chapters of this book: Kenneth Auchincloss, Steven Strasser, William Burger, and Mathilde Camacho.

I cannot say enough about the counsel and kindness of my friend Professor Ralph Buultjens of New York University. He was a wonderful guide throughout the writing of this book; no one knew Indira Gandhi better. And even though my assessment of her was often at odds with his, Professor Buultjens was generous in sharing his insights and anecdotes concerning his longtime friend and mentor.

And finally, but certainly not least, my deep gratitude to my wife, Jayanti, and to our son, Jaidev, for all their love and their forbearance. They deserve more than what they got in a neglectful husband and an absent father who constantly took off for India and then returned home to New York—only to stay maniacally glued to his word processor. I have always hoped that the India of Jaidev's adulthood will be a better, happier, and more stable society. But recent events—the mounting violence, the murder of Rajiv Gandhi—suggest otherwise.

Mother India

Prologue: The Funeral of Indira Gandhi (1917–1984)

Afterward, after the rituals of cremation and mourning, after the lighting of the sandalwood pyre doused with clarified butter in the traditional Hindu style, the dead woman's son would be proud that it was a funeral to which the whole world came on that cool November day in New Delhi.

The young man's grief had been overwhelming, and he had never really imagined that he would be called on so suddenly and tragically to mourn his mother. He had never imagined that he would be standing beside her terribly still, bullet-riddled body in order to light the pyre that would consign his mother to the ages. His mother, after all, was Indira Gandhi, "Mother India" to all the world, a legend in her own lifetime—and legends are supposed to be everlasting. Yes, there had been threats against his mother, the prime minister. Yes, the security situation in India had alarmingly deteriorated because of ethnic terrorism and separatist movements involving Sikhs and others. But the murder of a national leader was not what generally happened in India—although, as destiny would have it some seven years later, Indira Gandhi's assassination would not be the last tragedy to afflict her family. This was, after all, no Latin American banana republic headed by a caudillo. This was not some African dictatorship. Nor was this a fragile Middle Eastern state always fearing a leadership change by violence.

This was India, the world's largest democracy. Here people elected their leaders, and when they no longer liked them, they voted them out. That, at least, was the way it had been until the assassination of the young man's mother. Her murder ushered in a new era of unprecedented

1

violence in India—violence that was to claim the life of Rajiv Gandhi himself on May 21, 1991, in a bomb blast as he campaigned in southern India.

To the world that watched Indira Gandhi's funeral on television, the young man's inner turmoil and pain were not apparent. His deportment was extraordinary. He seemed composed, stoical, making the right gestures during the rituals as if the whole thing had been carefully scripted by a movie director from India's flourishing celluloid industry.* He comforted his pretty Italian-born wife, Sonia Maino, and their two young children, Priyanka and Rahul. He nodded at friends and acquaintances, and he was properly respectful toward the legions of priests and elders who presided over the funeral. There were moments, as he watched his mother's body crumble into ashes, when tears welled up in his eyes. But always the handsome—if slightly pudgy—aristocratic face regained control.

Much later, Rajiv Gandhi would recall the funeral as though it had been some fantasy. "I did not believe that this was happening," he said. Yet, on this day, his presence had been dignified and reassuring to a nation that had just lost a remarkable leader. The sympathy of the Subcontinent was with him every moment of the ceremony. The world wished him well in the challenges confronting the new, young prime minister—economic, political, and social challenges that seemed so formidable that even these well-wishers were not sure that Rajiv Gandhi could meet them successfully.

If the funeral was theater, then Rajiv Gandhi, at forty years of age, was its star. It was a funeral which marked the end of one woman's domination of the world's second biggest country, a nation larger in population than the United States, Soviet Union, and Europe put together. Only China was a bigger country, and China was no democracy.†

On this day, Rajiv Gandhi came to his mother's funeral as both her bereaved son and her successor as prime minister of the Third World's most powerful nation, a country with the world's fourth biggest military. He had inherited her office, her problems, some of her friends, and a lot of her enemies. He would later ruefully realize, as he struggled to wield power in post-Indira India, that the dead woman's legacy would certainly last beyond his own lifetime and that of the post-Independence genera-

---

* India produces nearly one thousand feature films each year in a dozen languages.
† China's population in 1984 was 1.1 billion; India's population was estimated by the United Nations at around 775 million. In 1991 these figures were 1.1 billion and 900 million, respectively.

tion he represented. More than a half of Indians were born after 1947—the year the British colonial rulers left after being subjected to a relentless "Freedom Struggle" that was led, among others, by the dead woman's father, Jawaharlal Nehru.

Wakes and funerals come to an end, the condolence calls cease, and sympathies recede. Rajiv Gandhi would later realize that from the moment he stepped off the platform hosting his mother's funeral pyre, he would be perceived as the inheritor of her mantle, that he would soon be measured against her performance as a politician and leader—and that the harsh judgments would be as numerous as the encomiums. The judgment of voters, in fact, would eventually remove his Congress Party from power and he from the post of India's prime minister.

Rajiv Gandhi would later understand that his mother had changed forever the political landscape of her vast Asian nation through her tough politics and her tougher style of managing men and matters. He would also realize years later, ruefully, that if it was his mother's toughness that invited her demise, then it was his lack of her political sophistication that invited his downfall. Indians are often prepared to excuse incompetence in their leaders, but perceived confusion is something else. Whatever Indira's shortcomings, she always conveyed the impression of being in full control. Rajiv, by contrast, generally seemed to be floundering in the turbulent sea of Indian politics.

The funeral was held in traditional Hindu style on Saturday, November 3, 1984, near Shantivana, within hailing distance of the Jamuna, the ancient but polluted river that flows sluggishly through Delhi. Just four days earlier, Indira had been murdered in her garden by two trusted Sikh bodyguards, Beant Singh and Satwant Singh. One of the assassins was killed by irate colleagues while they held him in custody, and the other would be tried and executed some years later.

Leaders from all over the world were present to pay their last personal tribute to her, and among them were royalty, revolutionaries, presidents, and prime ministers: Margaret Thatcher, Britain's prime minister, was tearful; so was Zambia's president, Kenneth Kaunda. Prince Claus of the Netherlands seemed shaken. Prime Minister Nikolai Tikhonov of the Soviet Union occasionally dabbed his eyes with a handkerchief. Soviet Vice President V. V. Kuznetsov and First Deputy Foreign Minister V. F. Maltsev also came with their prime minister. India and the Soviet Union had been political allies since Nehru's time, even though India formally espoused nonalignment. Indira Gandhi's foreign policy generally echoed that of Moscow's; Soviet leaders were grateful for India's support in international forums such as the United Nations.

Many Indians noticed that, in contrast to the Soviets, the American delegation was relatively modest in size and stature. Washington was represented by Secretary of State George P. Shultz. Indians had widely expected President Ronald Reagan to attend, or at least Vice President George Bush. Indira Gandhi, during her years in power, had deeply resented Washington's favoring of Pakistan. Mrs. Gandhi understood, of course, that this "tilt" was intended to offset the military, political, and economic closeness between India and the Soviet Union. Still, bitter wars had been fought between India and Pakistan—wars that Indira felt could have been avoided had the United States not fattened Pakistan's arsenal so relentlessly.

Many Indians felt that with Indira Gandhi gone, Washington should initiate a new chapter in bilateral relations between the two countries—and that one conspicuous way would be for either Mr. Reagan or Mr. Bush to attend the funeral. Former U.S. ambassador to India John Kenneth Galbraith, who was present at the funeral, privately said to friends how disappointed he was that neither Mr. Reagan nor Mr. Bush came to New Delhi. That sentiment was also expressed by two other former American ambassadors to India, John Sherman Cooper and Senator Daniel Patrick Moynihan, who came to the funeral.

A number of top Indian officials were disappointed that Fidel Castro, the Cuban revolutionary, did not attend Indira Gandhi's funeral. He was said to be held up in Havana by pressing official business. Only a year earlier, he had traveled to New Delhi to formally hand over to Mrs. Gandhi the chairmanship of the Nonaligned Movement. At the summit, he enveloped her in a huge bear hug: Mrs. Gandhi, never an emotionally demonstrative person, visibly recoiled from that hug, managing only a faintly polite smile in the interest of diplomatic niceties.

Other than the fact that Castro was absent, the Third World—that assorted grouping of 127 mostly poor countries—was especially well represented; after all, Indira Gandhi had been an able spokesperson for developing countries that, like India, had wanted to lift themselves out of the cycle of poverty and deprivation into the age of modernity. Not long before her death, in fact, Indira had been elected chairperson of the Nonaligned Movement. *

---

* The Nonaligned Movement (NAM), which enjoys a membership of some 101 Third World nations, holds its summit meeting every three years. The 1983 summit was originally scheduled to be held in Baghdad, but the venue was shifted to New Delhi because Iraq, the host country, was at war with neighboring Iran. Traditionally,

4

A conspicuous mourner was Yasser Arafat, chairman of the Palestine Liberation Organization (PLO), whom Mrs. Gandhi had supported. Indira Gandhi had long championed the Palestinian cause, and the PLO enjoyed a prestigious address, presence, and diplomatic status in New Delhi.

"My sister is dead," Arafat said, in Arabic, to mourners around him. "My sister Indira Gandhi is gone." Seven years later, he would be back in New Delhi, this time for the funeral of Rajiv Gandhi.

Another prominent dignitary was Sri Lankan president Junius Richard Jayewardene, whom Mrs. Gandhi despised as a Western puppet. The septuagenarian Jayewardene once called Indira Gandhi a "cow"—an epithet which she never forgot.

Another neighbor's presence caused some commotion among mourners. He was President Mohammed Zia ul-Haq of Pakistan. A military man by training and bearing, he appeared genuinely grieved—not an emotion many observers would have associated with a man who led India's mortal enemy. Indeed, Indira Gandhi had long suspected that Zia's intelligence agencies were secretly supporting the Sikh militants who wanted to carve out a separate theocratic state called Khalistan from India's strategic border state of Punjab. Zia had earlier placed a large wreath on Indira Gandhi's body at Teen Murti Bhavan, where her father had lived. Within four years, Zia himself would be dead—the victim of a bomb that blew up his airplane.

Near Zia sat the king of Bhutan, President Kenneth Kaunda of Zambia, and Prince Claus of the Netherlands. President Kaunda broke down repeatedly at the funeral. The Zambian's tears seemed uncontrollable. Like Indira Gandhi, Kenneth Kaunda had been active in the Nonaligned Movement. Years later he would say: "She was a beacon for the developing world. Her career spanned such history-making years."[*]

Yugoslav president Vaelin E. Djuarnovic and Ugandan president Milton Obote were among those in attendance at the funeral that morning. India was traditionally close to Yugoslavia; indeed, Nehru and the late Yugoslav president, Josip Broz (Marshal Tito), had been among the founders of the Nonaligned Movement. President Obote had promised Mrs. Gandhi that his country would welcome back the thousands of Indians who had been unceremoniously kicked out of Uganda by his dreaded—and subsequently deposed—predecessor, Idi Amin. Many of these Indians were Uganda-born, and had lost all their wealth and possessions to Amin. Moreover, India's government had been less than wel-

---

the host country becomes head of NAM for the next three years. Jawaharlal Nehru was among NAM's founders.

[*]Conversation with the author in New York City, December 1989.

coming to them, and consequently thousands of these Ugandan-Asians settled in Europe, Canada, and the United States, where they were to rebuild their lives and indeed even prosper.

From the Middle East came Sheikh Hamdan Bin Mohammed Al Nahyan of the United Arab Emirates, and Sheikh Khalifa Bin Suleman from Bahrain. A Saudi Arabian delegation also arrived with them. Arabs occupied a special place in India's foreign policy—not only on account of the Palestinian issue, but perhaps even more significantly because hundreds of thousands of Indians were employed in the oil-rich countries of the Gulf. Indira Gandhi knew that the money sent home by these workers was important to India's domestic economic development—some $2 billion annually. Economics, perhaps more than ideology or Third World solidarity, explained India's tilt away from Israel and toward the Arabs.

The Chinese also came to the funeral. Vice Prime Minister Yao Yi Lin led this delegation, and some observers remarked how times had changed. China and India had a long-standing border dispute over barren Himalayan territory, and the two countries had fought a bitter war in 1962. Jawaharlal Nehru, who had always believed that China was a genuine friend, had not expected the Chinese assault. He was so heartbroken that he died not long afterward.

As Yasser Arafat and Kenneth Kaunda did, many of the world leaders who came to Indira Gandhi's funeral offered personal remembrances of her, and some offered strong condemnations of her assassination. The international media took copious notes of their comments, which were beamed worldwide. NBC even carried the funeral live to American television viewers. Britain's Princess Anne was especially sought after by the media, although she did not make a formal statement. Former British prime minister James Callaghan was also sought after for his comments about Indira Gandhi. "An extraordinary leader, and an extraordinary woman," Callaghan said, as he arrived at Shantivana.

But it was Callaghan's successor, Prime Minister Margaret Thatcher, who made the strongest remarks that Saturday morning before arriving at the funeral site. Mrs. Thatcher had first visited Teen Murti Bhavan to lay a wreath. There she told reporters: "I learn that there is a great indignation and distress—rightly in my view—among the Government and the people of India about the outrageous behavior of a tiny minority of irresponsible people in Britain who have gloated over Mrs. Indira Gandhi's murder and the publicity they have received." The reference was to jubilation among many Sikhs residing in Britain after the news broke about Indira Gandhi's murder. Mrs. Thatcher, with her deeply conservative politics, was no ideological ally of Indira Gandhi, who always prided herself on her socialism. But the two leaders had become friends over the years. Their iron-fisted management style seemed similar, as did their impatience with political dissidence. "I will miss Indira Gandhi very much indeed," Mrs. Thatcher told reporters after paying homage at Teen Murti Bhavan. "She was a truly great leader."

Leaders from every part of India and of almost every political party were at the funeral, too. They had not always seen eye to eye with Indira Gandhi. Some of them had been imprisoned by Mrs. Gandhi during "The Emergency" in the mid-1970s, when she had ill-advisedly suspended India's constitution and imposed a dictatorship. Yet most had respected her political abilities and acumen, even admired her for her courage.

Among the chief mourners in the inner enclosure, next to the raised platform where the cremation took place, were men and women whom Indira had admired and who in turn had adored her. Mother Teresa, the charismatic Albanian-born nun who had settled in Calcutta, was present. The small, frail woman, who had been awarded the Nobel Prize for Peace in 1979 for her work in helping the poor of Calcutta, had earlier said a few emotional words to journalists, recalling how supportive the late prime minister had been of her efforts. Zubin Mehta, the world-famous conductor, sat solemnly in this enclosure, as did a number of Indian film stars such as Raj Kapoor, Sunil Dutt, and Amitabh Bachchan.* Some of these stars were keen political supporters of Indira Gandhi, and some of them also spoke to the media who covered the funeral. They noted her interest in the arts, and how she had channeled formidable sums of government money into promoting classical music and dance.

Indira Gandhi's close relatives were also present: Mrs. Vijaya Lakshmi Pandit, the irascible aunt with whom Indira had had a falling out, and Indira's cousin, Braj Kumar Nehru, the former Indian ambassador to the United States. Maneka Gandhi and her son, Varun, were in that inner gathering, too, virtually lost in the long rows of those seated on the ground in traditional Indian style. Maneka was the widow of Indira's deceased younger son, Sanjay, who had died in 1980 when a stunt plane that he was piloting crashed. Shortly after Sanjay's death, she had ill-advisedly launched a political campaign against her formidable mother-in-law.

---

* Eyewitness accounts of the funeral.

Beyond the special enclosure where these dignitaries sat were India's masses, the millions for whom Indira Gandhi was always "Mother India"—the embodiment of a thousand goddesses, the symbol of shakti, or divine strength. Down in the South, Indira was widely known as Indiramma—"Indira the Mother"—and so faithful were southern voters that they largely stood by her Congress Party even when it was routed in the North in the 1977 election. For these overwhelmingly poor people, Indira was India.

"Indira Gandhi aamar rahe!" they kept chanting in unison. "Long live Indira Gandhi!"

The concluding funeral rites began at 3:55 P.M. and were completed in about an hour. The body, swathed in flowers, was brought from the gun carriage in the funeral procession, which had started earlier from Teen Murti Bhavan, the stately mansion once occupied by the late Jawaharlal Nehru, Mrs. Gandhi's father and India's first prime minister after Independence in 1947. Teen Murti Bhavan had been converted into a museum following Nehru's death in May 1964.

The body was carried up to the platform by Rajiv Gandhi and others, including Field Marshal Sam Manekshaw—India's highest ranking military man—and placed on a rectangular bed of sandalwood logs and flowers.* That was in the Hindu tradition.

Later, Indira's ashes would be scattered from an airplane by her son, who would also immerse one urn of those ashes in the Ganges, which Hindus regard as their great holy river. The immersion would take place on the thirteenth day after her death, as called for by Hindu tradition.

Rajiv's son, Rahul, clad in a flowing white shirt known as a kurta and white pajamas, had, like his father, a long white towel around his neck. He brought his palms together in a namaskar, a last salute to his grandmother. Then, in what was another symbolic rite, Rajiv Gandhi and Rahul walked around the body, each holding an earthern water pitcher. After the circling, they dropped the pitchers on the ground at Indira's feet. The pitchers shattered, as they were meant to, symbolizing the crumbling of the body into dust. (In Hindu tradition, it is always the men of the family who participate in the final rites at funerals.)

Little Varun, the late Sanjay Gandhi's son, had by then moved up the steps to the platform to peer closely at his grandmother's face. How much

---

* Although Manekshaw had formally retired from the army a few years earlier, as field marshal he was still considered India's ranking military officer. However, his prominence at the funeral was resented by the active-duty military brass, who felt that they should have been given precedence.

of his grandmother would he remember? Indira had adored him, just as she had reportedly always favored his deceased father, Sanjay, over her older son, Rajiv. A short while later, Maneka Gandhi also joined him, standing for a few minutes close to the body, in what looked from afar like a belated reconciliation—although those near Maneka noticed a baleful expression on her face. The two women had never gotten along when Indira was alive. Later, Maneka would tell friends that Rajiv's entourage had deliberately tried to keep her away from the family rites. *
Not long after the funeral, she would step up her criticism of the Congress Party and especially ridicule Rajiv Gandhi. †

Some thirty-one pundits, supervised by Dr. Girdhari Lal Goswami, a prominent Hindu leader and astrologer, conducted the last rites. In addition, priests representing the Christian, Muslim, Buddhist, and Sikh faiths were present. Indira Gandhi had always prided herself on her ecumenism, and her funeral was a testimonial to her beliefs. The various priests had begun reciting from their respective scriptures at two o'clock. They used Sanskrit, the language of the ancient Aryans of central Asia who had conquered India thousands of years ago. One of the most prominent priestly presences near the pyre was Dhirendra Brahmachari, the somewhat murky and mysterious camp follower of Mrs. Gandhi. Brahmachari, a specialist in yoga and arcane religious practices, was a haunting figure whose gaunt demeanor suggested that his preoccupations were both spiritual and temporal. The holy man, who dabbled in power politics to the irritation of many, was watching his considerable influence disappear in the smoke emanating from the pyre. Never again was Brahmachari to walk the corridors of power, which his association with Indira Gandhi had facilitated.

Hindu funerals involve the use of mounds of material. There is the sandalwood for the pyre. There are the joss sticks, which emanate fragrance. There is ghee, the clarified butter. There are cloves and pine nuts. Fruits must be offered to the pyre, a symbolic propitiation to the gods. After these gifts had been carefully placed on and around the body, Rajiv Gandhi lighted a pair of long sandalwood joss sticks. He then went

---

* Account based on conversations between author and friends of Maneka Gandhi.
† Maneka Gandhi ran against Rajiv Gandhi in the Amethi constituency in Uttar Pradesh in the December 1984 general election. She lost overwhelmingly to her brother-in-law. But she was to make a political comeback in the 1989 election, when she won a parliamentary seat for V. P. Singh's Janata Dal. Maneka was made minister of state for the environment in the Singh government, a post she continued to hold in the successor administration of Prime Minister Chandra Shekhar. In the 1991 election, however, Maneka lost her race.

around his mother's body nine times, touching her head with the lighted end each time he passed by. Like the host of other rituals he was required to perform, this act, too, was rooted in thousands of years of Hindu culture and tradition. Hindu tradition is mostly oral, and it was not inconceivable that the rituals that Rajiv Gandhi performed on this November day in 1984 had been performed in exact fashion by his predecessors many millennia ago. After completing the ninth round, he thrust the joss stick under the pyre to ignite it, and piled sandalwood logs upon the body. Three volleys of staccato fire from a military honor guard pierced the still air. Buglers sounded the Last Post.

The irony of the military's presence did not escape some of the mourners: The dispatching of troops by Mrs. Gandhi in June 1984 to flush out separatist militants from Sikhism's holiest shrine, the Golden Temple in Amritsar, precipitated the crisis that ultimately led her assassins to swear vengeance.

Smoke rose from the pyre as immediate members of Indira Gandhi's family threw fistfuls of powdered unguents, or samagri, on the body. The Hindu priests seated on the ground chanted "*Om shanti, shanti, shanti*"—"Peace be upon you." Their chants provided an eerie soundtrack to the ceremony. A little while later, the priests recited the ancient Vedic incantation beginning "*Sangachadwam . . .*" to liberate the soul and set it on the path to the pitru-lok, the heavenly abode of one's ancestors.

Although the cremation rituals were technically completed with those chants, the ceremony continued for more than forty-five minutes afterwards. This was to allow close colleagues and longtime associates of Indira, her friends, officials, and even some diplomats, to come up to the pyre to sprinkle unguents on Indira Gandhi's ashes. They walked around the burning pyre, many of them in tears. No doubt the grief was real in some cases, but several mourners surreptitiously looked for the television cameras that recorded the historic event.

Trusted Indira aides such as Dr. P. C. Alexander—her private secretary—and H. Y. Sharada Prasad—Indira's phlegmatic press adviser —were in that seemingly endless procession of mourners. Some of their colleagues wondered whether Rajiv Gandhi would command their loyalty as fiercely as his mother had—and whether, indeed, Rajiv would retain their services at all. Both Alexander and Sharada Prasad came from a generation of bureaucrats whose orthodox sensibilities were quite in contrast to the impatience and drive of the younger men that Rajiv Gandhi favored, men like his fellow pilot friend Captain Satish Sharma. On this day, Sharma protectively hovered around Rajiv; his physical nearness to the young prime minister was to be sustained over the next five years, with Sharma accumulating vast power.

Another man who trekked up to the funeral pyre was N. T. Rama Rao, the fiery Opposition chieftain from the southern state of Andhra Pradesh. He was attired in his distinct saffron robe in the manner of the Hindu deities that Rama Rao used to portray in the films he once starred in, mythological epics in the Telugu language that made him a household name in southern India. A parade of other mourners, including Swraj Paul, a London-based industrialist, also filed past the funeral pyre. Paul, who had supported Indira's campaigns, seemed especially fidgety. He reflected on his biography of Indira Gandhi, which had been published in Britain only months earlier. Going through his mind were thoughts of whether history's view of Indira would coincide with his highly favorable evaluation of her. That evaluation had provoked some controversy in India.

Carefully and sadly observing Swraj Paul and others was Professor Ralph Buultjens. As he joined family mourners beside the pyre, sprinkling his share of unguents on Mrs. Gandhi's body, and occasionally comforting the young Gandhi children, he thought that this was the last hurrah of Indira Gandhi's courtiers. Around her rapidly disintegrating body was a small coterie of men and women whose proximity to the prime minister —while she was alive—had given them enormous clout. A word whispered in Indira Gandhi's ear might be translated into nation-changing policies and, as in the courts of ancient sovereigns, access was indeed power. Buultjens, a Sri Lankan professor of political science at New York University, was one of those whose closeness to Indira Gandhi was known to only a few. But those who knew had no doubt of his prodigious capacity to help shape her decisions and focus her interests: Indira Gandhi once affectionately—and teasingly—called Professor Buultjens "my intellectual Mephistopheles." Ralph Buultjens could not help thinking that Indira Gandhi's inner circle embraced an odd assortment of characters—some were buffoons, some were self-seekers, some were shrewd political operators, and some were simply devoted to their leader because they believed in her. There was very little in common among these men and women who pulled the levers of power during Mrs. Gandhi's time; yet they were all bound through some central, almost mystical, connection to Indira Gandhi. Never again, thought Professor Buultjens, would this tiny group of attendants assemble together. Unlike some of them, he realized how totally derivative and ephemeral their power had been—a fact that was borne out by subsequent events.

Like Ralph Buultjens on this day, Janki Ganju thought about the passing of an era. A longtime friend and associate of the Nehrus, Ganju had flown to Delhi from his home in Washington through the courtesy of an American friend who accommodated him on his corporate jet via Frankfurt. Ganju, a chubby man with silver hair, had worked as a lobbyist for India in Washington since 1960. A Kashmiri Brahman, like Indira Gandhi, he was devoted to her. Whenever Mrs. Gandhi came to the United States, Janki Ganju would be a ubiquitous presence near her. It was Ganju who arranged her meetings with the American media, and who quietly smoothed ruffled feathers of editors and writers who were sometimes treated brusquely by Indira.

"I couldn't imagine that death would really touch her," Ganju later said. "But it hit me—the fact that Indira was gone—when I saw her body crumbling on that funeral pyre, with those tongues of flame leaping up. It was unbelievable, her death. Here she was, disappearing into history—and I was seeing her body turn to ashes. For me, she was truly Mother India. She was Mother India for everybody."

India's constitutional president, Zail Singh, Vice President R. Venkataraman, and the former president, Neelam Sanjiva Reddy, were among the last to pay their tributes. The Indian president is the country's constitutional figurehead, and although he is technically elected by representatives of all of India's twenty-five states, it is the prime minister who usually handpicks the candidate. The hirsute Zail Singh—who wore a trademark red rose in a buttonhole of his long outer vestment—seemed especially distraught, no doubt because his political mentor and fellow conspirator in the Punjab crisis had passed away. The portly Sikh owed his largely ceremonial job to Indira Gandhi. Perhaps he had repaid the debt by giving his instant presidential approval to the appointment of Rajiv Gandhi as Indira's successor, within hours of the assassination. Reddy, who had major political differences with Mrs. Gandhi, seemed to be tottering—he had recently been ill. There were those who wondered about the nature of Reddy's grief.

Then followed Buta Singh. He appeared visibly haggard. He was a trusted associate of Indira Gandhi, and he had held several cabinet portfolios in her administration. His condition was doubtless the result of his exertions earlier that day. He had been entrusted by Rajiv Gandhi to supervise the final arrangements for the funeral from well before midday. Indian cabinet ministers are generally unaccustomed to strenuous labor, and certainly find alien the notion that good management often requires on-the-spot management. It could not have been pleasant for Buta Singh to have to supervise hundreds of workers of the Central Public Works Department who were engaged to prepare the funeral area. Indeed, some of the workers seemed surprised that a cabinet minister was mingling with them, personally giving instructions and occasionally inquiring about their welfare.

The area where Indira was cremated in the age-old Hindu tradition is regarded as sacred ground by Indians. Mohandas "Mahatma" Gandhi, Jawaharlal Nehru, and Lal Bahadur Shastri had been cremated here. Now Indira joined that extraordinary band of India's great leaders, those men who fashioned India's struggle for independence from the British, and who later guided this old land toward modernity.

It was Buta Singh's job to ensure that the funeral site be ready by the time the procession arrived from Teen Murti Bhavan. Well before he turned up on this Saturday morning for the final supervision, round-the-clock work was in progress at a hectic pace on the grounds between Shantivana and Rajghat. Jawaharlal Nehru was cremated at Shantivana in May 1964, and Mahatma Gandhi's funeral took place at Rajghat in January 1948. Shantivana was selected by Rajiv Gandhi for his mother's final resting place. The original suggestion for cremation was a plot near Sanjay Gandhi's funeral site, not far away from Shantivana. But Rajiv felt that the area was not large enough to accommodate the millions who were certain to gather for Indira Gandhi's funeral ceremony.

It occurred to Buta Singh many times on this Saturday morning that he was one of the few Sikhs in a sea of Indians who were surely mindful that it was two other Sikhs who had murdered the woman whose funeral was now being arranged. Perhaps Buta Singh was too tired to worry about what his workers were thinking. He knew that not far from the funeral site, Sikhs in poor Delhi neighborhoods were being massacred by vengeful Hindus. In the week following the assassination of Indira Gandhi, more than 5,000 innocent Sikh men, women, and children would be murdered in the Delhi area, and thousands more elsewhere in India. *

But on this day Singh had a job to do, and he was determined to do it well. He had a reputation to protect as the best organizer among Indian cabinet officials of public events. After all, it was Buta Singh who had arranged the acclaimed Asiad, the huge sports event in Delhi some years earlier. Indira Gandhi had offered fulsome praise then. Now this was the last thing he could possibly do for his mentor.

Buta Singh supervised the erection of a tall platform of bricks on which Indira Gandhi's body would be placed. A few feet away from this

---

* The question of Sikh separatism, exacerbated by the November 1984 massacres in Delhi and North India, is one of the most intractable aspects of Indira Gandhi's legacy. A solution to the Sikh problem has eluded three successive prime ministers.

platform, earth mowers and huge land rollers were being used to level the barren stretch of land. Trucks laden with building material and water tanks were busy plying to and fro. Electrical wirings and loudspeaker arrangements were being installed.

It occurred to Buta Singh that while most Indians had taken the day off to mourn for Indira Gandhi, these hundreds of poor workers were offering special tribute to her by putting in a long day of grueling manual labor. Buta Singh had been present at Shantivana since well before midday. He had waited anxiously for the funeral cortege to arrive from the elegant portals of Teen Murti Bhavan. Singh recalled that a little more than twenty years earlier, a procession of a similar nature had started from the very same place—Jawaharlal Nehru's funeral. On this November Saturday, the body on the gun-carriage was that of Nehru's daughter.

Teen Murti Bhavan had been closed to the public from six o'clock that morning. Thousands of mourners had flocked to the sprawling colonial building over the past few days to pay their last respects to Indira Gandhi. On this Saturday morning, however, the ordinary citizens of India were barred from entering the premises. Only foreign dignitaries and some VIPs were allowed to pay their last respects, before Indira's body was prepared for the funeral.

From dawn, Hindu priests chanted mantras and conducted religious ceremonies that preceded the funeral procession. Roses and jasmine were constantly heaped on the body. Hymns and prayers were recited from scriptures of many religions. Heaps of wreaths and marigold garlands which kept piling up were removed swiftly. Outside Teen Murti Bhavan, tens of thousands of people from different states chanted slogans such as "*Indira Gandhi zindabad!*" and "*Jab tak suraj chand chamkega, Indira tera naam rahega!*"—"Long Live Indira Gandhi!" and "Your name will shine as long as the sun and moon shine!"

But the somber atmosphere that descended on Teen Murti Bhavan earlier this Saturday morning soon turned ugly. Impatient crowds tried to force their way into the premises. They met with resistance from the police, who lashed out with lathiis, or small batons. Not spared were women and children outside the main entrance of the mansion where they had come to pay homage to an extraordinary leader.

It was not enough that the prime minister of India had died a violent death. Even Indira Gandhi's funeral had its own measure of violence.

Introduction:
Indira's India

In 1983, a year before her assassination, Indira Gandhi traveled to New York to address the General Assembly of the United Nations. It was a hectic visit, with speaking engagements before numerous diplomatic groups, Indian expatriate organizations, and student unions. The Indian prime minister had come to the United States in connection with an effort by developing countries to dramatize the growing disparities between rich and poor nations. India was head of the Nonaligned Movement, and Indira Gandhi, the most celebrated of the Third World's leaders, was chief spokesperson for the group.

One of my journalistic commitments in those days was to the *Indian Express*, India's biggest newspaper chain.* The paper had long been editorially critical of Mrs. Gandhi; the paper's politics did not necessarily match mine, but I wrote fairly regularly because I felt that it was good to appear in print before home audiences. The *Indian Express* had not been able to obtain a berth for an India-based staff correspondent on the prime minister's plane.† The editors phoned me from New Delhi and requested—rather desperately, I thought—that I cover the prime minister's visit on a daily basis. It turned out to be an exhausting task, because an exhausting schedule had been fashioned for Mrs. Gandhi.

While I marveled at her energy, I also questioned the judgment of her staff who had set up such a formidable program for her. The schedule

---

*The *Indian Express* has a dozen regional editions around India, with a combined circulation of nearly two million.
†Withholding plane seats during foreign journeys was one way that Mrs. Gandhi's

may have worn out the journalists and staffers, but Indira seemed fatigue-proof. Throughout her three or four days in New York Mrs. Gandhi always appeared composed, a doll-like figure in her exquisite, colorful saris. She always sported a faint, slightly bemused smile—or was it a mocking smile? Faced with tough questions on NBC's "Meet the Press," about the mounting Punjab crisis, Mrs. Gandhi remained unperturbed, coolly deflecting the questioners' aggressiveness. Her expression was sometimes stern, and occasionally her face would become hard as marble. As I sat in NBC's Rockefeller Center studios watching the show being taped, it occurred to me that there was a book to be done on Indira's style of leadership. Just how did this woman function, and what drove her? What sort of a person was she really, this woman who led the world's biggest democracy?

Indira Gandhi had never been a favorite of journalists and writers.* Many of them, Indian and others, distrusted her, charging that she was unnecessarily arrogant, an impatient woman with little regard for others' sensitivities. Sydney H. Schanberg, now a columnist for *Newsday*, once told me of his interview with Mrs. Gandhi when he was based in New Delhi as the correspondent for *The New York Times*. She signaled her impatience with Schanberg's questions by looking beyond his shoulders at the wall behind him, and drumming her fingers on her desk. It was a most disconcerting experience, even for the usually unflappable Schanberg.† Bernard Kalb, the veteran American television correspondent, recalls the time when he met Mrs. Gandhi briefly in a television studio. "The impression I got was that of remoteness," Kalb says.‡ The bored expression that Indira wore occasionally may have been copied from her father Jawaharlal Nehru. Arthur M. Schlesinger, Jr., the Pulitzer Prize–winning historian who served as special assistant to President John F. Kennedy, recalls that when Kennedy visited New Delhi in 1951, Nehru treated him with marked indifference. Kennedy, who was then an unknown young congressman, had been warned that, when Nehru became bored, he would tap his fingers together and look at the ceiling.

Some of the newspapermen in Indira's entourage during that New York visit told me that she rarely mixed with the journalists in her traveling party. One respected columnist said that the prime minister simply

---

aides "punished" newspapers who opposed her. Fair enough, I suppose, except that somehow the story always seemed to get covered.

* There were, of course, scribes who fawned on her; but such "journalists" would be obsequious toward anyone in power.

† Schanberg disclosed this to the author during a conversation in New York City in 1982.

‡ Conversation with the author, April 4, 1991, New York.

loathed members of the Fourth Estate, although he was unable to furnish any startling insights about why Mrs. Gandhi found journalists so distasteful. I ventured the opinion that perhaps the prime minister was merely reciprocating journalists' sentiments toward her.

That was the only time that I saw Indira Gandhi at close quarters. About a year later, she was dead. The next "Indira Gandhi story" that I covered as a newspaperman was my last bit of reporting for a daily newspaper. My longtime employer, *The New York Times*, sent me to Punjab—a border state that was the home of Sikhism—in the wake of Indira's assassination. I filed stories from there about how Sikhs perceived Mrs. Gandhi, whose troops just months earlier had stormed the Golden Temple to flush out terrorists who had holed up there.

I watched Mrs. Gandhi's internationally televised funeral at the home of a distant relative, Inder Mohan Khosla, in Amritsar. It was a moving ceremony, filled with the rituals of the ancient Hindu religion. Like other viewers in Khosla's living room that cold November day, I wept because an old woman had been murdered in her garden by men she had trusted with her life.

Indira Gandhi had always been one of those distant but ever-present figures in my life when I was growing up in India. I had seen Indira at scores of political rallies at Chowpatty Beach, not far from my parents' apartment in Bombay. I had seen her zoom by in motorcades. I had been exposed to countless documentaries in which she starred, films made by the fawning Films Division of India's Ministry of Information and Broadcasting. *

Indira had an admirer in my family. My mother, Charusheela Gupte, was a prominent social worker, writer, and academician in Bombay. She would often talk of Indira's sharp political skills. Those skills were increasingly on display as Mrs. Gandhi traveled the country on behalf of her father, Prime Minister Jawaharlal Nehru. My mother did not know Indira well personally, but she predicted that one day Indira would become prime minister of our country. It was inevitable, my mother would say, because Indians revered aristocracy—and Indira Gandhi was a thoroughbred. She was born to rule. In those days, it was fashionable to ask, "After Nehru, who?"† My mother never had any doubt about the answer.

Indira Gandhi, however, did not become prime minister when her

---

* The ministry runs the national radio and television networks in India.
† Welles Hangen, a former NBC correspondent, wrote a book with this title (London: Rupert Hart Davis, 1963).

father died in May 1964. Nehru's successor was a popular, homespun politician named Lal Bahadur Shastri (1904–1966). He governed all too briefly before dying of a heart attack in January 1966 during a visit to Tashkent in the Soviet Union. He had gone there to sign a truce with Pakistan after the Indo-Pakistan War of 1965. The Soviets had brokered a fragile peace between the two traditionally feuding nations. Before he left for the Soviet Union, Shastri had made an eloquent speech in New Delhi reminding Indians and Pakistanis that their nations had been born of the same womb of British colonialism. It was after Shastri's death that Indira Gandhi was chosen by Congress Party elders to become India's chief executive.* The rest, as they say, is history.

I have long been fascinated by that special history. My interest in Indira Gandhi was not the least on account of the fact that she seemed very hard to read. In that sense, she was the perfect political player who rarely tipped her hand and whose responses to events were always carefully calibrated and designed, always designed to further her own self-interest. Nothing wrong with that, I suppose. Indira played vigorously in the spirited arena of Indian politics. But that was exactly the problem: With Mrs. Gandhi, everything was always politics. Even interpersonal relationships came to take a second place to politics. She forfeited the love of her husband, Feroze Gandhi, not least because she had no time, nor any great inclination, for a conventional family life.

Indira Gandhi was also a leader of strong, all-too-obvious contradictions. Here was a woman who reigned over the biggest democracy in the world, yet she was not particularly a democrat at heart. The "Emergency" that she imposed on India during 1975–77 was ostensibly in the cause of ensuring national security, but in truth was nothing less than an ill-conceived experiment in introducing a form of controlled democracy to a country that she privately felt—her demurrals notwithstanding—was not quite capable of handling the clangor of an open society.

Here was a woman who controlled one of the most promising economies in the world yet was not especially interested in economics. In fact, it could be persuasively argued that the Indian economy would have fared much better had Mrs. Gandhi been more attentive to economics than

* There were murmurs that Shastri's death was somehow engineered by the Soviets, who were always partial toward Indira Gandhi. But that line of thought seems excessively speculative, and no evidence exists to back it up. At any event, the Kremlin would then have had to also engineer Indira's ascension to the prime ministership, which at the time of Shastri's death was not at all inevitable.

to politics. A good economic policy requires much more than political rhetoric to fuel it: it needs sound management, and sustained supervision. Mrs. Gandhi did not have it in her temperament to supply either. And so vague socialist shibboleths became the magic mantras of Indira's time; and her promises of an egalitarian society created instead an elite bureaucracy that prospered and perpetuated itself. Here was the first woman prime minister of the world's largest nation after China. Here was a politician who won elections hugely by promising India's overwhelmingly poor masses that she would reduce poverty—her catchy slogan was *"Garibi hatao!,"* or "Let's get rid of poverty!" But the standard of living for these masses certainly did not improve significantly in the aggregate during Indira's fifteen years in office.* How intriguing it is that even so trusted a lieutenant of Indira in those *"Garibi hatao!"* days as Chandra Shekhar later became one of her bitterest foes, accusing her of being power-hungry. As president of the Janata Party, Shekhar had the satisfaction of seeing Mrs. Gandhi's Congress Party routed in the 1977 elections. Equally interestingly, the same Chandra Shekhar became prime minister in 1990 at the indulgence of Indira Gandhi's son, Rajiv, who was not in a position to accept the reigns of office himself at the time. Rajiv Gandhi had hoped to stage a political comeback in the 1991 elections, but he was killed in a bomb blast on May 21, 1991, as he campaigned in southern India on behalf of a local Congress Party candidate.

Indira Gandhi was the leader of the key nonaligned nation of the world, yet she never quite made a profound impact—as her father had—on East-West issues. She was attracted to Moscow because of her own left-leaning politics, although she did not view Communism too kindly. Her attitudes concerning the United States were always ambivalent, shaped more by her personal dislike of figures such as Richard Nixon and John Foster Dulles than by any overarching anti-Washington sentiments. Mrs. Gandhi also felt—justifiably, I think—that successive administrations in Washington never really accorded her the genuine respect and support she deserved. In a business—politics—where self-interest is paramount, Indira Gandhi became an accomplished artist in the politics of survival and self-defense. She changed the way politics was practiced. In her time, what had been a strong tradition in India of selfless public service was weakened. She tolerated corruption and

---

*When asked about her *"Garibi hatao!"* pledge in the elections of 1971, Indira Gandhi once told Professor Ralph Buultjens: "Unfortunately, a series of international and domestic events caused many setbacks and we could not fulfill this pledge." There was always a reason—or an excuse—to explain Indira's failures.

violence—as long as those twin satanic forces were employed in the service of the Congress Party. Publicly, of course, Indira Gandhi condemned those forces; privately, she encouraged party stalwarts who subverted the Indian polity in the name of the common good. Indira Gandhi's role in splitting the monolithic Congress Party in 1969 was a defining event in Indian politics. The split led, inexorably over the years, to the disintegration of centrist, secular forces in India. The split thus became the biggest contributor to the cycle of political instability that followed at the center and in state after state. Today, when there is so much talk and effort about the reunification of centrist secular forces, all of whom were born out of the womb of the Mother Party—the Indian National Congress—one can see the far-reaching consequences of the 1969 split. * To a large extent, the 1969 split was a result of Indira Gandhi's personal and paranoid attachment to power; the split also reflected the dynamics of socioeconomic changes in post-independence India. Behind the outward drama of all this lay the extreme difficulty of getting scattered centrist secular forces to reunify into a new, post-Independence reincarnation of the Indian National Congress. And the person primarily responsible for this denouement was Indira Gandhi. Both she and her sons, Rajiv and Sanjay, emphasized the public service of their political dynasty. But that service was often peculiarly combined with selfishness.

Mrs. Gandhi was always a political creature. In an environment that breeds the nastiest and most personality fixated kind of politics, Indira Gandhi seemed to be able to hold her own. She became better at this as she "grew" in power. For example, she was part of the era in which it became customary to extort political contributions from businessmen. In the tightly regulated License Raj of Indira Gandhi, governmental permissions were needed for the most innocuous of commercial activities—and businessmen who sought licenses were now required to embellish the coffers of the Congress Party. This extortion went far beyond the standard practice in India's business community of making political contributions.

Indira Gandhi was India's biggest commercial brand name, and her associates in the Congress Party merrily exploited that advantage.† And so corruption spread through the system like a malignant metastasis. Foreign investors were required to pay hefty bribes. Defense deals carried

---

* In essence, Mrs. Gandhi broke away from the "old" moribund Congress Party and formed her own wing of the party, which she called Congress (I). The (I), obviously, was for Indira.

† Arun Shourie, the Indian author and journalist, wrote a celebrated article in 1982

huge premiums, payable of course to Mrs. Gandhi's Congress Party. Her supporters claimed that she personally never took a penny from anyone. She did not need to, because the prime minister of India—any prime minister of India—has virtually unquestioned and unrestricted access to material comforts and luxuries. Today, it is impossible to get anything done in India without bribery and commissions. The culture of corruption is Indira Gandhi's lasting—even if unintended—gift to India, even though her supporters argue that she could not have possibly foreseen how much political corruption would expand and extend into other areas of national life. A weak argument, at best.

As in many ancient cultures, the mother figure is highly venerated in India. Indira Gandhi was sometimes called Bharat Mata—Mother India —by her supporters and detractors alike.* For her fans, Indira was the bountiful mother figure, who radiated strength—shakti—and a leader who gave succor to her political party, granted patronage to backers, and who tried to improve the lot of luckless Indians, in the manner of a mother who is always—albeit sometimes sternly—supportive of her progeny. For her critics, Indira Gandhi was the smothering mother figure who always strove to dominate the political scene, one who harbored no dissent, least of all any questioning of her policies, programs, and personal style. For her critics, Indira Gandhi was more demon goddess than Bharat Mata.

I wanted to explore the career and contradictions of Indira Gandhi in a book—and so this political biography of the woman whom Henry Kissinger once ridiculed as "the Empress of India."† I set out to paint a portrait of a political woman in her cultural and historical setting. At one level, this is a political biography of contemporary India because Indira's life and legend were so intertwined with the life of the extraordinary country she ruled. Indira's personal and political ambitions were entangled with the national interest. Her life span, after all, encompassed India's tumultuous independence struggle against the British from the 1920s until almost the 1950s, through the key post-Independence years, and into the 1980s. Few national leaders anywhere lived through so many important phases of their country's history and development.

---

in the *Indian Express* entitled "Indira Gandhi as Commerce." In it, Shourie accused some of her Congress Party colleagues of high corruption.
* "Mother India" translates into "Bharat Mata" in Hindustani. Indians reverentially call India "Bharat Mata."
† The *Economist* also called her Empress of India, following the defeat of Pakistan by India in the 1971 war that resulted in the creation of Bangladesh.

In *Mother India*, I have tried to assess her legacy. Indira may be gone, but India and Indians will have to contend with her life and actions well into the next century. In my view, Indira Gandhi was the central character in India's modern history. Her fingerprints and footprints are all over contemporary India, and will not be easily erased no matter what government is in power. While her record as a "national manager" cannot be dismissed lightly, Indira exploited what sociologist Ashis Nandy of Delhi's Center for the Study of Developing Societies calls the "criminalization and commercialization of politics."* Her departure from the Indian political scene may not have been mourned as much as that of her son and successor, Rajiv, but Indira was a far more masterful political figure than Rajiv ever was. It could be argued, of course, that Rajiv served for only five years as India's prime minister whereas his mother had fifteen years in office. Still, Rajiv left no lasting legacy—positive or negative—as Indira did.

Despite the monumental impact Mrs. Gandhi had on her huge country, not much is known in the West about her management style and her politics. Indeed, India itself continues to be an enigma, an exotic mystery, for most Westerners. I have long held that the everyday drama of democracy and grass-roots development in India is presented only fitfully before foreign audiences. And so at another level this book is a story of the management of contradictions and conflicts. The management of resources, which should be the highest priority of India's politicians, increasingly appears to take a distant second place to the management of constant crises—crises that are largely of these politicians' own making.

The entity that is India today consists of twenty-five states and seven "Union" territories, or areas directly controlled by the Delhi government, which everyone calls "the Center"; some states, like Madhya Pradesh, are larger than France. When the British left in 1947 after ruling the Indian Subcontinent for 150 years, there were 565 princely states in the territory that was then partitioned into India and Pakistan. These states were given the option of joining either India or Pakistan; virtually all chose to be part of India, whose leaders vowed at the very outset to establish a secular state (as opposed to Pakistan, which was set up as an Islamic nation). The departure of the British was the culmination of a long and sometimes turbulent "freedom struggle" during which leaders like Mahatma Gandhi, Jawaharlal Nehru, and Nehru's daughter, Indira

*Interview with the author, New Delhi, September 1990.

Gandhi, were frequently arrested and jailed by their colonial rulers. It was during this freedom movement that Mahatma Gandhi fashioned his philosophy of ahimsa, or nonviolence. He urged his followers to counter the brute strength of the British Empire with passive resistance. It was a philosophy that decades later would influence the Reverend Martin Luther King, Jr., who adopted it for his civil rights struggle in the Deep South of the United States. *

The British finally left, but not before they had carved out from greater India a homeland for many of the Subcontinent's Muslims. The division of India into India and Pakistan was known as "the Partition," which to this day evokes memories among many Hindus, Sikhs, and Muslims of widespread bloodshed and rioting.† Although India became independent in 1947, it did not formally become a sovereign republic until January 26, 1950, when its constitution was promulgated.‡ Jawaharlal Nehru, who became prime minister of independent India in 1947, continued in that post until his death in 1964. The Nehru years saw India make important progress in industrialization. Those were also the years when the country was divided up into linguistic states. Nehru was succeeded by Lal Bahadur Shastri, a veteran of the freedom struggle. Shastri died in 1966, soon after India had defeated Pakistan in the second of three wars between the two states since Independence. Shastri's successor as prime minister was Indira Gandhi. She was to serve in that office almost exactly as long as her father had.

With 900 million people now and a spirited multiparty system, India is the world's largest free nation. More Indians qualify to vote in their elections, which have been held mostly on schedule every five years since Independence, than the combined populations of all the industrialized democracies of the world, including Britain, the United States, and Japan. In the May–June 1991 elections, for example, some 510 million

---

* Dr. King often acknowledged publicly that he had read Mahatma Gandhi's writings and had been deeply influenced by them.

† The Sikhs who have been clamoring for a separate theocratic state called Khalistan conveniently tend to forget that their Muslim supporters in Pakistan were the very ones who butchered Sikhs during the Partition.

‡ January 26 is celebrated as "Republic Day" in India. What many people do not know is that the date commemorates Jawaharlal Nehru's *Purna Swaraj*—"Complete Independence"—resolution that the Congress Party incorporated in its platform on January 26, 1930. "We believe that it is the unalienable right of the Indian people, as of any other people, to have freedom and to enjoy the fruits of their toil and have the necessities of life, so that they may have full opportunities of growth," Nehru wrote. "The British government in India has not only deprived the Indian people of their freedom but has based itself on the exploitation of the masses, and has ruined India economically, politically, culturally, and spiritually."

Indians were registered to vote. Unlike many Third World nations, India is an open society where foreigners and locals alike can go where they wish. Little men in little cars or bullock carts do not follow foreign correspondents around, monitoring all their movements—as frequently happens in other developing nations which do not share India's commitment to democratic values and institutions, and to human rights. * The Indian government does not censor transmissions to outside news organizations—although, of course, the work of foreign news organizations reporting out of India is closely monitored. Access to news sources in India is rarely a problem: indeed, Indians and their officials are garrulous to the point of verbosity. The Indian press is arguably the freest in the world, with more than 5,000 daily and weekly newspapers, and another 5,000 monthly magazines, in a variety of languages.

India is an old land, but it is also one of the giants of the modern postwar era. Among the myriad nations of the Third World, it is widely regarded as the first among equals. Since Independence, India has become the world's tenth most powerful industrial country, producing cars, computers, and satellites. India possesses the world's biggest group of scientists and engineers after the United States and the Soviet Union; India's military is the fourth biggest in the world, after the United States, the Soviet Union, and China;† India has exploded nuclear devices; and it produces more feature films—nearly one thousand annually—than any other nation. Ancient culture, modern nation.

Change has come with bewildering speed in the postcolonial period; yet, age-old customs and traditions remain a vital part of everyday life. Marriages are still arranged in many parts of India; elders are still venerated, not shipped off to distant nursing homes for the aged; religion reigns, if not supremely, then still powerfully. Color television is now enjoyed by the masses, and there are live satellite hookups for Wimbledon and World Cup Soccer, and cricket matches, of course. But the most popular programs remain operas and epics about mythological kings and queens.

I have long felt that this aspect of India—change in the midst of continuity—was not fully conveyed to their audiences by journalists reporting out of India. As a journalist of more than two decades' standing, I can appreciate the fact that my brethren must cater to their constituen-

---

* The notable exception to this occurred in 1975–77, when Indira Gandhi suspended the constitution and imposed the "Emergency." Harsh censorship was in force during that time, and civil liberties suffered.
† Data from the International Institute for Strategic Studies, London.

cies. Thus headlines about the Subcontinent that have raced across the front pages of British, American, and other Western publications are mostly about natural or man-made tragedies. Of course, Indira Gandhi's assassination—and her son Rajiv's—invited banner headlines and round-the-clock television coverage. Communal riots seem to be a special favorite of Western television and radio producers: nothing like a good story on bride-burning to win viewers. As with many other Third World nations, India is "news" mostly when there is bad news to report. * Otherwise, India often vanishes from the global radar screen. An adapted version of Gresham's Law seems especially applicable to India: The bad news drives out the good. And the availability of such news? Plentiful, if you are hunting for it. There are foreign journalists who argue that, even under the best of circumstances, India is a difficult place to cover. The sheer size of the Subcontinent poses a formidable challenge. Local transportation is not always reliable; the climate can be debilitating; rich curries can give you the runs; communications can pose a problem.

Finally, at still another level, this is a highly personal book written by an Indian about his native India. On a balmy October morning in 1984, I found myself in Bombay, where I was born. I had flown in from my home in New York to visit my father, who was terminally ill and confined to a hospital room. On that day, October 31, the news of the assassination of Prime Minister Gandhi hit us all like a thunderbolt.

Later that day, *The New York Times* telephoned to ask if I would travel up to the Punjab and report from there for the newspaper.[†] The editors diplomatically did not point out that for security reasons foreigners were forbidden from traveling to the Punjab since the Indian Army's invasion of the Golden Temple in Amritsar. This meant that the newspaper's American staff members could not travel to this troubled state. In my case, of course, it helped to look Indian in India and also to carry an Indian passport—facts that were implicit in the newspaper's request and which would enable me to journey without hindrance to the trouble-torn Punjab, the home state of Prime Minister Gandhi's assassins, Beant Singh and Satwant Singh.

When I told my father about my editors' request, he urged that I at once speed up north, never mind his condition, for this was history in the making. In the event, I was the only correspondent representing a

---

* Mort Rosenblum, the intrepid correspondent for the Associated Press, deals very ably with the question of how the Western media report the Third World. Please see his book *Coups and Earthquakes* (New York: Harper & Row, 1979).
[†] The author worked for *The New York Times* from 1970 to 1982. He also put in summer stints in 1968 and 1969.

foreign publication who was able to report from the Punjab in the wake of the assassination. * Even while I was in Amritsar, thousands of innocent Sikhs were being massacred in New Delhi and elsewhere in northern India by Hindu-led mobs, supposedly to exact retribution for the murder of Indira Gandhi. Yet there was a strange calm at the Golden Temple, where I worshiped in the company of Sikh friends.

I decided that I would write not only about the assassination of Indira Gandhi and its aftermath; I would write about where Indians, who had gone through the remarkable years of her political rule, now saw their country going. I would write a blend of narrative, anecdote, and analysis. I did not wish to be a soothsayer, but I did want to find out from ordinary Indians and from their leaders what sort of future they thought lay in store for them. And so I embarked on a fresh series of travels. That reporting trip took me between November 1984 and June 1985 from the northern Indian state of Kashmir to Kerala at the southern tip of the country. I traveled to India's great cities and bustling towns, and I journeyed to rural areas, where more than 70 percent of India's population lives. I interviewed politicians and peasants and political scientists; I talked with young professionals, movie stars, teachers, farmers, businessmen, technocrats, journalists, musicians, artists, village artisans, and social workers. I talked to people of many religions and ethnic persuasions.

Most of all, I looked up ordinary Indians. I wanted, if not a grand portrait, then at least a sense of where my country stood at a particular point in time. I wanted to write about the great changes that had occurred in national life during Indira's time—and about what lay in store under her son and successor. I observed firsthand the December 1984 national elections in which Rajiv Gandhi's ruling Congress Party won 401 out of 508 seats contested for Parliament, an unprecedented achievement for any political party since India became independent from Britain. I rediscovered the hugeness of my land—1,269,340 square miles, or one-third the size of the continental United States, nearly as large as all of Europe, its population constituting a fifth of all humanity. I heard the cadences and discords of India's fifteen major languages and of many of its estimated 874 regional dialects. India stretches 2,000 miles from the Himalayan heights of Kashmir in the north to the beaches of Kerala in the south, and 1,700 miles from the tea gardens and oil fields of Assam in the east to the scorched plains of Gujarat in the West. India's coastline is more than 3,500 miles long; its borders with Pakistan, Nepal, China, the

---

*Later, of course, other "foreign" correspondents slipped into the Punjab. But by that time, *The New York Times* had obtained a solid beat on the competition.

Soviet Union, Myanmar, Bhutan, and Bangladesh, ramble over 8,300 miles of deserts, mountains, and tropical forests.

Everywhere there are huge crowds: When India achieved Independence, there were 350 million Indians; in fifty years, there will be more than 2 billion. Indeed, India has already become the world's second most populated country, after China, which has 1.1 billion people. India keeps adding more than 18 million annually, or more than the entire population of Australia, and by the end of the century the number of people added annually to the population will exceed 20 million. Everywhere there are cattle: India has 200 million of them, or a quarter of the world's bovine population. More than seven-tenths of Indians depend on farming for their livelihood, but although agriculture constitutes almost 45 percent of India's gross national product of $250 billion, farmers enjoy a per-capita income of considerably less than the national average of $250. I found out that fewer than half of India's 650,000 villages are electrified. Literacy is also low in villages: Only one woman in four can read and write; only half of India's males have gone to primary school. I was told that more than a third of the world's illiterates live in India. * Hardly a heartening legacy for Indira Gandhi.

Despite the widespread availability of primary health care, the infant mortality rate in India is 91 per 1,000 live births—one of the highest in the world. Life expectancy is fifty-four years, according to the government, but Indians in many parts of the country survive fewer years than that. I discovered that there are 100 million "untouchables" in India, the economically backward and socially shunned people whom Mahatma Gandhi called Harijans, or God's children. Of India's total population, 85 percent are Hindus and 10 percent are Muslims; there are also 20 million Christians, 14 million Sikhs, 5 million Buddhists, and almost 4 million Jains, members of a sect who abhor violence so much that most would not even dream of crushing a cockroach. †

Listen to James W. Michaels, editor of *Forbes* and perhaps the most experienced of the "India hands" in American journalism:

> The differences between India and the West are profound. But so are the similarities, the common ground. India is a political democracy.

---

* The literacy rate has been on the rise, however. The government's 1990–91 census says that at least 50 percent of the population has basic reading and writing skills.
† Indeed, some Jains are so sensitive about the sacredness of life that they wear gauze over their noses and mouths so that they will not breathe in living organisms.

Toleration of cultural diversity is not foreign to India but deeply rooted in its culture and history. A Westerner's first impression of India is: How different this place is. But closer observation yields a quite different insight. Democracy in India is a living reality—blemished, but reality usually is. In India, as in most of Western Europe and the United States, people are free to be people—providing they do not too flagrantly break the law. Here are 900 million people, half of them under the age of twenty. They do not have a common language. It is not exceptional in Delhi and elsewhere to see a South Indian speaking in English to a North Indian waiter because it is the only language they have in common. Religions? Hindu and Muslim have a history of strife that makes Catholic and Protestant in Northern Ireland seem like a couple of neighbors squabbling over a back fence. Yet the polyglot, poly-racial, poly-religious mass of people has maintained under ferociously difficult conditions what I believe to be the only freely elected government among the dozens of countries which shed imperial rule after World War II. India's army has left its barracks only to fight foreign enemies or to restore order when the police were overwhelmed. Unlike in next-door Pakistan, the army in India does not pretend to embody national legitimacy; it exists only to defend that legitimacy. No matter how you cut it and for all her flaws, modern India is a magnificent and humane accomplishment. *

A traveler in those months following Indira Gandhi's death was struck by the high hopes that many Indians had for her son and successor, Rajiv Gandhi. People were liberally garlanding their new leader with goodwill. I was encouraged by their general optimism concerning Rajiv, who was widely perceived as a young and fresh-faced man untainted by the corrosive political practices of his predecessor and mother. He had an extremely telegenic family in his wife, the Italian-born Sonia Maino, daughter Priyanka, and son Rahul. "He was a basically decent man, and the decency showed," says Bakul Rajni Patel, a social worker in Bombay. "Everybody responded to that decency."

I was also encouraged by the fact that in a period of general political decline, missed economic opportunities, and authoritarian tendencies under Indira Gandhi, popular Indian culture nonetheless flourished. The fine arts and performing arts were thriving. Several grass-roots organiza-

---

* Conversation with the author, New York, 1985. Jim Michaels made his journalistic mark early in life when, as a young correspondent for United Press, he was near the scene of the assassination of Mahatma Gandhi. For more than forty years since his

tions had sprouted to serve everyday needs of deprived people in towns and villages, whether such needs concerned supplying potable water, providing legal advice, or generating employment for village artisans.

Parts of my reporting appeared in two books in 1985 and 1989. I was initially convinced that the Rajiv Raj would truly usher in a new era of peace, prosperity, and general progress, not only in India but the whole South Asia region. Rajiv Gandhi, after all, was starting with a clean slate; his view of politics was global, not parochial; his economic instincts were centrist, even favoring free enterprise over Indira Gandhi's preferred public-sector statism. He seemed keen to play a decisive role in resolving numerous local conflicts in the region. And Rajiv was anxious to make his mark quickly as a world leader, initially through the mechanism of the Nonaligned Movement.

Within four years, however, the political landscape of India had altered dramatically. The early promise of Rajiv Gandhi had withered. Gandhi's bold plans for economic liberalization were stymied by India's bureaucratic behemoth—and by his own inability to provide a strong implementation impetus. For decades India prided itself on the fact that, almost alone among major developing countries, it had not piled up major foreign debts. Since October 1984, when Gandhi had become prime minister, India's foreign debt grew from $23 billion to $35 billion.[*] Why? Partly because of rising imports and lavish borrowing to finance showcase projects; and partly because of the scale of India's budget deficit, which rose from 5.5 percent of the gross domestic product in 1979 to more than 9 percent in 1986. As in the case of many Latin American countries in the 1970s, the deficit contributed to the huge increase in foreign borrowing. Inflation was headed toward double-digit figures. Economic policies were bedeviled by inconsistencies of approach, frequent reshuffling of key aides entrusted with carrying out Rajiv Gandhi's vision, and by Gandhi's own failure to provide strong committed direction.

"The deterioration in India's fiscal position is likely to prove the most important legacy of Rajiv Gandhi's period as prime minister," says Martin Wolf of the London *Financial Times*.

His attempts at economic liberalization were not insignificant and led to substantial improvement in the country's rate of economic

---

initial assignment in India, Jim Michaels has been widely considered one of the most perceptive observers of the Indian scene.
[*] The World Bank estimates that India's external debt in mid-1991 was $70.3 billion. Of this amount, some $44 billion is owed to official creditors, and $11 billion to foreign banks.

growth. But liberalization is unsustainable in the presence of substantial macroeconomic imbalances, which show themselves in higher inflation, larger current account deficits and soaring international indebtedness. Furthermore, however dramatic it may have been by India's standards, the liberalization of 1985–87 was decidedly limited by those of almost any other country. The structure of official control was left intact—[control] over what can be imported, over who can import, over who can produce, over what can be produced, over where things can be produced, over the amounts that can be produced, over who can be employed and over who can be made redundant. . . . The way in which regulations were interpreted may have changed. The basic structure of control remained unaltered.*

In an interview in late 1990, Rajiv Gandhi acknowledged the problems he had concerning his economic liberalization program. "We did start out with a major liberalization program—what we didn't start out with was an understanding of how the system worked," Gandhi said. "Our first target should be to strengthen our industry so that we are internationally competitive. In the changing world order, it's becoming very clear that you will only survive if you are strong and competitive. And India cannot afford to be anything else—especially when we have the capability of being competitive."[†]

By 1989 Gandhi's leadership was being increasingly challenged by opposition leaders who were emboldened by a series of corruption scandals featuring Gandhi associates and friends. One of the biggest scandals involved the secret and illicit payment of millions of dollars in commissions by the Swedish arms manufacturer Bofors A. B., allegedly to people close to the Rajiv Gandhi circle. Bofors, a subsidiary of Nobel Industries, had been awarded a controversial $1.3 billion contract to provide India with 155mm howitzers.[‡] The Indian media, ever eager for a hot scoop, seized on the story along with Rajiv Gandhi's political opponents—at least in part because Gandhi's supporters had made such a big deal of his "Mr. Clean" image.[§] The scale of the Bofors affair suggested that politi-

---

*Martin Wolf, "Indian Economy Frozen in Time," *Financial Times*, May 23, 1991.
[†]Interview with Pranay Gupte and Bernard Kalb, New Delhi, September 1990.
[‡]The negotiations for the Bofors contract actually began when Indira Gandhi was still alive. No one really knows exactly how much was paid in commissions. There is general agreement among Indian law-enforcement officials that it was at least $100 million; some officials even suspect that the truer figure was $200 million.
[§]At the Congress Centenary celebrations in Bombay, in December 1985, Rajiv Gandhi sternly scolded his fellow party members about growing corruption in the Congress. He urged them to clean up their act—and their organization.

cal corruption had become more extensive than ever before and had also deepened its roots in the body politic. "Corruption—yes, there is corruption," Rajiv Gandhi said. "We tried a lot to remove it. We were successful in some areas. We weren't in others. But many of the charges made were unsubstantiated. In a developing economy, there are shortages by definition. And when there are shortages, there is a lot of money chasing those shortages—so you are going to have problems. The only real way out of this is fast enough development—so that enough is available and there are no shortages."* Shortages may well explain the small-scale corruption that Gandhi talked about—but not the high corruption, the millions of dollars in illegal commissions, that those around him reportedly pocketed. That was plain greed.

The arms scandal was not the only unpleasant story on the Indian scene. In the strategic border state of Punjab—a state long considered India's granary—Sikh separatists escalated their terrorist campaign to establish a theocratic state called Khalistan. Where did the Sikhs get their weapons? The Gandhi administration charged that neighboring Pakistan was a conduit for arms, and was also providing sanctuary to the rebels. Moreover, Indian intelligence officials seemed convinced that money raised by affluent Sikh expatriates in Britain, the United States, Canada, and Western Europe was being used to buy sophisticated weapons for the terrorists. These officials believed that the Sikh terrorists' "hit list" included not only Rajiv Gandhi but also his wife and children. The Gandhi children, in fact, were pulled out of school by their parents and tutored at home.[†]

By 1988 virtually the entire South Asian region was in the throes of turmoil. In Afghanistan the Indian government under Indira Gandhi had supported the Soviet invasion of December 1979; Pakistan, meanwhile, had joined hands with its patron, the United States, in backing the mujahedeen, the so-called freedom fighters whose beliefs did not prevent them from butchering dissidents within their ranks. More than 3 million Afghan refugees (out of the 5 million who had fled their country) were camped in Pakistan. The Soviet invasion of Afghanistan proved to be of unusual value to Pakistan: Washington began to perceive Pakistan as a front-line state against Soviet expansionist ambitions in Asia, and funneled more than $2 billion in economic and military assistance to the mujahedeen through the Pakistani government. Moreover, the United States initiated a six-year, $3.2 billion aid package to Pakistan

---

*Interview with Pranay Gupte and Bernard Kalb, New Delhi, September 1990.
[†]There were reports, which proved false, that the Gandhi children had been sent to school in the Soviet Union.

in 1981—a package that included forty F-16 fighter-bombers—and in 1988, after considerable debate, the U.S. Congress agreed to a second six-year aid package, this one amounting to $4 billion.* By early 1988, the Soviet Union's reformist leader, Mikhail S. Gorbachev, had decided to pull his troops out of Afghanistan, where 13,000 Soviet soldiers had died in guerrilla combat with the mujahedeen, and another 37,000 had been wounded. The incursion into Afghanistan had obtained for Moscow widespread international condemnation, especially from the Islamic countries, although Indira Gandhi had not conspicuously lent her voice to those criticisms.

Moreover, despite the massive investment of manpower, munitions, and money, the Soviets were not able to sustain a strong local government in Kabul, the Afghan capital. The dynamics of President Gorbachev's *glasnost* and *perestroika* obviously meant that the Afghan adventure had to end soon. Moscow could not afford the economic price to a prolonged stay in Afghanistan, and world opinion would not favor such a stay anyway. Better to cut one's losses and exit gracefully. Gorbachev's "savior" turned out to be the United Nations, which had tried for six years to end the Afghan war. On April 14, 1988, an agreement was signed in Geneva under the aegis of the UN; the agreement was guaranteed by both superpowers. Under its terms, the Soviets agreed to pull their 115,000 troops out of mountainous Afghanistan; the United States and the Soviet Union, however, reserved the right to resume military assistance to the mujahedeen and the Kabul government respectively.

Because India—under Indira Gandhi as well as her son—had been such a strong supporter of the Soviet-backed Kabul regime, there was now a general feeling that if the mujahedeen resistance leaders grabbed power in Kabul, India's influence would be diminished in Afghanistan. It was not just India's western border that Rajiv Gandhi had to worry about. In the south, after a peace treaty that Gandhi signed with neighboring Sri Lanka in July 1987, India sent peacekeeping troops shortly thereafter to help resolve a bitter civil war between that island nation's majority Sinhalese and minority Tamils. The exercise proved costly, and by no means conclusive: More than 1,000 Indian troops were killed by the Tamil separatists, who had earlier received alms and arms from India. Some of Gandhi's critics called the Sri Lankan situation India's Afghanistan or Vietnam. Rajiv Gandhi himself was to become a casualty of the Tamil crisis: A Tamil woman of Sri Lankan origin was his assassin. To the east, in Burma, students clamored for democracy, and after some

* The American aid package was temporarily suspended in 1990, after news reports concerning Pakistan's efforts to build a nuclear bomb.

initial concessions the military was once again in charge, bloodily crushing dissent. In Nepal and Bhutan, there were new, popular challenges to feudal monarchies. The military-led government of Bangladesh was mired in corruption, and the country's economy continued to be bedeviled by natural disasters and inept management.*

The overall geopolitical situation in South Asia had changed considerably since my reporting trips of 1984–85, and so I embarked on new reporting trips in the region that extended through early 1991. Two of the most dramatic developments occurred in 1988:

- President Mohammed Zia ul-Haq of Pakistan was killed when his plane blew up.† Despite being a military dictator who could not resist occasional saber-rattling at India, Zia was essentially a moderate man who did not feel that war was the best way to arrive at an accommodation with his huge neighbor. He was a shrewd and masterly politician who held his ethnically tumultuous country together over two difficult decades. If Zia tried to destabilize India's Punjab and Kashmir states—as Indira Gandhi believed—then he was certainly paying Indira back in kind for what he perceived as her own meddling in Pakistan's internal affairs.

- In Sri Lanka, President Junius Richard Jayewardene decided in September 1988 that he would retire from public life, thereby ending one of the most remarkable careers in Third World politics. His retirement created another imponderable in India's relationship with this troubled island neighbor. Jayewardene had shifted from an anti-Indian to a strongly pro-Indian stance in recent years, bringing Sri Lanka's foreign and domestic policies into alignment with India's strategies. However, Jayewardene's expectations that this demarche would ease the separatist and other tensions in his country remained unfulfilled—more than 15,000 Sri Lankans had died in the civil war since 1985. India now had no guarantee that Sri Lanka's new leader, Ranasinghe Premadasa, would be as favorably disposed toward New Delhi as Jayewardene, creating another gray area of uncertainty for Indian policymakers. Eventually, Indian troops were withdrawn from Sri Lanka at Premadasa's insistence.‡

---

* Bangladesh held elections in March 1991, and an opposition figure, Begun Khaleda Zia, became prime minister.

† The mystery of his death has yet to be solved. One widely held theory has it that the Soviets were behind the blowup of Zia's plane. And the cloud of suspicion still hangs over India, at least in the minds of many Pakistanis.

‡ The separatist threat posed by Sri Lanka's Tamils has continued into 1991. The Tamil movement, of course, has found resonance and support in the southern Indian

These developments restructured an entire region that had become increasingly important in world affairs, a region increasingly wooed by the superpowers because of its strategic location and its potential as a huge market. More than a quarter of the global population, which was squeezed into this region, now faced the 1990s with uncertainty and insecurity. South Asia's problems were exacerbated in 1990, when President Saddam Hussein of Iraq invaded and annexed neighboring Kuwait on August 2. For India and other Third World nations, this development had tragic consequences: more than a million Indians lived and worked in Kuwait, Iraq, and other Gulf countries, and they remitted some $2 billion annually to India. Moreover, India obtained a formidable portion of her crude oil from Kuwait and Iraq, and these supplies were virtually cut off, along with income from the expatriate Indians who fled the region in droves. As a result of the Iraqi invasion, and the subsequent Gulf War of January–February 1991 in which Iraq's economy was virtually destroyed by the United States and allied countries, India's own economy plunged into a severe depression.* Its annual oil-import bill rose by billions of dollars, its trade with the Gulf countries was dramatically shrunk, and the economic gains of the 1970s and 1980s were greatly endangered.†

The speed and fluidity of local developments illustrated how quickly things change in regional and world politics; the changes underscored the need for local and world leaders to act swiftly and shrewdly to cope with exigencies and emergencies. Perhaps more than ever before in the postwar, postcolonial era, the Subcontinent now constituted a test case of whether Third World countries could ensure a satisfactory life for their people in a world where economic growth and social progress are increasingly hard to fashion.

By 1989 it was by no means clear that the countries of the region were meeting their challenges adequately. It was amply evident that the new

---

state of Tamil Nadu, the home of more than 50 million Tamils, who enjoy cultural, linguistic, and sentimental links with Sri Lankan Tamils. Successive Sri Lankan governments have accused Indian Tamils of harboring and helping Sri Lankan Tamil guerrilla groups.

* A study by the United Nations in March 1991 said that the allied bombing of Iraq had reduced that country to a "preindustrial" state. Iraq's economic condition, the UN said, had become "near-apocalyptic."

† President George Bush announced on Wednesday, February 27, 1991, that the Allies had liberated Kuwait. The economic and political repercussions of the Gulf War, however, are likely to affect Third World countries such as India for years to come.

rulers of India, who had promised change, were confounded by it. It seemed to me that 1989 would be an especially critical year, a time when vital concerns, issues, and a clash of heritages would converge. The axis of confluence would, of course, be India's general election which was scheduled to be held during 1989, since the constitution mandates that national elections be held every five years. It would be the greatest political show on earth when more than 400 million voters would pour their frustrations, concerns, and hopes into the ballot box.

I felt in late 1989 that the noisy clamor of democracy at work would be, in truth, a vast referendum on the future direction of India and the performance of its rulers, successors of Indira Gandhi. In the event, the 1989 election, coming as it did at this juncture of Indian history, produced an indictment of Rajiv Gandhi and his policies for a "New India." Rajiv Gandhi's exit from power in the November 1989 election represented more than a defeat for his Congress Party.* The event was a stunning setback for the remarkable Nehru-Gandhi political dynasty; there was even a sense that the dynasty was now in eclipse. How permanent would that eclipse be? Would Rajiv be able to revive his dynasty's fortunes? Would he be able to finally shrug off his mother's shadow and emerge as a genuine political leader in his own right? Would Rajiv be chastened by his defeat, as his mother had been back in 1977 when she was uprooted from power?

We will now never know the answer to these questions. The murder of Rajiv Gandhi effectively ended the domination of Indian politics by the Nehru-Gandhi dynasty. If his widow, Sonia, decides to carve out a political career for herself in India, or if his children emerge in due course as political players, they will have to do so in their own right. They will have to contend with the fact that none received political tutelage or grooming from their predecessor. In contrast, Nehru had helped facilitate Indira's entry into Indian politics; and Indira, however briefly and however against his own initial wishes, groomed Rajiv for public life. The death of Rajiv Gandhi was certainly a stunning tragedy for his family and

---

* Rajiv Gandhi was reelected to parliament, but his Congress Party could bag only 197 seats out of the 545-seat Lok Sabha, or lower house of Parliament. The Congress's control of 197 seats was not enough to enable it to form a government. The Janata Dal—or National Front—of V. P. Singh, once Rajiv's finance and defense minister, had won 150 seats. The Janata Dal formed a government with the parliamentary support of the pro-Hindu Bharatiya Janata Party (BJP). The Left Front, a group of Communist and left-leaning parties, won about fifty seats. About 508 seats were contested, and the rest were allocated by nomination to economically backward communities and minorities.

supporters. But in a political sense it does not mean much because Rajiv Gandhi did not leave behind a special legacy.

The men who replaced Rajiv Gandhi in the prime minister's chair after the 1989 elections turned out to be inept, and incapable of holding together for long the parliamentary arithmetic necessary for governing in India.* And so, in early March 1991—barely 420 days after Indians went to the polls in 1989 to elect a new government—it was announced that there would be new elections. Some 510 million voters were eligible to vote.† The 1991 elections had been scheduled for May 20, 23, and 26. But after Rajiv Gandhi's murder on May 21, the remaining two days of balloting were shifted to June 12 and 15. The Congress Party won the largest number of seats—although not a majority—and formed a government, which was headed by P. V. Narasimha Rao.

Indira Gandhi's life and career, more than anyone else's, continue to be the touchstone against which all contemporary political activity in India must still be measured, rated, and reflected. It will not be easy for post-Indira leaders to step out of her shadow. Her ghost will not go away so readily. In death, as in life, Indira Gandhi is Mother India, refusing to let go of the forces and fruits of her political womb that affect—and afflict—the modern nation-state. Try as they might, leaders of contemporary India cannot shake away—nor will away, nor wash away—Indira's legacy.

It is now more than seven years after Indira Gandhi's murder. I believe that her legacy continues to inhibit India's economic growth and social progress because the bureaucracy that ballooned and blossomed during her time refuses to yield its power: it is, after all, highly profitable for bureaucrats and politicians to maintain the License Raj, that suffocating system of controls and permits that zestfully extracts bribes from those

---

*V. P. Singh's government fell when the BJP withdrew its support after its leader, L. K. Advani, was arrested as he led a pro-Hindu march toward the site of a religious shrine in Ayodhya—in Uttar Pradesh State—claimed by both Hindus and Muslims. Singh was succeeded by his archenemy, Chandra Shekhar. Shekhar obtained the legislative backing of Rajiv Gandhi and the Congress Party. In March 1991, however, Rajiv withdrew his support in a fit of pique over alleged surveillance of his home by police from neighboring Haryana, a state controlled by political allies of Shekhar. Rajiv's action meant that Shekhar could not summon a working majority in Parliament. The president then dissolved Parliament and ordered fresh elections.

†The voter registration list had increased by almost 20 million since the 1989 election. The May national elections were the tenth since 1952, when the first were held.

wishing to be in business or to expand production. Meanwhile, many Third World countries are today going through a process of transition from public-sector-based socialism to private-sector-led economic growth. These countries—many of them with far fewer natural and manpower resources than India—are also moving from the traditional narrow focus of "self-reliance" to participation in the global market through export-led growth. But India, the "socialist" India fashioned by Jawaharlal Nehru and encouraged by Indira Gandhi, still disappointingly lags in such economic growth.* Not long ago, the *Economist* had this to say about India's plight: "The socialist and protectionist dogma fastened on the country in the 1950s has kept it far poorer than it should be. India sparkles with entrepreneurial and commercial verve. . . . Yet a thick swaddling of red tape strangles the economy."†

In the early part of the next century, India will most certainly become the world's most heavily populated country. No amount of accelerated economic growth can possibly keep pace with the rising demands and expectations of India's masses unless there is major structural reform in the economy. And, as we all know, the first requirement for any economic reform is political commitment.

Such political commitment is also needed to rid India of the communalism that is eating at its entrails.

James W. Michaels says:

> One of the greatest obstacles to forward movement is what Indians call communalism and we, in a slightly different context, call racism. Both are more often swear words than accurate descriptions of attitudes. When an Indian deplores communalism he means the practice of favoring one's own community over other communities, putting community before nation. Communalism, carried to extremes, leads to bloody riots. In practice, the term is almost always coupled with "Hindu," since the Hindus, being 80 percent of the population, are expected to be more tolerant than the minorities—for whom one is supposed to make allowances. One is supposed to be particularly gentle with Muslims and solicitous of their sensibilities. Since the central government is bound by the very Constitution to secularism,

---

* In a conversation at his Washington office in February 1991, Sir William Ryrie, head of the World Bank's International Finance Corporation, told me that he thought India was frittering away its economic potential through the continuation of heavy bureaucratic regulations. In July 1991, the Indian government announced a major economic liberalization plan. How successful it will be remains to be seen.
† *Economist*, March 9, 1991.

any assertion of Hindu rights or of Hindu virtues tends to be regarded as communalism.

Thus we see the spectacle of an overwhelming majority having to behave with great restraint in its own land. When Sikh extremists massacred innocent Hindus in the Punjab, throwing bombs into wedding parties and pulling travelers from buses and hacking them to pieces, a devotion to secularism forced many Indian intellectuals into a position of criticizing Mrs. Gandhi's government for ignoring the "legitimate demands" of the Sikhs—although nobody articulated with any precision just what these demands were. But when Mrs. Gandhi sent the Indian Army into that nest of murderers that the Golden Temple had become—well, some people considered that a communal act. Ridiculous as these arguments sometimes become, there is virtue in them. They force the majority to lean over backward to protect the rights of minorities. That India's overwhelming Hindu majority accepts, though sometimes grumblingly, these restraints is one more sign of how basic is India's underlying commitment to tolerance and to democracy. Nobody can negotiate with the IRA provos, the Red Brigades, or Middle East terrorists—and nobody could conduct rational negotiations with the Sikh killers. Too bad that so many innocent Sikhs suffered; their real tormentors were fellow Sikhs. Remember this about the Sikhs: they are no downtrodden minority but a group who by dint of hard work and common sense have earned an economically and politically privileged position in India. They are an admirable people ill-served by a rotten leadership; one is tempted to think of Germany in the 1930s. What is said is that many Sikhs in Britain and North America, secure in their sanctuaries, egged on and financed the fanatical leadership and helped bring suffering on their people in India. *

Not long ago, I spoke with Russi Mody, chairman of Tata Steel, which is the largest private-sector company in India. Mody was visiting New York, and his natural ebullience seemed muted this time. He was deeply worried, Mody said, about the growing sectarian violence in the country.

India is being torn asunder—on caste lines, on religious lines, on class lines. Unless this particular matter is urgently tackled, there is

---

* "From Mahatma Gandhi to Rajiv Gandhi," foreword by James W. Michaels to *Vengeance*, by Pranay Gupte (New York: W. W. Norton and Company, 1985), pp. 20–21.

no future for the country. The rarest commodity in India today seems to be the genuine Indian. We have got millions of Sikhs, millions of Muslims, millions of Christians, millions of Hindus. Everybody is either from Punjab or Tamil Nadu or Bengal or wherever. But we can't find the Indian. If we had a true and genuine Indian, there would be no problem in Punjab, no problem in Kashmir, no problem in Assam. Why has the Indian disappeared? He has disappeared at the altar of religious fanaticism. The politician is bent on creating a vote bank through the medium of religion. The immediate need today is to find that real Indian. If you don't have Indians in India, then you won't have India. *

I think Russi Mody said it very well indeed. When I look at my India, the land that spawned Mahatma Gandhi and Jawaharlal Nehru—even Indira Gandhi—I get terribly disheartened these days. Surely India deserves much better than the politicians—and their swamis and gurus—who rule the roost today and who have invited upon India such misery and calamities.

Yet one should not overlook some hopeful signals. Never before in history have one-sixth of the world's population lived together in a single democratic state. This is an extraordinary achievement that has been sustained for more than four decades now. There are large numbers of enterprising and vibrant individuals committed to making India a better place in which to live. Precisely because India has so much potential, one is disappointed in its performance. What, after all, is promise if it remains unfulfilled?

In the larger crucible of history, perhaps Indira Gandhi's greatness lay not so much in what she did but in what she wanted for her country. She was confident that India would make it. And that confidence resonated through the system and across the land—at least during the early years of Indira's stewardship. That confidence may have excessively camouflaged some of the warts of India's body politic—but it remains a testimony to her patriotism, vision, and belief in her compatriots. Measured by statistical yardsticks, India's record during the Indira era may not have been great at all. Yet Indira Gandhi always maintained that these were the foundation years—and that the fruits of her enterprise and that of ordinary Indians would grow once the tree of nationhood was firmly rooted.

* Conversation with the author, New York City, January 1991.

I

The End

I

The Assassination

On Wednesday, October 31, 1984, Indira Gandhi woke up, as usual, at around six o'clock in the morning. Her longtime valet, Nathuram, fetched her a customary pot of piping hot tea. Mrs. Gandhi, barely a month short of her sixty-seventh birthday, then quickly scanned several local Hindi and English-language newspapers—another daily practice.* Many of the papers carried front-page articles about her trip, the previous day, through the eastern state of Orissa, where she had made a number of appearances at political rallies.

At a place called Gopalpur, she had laid the foundation stone of a new military school for guided-missile training. That same day Indira Gandhi had spoken at a rally in Bhubaneshwar, the capital of Orissa State.† It was a typical political rally, which is to say that hundreds of thousands of people had gathered on an open-air parade ground to glimpse and applaud her, no matter what she said. Many of these people had been brought from their remote rural homes in buses hired by the local Congress Party. The party always seemed to have plenty of cash for such things; it was also blessed with a cadre of skilled advance men who traveled from state to state ensuring that Mrs. Gandhi's public appearances went off well.

---

* There are a dozen English-language and Hindi newspapers published every day in New Delhi alone. Mrs. Gandhi insisted on having all of them delivered to her on a daily basis.
† Orissa is on the eastern coast of India.

In her thirty-minute speech in Hindi, Mrs. Gandhi spoke about the dangers of communalism and about external threats to India's security. Then she recalled that in some quarters there was considerable political hostility to her and that sometimes the situation got out of hand. She recalled that only the previous day, someone had hurled a stone at her at a rally.

"But I am not afraid of these things," one newspaper quoted Mrs. Gandhi as saying. "I don't mind if my life goes in the service of the nation. If I die today, every drop of my blood will invigorate the nation. Every drop of my blood, I am sure, will contribute to the growth of this nation to make it strong and dynamic."

It was cold in her bedroom—few Delhi homes, including Mrs. Gandhi's, are equipped with central heating—and the portable electric heater seemed to work unsatisfactorily. Mrs. Gandhi rose and spent a few minutes on limbering yoga exercises, bathed, put on a bright orange sari, and joined her grandchildren Priyanka and Rahul, and their Italian-born mother, Sonia, for breakfast. Rajiv was in West Bengal that morning on a political mission for his mother, who was widely expected to announce soon the date for India's national parliamentary elections.*

The morning meal consisted of toast, cereals, freshly squeezed orange juice, eggs, and tea.† After that the children would set off for school. Mrs. Gandhi asked Rahul and Priyanka how they felt. The previous evening, the car in which they had been riding was rammed by a van that shot through a red traffic light not far from the prime minister's residence, at One Safdarjung Road. The children were not hurt, and the prime minister's security staff reported that there was nothing sinister about the accident.

As Mrs. Gandhi talked to the children, an aide entered the dining room. He was Rajendra Kumar Dhawan, a short, pleasant, forty-seven-year-old man with slickly oiled hair that appeared permanently plastered down on his scalp. Dhawan had served Mrs. Gandhi for almost twenty years and was probably her most trusted subordinate and certainly her most powerful one.‡ Dhawan advised the prime minister about everything

---

*Under the Indian constitution, elections are to be held every five years. But the president—India's constitutional head of state—has the power to dissolve Parliament and order fresh elections. The president usually acts on the advice of the head of government, the prime minister.

†Mrs. Gandhi herself generally ate very little at breakfast.

‡R. K. Dhawan was born in Chanyot, in what is now Pakistan. In 1947 Dhawan and his family came to Delhi as refugees. They stayed with Yashpal Kapoor, who was to become a close associate of Indira Gandhi. Dhawan started his career as a

from political appointments to foreign policy, and there were those who contended that he, as much as Mrs. Gandhi, ran the country.

Dhawan told the prime minister that it was nearly time to leave for her first appointment of the day. She nodded, then kissed and hugged her grandchildren. As they left her, she, quite unusually, called them for a second farewell. Then she walked into her small study to flip through a pile of government files that Dhawan had already placed on her desk. On her desk was something that Mrs. Gandhi had written in her own hand. It was a sort of last will and testament. Of her aides, only Dhawan had seen it. Mrs. Gandhi had not quite finished working on her will.

He had once asked her about it, and Mrs. Gandhi had shrugged the question away. But Dhawan, like some others who worked in close proximity to the prime minister, was aware that she had lately seemed rather distracted. A longtime friend and adviser, Professor Ralph Buultjens of New York University, had even heard her reflect often about the possibility that some harm might befall her. Professor Buultjens had tried to reassure Mrs. Gandhi, but she seemed extremely despondent.[*] Once before—in 1978, when she was out of power—Indira Gandhi had shown Professor Buultjens a draft of a statement that she had prepared for public release if she was violently killed.

Mrs. Gandhi's mood worried both Buultjens and Dhawan, who had been concerned about her safety since the Indian Army's assault in June on the Golden Temple in Amritsar. The army had flushed out Sikh terrorists who had been holed up in the temple, but not before more than a thousand men, women, and children, who had come as pilgrims to Amritsar, died in the cross fire between the terrorists and the military.[†] Mrs. Gandhi had been determined not to yield to the terrorists' demand for a separate nation, which they wanted carved out of the northwestern state of Punjab, India's granary. Although the majority of the country's 14 million Sikhs did not support the separatists, the army's action in

---

stenographer with All-India Radio, the government-owned broadcasting network. He later became a typist for Mrs. Gandhi when she headed a government agency that organized India's booth at the 1962 New York World's Fair. Dhawan continued working for Mrs. Gandhi when she became minister of information and broadcasting under Lal Bahadur Shastri. He became her closest confidant and, indeed, henchman. A canny political operator, Dhawan was widely regarded as the "secret" of Mrs. Gandhi's successes in dealing with Congress Party maneuvers in India's states. Dhawan later played a similar role for Rajiv Gandhi, and for P. V. Narasimha Rao, who became prime minister in June 1991.
[*] Conversation with the author, New York, December 1984.
[†] To this day the exact number of casualties remains a mystery.

Amritsar was widely deplored in the Sikh community. Sikhs—and other Indians—had been shocked by the loss of lives, and by reports of the extensive damage to the venerated Sikh shrine.

Among Mrs. Gandhi's aides, as among Indians all across this vast country, there had been, since the Amritsar event, a growing conviction that it would be only a matter of time before Sikhs took action against the prime minister. They feared that Indira Gandhi would be killed in vengeance.

Was she herself seized by some premonition? Dhawan glanced quickly at the handwritten note. This is what Mrs. Gandhi had written:

> I have never felt less like dying and that calm and peace of mind is what prompts me to write what is in the nature of a will. If I die a violent death as some fear and a few are plotting, I know the violence will be in the thought and the action of the assassin, not in my dying—for no hate is dark enough to overshadow the extent of my love for my people and my country; no force is strong enough to divert me from my purpose and my endeavor to take this country forward.
>
> A poet has written of his "love"—"How can I feel humble with the wealth of you beside me?" I can say the same of India. I cannot understand how anyone can be an Indian and not be proud—the richness and infinite variety of our composite heritage, the magnificence of the people's spirit, equal to any disaster or burden, firm in their faith, gay spontaneity even in poverty and hardship.

Dhawan reminded Mrs. Gandhi of her first appointment of the morning, with Peter Ustinov, the British actor. Ustinov planned to produce a documentary on her and, indeed, had accompanied the prime minister during some of her travels across India. The feature on Mrs. Gandhi was to be part of a series tentatively called "Ustinov's People." Now he had scheduled a final interview with Mrs. Gandhi and was waiting with his film crew on the lawns behind the Safdarjung Road residence, on the side facing Akbar Road. Mrs. Gandhi had a special fondness for men and women in the arts, and Peter Ustinov was one of them.

Moreover, Ustinov, a stout Santa Claus in mufti, was heavily involved in a cause that the prime minister herself vigorously supported—the plight of children. In fact, Ustinov had come to India wearing two hats: as a film producer, and as a fund-raiser for UNICEF, the United Nations Children's Fund. Later Ustinov would say that he had wanted to ask Mrs. Gandhi how as an only child she came to terms with loneliness.

Ustinov's interview was scheduled for 9:20 A.M. He thought the Akbar Road lawn would be an ideal spot because of its picturesque location. It was a cool, late fall morning, with just a nip in the air, and the roses in Mrs. Gandhi's garden were in full bloom. Behind the lawn was the prime minister's residential office, where she often received visitors in the morning before her usual journey to the more formal prime-ministerial office in South Block, near the ornate Parliament House; this building, and a tall hedge next to it, separated the Akbar Road area from Mrs. Gandhi's living quarters on Safdarjung Road.

At nine-fifteen, Mrs. Gandhi stepped out of her house, with Narayan Singh, a New Delhi policeman, holding an umbrella over the prime minister's head to shield her from the sun. Dhawan followed. Behind them were Rameshwar Dayal, a local police subinspector, and Nathuram, Mrs. Gandhi's valet.

She walked briskly, as was her custom, toward the Akbar Road office. As she neared a hedge, she spotted Beant Singh, a Sikh policeman who had been part of her security guard for six years. She smiled at the twenty-eight-year-old Beant, a tall, bearded man. The prime minister had resisted pleas from aides to have him transferred in the wake of the assault on the Golden Temple. "I have nothing to fear from Sikhs," Mrs. Gandhi told them.

Beant moved up to Mrs. Gandhi, whipped out a pistol, pointed it at her, and fired three shots into her abdomen. Without a word, Mrs. Gandhi started to fall to the ground. There was a nonplussed look on her face. But before her body slumped, another Sikh guard, Satwant Singh, twenty-one years old, emerged from the hedge and opened up with a Thompson automatic carbine.

Mrs. Gandhi's body was nearly lifted from the gravel pathway by these powerful bullets; she was spun around by the velocity of the bullets, and then she crashed to the ground. In the space of twenty seconds, thirty-two bullets had been pumped into her small, frail body. By the time Indira Gandhi's body fell on the ground, she was quite possibly dead. It was now 9:17 A.M. The body lay on the ground for nearly a minute before anyone took action. Her bodyguards had dived to the ground, while some others who had accompanied the prime minister scurried for cover. Not long before her death, Indira's security adviser, Ramji Nath Kao, had urged that he be allowed to landscape the prime minister's garden in such a way as to guard against explosives or bombs tossed in from the outside. [*]

[*] Kao, Rajiv Gandhi, and Dr. P. C. Alexander were among the "hawks" around Indira Gandhi who had urged her to take firm action against the Sikh militants—in-

But Indira had laughed the suggestion away, saying: "When they come to kill me, nothing would help. Those supposed to save me will be the first to run away."[*]

Rameshwar Dayal had been shot in the thigh from the round fired by Satwant Singh. When Dhawan and the others rose, they saw Beant and Satwant standing with their hands raised; they had dropped their weapons.

"We have done what we set out to do," Beant Singh said, in Hindi. "Now you can do whatever you want to do."

But no one attempted to grab the assailants. Mrs. Gandhi's aides looked at her body and started shouting orders to one another. At this point, Sonia Gandhi ran out of the house barefoot and still in her dressing gown, her brown hair still wet from a shampoo.

"Get a car!" Sonia shouted. "Get a car!"

"Madam, there is an ambulance here," someone responded. A specially equipped ambulance was parked near the Safdarjung Road exit; the vehicle was kept there on a twenty-four-hour standby for emergencies.

But on this morning, with Mrs. Gandhi bleeding profusely and bits of her bones and flesh spattered on the ground, no one could find the ambulance driver. Someone said he had gone off to get some tea; someone else said the driver hadn't reported for work at all; there were no keys in the ignition switch.

Sonia Gandhi and Rajendra Kumar Dhawan then lifted Mrs. Gandhi's body, with the assistance of Narayan Singh, Nathuram, and Dinesh Bhatt, a security official, and carried her toward an Indian-made Ambassador car that was parked nearby. She was placed on the back seat, with Sonia cradling her head while crouched on the floor. Dhawan, Bhatt, a physician named Dr. K. P. Mathur, and an aide named M. L. Fotedar also got in. Dhawan ordered the driver to rush to the All-India Institute of Medical Sciences. The Institute was a good twenty minutes away by car in moderate traffic; there were other medical facilities closer to the prime minister's house, such as the Ram Manohar Lohia Hospital on Baba Khark Marg.[†] But the Institute, known locally as AIIMS, kept a special supply of Mrs. Gandhi's Type O–group Rh negative blood; her complete medical records were also maintained there.

The Ambassador darted toward AIIMS, but the traffic this morning

cluding the army's attack on the Golden Temple, according to sources close to Mrs. Gandhi. Her own instincts were more cautious.
[*]Anecdote recounted by Inder Malhotra in his biography, *Indira Gandhi* (London: Hodder & Stoughton, 1989), p. 19.
[†]This hospital was named after a prominent socialist leader who, during Indira's

was heavier than usual, and it was ten o'clock before the vehicle finally reached the hospital, some four kilometers away from the prime minister's house. Dr. Mathur tried to administer artificial respiration, but he could already see that there were few signs of life in Mrs. Gandhi.

It had not occurred to anyone to telephone AIIMS to warn hospital authorities that Mrs. Gandhi was being brought there. Various security guards scurried about the area where Beant Singh and Satwant Singh still stood, their weapons on the ground. Then someone suggested that the two men be arrested. They were led off to a nearby guardhouse by members of the elite Indo-Tibetan Border Police. Within twenty minutes, shots were heard inside the guardhouse. Beant and Satwant both had been shot by their guards; Beant died instantly, while Satwant suffered serious injuries to his spine and kidneys. It was later explained by the government that the two Sikhs had tried to wrest away their guards' weapons in an effort to escape. But at least three officials present at the scene have testified that the Indo-Tibetan guards abused the Sikhs verbally and then shot them.*

Peter Ustinov, meanwhile, had been waiting with his television crew barely seventy yards away from where the shooting occurred. He later recalled:

> We were ready with the mike and the camera. A secretary had gone to fetch her, and then it happened. I heard three single shots. We looked alarmed but the people in the office said it must be firecrackers. Then there was a burst of automatic fire as if the attackers were making sure of it. I didn't think she had a chance in hell. We saw soldiers running. They kept us there for five hours. It became like a prison.†

When the prime minister's car arrived at the emergency entrance of the Institute, there was no reception committee. In fact, it took the sentries more than three minutes to open the gates leading up to the emergency section, for the guards had not been informed that a VIP was in critical condition.

---

early days as a government minister and prime minister, had mocked her parliamentary skills.

* It is unlikely that Satwant Singh and Beant Singh could have escaped the premises, even if they had tried vigorously. Moreover, both assassins were said to be in shock following their shooting of Mrs. Gandhi.

† Peter Ustinov's comments in *The Guardian* (London), November 1, 1984.

Once at the emergency unit, Dhawan and Fotedar jumped out to alert medical personnel that Mrs. Gandhi lay gravely wounded outside. But no stretcher could be found. Someone got hold of a hospital gurney. As the body was placed on the gurney, the young intern in charge of the emergency room became hysterical.

"Madam! Madam!" he started shrieking, nearly collapsing over Mrs. Gandhi's crumpled, blood-covered body.

Another physician who was present in the room said to himself: "This cannot be Indira Gandhi. She looks like a child wrapped in a washerwoman's sheet. Is this really the prime minister of India?"

This doctor rushed to a house phone and dialed the number of the Institute's senior cardiologist. Within five minutes, a dozen of the Institute's top physicians gathered in the emergency room, including Dr. J. S. Guleria, a veteran professor of medicine, and Dr. S. Balaram, the senior cardio-thoracic surgeon on duty that morning. They tried to massage Mrs. Gandhi's heart. An electrocardiogram showed faint traces of a heartbeat.

"Her pupils were dilated—so we knew that her brain was already affected," one physician recalled later. "Even if we had clinically revived her, there already was permanent brain damage."

There was no pulse. One medical aide inserted an endotracheal tube—a rubber tube that is pushed down the mouth and windpipe—to pump oxygen to Mrs. Gandhi's lungs, mainly to keep the brain alive. Two intravenous lines were set up for blood transfusion. At this point, the decision was made to take Mrs. Gandhi to the eighth-floor operating theater. There, in Operation Theater Number Two, surgeons labored mightily to remove bullets from her body. More than eighty pints of blood were pumped into her, or four or five times the body's normal blood content.

The surgeons linked Mrs. Gandhi's body to a heart-lung machine, which assumed the function of pumping and purifying her blood. The surgeons wanted to ensure that her body's metabolism rate slowed down and that her blood pressure dropped—this was done through the heart-lung machine, which cooled the blood from the normal 37 degrees Centigrade to 31 degrees. Present in Operation Theater Number Two were the leading physicians and surgeons attached to the Institute, which has long been the country's showcase medical teaching and research facility. In addition to Dr. Guleria and Dr. Balaram, there were cardio-thoracic surgeons P. Venugopal and A. Sampat Kumar; and general surgeons J. Shukla, and M. M. Kapoor. The anesthetist was G. R. Gode. *

* The use of initials by Indians in their names can be sometimes confusing to

50

They found that the bullets Beant Singh and Satwant Singh pumped into Mrs. Gandhi had ruptured the right lobe of her liver. There were at least twelve perforations in the large intestine and there was extensive damage to the small intestine. The heart was intact, but one lung was shot through. Blood vessels, arteries, and veins had burst. Bones and vertebrae were shattered. The spinal cord was severed.

Nothing that the surgeons could do would bring Indira Gandhi back to life. "She was already far, far gone by the time she was brought to the Institute," one surgeon said later. "In fact, Mrs. Gandhi probably was dead by the time she hit the ground in her garden at Safdarjung Road."

At two-thirty that afternoon, five hours after she was shot by Beant Singh and Satwant Singh, Indira Gandhi was officially declared dead. An extraordinary era that spanned much of modern India's history had ended on a cold October day in 1984.

---

outsiders. Indians hailing from the South, in particular, use first initials to denote their region or their particular community. Thus, the last name is actually often their first name. In some instances, Indians use only one name—i.e., a single name that incorporates both the family name, which Indians call "surname," and the Christian first name.

2

The News

On the morning of Wednesday, October 31, 1984, Vichitra Sharma was preparing to leave her home in New Delhi's Maharani Bagh for her office in Connaught Place, the capital's bustling downtown section.

Sharma, then thirty years old, lived with her parents in one of Delhi's wealthy residential neighborhoods; it is still uncommon for single women to live away from home, even in sophisticated urban India, and besides, Delhi at the moment was experiencing a serious housing shortage.

Vichitra Sharma was what her colleagues called a "rising star." Her star shone at *The Hindustan Times*, one of Delhi's leading English-language dailies. At *The Hindustan Times*, Sharma's star was a fiery one because she often challenged governmental policy at a newspaper widely known for its general allegiance to the ruling Congress Party. *

She was a small woman, with large expressive eyes. Her reporting assignments had taken Sharma all over India, but in the last year or so she had been focusing especially on labor and political issues in Delhi. She had recently written an acclaimed series of articles on medical politics at the prestigious All-India Institute of Medical Sciences. For that series, she was to win several awards.

* Vichitra Sharma now works for the Observer Group of Newspapers in New Delhi. Her journalism has continued to be acclaimed by Indian audiences. Not long after the assassination of Indira Gandhi, Vichitra Sharma took a leave of absence from journalism and enrolled at Columbia University's School of International Affairs in New York. She spent nearly three years in the United States, and received a master's degree.

At ten-thirty on this morning, Sharma was just about to step out of her parents' two-story house when the telephone rang. The caller was A. R. Wig, Sharma's immediate superior and the newspaper's chief reporter.* Wig asked Sharma to go immediately to the All-India Institute.

"Indira Gandhi's been hurt," he said. "We think she was taken to the Institute. You know a lot of people there. Why don't you try and get in there and see what you can find out?"

Sharma's first reaction to Wig's call was that perhaps the prime minister had been injured at some political rally. She was scheduled to cover one of Mrs. Gandhi's forthcoming campaign swings through the neighboring state of Uttar Pradesh, and a colleague at *The Hindustan Times* had cautioned her to expect stone-throwing incidents in that politically volatile province where Mrs. Gandhi was not universally popular.

Sharma hailed a taxi outside her house. The thirteen-kilometer ride to the Institute took nearly thirty minutes. There were no signs of any unusual activity at the hospital's gate, no crowds had gathered. Sharma wandered for a few minutes around the Institute's teaching college, hoping to spot a familiar face.

She saw a young physician who had been a source for her recent articles on the Institute. He told her that he had just come out of the emergency room assisting the surgeons who were trying to revive the mortally wounded prime minister.

"Look, the whole eighth-floor area has been sealed off by security guards," the physician, Dr. Ali Rizvi, told Sharma. "If you want to go anywhere near the area where Mrs. Gandhi is, then go as a blood donor."

"She's not dead, then," Sharma said.

"She's in very bad shape," Dr. Rizvi said.

Vichitra Sharma slipped into the Institute's main building. She was stopped by a security guard on the main floor.

"No one allowed," the guard said.

"But I'm going to give blood," Sharma said.

"Then you may enter," the guard said. "The blood bank is up ahead."

Sharma knew enough about the building's layout so that she could circumvent the blood bank and head toward the stairwell that would take her to the eighth floor.

Over the next ten hours, this stairwell, which surprisingly was unmanned by security guards, would be Sharma's repeated route back and forth from the eighth-floor operation theater to the main floor, where

---

* Titles in Indian journalism don't necessarily reflect power or responsibilities. At most newspapers, for example, the "chief reporter" is usually the person who gives out assignments.

Delhi's VIPs gathered. These VIPs generally got access wherever they wished, including to intensive-care units of hospitals not normally open to the public.

As Sharma climbed the stairs, she ran into a woman who was rushing down. The woman was in tears.

"She's gone, she's gone!" the woman cried.

"How could it be?" Sharma said.

"I saw it upstairs. The doctors have given up."

Once upstairs, Sharma found the eighth-floor corridor outside Operation Theater Number Two filled with guards and various hospital personnel.

No one tried to stop her. She surreptitiously took notes. Now there was a crescendo of murmurs. Delhi's VIPs had started arriving. Sharma recognized a woman named Shehnaz Hussain, Mrs. Gandhi's personal beautician. Miss Hussain wore a long, flowing yellow evening dress. Sharma also recognized several members of Parliament belonging to Mrs. Gandhi's Congress Party. Delhi socialites started showing up; some junior cabinet ministers followed.

Sharma decided to take in the scene downstairs on the main floor. There she found that many senior cabinet ministers were ensconced in a conference room. Some of them were weeping, most seemed numb. Outside the conference room someone tapped Sharma's shoulder.

"Excuse me, but can you do me a favor?" a man asked. "My boss, the health minister Shri Shankaranand, * is in that room. Can you tell him that his driver is waiting outside and wants to know if the boss will come home for lunch?"

"Why don't you go in yourself?" Sharma said.

"I cannot do that. I am only a lowly employee."

Sharma delivered the message, but Shankaranand seemed too distraught to understand what she was saying. It struck Sharma that these cabinet ministers had slid into a kind of collective coma.

"What kind of men were these?" Sharma would say later. "I realized then that she had made puppets out of every one of them—and now she was no longer around to pull the strings. In her years of power, she had taken away the manhood from every one of these men—so now they were like zombies, not knowing what to do, no initiative coming from them. It occurred to me how propitious a time it was for some determined military man to seize power at this very moment."

Upstairs, the surgeons kept pumping blood into Mrs. Gandhi's body.

---

* "Shri" stands for "Mr." It is quite common for subordinates to use the Hindi honorific, even when they are speaking in English.

They kept furiously trying to remove the bullets, trying to revive her—knowing full well that she was long dead. But no one had ordered them to desist—so they kept up their efforts.

At four o'clock in the afternoon, Rajiv Gandhi, Mrs. Gandhi's son and heir-apparent, arrived at the All-India Institute of Medical Sciences.

At the time that Mrs. Gandhi was brought into the eighth-floor operation theater, her forty-year-old son, Rajiv, had been almost a thousand miles away in Contai, not far from Calcutta in the state of West Bengal. As general secretary of the All-India Congress Committee, Rajiv had traveled to the Communist-led state to develop a better grass-roots organization for his party.* These travels were part of his political education, an education that had been urged by his mother, the prime minister.

It was an hour or so later, on his way to yet another political rally, that Gandhi's motorcade was stopped by a police Jeep at a place called Heria. It was there that a police inspector told him about the assassination attempt. A number of Congress Party workers around him started to weep, but Rajiv Gandhi kept his poise and even comforted some of them. A police officer told him that an Indian Air Force helicopter was waiting at a place called Kolaghat to transport Gandhi to Calcutta, or some nearby military air base, where an Indian Airlines jet would speed him back to New Delhi. But when Gandhi's motorcade reached Kolaghat, there was no helicopter there. Apparently it had already been despatched to Mahisadal, which would have been the next destination on Gandhi's schedule that morning. A policeman rang Mahisadal urging that the helicopter be sent back to Kolaghat.

While he waited, clad in a khadi homespun flowing white shirt called the kurta, and in loose pajama trousers, with his trademark Kashmir woolen shawl draped around his shoulders, Rajiv Gandhi appeared to the men and women around him a picture of cool composure. He fiddled with the dials of his portable Sony transistor radio and finally raised the BBC. The British Broadcasting Corporation's overseas service was already saying that Indira Gandhi was dead. But Rajiv Gandhi had also tuned in alternately to All-India Radio, the government network, which was playing Hindi film music.

"It's all very confusing," Gandhi said, to no one in particular.

Months later, in a conversation with journalist M. J. Akbar,† Rajiv

---

* West Bengal was one of two Indian states where Communist governments were elected, the other being the southern state of Kerala.

† M. J. Akbar subsequently became very close to Rajiv Gandhi. In the 1989 election, he won a parliamentary seat from Bihar State on a Congress Party ticket. He then

Gandhi noted with some concern that there had been reports that he'd broken down when he heard about the shooting.

"Let me say that some newspapers or magazines reported that when I heard the news I went to the loo and had a bawl," Gandhi told Akbar. "That's all rubbish. I was fairly upset but that is not the way I give expression to my emotions."

On this particular trip to West Bengal, Rajiv Gandhi had been accompanied by several Congress Party heavyweights, including Finance Minister Pranab Mukherjee and Railways Minister A. B. A. Ghani Khan Chowdhary. Both officials were natives of West Bengal. Each saw himself as a sort of political tutor for the inexperienced Rajiv. Mukherjee and Chowdhary hopped aboard the helicopter that ferried Rajiv to Calcutta's Dum Dum Airport. Since no one knew the precise situation in New Delhi, not much was said during the short flight. At the Calcutta airport, the group was joined by other Congress Party luminaries who had also been in West Bengal that week for politicking: Balram Jakhar, the Speaker of the Lok Sabha, or lower house of Parliament; his secretary, S. Bali; Uma Shankar Dikshit, the governor of West Bengal; and Dikshit's daughter-in-law, Sheila Dikshit. *

Minutes after the Indian Airlines Boeing 737 took off from Calcutta, Rajiv Gandhi strode into the cockpit. Jakhar dispatched his secretary, Bali, to the cockpit to find out whether Rajiv intended to fly the plane himself.

"I am not here for flying," Rajiv said to Bali. "I just want to be close to the radio and be in touch with Delhi."

About forty-five minutes later, at around 2:30 P.M., Rajiv emerged from the cockpit. His face was ashen.

"She is no more," he said.

There was an audible gasp from Rajiv's group. Someone started sobbing loudly. Then there was silence.

Balram Jakhar gently put his arms around Rajiv and took him toward the rear of the aircraft. They sat down.

"You are the man of destiny," Jakhar said to Rajiv. "You be the prime minister now."

---

became Mr. Gandhi's spokesman, and quickly established a reputation for rapier-like wit. Mr. Akbar continues to write opinion columns, magazine articles, and books. He lost his reelection bid in the 1991 election.
* The governor of a state is appointed by the president of India, on the recommendation of the prime minister. This job is really a sinecure, and most governors spend their time at opulent state dinners or at ribbon-cutting ceremonies. The chief executive in Indian states is the chief minister, who is usually the leader of the majority party in the state assembly.

"How can I become PM? There could be an acting PM. The constitutional provisions have to be followed," Rajiv replied.

Governor Dikshit, a veteran Congress Party hand, quickly suggested that the constitution should be consulted.* As it turned out, Sheila Dikshit had a copy with her. The book was carefully scrutinized, and it was agreed that the president of India—technically the head of state —had the authority to nominate anybody he wanted to become prime minister. There was a general feeling that the current president, Zail Singh—who had been given the job by Indira Gandhi—was hardly likely to oppose the nomination of Rajiv Gandhi.

At this point, Finance Minister Pranab Mukherjee broke in. He was the most senior member of Indira Gandhi's cabinet, a man widely regarded as a future prime minister and certainly not one to drive such notions out of others' minds.

"It is not the constitution which makes the prime minister," Mukherjee said to Rajiv Gandhi. "I am number two in the cabinet. I can take over as acting prime minister. We will then see what can be done after the state mourning is over." Mukherjee was to later deny that he ever suggested that he become caretaker prime minister; indeed, he insisted that it was he who repeatedly advised Rajiv to take over as prime minister immediately.

When Rajiv Gandhi landed at Delhi, he was met by several friends and associates, including Amitabh Bachchan. Bachchan was one of India's best-known movie stars, and was also a childhood friend of Rajiv's.† Bachchan had been seriously ill some months before and had only recently recovered.

The two men embraced.

"First of all he wanted to know whether his wife and children were all right," Amitabh Bachchan later recalled. "Then he turned to me and asked me about my illness.

" 'How are you?' he asked. 'When I was in Calcutta, I met someone who said he had a cure for your illness. I want you to meet him. I will tell you about him.'

"It is a marvelous thing that he was able to think about the person

---

* Uma Shankar Dikshit was an early supporter of Indira Gandhi when she became prime minister in January 1966. He was part of her "kitchen cabinet," an informal group of close advisers.
† Amitabh Bachchan was later to be accused by Opposition leaders of profiting by his association with Rajiv Gandhi, charges that were not substantiated. Bachchan won a parliamentary seat from Uttar Pradesh State in the 1989 election, but later resigned from the Lok Sabha during the controversy.

next to him, about his friend, in spite of everything that had happened to him. His spirit was unbowed, and he could still think about his friend."

Amitabh Bachchan got into a car with Rajiv Gandhi, as did Arun Nehru, a second cousin of Gandhi's.* Nehru, a former top executive with the paint-manufacturing company of Jensen and Nicolson, had been inducted into politics by Indira Gandhi. Others who had accompanied Rajiv on the flight from Calcutta were herded into various cars. The caravan sped toward the hospital where Indira lay dead.

After a few miles, the car carrying Rajiv suddenly screeched to a halt. Arun Nehru, a giant of a man, squeezed out of the car, walked toward one of the rear cars, and asked for Balram Jakhar. Nehru invited Jakhar to join him in Rajiv's car, and the motorcade once again took off.

"There is no question of having an acting prime minister," Arun Nehru said, clearly alluding to Pranab Mukherjee's comments during the flight from Calcutta to Delhi. Presumably, it was Rajiv Gandhi who had told his cousin about Mukherjee's view.

Years later, after the cousins had gone their separate ways following an acrimonious dispute, Arun Nehru would tell a reporter from *Onlooker*, a Bombay-based journal: "Rajiv wanted the job rather badly. . . . The fact is, Rajiv was dying for the job. Rajiv told me that he did not want an interim prime minister, but instead he himself wanted to be sworn in as PM straightaway."

There was confusion at the All-India Institute of Medical Sciences when Rajiv Gandhi eventually arrived from Delhi's Palam Airport. Government officials were fluttering about like pigeons, arguing among themselves whether the government-owned radio and television networks should announce the prime minister's death. There were angry comments about Sikhs in general, and about Mrs. Gandhi's Sikh assailants in particular. There was some discussion also about whether Indira Gandhi's body should remain at the hospital or be taken back to One Safdarjung Road.

Rajiv Gandhi stayed inside Operation Theater Two until about six o'clock in the evening. By now the corridor outside was thick with Congress Party workers, cabinet ministers and their families, and assorted hangers-on.

Vichitra Sharma stood next to a group of wealthy Delhi socialites,

---

* Arun Nehru and Rajiv Gandhi parted company some years later, and Nehru teamed up with Gandhi's bitter opponent V. P. Singh.

men and women who savored proximity to the politically powerful, who, in turn, granted them favors which thickened their treasuries.

"I must go inside to show my face to Rajivji," one of these socialites said. "He must know we took the trouble to come here at a time like this." Sharma thought: In India it is so important to be seen doing the right thing in front of the powers-that-be.

When Rajiv Gandhi left, the corridor was quickly emptied of people. A physician who knew Sharma told her that Gandhi had said he would return at 7:30 P.M. to collect his mother's body.

By 9:30 P.M., he had not come back.

Sharma went into the operation theater to look at the body. Indira Gandhi lay there, alone and dead and unattended, on a cold steel table. No family member was present, just some curious medical orderlies who occasionally slipped into the room.

"I was in tears," Sharma said later. "Here was a woman who ruled India, who was so powerful until that very morning. And now she lay there cold and lifeless. And no one was there to pay her the courtesy of guarding her body. It was pathetic.

"I felt numb. Before me lay a woman who once was so majestic. Now she was a mere body, crusted with blood and surrounded by ugly tubes and bottles and equipment. Right before my eyes I saw that an era had ended, that something had gone from our lives for all time."

The prime minister was dead, and the minions who fawned over her while she was alive were already applying their attention to her son, Rajiv Gandhi, who would succeed her.

At 9:40 A.M. on Wednesday, October 31, 1984, Murli Deora was saying farewell at Bombay's cavernous Victoria Terminus to nearly a thousand elderly citizens who were about to board a train for the northern city of Allahabad. They were all "freedom fighters," men and women who had struggled alongside Mahatma Gandhi and Jawaharlal Nehru and Indira Gandhi against India's British colonial rulers.

On this morning, they were about to travel to Mrs. Gandhi's home-town of Allahabad to observe the fiftieth anniversary of the founding of their particular freedom fighters' unit. In his capacity as president of Bombay's Congress Party organization, Deora had arranged the financing of the trip.

Deora was a short, slim man with a ready smile and quick wit. He was a self-made businessman who parlayed his high school savings into a personal fortune that was said to run into the millions. He had served as Bombay's mayor, a ceremonial position with no executive power but one that fetched a great deal of media exposure for whoever occupied the mayoral chair for the standard one-year term. Married to a former interior decorator named Hema Phansalkar—who bore him two sons—Murli Deora was seen at every event that mattered in Bombay, especially those events that attracted the city's political and commercial elite, whose darling he had become, and from whom he raised money to finance election campaigns not only in Bombay but elsewhere in India for the ruling Congress Party. *

His popularity with this elite, Deora often told visitors with a twinkle in his eyes, was largely because of his own personality and charm. Not entirely so. Bombay's high and mighty were fully aware of Deora's powerful connections in New Delhi. He was very close to Indira Gandhi; and he had taken her son, Rajiv Gandhi, to participate in management seminars in Western Europe, where Deora had business associates. Deora maintained an extensive national and international network of contacts, which benefited the Congress Party as well. He stayed in touch with key people in this network through regular telephone calls, personal letters, and, of course, greeting cards during festive seasons. Moreover, Deora often took time out to visit constituents in hospitals, and he made it a practice never to miss a funeral in his election district. As a result, this whirling dervish of political energy and commitment frequently put in eighteen- or twenty-hour days. That Deora had survived as a Gandhi friend was the subject of much discussion in Bombay society. Indira Gandhi had a way of exiling from her inner circle those who capitalized excessively on their friendship with her. And there was no shortage of such people. A former chief minister of Maharashtra State, A. R. Antulay, even collected millions of rupees for a dubious social welfare society, telling his industrialist donors that his friend, Mrs. Gandhi, had blessed his endeavor. Antulay was eventually cut adrift by the prime minister. † But Deora was a shrewd political operative who always managed to stay on the right side of most issues—and of his political patrons, the Gandhis. On this morning, Deora mingled with the "freedom fighters," and addressed the group briefly in Hindi.

"You are going to a historic place to observe a historic anniversary," Deora said. "You are going to the very home of Nehru and our beloved leader, Indiraji."

The group applauded vigorously. Deora wished them well on their

---

* The Bombay wing of the Congress Party has long been the source for much of the national organization's funds. That is because Bombay is India's commercial capital, and home to many of its wealthy industrialists.

† Antulay later wriggled back into favor with Rajiv Gandhi.

journey and left for his business office in Khetan Bhavan, a blue-façaded building located in Bombay's commercial district of Churchgate.*

He ordered a cup of tea, then settled back in his high-backed vinyl chair to scrutinize the morning's mail. Behind his chair was a large montage showing a sylvan setting of green woods and sun rays streaking through foliage. The office had a yellow sofa and armchairs to match, and little else. A friend had once suggested that Deora install a bookcase, but the Congress Party boss had replied, "What for? Books are not part of my personality."

At 10:15 A.M., one of the four telephones next to Deora's desk rang. It was Girilal Jain, the Bombay-based editor-in-chief of *The Times of India* chain.†

"I've just learned that the prime minister was shot in her home," Jain said. "She's not dead, as far as I know. I thought I should inform you."

Deora leaped out of his chair.

"Thank you for telling me," he said, replacing the receiver in the cradle.

As Deora recalled later, his first reaction was of total disbelief. He thought of telephoning a local physician friend, Shantilal Mehta. The physician had long ago operated on both Nehru and on Indira, and was still occasionally consulted by the prime minister.

Deora reached Dr. Mehta at Bombay's Jaslok Hospital and gave him the news.

"You are familiar with Indiraji's health," Deora said to Mehta. "Perhaps you can be of assistance to the doctors in Delhi."

The two men decided they would fly to Delhi at once. Deora told Mehta that he'd collect him at the hospital in thirty minutes and that meanwhile he would book them both on whichever flight was available.

As it turned out, while Deora was on the phone with Dr. Mehta, someone called Deora's office on behalf of two key Gandhi aides, Dr. P. C. Alexander, her principal private secretary, and Dr. Krishnaswamy Raosaheb, the cabinet secretary. These two men were in Bombay that morning, and now a special Indian Airlines plane was being readied to transport them to Delhi. The caller urged that if Deora wanted to fly to Delhi, he should be at Bombay's Santa Cruz Airport no later than eleven o'clock that morning.

Deora informed his wife, Hema, that he was on his way to Delhi. She

---

*Many neighborhoods in Indian cities still retain names bestowed on them during the British Raj.

†Girilal Jain has since retired from the editorship of *The Times of India*, but continues to write editorial-page columns.

had herself just heard the news of the shooting from a family friend, Harry Cahill, who was the U.S. consul general in Bombay, and she had been trying unsuccessfully to reach Deora by phone.*

Deora collected a small overnight suitcase that was kept fully packed with clothes and accessories in his office closet, then drove off to Jaslok Hospital, where Dr. Mehta was waiting for him with his own overnight attaché case. Deora's driver sped to the airport. But by the time they reached Santa Cruz, which is located in the northern suburbs of Bombay, some thirty kilometers from Deora's South Bombay office, it was almost eleven-twenty. The Boeing 737 jetliner chartered by Dr. Alexander and his colleague had already taken off. No regular flight from Santa Cruz to Delhi was scheduled until 5:00 P.M.

Deora found out, however, that there was a Kuwait-bound flight out of nearby Sahar Airport—which is actually the international wing of Santa Cruz—that was scheduled to stop in Delhi. That Air India flight would leave at 1:30 P.M. So Deora and Dr. Mehta rushed to Sahar. There they found an assembly of other local dignitaries who had already booked themselves on the flight to Delhi. Among those gathered at the check-in counter were Vasantdada Patil, the chief minister of Maharashtra State (of which Bombay is the capital), and Margaret Alva and Saroj Kharparde, both members of parliament.

"Somebody had a transistor radio, but All-India Radio was still giving no news about the shooting," Deora recalled later. "They were still playing Hindi film songs."

The men and women gathered at the airport exchanged views about the shooting. There was general agreement that the assassination attempt was part of a conspiracy by the Sikhs.

"Among us, there was gloom, sadness—and growing anger that something like this had been allowed to happen," Deora said later.

Everybody aboard the Air India flight was tense during the ninety-minute ride to Delhi. Deora walked up to the cockpit several times to request the pilot to radio for additional news concerning Mrs. Gandhi. Virtually everyone on board refused the meal offered by Air India's stewardesses.

"When we landed in Delhi, the atmosphere of gloom at the airport was so heavy that I just knew she had died," Deora recalled. "I just broke down and cried."

Dr. Shantilal Mehta, who was almost forty years older than Deora, put

---

* Phone connections in Bombay, as in most Indian cities and towns, are extremely unreliable. Although Murli Deora had several phone lines, his wife was unable to talk to him until he called her.

his arm around the younger man and consoled him. The two men were driven by Saroj Kharparde in her chauffeur-driven car to the All-India Institute of Medical Sciences. * It was her driver who had told them about Mrs. Gandhi being taken there. Deora saw that several foreign embassies, including the U.S. Embassy, had already lowered their flags to half-mast—but the flags at Indian government offices were still flying loftily.

Huge crowds had gathered in front of the Institute. Security guards were using lathis—the bamboo sticks favored by Indian policemen—and batons to keep people from entering the hospital's compound. But in India, dignitaries such as members of Parliament enjoy near-divine status, and so Mrs. Kharparde's car was allowed to enter the premises. It was 4:15 P.M. Deora, Dr. Mehta, and Mrs. Kharparde went up to the eighth-floor operation theater where surgeons had tried to revive Mrs. Gandhi. They were informed that the prime minister had been officially declared dead at 2:30 P.M. Deora was crying without control. He saw Rajiv Gandhi disappear into Operation Theater Two, where Mrs. Gandhi's body was kept, and then reappear to comfort some friends who waited outside in the corridor.

"But I just did not have the heart to go up to Rajiv," Deora recalled.

Deora composed himself and continued to linger in the area outside Operation Theater Two. At 5:15 P.M., there was some commotion. President Zail Singh, who had been in North Yemen on an official visit, had arrived directly from Delhi Airport. Rajiv Gandhi greeted him and escorted the bearded Sikh head of state into the room where Mrs. Gandhi's body lay. Deora spotted Karan Singh, the Hindu former Maharaja of Kashmir, and Pupul Jayakar, India's cultural czarina and probably Mrs. Gandhi's closest friend. He saw Rajiv Gandhi's close friends and aides, Arun Singh and Arun Nehru.

"Rajiv Gandhi was the most calm and collected person there," Deora recalled much later. "Everybody else was weeping or howling. He was comforting others."

As Deora waited, he thought about the last time he had seen Indira Gandhi alive. It was during her visit to Bombay on October 5. He had arranged a public rally for her, and then, before she took off for New Delhi from Santa Cruz Airport, he accompanied her to the home of her elderly uncle, Gunottam "Raja" Hutheesing. Hutheesing had married Nehru's sister, the late Krishna, and was grievously ill and confined to his home in Navroj Apartments on Altamount Road.

* All members of Parliament are given use of a free car, and also free housing in New Delhi. Other perks include free air tickets, and a generous staff allowance.

"He will be very happy to see you," Deora said to the prime minister. "With someone as old as he is, you never know what can happen, how long he will last."

"You're right," she said to Deora. "You never know what's going to happen to any of us. Let's go and see him." The prime minister hugged Hutheesing warmly. As she left, after a ten-minute visit, she said to him, "Get well soon!"

Was it a premonition of her own death that made her decide to squeeze in a visit to Raja Hutheesing? Deora pondered this as he waited outside the operation theater.

It was now well after six o'clock. Saroj Kharparde suggested to Deora that they go to her home so that he could rest for a while. Deora decided instead that he would stop off at the luxurious Taj Mahal Hotel on Mansingh Road, where a room had been booked for him by his Bombay office. He showered, napped briefly, then went to Maharashtra Sadan —the Delhi bureau of the Maharashtra State government—to meet Chief Minister Patil. At around 10:30 P.M., the two men drove to One Safdarjung Road to meet Rajiv Gandhi. They did not know that Rajiv had already been sworn in as the new prime minister of India.

"Rajiv was very composed," Deora recalled. "He was consoling every visitor. The torch had been passed to a new generation."

Gandhi told Chief Minister Patil that he should at once return to Bombay.

"I want every state chief executive to be at their station," the prime minister said. "If any trouble occurs around the country, I want you all to be back where you belong." The directive obviously applied to Deora as well, for he was head of the influential Bombay unit of Rajiv Gandhi's Congress Party.

As Patil and Deora left One Safdarjung Road at around 11:15 P.M., they ran into B. K. Nehru, an uncle of Gandhi's and a former ambassador to the United States.[*] Many years ago, One Safdarjung Road had been Nehru's private residence when he held a government post in Delhi; Nehru was now governor of the western state of Gujarat.

"Why did she reinstate those Sikh guards?" Deora recalls Nehru asking. Mrs. Gandhi had insisted that the two men who later killed her, Beant Singh and Satwant Singh, be brought back as her personal security guards

---

[*] The Nehrus are a big clan. B. K. Nehru was actually a distant cousin of Jawaharlal Nehru. Before serving as Indian ambassador to the United States, he enjoyed a distinguished career in the elite Indian Civil Service (ICS), which had been established by the British.

after they had been transferred in the wake of the Indian Army's assault on the Golden Temple.

That night, at the Taj Mahal Hotel, Murli Deora slept fitfully. He was, of course, pleased that his friend Rajiv had become prime minister, and not someone else. But Deora wondered what sort of chief executive Rajiv Gandhi would make. He worried that there would be a backlash against India's minority Sikhs. Would there be trouble in Bombay? And in Delhi?

Deora fell asleep not knowing that the massacre of Sikhs in India's capital city had already started.

At about the same time that Murli Deora fell into his troubled sleep, Swraj Paul was disembarking from Air India's Flight 104, which had brought him nonstop from London to New Delhi. The journey had taken ten hours, and Paul had sat through most of it in uncharacteristic silence. He was ordinarily an extrovert, an irrepressible man, given to loud laughter and chatter. At fifty-three, he had established himself as one of the wealthiest Indian immigrant entrepreneurs in Britain; he owned steel mills and foundries, and now was involved in electronics, real estate, and shipping.* But it was not because of his self-made millions that Paul had become well-known in both Britain and India. His fame—some would say notoriety—was more the consequence of his much-publicized friendship with Indira Gandhi and her family.

There were those who apportioned unsavory underpinnings to that friendship, whispering that Paul was the foreign-based manager of the Gandhi family's ill-gotten fortune.† But Swraj Paul would insist that he did nothing illegal on behalf of Indira Gandhi, and there was no evidence to prove him wrong. He often said that he simply demonstrated unswerving loyalty to the Nehru-Gandhi dynasty because he believed in its greatness. His explanations did not silence critics, some of whom wondered in print whether Paul's close ties with the Gandhis had resulted in any financial gains for him; some uncharitable critics said that Swraj Paul did nothing for anyone unless there was a heavy measure of personal gain in the transaction, a charge which Paul cheerfully refuted with ready references to his many benevolences.

* Swraj Paul was, and continues to be, chairman of a business group called Caparo Industries. In April 1991 his net worth was put by British newspapers at more than $300 million.
† These rumors persist. Rajiv Gandhi was accused by detractors of using the family

Indira Gandhi's relationship with Swraj Paul was mutually advantageous. Between 1977 and 1980, when she was out of office and a political pariah during the opposition Janata Party's years in power, it was Paul who invited her abroad and arranged many public appearances for the former prime minister. Those appearances helped sustain her confidence in her own appeal as a public figure; Mrs. Gandhi also used these occasions to keep abreast of international affairs. And the foreign contacts got her widespread media coverage, always a restorative for a politician's spirits, especially a politician who was then being vilified in her native land by politicians who did not have a fraction of her experience and pedigree. *

Swraj Paul did not abandon Indira Gandhi during the years of her political wilderness. Indeed, hardly a week went by without some sort of communication between them. Mrs. Gandhi had a habit of telephoning Paul when it was very early in the morning in London.† So when the phone rang in Swraj Paul's bedroom in his fourth-floor apartment on Portland Place at four-forty-five on the morning of October 31, 1984, he instinctively assumed that the caller was his friend and patron Indira Gandhi.

"Swraj, I have bad news to tell you—the prime minister has been shot," the caller said to a sleepy Paul.

Paul's first reaction was to assume that Prime Minister Margaret Thatcher of Britain had been shot. The caller was a friend named Ralph Buultjens, who was telephoning from New York. Buultjens was at least as close to Indira Gandhi as Paul was; Buultjens, in fact, was widely said to be her most influential foreign policy adviser, even though he was born a Sri Lankan. He made his living as a university professor, lecturer, and author in the United States. Buultjens had heard the news of the shooting through a telephone call from a friend in New Delhi around eleven-thirty in New York on Tuesday night.‡

Swraj Paul woke up his wife, Aruna, who had slept soundly through his brief conversation with Ralph Buultjens. Her response to the news was one of disbelief. She suggested that Paul at once telephone New

---

of his Italian-born wife to shelter illegal millions in Europe and elsewhere. No one has come up with a shred of evidence to support these accusations.

* The Janata Party, which was in power between 1977 and 1979, tried hard to indict Mrs. Gandhi on charges of misuse of power and corruption. But the charges did not stick. Moreover, the Janata government, headed by a irascible man named Morarji Desai, got caught up in internal dissension. Desai was replaced as prime minister by Charan Singh, and not long after that, the government collapsed.

† Indian Standard Time is five and a half hours ahead of Greenwich Mean Time.

‡ Eastern Standard Time is ten and a half hours behind Indian Standard Time.

Delhi. Paul then direct-dialed a private number at the prime minister's residence. The phone was picked up by Mrs. Gandhi's information adviser, H. Y. Sharada Prasad.

"Is it true?" Swraj Paul asked.

"Yes, I'm afraid," Prasad said, glumly. "The news is very, very bad."

Paul recalls that he took this to mean that Mrs. Gandhi was dead, although even as Prasad spoke with him the prime minister was being attended to by physicians at the All-India Institute; there were faint flutters of a heartbeat in her at that point.

Paul started to cry. So did Aruna. They both decided to catch the next available flight to New Delhi. Later that morning, Aruna was still so overcome with emotion that she could not make the journey to New Delhi.

Air India's Flight 104 left London's Heathrow Airport at nine-thirty-five that morning. As Swraj Paul lowered his six-foot frame into his first-class seat, he wondered if Rajiv Gandhi had been selected by the ruling Congress Party to succeed his mother. A special car from the prime minister's house awaited Paul at Delhi's international airport. Paul went straight from the airport to One Safdarjung Road. He saw Rajiv Gandhi and embraced him. Not a word was exchanged between the two men. Paul was led by a Gandhi aide to the dining room, where Mrs. Gandhi's body now lay, smothered in flowers. Incense wafted from joss sticks. Paul thought about the last time he had met with Indira Gandhi. That meeting was in August, when he'd flown in from London to present Mrs. Gandhi with a copy of his pictorial biography of her.[*]

"I hope you like the book," Swraj Paul said to Mrs. Gandhi.

"I'm sure I will," she had replied, with a soft smile, turning the pages of the lavishly illustrated volume. "I appreciate what you have done here."

The conversation had taken place in the same dining room where Indira Gandhi now lay lifeless.

On that Wednesday morning, Ralph Buultjens, like Swraj Paul, spent many hours remembering Mrs. Gandhi. Swraj Paul's friendship with Mrs. Gandhi was of relatively recent vintage: In 1969, she had helped with arrangements to transport Paul's young daughter, Ambika, to London for treatment of leukemia.[†] But Buultjens had known the Nehru family for

---

[*] *Indira Gandhi* (London: Heron Press, 1984).
[†] Ambika Paul subsequently died. Swraj Paul has named his house in London after her.

nearly thirty years, ever since traveling to New Delhi after his education in Colombo to obtain an interview with Mrs. Gandhi's father, Prime Minister Jawaharlal Nehru. So close did Buultjens and Mrs. Gandhi become that they would speak on the phone several times a week: Buultjens has voluminous notes of their conversations.

They would meet up in New Delhi, which Buultjens visited frequently, or during one of Mrs. Gandhi's periodic travels abroad. They discussed not only foreign affairs and politics but also history, literature, poetry, and the theater. Buultjens would arrange for Mrs. Gandhi private meetings with Western intellectuals, whose company she relished. Buultjens, a tall, striking man with a high forehead, thick graying hair, and a tendency toward heaviness, was often conspicuously near Mrs. Gandhi whenever she made public appearances in Britain and the United States. Unlike others who enjoyed far less access to her, he never flaunted his relationship with Indira Gandhi. In fact, even with close friends Buultjens seemed reticent about discussing his dealings with the Nehrus and the Gandhis. Buultjens, of course, did not need to exploit his access to the prime minister because he was never dependent on this privilege for his livelihood. He taught political economy and comparative religions at New York University, and at the New School for Social Research in New York, and was also a visiting professor at many institutions around the world. The forty-six-year-old Sri Lankan–born scholar was regarded by his peers as one of the most brilliant political scientists of his generation. His views on world affairs were frequently sought by business and social leaders.

Buultjens was also often invited by international figures to offer his counsel and analyses on global topics. His writings appeared regularly in the opinion pages of such major publications as *The New York Times*. And Buultjens had also authored nearly a dozen books on international affairs.* When Buultjens was first informed about the Gandhi shooting, he could not believe the news and thought it was a very bad joke. But then a producer from ABC telephoned him, asking that Buultjens appear on a television news show on Wednesday morning. Shortly thereafter, a producer from NBC called, and after that someone from CBS. On Wednesday, Buultjens, who was already known to television and radio producers as an authority on the Indian subcontinent, would be one of the most sought-after sources for the American media. In between the media queries, Buultjens—still wearing night clothes—continuously telephoned friends in India to get the latest news concerning Mrs. Gan-

* Please see bibliography.

dhi. His phone bill for the night of October 30–31 would eventually amount to nearly nine hundred dollars.

"I kept wondering what was going to happen to the whole region now," Buultjens said later. "I was always telling Mrs. Gandhi during our phone conversations to be careful."

He recalled being in her Delhi office on June 1, when the prime minister was giving her generals the go-ahead for Operation Bluestar—the army assault on the Golden Temple in Amritsar. Mrs. Gandhi had said to Buultjens, "You know, this is the most difficult decision of my political career. This is war on your own people."

A couple of months later, Buultjens had accompanied Mrs. Gandhi to Delhi's Red Fort, from whose ramparts she delivered her annual Independence Day speech on August 15. He noticed that the sixty-six-year-old prime minister became breathless as she climbed the steep stairs to the rostrum, and the longtime tick in her right eyelid had become more pronounced.

"It must be very tiring to go up all those steps," Buultjens said to Mrs. Gandhi.

"I may never have to do it again," she replied cryptically.

And only two days before the assassination, Buultjens had spoken with Mrs. Gandhi on the telephone about the continuing controversy concerning the army action in Amritsar. Although Sikhs generally had not supported the terrorists—who agitated for a separate Sikh state which they wanted to call Khalistan—there was almost universal condemnation in the Sikh community of Operation Bluestar.

"We're all besieged," Mrs. Gandhi said to Buultjens. "But we will pull through this one."

A few weeks before that conversation, Buultjens had telephoned the prime minister to relay the news that he had been selected as a recipient of the prestigious Toynbee Prize, given annually to an outstanding social scientist. Buultjens requested that Mrs. Gandhi formally hand out the award. *

"I would be delighted," Mrs. Gandhi said to Professor Buultjens. Then she mysteriously added, "But I may not be around to give it to you." In fact, that proved to be the case.

The evening of the assassination, Ralph Buultjens boarded an Air India flight in New York for New Delhi. As the Boeing 747 jetliner took off, it struck Buultjens how Orwellian a year 1984 had turned out for

---

* A similar request had already been made by the Paris-based Toynbee Committee to Mrs. Gandhi's office.

India: There were communal problems in Assam; there were growing tensions in the Punjab; there was the army assault on the Golden Temple; there were assorted political crises in Kashmir and Andhra Pradesh. And now there was the assassination of Indira Gandhi.

He thought of something else. How ironic it was that once again, as at Independence in 1947, people were asking aloud if India would survive as one nation. Ralph Buultjens had been long associated with the Nehru family, and with Indira Gandhi in particular. He had seen her in moments of triumph and tragedy, victory and defeat. In recent years, Indira Gandhi had shared many confidences and major decisions with him—an unusual trust from someone so habitually suspicious.

"When I retire," she once said to Buultjens, "I will go to Cambridge as a visiting professor—if they will have me. You will have to come and help me there, because I am not much of an academic. And I have another job. You will have to help me with my memoirs. I must tell my story."*

That story, thought Ralph Buultjens, would never be told. Death had snatched away Indira Gandhi's chance of explaining herself to the world, and to history. Once again, as he had often done before, Buultjens reflected on the shimmering and sinister sides of her character—both so real and so quickly interchangeable. Now, nobody would ever know the truth about this coruscating person, probably the single most powerful woman of the twentieth century. Sitting restlessly in his airplane seat, Buultjens recalled a quotation that Indira Gandhi had once given him from one of her favorite works, George Bernard Shaw's drama *Saint Joan*:

> "Must then a Christ perish in torment in every age
> To save those that have no imagination?"

Some hours later, disembarking from his painful flight, Ralph Buultjens encountered a Delhi different from the city he had known so well for so many years. The capital, long a place of pleasant association and political activity for him, now seemed a mausoleum of memories. Buultjens could scarcely believe that he was here to attend the funeral of his closest friend.

---

*Quotation from notes maintained by Professor Ralph Buultjens.

3

The Aftermath

At ten o'clock on the morning of Wednesday, October 31, 1984, Payal Singh and several other Sikh friends and relatives boarded a train in the eastern metropolis of Calcutta. Singh, a journalist, and her group, were headed for Delhi to attend a wedding. It was not until six o'clock that evening that the group heard about Mrs. Gandhi's death—and the fact that her assassins had been Sikh.

"Every passenger irrespective of his religion was in a state of shocked silence," Singh later recalled. *

At eleven o'clock the next morning, the train reached Ghaziabad. Delhi was still more than fifty miles away.

"That was the beginning of two harrowing hours for us, when we were suspended between life and death," Payal Singh said later.

She continued:

A bloodthirsty mob, almost like a pack of hungry wolves hunting for prey, went from coach to coach in search of Sikhs. In a frenzy of madness, the mob, armed with iron rods and knives, brutally dragged out Sikhs, burned their turbans, hacked them to death, and threw them across the tracks. Even the old and feeble were not spared. The barbaric mob, totally devoid of rationality, declared that women would be spared. But in what sense were they spared? After all, what

* Payal Singh later wrote movingly about her experiences in *The Illustrated Weekly of India.*

73

can be more torturous for women than seeing male members of their family hacked to death in front of their eyes?

The only sardars* who were spared were the six with us. And all because of the concern and cooperation of the passengers in our coach. Before the train even halted at Ghaziabad, the hysterical mob had caught a glimpse of the six sardars with us. A fusillade of stones followed and the glass windows were smashed to bits. Shutters were hastily put down for protection. The police, we were told, could not control the wild mob and so they just turned their backs and walked away.

We had a ladies' compartment and the other passengers in our coach, realizing there was more trouble ahead, suggested that the sardars in our group occupy it. At first, they were reluctant but we literally forced them to stay inside. It was ironic. Sardars, who were historically known for their valor, now had to protect themselves by hiding in a ladies' compartment or else become victims of a hysterical horde.†

The main doors of our coach were locked from inside. And we waited with bated breath. The mob, hell-bent on destruction, was not to be deterred. They pounded on the heavy metal door for over fifteen minutes. The incessant pounding was accompanied by threats to set the train on fire. One non-Sikh passenger shifted uncomfortably in his seat and said he felt all of them would lose their lives if the door was not opened. But he was sternly reprimanded by the others, who declared that under no circumstances would the door be opened.

But the mob finally broke open the door. Their violent mutilation of the train had only whetted their appetite for more destruction. The mob stormed into our coach. And walked past the ladies' compartment. But before we could even sigh with relief, they turned around and demanded that the door of the ladies' compartment be opened, so that they could check it. By now our nerves had reached breaking point. Yet we couldn't lose our composure lest they suspect that something was amiss. We tried to convince them that there were just women inside but the mob was adamant, and began to bang on the door. The petrified screams of two women inside our compartment, our own pleas, and the persuasion of the other non-Sikh

---

* The word "sardar" is widely used in India to denote a male Sikh. The term for a female Sikh is "sardarni."

† Indian trains still have segregated coaches for women. The sexes can also travel together, of course, but women who wish to book themselves in "Women Only" compartments can generally do so.

passengers finally seemed to convince the mob that there were no sardars inside. The mob retreated.

When Payal Singh's train reached Delhi at three o'clock that afternoon, its surviving Sikh males helped carry out corpses from compartments. By then other trains were also arriving in Delhi from northern Indian cities. Scores of Sikh males lay dead in them.

"The bodies had been battered," Payal Singh said. "Those Sikhs were innocent people who had done nothing, except for being Sikhs and traveling toward Delhi on that fateful day."

By 2:00 P.M. on October 31, All-India Radio's hourly news bulletins began referring to the fact that Indira Gandhi had been shot in the garden of her home and that she was being treated at the All-India Institute. By four o'clock that afternoon, a large crowd had gathered in front of the Institute's main entrance. Dev Dutt, a Delhi-based journalist, happened to be in that crowd. "There were slogans mostly in praise of Mrs. Gandhi, and a few slogans threatening revenge," Dutt later recalled in testimony given to investigators from the People's Union for Civil Liberties.

But there was no tension. There were a number of Sikhs in the crowd. Their faces showed no fear or apprehension.

We talked to some of them in order to gauge their state of mind. The Sikhs seemed to be supremely confident about the goodwill of their Hindu brethren. It seems they nursed no suspicions against the Hindus. They did not show any traces of nervousness of any kind. The non-Sikhs in the crowd did not seem even to notice the presence of Sikhs and took their presence as normal.

While this crowd waited patiently, the flow of traffic and the normal business around nearby kiosks continued. I was standing near the street crossing in front of the Institute when thirty or forty young men emerged out of the crowd and formed a neat column three or four men deep and ran toward the crossing near a traffic island. They caught hold of a scooter that was parked on the other side and set it on fire. Then these young men moved toward some nearby buses that had been slowing down on account of the fire. They began to pull Sikhs out of buses. They started to pull off their turbans and beat them relentlessly. I saw five turbans burning in a row on the road. There were no policemen in the area. The group had a free hand.

After about twenty minutes, a group of khaki-clad men arrived and began to chase away the miscreants.

It is difficult to explain the sudden eruption of violence in the Institute area that afternoon. But the question is: Who were these people who came out of the crowd and went on a rampage?

The incidents near the All-India Institute were reportedly the first in Delhi in which Sikhs were targeted and manhandled. By late evening, non-Sikh mobs were rampaging through Sikh neighborhoods elsewhere in the capital. Led by men identified by some of the victims as local Congress Party leaders and Delhi administrative officials, these mobs burned down houses, raped women, looted homes, and murdered Sikh males. A senior member of Mrs. Gandhi's cabinet was seen directing some of the rioters.* Satish Jacob, a Delhi correspondent for the British Broadcasting Corporation, saw charred bodies on the verandas of nearly every house in the Trilokpuri section of Delhi, a working-class neighborhood. Most of the bodies were of Sikh men, whose hair—according to eyewitnesses—was cut after they were killed and placed in heaps near the bodies. Jacob, a highly regarded reporter, said later that he could smell the fumes of the kerosene which had been used to burn the bodies.[†] Rahul Bedi, a reporter for the *Indian Express*, saw a truckload of charred bodies parked in front of a local police station on the afternoon of November 2. A junior police officer told Bedi that his superiors knew about the situation and would deal with it. Bedi later recounted how he found even army officers least helpful or even not much bothered about what was going on.

Looking back over these sad years at the Sikh tragedy, it is clear that the violence was not so much popular rage—or even chauvinistic Hindu rage—over the murder of Mrs. Gandhi. The attacks against Sikhs in Delhi and elsewhere largely stemmed from other reasons. There were personal vendettas to be pursued; there was the simple, primal matter of looting and rape. And there was pent-up fury on the part of Delhi-ites over the whole Khalistan issue. Innocent Sikhs were now being made to

---

* The official has been identified by several witnesses as H. K. L. Bhagat, who denied his involvement. Rajiv Gandhi thought highly enough of Bhagat to appoint him to several important ministerial positions. Another Congress chieftain who allegedly was involved in attacks against Sikhs was Jagdish Tytler, who was also selected by Rajiv Gandhi for a ministerial position. Tytler, like Bhagat, denied any wrongdoing, but Sikhs remain unconvinced.

[†] Satish Jacob's account appears in the book he coauthored with his BBC colleague, Mark Tully: *Amritsar: Mrs. Gandhi's Last Battle*.

pay the price for brutal attacks against Hindus by Khalistani militants in the Punjab in the early 1980s.

Not long after the November 1984 massacres, I visited Sikh neighborhoods in Delhi. It was hard to believe that people in countries that call themselves civilized were capable of inflicting such gruesome atrocities on innocent men, women, and children.* Dhanwat Kaur, a twenty-eight-year-old woman in Trilokpuri, recounted for me how the rampaging mobs invaded her one-room tenement, dragged her husband, Manohar Singh, by his genitals, and hacked him to death in front of her. Her three small daughters and a son were present when this brutality occurred. For an hour afterward, the son, three-year-old Jasbir, clutched what remained of his father's body and refused to let go. Dhanwat's neighbor, Amir Singh, a carpenter, told me how he had gathered a group of women and children and sequestered them in a nearby Sikh gurdwara, or temple. But a large group of marauders set fire to the temple. Most of the women and children managed to escape, Amir Singh said, but a dozen Sikh men remained trapped inside the inferno and perished.

"The sad thing was, the people who set fire to our temple included those very men who had helped us to raise money for building the temple," he said.

Over the next four days, more than 2,000 Sikhs died at the hands of these mobs in Delhi. Most died terribly: They were often burned alive, or were hacked to pieces. Female members of their families were often stripped and made to watch, or they were raped. Prepubescent boys were castrated by mobs. The carnage spread to neighboring states as well. In Uttar Pradesh, more than a thousand Sikhs were reported to have been killed in cities such as Kanpur, Lucknow, and Ghaziabad. In Haryana, the death toll exceeded a hundred. In Bihar, the toll rose to 300. Sikhs were also slaughtered by well-armed mobs in Madhya Pradesh, West Bengal, and parts of Himachal Pradesh. Most of those states were governed by the Congress Party.

It is impossible to say with certainty how many Sikhs died in the five-day period following the murder of Indira Gandhi. But officials of the

---

* It was remarkable that no policemen came to the rescue of Sikhs during these attacks. No one was arrested, there were no trials, and there wasn't even an official commission of inquiry into the atrocities until much later. The commission's work led to no indictments. To this day, Sikhs remain angry that the Indian government has done little to bring to justice those who killed innocent men, women, and children. Only a few cases have been prosecuted. On March 30, 1991, the Sessions Court in Delhi sentenced three men to life imprisonment for murdering three Sikhs and looting their property during the November 1984 riots in the capital.

Delhi-based People's Union for Democratic Rights (PUDR) and the People's Union for Civil Liberties (PUCL)—who investigated many of the incidents in the capital and who produced a well-documented report—say that the national death toll probably exceeded 3,000. Professor Rajni Kothari thinks that the actual toll was double that figure. To this day, there is disagreement over the casualties of the attacks against Sikhs. Some Sikhs have said that more than 20,000 of their brethren were killed in Delhi and across northern India. The BBC's Mark Tully and Satish Jacob quote government figures that put the number of people killed in the anti-Sikh riots at 2,717, of whom 2,150—virtually all Sikhs—died in Delhi alone. While the actual property loss may never be known, many estimates suggest that between October 31 and November 5, more than $250 million worth of property was destroyed in Delhi alone.

The report by PUDR and PUCL is still widely considered the most reliable document on the tragedy. It has been used by numerous official commissions and private organizations as the basis for further investigations into the massacre. Entitled *Who Are the Guilty?*,* it sold briskly. The report charged that the Delhi government of Rajiv Gandhi had in effect encouraged Hindu and Sikh communalism to "feed upon each other" in the Punjab, and that the repercussions of the Punjab situation were being felt in Delhi. The Sikh community must be reassured in the aftermath of the holocaust in Delhi, the report said. Investigators from the PUDR and the PUCL found that the attacks against Delhi's Sikh community were hardly spontaneous expressions of grief and anger over Mrs. Gandhi's assassination—as the Delhi authorities have asserted they were. The rampaging mobs were well-led, well-armed, and well-informed about just where Sikh families lived. Congress Party leaders were seen turning up with lists of residents not only in poor localities such as Munirka, Mangolpuri, and Trilokpuri, but also in rich neighborhoods such as Friends Colony and Maharani Bagh. Thugs—or goondas, as they are commonly known in India—turned up in Delhi Transport Corporation (DTC) buses, or in vans and trucks and Jeeps ordinarily used by local Congress Party workers.

Throughout the carnage, Delhi's policemen were either totally absent from the scene; or they stood by while mobs freely burned Sikhs alive; or they themselves participated in the orgy of violence against innocent

*Who Are the Guilty? Report of an Inquiry into the Delhi Riots of October 31–November 4, 1984. People's Union for Democratic Rights and People's Union for Civil Liberties. Published jointly by Gobinda Mukhoty and Rajni Kothari (Delhi: Sunny Graphics, 1984).

Sikhs. But in Lajpat Nagar, on November 1, when a group of concerned citizens tried to organize a peace march in support of Hindu-Sikh amity, a police Jeep blocked the way and police officials demanded to know if the marchers had official permission.* In areas such as Trilokpuri, policemen were seen supplying diesel oil and petrol to arsonists. In Kotla Mubarakpur, several witnesses heard a police inspector say to a group of rioters: "We gave you thirty-six hours. Had we given the Sikhs that amount of time, they would have killed every Hindu."

A number of Hindu residents of areas such as Mangolpuri tried to hide their Sikh neighbors from the marauding mobs. But when two Hindus, Dharam Raj Pawar and Rajvir Pawar, went to a police station at Ber Serai and asked for police protection for their Sikh friends, a policeman said to them: "You, being Hindus, should have killed those Sikhs. What are you doing here? Don't you know a train has arrived from Punjab carrying bodies of massacred Hindus?"

On the evening of October 31, Atal Behari Vajpayee, an Opposition leader, called on Home Minister P. V. Narasimha Rao to express outrage over the mounting attacks against Sikhs.

"Everything will be brought under control within a couple of hours," Narasimha Rao told Vajpayee, a former foreign minister.

But Narasimha Rao did not impose a curfew until two days later, and he belatedly called the army in to restore law and order. But even then, the violence against the Sikhs continued, aided and abetted by those in power. To this day, the delay remains unexplained.

One eyewitness to these events was Ashwini Ray, head of the department of political science at Delhi's Jawaharlal Nehru University. "There was a police vehicle with four policemen parked near Bhogal market," Ray recalled. "I came out of my house and saw smoke billowing out. I heard the sound of a tire bursting. Policemen were reading newspapers and drinking tea inside their car while arson was going on all around.

"I went to the police car to ask why they were not stopping the arson and was told to mind my own business. I then saw several looters carrying off radio and television sets from stores right in front of the parked police vehicles. Some of the policemen asked the people to hurry with the loot."†

None of the looters or rioters was arrested during the carnage. But the police did take into custody several Sikhs who defended themselves and

---

* Even though the Indian constitution provides for the right to free assembly, police permission is generally required to march in the streets or to hold rallies.
† Ray's testimony was given to investigators from the People's Union for Civil Liberties.

their families with weapons. The Rajiv Gandhi government dragged its feet in providing relief money to Sikh victims, authorizing the equivalent of no more than $300 per family. Few of the victims have received this money to this day.

The report prepared by the PUDR and the PUCL makes dramatic points in its conclusion:

> The social and political consequences of the government's stance during the carnage, its deliberate inaction and its callousness toward relief and rehabilitation are far-reaching. It is indeed a matter of grave concern that the government has made no serious inquiries into the entire tragic episode which seems to be so well planned and designed. It is curious that during the several hours the government had between the time of Mrs. Gandhi's assassination and the official announcement of her death, no security arrangements were made for the victims. The riots were well-organized and were of unprecedented brutality. Several very disturbing questions arise that must be answered: What were the government and the Delhi administration doing for several hours between the time of the assassination and the announcement of Mrs. Gandhi's death? Why did the government refuse to take cognizance of the reports of the looting and murders and call in troops even after the military had been "alerted"? Why was there no joint control room set up and who was responsible for not giving clear and specific instructions to the army on curbing violence and imposing curfew?
>
> Who was responsible for the planned and deliberate police inaction and often active role in inciting the murders and the looting? Who was responsible for the planned and well-directed arson? Why were highly provocative slogans (such as "*Khoon ka baadla khoon*": "Blood for blood") allowed to be broadcast by Doordarshan during the televised transmissions depicting the mourning crowds at Teen Murti Bhavan, where Mrs. Gandhi's body was kept on display? Why has the Congress Party not set up an inquiry into the role of its members in the arson and looting?*

Now, years after the assassination and its horrendous aftermath, these questions remain to haunt India and Indians because—notwithstanding

---

*Former chief justice of India S. M. Sikri prepared a document titled *Report of the Citizens' Commission*. It was published by the Tata Press in Delhi in January 1985. The findings of the report were, of course, largely ignored by Rajiv Gandhi's government.

some government inquiries—those who wreaked havoc on the Sikhs remain unpunished and, indeed, have even been rewarded. Many Indians find this situation difficult to understand.

Late in the evening of Wednesday, October 31, Rajiv Gandhi appeared on Doordarshan, India's government-run television network, to address the millions of people whose prime minister he had so suddenly become. He spoke from One Safdarjung Road, with a garlanded portrait of his mother in the background.

He spoke slowly, in English first, then in Hindi, and his face was composed. He did not even look tired, although his day had begun this Wednesday at four o'clock in the morning in distant West Bengal.

"Indira Gandhi, India's prime minister, has been assassinated," the new prime minister said.

> She was mother not only to me but to the whole nation. She served the Indian people to the last drop of her blood. The country knows with what tireless dedication she toiled for the development of India.
>
> You all know how dear to her heart was the dream of a united, peaceful, and prosperous India. An India in which all Indians, irrespective of their religion, language, or political persuasion, live together as one big family in an atmosphere free from mutual rivalries and prejudices.
>
> By her untimely death, her work remains unfinished. It is for us to complete this task. This is a moment of profound grief. The foremost need now is to maintain our balance. We can and must face this tragic ordeal with fortitude, courage, and wisdom. We should remain calm and exercise the maximum restraint. We should not let our emotions get the better of us, because passion would cloud judgment.
>
> Nothing would hurt the soul of our beloved Indira Gandhi more than the occurrence of violence in any part of the country. It is of prime importance at this moment that every step we take is in the correct direction.
>
> Indira Gandhi is no more, but her soul lives. India lives. India is immortal. The spirit of India is immortal. I know that the nation will recognize its responsibilities. The nation has placed a great responsibility on me by making me the head of the government. I shall be able to fulfill this responsibility only with your support and cooperation. I shall value your guidance in upholding the unity, integrity, and honor of the country.

If his speech seemed a bit disjointed, that was because at least half a dozen aides had been responsible for it. One draft was written by H. Y. Sharada Prasad, Mrs. Gandhi's information adviser and chief speech-writer; other contributors included Rajiv Gandhi's closest friend at the time, Arun Singh, a former corporate executive and scion of a royal family; and Arun Nehru, Rajiv Gandhi's third cousin and his adviser on Congress Party affairs.* Gopi Arora, a powerful bureaucrat attached to the prime minister's secretariat, made important contributions.† Even Sonia Gandhi pitched in.

Even though the speech was broadcast close to midnight, millions of Indians—perhaps as many as 75 million, according to several estimates —were believed to have watched Rajiv Gandhi on television. Few Third World leaders ever had such a large audience. He had been sworn in as prime minister barely five hours before the speech at a simple ceremony at Rashtrapati Bhavan, the residence of India's constitutional head of state, President Zail Singh, generally known as "Giani"—the learned one. There, under a glittering chandelier in a vast chamber called the Asoka Hall, Rajiv Gandhi had become India's seventh and, at forty years, its youngest head of government. Zail Singh, an amiable Sikh who had been selected for the job by Indira Gandhi mostly because of his total loyalty to her, fawned over the new prime minister, who didn't seem inclined toward much small talk. Members of the cabinet waited around.

Zail Singh had risen that day in Sanaa, the capital of the Yemen Arab Republic. Yemen was the last stop on a two-nation official tour that had included Mauritius. It was his secretary, A. C. Bandopadhyay, who conveyed to Singh the news of the shooting of Indira Gandhi. The

---

* All three men eventually had a falling out with Rajiv Gandhi. Sharada Prasad served as the new prime minister's spokesman for a couple of years, then was eased out and appointed head of the Indira Gandhi Memorial Trust. He was dismissed from that sinecure after disagreements with Rajiv Gandhi over how best to preserve Mrs. Gandhi's memory. Arun Singh served in Rajiv's cabinet, but later resigned in protest against the prime minister's handling of a controversial $1.3 billion arms deal with Sweden. And Arun Nehru stormed out of Rajiv Gandhi's Congress Party and joined hands with Rajiv's bitterest rival, V. P. Singh. Nehru served as tourism and commerce minister in the Singh government, which came into power in December 1989 and lasted barely eleven months. After the fall of the Singh government, there was widespread talk that Arun Nehru would rejoin the Congress Party and make his peace with Rajiv Gandhi.
†Gopi Arora was assigned by the V. P. Singh government to the International Monetary Fund in Washington, D.C. He became an executive director, a high-paying job.

president decided at once to abandon his tour and leave for India. He asked that the formal guard-of-honor ceremonies at the airport be dispensed with. His chartered Boeing 707 would ordinarily have flown from Sanaa to Bombay for a refuelling stop, but Singh requested that the pilot fly directly, if possible, to New Delhi. The plane's crew were not happy with the request, but under the circumstances they said they would oblige.

During the five-hour plane journey, Singh's aides—Bandopadhyay, Special Assistant I. S. Bindhra, and Romesh Bhandari, a senior secretary in the external-affairs ministry—kept in touch with Delhi by radio. Singh himself declined lunch and lay in his bed for more than three hours.

He reflected on the years he had served Indira Gandhi. He once said to journalist Hari Jaisingh: "I owe everything to Biwiji (the affectionate sobriquet he had given to Indira: "Biwiji" meant big sister). Even if she asks me to sweep the floor, I would do it. I am very fortunate to have her blessings. I have eaten her salt, and I will never betray her. I am a loyal servant of the Nehru family." And Zail Singh reflected on his own years as chief minister of the troubled Punjab, where he was Mrs. Gandhi's emissary to Sikh leaders who agitated for greater autonomy for the state. Zail Singh had failed to bring about a lasting solution to the Sikh crisis, and indeed there were some critics who felt certain that he had contributed to escalating that crisis. And now Indira Gandhi was dead, killed by Sikhs, and Zail Singh wondered whether history would have changed had he and his Punjab Congress associates acted differently.

Singh was met at Delhi's Palam International Airport by Vice President R. Venkataraman, Rajendra Kumar Dhawan, Balram Jakhar, the speaker of the Lok Sabha, Dr. P. C. Alexander—who had served as principal private secretary to Mrs. Gandhi—and Arun Nehru. During the twenty-minute ride from the airport to the All-India Institute, Arun Nehru raised the question of succession. Nehru's message was clear: Zail Singh would invite Rajiv Gandhi to become prime minister.

"The Congress parliamentary board has decided that Rajivji should become PM," Nehru, a giant of a man with a permanent scowl bolted to his face, said to Singh. Zail Singh was to say much later that even if Arun Nehru had not suggested Rajiv's name, he had already decided in the privacy of his mind to invite Indira Gandhi's son to succeed her as India's prime minister. "It was perfectly natural for Rajivji to become prime minister," Zail Singh said.

The board currently had just four members instead of the normal nine: Home Minister P. V. Narasimha Rao (later to succeed Rajiv as prime minister); Finance Minister Pranab Mukherjee; Maragatham Chandrasekhar; and senior Congress Party aide Kamlapati Tripathy. Mrs. Gandhi had been a member of this board, which served as the highest policy-making unit of the ruling Congress Party. When the assassination occurred, Narasimha Rao was politicking in his home constituency of Warangal, in Andhra Pradesh, and Pranab Mukherjee was accompanying Rajiv Gandhi in West Bengal, his own home state. Tripathy and Chandrasekhar were also out of Delhi. It did not matter, of course, that these men were out of station. Arun Nehru—who had muscled his way to preeminent power in the Congress Party—had already resolved that his cousin, Rajiv Gandhi, would become India's next prime minister. He was supported in this by Sitaram Kesari, treasurer of the Congress Party. Nehru and Kesari met with top Congress officials in a sixth-floor conference room at the All-India Institute and declared that the party had no other choice but to name Rajiv Gandhi to succeed his mother. Concurring with this were Chief Ministers Chandrasekhar Singh of Bihar, Janaki Ballav Patnaik of Orissa, Arjun Singh of Madhya Pradesh, and Shiv Charan Mathur of Rajasthan. The Nehru-Kesari decision was conveyed to other senior Congress Party officials all through the afternoon.

A formal letter advising President Zail Singh of the Congress parliamentary board's "decision" was drafted by G. K. Moopanar, general secretary of the All-India Congress Committee. The letter also formally requested Singh to appoint Rajiv Gandhi as prime minister. *

Rajiv Gandhi and Zail Singh linked up with each other on the eighth floor of the Institute. Singh hugged Gandhi. Then he plucked his trademark red rose from the buttonhole of his achkan, or long fitted jacket, and gently placed it on Indira Gandhi's body. He asked Rajiv Gandhi to come to Rashtrapati Bhavan at 6:30 P.M. for the formal ceremony during which Indira Gandhi's son would be sworn in. When Gandhi turned up at the president's sprawling sandstone home—where Britain's viceroys had once resided and ruled—most of the Congress Party's top officials had already assembled in the Asoka Hall. Gandhi wore a white kurta and tailored pajama trousers. He had shaved. His eyes seemed slightly red, but otherwise he looked remarkably self-controlled.

At 6:40 P.M., nine hours after his mother was felled, former pilot Rajiv Gandhi was sworn in as the sixth prime minister of India since Independence. He had never held a cabinet portfolio before; he had been a member of Parliament only since 1982.

The myth that Rajiv had entered politics only reluctantly had been widely accepted. Conventional wisdom held that all Rajiv Gandhi ever

---

* Under India's constitution, the president is required to name the prime minister.

wanted to do was fly planes for Indian Airlines. Only after his mother applied much emotional pressure on him following the death of her initial heir-apparent and younger son, Sanjay, did he coyly venture into public life. Now he was in charge of 800 million Indians.

There is, however, another perspective to consider. Rajiv Gandhi was consciously and consistently excluded from politics by his ambitious younger brother, Sanjay. Sanjay, who at times was barely on speaking terms with Rajiv, monopolized the political attention span of his mother. Rajiv saw the power and the perks of political life from the sidelines. At times, when he wanted some small favor for a friend, Rajiv had to wait in line outside his forceful brother's living quarters at One Safdarjung Road before deferentially making his request. All this must have been immensely frustrating. In the months immediately after Sanjay's death, the story of "reluctant Rajiv" was convincingly woven.

Yet in the waiting period before his resignation from Indian Airlines and entry into Parliament in mid-1981, Rajiv Gandhi showed no reluctance whatsoever to heavily involve himself in back-door politics. Favor-seekers, political notables, commission agents, and other cronies flocked around him and readily received an audience. Around Rajiv clustered a group of friends who supported his veiled political activities. These friends included Arun Nehru, Vijay Dhar, Romi Chopra, Satish Sharma, and Arun Singh. For someone reportedly hesitant to immerse himself in what he frequently called "the dirty game," Rajiv Gandhi was remarkably active in all phases of political work. A significant element of that work involved trading favors, always under the rubric of "helping Mummy." This was scarcely the behavior of a political wallflower. And yet the myth of "reluctance" continues.

By a stroke of fate, Rajiv had become the leader of the world's largest democracy, the most powerful nation of the Nonaligned Movement. He was now chief executive of a country with the biggest military force in the world after the United States, the Soviet Union, and China. His theater would no longer be the cockpit of the turboprop planes he had piloted for Indian Airlines, nor even just the great land mass of the Subcontinent. From now on, Rajiv Gandhi's stage would be the whole world itself.

Vir Sanghvi, a slim man with an intense face and large, soulful eyes, was a whiz kid of Indian journalism, and I met him and his writer-wife, Malavika, for lunch on the day of the assassination. A product of Bombay's exclusive Campion School and Ajmer's Mayo College, he had gone on to the Mill High School in London, and then obtained a master's degree in politics, philosophy, and economics at Oxford University's Brasenose College. He had started writing for Indian publications while he was still an undergraduate at Oxford. Upon his return to India, Sanghvi helped start Bombay's first city magazine, one modeled vaguely after *The Tatler* and *New York* magazine. The magazine, which he guided for three years before moving on to the editorship of another magazine, was called *Bombay.* *

"Are you going to miss Indira?" I asked.

Vir Sanghvi offered an incisive assessment of the dead prime minister, one that is as valid today as it was when he spun it out for me on that strange afternoon.

"I think it's fair to say that most people of my generation were ambivalent about Indira Gandhi," Sanghvi said. "In 1966, when she first became prime minister, we were too young to realize what she stood for—I was only ten then. But by 1971, when she fought a national election and won by a landslide—after having first broken away from the Congress Party bosses who had installed her in the first place—we were all on her side. Then she won state assembly elections all across the country in 1972 and established her credentials as India's most powerful leader—one who did not need the support of any party machine.

"My disillusionment came later. By 1974, things had begun to go badly wrong: inflation, lawlessness, corruption—these were all on the rise. Still, I retained a sneaking admiration for her until 1975, when she declared the Emergency and suspended the constitution and jailed thousands of her political opponents. Even then, I was prepared to buy her story: that the Opposition, through its unruly, disruptive agitations, had left her with no choice. By late 1976, though, when her younger son Sanjay rose to be heir-apparent, it was impossible to defend Indira Gandhi.

"She was clearly establishing a dynasty, and this became even clearer after Sanjay's death in 1980—Indira insisted that Rajiv give up his pilot's career and enter politics, even though he seemed extremely reluctant to do so at that point. For most of the last eight years of her life, I was opposed to Indira Gandhi and much of what she stood for."

Did he feel any sadness at all at her death?

"Of course," Sanghvi said, "an old woman was shot to death in her

---

* *Bombay* is still flourishing as a guide to events in the metropolis, and as a social monitor of the city's privileged. Vir Sanghvi, meanwhile, has moved on to *Sunday* magazine, a Calcutta-based weekly that specializes in polemical reporting. He also appears frequently on television talk shows.

own garden. There is sorrow in that. Indira did contribute to India. She provided firm, strong leadership, she ran a shrewd and intelligent foreign policy, and she believed in India as an entity, often rising above caste and communal divisions."

What impact did she have on Indian life? I asked Sanghvi. How would he assess her legacy? I realized that it was probably premature to ask such a question, but I wanted to try it out on him.

"She did a lot of damage," Sanghvi said, as if he had already expected the question. "In retrospect it seems clear that she either destroyed or subverted most of the institutions of Indian democracy. She pretty much killed the Congress Party, which was one vehicle, especially under her father, Nehru, of ensuring that a vast country like India was ruled by consensus. She destroyed the powers of state chief ministers and damaged the federal structure.

"She pressurized the judiciary and sapped its independence by appointing mediocre judges and transferring to inconsequential and uncomfortable outposts those judges who dared to assert their independence. She damaged the independence of the bureaucracy by calling for a 'committed civil service.' She politicized the army by using it for civilian purposes and by manipulating promotions. She turned the cabinet into a joke by vesting unprecedented and sweeping powers in her personal staff and in her sons. And she prevented any rivals from emerging within the party—peopling it, instead, with thieves and scoundrels, in comparison to whom her older son, Rajiv, seems positively angelic."

What impact did Indira Gandhi have on his own life? I asked Sanghvi. He reflected on that a bit, fiddled with the fried rice on his plate, then said: "I feel tremendously let down. I came back to India with great hopes and a sense that good would prevail. But what I encountered was a cynical leader whose only concern was political survival.

"I think people now, and certainly myself included, simply have no faith in their national government. We've seen how corrupt those in government have become. It seems to me that if Rajiv becomes prime minister, he simply will have to institute major political reforms—he will have to fashion a new climate of hope and political cleanliness—if people are to trust their leaders again.

"I don't think his task is that difficult. Unlike a lot of other Third World countries, we still have such institutions in place as a judiciary, a parliament, a strong press. We have the two-thousand-odd officers of the Indian Administrative Service who can be galvanized into selfless service.* The answers are already there—no need for Rajiv, or whoever

---

* The Indian Administrative Service, better known in India by its acronym IAS, is

becomes prime minister, to appoint commissions to search for solutions. I say, stop interfering with the judiciary, depoliticize the bureaucracy, lift the stifling controls over industry—and stop trying to run every little thing directly from the prime minister's office in Delhi. Let people be."

Malavika Sanghvi, an established writer in her own right, had been listening attentively to her husband. I asked her how she viewed Indira Gandhi's death and the likely ascension of Rajiv Gandhi to India's political throne.

"I can't help but feel in my bones that exciting times lie ahead," she said. "I know, of course, that Indira herself had a wonderful opportunity back after the 1971 elections to bring about massive changes. She blew it. So I'm cautious about the prospects of any leader to succeed. But there is one side of me that desperately wants Rajiv to succeed—and I hope it will be him in the prime minister's seat. After all these years of bad news, we need good things to happen in India."

Vir and Malavika Sanghvi, each in their own way, were being terribly prescient. The years ahead would bear them both out, Rajiv Gandhi would initially prove an exciting political prospect. Within five years, Vir and Malavika would feel very let down, as would much of India. * The hopes they had invested in Rajiv Gandhi would not be fulfilled. Vir Sanghvi would become one of Rajiv Gandhi's bitterest critics in the media, and much of what Sanghvi said would echo the disappointments of millions of Indians who had genuinely believed that Indira Gandhi's son would overcome the past and usher in an era of prosperity and progress.

Late in the evening of Wednesday, October 31, 1984, I dined with Dilip and Nina Sardesai at the Cricket Club of India in Bombay. I was scheduled to fly the next evening to Delhi, and on to Punjab after that on assignment for *The New York Times*. Nina Sardesai, a professor of sociology at St. Xavier's College, was a cousin of my wife, Jayanti; her husband, Dilip, was a businessman and a former cricket star who represented India in international tournaments. We were joined by Nina's sister, Jaymala Bhandarkar, and her husband, Anil, Pan Am's marketing director in Bombay. The occasion was Nina's birthday. The Sardesais had insisted I eat with them.

---

the country's elite civil service cadre. Admission requires a stiff competitive exam, rigorous interviews, and a difficult training course. The diplomatic counterpart of the IAS is the Indian Foreign Service (IFS). There is also the Indian Police Service (IPS).

* During the 1989 and 1991 elections, Vir Sanghvi was frequently seen on national television. His analyses were widely considered to be astute and even prophetic.

I had always enjoyed their company, not the least because Dilip Sardesai had been one of my cricketing heroes. He was a great raconteur, reenacting cricket matches and offering funny insights about the sport's stars. His wife, of course, always listened to these stories attentively, seldom letting on that she had probably heard them hundreds of times before.

Ramchandra Moray, a local taxi owner, drove me to the club, an elegant structure in a fancy, mostly residential neighborhood of Bombay. Traffic was thin, and few people were out on the streets. It was as if the sidewalks of Bombay had been rolled up. Restaurants were shut. No shops seemed open. In this southern part of Bombay, I didn't see any policemen. Unlike some other Indian cities, Bombay was to be spared the tragedy of massacres against Sikhs.

"Everybody is home watching television or listening to the radio, sahib," Moray said. "What a day this has been for India!"

At the club, dinner had been laid out on a veranda overlooking a vast cricket field. The cuisine was Chinese. No one, however, felt like eating much, and Nina Sardesai seemed a little embarrassed that her birthday celebration was even being held on a day such as this. Later, the conversation at the table was about what would happen to India's Sikhs.

"I'm telling you—there's bound to be a massacre of the Sikhs," Dilip Sardesai said. "At times like these, good sense does not prevail in India."

"I hope Bombay is spared," Anil Bhandarkar said.

"Unlikely," Jaymala Bhandarkar said, tersely.

"Too many goondas here who would like nothing better than to bash some Sikh heads," Nina Sardesai said.

After dinner, we retired to the club's lounge to watch Rajiv Gandhi address the nation. It was approaching midnight. Half a dozen Sikhs sat quietly in one corner. The non-Sikhs in the room looked furtively at them. I thought: here we go. The Sikhs are already aliens in their own country.

When Rajiv Gandhi's speech was over, someone in our group pointed out that we had forgotten to sing "Happy Birthday" to Nina Sardesai. In the gloomy atmosphere of the club's lounge, that seemed quite an inappropriate thing to do. Nina Sardesai understood; I did not think she really expected that we would suddenly switch to revelry.

It was Anil Bhandarkar, a relative of mine, who suggested that I visit some Sikh neighborhoods in Bombay the following morning to assess their mood. There are an estimated 300,000 Sikhs in this city, which has long been known for tolerance among religious groups. Neighborhoods such as Sion, Koliwada, and North Dadar contain significant Sikh enclaves. Bombay may have a mottled history of strife between Hindus and Muslims, but Sikhs have traditionally lived in harmony with non-Sikhs here. Many Sikhs own automobile shops or work in the automobile spare-parts business. Some operate restaurants; still others are carpenters or handymen. Some drive taxis. In this city of much unemployment and poverty, few Sikhs are jobless. And so it was that I found myself the next morning in a neighborhood known as Sion. I had been given the name of a man named Bhupinder Singh Chatwal, a dealer in automobile spare parts. He lived in a three-room apartment not far from the Sion railway station. I had telephoned him to say I was coming. But when I rang the doorbell, he let me in only reluctantly. I could hear his wife, Surinder Kaur, speaking to her four small children in the bedroom next to the living room.

"You are not to step out of this home," she said. "Under no circumstances are you to leave the safety of these four walls."

She joined her husband in the living room, and offered me tea.

"Have you bought the padlock yet?" she asked Bhupinder Singh. She had slept late this morning, but the previous night had asked her husband to buy one.

"No," Bhupinder Singh said.

"And why not?" Surinder Kaur said, her voice rising just a fraction.

"Because I didn't think it was safe to go out this morning."

I was aghast at hearing this. I was brought up believing that Sikhs were the proudest, most courageous people of all Indians. They were tall, they walked with their heads in high heaven, and they were fearless. There were some 120,000 Sikhs in the Indian armed forces, and 22 percent of the officer corps was Sikh. Sikhs were brave in battle; and in civilian life they had for centuries been the traditional protectors of the meeker and mostly cowardly Hindus. And now Bhupinder Singh was saying he was afraid to go out of his home?

"We know we will be the victims," he said to me, his deep voice cracking a bit. "It is only a matter of time."

We were visited by his next-door neighbor, Mahinder Singh, who owned an electric goods store. He had just received a telephone call from relatives in Delhi who had told him about the mounting violence against Sikhs in the capital.

"Our fear is that we will be made scapegoats," Mahinder Singh said. Like Bhupinder Singh, he seemed to be in his late thirties. "And once any rioting or violence starts, then the antisocial elements take over soon. I dare not keep my shop open."

He paused to sip tea.

"Tell me," he said, his eyes welling with tears, "why should all Sikhs bear the responsibility for the horrible event in Delhi yesterday?"

What could I say to Mahinder Singh? That the weak will always prey on the strong when given a chance? That the "tolerance" of India's majority Hindus was a fiction? That the death of Indira Gandhi showed how fragile our secular structure was, how easily it could be shaken and abused?

I didn't say any of this to him.

"Look," I said, "if there's any trouble here at all, please contact me. I'm staying at a friend's apartment. It's large enough to hold all of you. Please come there. I promise you complete safety."

I later reflected on what I had just told the Sikhs. If indeed there was violence against them in Bombay, could I, a Hindu-born man, really protect them against a mob's blind fury?

In those hours and days of terror, some Hindus came to the assistance of besieged Sikhs. A number of young people got together in Delhi and formed an umbrella organization called the Nagarik Seva Manch, which translates as Citizens' Service Group. A Sikh named Tejeshwar Singh—a publishing executive who also anchors the government's evening network news program—defiantly led a procession of Hindus and Sikhs through Delhi's streets.* The participants urged Indians to shun violence and renew their commitment to communal harmony.

"*Hindu-Sikh bhai!*" the marchers shouted. "Hindus and Sikhs are brothers!"

But as the procession moved through low-income neighborhoods, crowds sometimes heckled them. Stones were thrown at Tejeshwar Singh. The marchers were threatened with bodily harm.

A number of Hindus offered shelter to their Sikh friends. My brother-in-law, Ajai Lal, and his wife, Indu,[†] went across to the home of their Sikh neighbor, Anand Singh, and invited the former army colonel to pack up and stay with them until the trouble subsided. When Hindu friends found out that Khushwant Singh, the well-known Sikh writer and historian, had sought refuge in the Swedish Embassy, they implored him to come to their homes. Some 50,000 Sikhs sought sanctuary in

---

* Tejeshwar Singh, called "Bunny" by his friends, has one of India's most recognizable faces because of his anchoring of the national news program. He also does modeling for a textile manufacturer.

† Ajai Lal is a successful producer of audiovisuals and films in New Delhi; Indu Lal works for British Airways.

special refugee camps set up by the government and by private voluntary agencies.

Scores of Sikh men in Delhi cut their long hair, threw away their turbans, and shaved their beards so that they would not be singled out as Sikhs. The barber shops in Delhi's luxury hotels did roaring business. Noni Chawla, a young executive with the ITC–Sheraton Hotel group, moved to his employer's flagship hotel, the Maurya-Sheraton, with his wife, Nilima, and their two children.* The homes of a number of Sikhs in the Chawlas' affluent neighborhood in the Vasant Vihar section of Delhi had been attacked by mobs who came armed with voter lists. Several Sikhs were dragged out of their houses, stripped in the streets, beaten, then burned alive. Some Sikh children were hanged in front of their parents, while others were castrated and their genitals stuffed into the mouths of their mothers and sisters. "What kind of a country has this become?" asked Noni Chawla, who refused to doff his turban in public or cut his hair.

"I've never felt discriminated against in India," Chawla said. "But clearly times are changing. Among many young Sikh professionals I now hear increased talk of emigrating to the West. We don't want our children taunted in school. A lot of us feel a sense of alienation, of separation. I think Sikhs will increasingly have a difficult time in India."†

I read an extraordinary essay by Pritish Nandy, editor of *The Illustrated Weekly of India*. Nandy, a Bengali Hindu, had this to say:

> The assassination of Prime Minister Indira Gandhi was a brutal and reprehensible act, condemned by everyone. An act of murder that laid to rest all our pretensions to civilized politics. What the assassination brought in its wake was equally brutal. A retaliation quite unthinkable. Rampaging mobs went berserk. Particularly in Delhi, where they took upon themselves the divine right to avenge the prime minister's murder. Just because those who killed her owed allegiance to the frenzied fringe of the Sikh community, who were seeking vengeance against those whom they saw as responsible for the sacrilegious act of sending the army into the Golden Temple in Amritsar, the entire community became the victims of organized violence and sheer butchery. Marauding gangs went around, report-

*The Maurya-Sheraton is situated not far from the Diplomatic Enclave, an exclusive section of New Delhi.
†Noni Chawla has since prospered at his firm, rising to the highest executive echelons. He is now based in Bombay.

edly with voters lists in their hands, burning down Sikh homes, looting, maiming, killing, and setting them ablaze. Even defense personnel were not spared. Trains reached stations with people lying dead inside. Trucks and lorries lay charred on the highway. People were beaten to death and burned as torches, doused in kerosene.

Thousands fled, leaving behind their homes, their families. But where could they go? The *lumpen* mobs ruled the streets, led by men in power. The police, as always, quietly stood by and watched. As homes went up in flames. As dead bodies littered the streets. As train after train rolled in, with unidentified corpses. It was incredible. A shocked and bereaved nation watched with dismay the collapse of the entire law and order machinery in the face of such savagery.

The riots are now over. But who will put out the fires that still burn? Thousands lie dead. Many more are alive, but destroyed forever. We all see the victims. And we all know who the people responsible are. And why they did it. But what are we going to do about it? Let it pass again into books of history and old newspapers as yet another tragic episode to be quickly forgotten, healed with easy charity—so that we can get back to our comfortable cliches? Can a stupid and barbaric act committed by a few people owing allegiance to a lunatic fringe destroy our faith in our own ability to live together as a single nation, irrespective of religion, caste, and community? For the faults of a minuscule minority, who may or may not have celebrated the prime minister's death, shall we humiliate an entire community whose loyalty to the nation has never been in question before? Is this the way we, as Indians, ought to behave with each other? Is this the secularism we preach and pretend to practice?

I went to Amritsar, where I was introduced to a man named Bhagwant Singh Ahuja, a tall, stocky Sikh who ran a profitable trading business, with shops in the Punjab, Delhi, and Bombay. I had been told that Ahuja had links to Sikh priests and others who were sympathetic to some militants. Ahuja turned out to be exceptionally generous with his time and thoughts, offering to take me to the Golden Temple—but only after the priests' meeting had ended. Implicit in what he said was the caution that perhaps it would be inflammatory for a non-Sikh such as myself to be seen in the precincts of the temple while a religious-political meeting was going on. That meeting would last through much of the night.

"This is a very dangerous time," Ahuja said. "People's emotions are very raw. We now more than ever need to get across the message that

Sikhs and Hindus are brothers, that we have such great common links. But what's happening in Delhi now, this slaughter of innocent Sikhs—this is wrecking people's faith here in amity. The feeling among Sikhs is that a minority community is being held to ransom because of the actions of two misguided madmen."

We were having dinner at Ahuja's home, a large bungalow with a glass wall that overlooked a neat lawn. The house itself nestled under mango and eucalyptus trees. On the mantlepiece above a fireplace were porcelain figures and bronzes of various Hindu gods. There was a stone Buddha, and there was an exquisite wooden cross with the crucified Jesus.

"We need the healing touch," Ahuja said. There was a murmur of agreement from around the mahogany dining table. With us were Ahuja's wife, his daughter, and two sons. Also present were a local judge named Gurdial Singh and his wife, and a couple of other Sikhs from the neighborhood. The round table easily accommodated a dozen diners. In the middle of the table were enormous dishes of tandoori chicken, curried lamb, parathas, or roasted bread, and spicy eggplants and potatoes. There was also a mound of saffron rice.

"Bhindranwale was spitting poison, he was propagating things that were not normal for the people of the Punjab," Ahuja continued. "The whole atmosphere was polluted here. People had lost faith in the Akali leaders as well. And Mrs. Gandhi was not applying the healing touch. So what were we left with? Bitterness, anger, sorrow. The joy of life, our hopes, these were all being darkened."

"Nothing justifies the atrocities in Delhi," Gurdial Singh, the judge, said. "I really question the allegations that Sikhs were distributing sweets to celebrate Mrs. Gandhi's death."

"I want to show you something," Ahuja said, getting up suddenly.

He returned shortly with a newspaper clipping and started reading extracts. It was an article by Dharma Kumar, a well-known economic historian in Delhi. It had appeared on the editorial page of *The Times of India,** and Mrs. Kumar, a Hindu, had said: "If all the sweets in India had been distributed, that would not have justified the burning alive of one single Sikh. If burning alive were the punishment for vulgarity and folly, there would be few people left in India. Why should every Sikh be responsible for the doings of all other Sikhs?"

Earlier that evening, Ahuja and his friends had met with some Hindu neighbors. They had decided to form citizens' groups to patrol neighborhoods in the event of trouble. They also agreed to telephone and visit

*November 15, 1984.

as many Sikh and Hindu families as they could to urge everyone to keep cool.

The bazaars near the Golden Temple were packed with people next Sunday morning. We parked outside one of the four main gates, in what seemed to me to be an extension of a bazaar: Ahuja's station wagon had to be squeezed in between a vendor of oranges and a man who had set up a stall of spicy savories. Ahuja's wife and mother went in separately. He and I checked in our shoes at a booth near the entrance, and Ahuja rented for me a patka, or a sort of cap to cover my head—everyone must have their head covered when inside the Golden Temple. We washed our feet in a small basin and then walked down a flight of marble steps into the courtyard of the temple.

The Harimandir sparkled in the brilliant sunshine. The sacred pool in which it sat was lightly ruffled by a cool breeze. I looked around. I was the only non-Sikh male in the vast courtyard. The temple's public address system was broadcasting hymns in the Punjabi language that were being sung inside the Harimandir by granthis, or acolytes. Ahuja and I walked on the marble-floored perimeter, known as the parikrama. We occasionally weaved through columns and under doorways. Ahuja kept very close to me physically. I thought: this is a gesture of protection, this Sikh wants to make sure that his Hindu companion comes to no harm. If I was being bold turning up inside Sikhism's holiest shrine even as Sikhs were being butchered not far away in Delhi by non-Sikhs, then Bhagwant Singh Ahuja was even more courageous in escorting a Hindu to the temple. Several Sikhs stared at us as we walked by. Ahuja sometimes would stop at a ghat, or steps that led into the sacred pool, and sip holy water: I replicated his motions. The water was cool, even sweet.

We bought a tray of flowers from a vendor who had parked himself not far from the Harimandir. "The very fact that you are here must tell you how tolerant Sikhism is," Ahuja said, as we walked on. "You are my brother. That is why you and I are here together. Even if you were my political enemy, I would still bring you here. Why not? The temple is one place where we must all leave our politics and social differences outside." He paused to bow before an ancient tree in whose shadow a Sikh saint, long ago, once lived and preached.

"But there are people who brought their politics and weapons into this temple," Ahuja said. "Look around you. Look carefully." I was startled by what I saw. Abutting the parikrama were mounds of rubble. Marble flooring had caved in. Bullet holes pocked many buildings. The sunburst of shells marked several structures. Even the Akal Takht, which had been restored by the Indian government at a cost of $40 million since the June storming, somehow looked hastily patched up. Heavy tanks had been brought in during that military operation to counter Bhindranwale and his terrorists. * The man in operational charge of the military assault was himself a Sikh—Lieutenant General Ranjit Singh Dayal, chief of staff of the army's prestigious Western Command. General Dayal's main adversary was not Sant Jarnail Singh Bhindranwale, who had no formal military training, but another highly decorated war hero like Dayal himself—Major General Shahbeg Singh. Shahbeg Singh had been among those who trained the Mukti Bahini guerrillas who fought to establish the state of Bangladesh in what was then East Pakistan. But he was later cashiered from the Indian Army on corruption charges. Singh was subsequently recruited by Bhindranwale to train his growing band of militants. It was Shahbeg Singh who had planned the fortification of the Golden Temple. It was he who had trained Bhindranwale's motley band of militants in the use of highly sophisticated weapons such as antitank cannon. Those weapons were fired by the terrorists with deadly accuracy on June 5 and 6. Scores of Indian soldiers died. Officials in Delhi said that the army had been surprised to confront sophisticated weaponry in the Golden Temple. Obviously, the government's intelligence system —seldom an especially reliable one—had let it down again.

As I looked at the temple on this lovely November morning, it seemed inconceivable that anyone could have dared to defile its serenity and sanctity—whether it be Bhindranwale or Shahbeg Singh or the Indian Army. Temples are our last sanctuaries for peace and reflection. Punjab's Sikh terrorists had infiltrated not only the Golden Temple, but also forty-two other gurdwaras across the state. Why had not those temples' priests protested? The lines between the spiritual and the temporal in the Punjab had blurred.

I wept.

Inside the Harimandir, the prayers were for peace and brotherhood this morning, as they are every day of the week. Granthis played on harmoniums. Priests chanted hymns in front of the holy Granth Sahib —the collection of sayings and songs of Guru Nanak—which lay covered by a burgundy-silk shawl. The gold-sheathed walls glistened. There was a powerful fragrance of incense. I followed Ahuja in circumambulating the inner shrine, then I knelt in front of the Granth Sahib, and applied

---

* A complete and accurate list of fatalities was never released. As noted earlier, more than a thousand people are believed to have died, although the Delhi government insists that it was no more than 400. Many Sikhs believe that more than 3,000 men, women, and children were killed during the Indian Army's assault on the Golden Temple, although this figure is somewhat hard to believe.

my forehead to the floor. A hand touched my head. I looked up. It was a Sikh priest, and he was blessing me. I rose, and he handed me some marigolds. He was an old man, and there was a gentle smile on his face.

Ahuja and I walked up to the balcony of the Harimandir. I looked out at the Golden Temple's courtyard, and beyond it toward an entire residential block that had been razed during the June military operation. So much history here, I thought, so much violence, and now what? Will Sikhs and Hindus ever again worship here without mutual suspicion? Will they intermarry with the same zest and enthusiasm? Will Hindu families, who had traditionally converted their eldest sons to Sikhism, continue the practice? Or will Sikhs now be a besieged minority in a country for which so many had shed their blood and perished in battle over the years? Ahuja and I looked at each other, as if the same thoughts rushed through our minds, but we said nothing to each other. What was there to say?

We started toward the parikrama again. On the way, Ahuja lingered near a blackboard on which was handwritten, in chalk, the daily quotation from the Granth Sahib, which serves as Sikhism's bible. The script was Gurumukhi, which had been devised by Guru Nanak's successor, Guru Angad. The script was one of the very first steps toward establishing a separate Sikh identity.

"*This world is a transitory place,*" the quotation read. "*Some of our compatriots have already gone, and someday the rest of us also have to go. This world is only a temporary abode.*"

It was an astonishing quotation to have put up at a time of such crisis, I thought. It was freighted with humility and fatalism. I wished I could have broadcast it to those rampaging Hindus in Delhi: The quotation would have put them to shame.

We climbed the stairs that led away from the parikrama. A fresh hymn was being broadcast now, sung in Punjabi by a granthi. He sang softly at first, then his voice rose clear and sharp.

"If God is with me," came the granthi's words, "what do we have to fear? Nothing."

In the weeks following my first visit to Amritsar, the arithmetic of population in the Punjab began to change. More than 50,000 Sikhs emigrated to the state from other parts of India. They came here from Himachal Pradesh and Uttar Pradesh and Haryana, even as far away as Bihar and Orissa. They fled their homes to escape further harassment. Many of the émigrés were widows and orphaned children. There are still some 7 million Sikhs spread across states other than the Punjab—but the 50,000 men, women, and children who poured into this already troubled state brought with them tales of horror. These tales were narrated every day, and the narrations exacerbated tensions.

One evening near Amritsar, I listened to Amrik Singh, a young carpenter who had transplanted himself from his home in Delhi. He spoke before a small gathering of friends and relatives in a dhaaba, a roadside restaurant. People squatted on the floor, huddled in blankets to keep out the bitter December cold. Singh was a tall, thin man, with a mustache and narrow eyes that looked at you with pain. His voice was so low that the slightest rustling of someone's blanket would smother a sentence. But everyone's attention was riveted on him. He said he had lost his father, five brothers, and two sons during the riots following Indira Gandhi's assassination. They were hacked to death, he said. His wife was gang-raped while he was made to watch, his seven-year-old daughter was molested. He himself was repeatedly stabbed, almost castrated, and left for dead. Now he and his wife were starting all over again in the Punjab.

His audience seemed stunned as he spoke. It is not often that a Sikh male will volunteer information that his wife's honor was violated. Women started weeping. Men began to shout in anger. I thought: These tales will be told and retold until they become part of the Punjab's mythology. How many young men like Amrik Singh would swear revenge? How could Sikhs ever forgive Hindus? How would the bitterness and anguish ever disappear from this land? We need the healing touch, Bhagwant Singh Ahuja had said to me that November evening not long after the murder of Mrs. Gandhi. But who would bring a healing hand to these proud and wounded people of the Punjab? Rajiv Gandhi? Would he be able to forget—and forgive—the fact that his mother was murdered by two Sikhs? His December election campaign was not especially heroic: His ruling Congress Party appealed shamelessly to the sentiments of India's overwhelming Hindu majority by charging that the Sikh leadership had balked at resolving the Punjab problem. He charged that Opposition leaders were in collusion with antinational elements in the Punjab. A "foreign hand" was working actively to destabilize the Punjab, Gandhi said. He did not elaborate. This was not the sort of rhetoric that would reassure Punjab's Sikhs. But then, the Punjab was not voting in the 1984 election.

In Delhi I came across posters put up by Congress Party candidates that said: "Would you trust a taxi driver from another state? For better security, vote Congress." Since a large number of Delhi's taxi drivers were Sikh, the message was clear. Even clearer, and more sickening, were billboards commissioned by Congress candidates in states like Andhra Pradesh and Kerala. These depicted a slain Indira Gandhi, blood gushing from her body, being held by her son Rajiv. Two Sikhs crouched at one side, their guns smoking. Indians rewarded Rajiv Gandhi's Congress Party with 401 out of 508 seats contested for the national parliament.

During my travels around India, I was astonished at how many non-Sikhs, particularly educated and affluent Indians, voiced the view that the Sikhs "had it coming" to them. One very cold January evening in Delhi, I sat in the drawing room of my brother-in-law, Ajai Lal. The mood in Lal's home was one of general jubilation over Rajiv Gandhi's unprecedented victory. Gandhi and some of his top aides, such as Arun Singh, had studied at the exclusive Doon School in North India—and most of the males present this evening also were Doon graduates (they called themselves Doscoes). In fact, thirty-two newly elected parliamentarians had attended the Doon School in Dehra Doon.

One particular guest did not, however, dwell too much on the old-boy angle. He was a young local businessman, and he consumed several glasses of whiskey and kept up a harangue about the Punjab. He himself was a Punjabi Hindu. "We will fix them now," he said. "They thought they were God's gift to India, eh? They thought they were the only strong, virile ones around, eh? Well, they sure showed themselves to be cowards recently, didn't they? How many faced the mobs with courage, eh?"

"Would you have faced a mob like that?" I asked.

The businessman shrugged. He helped himself to another whiskey.

"Those bastards," he said, presently, "those Sikh bastards. If I had my way, I would rip their bowels out. I would slaughter every last one of them. I would decimate them. Those arrogant, filthy bastards. Who do they think they are? They have destroyed India."

I shivered, and it was not because of the cold.

I returned to the Punjab in December that year, more than a month after my first trip, to see for myself what changes had taken place in the state. The assassination, although less than two months old, was no longer the main item for discussion in most people's homes. One of her assassins, Beant Singh, had died within an hour of shooting the prime minister: He was killed by troops of the Indo-Tibetan Border Force in a guardhouse just yards from where Mrs. Gandhi was felled. Satwant Singh, too, had been shot by his captors, but he survived and was now being questioned by the authorities. Officials were soon to arrest another alleged conspirator, Kehar Singh. In the event, Satwant and Kehar—who once worked as a minor official in the government's supply office in New Delhi—were found guilty after a long trial; both men were sentenced to be executed, although their lawyers began what appeared to be an uphill campaign for clemency.* (Meanwhile, Ram Saran and T. S. Jambhal, two of the guards who had allegedly shot Mrs. Gandhi's assassins, were also being tried in a Delhi court.)

All sorts of theories were being advanced about conspiracies. The American Central Intelligence Agency—always a convenient scapegoat in most of the Third World, but particularly in India—was said to be behind the assassination of Mrs. Gandhi, whose political alignment with the Soviet Union had long been resented by Washington. Pakistan, which was said to support the separatists who wanted to establish Khalistan, was also believed to have been behind the plot. Relatives of Beant and Satwant were arrested in their Punjab villages, then freed, then rearrested, and let go again. The investigators appeared to be making little progress.

Many Indians were coming around to the view that rather than being a major international conspiracy, the murder of Indira Gandhi had been a case of vengeance by a handful of Sikhs who were maddened by the invasion of the Golden Temple in Amritsar. Beant and Satwant were reported to have taken vows of revenge at the Bangla Sahib Gurudwara in New Delhi. By mid-December, few Indians I encountered bothered to speculate much about conspiracies and the motives of the killers. Their attention, instead, seemed focused on the political future of India. A national election campaign was in full swing in India, but the Punjab had been excluded from the parliamentary poll because of the political instability here. The army was still out in force around the state, but places like Amritsar were no longer under curfew. Rajiv Gandhi, as the new prime minister, was going around the country saying that Sikhs would have no reason to fear their for their safety under his administration—but few Sikhs had been compensated for the frightful loss to their property during the riots after Mrs. Gandhi's assassination. And not one rioter had been arrested and brought to justice following the murder.†

The Hindus and Sikhs of the Punjab continued their dangerous drift away from one another. Few civic leaders in this troubled state dared to call openly for rapprochement. No one issued calls for national unity:

---

* Satwant Singh and Kehar Singh went to the gallows in Delhi on January 6, 1989.
† It was not until 1991 that some rioters were convicted.

There were already two countries within this single state. More than 8,000 men and women, suspected of being terrorists or of sympathizing with Sikh terrorists, were in the Punjab's jails; few of them had been allowed to see lawyers. Among those behind bars were said to be boys and girls under eleven years of age.

"It is very difficult now to go to the Punjab and talk to the masses about any reconciliation," Manmohan Singh, the chairman of Frick India and one of India's most respected Sikh industrialists, said to me. "There are thousands of Sikh students now in jail on what are at best vague charges. Their parents won't even hear of reconciliation. So what does one do? You bide your time."

I found that Hindus were even more angry that Sikhs hadn't, as a community, formally condemned the assassination of Indira Gandhi. And Sikhs were bitter that not one of those who had murdered their brethren across North India and looted their homes had been arrested or punished.

"This is justice?" asked Mickey Singh, Bhagwant Singh Ahuja's son. "You call this a free, civilized society?"

He was echoing outrage being expressed around the country. I asked Mickey, a tall, sturdy Sikh who is only twenty-three but who appears much older, what he thought Mrs. Gandhi's legacy was for the Punjab.

"Legacy?" Mickey Singh said. "You ask about legacy? Just look around you. Look at the army, and the unhappiness. You want to find out about her legacy?"

In Britain, where there are said to be nearly 500,000 Sikhs, there was jubilation in the Sikh community over Indira Gandhi's death. Jagjit Singh Chohan, the self-appointed "president" of Khalistan, gave several television interviews when the news of the assassination broke in London.

"She was doomed to die," Chohan, a physician with a long white beard and a gentle manner, said. "She deserved to die."

What about Rajiv Gandhi? an interviewer asked. Would he now also be killed?

"He's definitely a target," Chohan said, "and he should be."*

Sikhs marched in processions in Southall, the London neighborhood that Britons call "Little India." They distributed chocolates. Sikh women danced in the streets. Not everybody shared these sentiments. Non-

*Chohan later denied making some of these remarks, but the videotapes contradict him.

Sikhs recoiled in horror. Hindus conducted special mourning services in temples. In New York City, too, many Sikhs were ecstatic over the event. They bought hundreds of dollars' worth of candy and sweetmeats, and distributed them to passersby in front of Asian grocery stores on Lexington Avenue in Manhattan. They drank champagne. They gave out roses. They tore up photographs of Indira Gandhi and spat on the Indian flag. Like Chohan across the Atlantic, they appeared on television programs and said they were delighted about Mrs. Gandhi's death.

If tensions between Hindus and Sikhs had built up in India because of the Punjab problem, these frictions until now were rarely mirrored in relations between the two communities in Britain. Hindus and Sikhs had mostly lived in harmony here. They were, after all, both strangers in a land where white attitudes concerning nonwhite immigrants were becoming guarded, even hostile. Britain, which once hired the poor men of its former tropical possessions in the West Indies and India for its textile and metal-fabricating industries, now was withdrawing such welcome. Why? Because Britain's once flourishing economy was languishing; the great foundries of the Midlands were shutting down, as British metal products lost out in the face of sharp competition from Western Europe, Japan, Taiwan, even Singapore; unemployment was in excess of 12 percent—in a country of barely 53 million people.* The immigrants from the Indian Subcontinent labored especially hard. Sikhs, particularly, had become the single most affluent ethnic community in Britain. Many of these wealthy Sikhs had started off as farmers in the Punjab.

It was in Britain that the Khalistan movement initially gathered steam. Men like Jagjit Singh Chohan, who became unhappy with Indira Gandhi's stonewalling tactics concerning Sikh demands for greater autonomy in the Punjab, decided that the time was propitious to start agitating for not an autonomous state but an independent and theocratic nation—Khalistan.†

Chohan raised millions of dollars for his cause from rich Sikhs all over the world. Khalistan cells were created in Canada and the United States, where there are significant Sikh enclaves. The Khalistan supporters issued their own fancy passports and their own currency, which, of course, were only "legal" in Chohan's modest home in London. The Khalistanis feared that Sikhism was on the decline: Sikhs were freely intermarrying with Hindus; Sikh males were cutting off their long hair and beards;‡ some

---

*According to British government figures, total immigration into Britain in 1983 was 12,000, the lowest figure in more than a decade.
†"Khalistan" means "Land of the Pure." So does the name "Pakistan."
‡Sikhism requires males not to cut their hair. That explains why Sikh males wear turbans.

Sikhs were returning to the folds of Hinduism—Hindus viewed Sikhism not as a separate religion but as a variation of Hinduism, much as Hindus hundreds of years ago had initially tended to regard Buddhism as a branch of their own faith.

(Eventually, Buddhism established itself as a major religion outside of India; in India, the Hindus' priestly caste, the Brahmans, declared, in a theological *coup de grâce*, as it were, that Buddhism's founder, Gautama Buddha, had actually been the ninth avatar, or reincarnation, of the god Vishnu. The Lord Vishnu, the priests would explain, periodically came down to earth in the guise of a mortal so that he could offer salvation to sinning human beings. Centuries later, Hindu clergymen countered the growing influence of Christian missionaries in much the same way: They said that Jesus Christ was also an incarnation of Vishnu.)

The Khalistanis' fears were exacerbated by reports that orthodox Hindu proselytizers in the Punjab were proclaiming that Sikhs were only Hindus by another name. The Khalistanis were aware of Hinduism's great modus operandi—triumph not by coercion but by cooption; Hinduism assimilated and absorbed, it did not convert by the sword as Islam did. Chohan and his supporters felt that the purity of Sikhism could only be preserved in a totally independent Sikh nation. They began to solicit and receive the endorsement of many Sikh clergymen in the Punjab, who shared Chohan's apprehension that unless something dramatic was done soon —like creating a new Sikh nation—Sikhism would be completely absorbed by Hinduism in the not-too-distant future.

Supporting Chohan, too, was the fiery Sikh fundamentalist Sant Jarnail Singh Bhindranwale. Bhindranwale, once an ally of Mrs. Gandhi, holed up in the Golden Temple. From there he directed a terrorist movement that would result in the deaths of hundreds of Hindus and moderate Sikhs in the Punjab who did not support him. Indian intelligence officials were convinced that Bhindranwale's terrorist activities were financed by Sikhs living abroad, including Jagjit Singh Chohan. These officials also seem convinced that the Sikh separatists were somehow being helped by the American Central Intelligence Agency.*

---

* To this day, senior Indian officials maintain that the CIA has actively helped the Khalistan movement by funneling arms and ammunition into the Punjab. Why would the CIA interfere in India's domestic affairs? Indian officials say that Washington has never been happy with India's left-leaning nonalignment, and therefore has used every opportunity available to destabilize the country. Of course, such perceived interference by Washington has also driven New Delhi closer to Moscow, both politically and also in terms of obtaining military assistance. India and the Soviet Union signed a friendship treaty in 1971, and both countries said in early 1991 that the treaty would be renewed.

Indira Gandhi viewed the Khalistan "struggle" not only as a secessionist movement but also one that directly and immediately threatened the unity and integrity of India. If Sikhs were allowed to break away into their own nation, then would not the people of another strategic border state, Kashmir, also accelerate their simmering movement to gain independence from India? Mrs. Gandhi was aware that in the cases of both Punjab and Kashmir, neighboring Pakistan, India's bitter foe, was providing moral support, and maybe more. Sikhs were in the majority in the Punjab; Muslims enjoyed a majority in Kashmir. If the Punjab became Khalistan and Kashmir became independent—or was annexed by Pakistan, as was possible—then, as journalist M. J. Akbar said, the Indian capital of Delhi would "end up as a border city."[*]

This Mrs. Gandhi could never allow. After much hesitation, she sent in her troops in June 1984 to flush out Bhindranwale's terrorists from the Golden Temple. Professor Ralph Buultjens recalls her anguish over the military action. He had been in New Delhi the day that the prime minister gave her military commanders the green light, and to the very end Mrs. Gandhi pondered the toll that the military action would inflict.[†] To this day, those close to Mrs. Gandhi feel that she may have been pressured into such action by a small group of hawks around her, against the cautionary signals flashed by her own political instincts.[‡] Awesome damage was done to the historic shrine during the military operation; not only Bhindranwale and his key lieutenants but also hundreds of pilgrims, including women and children, were killed. Sikhs all over the world were horrified. The Khalistan leaders swore they would take revenge. So on this October morning in London, Chohan and his friends were beside themselves with joy when they heard that Indira Gandhi had been murdered. "In June, when we said we would kill her, no one believed it," said a Sikh who identified himself as Baldev Singh. "We've done it. And we will continue until Khalistan is formed."

Later on the day of the assassination, various television programs recapped Prime Minister Gandhi's turbulent career. The BBC ran snippets from one of her last television interviews. Did she fear being killed by the Khalistanis who had vowed vengeance, an interviewer asked Mrs. Gandhi? "I've lived with danger all my life," she replied, "and I've lived

[*] M. J. Akbar was a member of Parliament from 1989 to 1991, representing the Congress Party from the eastern state of Bihar. Akbar continues to write, having served for several years as Rajiv Gandhi's spokesman.
[†] Ralph Buultjens frequently visited Mrs. Gandhi in Delhi. On this occasion, his visit followed several telephone conversations with her from New York.
[‡] These hawks reportedly included Rajiv Gandhi and P. C. Alexander.

a pretty full life. And it makes no difference if I die in bed or die standing up."

Not long after Indira Gandhi's assassination and the murderous aftermath, her close friend Pupul Jayakar* wrote a letter to another longtime Indira friend, Dorothy Norman. Miss Norman, a New York-based writer and photographer, had maintained a correspondence with Indira for nearly four decades.[†] Whenever Indira visited New York, she would spend time with Miss Norman. This is what Mrs. Jayakar, an art historian and collector, wrote to Dorothy Norman:

> The horror of the whole thing! She had such élan, such grace, such lightness of foot. She had a fluid mind, could look with clear eyes into the situation around her, could find time for the significant things of life even though the pressures of the immediate were so complex.
>
> Three days earlier I had met her. She was going the next day to Srinagar. She said she wanted to go as she had never seen the Chinar leaves turn brilliant red and orange in autumn. She spoke of one of the oldest Chinar trees in the Valley; she had just heard that it died.
>
> The last time I saw her, she spoke at length of death. I am glad that her face was untouched by the assassins' bullets. She looked extremely beautiful and at peace.

---

* Pupul Jayakar has long been known as India's "czarina" for culture. She is credited with reviving the handicrafts industry, and with revitalizing village communities that depended heavily on artisans' revenues for general economic sustenance. Along with S. K. Misra—a top civil servant—Mrs. Jayakar also initiated the "Festival of India" series under which massive celebrations of Indian art and culture were organized during the 1980s in Britain, the United States, France, Japan, and the Soviet Union. Doubtless, her friendship with Indira Gandhi enabled Mrs. Jayakar to expedite her plans; but she has certainly done more to positively project India's image abroad, and to help India's languishing artisans and rural craftsmen, than almost anyone else in recent memory.

[†]Dorothy Norman has written extensively about her correspondence with Indira Gandhi. See *Letters to an American Friend* (New York: Harcourt Brace Jovanovich, 1985), p. 178.

4

The Legacy
of Indira Gandhi

The murder of Indira Gandhi altered the political landscape of India, and arguably of the Third World as well. It touched off a holocaust in which several thousand innocent Sikhs were massacred by Hindu mobs who were blessed, if not led, by factotums of the ruling Congress Party.[*] The very idea of secularism, ardently espoused by Indira Gandhi's father, Jawaharlal Nehru, and so eloquently enshrined in the Indian constitution, was suddenly threatened.[†] Government in the capital city of New Delhi was paralyzed. No officials seemed able, or willing, to give orders to police and soldiers to stop the carnage of Sikhs by vengeful Hindus.

The questions on everyone's mind were: Would India, the world's

---

[*] Few of those suspected of wreaking havoc against the Sikhs have been brought to justice. Indeed, some of the Congress Party politicians who were allegedly behind the attacks in North India have even prospered. On March 30, 1991, Judge J. B. Goel in New Delhi's Sessions Court convicted Tribhuvan Nath, Sita Ram, and Wazir Nath—all slum dwellers in Delhi's Sultanpuri Resettlement Colony—of the murders of three Sikhs, Himmat Singh, Sunder Singh, and Wazir Singh. They were sentenced to life imprisonment. The culprits, Judge Goel said in his fifty-five-page judgment, "had no personal enmity or vendetta" against their victims. They were "swayed by the grave mob fury." The judge noted that the victims were attacked with sticks and iron rods, and later burned in the presence of their relatives. It was the first time that anyone had been convicted for participating in the riots following the assassination of Indira Gandhi.

[†] By "secularism," Indians mean tolerance of all religions and creeds. Even though India's population is predominantly Hindu, there are still some 110 million Muslims, a little more than 10 percent of the population. Put another way, India has the third largest Muslim population in the world, after Indonesia and Bangladesh.

biggest democracy, survive as one nation? Would the center hold? Today those questions remain. India is racked by more violence, and more political and social turbulence, than ever before—and more seized by uncertainty about its future than at any other time since Independence. The murder of Rajiv Gandhi raised anew the question of the survival of democracy. This is certainly not a legacy that Indira Gandhi would have wanted to bequeath to her nation. But, given her policies, and the divisive social forces she released, it is hardly a surprise that the conditions and contours of today's India have turned out this way.

The debate over Indira Gandhi's legacy continues—albeit fitfully—to this day, just as it began the morning of her assassination. The death of Rajiv Gandhi, in fact, has deepened that debate—and it has introduced new and troubling questions: When leader after leader in a democracy gets assassinated, what does it do to the psyche of a nation? If democracy is to function in an atmosphere of constant violence and turmoil, then is democracy worth it? On balance, has the Nehru-Gandhi dynasty done more good or more harm to India?

While Indira Gandhi still continues to puzzle many people even from the grave, there are those who believe that her leadership will stand the test of time. Professor Ralph Buultjens believes that the real test of a political leader was how he tackled his society's problems.

"Did the leader leave his country behind in better shape than when he found it?" Professor Buultjens says. "In a larger sense, Indira Gandhi meets this test well."

According to the professor, India coped well with many difficulties under Indira's helmsmanship: the Bangladesh war of 1971; the global oil crisis of the 1970s; the economic slump that followed; the Emergency of 1975–77. "She managed to sustain the unity and integrity of India," Buultjens said. She was responsible for making India a self-sufficient country in food, he went on, and she instilled in the country's poor a consciousness that they had the right to a better life. Mrs. Gandhi, Buultjens said, took personal interest in promoting such things as science, technology, and higher education, items she saw as the "bedrocks" of India in the future.

"She was also a real secularist," Buultjens said. "She really believed that people of all religions could coexist within the boundaries of a modern state."

"She was the single most exposed and heard political figure in all of history," Buultjens said. "Just think of the millions in India who saw her at rallies, on television, who heard her voice on radio. And think of her own life—she met virtually every major political figure of this century: Gandhi, Nehru, Churchill, De Gaulle, Adenauer, Monnet, Kennedy, Eisenhower."

It was largely because she was her father's daughter that Indira gained such exposure. Between 1947 and 1964, she served as Prime Minister Nehru's official hostess. Her mother, Kamala, had died in 1936. Nehru never remarried, although he enjoyed dalliances with a number of women. Indira Gandhi's own marriage in 1942 to a Parsi named Feroze Gandhi floundered: She and her two sons, Rajiv and Sanjay, now lived with Nehru at the prime minister's official residence in New Delhi—Teen Murti Bhavan—while Feroze Gandhi camped in a house reserved for parliamentarians. An alcoholic—and a workaholic—Feroze died in 1960 of a heart attack.* Those years at Nehru's side were invaluable. She learned statecraft. As president of his Congress Party, Mrs. Gandhi—just barely in her forties—played a leading role in forging a coalition in Kerala that defeated that state's ruling Communist government. She traveled the length and breadth of India, getting to know grass-roots party workers everywhere. She often accompanied her father on his frequent trips abroad; she attended summit meetings, she sat in on his sessions with such Third World leaders such as Marshal Tito of Yugoslavia and Gamal Abdel Nasser of Egypt, who had founded the Nonaligned Movement. This experience more than made up for her lack of a completed university education.

It was not until after Nehru's death in 1964 that Indira Gandhi fully came into her own. She was selected by Nehru's successor, Prime Minister Lal Bahadur Shastri, to serve as minister for information and broadcasting. Shastri died in Tashkent of a heart attack on January 10, 1966, while visiting the Soviet Union to sign a treaty that would formally end a bitter war with Pakistan; fourteen days later, Indira was sworn in as prime minister. She was initially chosen because the Congress Party's aging but still powerful leaders—known collectively as the Syndicate —thought Indira Gandhi would be extremely amenable to their manipulations. No one suspected her of possessing a steely will. She outmaneuvered these party bosses, broke away from the old Congress to form her own Congress Party, and flourished. But the years in office were not free of controversy. She imposed a national "Emergency" in 1975, contending that Opposition leaders had brought India to the brink of disintegration.

* Feroze Gandhi was not related to Mohandas "Mahatma" Gandhi. Feroze belonged to the small Parsi community, followers of the Persian-born Zoroaster. Mahatma Gandhi was a Hindu from the western state of Gujarat. It was simply a coincidence that Indira came into such close contact with two Gandhis during her lifetime, each man playing a major role in her personal life and career.

Thousands of her political opponents were incarcerated during the two-year period, when the constitution was suspended.

When she decided to hold general elections in March 1977, her party was routed. During her three years in political exile, however, she meticulously planned her return to office. The opposition Janata Party, which had defeated the Congress, collapsed because of internecine squabbling, paving the way for new elections in January 1980. Once again, Indira became prime minister of India.

How would Indira Gandhi be remembered?

"As a political giant," Ralph Buultjens said. "As a superb political strategist. As a leader who genuinely cared for her people and worked selflessly for them."

Some weeks after the assassination, the British writer Marie Seton spoke at length with Ian Jack of the London *Sunday Times* about her long years of friendship with Indira Gandhi. The London-based Seton would meet up with Indira either in Britain or in India at least once a year.* She had enjoyed a private lunch with Mrs. Gandhi in New Delhi a few days before the Indian Army's storming of the Golden Temple.

"She seemed like a woman who had run out of steam," Miss Seton told Ian Jack. "She'd always been a private person, an introvert rather than an extrovert, instinctive rather than empirical, but now she seemed to be genuinely at a loss and more melancholic than I'd ever known her. I took away the impression that she no longer knew whom to trust, or what advice to act on. I think she'd begun to doubt her own judgment. I felt worried and sorry for her."

On the day that the prime minister was assassinated, there was no massive outpouring of grief for Indira in most places across this huge country.

There was, of course, alarm over the brutal manner in which she'd been murdered, but about Indira Gandhi herself there was a noticeable ambivalence. Shops and offices shut down, and people welcomed the opportunity to go home early. Other than her Congress Party associates and sycophants who now stood to be deprived of her patronage, most people simply did not shed tears for her.

I recalled the day Indira's father died in 1964. I was in high school then. The whole nation shook with shock and sadness when the news spread on May 27 that Jawaharlal was no more; people cried openly. Nehru, the father of modern India, drew hero worship and affection from

---

*Marie Seton was a long-standing friend of the Nehru family. She had written an acclaimed biography of Jawaharlal Nehru. Miss Seton died in London in 1985.

the masses as no one before him, perhaps not even Mahatma Gandhi, Nehru's mentor and the man who more than any other helped India obtain independence. Nehru's daughter was far less loved by everyday Indians, although there were periods—after the 1971 victory in the Bangladesh war, for instance—when Indira Gandhi enjoyed overwhelming popular support. She lacked her father's capacity for demonstrating affection openly, his affability and his gift of laughter in public. Those better acquainted with her claimed that Indira could be warm and share in laughter with her intimates—a side of her personality that she rarely revealed in public.

Throughout her years of stewardship of India, Indira Gandhi came across to people mostly as a grim woman of unbridled ambition who would stop at nothing to gain and consolidate power. There was more to it than that: Both Nehru and Mahatma Gandhi gave enough play to the essential plurality of India; they sought consensus, they solicited diverse counsel, including advice from those politically and ideologically opposed to their own positions. These tactics obtained for Nehru, especially, widespread popular admiration. His daughter, instead, had imposed on the national scene the will of one person. It was, of course, a matter of style, and maybe of circumstance. As with most people, the key to Indira's personality lay in her childhood—a privileged childhood, to be sure, but a very lonely one. Indira grew up with virtually no close friends, surrounded by a sea of people whose focus was not Jawaharlal and Kamala Nehru's only child but the dramatic struggle for freedom going on at the time.

That she wanted national unity and strove for it there need be no doubt. But the politics that she pursued to achieve her goal left deep scars on the country's communal, regional, and political framework. During her reign, well-established institutions began crumbling. One reason why many of her admirers, as well as some among her critics, thought that there was no alternative to Indira was that she had so managed a number of political problems, such as the Punjab crisis, in a way that convinced everyone that only she could handle them. I think it is quite legitimate to ask, now that both Indira and Rajiv are dead, whether traditional societies of a heterogenous nature such as India need dynastic figures to hold a nation together. For implicit in the notion of hereditary rule is the question of indispensability—and that, in a democracy, can always constitute a danger.

What Indira Gandhi did following her swearing-in as prime minister was to undertake a definite transformation in the manner in which political power was exercised in India. Rather than seek popular and secular appeal as Nehru had, she sought to rouse—however subtly—the chauvinistic sentiments, especially in her last years, of the country's Hindu majority whose electoral support she considered vital to her political survival.

"My father was a statesman, I am a politician—my father was a saint, I am not," Indira once said, in a rare moment of candor. "He was not a politician in the sense that the word is understood in the West or, unfortunately, in India. For most of us who grew up in the freedom struggle, politics was not a career. It was not a job or a question of getting something for yourself. It was working, sacrificing, and struggling for your country. My father exemplified this. When I said he was a saint, I meant he was a very good man—a basically good man. Winston Churchill once said that he was a man who had conquered hatred and fear. He had no viciousness or spite in him."[*]

She might have added that her father was everything that Indira Gandhi was not. Much of her energy was concentrated on the politics of survival. She moved from her father's policy of seeking national consensus to one of confrontation. Confrontation, of course, was her way of keeping her opponents constantly off guard. She refused to accept the legitimacy of an opposition government in another strategic border state, Kashmir, and actively undermined and subsequently toppled that administration. She alienated the sensitivities of southerners when she authorized a clumsy—and unsuccessful—attempt to overthrow a legitimately elected Opposition government in the state of Andhra Pradesh.[†] In short, Indira Gandhi could tolerate no opposition of any kind: She wanted to be unchallenged. It was not necessary to create these problems, and Indira was not able to manage them—they remained to haunt Rajiv Gandhi. She informally groomed Rajiv for the office of prime minister, but she also left him a legacy of central management in a troubled nation. This legacy will haunt Indian leaders well into the next century. V. P. Singh and Chandra Shekhar—the men who followed Rajiv Gandhi as prime minister in 1989 and 1990, respectively—quickly found out how the Punjab and Kashmir would consume their government and their guts. In the end, Indira Gandhi fell victim to the very poisons she injected into the Indian system. And so, in the days following her assassination, India mourned, but it did not weep for Indira.

[*] Conversation with Professor Ralph Buultjens, New Delhi, August 1977.
[†] Rajiv Gandhi, who was then general secretary of the Congress Party, helped to shape this attempt to oust the legitimate Andhra Pradesh government—one of Rajiv's first major strategic ventures in politics.

It occurred to me that October day that the murder of Indira Gandhi nevertheless brought to an end a special era, just as Nehru's death had. It was an era dominated by an ongoing confrontation between Indira and the opposition parties, but it was also an era of a charismatic leader whose style and character had been forged in the freedom struggle against the British. Sudheendra Kulkarni, a distinguished writer and editor with the *Sunday Observer*, has this to say about Indira Gandhi's legacy:

> I believe that Indira Gandhi left behind a complex legacy which I can neither fully condemn nor fully praise. But on balance her legacy has been negative, especially as it affects Indian politics. She killed the spirit of dissent and democracy in the Congress Party. And since that party also happens to be the largest, oldest and, in many ways, the only national political organization in the country, the erosion of democracy in the Congress also meant grievous injury to the democratic process in India as a whole. Indira tolerated corruption—and she nurtured, indeed even encouraged, the notion of the indispensability of dynastic rule by the Nehrus. *

James Michaels, editor of *Forbes*, offers a different assessment:

> How will history judge Indira Gandhi? Her flaws were obvious: her tendency to surround herself with nonthreatening nonentities, her ruthlessness. She was political to her very soul; while campaigning on an "eliminate-poverty" platform, she did little to stimulate the economic growth that can alone reduce poverty in a developing economy. Politics interested her; economics was secondary. Grant all this, but examine the other side of the balance sheet. This fragile woman held India together. Given the centrifugal tendencies, she may have been right to emphasize politics over economics. She had a shrewd sense of timing, rarely making major moves until she felt the swell of public opinion behind her. When she did move, it was with overwhelming force. Take the war with Pakistan over Bangladesh. She held her hand while millions of refugees poured into India, while Pakistani troops committed atrocities in what was then East Pakistan; she seemed to remain passive despite the clamor for action from the electorate. But she was not being passive; just waiting for her case to build. India won an overwhelming victory.
>
> Indira Gandhi has been faulted, unjustly I believe, for the Indian

* Conversation with the author, New York City, February 1991.

Army's bloody and partly bungled attack on the Golden Temple in Amritsar. Whoever was to blame for the political impasse between the Sikh community and the government, by the time she sent the army in there was really no alternative to the use of overwhelming force. The place was no more a temple; it was an arsenal and a hiding place for assassins and cutthroats. The worst element of Sikh terrorists had taken it over; these terrorists were sallying forth to kill women and children and old men, then scurrying to the temple for refuge. People now say: Perhaps she used excessive force. But at the time the Hindu majority and the moderate Sikhs were wondering what she was waiting for. In the event, the attack on the Golden Temple cost Indira Gandhi her life. To have failed to act would have cost her and India worse: a total breakdown of authority.

I interviewed her in early 1984 when she had less than a year to live. She was in a philosophical mood, dwelling on the difficulties of working needed change in an ancient, impoverished society. I shall never forget her words: "Although India doesn't present the tidy picture we would like to have, you can't deny the forward movement." No, you can't. Nor can you deny her dominating presence in that movement. *

There are many others who will agree with Jim Michaels. Their assessment of Indira Gandhi claims that she had a deep and genuine commitment to the poorer segment of Indian society and did whatever possible to help the dispossessed. Her capacity to win elections—she lost only one during her lifetime, in 1977—indicates that a large portion of the Indian masses agreed with this judgment. Says Professor Buultjens: "Whatever the intelligentsia may theorize, the ultimate proof of a leader's resonance with the people lies in the ability to win elections in democracies. In or out of power, Indira Gandhi consistently remained the single most popular political figure in India during her years of public life. We should not massage facts to support intellectual theories that the people themselves rejected. This is not such a bad achievement, after all."

The ascension of Rajiv Gandhi as prime minister opened the door for a generation of political leaders who were born or who grew up after Independence in modern India and who were likely to be more technolog-

* "From Mahatma Gandhi to Rajiv Gandhi," by James W. Michaels. The essay appeared as a foreword to *Vengeance*, by Pranay Gupte, pp. 19–20.

ically oriented and receptive to modern business strategies than Mrs. Gandhi and the politicians of her generation.

On December 24 and 27, 1984, nearly 300 million voters participated in elections for the national Parliament—and Rajiv Gandhi's ruling Congress Party won an unprecedented 401 out of 508 seats contested. The young Gandhi had campaigned promising change, but he provided few specifics. When the election results were announced on the morning of December 29, the stunning majority that Indian voters handed to Rajiv Gandhi was widely interpreted not as an endorsement of Indira Gandhi's policies, nor as a sympathy vote. Rajiv Gandhi was seen as having received a mandate to institute accelerated change; he was seen as the man to fulfill the aspirations of a young population, 75 percent of whom were born after Independence.

For this post-Independence generation, Rajiv Gandhi, despite his political inexperience, was clearly India's hope for the future. His triumph also reflected the widespread disenchantment of Indian voters with the national Opposition parties, which they saw as being disunited, petty-minded, and aimless. It was the first time since Independence that a massive negative vote was cast by Indians not against a government in power but against an Opposition. It was not an especially heartening campaign: More than $300 million was said to have been spent by Gandhi's ruling Congress Party, among other things on an advertising spree that stirred up voters against any public dissidence by raising the specter of disintegration.* The Opposition parties were cleverly portrayed as promoting discord at a time of deepening national crisis over issues such as the Punjab and Kashmir; the Congress message was that the Indian nation was in danger and that Rajiv Gandhi's party alone was capable of saving India from anarchy. As Professor Rajni Kothari of New Delhi's Centre for the Study of Developing Societies said to me, this was a big coup by a party that had brought the country to the brink of disintegration yet successfully sold the line that the Opposition was actually responsible for it.† The Congress Party, with less subtlety, appealed to the deep-rooted communal instincts of India's Hindu majority, particularly in the Hindi-speaking belt in the northern states of Uttar Pradesh, Haryana, Bihar, Madhya Pradesh, and Rajasthan. It was not just India's 14 million Sikhs who felt alienated; India's large Muslim population felt similarly shut out of the political process. No doubt a major factor

---

* The bulk of Rajiv Gandhi's political advertising was handled by a Bombay-based company called Rediffusion.
† Conversations with the author in New Delhi, 1985.

underlying the "Rajiv Wave" was the growing assertiveness of the Hindu voter. According to many Indians, a long period of pluralistic, segmented existence was leading to a slow sense of uneasiness with mainstream politics. Many Hindus were beginning to feel cheated: They entertained a feeling that the very spirit of accommodation and tolerance on which the Hindus prided themselves was being misused, that India's "minorities"—from Muslims and Sikhs to tribal communities in Assam—were being pampered by the federal government. These minorities seemed to have obtained generous state patronage—and here were the Hindus, the so-called majority, left high and dry.

Many Indians saw the communal vote for Rajiv Gandhi's Congress Party as less a result of the alienation of minorities from it than one of assertion of the Hindu, responding to the call for unifying the disparate groupings and identities, for homogenization, for a strong India—for a strong Hindu India. "All of this was reflected in the so-called Rajiv Wave—the rest was rationalization," said Professor Kothari. An ominous development in the years since Rajiv's first election campaign has been the rise of militant Hinduism. Nowhere in the world is more violence sustained on a daily basis than in India because of religious differences. Far from trying to soothe these divisions, irresponsible Hindu politicians, determined to divert attention from their own economic failures, are cynically stoking the fires of communalism. These men know only too well that despite the emergence of a dynamic middle class and the development of a sizable industrial base, deep-rooted antagonisms between majority Hindus and minority Muslims continue. These tensions are easily exploited on the electoral trail, and not readily contained once the ballots are counted.

Rajiv's message to the electorate in 1984 was not just of "Mr. Clean" but of a shrewd combination of that image with the rhetoric of confrontation of a nation in peril. His election rhetoric had it all: The Opposition was illegitimate, India could do without one; there were serious threats from Pakistan and China, India's traditional enemies, and from the unidentified "foreign hand" that guided antinational forces. His tactics made Rajiv the darling of both the communalists and the progressives, and that gave him his massive mandate, according to Professor Kothari. *
Indira Gandhi's death had brought Rajiv to leadership and given him his

---

* Professor Kothari was appointed to the Indian Planning Commission by Prime Minister V. P. Singh. The agency draws up the country's spending priorities on a five-year basis. But the professor resigned from the Planning Commission soon after Singh lost power in late 1990 to Chandra Shekhar.

massive mandate. Had Indira voluntarily retired from politics, and had the trauma of her death not gripped the nation, such a mandate would not have been possible. But the challenge Rajiv Gandhi faced was how to overcome his mother's political legacy of communal discord and regional hostilities.

Rajiv Gandhi did not possess his mother's overwhelming personality, nor her charisma, and certainly not her ruthlessness. So how was he going to do it? How was he going to tackle the problem of Sikh separatism in the Punjab? Of tribal discord in Assam? Of dissatisfaction in Kashmir? How was he going to reassure India's diverse minorities that their welfare would be looked after? How was he going to arrive at some working accommodation with Pakistan and Bangladesh and Sri Lanka, neighboring nations that had long felt that Big Sister India behaved like a bully and actively worked to destabilize their own nations under one pretext or another? And what about the thorny business of relations between the central government and the states? India's twenty-five states were certain to demand greater devolutionary powers, and they were certain to ask for a larger share of tax revenues. These states, after years of being treated like stepchildren by Indira Gandhi, were certain to demand more equitable treatment. The only way for Rajiv Gandhi to deal effectively with such demands would be to federalize India's political system even more, and to decentralize authority. But his mother did not much care for states' rights. Her idea of governing India was predicated on a strong central government.

In the event, the five years of Rajiv Gandhi's rule showed that of all the Nehrus and Gandhis, he was the least equipped to lead India well. He was a singularly ill-formed character—personally charming and always courteous, to be sure, but not especially inventive or imaginative or consistent in his leadership. "Rajiv's general initiatives were good," says Nikhil Chakravarty, editor of the left-wing magazine *Mainstream*. "But he did not have the tenacity of a great political leader. He started without having any great interest in politics. Later, he developed a flamboyant way of looking at problems superficially, suggesting solutions that were not followed through."*

Just two months short of the first anniversary of Indira Gandhi's assassination, there was another startling murder of another well-known Indian. It, too, rocked India. The victim this time was Sant Harchand Singh

---

*Interview with Barbara Crossette of *The New York Times*, May 26, 1991.

Longowal, president of the Akali Dal, who had signed a ground-breaking pact with Prime Minister Rajiv Gandhi on July 24, 1985, that appeared to offer solutions to the Punjab crisis. Under the terms of that accord, Gandhi had agreed to local elections in the Punjab. More significantly, the Gandhi administration conceded a number of long-standing Sikh demands concerning regional autonomy. Chandigarh, which doubled as a capital for both Haryana and the Punjab, would be the sole capital of the latter (Haryana would get its own new capital). The Punjab would get a greater share of the waters of the "Land of the Five Rivers." Gandhi also agreed to step up the promotion of industrialization in the beleaguered state. In return, Longowal committed himself to finding a peaceful solution to the Punjab's problems within the framework of the Indian constitution.

The Gandhi-Longowal accord was widely hailed in India, especially by moderate Sikhs. The very fact that Gandhi and Longowal had sat across the negotiating table and worked long and hard to accommodate each other was seen as a historic development indeed. It was the first political settlement that Sikhs had agreed to sign publicly; moreover, they agreed to police the enforcement of the pact—particularly the antiterrorism component—themselves.

Not everyone, of course, thought highly of the accord. Barely had it been signed when rumors started swirling that Khalistan terrorists had vowed to kill Longowal. The terrorists put out the word that Longowal had caved in to pressure from Gandhi, that he had sold out. The Sikh leader, a cheerful man whose optimism about the Punjab now seemed increased because of the accord, didn't seem perturbed by the criticism; he shrugged away the rumors about his being the number-one target of the terrorists. He had a fatalistic view of life, and if his time was up, Longowal told associates, then, notwithstanding the heavy security around him, there was nothing that he could do.

Late in the afternoon of Tuesday, August 20, 1985, Longowal walked into a gurdwara near Sangrur, his home village in the heart of the Punjab, to offer prayers for peace. He had spent the earlier part of the day in Chandigarh, where he conferred with party colleagues on how to contest state and parliamentary elections that had been set for September. The elections were intended to restore political normalcy in the Punjab, which had long been under direct rule from New Delhi. Gandhi also seemed keen on transferring to local authorities in the Punjab the responsibility of tackling the escalating terrorism. The prime minister was aware, of course, that it was by no means certain that his Congress Party would win the Punjab elections; in fact, the strong likelihood was that the Akalis would be swept into power.

In the gurdwara, Longowal, a fifty-four-year-old man with a long beard and a gentle face, bowed before the Granth Sahib and then began speaking to the mostly Sikh congregation, urging reconciliation between Sikhs and Hindus. Suddenly, a Sikh youth seated in front of Longowal pulled out a pistol and started firing. The assailant was grabbed by a teenage boy next to him, and the bullets intended for Longowal tore into the boy, killing him on the spot. In the confusion, another Sikh man—whom many took to be one of Longowal's bodyguards—rushed toward the Sikh leader, shouting for order and urging the congregation to remain calm. But this man then spun around toward Longowal, produced a pistol from his jacket, and pumped several shots into the Sikh leader at point-blank range. Longowal was taken to a nearby hospital, where he died within minutes of arrival.

The cause of peace in the Punjab was dealt a devastating blow by the tragedy. Many Indians feared that by removing the one moderate Sikh leader courageous enough to conclude an agreement of reconciliation with the Indian government, Longowal's assassination would provoke a still deeper crisis for the trouble-torn Punjab. The Akali leader had begun to create a middle ground where Sikhs could indeed reconcile their own internecine political differences and also begin to deal collectively with an Indian government that many of them felt continued to be insensitive to their community. Even more important, perhaps, Longowal had attempted to reach beyond politics alone to urge broader reconciliation between Hindus and Sikhs. For that reason, his death was not only a blow to peace in the Punjab but also a setback to a deeper healing of communal differences throughout the country. The carefully planned assassination was also seen widely as a warning to other Sikh moderates who may have wished to speak out against terrorism and find a peaceful solution to the worsening crisis.

A month after the Longowal assassination, the Akali Dal won an overwhelming majority in the elections for the Punjab's 117-seat legislative assembly. The Akalis named Surjit Singh Barnala to head the Punjab cabinet, and there was much expectation—perhaps too much expectation—that the Akalis would be able to curb, if not entirely eliminate, terrorism in the state. The Barnala government was to last only eighteen months, however, before Rajiv Gandhi once again imposed President's Rule in the Punjab. Why? Because, said Gandhi, the law-and-order situation had deteriorated hopelessly under Barnala. The state government was incapable of combating terrorism, Gandhi said—an assertion that was vigorously but vainly challenged by the Akalis.

In October 1988, Governor S. S. Ray—the man who administered the Punjab on behalf of the central government—announced with a flourish that during the first sixteen months of President's Rule, 469 terrorists had been killed, compared to 118 killed during the eighteen-month tenure of the Barnala administration. Ray also said that during this period, there had been a sharp increase in the seizures of terrorists' weapons, and that there had been 580 encounters between the Punjab police and terrorists, compared to 192 such encounters in Barnala's time. Of course, statistics can be misleading. Notwithstanding the figures supplied by Governor Ray, terrorism had hardly abated in the Punjab. Indeed, during the same sixteen-month period of President's Rule cited by Ray, more than 3,000 civilians were killed by Khalistani terrorists, compared to about 850 during the Barnala administration. In October 1988, Prime Minister Gandhi toured a couple of rural communities in the Punjab in a show of personal courage and governmental resolve not to be intimidated by the terrorists—but he was shielded by such heavy security that this protection underscored the continuing tenuousness of life in the Punjab. The Khalistanis continued to demonstrate that they could strike at will anywhere.

When I visited the Punjab a third time in 1985, I was struck by how gloomy the overall situation seemed. The most powerful impressions that an outsider has these days of the Punjab are not of its prosperity, as spelled out by the shiny tractors and the television antennae and sleek motorcycles and the Japanese cars and trucks. It is not the greenness that dazzles the visitor, but the tens of thousands of bright saffron turbans worn by Sikh men, young and old alike. Saffron has become the color of protest against what many Sikhs believe is needlessly authoritarian rule in their Sikh-majority state by the central government. The saffron turbans, and the saffron duppattas, or long shawl-type garments, worn by Sikh women, are meant to convey how terribly hurt and humiliated Sikhs feel at their alienation from India's majority Hindus.

Lieutenant General Gauri Shankar, who was the chief military officer for the Punjab based in Chandigarh, felt, however, that many Sikhs and their leaders had simply abandoned reason. "They have dropped their shutters," he said, wearily. "They have imaginary fears and their total distrust of the Indian government is often based on wild rumors. They seem to have transferred guilt to the 'other side.' Which is to say that nothing in Punjab is ever their own fault. That it is always us, the outsiders or Hindus, who are to be blamed. And Sikhs abroad get excited by such wild charges. The Sikhs abroad have seen how tiny territories obtained independence—like Djibouti and Bangladesh—so now they feel that they, too, have a chance."

The general said that what really worried him was the fact that more and more young Sikhs seemed to be attracted to the terrorist cause—into a state of fanaticism about their religion. He said that while "Khalistan" was still a knee-jerk concept for many young people, one espoused mostly to annoy the authorities, an expression of frustration not unlike teenagers' tantrums, there now appeared to be a growing hardcore of rabid terrorists in the Punjab. Little wonder, then, that the districts of Ludhiana, Patiala, and Ropar, which were considered quite peaceful when Surjit Singh Barnala was the state's chief minister, were now plagued with murders and bomb blasts.

The general, one of India's most decorated soldiers, told me that the terrorists found it easy to slip into neighboring Pakistan because the 375-kilometer-long border with the Punjab was porous and inadequately patrolled. He said that he had no doubt that these Sikhs received training in Pakistan. And once back in India, the terrorists were sheltered by relatives in their villages. The aim of these terrorists was not only to disrupt government activity, indeed even make the Punjab impossible to govern, but also to drive a wedge between Sikhs and Hindus. In time, as the situation deteriorated beyond repair, New Delhi would have no choice but to yield to the creation of an independent Khalistan. I was convinced it was unlikely that any central government would let this happen, but I was astonished at how many Sikhs believed in this scenario.

As I traveled through the Punjab this time, I thought of how things there increasingly fitted into a vicious cycle: Terrorism begat rigorous antiterrorist campaigns by the authorities, which in turn alienated Sikh youths even more. Many Sikh moderates now felt that all Sikhs were, implicitly at least, under suspicion. Parkash Singh Badal, a former chief minister of the state and a top Akali leader, said to me: "All ordinary Sikhs are having to pay the price of the government's dispute with the terrorists."

One evening in Chandigarh, I saw for myself what Badal was talking about. I had been invited to dinner at the home of a businessman named Shivinder Singh. At one point before the food was served, the doorbell sounded, and Shivinder, who happened to be near the door, opened it.

A group of policemen were at the door.

"We have come to impound your Jeep," one of the policemen said to Singh.

"Why?"

"Because its color is olive-green—and it can be easily mistaken for a military Jeep," the policeman said.

Shivinder argued unsuccessfully that he only used his Jeep to hunt partridges in the bush. But the policemen were adamant, producing documents that authorized the seizure. They took the keys of Shivinder's Jeep and drove it away. Afterward, Shivinder's two little children kept asking why the police had come to their home.

Later, Shivinder said to me: "You see what has happened here—the Punjab situation is already affecting the minds of our children."

A couple of days after that, I was introduced to Sukhinder Singh, another young businessman, and his wife, Kunal. They spoke with despondency about how a great social divide had already occurred in the Punjab between Sikhs and Hindus. What also especially bothered Kunal was the constant security searches. Whenever her children saw security checkpoints, they now reflexively opened the glove compartment of their car, switched on the interior lights, and raised their hands.

"What sort of a place has this become?" Kunal said to me, ruefully. "I used to be the greatest ambassador for India. But now we Sikhs are being suspected at every turn. I want my kids to grow up in a place where they feel proud of belonging. But it's become really frightening these days. I see no future in India for my children."

Her husband added: "We used to laugh at the notion of Khalistan. But today it may very well become a reality."

I listened to Sukhinder Singh—and I hoped fervently that he was wrong. I would like to think that, despite all his travails and those of other decent Sikhs like him, Sukhinder would still like to live in the entity that is known as India—and not in Khalistan. For some people, particularly misguided Sikh expatriates who don't have to contend with the consequences of their folly, Khalistan may be a legitimate political dream. In truth, that dream is a dangerous illusion that can only harm Sikhs and Sikhism. No India government is likely to grant independence to the Punjab. Nor is it likely that the Hindu population—about as large as the Sikh population—will move out voluntarily.

In the months and years following Indira Gandhi's assassination, I felt that the great theme in India in the years ahead was likely to be one of the management of power in a multicultural nation-state given to what the Indian press likes to call "fissiparous tendencies." Would Rajiv Gandhi be willing to devolve power when his mother had left him a heavily centralized administration? Would he interpret his huge election victory as a justification for more concentrated authority in New Delhi, or as an opportunity to share power with the states? Would the Delhi-states power nexus consist of an iron chain emanating out of the prime minister's office? Or would this nexus consist of a silken thread?

During my travels across India in the years since Indira Gandhi's murder, I have repeatedly asked Indians about the effect that her helmsmanship had on their individual lives. One bitterly cold evening in New Delhi, Romesh Thapar, one of India's most incisive political and social analysts, shared tea and his thoughts with me. "Indira Gandhi has left behind an extraordinary record of mercurial, manipulative, conspiratorial, and brilliant leadership," he said. "Everything she did affected the entire political system."*

But how did her actions touch India's everyday people? Had she been an agent of change for the better? One answer was provided by Professor Ashis Nandy of Delhi's Centre for the Study of Developing Societies: "Indira bequeathed to us a legacy of corruption and violence. She subverted the state for her own sinister purposes."

There were other questions I posed as well, or that rose out of conversations as I moved through the country: How did a society that set out on a particular model of integration find its secular vision collapsing? How had popular disenchantment with traditional politics led to a growing belief in the value of modern managerial techniques to bail the country out of its woes? Would "technology and science"—the new buzzwords in India—really clean up the country's sociopolitical mess? I looked into the economic "liberalization" that was being instituted. Would India open itself to the West? Would Rajiv Gandhi allow free enterprise to thrive? I asked whether the enormous problems of poverty were being tackled correctly. Had "development" failed in India? Had land reform worked? Had the emphasis on rapid heavy industrialization led to intolerable deforestation and destruction of the ecology? How could such institutions as Parliament, the police, and the judiciary, which were weakened during Indira Gandhi's rule, now be revitalized and strengthened?

A big question: With India expected to contain more than 2 billion people within the next fifty years, what urgent steps would be taken to slow down population growth without violating human rights? And the biggest question still was: Would India hold together?

Nations, like people, do overcome tragedies, of course, and life does go on. There was a definite sense in the country that a new era of rejuvenated political leadership had arrived under Rajiv Gandhi. But would a post–Indira Gandhi India bring better times for the country's tens of millions of poor people, so many of whom had been kept hoping and waiting for so long? And when would the better times arrive?

In the seven years since Rajiv Gandhi took power—and lost it—and

---

*Conversation with author, New Delhi, December 1984.

lost his life in a bomb blast, there have been few reassuring answers to those central questions. While there were some striking economic gains—India became the world's tenth largest industrial nation, for example—the principal beneficiaries of Rajiv Gandhi's economic liberalization programs were the already privileged upper classes. Rajiv Gandhi lost the December 1989 general election largely on the corruption issue: V. P. Singh and his Janata Dal coalition successfully persuaded the electorate that Gandhi's Congress Party had encouraged high corruption in lucrative arms deals. Gandhi, who had come into office as "Mr. Clean," was convicted at the polls of being "Mr. Dirt."

Rajiv Gandhi's successors, however, seemed muddleheaded, and certainly incapable of projecting a vision for the India of the 1990s and beyond. His immediate successor, Vishwanath Pratap Singh, for instance, seemed to slide from one crisis to another without any great assertive leadership. Singh's style of management suggested that he protected himself politically with much astuteness but that he governed ineffectively. Chandra Shekhar, who briefly succeeded Singh, hardly seemed to govern at all. By the time Shekhar took office in November 1990, India's ninth Parliament was in such a state of paralysis that he could not even fill all cabinet positions during his short stewardship.

To be sure, India's middle class, estimated to number nearly 200 million, is growing along with the economy; but inflation has also eaten into the purchasing power of this middle class. Down near the bottom of the social structure, India's impoverished millions—the majority of Indians—are still waiting for better times. Meanwhile, India continues to muddle along, with increasing threats to its secularism and its territorial integrity. Faced with a rapidly changing world where state-sponsored socialism has been discredited, India still seems unable to massively reorient its economic policies in order to ensure accelerated growth for its overwhelming poor masses. That fact—the inability to fully make the transition from public-sector-based socialism to private-sector-led economic growth—is a major and irritating legacy of Indira Gandhi. Why? Because she expanded the behemoth that is India's bureaucracy in the name of socialism to the extent that, I fear, it is now virtually impossible to dismantle the demon. It is in the bureaucracy's interest to sustain the "License Raj" because a restrictive economy means more power and more money in their own pockets. *

---

* The "License Raj" denotes an administrative system where bureaucratic permissions are required for virtually all forms of economic activity. Because the Indian bureaucracy is vested with so much power of patronage, corruption flourishes. It is not

*   *   *

Long hailed as a model of nonsectarian development and democracy in the postcolonial Third World, India today seems infected by political pneumonia that could be terminal for its great democratic experiment. The agents of this illness are native bacteria posing as politicians. The illness has affected India's national government itself, causing the toppling of Prime Minister V. P. Singh in November 1990, after a lackadaisical tenure of barely eleven months. The emergence of yet another fragile coalition government, headed by Singh's adversary, Chandra Shekhar, underscored that coalition governments in India simply don't last long enough to ensure good government. At least it could be said of Indira Gandhi that she held together her administration. Because he was beholden to certain vested interests in the business and political communities who were being investigated by Singh, Shekhar did not enjoy the flexibility to pursue three of the biggest scandals that surfaced in recent years:

- The $1.3 billion arms deal with Bofors A. B., the Swedish company, in which more than $100 million in illegal commissions was paid by the Rajiv Gandhi administration that Mr. Singh defeated in the November 1989 election. The practice of demanding and receiving huge commissions for government-blessed agents began during the time of Indira Gandhi.
- The HDW submarine deal with Germany, in which millions of dollars of illegal commissions were also paid by the Indian government to foreign-based middlemen. This deal was initiated during Mrs. Gandhi's last administration.
- The "frame-up" of Mr. Singh's son, a New York–based employee of Citibank, in which the Gandhi administration clearly conspired with a peripatetic and politically well-connected Indian swami to establish that Mr. Singh had squirreled away millions of dollars in a secret bank account in the Caribbean haven of St. Kitts. The swami received assistance from Indian Foreign Service personnel. It was subsequently shown by enterprising Indian journalists that no such account existed, but the Gandhi government did not apologize or retract its accusations. *

---

uncommon for Indian officials to demand—and receive—commissions of up to 25 percent on business deals that they are requested to authorize.
* Indira Gandhi often turned for spiritual comfort to an assortment of swamis and gurus. Some of these men turned out to be charlatans, more interested in exploiting

No wonder that among the initial demands that the Gandhi coterie reportedly imposed on Mr. Shekhar, in exchange for offering the Congress Party's support to his minority government, was the right to replace personnel who had been investigating—however ploddingly—these scandals. Mr. Shekhar's slithering into power was made possible by support from Rajiv Gandhi, raising disturbing questions: Is India forever destined to be ruled, openly or covertly, by the Nehrus and the Gandhis? Is dynastic reign inevitable in a country whose political system appears incapable of turning out alternative leaders of national stature? Prime Minister Chandra Shekhar was widely perceived as a "caretaker," a politician who sat in the prime minister's seat only long enough to allow Mr. Gandhi to energize the Congress Party's debilitated grass-roots organization, engineer a new election, and ensure his return to power. The assassination of Rajiv Gandhi effectively ended the Nehru-Gandhi political dynasty.

---

their access to her for their own financial gains. For a woman brought up in the "scientific tradition" of her agnostic father, Jawaharlal Nehru, it was astonishing how much Mrs. Gandhi relied on astrologers and soothsayers for advice.

II

The Beginning

II

The Beginning

5

Daughter of Privilege

Indira Priyadarshini Nehru was a child of privilege, born to parents of pedigree Kashmiri lineage. "It's a bonnie lass," announced the Scottish doctor who brought Indira Nehru into this world in Allahabad, India, on November 19, 1917, just twelve days after the Russian Revolution started—and right in the middle of World War I. Her birth occurred twenty months after the marriage of her parents, Jawaharlal Nehru and Kamala Kaul, both children of privilege themselves whose parents were affluent and aristocratic.

The local astrologers said that it was an auspicious birth; it is hard to imagine that they would have said anything else to Allahabad's most prominent family.* The infant's mother, however, had not been entirely happy with the birthplace. Kamala Nehru had been keen that her first child should be born in her own parents' home in Delhi: Indian tradition calls for the first child of a family to be born in the home of the mother's parents.

The matter of tradition side, there was another reason why Kamala did not wish to give birth in her in-laws' home. The fact was that the Nehru women were not particularly well-disposed toward her, especially Jawaharlal's acid-tongued sister Vijaya Lakshmi Pandit. Mrs. Pandit's

---

* In virtually every Hindu household, it is customary to invite astrologers to draw up a newborn child's horoscope. That horoscope often serves as the central guiding reference to the child's life: education, even engagements and marriage, are arranged according to interpretations extrapolated from the horoscope.

antagonism would later fall on Indira as well, and Indira's early memories of her aunt's behavior toward her mother would darkly color her feelings toward Vijaya Lakshmi throughout her life. Mrs. Pandit—who was to become the first woman president of the United Nations General Assembly—was later to even campaign against Indira Gandhi, and Rajiv Gandhi never forgave her.*

Vijaya Lakshmi frequently ridiculed Kamala Nehru; she accused her of being unsophisticated, of not being conversant enough with the "Western ways" of Motilal Nehru's affluent household, of being a *dehaat*—a country bumpkin. These were unfair and hurtful accusations, for Kamala herself came from a family that was at least as aristocratic as the Nehrus, although certainly not as Westernized. Like the Nehrus, the Kauls were Kashmiri Brahmans.[†] Unlike the Nehrus who made their home in Allahabad, not far from the Hindu holy city of Benaras, the Kauls had settled in Delhi.

Perhaps the Nehru woman with whom Kamala got along best was Krishna Hutheesing, the youngest daughter of Motilal Nehru, grand patriarch of the family. Years later, Krishna was to write:

> At first poor Kamala was completely confused and uncomfortable in a place so different from her home. The big dinners with crystal and china on the long table and rows of wineglasses at everyone's place, the strange food, and, most of all perhaps, the quick loud voices of our many British guests, made her feel lost and lonely.
>
> But all the family liked her and did their best to help. Being very intelligent, she soon learned how to handle things. When eventually she came to live at Anand Bhavan as a daughter-in-law, she won all our hearts.
>
> My father doted on her, and my mother was very fond of her. They had their disagreements, though, because mother was quite a queen in her own domain and Kamala, for all her sweetness, was a spirited girl—as she was to show when the going got rough in our long fight for independence [from the British]. My sister Nan [Vijaya Lakshmi] who was almost exactly her age, felt the usual complicated sister-in-law's feelings toward her.[‡]

*Vijaya Lakshmi Pandit died of natural causes at the ripe old age of ninety in December 1990. To the end of her life, she remained critical of Indira Gandhi, and of Rajiv as well.
[†]For a brief description of India's caste system, see note on page 192.
[‡]These remarks are drawn from Krishna Hutheesing's book, *We Nehrus* (New York: Macmillan, 1965).

Vijaya Lakshmi Pandit has acknowledged that she adored her brother Jawaharlal, and that she felt possessive about him. "A brother occupies a very special position in the Indian family, and the brother-sister relationship is a cultivated and meaningful one," she said. "He is the 'protector' of his sisters, and in many cases their hero. To me Bhai [meaning "brother"] was a knight *sans peur et sans reproche.*"*

About Kamala Nehru, Vijaya Lakshmi had this to say:

> It was hard for her to adapt herself to surroundings totally different from those in which she had grown up. Her whole approach to life prevented her being able to enjoy the situation in which she now had to live and make a home. The excessive lavishness by which she was surrounded as well as the Westernized way of living were foreign to her, and she did not fall into the pattern easily.
>
> There must have been many conflicts in her mind in those early days in which she did not even have the opportunity of being alone and coming to grips with her problem, because she was surrounded by the family and, to what any normal young woman must have seemed a madhouse, with streams of guests coming and going.

Years later, when the distinguished Indian columnist Inder Malhotra asked Vijaya Lakshmi Pandit about reports that she and Kamala Nehru did not get along, Mrs. Pandit vigorously denied ill-treating her sister-in-law. She said that the allegations were spread by Indira. But Malhotra writes: "If Mrs. Pandit's vehement denials are usually disbelieved it is because too many friends and acquaintances of the family witnessed the taunts Kamala had to endure."

Indeed, Indira herself was to say this later about the treatment her mother received at her in-laws' home: "I loved her deeply and when I thought she was being wronged I fought for her and quarreled with people."†

Motilal Nehru, Jawaharlal's father, was personally very fond of Kamala, his only daughter-in-law. He refused to allow her to travel to Delhi for the birth of his first grandchild. Motilal prevailed, of course. Motilal took special pride in his daughter-in-law because he had been responsible for selecting her as Jawaharlal's bride. His son had been studying in Britain, at Harrow and Cambridge, and later obtained a law degree in London.

---

* Mrs. Pandit's comments are drawn from her book *The Scope of Happiness* (New York: Crown, 1979), p. 51.
† Interview by Inder Malhotra with Indira Gandhi in New Delhi, 1982.

Motilal often wondered whom he would marry. Notwithstanding the fact that Motilal had himself enjoyed dalliances with Western women during his own youth, the thought that his son might end up with a foreign wife did not please him.

He was concerned that Jawaharlal's British exposure had made him a bit more Western than even the Westernized Motilal would have liked. Motilal confided to a friend that he thought Jawaharlal had become "more an Englishman than an Indian." In Motilal's view, marriage to a traditional Indian woman would certainly "Indianize" his son. Motilal viewed his own marriage to Swarup Rani, another Orthodox Kashmiri Brahman, as a kind of model union. Could a similar kind of home-loving, generally compliant bride not be found for Jawaharlal?

So Motilal Nehru searched around for a suitable wife for his son. He would occasionally mail Jawaharlal photographs of prospective brides, which initially amused him but later became a source of friction with his father. At a wedding in Delhi in 1912, Brajlal Nehru, a member of the Nehru family, caught the eye of a thirteen-year-old girl named Kamala Kaul, and suggested to Motilal that he might wish to consider her as a bride for Jawaharlal. Kamala was pretty and dainty, and, according to Brajlal Nehru, she had excellent Kashmiri pedigree.

Jawaharlal was still in England, and Motilal didn't think his son would be averse to an arranged marriage. In those days, as indeed even today in India, parents of young girls and boys often scout for spouses for their progeny at weddings. Jawaharlal himself did not exactly force the issue of an arranged marriage with his father. In one letter to him, Jawaharlal wrote: "You express a hope that my marriage will be romantic. I should like it to be so, but I fail to see how it is going to come about. There is not an atom of romance in the way you are searching out girls for me and keeping them waiting till my arrival. The very idea is extremely unromantic. . . . But I have left the matter entirely in your hands."*

Motilal wrote to his son about Kamala Kaul. "The day after I wrote last, I suddenly made up my mind to go to Delhi for a day and see the little beauty," Motilal wrote. "Brajlal had managed to have the little girl invited at a get-together given to us by a relation. From what I could see of the girl, I found that Brajlal's description of her was perfectly accurate. So far as features go, there is no other girl to approach her. She seemed to be extremely intelligent. The net result of my visit to Delhi is that one more girl is waiting for you."

---

*Extracts from correspondence between Jawaharlal Nehru and Motilal Nehru. The correspondence is available at the Nehru Memorial Trust in New Delhi.

A photograph of Kamala Kaul was sent to Jawaharlal, and the young Nehru wrote back to his father: "As regards the Delhi girl, surely she is too young for me. I am ten years her senior and that is rather a big difference. I could not possibly marry her before she was eighteen or nineteen, that is six or seven years hence. I would not mind waiting as I am not in a matrimonial state of mind at present.

"As for looks, who can help feeling keen enjoyment at the sight of a beautiful creature? And I think you are quite right in saying that the outer features generally take after the inner person. And yet sometimes this is not the case. Beauty is after all skin deep. . . ."

Motilal wasn't one to encourage child marriage, but he certainly felt that perhaps an engagement between his son and Kamala Kaul might be in order. Could the period between the engagement and marriage not be "usefully employed" to educate Kamala in the Western ways of the Nehru household? After all, Jawaharlal had spent seven years in England, and he would surely expect his wife to be sophisticated and capable of entertaining lavishly in the Nehru style.

And so Kamala Kaul was invited to spend some months in Allahabad. She traveled in the company of her uncle and aunt, the Mushrans, and they frequently visited Anand Bhavan. Motilal Nehru assigned Cecilia Hooper, an English governess who attended to his own two daughters, to teach Kamala the language and life-style of the West.

Kamala became instantly popular in Allahabad, not the least because everybody knew she was being groomed to marry Motilal Nehru's only son. Kamala wore simple cotton saris, and virtually no jewelry. Krishna Nehru, known around her parents' home as Betty, was quite impressed the first time that Kamala Kaul came to Allahabad from Delhi. This is what she wrote: "She was sixteen and very lovely: slim and rather tall for an Indian girl, with the typically fair skin of Brahmans of Kashmiri descent. Her hair was dark brown and she had large brown eyes and a very gentle disposition.

"She was one of the most beautiful women I knew or ever have known. What made father like her, apart from her sweetness and beauty, was that she looked very healthy. My mother had been a semi-invalid most of her life and, though father treated her and taught us to treat her as a very precious delicate piece of china, he wanted a strong wife for his son."[*]

Kamala Kaul's family knew that Jawaharlal was one of the most eligible bachelors in the Kashmiri community. Kamala's grandfather, Pandit Kishan Lall Atal, had been a key adviser to the royal families of Jaipur,

*Hutheesing, *We Nehrus.*

Jodhpur, and Rewa, and he was determined that the girls in his family should marry well. Kamala Kaul's "education" in Allahabad, therefore, was encouraged by her own family.

This was in 1915, and by this time Jawaharlal Nehru, back in Allahabad from England, would frequently escort Kamala through the city in one of his father's three cars. A uniformed chauffeur drove them, and there was usually a chaperone as well. Kamala traveled back and forth between Allahabad and Delhi. With such a long engagement period, the couple got to know each other well, although Jawaharlal told his sisters that he often found Kamala's shyness to be a real barrier in establishing a warm relationship. Needless to say, their relationship was chaste; the chaperone did not even permit the holding of hands.

On February 8, 1916, Jawaharlal and Kamala were married in Delhi, on a day that Hindus regard as extremely auspicious: Vasant Panchami, a day that heralds spring. Jawaharlal Nehru was twenty-six years old, a freshly minted lawyer with an assuredly lucrative practice because of his father's success; Kamala Kaul was seventeen, and lovely. The wedding festivities lasted a week. And what a week it was. A specially chartered train brought more than 500 guests of the Nehru family from Allahabad to Delhi. Since Kamala Kaul's family could not possibly accommodate all of them in various houses that had been rented for the occasion, a tent city was erected not far from the family home. A sign, fashioned in flowers, announced that this city was the "Nehru Wedding Camp." There was much dancing, dining, and drinking throughout the wedding week, and indeed even for days beyond.

Jawaharlal Nehru and Kamala Kaul made a smart couple at their wedding. The bridegroom wore a brocaded sherwani—a long, traditional jacket that reached below the knees—and a striking turban. * Kamala's pearl-studded sari had been prepared in Allahabad, where artisans worked at Anand Bhavan for several months on the design and motifs. Not long after the wedding, Motilal Nehru took the newlyweds to mountainous Kashmir for a holiday. There Jawaharlal Nehru narrowly escaped death after slipping down a steep gorge. India's history would have been very different indeed had tragedy struck the Nehru family then. Vijaya Lakshmi Pandit recalled the incident:

> My brother made light of it in his usual way, but it was a near thing. Bhai and some friends had gone on a trek in Ladakh. Beyond

---

* This sherwani-style garment later came to be known as the fashionable "Nehru jacket."

the Zoji-la Pass, at a height of over 11,000 feet, they were informed that the famous Amarnath Cave, an ancient place of pilgrimage and a breathtaking sight, was only a few miles away cross-country. Guided by a shepherd, they decided to climb a snow-covered mountain to reach it. On the way they passed several glaciers, and in crossing one of these Bhai fell into a deep crevasse of fresh snow. Fortunately, the members of the party were roped together and he was rescued. In spite of the accident, the party continued but eventually had to turn back without reaching Amarnath. *

Many years later, Jawaharlal Nehru had this to recall about Kamala's entry into his life:

Except for a little schooling, she had no formal education; her mind had not gone through the educational process. She came to us as an unsophisticated girl apparently with hardly any of the complexes which are said to be so common now. She never entirely lost that girlish look, but as she grew into a woman her eyes acquired a depth and a fire, giving the impression of still pools behind which storms raged.

She was not the type of modern girl, with the modern girl's habits and lack of poise; yet she took easily enough to modern ways. But essentially she was an Indian girl and, more particularly, a Kashmiri girl—sensitive and proud, childlike and grown-up, foolish and wise. She was reserved to those she did not know or did not like, but bubbling over with gaiety and frankness before those she knew and liked. She was quick in her judgment and not always fair or right, but she stuck to her instinctive likes and dislikes. There was no guile in her. If she disliked a person, it was obvious, and she made no attempt to hide the fact. Even if she had tried to do so, she would probably not have succeeded. I have come across few persons who have produced such an impression of sincerity upon me as she did. †

Twenty months after Jawaharlal and Kamala were married, Indira Priya-darshini was born. Krishna Nehru Hutheesing, Jawaharlal Nehru's sister, recalled that on the night of Indira's birth "the family house, Anand Bhavan, was brightly lit, people were going in and out, servants were

* Pandit, *The Scope of Happiness*, p. 56.
† Jawaharlal Nehru, *The Discovery of India* (New York: John Day, 1946).

rushing around serving soft drinks to women and scotch to men." Had the proud grandfather, Motilal Nehru, not been so excited at the prospect of a grandchild, the child of his beloved Jawaharlal, he would have remembered to celebrate the occasion with champagne.

There was at first some confusion among servants as to the sex of the child because Indira was heavily swaddled. One ancient retainer congratulated Jawaharlal on the birth of a son. "Eagerly awaited by the expectant grandparents, it was presumed that it would be a boy," recalled Vijaya Lakshmi Pandit.

> The baby was born in one of the rooms across the courtyard from Father's room, and several of us were standing in the veranda awaiting the announcement.
>
> Presently Mother came out of the room and said, '*Hua . . .*' ["The event has happened."] Before the others realized the implication, Father laughed and said, '*Baccha hua?*' ["A child is born?"] Mother had not said a son is born but "it" has been born. In the traditional way she could not bring herself to announce the birth of a daughter!
>
> Father wanted the baby to be called after his mother, Indrani, but it was considered old-fashioned by some, and finally the name Indira, then much in vogue, was chosen. Because of his love of things Buddhist, Bhai [Jawaharlal] added Priyadarshini, meaning "pleasing to behold." The Buddha, the Enlightened One, was also known as Priyadarshini. The two names together suited Indu, as the family soon began to call her.

The city in which Indira Priyadarshini Nehru was born was once known as Prayag. Prayag dated back to A.D. 600, and its significance lay in its location, at the confluence of two of Hinduism's most sacred rivers, the Ganges and the Jamuna. Hindu mythology also held that there was a third river in Prayag, the Saraswati, but in contemporary times, at least, this river existed only in the historical imagination. The rivers that did actually flow through Prayag—the Ganges and the Jamuna—enjoyed their source in the mighty Himalayas. Prayag was renamed Allahabad, or Allah's abode, by the Mughal Emperor Akbar. Allahabad was situated on the banks of the River Ganges. This made transportation of goods an easy task for the enterprising merchants of northern India. Trade flourished here, making Allahabad a center of administration policies, education, and commerce. Allahabad continued to be a premier commercial and religious city at the time of Indira's birth.

For Hindus, dating back to the era of the ancient Aryans, Prayag—or

Allahabad—was a holy city indeed. They came from all over India to bathe in the river waters, to cleanse themselves of sin. Like most cities that grew exponentially during the 150-year-old British Raj, Allahabad had two sections: the old city of bazaars and ancient crumbling houses; and the modern "civil lines"—neat, tree-lined neighborhoods containing one- and two-story bungalows built mostly by British architects—where the British and wealthy Indians lived.

Jawaharlal Nehru wrote about Allahabad's "civil lines":

> It is in these . . . that the English officials and businessmen, as well as many upper-middle-class Indians, professional men, and officials live. The income of the municipality from the city proper is greater than that from the civil lines, but the expenditure on the latter far exceeds the city expenditure. For the far wider area covered by the civil lines requires more roads, and they have to be repaired, cleaned up, watered, and lighted; and the drainage, the water supply, and the sanitation system have to be much more widespread.
>
> The city part is always grossly neglected, and, of course, the poorer parts of the city are almost ignored; it has few good roads, and most of the narrow lanes are ill-lit and have no proper drainage or sanitation system. It puts up with all these disabilities patiently and seldom complains; and when it does complain, nothing much happens. Nearly all the "Big Noises" and "Little Noises" live in the civil lines.

The Nehrus were not originally from Allahabad. They were Kashmiri Brahmans whose ancestors could be traced back to Raj Kaul,* a highly distinguished Persian and Sanskrit scholar who left his abode in the Himalayan heights of Kashmir, and migrated to Delhi, the capital of the imperial Mughal dynasty, in 1716. Raj Kaul had hoped to make a fortune, since the Delhi of the time was said to be a place where clever men could talk their way into the Imperial Court and gain access to all sorts of business opportunities.

Raj Kaul came to the court of the Emperor Farrukh Siyar. The emperor was so charmed with the Kashmiri scholar's learning that he gave him a house in Delhi on the banks of a nehar, or canal. But the Kauls' imperial patronage ended when Farrukh Siyar was murdered by his rivals, the Sayyid brothers. Though they were originally known as Kaul, the name Nehru presumably was adopted to distinguish themselves from other Kauls who had trekked to Delhi from the heights of Kashmir. "Nehru"

---

*Raj Kaul was not related to the Kaul family from which Kamala hailed. "Kaul" is a fairly common name among the Kashmiri Pandit clan.

was a name taken from the Urdu word "nehar," or canal, adjoining their house. "Nehru" thus meant "he who resides by the banks of the canal."

Notwithstanding the termination of imperial patronage, the Kauls prospered because they retained possession of a few farming villages and other property that Farrukh Siyar had given to them as gifts. The French traveler François Bernier, who visited Delhi in 1656, described the sort of architecture characterizing houses in which the Kauls probably lived: "Very few houses are built of brick or stone, and several are made of clay and straw, yet they are airy and pleasant, most of them having courts and gardens, being commodious inside and containing good furniture. The thatched roof is supported by a layer of long, handsome, and strong canes, and the clay walls are covered with a fine white lime."

There is not much recorded history available today of the fate of the possessions of the Kaul-Nehrus in Delhi after the death of Farrukh Siyar. Indeed, Delhi itself was turbulent for almost 200 years, with a succession of coups, invasions, and wars. The Mughal dynasty had practically ended, and a scion of the Nehru family, Lakshmi Narayan Nehru, now worked for the British East India Company as a scribe in the early part of the nineteenth century. His son, Gangadhar Nehru, was a police officer in Delhi in 1857, a fateful year for India.

It was a fateful year because restless native Indian soldiers launched the Sepoy Mutiny. They butchered British soldiers of the East India Company in a rebellion that was intended to drive the foreigners from Indian shores. The Indian writer Dom Moraes has supplied a fascinating account of the origins of the Sepoy Mutiny:

> When, in 1857, the East India Company issued a new type of cartridge, the end of which had to be bitten off before it could be fired, the Hindu soldiers were told by intelligent agitators that it was greased with beef fat; the Muslims were told that the unguent employed was pork fat. *
>
> Both Hindus and Muslims would have been, so to speak, excommunicated from their religions, had the Hindus eaten beef or the Muslims

---

* Muslims are forbidden to eat pork, and devout Hindus do not consume beef, since the cow is worshiped in Hinduism as a sacred animal. The term "sepoy" means soldier. The East India Company, a private agency at the time, simply hired mercenaries to fight its wars of annexation. These wars were directed against local princeling, who ruled some 500 fiefdoms all across India. Most of these princes and maharajahs yielded without a fight against the British, in exchange for fat annual retainers to sustain their often debauched life-styles. But some native rulers fought the East India Company. The sepoys were often put in a position where they were arrayed against fellow Indians.

pork. And so they did not believe their British officers when they were told by them that no animal fat was employed in the greasing of the new cartridges. What subsequently took place was, in microcosm, typical of the entire history of India.

The British understood India more than any previous conqueror had done. What they did not understand, however, was that popular gossip in India plays a very important role in the politics of the country. The rumors and whispers among the sepoys were disregarded because by this time Indians were regarded as a lesser breed than white Englishmen. Meanwhile, a confederation of rulers, none of whom much liked the other, had collected to drive the British out of India. It was from their employees that the rumors and whispers came: unheard by the East India Company, but heard loud and clear by the sepoys.

The word that came was that they should rise and slay the British. They rose and slew. Delhi fell to the mutineers. *

When Delhi fell to the sepoys, who raped and plundered the capital mercilessly, hundreds of thousands fled the city. Among the refugees were Gangadhar Nehru; his wife, Jeorani; their two sons, Bansi Dhar and Nandlal; and their daughters, Patrani and Maharani. Their house in Delhi was destroyed, and with it all family records.

The Nehrus landed in Agra, some 200 miles from Delhi, the home of the Taj Mahal, the mausoleum that the Mughal Emperor Shah Jehan built in memory of his beloved wife, Mumtaz Mahal. There Gangadhar Nehru obtained a succession of civilian jobs for himself. In 1861 Gangadhar died in Agra, leaving behind a wife who was six months pregnant.

Motilal Nehru, the last son of Gangadhar, was born after his father's death in Agra. His older brothers, Bansi Dhar and Nandlal, helped raise him. † Motilal was schooled in Arabic and Persian to obtain a broad secular outlook, which was the fashion of the time. Such education was deemed essential in order to obtain competitive civil jobs in the Raj. Nandlal Nehru, meanwhile, had become a schoolteacher. He then became a lawyer, one of the first to so qualify under the new educational system that the British had instituted in India.

Because the high court of the state—known then as the United Provinces, and now as Uttar Pradesh—had been shifted to Allahabad,

---

* Dom Moraes, *Mrs. Gandhi* (Delhi: Vikas Publishing House, 1980), pp. 22–23.
† Bansi Dhar obtained the Nehru family's first look at the West when, in 1897, he undertook a ship voyage around the world. He was able to witness the diamond jubilee celebrations of Queen Victoria's reign in London. Bansi Dhar also went to Washington, D. C., where he met briefly with President William McKinley.

Nandlal moved there. Meanwhile, Motilal Nehru received a law degree in Kanpur, not far from Allahabad. After practicing law for a few months in Kanpur, Motilal then moved in with Nandlal in 1886 as a junior member of his brother's law firm in Allahabad.

Nandlal Nehru died a year later, and Motilal took over the lucrative law firm. He was twenty-five years old. He had been married briefly at the age of twenty to a Kashmiri woman from Lahore, but she died soon after giving birth to a son. The infant, too, died shortly thereafter. Motilal Nehru then married a fifteen-year-old girl named Thussu, who was also from Lahore. After the marriage, she changed her name to Swarup Rani: Indian women often change their names to please their husbands. On November 14, 1889, Swarup Rani gave birth to Jawaharlal Nehru.

The birth was a major event in Allahabad. The infant was weighed publicly, and the weight equivalent in wheat and savory foodstuffs was distributed to the city's poor. Such food distribution became an annual custom in the Nehru household. The name "Jawaharlal" means "precious stone," and the boy was certainly regarded as that by his parents and community. Jawaharlal's birth brought Motilal enormous good fortune. His law practice flourished. In 1900, he bought a huge house called Anand Bhavan—"the Abode of Bliss"—and remodeled it with English and French furnishings. There was a spacious garden, an indoor swimming pool, a riding ring for children, and tennis courts. Anand Bhavan also had Western and Indian kitchens, so that all kinds of culinary preferences could be accommodated. Entertainment was always on a large scale. Motilal's three children thrived in the atmosphere of goodwill and congeniality.

"Our home . . . lived up to its name for it was a happy house, a place where all were welcome, and it was always bustling with activity," recalled Vijaya Lakshmi Pandit. "Everyone seemed to be involved, and happily so, in work and play or whatever the interest might be, and the sound of laughter was what guests always associated with Anand Bhavan. . . . Parties in Anand Bhavan were popular whether they were informal ones in the courtyard or formal ones in the dining room. The reason was father's meticulous attention to detail and his talent in getting the right people together."

Motilal Nehru was one of those Indians who took to Western ways very avidly. His success at the bar subsequently enabled him to acquire a great deal of wealth and popularity. It was reported that his law practice brought him the equivalent of $200,000 annually—an astronomical figure in those days. As Motilal's wealth increased so did his desire to be further Westernized. He became an Anglophile and was proud that his life-style resembled that of an English aristocrat. In a speech that he made in 1907, Motilal said: "England has fed us with the best food that her language, her literature, her science, her art, and, above all, her free institutions could supply. We have learned and grown on that wholesome food for a century and are fast approaching the age of maturity." Motilal may not have intended it at the time, but there was high irony in what he said: The "age of maturity" that he spoke of would soon translate into a dramatic struggle for India's independence from the British Raj.

Motilal's household revolved around him. His exuberant personality made him a natural leader. Heavyset and thickly mustached, he resembled a Victorian squire. He was a man with great zest for life, but he also had a volatile temper which erupted easily. He stood for the old-fashioned values that keep an Indian home and family together: The husband earned a livelihood, and the wife stayed at home tending the children. The term "brown sahib" could certainly have applied to him. *

Motilal Nehru was very fond of his elder daughter Vijaya Lakshmi, but the major part of his devotion was directed toward his only son, Jawaharlal. He employed English governesses for his daughters and spared no expense to make an Englishman out of Jawaharlal, educating him at Harrow, Cambridge University, and the Inner Temple, making him "more an Englishman than Indian"—as Motilal himself would later acknowledge.

Motilal and his immense family, including the widow of his brother Nandlal, and her five sons and two daughters, represented a typical Indian joint family—although, of course, a family that lived in greater grandeur than most other ones. Anand Bhavan, already a huge property in the Civil Lines "antiseptic" area of Allahabad ("Hidden from the public gaze by the spreading branches of magnificent old trees" was how Motilal himself once characterized the property), kept growing as Motilal added new wings to the sprawling house.

The Reverend Charles Freer Andrews, who was associated with Mahatma Gandhi in India's freedom struggle against the British, and was a great friend of Motilal as well, described the house: "A family residence of this type is like the ancestral house of a clan in the highland of Scotland." He added that it was "like one of the stately country houses

---

* The provenance of "brown sahib" is disputed by linguists, but many believe that the term was popularized by the Sri Lankan writer and editor Varindra Tarzie Vittachi. "Brown sahib" means someone from the Indian Subcontinent who tries hard to emulate Western life-styles and who puts on superior airs when in the company of fellow brownskins who might be less privileged.

in England owned by the aristocracy." He might have also added that, unlike stately homes in England, Anand Bhavan sat in a sea of general poverty. Then, as indeed now, Allahabad was a microcosm of urban India, a teeming city where people scratched for a living. Perhaps there weren't as many beggars and street urchins then as there are today, but anyone looking out of Anand Bhavan's windows could at once spot the poverty around the estate. Motilal was not insensitive to this poverty, and he frequently made donations to local charities. He was also keen on those social welfare programs that generated jobs in poor neighborhoods. *

In those days, as now, India was a male-dominated society. On hearing that Kamala had given birth to a girl, Swarup Rani, Motilal's wife and Jawaharlal's mother, couldn't restrain from blurting out: "It should have been a boy." Motilal Nehru was upset at hearing his wife speak in this manner. "What's the matter with you?" he said, in a loud voice that startled the legion of servants who hovered in the background. "Have we made any distinction between our son and daughters in their upbringing? Do you not love them equally? This daughter of Jawaharlal, for all we know, may prove better than a thousand sons."

Motilal's words were to prove prescient. Even if Motilal had secretly hoped for a grandson to continue the family line, to his credit he never showed it. Indeed, a boy might have had difficulty flowering in the awesome shade of Motilal and Jawaharlal; perhaps because Indira was female, she was not intimidated by the towering achievers of the family and went on to make her own mark in life.

At Indira's birth, congratulatory telegrams and letters flooded Anand Bhavan. One of these was from Sarojini Naidu, the poetess who was hailed as the nightingale of India. She described the baby as "the soul of India." Recalling her first meeting with the little Indira when she was six months old, Sarojini Naidu said that Jawaharlal Nehru's daughter was "the proudest baby I have ever seen."†

Right from the start, Indira Priyadarshini was a special favorite of Motilal Nehru. He might vent his spleen on others, but never on Indira. The young granddaughter was an absolute favorite of everybody else as well. She later recalled that in her early years she admired her grandfather more than her own father, whom she hardly knew as he was always out of the house, politicking and plotting against the British. Her early years

---

* Motilal Nehru was fond of telling visitors that he himself ran one of Allahabad's biggest labor agencies—Anand Bhavan itself, where more than fifty servants were employed.
† Sarojini Naidu, a doughty freedom fighter, was a close family friend of the Nehrus and a distinguished literary figure who wrote in English.

were generally happy in the huge sprawling house where a child had a lot of space to run around and play hide-and-seek.

Motilal had a very volatile temperament and everyone was scared of his fiery temper, yet Indira was never on the receiving end of it. On the contrary, he indulged in her totally and spoiled her endlessly by meeting her every whim and fancy. Jawaharlal Nehru had a different experience growing up as Motilal's son. "One of my earliest recollections is of his temper, for I was the victim of it," Jawaharlal wrote.

> I must have been about five or six then. I noticed one day two fountain-pens on his office table, and I looked at them with greed. I argued with myself that father could not require both at the same time, and so I helped myself to one of them. Later I found that a mighty search was being made for the lost pen and I grew frightened at what I had done, but I did not confess.
>
> The pen was discovered and my guilt proclaimed to the world. Father was very angry and he gave me a tremendous thrashing. Almost blind with pain and mortification at my disgrace I rushed to my mother, and for several days various creams and ointments were applied to my aching and quivering little body.

According to Krishna Hutheesing, Indira was exposed to no capital punishment of any kind. No one in the Nehru household could even remember Motilal ever scolding the little girl. There was no fixed bedtime for her. The discipline that Motilal Nehru had inculcated in his own children was conspicuously absent in the case of his first grandchild. In an interview with Dom Moraes in New Delhi, Indira Gandhi said that despite the attention and affection lavished on her by Motilal Nehru, she was not really a spoiled child.

"I certainly think I wasn't spoilt," Mrs. Gandhi said. "On the contrary, I felt rather deprived of everything. My aunts and other relatives had a very carefree, happy childhood in my grandfather's house, but by the time I was three years old, life there was very austere and very unsettled, at least for me."

Throughout her life, Indira Gandhi would cherish wonderful memories of her grandfather. In an article written in 1961 to commemorate Motilal Nehru's birth centenary, Indira wrote: "In days of affluence or in days of hardship, the household was sternly governed by my grandfather—his awe-inspiring temper softened by quick forgiveness and infectious laughter, his strict discipline tempered by his love for his family and his enormous zest for life."

* * *

Indira Priyadarshini was a quiet and solemn child. She flounced around freely in the huge house, free to listen with curiosity to grown-ups who were to have a vital role in the history of India. Having no one of her own age to play with, she exaggerated her own role in a household buzzing with political activity. Indira was exposed to many different cultures. From a family maid in the house she acquired a taste for South Indian food. From a Goanese cook, she learned about Portuguese cuisine. Since in those days ladies rarely left the house, sari sellers from Old Allahabad brought to Anand Bhavan all the cloth that the women wished.

Indira would be left free to allow her own imagination run wild by dyeing rags for her dolls or printing material with blocks. She would sit and chat with vegetable sellers and learn stories of the outside world and their villages. They celebrated all local festivals with great pomp and splendor.

Indira was born at a time when India was awakening to the cause of independence. Jawaharlal Nehru soon became an absentee father, as his involvement in India's freedom struggle increased. Indira grew very close to Kamala Nehru, even as her mother's health began to deteriorate—not the least because of inattention from Kamala's husband. Husband and wife fought a great deal, and they often sulked.

Much later, Indira Gandhi was asked about the tenuous relationship between her parents. "Everybody is maladjusted in early married life," she said. "Even in love marriages there has to be adjustment. My mother came from a relatively less well-to-do home where living was very simple. She was suddenly catapulted into an Anglicized house where she had to play hostess to high-ups in an entirely different, Westernized type of atmosphere. So naturally it was a very great strain and uprooting."

Jawaharlal Nehru himself was to write later: "In spite of the strength of my family bonds, I almost forgot my family, my wife, my daughter. It was only long afterward that I realized what a burden and a trial I must have been to them in those days, and what amazing patience and tolerance my wife had shown toward me."

Years later, when the writer Promilla Kalhan asked Indira Gandhi about the treatment her mother had received at Anand Bhavan from the other Nehru women, Mrs. Gandhi replied: "In most Indian homes you have jealousy. But in my mother's case, I don't think it was only a question of jealousy directed toward her. It was a sort of clash of personalities. People find it difficult to understand somebody who is entirely different."

144

*   *   *

In those days, Jawaharlal was also fretting at the slow progress of the Indian Congress in ridding India of the British. He was a man of ideals who was impatient. Motilal Nehru had watched his son's impatience at the slow pace of events. He had hoped it was only a passing phase, blaming it on youth. He hoped that his son would finally settle down into the practice of law. After all, Motilal had made a huge fortune as a lawyer, and Jawaharlal had a ready-made law practice to slide into.

But Jawaharlal Nehru would never practice law. A huge storm was brewing in the form of a little, soft-spoken man who would eventually lead India to freedom. He was Mohandas Karamchand Gandhi (1869–1948)—also a lawyer like Motilal Nehru. He hailed from a merchant caste family in Gujarat state in western India. His father, Karamchand Gandhi, was a privileged official—known as a diwan—of the small principality of Porbandhar.* His father sent him to be educated in Britain, where Gandhi read law and was admitted to the Inner Temple. He then moved to South Africa where he championed the cause of Indian indentured laborers for twenty years, fighting against the tyranny of racism. He called for Satyagraha, or the "path of truth," a form of civil disobedience. Reports of Gandhi's defiance of the white minority regime in South Africa fired the imagination of the Indian youth, including Jawaharlal. In 1915 Gandhi returned to India and made contact with a group of moderate social reformers in the Indian National Congress, and soon began agitating against such injustices as the Rowlatt Bill.† Gandhi also championed the cause of poor landless peasants. Not long after he returned to India, Gandhi abandoned his Western-style clothes for the simple homespun loincloth—prompting Winston Churchill to call him "that seditious fakir."

Motilal Nehru was not enamored of Gandhi at first. He dismissed Satyagraha as "midsummer madness." The very idea of lawbreaking was inconceivable to him. Anand Bhavan in those days was like a veritable firecracker, full of tension and ready to explode. Motilal would not allow his son to start agitating against the British. He knew that agitators almost certainly faced imprisonment. Tension between father and son was at its peak. Much later, Jawaharlal would say this about his father's political attitudes in those days: "He was, of course, a nationalist in a

---

* Porbandhar was among the 565 princely states that formed Royal India. Rulers were given a small measure of autonomy by the British, but none could truly consider himself independent of the British Raj.
† The Rowlatt Bill was designed to fight terrorism, and gave the British authority to crack down against freedom fighters who were branded as militants.

vague sense of the word, but he admired Englishmen and their ways. He had a feeling that his own countrymen had fallen low and almost deserved what they had got. And there was a trace of contempt in his mind for the politicians who talked without doing anything, though he had no idea at all as to what else they could do."*

The family did not know how the conflict could be resolved. Then a great tragedy occurred in Punjab. On April 13, 1919, some 20,000 people assembled in a large compound called Jallianwalla Bagh in the holy city of Amritsar for a peaceful demonstration against the martial-law restrictions that the British had imposed. An arrogant British officer named Brigadier General R. E. H. Dyer—the martial-law commander in Amritsar—arrived with 150 armed soldiers, and blocked the only exit. Dyer ordered his soldiers to fire point-blank at the crowd. The British general had reportedly been upset because a female missionary had been beaten by Indian agitators and left for dead in the preceding week. General Dyer placed fifty troops at the entry. In ten minutes, the soldiers fired 1,650 rounds with their machine guns.

Dozens of innocent men, women, and children were killed by the bullets or crushed to death in the stampede to get out of the area. The casualty figures reached almost 2,000. The general was unrepentant during a formal government inquiry, insisting that he had "done a jolly good thing." While General Dyer was reprimanded for his action, the inquiry implicitly cleared him of any wrongdoing. Sikh priests even honored him at the Golden Temple in Amritsar—infuriating thousands of ordinary Sikhs who had joined Mahatma Gandhi's nonviolent movement to drive the British out of India. General Dyer retired from the British army soon thereafter. He became a hero to fellow Britons, and as a going-away gift, Englishmen stationed in India raised nearly 30,000 pounds for him. That sum, plus his generous pension, ensured a comfortable retirement in England. The whole country was enraged.

The Jallianwalla Bagh massacre was a critical turning point in India's struggle for independence from the British. Until then, the British were generally perceived as tough but benign rulers, foreign conquerors who administered India civilly. The wars that the East India Company had fought in the nineteenth century to annex territories of Indian princes had been generally relegated to the dust heap of history. The British were never regarded as people who would authorize troops to fire on unarmed civilians.

But General Dyer's actions in Amritsar dramatically changed the way Indians viewed the British. It was the Jallianwalla Bagh tragedy that

* Jawaharlal Nehru, *Autobiography* (London: Bodley Head, 1936).

finally persuaded Motilal Nehru that the time had come to work for India's independence from the British. According to Krishna Hutheesing: "My father's reaction to the massacre of unarmed and peaceful people led him to an entirely new position. He was now on Jawaharlal's side and had only profound admiration for Gandhi. In a dramatic shift of attitude, he gave up his lucrative law practice and threw his whole being into politics. When the Congress undertook an inquiry into the massacre, father and son joined Gandhi as members of the committee sent to Amritsar to make an official probe."

Indira's first memory at five was a highly political one. The whole country was seized by a fever of patriotism. Mahatma Gandhi had called for a civil disobedience movement. He asked everyone to boycott the British law courts, schools, colleges, and foreign-made goods. He asked people to discard their fashionable Western clothes and wear the home-spun khadi. As a token gesture, everyone was to light a bonfire of their foreign attire. One such bonfire was lit on the terrace of Motilal's house as well. Motilal's expensive and expansive British and French wardrobe was conspicuously laid out on the terrace, soon to be fed to the fire. Jawaharlal's Western suits were similarly displayed. The parents of five-year-old Indira wanted her to go to sleep before the bonfire was lit. But she appealed to her grandfather. He relented, and she was allowed to stay up at that late hour. She never lost the memory of blazing stacks of bright foreign-made clothing.

Indira was being made conscious of the importance, and the symbolism, of discarding English garb. An aunt who had just returned from Paris had bought her a beautiful embroidered frock. Kamala Nehru told the lady that the women of the household had stopped wearing foreign clothing. The visitor suggested the choice be left to young Indu. Any young child would easily have succumbed to the desire for the pretty material. Indira felt torn between what was been inculcated in her and wanting to own the pretty garment. Her timid hand felt the garment; it then moved back swiftly. Indira returned the frock saying, "Take it away, I shan't ever wear it." The aunt thoughtlessly pointed toward Indira's foreign doll, and said: "All right, Miss Saint, how is it you have a foreign doll?"

It was a remark that tore through Indira's heart. Like any little girl, she loved her doll and was deeply attached to it; it was her friend, she had given it a series of intimate names. "For days on end—or was it weeks?—the struggle went on for love of the doll and pride in the ownership of such a lovely thing," Indira would later say. "At last I made my decision and quivering with tension, I took the doll up to the roof and set fire to it. Then the tears came as if they would never stop, and for some days I was ill. To this day, I hate striking a match."

Indira matured at a very early age. One reason was the pain and suffering that her mother was going through. Even though Motilal Nehru employed a governess to teach Kamala English, it did not help much because of her lack of ease and sophistication.

Kamala might have borne her suffering more stoically had Jawaharlal stood by her through all this and come to her defense. But he was always preoccupied with other things, particularly the freedom movement. He was more or less indifferent to his wife, perhaps because it had been an arranged marriage forced on him by his parents. It was not until much later that Jawaharlal would understand his wife's anguish during those early years of marriage. "I hardly realized that this delicate, sensitive girl's mind," Nehru wrote in his autobiography,

> was slowly unfolding like a flower, and required gentle and careful tending. We were attracted to each other and got on well enough; but our backgrounds were different, and there was a want of adjustment. These maladjustments would sometimes lead to friction, and there were many petty quarrels over trivialities, boy-and-girl affairs which did not last long and ended in a quick reconciliation. Both had a quick temper, a sensitive nature, and a childish notion of keeping one's dignity. In spite of this, our attachment grew, though the want of adjustment lessened only slowly.

Indira suffered along with her mother at every rebuke she received from the Nehru women. Seeing the treatment meted out to Kamala made her determined not to ever let anyone treat her the same way. She also resented her father's indifference toward her mother. The impression Kamala Nehru made on her daughter proved to be the most lasting influence of her childhood. She watched her grandmother, Swarup Rani, and her grandmother's widowed sister who stayed with them, create trivial family problems for her. Indira would always come to the defense of her mother even as a little child. She took an intense dislike to Swarup Rani's sister.

Kamala, lovely yet truly unhappy, with no one really to rescue her from constant ridicule, retreated into religion. It was she who taught Indira Priyadarshini to appreciate Hindu mythology. They would have sessions in the morning when Jawaharlal, Kamala, and Indira would read the *Bhagavad Gita*, the ancient Hindu epic.* It was also Kamala who

---

* The origins of the *Bhagavad Gita* are uncertain. It is part of the *Mahabharata*, the long epic said to have been handed down orally from the time of the ancient Aryans who invaded and settled in northern India thousands of years before Christ. The *Gita* is supposed to be a sermon of advice that the Lord Krishna, a Hindu god, recited

taught Indira her Hindi. In fact Kamala, though a quiet-mannered woman, had very strong ideas about independence and was the first person to become Jawaharlal's political ally. She, too, was intoxicated by the drug of independence. Since she had been brought up in a simple atmosphere, she easily imbibed the austerity prescribed by Gandhiji. In Indira's own words: "When my father wanted to join Gandhiji and to change the whole way of life . . . the whole family was against it. It was only my mother's courageous and persistent support and encouragement that enabled him to take this step which made such a difference not only to our family but to the history of India." Jawaharlal was also thrilled to see his wife working by his side. For once, he found time even to appreciate her qualities.

"It was really all very unsettled," Indira would later tell Dom Moraes. "There was no regularity about meals, and I never knew where my parents were or when or if they would come home. . . . I used to want to be with them whenever they went out, but I was never allowed to." At the age of four, Indira watched proceedings against her father and grandfather, saw them being sentenced to jail terms on charges that included civil disobedience. The British authorities believed that by imprisoning the Congress Party leadership, the backbone of India's independence struggle would be broken. But such tactics only stiffened the resolve of leaders such as Motilal and Jawaharlal Nehru.

Vijaya Lakshmi Pandit would later write of this time:

> Besides the jail sentences for Father and Bhai [Jawaharlal], fines were also imposed. The rules of the National Movement forbade us to pay these, and we expected the police to come and take away whatever they wished in lieu of the money. Gandhiji's instructions on this point were clear. The police must not be obstructed in the performance of their duty, and should be allowed to take whatever they wished.
>
> Mother could not reconcile herself to this invasion of her home and, by the time the police arrived a few days later, she was seething with anger. Kamala, on the contrary, was quite serene and kept trying to persuade Mother [Swarup Rani] that we must let the men who were present in the house deal with the situation. I insisted on standing around watching all that happened, and it was a bitter experience to see the conduct of the police and their manner of handling the things we had loved and which had become part of our lives.

---

to Arjuna, a warrior whom he had befriended. The *Mahabharata* was put in writing some 2,000 years ago.

The word "police" was synonymous with terror. They were symbols of the foreign ruler and, in most cases, brutal men who behaved ruthlessly.

Indira had only her mother to rely on, and Kamala Nehru as well was now in and out of jail. No one really had time for the fears and anxieties of a little child. They remained embedded in her, and the experience led her to keep all her fears to herself throughout her life.

There were several incidents in Indira's early childhood that she would never forget. In December 1921, for instance, Motilal and Jawaharlal Nehru had been put into prison for refusing to pay minor fines for having participated in a demonstration. When local police came to Anand Bhavan to seize property that would have been the equivalent of those fines, Indira found that the constables were carting away far more. She pummeled some of them with her tiny fists, and shouted at them. "This continuous process of despoliation was irritating enough, but to watch it impotently was beyond the patience of a strong-willed child such as I was," Indira later wrote. "I protested to the police and indicated my strong displeasure in every way I could, once nearly chopping off an officer's thumb with a bread-slicing gadget." In later life, of course, Prime Minister Indira Gandhi often chopped off her adversaries' political prospects, and even the livelihoods of those whom she did not like.

Indira wanted to share her feelings about policemen and the British authorities with her father, and a great part of her childhood relationship with her father was carried out in letters. Her father started going to jail very frequently when she was barely five years old; he would be taken away to "the other home" for long periods where he would correspond very frequently with her. There was, at least, time for written dialogue, which to a great extent shaped her personality.

"Those were lonesome days," Indira recalled later in life. "I did resent the fact, perhaps, that my parents were not with me in the way other children had their parents. But otherwise I was very proud of them, and I did not really envisage having another kind of life."

To overcome her loneliness, Indira often gathered the Nehru servants around her, jumped atop the dining table, and delivered speeches—in her own words, "repeating disjointed phrases that I had picked up from grown-up talk." Even in her childhood, the politician in her was emerging, although it would be many years before Indira would actually deliver an authentic political speech.

6

The Education
of Indira Nehru

There were few children in Indira Nehru's Allahabad neighborhood, and so she found herself mostly in the company of grown-ups.* When it was time for her to start school there was a tussle between Jawaharlal and Motilal about where she should go. Her mother had sent her to kindergarten in Delhi, where Kamala Nehru's mother looked after Indira for nearly a year. But it was decided that Indira be brought back to Allahabad to enroll in the Allahabad Modern School, the Indian equivalent of a junior school. But Motilal thought it wasn't good enough for his grandchild. The school, started by a group of local educators as an alternative to the British schooling system, lacked resources; there were not enough books, and even a startling lack of space so that children from various grades had to attend school in shifts in order to use the limited number of classrooms.

Motilal thought that it was humiliating for a girl of aristocratic background to be subjected to such indignities. To this day, it is not uncommon for privileged Indians to send their children to exclusive—and expensive—private schools, sometimes overseas, largely to shelter them from perceived deficiencies of the public school system in India. Perhaps Motilal secretly envisioned private tutorials from British educators for

---

* It was unusual that Indira Nehru did not have many childhood friends. There are always lots of children in Indian neighborhoods, and Allahabad was—and continues to be—a heavily populated place. Perhaps the Nehru family purposely kept local—and less privileged—children away from Indira, on the grounds that children of aristocrats should not mingle too freely with the lower classes.

Indira, something that would have been difficult for him to implement in any case because of the rising anti-British sentiments in the country and in the Nehru household. Or perhaps no such tutors were available in Allahabad.

Indira was then put in St. Cecilia's School, run by three English-women, the Cameron sisters. This led to a fight between father and son as Jawaharlal felt that the ban against British schools should be implemented. That ban grew out of a resolution adopted by the Indian National Congress at its 1920 Calcutta session. The Congress Party resolved that its members should not send their children to schools run by Britons or financially assisted by the government of the Raj. Ironically, Motilal Nehru had withdrawn his younger daughter, Krishna, from one such school in Allahabad.

Years later, Indira was to say that she never enjoyed being at the Cameron sisters' school. "All the other girls wore—well, other kinds of clothes," she said. "I had to wear khadi, homespun cloth. It was very rough and stiff, and very uncomfortable. And I always felt out of place."

The row concerning Indira's admission to St. Cecilia's School was settled by Mahatma Gandhi, in itself a remarkable matter because it represented the first time—but not last occasion—that India's saintly national hero entered into domestic issues of the Nehru family. Gandhi was invited by Indira's father to adjudicate the dispute between Motilal and Jawaharlal. One Western correspondent joked in his dispatch to his newspaper that the three men were "Allahabad's Trinity: Motilal, the Father; Jawaharlal, the Son; and the Mahatma, the Holy Ghost." Gandhi upheld Jawaharlal's view that he didn't want Indira turned into a "little Miss Muffet," although he also expressed some reservations about having been asked to take sides between two men who were his friends.

"I don't want to be the cause, direct or indirect, of the slightest breach," Mahatma Gandhi wrote to Motilal. Still, said Gandhi, his letter urging that Motilal pull Indira out of St. Cecilia's School was "meant to be a plea for Jawaharlal, since he is one of the loneliest young men of my acquaintance in India."

Although Motilal Nehru withdrew Indira from St. Cecilia's School, he was clearly upset by what had happened. He felt that what should have been a simple family matter had been needlessly dragged into the public realm, not the least because of his willful son's insistence on consulting Mahatma Gandhi. Indira wasn't enrolled in any school at all at this point, and private tutors were kept for her at Anand Bhavan. This led to complete isolation from young people of her own age. Perhaps such isolation spawned in Indira's own mind a sense that she would always be a loner.

One childhood incident stuck in her mind because it was Indira's first exposure to open violence. Her parents frequently sheltered fugitives from justice, Indian patriots who were wanted by the British authorities on charges of sedition or anti-Raj agitation. One evening, as Indira was to recall years later, she was looking out her window at Anand Bhavan when she spotted police chasing a man. He was a self-styled revolutionary named Chandrasekhar* who, according to the newspapers, was allegedly involved in a plot to kill a local British administrator.

Chandrasekhar was surrounded by policemen in a park just outside Anand Bhavan. "I don't think I actually saw the last shot," Indira recalled. "But I saw the flashes and heard the shots. Violence is terrifying, you know. I saw all this from the house, and I felt numb, as though I had been dropped in very hot water or very cold water."†

Soon thereafter, when Indira was nine years old, she left Allahabad on a long journey overseas. Kamala Nehru had contracted pulmonary tuberculosis as early as 1919; in India, as elsewhere, TB was considered a killer disease at the time. Her health had always been delicate, but it was thought that the disease had been in remission. In November of 1925, however, doctors advised Kamala to go for treatment at a Swiss sanitorium, although they cautioned that a cure was by no means assured. A year earlier, Kamala had given birth prematurely to a son who died when only two days old. Indira was particularly upset because she had looked forward to the presence of another child in the Nehru household.

Although Jawaharlal, as well as Motilal, was keen that Kamala be taken at once for treatment to Switzerland, there were several obstacles. For one thing, the British authorities seemed reluctant to issue Jawaharlal a new passport, perhaps fearing that he would launch anti-Raj agitations abroad. For another, Jawaharlal had just succeeded Motilal Nehru as head executive of the Congress Party. It was Mahatma Gandhi who convinced Jawaharlal that he should take some time off and go with his family to Europe. At any rate, the "freedom struggle" seemed generally in low gear at this particular juncture, and Jawaharlal himself was clearly depressed over the death of his son and the worsening condition of Kamala.

* This Chandrasekhar was not related to Chandra Shekhar, also from the region, who became prime minister of India in late 1990.
† The incident was remarkable in that there were very few exchanges of gunfire between British and Indian revolutionaries during this period. Mahatma Gandhi had advocated a strategy of nonviolence, and the Congress Party was convinced that the moral weight of such a strategy would eventually force the British out of India.

The trip was finally undertaken in March 1926. Jawaharlal, Kamala, and Indira sailed from Bombay on an Italian cruiser to Venice. As they passed through the Suez Canal, Jawaharlal spoke to Indira about the great Egyptian civilizations, about the pharaohs, the Sphinx, and the pyramids. This clearly excited the little girl's imagination. As their ocean liner passed Crete, Nehru told his daughter about the ancient civilization of that island, about the ruins of the palace in Knossos and its bathrooms and toilets "which some people think are modern inventions but were really devised centuries ago."

From Venice, the Nehrus went to Geneva by train, and then by car to Montreux, where Kamala Nehru was admitted to a sanitorium. Indira was admitted to a school, L'Ecole Nouvelle at Bex. The school's motto was: "Do your best!" She picked up French, and learned music and skiing. Indira later recalled her clumsy efforts at learning how to ski, how both she and her father "took innumerable falls." But in the end, Jawaharlal and Indira both became accomplished skiers. Skiing was a sport that father and daughter often enjoyed together later in life.

One of Indira's teachers at L'Ecole Nouvelle, Mrs. Ernest Gosnell—a graduate of the University of Chicago—remembers that Indira was always anxious to participate in classroom discussions. "She was a very bright child," Mrs. Gosnell said. "Her slender long hand was frequently going up in the class."*

For the very first time in her life, Indira had her parents to herself: Jawaharlal and Kamala spent long hours with Indira. She stayed with her parents in a small chalet that Jawaharlal had rented. As a result the three became a closely knit family. At one point, Jawaharlal Nehru wrote to Vijaya Lakshmi Pandit: "Indu's English is becoming infected with her French, and she talks of going *jusqu'à* the post office and it being *presque* ten o'clock! As for Hindustani, she tries to avoid talking in it. I insisted on talking to her in Hindi, and I always write to her in Hindi."

The Nehrus also traveled in Europe a great deal.† Jawaharlal escorted Indira around the South Kensington Museum in London, talking excitedly about extinct creatures such as dinosaurs. In London's Kew Gardens, he told her about experiments conducted by the Indian scientist Sir Jagdish Chandra Bose that established the life cycle of plants, and even showed that stones enjoyed a life of their own. Father and daughter went

---

*Mrs. Gosnell later taught school for many years in Washington, D.C. Indira Gandhi kept in touch with her over the years.
†Indira Gandhi, later in life, accompanied her father virtually everywhere he went to represent India. Because Nehru never remarried, Indira served as his official escort and hostess on foreign trips.

to Heidelberg, then traveled in France. It was all very head[,] Indira, the pleasures of travels exceeded only by the proximity who doted on her and devoted so much time to her.

Kamala Nehru's treatment for tuberculosis in Switzerland was expen-sive, and she had to sell her jewelry. This pained Motilal, who wrote his son several letters in which he chastised Jawaharlal for not taking ade-quate care of his wife. Indeed, Motilal Nehru even sent Kamala some money to defray expenses. Jawaharlal occasionally took off by himself to visit various European capitals, meeting with political leaders of assorted persuasions and philosophies. Already a Fabian Socialist, he was naturally drawn to socialists and Communists in European cities in those years. *

He even took Kamala, as well as Motilal, with him to the Soviet Union, a trip that was to make Jawaharlal forever enamored of the Russians. The Russian Revolution was then just a decade old, and ideal-ism was still in the air. Nehru, an unreconstructed idealist, got carried away by what he saw: the development of industries, the establishment of agricultural communes.

When he became prime minister of India in 1947, Nehru was quick to adopt a paternalistic type of socialism as the country's official economic and political philosophy. Indira Gandhi would continue in that mold. Would India's economic record have been different had Jawaharlal Nehru not visited the Soviet Union in 1927? Quite possibly.

"The mere fact that English politicians are never tired of showing that the Russians are monsters need not frighten us or prevent us from associating with them where it is manifestly to our advantage to do so," Jawaharlal Nehru wrote in a report to the Indian National Congress. "Insofar as we are up against British imperialism, we must recognize that Soviet Russia is also very much against it."

To his sister, Vijaya Lakshmi Pandit, Jawaharlal Nehru wrote: "The picture I carry away from Russia is one of admiration for the men who have accomplished so much within a few years in spite of all the disadvan-tages that one can imagine. We are always complaining of the poor human material we have in India. Yet in Russia it is, or was, no better."

Another trip that Jawaharlal took with his wife was to England, fount of the Raj.[†] Kamala, in particular, was troubled by what she perceived

---

* Fabian Socialism was a democratic socialist variant of Marxism fashionable among British intellectuals during the first half of the twentieth century. Among its leading proponents were Sidney and Beatrice Webb, Harold Laski, and George Bernard Shaw.
† "Raj" is actually a Hindi word that means "kingdom." It came to be incorporated into English usage to denote the British Empire, not only in India but also elsewhere.

to be class-and-color consciousness in British society. She became a self-styled feminist.

"We have degraded ourselves beyond limits," she wrote to a friend in India. "Women are even less enlightened than men due to lack of education. When I think of the plight of my sisters, my heart bleeds because they are indifferent to the question of their own rights.

"Day by day I am getting more and more determined that on my return home, I shall take my sisters along with me. I shall urge them to place their trust in God and fight for their own freedom, educate their daughters so that they are not in trouble like us, and join the struggle for independence so that we do not have to spend our lives in shame."

Kamala Nehru most certainly passed on her impulses to her daughter, who would show later in life that she had learned well from her mother.

The Nehrus returned to Allahabad from Switzerland in late 1927. The Swiss doctors thought that Kamala's TB was under control, although she herself did not feel appreciably better. At any event, the Nehrus had run out of funds that Motilal had accumulated during his career. Jawaharlal had been living on family money, since he had not held any job since his return to India from England years earlier.

In India, anti-British sentiment was rising dramatically, and Jawaharlal was yearning for action. He resumed his post in the Congress Party, and made fiery speeches all across the country. Jawaharlal was even set upon by policemen as he marched in an anti-British demonstration in Lucknow in February 1928. Nehru also tried to spread the notion of socialism among his Congress colleagues. Kamala Nehru organized women's groups in Allahabad, and also did social service in poor neighborhoods.

Indira, meanwhile, was sent to St. Mary's Convent School. Jawaharlal Nehru had withdrawn his objection to missionary school education. He insisted, however, that a Hindi tutor be retained for her. The presence of this tutor proved unnecessary since Kamala had already started teaching Indira both Hindi and Hinduism.

When Indira turned thirteen, her father realized that he, too, had a further contribution to make toward her education beyond his "lecture tours" in Europe. He was in Naini Prison in late 1930 when he started writing a series of letters that were published much later as *Glimpses of World History* and *Letters from a Father to His Daughter*. The appearance of Nehru's letters in book form was the result of a suggestion by Mahatma Gandhi that they be published. Jawaharlal's first letter was received by Indira on November 19, 1930, her thirteenth birthday:

"On your birthday you have been in the habit of receiving presents and good wishes," Jawaharlal wrote. "Good wishes you will have in full measure, but what present can I send you from Naini Prison? My presents cannot be very material or solid. They can only be of the air and of the mind and the spirit, such as a good fairy might have bestowed on you—things that even the high walls of the prison cannot stop."

Nehru's letters were written without the benefit of a reference library, and therefore contained many historical mistakes. Yet, to this day, these letters are hailed as some of his best writings, simplified to be comprehensible to a thirteen-year-old. In all, Jawaharlal Nehru would write nearly 200 letters to his daughter. Vijaya Lakshmi Pandit's daughter, the novelist Nayantara Sahgal, would later say this about the correspondence from Nehru which formed the two books of letters:

> Those books did more than explain the scientific beginnings of the world, or the procession of men and events constituting its history. These pages held an approach to life compounded of buoyancy and optimism, a humorous tolerance toward life's foibles and even its trials. Indira saw life in another more solemn perspective, cast in an austere mold, shorn of lightness, as if lightness were a weakness, a trap to be avoided.
>
> Nor, apparently, could the written word take the place of flesh-and-blood human beings to turn to. Absent parents, though absent from well-understood and admired reasons, left a void that was never quite filled.

To young Indira, however, Nehru's missives were just letters which were penned by her father. She did not know this then, but these letters helped to form her thinking as no other education could have. A major part of her childhood relationship with her father was through letters. Jawaharlal was weighed down with the pressure of fighting for freedom, yet he tried to make a conscious effort to make a mark on his daughter's young mind.

In his letters, Nehru often emphasized that India's history and political development constituted a remarkable story. Indian civilization had been around continuously since at least 2900 B.C. Inhabitants of the Indus River valley developed an urban culture based mostly on commerce and trade. Around 1500 B.C., Aryan tribes rode in from central Asia and drove the Indus inhabitants—known as the Dravidians—southward. During the next several centuries, various indigenous Hindu and Buddhist kingdoms flourished in India; the land also attracted waves of invaders from Persia and Muslim Asia, marauders whose greed was stirred by accounts of travelers such as Marco Polo and Vasco da Gama about fabulous wealth in India's temples and royal courts. Most of these invaders foraged, pillaged, raped, and then left. But some stayed on, the most prominent of these being the Mughals. They established a dynasty that ruled most of India until the British conquered the Subcontinent in the nineteenth century. It was the Mughals who accelerated the conversion of millions of Indians to Islam, often accompanied by great cruelty toward those who resisted such conversion. But the Mughals also left behind extraordinary architectural achievements—the Taj Mahal in Agra, the Shalimar Garden in Kashmir, the sandstone city of Fatehpur Sikri, the Red Fort in Delhi. And it was the Mughals who established ateliers where miniature paintings were produced—paintings that survive to this day and which can command hundreds of thousands of dollars at international auctions.

The British did not enter India as the Mughals did, which is to say that they did not come with swords unsheathed and war cries on their lips. They came instead as traders and established a warehouse in Surat in 1619. They came under the auspices of the East India Company, which had been formed in London to promote trade in spices. Various native rulers, flattered by gifts given to them by the foreigners and perhaps intrigued by the sight of white skins, offered the traders "protection." Christian missionaries arrived in force, too, to introduce British-style education and to "convert the heathens." The traders steadily expanded their influence by subterfuge sometimes, and sometimes by outright conquest. Local kingdoms, already beset with internecine succession problems and family squabbles, fell like kingpins. By the 1850s, the British East India Company controlled most of the land area that today covers India, Pakistan, and Bangladesh. But in 1857, much of northern India revolted against the British. The revolt, known as the Great Mutiny, was largely the work of Indian foot soldiers, or sepoys. Their mutiny sparked riots in cities such as Lucknow, Meerut, and Cawnpore, and there was considerable savagery against Britons. But in the end there were simply too many poorly led and disorganized groups in too many places, and the mutiny was put down by the better-equipped British troops, who were ably assisted by Sikh regiments. The Great Mutiny resulted in the formal takeover of Indian territories by the British Crown. India was now part of Britain's Empire.

The Welsh writer James (later Jan) Morris—a great favorite of Indira Gandhi in later years—has a particularly eloquent passage in *Heaven's Command*, which forms part of Morris's trilogy on the British Empire:

Swept away with the carnage of the Indian Mutiny were the last dilettante deposits of England's eighteenth-century empire. There had been a pagan, or at least agnostic charm to that old sovereignty—short on convictions, rich in gusto and a sense of fun—but there would be little that was airy or entertaining to the new empire emerging from the shambles of Lucknow and Cawnpore. It knew its values now, stern, efficient and improving, and it recognized as its principal duty the imposition of British standards upon the black, brown and yellow peoples. The Mutiny had demonstrated indeed that not all the colored peoples were capable of spiritual redemption, as had earlier been supposed, but at worst the British could always concentrate on material regeneration—the enforcement of law and order, the distribution of scientific progress, and the lubrication of trade.

That was exactly what Queen Victoria's minions proceeded to do. They fashioned regional police forces; they whipped into shape an impressive national army; they introduced telegraph communications; they built more than 25,000 miles of railway tracks; they established a nationwide postal service; they raised schools and churches; they constructed roads through thick jungles and tall mountain ranges; they started the elite Indian Civil Service to which educated Indians eventually began to be admitted.

But the British also bled India dry. India's fine cotton fed the looms of Lancashire; the indigenous textile industry was crushed by the import of British fabrics fashioned from Indian cotton and silk. Indian iron ore went to Britain's steel mills, only to reappear in India in the form of locomotives and vehicles and machinery. The British barred industrial development in India because it would compete with their own factories and furnaces. Poverty widened in India. Joblessness increased.

In 1885 an Englishman named Allan Octavian Hume started an organization he called the Indian National Congress. Hume was a liberal-minded man who had served in India for many years as a British bureaucrat, and it was his feeling that the country's colonial rulers were dangerously out of touch with ordinary people's feelings. Hume was keen that his new organization should serve as a vehicle of communication between the rulers and the ruled. Unlike the overwhelming majority of Britons of his time, Hume did not subscribe to the theory that India's white rulers were racially superior to its brown masses.

The Indian National Congress quickly became a forum not only for ideas concerning relations between the British and their subjects but also a platform from which India's struggle for independence was launched.

Starting in 1920, Mohandas Karamchand Gandhi—later to be known as the Mahatma, or "saintly soul"—transformed the Congress into a mass movement. He used it to mount a popular campaign against the British. Jawaharlal Nehru wrote movingly and passionately about the Congress's struggle for independence.

Scholars now agree that in his letters to Indira, Jawaharlal Nehru brought a new approach to history that, for the first time, centered on Asia. Of Nehru's writing, the historian Anand Mohan says: "More than being merely narrative history, it was a materialistic interpretation of history along the lines of Marxist methodology. Its chief virtue as history was to correct the distortion caused by the Europe-centered view of Western scholars, and to reestablish the primacy of Asia, the loss of which Jawaharlal deplored."*

In one of his letters from prison, Jawaharlal wrote to Indira: "Ordinary men and women are usually not heroic. They think of their daily bread and butter, of their children, of their household worries, and the like. But a time comes when a whole people become full of faith for a great cause, and then even simple, ordinary men and women become heroes, and history becomes stirring and epoch-making. Great leaders have something in them which inspires a whole people and makes them do great deeds. May you grow up into a brave soldier in India's service."

In another letter, Jawaharlal wrote: "Through these letters you shall silently come near me and then we shall talk of many things." And in still another letter, he said: "Do you remember how fascinated you were when you first read the story of Joan of Arc and how your ambition was to be something like her? Often we may be in doubt as to what to do. One little test I shall ask you to apply whenever you are in doubt: Never do anything in secret or anything that you would wish to hide. For the desire to hide anything means that you are afraid, and fear is a bad thing and unworthy of you. . . ."

Yet at her young age, Indira was quite unresponsive to this great effort by her father. This not-uncommon reaction on a daughter's part frustrated Jawaharlal. Years later, after she had become prime minister, Indira Gandhi would say: "Now I realize that my father's letters helped to form

---

* Professor Anand Mohan teaches political science and history at Queens College, New York. A longtime student of the Nehru-Gandhi dynasty, he believes that Nehru's brand of Marxism was a benign and diluted one. Professor Mohan points out that Nehru subscribed to Fabian Socialism, a dogma that endorsed the welfare state and advocated a strong role for government in economic development. Nehru, however, did not condone Marxism's excesses, especially the abuses that Josef Stalin perpetrated on the Soviet Union.

my mind in a way that no other education did because they helped me to see things in perspective."

In a letter to his sister Vijaya Lakshmi, when Indira was fifteen, Jawaharlal Nehru wrote:

> During the last fourteen months or more I have written to Indu regularly and have hardly missed a fortnight. It has been a very one-sided correspondence as my letters have evoked practically no response. After a couple of months of silence on her part a hasty letter would come with many apologies and excuses, and with no reference at all to my letters or the questions I had asked in them.
>
> I have sent books on her birthday and on other occasions. These are not acknowledged and I have no definite knowledge if they reached her. I gather that Kamala is treated in much the same way. Now it does not matter if an odd letter comes or does not come. Nor does it matter fundamentally if a joy that I might have is denied to me or Kamala. I can get used to that as to other things that I do not like. But I am naturally led to think why this should be so. It is not casual; it is persistent. And in spite of numerous efforts it continues.
>
> I know that Indu is fond of me and Kamala. Yet she ignores us and others completely. Why is this so? Indu, I feel, is extraordinarily imaginative and self-centered or subjective. Indeed, I would say that, quite unconsciously, she has grown remarkably selfish. She lives in a world of dreams and vagaries and floats about on imaginary clouds, full probably of all manner of brave fancies.
>
> Now this is natural in a girl of her subjective nature and especially at her age. But there can be too much of it and I am afraid there is too much of it in her case. . . . I feel she requires a course of field or factory work to bring her down from the clouds. . . . She will have to come down, and if she does not do so early she will do so late, and then the process will be painful.

Indira had watched history in the making within her own family, but she didn't see it that way. Motilal and Jawaharlal had often differed in their political opinion and in their ways of going about making India independent. The younger Nehru wanted nothing less than a complete withdrawal, instantly, by the British. Motilal shared his son's goal, but felt that Jawaharlal was being unrealistic and impatient. Motilal felt that the Raj, assembled over nearly 200 years by the British, was hardly likely to be abandoned by them in a hurry.

In 1928 the Congress Party held a session in the southern city of Madras; among other things, delegates hotly debated who should succeed Motilal Nehru as party president. Motilal's health was deteriorating, and he also seemed despondent about the Indians' prospects of kicking the British out of India. Indeed, in a letter to Mahatma Gandhi, Motilal wrote: "As for myself, I feel I have lost much of the confidence I had in myself, and am more or less a spent force."

Motilal Nehru had suggested initially that the title of party president be passed on to Vallabhbhai Patel, a fiery leader from Gujarat, who believed passionately in the importance of the private sector as the key engine of economic growth.* He also suggested to Mahatma Gandhi that Jawaharlal Nehru would make an excellent president. And so it was that the title of Congress Party President ultimately went to his son. Professor Ralph Buultjens believes that the Nehru-Gandhi political dynasty was consolidated right there. "It was as though the Nehru clan had been born to rule," he says. "The father's mantle was passed on to the son—a process that became a family tradition in the next two generations."†

It was rapidly becoming a time of great turbulence in India. In 1930, the political unrest against British rule in the country increased; hundreds of thousands of people took a pledge that they would not rest until they attained independence. Mahatma Gandhi decided to go ahead with satyagraha and to defy nonviolently the salt tax imposed by the British.‡ On April 6, the anniversary of the Jallianwalla Bagh massacre, Gandhi led a huge march from his ashram in Sabarmati to Dandi, a small seaside village in Gujarat, in which several million people participated. In Dandi, Gandhi violated British law by making salt from seawater. Gandhiji's tactics of nonviolent protest managed to capture the imagination of the Indian masses. The authorities, of course, arrested tens of thousands of Indians as unrest spread across the country. Among those jailed were Mahatma Gandhi and Jawaharlal Nehru.

---

* There was some talk among Congress Party members at the time of Independence that the party should be broken up into two separate entities: The left wing would be led by Jawaharlal Nehru, and the right wing by Vallabhbhai Patel. The idea behind this proposal was to create a two-party system, since at the time the Congress was about the only viable political mechanism in India. Many Indians wish that the proposal—which Mahatma Gandhi endorsed—had been enacted: The Congress, unfortunately, was allowed to flourish as a behemoth, with all the resulting corruption and abuses that it imposed on the country in the years since Independence.
†Conversations with the author, New York City, 1990.
‡Salt was the one commodity that every Indian required, but its production remained an official, heavily taxed monopoly. It was illegal for private individuals to manufacture or sell salt. If a peasant living near the sea dared to pick up and use natural salt, he could be arrested.

Indira at this point was too young to take part in active politics, or to follow her parents to jail. She joined the female members of the household in nursing the victims of police brutality. She was a volatile little girl, and when told by her elders that she could not be a member of the Congress Party, she was very angry and decided to organize a party of her own.

She decided to call it the "Vanar Sena" or monkey brigade. This was modeled after the legendary monkey army that had helped Lord Rama, hero of the Indian epic *Ramayana*, to bring back Sita, his queen, who had been captured by an evil marauder from Sri Lanka named Ravana. An account of how she set about this is given by her aunt Krishna Nehru Hutheesing in her portrait of Indira Gandhi entitled *Dear to Behold*:

> She rallied the children of the neighborhood—boys and girls, rich and poor and asked them to bring all the children they could collect to our own back lawn for a meeting, at which she would expose a thrilling plan. The next day our lawn teemed with several hundred youngsters. Indira addressed them like a veteran speaker. Her proposal was to set up a children's volunteer organization to work for the Congress, which she said was fighting for the freedom of the country. They were to be of use to the Congress in mysterious ways that she had devised. She asked them if they were prepared to serve their motherland. For the assembled boys and girls it was a call to arms.
>
> Thousands joined her monkey army. She drilled them, marched them, and instructed them in their allotted duties. They worked as an auxiliary to the Congress—making flags, addressing envelopes. The more daring youngsters went around sticking up notices of meetings and processions when it was dark. They bravely carried messages from one group to another in a truly underground system.

At this point in life Indira was truly happy. To be of some use made her less disturbed and more alive. Years later, she would say: "I belonged to a generation that spent its childhood and youth fighting every inch of the way for our basic human rights as citizens of an ancient and honorable land. It was a hard life, of sacrifice and insecurity, of anger and impatience. Yet the hope in our eyes and our hearts never dimmed, for we were beckoned by the star of freedom, by the bright promise of a world without want and exploitation."

While Indira was developing political consciousness, the health and well-being of her mother and of her grandfather were on the wane. Kamala had never quite conquered her tuberculosis. Motilal Nehru was becoming increasingly despairing about India's prospects for independence. He missed the grandeur of the old days, when his law practice thrived and Anand Bhavan was the center of the universe. Now Anand Bhavan served as an office for the local Congress Party—a gift from Motilal—and Jawaharlal's parents lived in a small cottage in the compound. When an old family servant asked permission to return to his village, Motilal said to him: "Yes, by all means, leave. How can I ask you to stay? The wine, the cup, the party—all, all are gone."

Motilal was also dismayed that Kamala had been arrested on January 1, 1931, by the authorities for anti-British agitation.* It was no solace to him that she, like Jawaharlal and other Congress Party leaders, were never tortured or mistreated during captivity; on the contrary, these Indians were given reasonably comfortable quarters, were permitted books and allowed to write. The prisoners were occasionally permitted visitors as well. Such visits were always welcomed, especially by Jawaharlal, who was imprisoned several times by the British for a total of more than fourteen years.

One such visitor in early 1931 was Motilal, who went to Naini Prison to see his son. Later, Jawaharlal would say how shocked he was over his father's physical condition: "He had now changed for the worse, and his face was swollen. He had some little difficulty in speaking, and his mind was not always quite clear. But his old will remained."

Back at Anand Bhavan, Motilal would himself receive Congress Party members, many of whom were tearful in his presence because it was clear that the old man had not long to live. He was suffering from piles and a chronic asthma that had resulted in fibrosis of the lungs and a tumor in the right side of his chest. Of this period, Jawaharlal would write:

> There he sat, massively and rather expressionlessly, for the swelling on his face prevented much play of expression. But as one old friend came after another, and comrade succeeded comrade, there was a glitter in his eye and recognition of them, and his head bowed a little and his hands joined in salutation.
>
> And though he could not speak much, sometimes he would say a few words, and even his old humor did not leave him. There he sat like an old lion mortally wounded and with his physical strength almost gone, but still very leonine and kingly. . . . Even when a constriction in his throat made it difficult for him to make himself

---

*Kamala Nehru was released from Lucknow Prison after serving only twenty-six days, mainly because of her ill health.

understood, he took to writing on slips of paper what he wanted to say.

One of the last things Motilal said to anybody was to Mahatma Gandhi. "I am going soon," he told Gandhi, "and I shall not be here to see independence. But I know that you have won it, and will have it soon."*

On February 5, 1931, Motilal's family decided to drive him 150 miles from Allahabad to Lucknow for further medical treatment. The car trip exhausted the old man. The next morning, it was certain that he would not last much longer. Jawaharlal and his mother were at Motilal's bedside. Jawaharlal later remembered his father's death:

"Suddenly I noticed his face grew calm, and the sense of struggle vanished from it. I thought he had fallen asleep, and I was glad of it. But my mother's perceptions were keener, and she uttered a cry. I turned to her and begged her not to disturb him, as he had fallen asleep. But that sleep was his last long sleep, and from it there was no awakening."

Indira was deeply shaken by her grandfather's death. Perhaps it was he who influenced her most in her childhood. "I admired my grandfather as a strong person and I loved his tremendous zest for life, which he had and which my father also developed later on," Indira Gandhi told Arnold Michaelis, the American television journalist, years later. "But I was tremendously impressed with my grandfather's bigness—I don't mean physically—but, you know, he seemed to embrace the whole world. I loved the way he laughed."†

Jawaharlal and Indira often talked about Motilal. Later, in a letter to Indira, Jawaharlal wrote this about his father:

We sorrow for him and miss him at every step. And as the days go by, the sorrow does not seem to grow less or his absence more tolerable. But, then, I think that he would not have us so. He would not like us to give in to grief, but to face it, as he faced his troubles, and conquer it. He would like us to go on with the work he left unfinished. How can we rest or give in to futile grief when work beckons and the cause of India's freedom demands our service? For that cause he died. For that cause we will live and strive and, if necessary, die. After all,

---

* It would be another sixteen years before the British finally granted India independence, on August 15, 1947.
† Arnold Michaelis, *"An Interview with Indira Gandhi,"* McCall's, April 1966.

we are his children and have something of his fire and strength and determination in us. *

Indira's parents knew that their own life-style was getting more and more unpredictable, with both of them going in and out of jail. With Motilal gone, there was no one at Anand Bhavan who could properly look after Indira's education. Jawaharlal and Kamala felt that Indira should be placed in a boarding school. After a trip to Ceylon,† the Nehrus enrolled Indira in an experimental school in the small town of Poona, 120 miles southeast of Bombay in western India.

The Children's Own School was run by Jehangir and Coonverbai Vakil, a Parsi couple who were known to the Nehru family. The Vakils believed in the value of establishing and evolving a new educational system that blended the study of ancient Indian scriptures with modern Western subjects. The Vakils also believed that the educational system that the British had set up in India was an insidious effort to turn Indians into cheap clones of Westerners; the system would eventually rob the country of its cultural identity. Jawaharlal Nehru enthusiastically endorsed the Vakils' views.

With "Aunt Vakil" Indira was to develop a lifelong relationship.‡ Even so, Indira's stay in Poona—now known as Pune—was an unhappy one. She was very lonely and often cried at night. The Vakils were demanding disciplinarians. The school was housed in an ancient colonial bungalow that was once reputedly occupied by Lord Wellesley, the Briton who annexed Indian territory for the East India Company and set the stage for the establishing of the British Raj. So inadequate were the facilities that the rooms of the boarders were converted into classrooms during the day.

Moreover, Indira, now nearly fourteen, was the oldest girl at the school. When some younger cousins were also placed in the boarding school, Indira was put in a position of being, in effect, their guardian. The cousins were much too young to be real friends, and Indira was very

---

* *Glimpses of World History* (New York: John Day, 1960).
† Ceylon was the name the British gave to the ancient island of Lanka. The Ceylonese changed their country's name back to Lanka, adding the prefix of "Sri," in 1972. Sri Lanka's main export, tea, however, continues to be marketed internationally as Ceylon Tea because of consumer familiarity with the brand name.
‡ Many decades later, when Prime Minister Indira Gandhi suspended India's constitution and imposed the two-year Emergency, Mrs. Vakil publicly scolded her for violating democracy. The old schoolteacher was probably the only person in the whole country who could have done such a thing and gotten away with it.

lonely. Her beloved grandfather was dead, her father was in jail, and her mother was wasting away in a sanitorium a thousand miles away in northern India. At one point, Indira trekked to nearby Yeravda Prison, where Mahatma Gandhi was incarcerated, and demanded to meet with him. The authorities reluctantly allowed her to spend a few hours in Gandhi's company.

When Jawaharlal Nehru came to see her after being released from prison in September 1933, Indira insisted on returning home to Allahabad with him.

Indira's games as a child were politically oriented, as were those of many Indian children in those days. She divided her toys into freedom fighters—meaning native Indians—and the British. Naturally, the freedom fighters always won. The house was always buzzing with political talks; meetings with all the famous Congress men were held in her house.

Her father, though not being around most of the time, always wrote her about what books to read; a lot of them were serious books meant for an older age group. She admitted that a lot of what she read went over her head. She read blindly without any comprehension of the deep philosophy hidden within the lines. What really impressed her were the visions of heroism and martyrdom.

As an adult, Indira was to appreciate the true value of books. "What are books if they are not ideas, experiences, and emotions expressed in language at once authentic and moving and memorably beautiful?" she would say. In fact, she would seek out the company of authors and artists all over the world. During her New York visits, for instance, she would ask Ralph Buultjens to arrange small dinners with leading writers and scholars in order to discuss contemporary issues.*

Her aunt Krishna saw her striking a pose and muttering fervently to herself. On asking her about what she was doing, she was told that she was pretending to be Joan of Arc, and that one day she, too, would lead her people to freedom as had the Maid of Orleans. It was a childhood fantasy of heroism, a desire to do something. Ironically, the Joan of Arc syndrome was to remain with her to the end, in martyrdom.

Her father forced her to read books by H. G. Wells, George Bernard

---

* Among those who attended Professor Buultjens's dinners were Arthur Schlesinger, Jr., the historian; Betty Friedan and Gloria Steinem, the feminist writers; Dr. Jonas Salk, the inventor of the polio vaccine; Professor Ainslee Embree of Columbia University; and Theodore C. Sorensen, an international lawyer and former aide to the late President John F. Kennedy.

Shaw, Nietzsche, Charles Dickens, and Robert Frost. Indira often wanted to read fairy tales, of which Jawaharlal sternly disapproved, and so she had to read *Grimm's Fairy Tales* in the bathroom or under a blanket. Sometimes the books Jawaharlal told her to read made no sense to the little girl, but he still insisted that she read them. Sometimes the meaning came to her many years later. On one occasion, Nehru asked his daughter to read H. G. Wells's *Science of Life*. He had given the huge tome to her as a gift on her tenth birthday. "Do not get frightened by its size" was Jawaharlal's inscription.*

As Indira grew older, her major interest was freedom struggles everywhere. She read biographies and stories about liberation efforts. She read about William Tell, Simon Bolivar, Mazzini, and Garibaldi. Jawaharlal was clearly delighted that his daughter had finally embraced books so fervently. Books were to become Indira's passion in life, although she would tell a group of Delhi students years later: "As knowledge grows, so does ignorance. Lost in statistics and masses of information, we miss the real meaning or ultimate purpose. We oversimplify situations, attaching labels, and shoving people and ideas into pigeonholes."†

As a child under Gandhiji's influence she started the Bal Charkha Sangh,‡ though all she remembered of it was that she did some very bad spinning. It was the Mahatma who encouraged Indians to toss away foreign-made garments and instead wear homespun clothes from the rough material known as khadi. Although Indira continued her schooling in Allahabad, Jawaharlal and Kamala both felt that their daughter needed her mind challenged more. During a visit to Bengal in 1934, they were impressed by Visva-Bharati, an unusual academy at Shantiniketan that was presided over by Rabindranath Tagore, India's leading poet-philosopher and only Nobel laureate in literature.§ The academy, situated in idyllic surroundings not far from Calcutta, exuded tranquility and peace. Tagore had established the school in 1921.**

* Indira Gandhi was to become an avid collector of books, and whenever possible she would ask authors to autograph copies of their own books for her.
† During her visits to New York and London, Indira Gandhi always made it a point to go to local bookstores. She was often accompanied by Professor Ralph Buultjens, or by two longtime friends, Janki Ganju and Asoka Dutt.
‡ This was an organization that encouraged children to spin yarn and make clothes for themselves. The idea was that these homespun clothes would replace British-made garments, which the Congress Party boycotted.
§ Tagore was also knighted by the British. He later "returned" his title as a protest against the British occupation of India, but the British refused to take back Tagore's knighthood. Tagore never used the honorific "Sir" after he returned his knighthood.
** The Vakils' Children's Own School in Poona was modeled after Shantiniketan.

And so Indira was enrolled at Shantiniketan. Indira lived there as prescribed by "Gurudev"—the respectful honorific given to Tagore —dressing in plain cottons, barefoot, rising at five-thirty in the morning, with classes at six o'clock. She took classes in art and music. Twice daily, at sunrise and dusk, everyone at Shantiniketan was required to meditate. "I was in a quiet place for the first time in my life," she would say later. "I was brought up in a home which was going through a lot of political activity. Being away from all that at Shantiniketan I could live close to nature for the very first time in my life. My own inclination was towards nature and quiet living."

She admired Rabindranath Tagore very much and was very keen on different aspects of his personality, his poetry, his painting, his environmental concern, as well as his vision in general. "Tagore influenced me profoundly and helped me in molding my personality," Indira recalled years later. "We had a glimpse of the universality of his spirit, the broadness of his vision, and his strong sense of purpose. These were moments of serene joy, memories to be cherished forever."

Tagore himself wrote to Jawaharlal Nehru about Indira: "She is such an asset to our place. I have watched her very closely and have felt admiration for the way you have brought her up. The teachers, all in one voice, praise her, and I know she is extremely popular with the students." Gandhi told Nehru that Indira would blossom at Shantiniketan because Tagore's institution was "like a joyful garden of ideas."

Comments such as these pleased Jawaharlal, not least because Tagore and Mahatma Gandhi were icons for Nehru. Jawaharlal would write this about the two men:

> Tagore and Gandhi, each in his different way was a symbol of India, steeped in her ancient culture and drawing strength and sustenance from her. How typical they were of India, and how utterly different from each other! Possibly no other country could have produced them, and they had their roots deep down in the Indian soil and their minds roamed over the many thousands of years that have gone to make India what she is. And yet they were men of the present day, intensely alive to the day's problem. Both of them, in their respective and wholly different ways, represented that wonderful continuity of India's cultural tradition which has known no break though disaster has so often laid her low.

Jawaharlal was confident that under Tagore's guidance Indira would learn more about Indian culture. Shantiniketan also reinforced in Indira certain traditions, mainly of solitude and self-reliance, that she had known in her childhood. Indira would later say: "I think what I learnt most at Shantiniketan was the ability to live quietly within myself no matter what was happening outside. This has always helped me survive."

At this point Indira was most at peace with herself and the world. She had a lot of international friends. People from Hungary, China, Japan, and other countries would visit Tagore's educational sanctuary. Indira sought out these foreigners, always inquisitive about their cultures. Perhaps at Shantiniketan she formed what was to be a lifelong interest, indeed even a preoccupation, in international affairs. Indira and her friends would sit at the feet of the robed seventy-three-year-old white-haired figure and "talk of diverse subjects, watch him paint; often he would recite or read aloud."* For once in her life she no longer felt as lonely as she did in Allahabad.

"I seemed suddenly to have landed in another world," Indira would say of her time at Shantiniketan.

It was a world in which she developed what would be a lifelong love of poetry. That love was ignited doubtlessly by Rabindranath Tagore, whose writings Indira devoured. Indeed, she expressed dismay at the poor quality of an English translation of one of Tagore's poems in the Bengali language. So she rewrote the translation as follows:

> If no one listens to your call,
> Walk alone.
> If in fear they cower, mutely facing the wall,
> O hapless one,
> Open your mind and speak out alone.
> If, as you cross the wilderness, they turn away and desert you,
> O hapless one,
> Tread firmly on the thorns along the bloodlined track and
>   travel alone.
> If, in the storm-troubled night, they dare not hold aloft the
>   light,
> O hapless one,
> Ignite your own heart with the lightning and pain, and yourself
>   become the guiding light.†

---

*Rabindranath Tagore died of natural causes at the age of eighty. He is the only person who wrote songs that became two national anthems: for India ("Jana Gana Mana") and Bangladesh ("Amar Sonar Bangla").
†Translation courtesy of Mr. H. Y. Sharada Prasad.

7

The Death
of Kamala Nehru

Most Indians are devout believers in destiny, in the cosmic chakra*
which spins out the threads of an individual's life from the moment of
birth, or maybe even before conception. For Indians—or Hindus, to be
precise—life is preordained, and destiny is often a function of astrology.
Much is written in the stars. Indira Gandhi was no exception to this
tradition. She steadfastedly believed in astrology all her adult life. Perhaps, as Indira told friends years later, her pleasant stay at Shantiniketan
was destined to be cut short.

Even as Indira was savoring Rabindranath Tagore's tutelage and expanding her intellectual borders, she started receiving disturbing reports
from Allahabad that Kamala Nehru's health was deteriorating. Indira's
worst nightmares about her mother were coming true. She had never
been convinced that Kamala would fully recover from her tuberculosis.
Despite her happiness at being at Shantiniketan, Indira sorely missed her
mother. She often wished that she could be with her when Kamala
was taken by relatives to various hospitals in Bombay and Calcutta for
treatment of her disease.†

Kamala, weakened though she was, found time to write to her daughter. "She said it was 'important to get educated, to stick to principles,' "

* "Chakra" means "wheel." Most Indians use the word in reference to the "cosmic
wheel," or the "wheel of life."
† Tuberculosis remains a major disease in India, accounting for untold fatalities each
year. Primary health care, through which the disease can often be diagnosed early,
is still not available widely in rural India.

Indira recalled her mother writing in one letter. And despite her tubercu-losis, Kamala Nehru continued to participate in the freedom struggle by attending rallies and organizing women's groups in Allahabad. She also helped out with preparations for Krishna Nehru's wedding in October 1933, at Anand Bhavan. Krishna, Jawaharlal's youngest sister, married Gunottam "Raja" Hutheesing, a barrister who hailed from a well-known industrialist family in the western city of Ahmedabad. Later, Krishna Hutheesing would say this about Kamala: "Though she was far from well that autumn of 1933, Kamala took enormous pains with my trousseau, and saw to all the details of the wedding. The one thing that upset her was that our family had very little money left. Nearly all her jewelry, and mother's too, had been sold; there was not much left for me. But still she gave me part of what little jewelry she still had; and mother gave me a little of hers. It was Kamala, more than anyone else, who made my wedding a gay and happy occasion."

Everyone who attended the glittering wedding could see quite plainly that despite Kamala Nehru's brave front, she was not at all well. She was given to fainting fits, and she coughed continuously. Doctors in Allahabad suggested that Kamala be taken immediately to a sanitorium in Bhowali, a small resort near Kumaon, in the foothills of the Himalayas. Even in those days, Allahabad's environment was considered polluted because of a rapidly growing population, and increasing industriali-zation.*

Among those who accompanied Kamala to Bhowali was Dr. Madan Atal, a fellow Kashmiri and a physician who had treated her in Allah-abad. Dr. Atal enjoyed a lucrative practice in Allahabad, but he left it in the care of an assistant in order to be with Kamala.† Also in Kamala Nehru's entourage was a young man named Feroze Gandhi. The son of a naval engineer, Feroze belonged to the small Parsi community, followers of the ancient prophet Zoroaster. The Zoroastrians had fled Persia to escape persecution, and established an enclave in India.‡ Feroze's

* Today, Allahabad is a congested city whose chaos would have bewildered Kamala Nehru.
† Kashmiris are considered among the most clannish people, even in a country where communities tend to stick together.
‡ The Parsis are a remarkably close-knit community, numbering no more than about 110,000. They generally marry within the community. Parsi women who marry non-Parsis are automatically excommunicated, and their children forbidden from worshiping at the Parsis' traditional fire temple. Parsis also have a curious funeral

Allahabad-based relatives, who ran a general supplies store, had struck up a friendship with Indira's ailing mother.* Feroze, in fact, had been sent to Allahabad at the age of two because his father traveled a great deal. Feroze, his mother, Rattimai, a sister, Tehmina, and a brother, Faredun, lived with his father's sister, who was a surgeon at the Lady Dufferin Hospital in Allahabad.

Feroze Gandhi was an exuberant child, perhaps even a hyperactive one. His first three years as a student were at a local girls' school, where he terrorized the population with pranks. He was then transferred to the Anglo-Vernacular School for Boys, where he was no less of a miscreant. At the age of twelve, Feroze joined the Boy Scouts, where he came under the tutelage of a man named K. D. Malaviya, who later became a powerful minister in Jawaharlal Nehru's post-Independence cabinet.† Feroze was not terribly interested in studies, and his teachers often complained that he was inattentive in class. Perhaps that was because the Indian Freedom Movement was in full swing, Allahabad was in the thick of things in those years, and even though Feroze had not been especially oriented toward politics, the anti-British agitations must have been intriguing for an impressionable boy.

There were many demonstrations against the British, and Feroze was caught up in one of them—an incident that proved to be his political baptism. One afternoon, Feroze, then sixteen and a first-year student at the local Ewing Christian College,‡ was on his way home when he came upon a street demonstration against Sir John Simon and his Royal Commission. The Simon Commission had been set up by the British to study the question of constitutional reform in India.§ The Congress Party protested against the Commission on the grounds that it was yet another way for the British to delay granting independence to India. Wherever the commissioners went in India, there would be large demonstrations, even strikes. The protests in Allahabad were ironic because

---

custom: Bodies are not buried, as with Christians, Jews, and Muslims; nor are they cremated, as with Hindus. The corpse is laid out in a special "Tower of Silence" for vultures to consume.

* To this day, one finds Parsis owning and operating small general stores all over India. Parsi-run stores invariably carry at least some Western-style items such as ginger biscuits.

† Malaviya was to become Feroze Gandhi's political patron in Parliament.

‡ The college was run by American missionaries.

§ The Simon Commission's members included Clement Atlee, who was to become British prime minister after World War II. It was during Atlee's tenure that India was granted independence.

Sir John Simon and Motilal Nehru were good friends and occasionally corresponded. Feroze had been bicycling home that afternoon and upon encountering a charge by the police, he parked his bicycle on the curb and watched the proceedings. A couple of police, however, seized him and beat him up with their lathis, or batons.

When Feroze returned home, bruised and bloody, there was more beating—this time from his older brother Faredun, who was convinced that Feroze had joined the agitation against the British. Faredun was especially concerned because in those days the British authorities would be vengeful against civil-service employees whose relatives participated in antigovernment demonstrations: The Gandhis' aunt was nominally a government employee since she worked in a British-run hospital; the bungalow in which she and the Gandhis lived had been allocated to them by the government. Faredun was also worried that Feroze's participation in demonstrations would adversely affect Faredun's prospects for joining the civil service. Faredun's arguments, ironically enough, instilled in Feroze not only rebelliousness but also a resolve to become active in the Congress Party's anti-British agitations.

By 1930 Feroze Gandhi had become a prominent fixture in Allahabad's anti-British demonstrations. He was arrested during one such protest, and imprisoned briefly. While he was in jail, his mother, Rattimai, visited Anand Bhavan to plead with Mahatma Gandhi to persuade Feroze to refrain from anti-British activity. She told him, tearfully, that without a college degree Feroze would amount to nothing. The Mahatma listened patiently, then said that in independent India "the number of times one had courted imprisonment" would matter far more than college degrees. "Give me seven young men like Feroze and we shall achieve independence in seven days," Mahatma Gandhi said to Rattimai Gandhi. Seeing that she was less than won over, the Mahatma added: "Don't be afraid for Feroze's safety. Not a hair of his will be touched. I assume personal responsibility for him."

Even though Gandhi spoke to Rattimai mainly to reassure her, word quickly got around in Allahabad that the Mahatma had begun to take special interest in Feroze. When he turned eighteen, Feroze joined the Allahabad City Congress as a full-fledged member. He found that his old Boy Scout tutor, K. D. Malaviya, held a senior position in the Congress Party. It was through Malaviya—a longtime friend of Jawaharlal Nehru—that Feroze eventually came to meet the Nehrus. Feroze then became a constant visitor to Anand Bhavan, particularly solicitous of Kamala Nehru. His ebullient manner and his ever-handy sense of humor made Kamala laugh a lot. He even performed such chores as cleaning out Kamala's spittoon, something that even the servants resisted because of the contagious nature of tuberculosis. Relatives often kept their distance from Kamala, fearing her disease, and their visits to her room would be brief. Feroze, however, would sit by her bedside and spend long hours entertaining Kamala with jokes and local gossip. The sick woman appreciated such attention from the handsome nineteen-year-old boy, especially with her own husband incarcerated, and her only daughter hundreds of miles away at Tagore's sylvan school in Calcutta.

Feroze Gandhi was ever attentive to Kamala but secretly in love with her daughter. Because Indian society was conservative—it still is—he could hardly demonstrate openly his increasing obsession with Indira. And so when he proposed marriage to Indira, Feroze triggered reactions of amazement and alarm among the occupants of Anand Bhavan. That he was not reprimanded for this bold act, or thrown out of Anand Bhavan, was probably explained by the fact that Indira did not take the proposal seriously—and because Kamala's affection for Feroze offered a sort of protection for him. At any rate, Feroze learned to keep his feelings about Indira to himself after that.

His obvious attachment to the Nehrus was frowned upon by his own relatives, who criticized him for the huge amounts of time he spent at Anand Bhavan, and for his subsequent long stay at Bhowali. News of the concern on the part of the Gandhis—who may have been troubled over the fact that their lower-middle-class son was perhaps aspiring excessively to be accepted by the aristocratic Nehrus—reached Jawaharlal Nehru. He had had reservations about Feroze, but these had to do with natural feelings of resentment that a father would harbor toward his daughter's first suitor. Notwithstanding his reservations, Jawaharlal was supportive of Feroze in his contrempts with the Gandhis of Allahabad. Nehru wrote to his sister, Vijaya Lakshmi Pandit, asking her to mollify them:

> It appears that Feroze Gandhi has got into hot water with his people because of his association with us. . . . It is difficult to understand other people's family quarrels and even more difficult to interfere in them. Still, something has to be done to save the boy from endless trouble (he is so downcast that he talks foolishly of entering some wretched ashram!)—and to put ourselves right with his family.
>
> We have grown fond of the boy because he is a brave lad and has the makings of a man in him. He has our good wishes in every way and we hope that he will train himself and educate himself in accordance with his own wishes and those of his family for any work that he chooses. It is not for us to interfere. . . .
>
> This is rather a ticklish job but yet there should be no difficulty

about it as really the chief trouble is a phantom of the imagination. But phantoms are often troublesome. . . .

Vijaya Lakshmi Pandit did indeed visit Rattimai Gandhi, whose attitude toward the Nehrus seemed to soften afterward. Ironically, Mrs. Pandit would later advise Indira not to marry Feroze. *

While Kamala Nehru found comfort in the company of a few friends such as Feroze Gandhi and Dr. Madan Atal, she also drew considerable solace from religion and philosophy. She had, in 1932, been initiated into the Ramakrishna Mission, a religious society that stressed meditation and yoga. The society was named after a famous Indian seer and teacher, Shri Ramakrishna, who subscribed to the Bengali Vaishnavite school of Hinduism.† One of Ramakrishna's greatest disciples—and certainly one of the society's best-known leaders—was Swami Vivekananda (1863–1902). His philosophical writings were widely popular in Asia, and indeed are still required reading in theological schools in India and even in the West.‡ Vivekananda—whose family name was Narendranath Datta—was a charismatic figure in modern Indian religion, a man who encouraged Indians to turn back to Hinduism's monotheistic roots. In 1882 he became Ramakrishna's disciple. Vivekananda helped build an extensive network of "missions" which drew young men to a life of penury, social service, and religious devotion.

Kamala did not want it to be widely known that she had undergone diksha, the initiation ceremony of the Ramakrishna Mission. Swami

---

*See Chapter 8.

†Shri Ramakrishna's philosophy owed its provenance to the Brahmo Samaj, founded in 1828 by Raja Ram Mohan Roy (1772–1833). The Samaj was intended to propagate a purified and monotheistic Hinduism; indeed, Roy was greatly influenced by Christianity, European Deism, and Islamic Monotheism. In time, Roy became a great social reformer as well, enlisting the allegiance of elite Indian families who were disenchanted with such coercive Hindu practices as sati, or self-immolation of widows on their husband's funeral pyre. The vigorous debates between members of Roy's Brahmo Samaj with British missionaries and orthodox Hindu pandits (learned men) helped generate wide public awareness of social and political issues during the nineteenth century in India.

‡Swami Vivekananda visited the United States to attend the World Parliament of Religions in 1883. He spoke there on the antiquity and beauty of ancient Indian religion. Vivekanada told delegates: "Let your country be the only God for the coming fifty years."

Abhayananda later recalled: "Kamalaji felt that her initiation should be kept a secret because some people would look upon it as a conversion and raise unnecessary criticism. She also thought that others might construe it as a spiritual achievement and perhaps shower undue praise on her. The initiation, she said, was her personal affair which she wanted to keep as a sacred treasure in the innermost recesses of her heart."

In May 1935, Kamala Nehru wrote to Swami Abhayananda: "I have full confidence in your assurance that Lord Krishna* will appear to me, but I wish to see Him soon. At times I feel that I myself am Krishna. It has now become a practice with me to offer Him whatever I think or do. . . . I feel the presence of God, only I cannot see or touch Him. I do not know when I will be able to place my head at His feet. If only He could appear to me. . . ."

Jawaharlal Nehru, a strong believer in the right of people to choose their beliefs, encouraged his wife when she became involved with the Ramakrishna Mission. But Nehru was himself an agnostic, and he could not have been pleased with the notion that Kamala sought visions of Krishna. There were those around Kamala who felt that as her physical condition deteriorated she became increasingly obsessed with the idea that only religion could cure her.

Indira, meanwhile, pursued her studies at Shantiniketan. She visited her mother in Bhowali whenever she could. Feroze Gandhi, as much as Kamala Nehru, looked forward to those visits. He had become infatuated with Indira, who was not especially impressed with his ardent pursuit of her. Indira may not have encouraged it, but Feroze was determined to marry Indira. In 1933, around the time of Krishna Nehru's wedding, Feroze had proposed to Indira. Somewhat surprised and indeed even startled, Indira declined to marry him. "I thought I was too young," she said later. "And I wanted to continue my political work. Actually, I had lots of proposals."† Kamala knew that Feroze was enamored of her

---

*Lord Krishna is regarded by Hindus as one of the many avatars of Vishnu, the god who forms part of the Hindu Holy Trinity: Brahma, the Creator; Vishnu, the Protector; and Shiva, the Destroyer of Evil. Hindu mythology depicts Krishna as someone who was not celibate.

†Indian families with eligible boys and girls usually start receiving marriage proposals while the children are still in their teens. Affluent or well-known families are especially sought after—or families whose children have received foreign education and are domiciled in the West. Modern times have generated much technological change in India, but many social customs remain bound in tradition.

daughter, and she seemed to approve of his romantic interest—even though she had staunchly opposed an effort by Swarup Rani, Jawaharlal's mother, to get Indira married off at the age of sixteen. *

In 1935 doctors at the Bhowali sanitorium advised that Kamala Nehru should be taken to Europe for intensive treatment. Since Jawaharlal was in jail, Indira, then seventeen years old, was asked by Nehru's mother to leave Shantiniketan and accompany her mother to Germany.

Rabindranath Tagore, who had become very fond of Indira, was sad-dened to see her leave his academy. She had stayed at Shantiniketan for only nine months. In a letter to Jawaharlal Nehru, he wrote: "It is with a heavy heart we bade farewell to Indira, for she was such an asset in our place. I have watched her very closely and have felt admiration for the way you have brought her up. Her teachers, all in one voice, praise her; and I know she is extremely popular with the students. I only hope things will turn for the better, and she will soon return here and get back to her studies."

Indira herself later acknowledged that Shantiniketan had broadened her perspective on life. "I had always regarded poetry as something separate from life," she said. "But Tagore showed that all the arts were integrated. I was very deeply influenced by Tagore. I think it was a sort of unfolding of my personality. In fact, I would say he completely changed my life."

Indira would never return to Shantiniketan to resume her studies. While Kamala stayed in Badenweiler, in Germany's Black Forest, where there was a fine sanitorium, Indira attended a school in Chézières, Switzerland. She hated the school, she would later say, because "a horrible woman ran it." Perhaps the contrast with Shantiniketan was still fresh in Indira's mind. At any rate, Indira was soon shifted to her old Swiss school at Bex—not because she wished it but because Kamala Nehru's doctors advised that she be taken to a sanitorium in Lausanne.

The move to Lausanne did not much help Kamala Nehru. Jawaharlal had just been released from Almora Jail by the British in a rare humanitarian gesture so that he could be near his wife. He hastened to be at Kamala's side, and rented a tiny room in a pension near the sanitorium. Jawaharlal would spend several hours every day with his wife—more time, in fact, than he had given her in many years. He knew that Kamala

* For more on this, please see Chapter 8.

did not have long to live: Physicians at the sanitorium told Jawaharlal that it was only a matter of time before her system would collapse.

Jawaharlal would often reflect on his unusual relationship with Kamala. "In the long autumn evenings I sat by myself in my room in the pension, where I was staying, or sometimes went out for a walk across the fields or through the forest," he wrote later.

> A hundred pictures of Kamala succeeded each other in my mind, a hundred aspects of her rich and deep personality. We had been married for nearly twenty years, and yet how many times she had surprised me by something new in her mental or spiritual makeup. I had known her in so many ways and in latter years, I had tried my utmost to understand her. That understanding had not been denied to me, but I often wondered if I really knew her or understood her. There was something elusive about her, something fay-like, real but unsubstantial, difficult to grasp. Sometimes, looking into her eyes, I would find a stranger peeping out at me.

Both Jawaharlal and Kamala received dozens of letters from friends and relatives. She was much too weak by now to respond personally, and so her husband took it upon himself to write to these well-wishers. Here is what he said in a letter dated February 26, 1936, to Swami Abhayananda: "I read it out [the swami's letter of February 17, 1936, to Kamala] to Kamalaji, and it gave peace and joy, and a forgetfulness of pain for a while. . . . Her body, after the terrible long fight it has put up with, seems to have exhausted all its strength and is deteriorating. It cannot cope with little ills even, and they grow. One never knows what she may not be capable of even now but, ordinarily speaking, there is no hope. . . ."

When he was not replying to the voluminous mail, Jawaharlal took short trips to London and Paris. Those journeys enabled him to stay in touch with friends who supported his struggle for India's independence, but there were also reports of dalliances with winsome women. Still, Jawaharlal also managed to spend considerable time with Indira on weekends. He would read out aloud from books. One book that Indira seemed especially to enjoy was Pearl Buck's *The Good Earth*. Years later, Indira mentioned this to the American Nobel laureate, which pleased Miss Buck enormously.

Meanwhile, Congress colleagues in India were imploring Jawaharlal to return home. His leadership was needed. The struggle against the British was moving into a dramatic phase of agitations. It was a difficult decision for Jawaharlal to make, because there was no telling when his wife would die. But he decided that he must return to India, and fixed his departure for the afternoon of February 28.

Jawaharlal was destined not to leave for India as planned. On February 28, Kamala Nehru died at five o'clock in the morning. Jawaharlal Nehru and Dr. Madan Atal were at her bedside. Indira was in an anteroom when Kamala took her last breath. Mother and daughter had been together almost until midnight the previous day. Years later, recalling the last time that she saw Kamala alive, Indira would say: "I do not think there was much conversation. She just asked where I had been."

Kamala was cremated in a private ceremony near Lausanne. Jawaharlal and Indira placed the ashes in an urn that they planned to immerse in the Ganges River near Allahabad.* Jawaharlal was terribly affected by Kamala's death, much more so that either he or his relatives had expected. He had finally begun to feel that he owed his wife more than just occasional attention. Despite his neglect of her, Kamala had been—as most Hindu women are brought up to be—unfailingly supportive of him. She had been a strong pillar in his life, utterly devoted to him, standing by him when even the entire Nehru household, including his formidable father, had been against the notion of Jawaharlal getting involved in politics. Kamala had been his political ally and had encouraged him at every step of his political life.

Years later, remembering the sad period when he watched his wife waste away before his eyes, Jawaharlal was to write this about Kamala —and about himself:

> My past life unrolled itself before me, and there was always Kamala standing by. She became a symbol of Indian women or of Woman herself. Sometimes she grew curiously mixed up with my ideas of India, that land of ours so dear to us, with all her faults and weaknesses, so elusive and so full of mystery. What was Kamala? Did I know her? Understand her real self? Did she know or understand me? For I too was an abnormal person with mystery and unplumbed depths within me, which I could not myself fathom.
>
> Sometimes I had thought that she was a little frightened of me because of this. I had been, and was, a most unsatisfactory person to marry. Kamala and I were unlike each other in some ways, and yet in some other ways very alike; we did not complement each other. Our very strength became a weakness in our relations with each other. There could either be complete understanding, a perfect union

---

*Hindus believe that if the deceased person's ashes are consigned to the Ganges, that person is assured of a place in heaven.

of minds, or difficulties. Neither of us could live a humdrum domestic life, accepting things as they were.*

Before he left for India with the urn containing Kamala's ashes, Jawaharlal took Indira with him to a quiet resort near Montreux. Father and daughter took long walks in the cold but lovely Swiss countryside, consoling each other and recalling the few happy times they had had together as a family. He later dedicated his autobiography, which was released not long after his wife's death, as follows: "To Kamala, who is no more."† He told friends and relatives that he had simply not realized how much a woman of substance his wife had been.

"Those who have had similar experiences, and I am one of them, can understand to some extent the sorrow that comes to one," Jawaharlal later wrote to a friend. "The only way to deal with it, so I found, is to apply oneself with greater earnestness to the causes for which one has stood." On his way to India, he stopped off in Rome, where Benito Mussolini, the Fascist leader, unsuccessfully sought a meeting with him. The next ten years were to prove frenetic for Jawaharlal, as he rededicated himself with a vengeance to the cause of India's freedom, but there were many occasions when he seemed unable to suppress his grief.‡

For Indira, the death of her mother, who was barely thirty-six years old, came as a major blow. Even though later in life she was to become intensely close to the "Papu" she adored, her bond with her mother had been very strong. She had suffered with her mother through all the humiliations that the Nehru women had heaped on Kamala from a very young age. Even as a young child, Indira realized that her famous father did nothing to lessen the humiliations and hurt that Kamala had been subjected to in the Nehru household. Jawaharlal was much too preoccupied with fighting the British for independence. Kamala had introduced Indira to the Vedanta philosophy derived from the ancient Hindu scriptures.§ She had also introduced Indira to Anandmayee Ma, a sagacious

*Nehru, *The Discovery of India.*
†The dedication was dictated over the telephone by Nehru to his publisher in London during a brief stopover in Baghdad, Iraq. Nehru was on his way to India at the time.
‡At the concluding session of the Congress Party convention in Lucknow, in April 1936, Nehru openly wept when someone mentioned Kamala. His speech at the closing ceremony was abrupt. Jawaharlal rushed to his quarters and fell asleep. A detailed account of this incident appeared in the *Bombay Chronicle*, April 15, 1936.
§The Vedanta philosophy is based on teachings that Hindus believe were crafted by the Aryans who poured into India from Central Asia and established a flourishing civilization in the Subcontinent. These Aryans are credited with composing the *Vedas*, a litany of poems and legends that were originally handed down orally from generation to generation. Indian scholars are still uncertain about the specific author-

mystic whose counsel was to be an important influence on Indira's later life. Kamala had been with little Indira through all the years when Jawaharlal was too busy to spend much time with his only child because of his preoccupation with India's independence.

Years later, when the author Promilla Kalhan asked Indira Gandhi how she remembered her mother, her eyes half-closed and she replied softly: "I loved her deeply."[*] Even some of the other women in the Nehru household—with whom Kamala had little in common—acknowledged that she had been a very special person indeed. Krishna Hutheesing wrote this about Kamala: "Her life was like the luminous flame of an oil lamp. It wavered, it brightened, it grew in intensity all the time, and then quietly when the oil got drained, the flame flickered and died."

Kamala had a very strong impact on Indira's mind during her formative years, even though it was Jawaharlal who would later pride himself on influencing his daughter more than his wife had. Nehru certainly had an impact on Indira's intellect, but her values and the way she regarded the world were definitely molded by Kamala. Seeing the harsh treatment meted out to her mother in her own household in Allahabad had made Indira determined that she would never allow anyone to humiliate her in this way. "I saw her being hurt and I was determined not to be hurt," Indira wrote many years later.

Her pain at her mother's suffering came out in the form of bitterness especially toward her aunt Vijaya Lakshmi Pandit, from whom she was to be estranged in later years. Indira had seen a loveless marriage between her parents, her father indifferent toward his wife. One would have thought that her early experiences would have somehow made Indira more sensitive to others after seeing the suffering in her own mother's life. Yet her own marriage to Feroze Gandhi—and her personal and political relationships with most men—were to be failures.

Nayantara Sahgal, Mrs. Pandit's daughter, says that despite strong attempts on Jawaharlal's part, father and daughter never quite bonded. "The parent-child relationship has its unanalyzed loves and hostilities, but, given the keen awareness Nehru had of his daughter, this relationship might have become a close mutual bond," she says. "That it did not partake of real human response and sharing, though it did of attachment, may have been because, though she spent most of her adult life in her

---

ship of the *Vedas*, but there is general agreement that these scriptures constitute a rich store of mythology.

[*] An interview with Indira Gandhi, by Promilla Kalhan, November 29, 1972, at Parliament House in New Delhi.

father's house, there was a point beyond which Indira could not go in simple give-and-take. It seemed fraught for her with hazards. The intellectual and emotional labor her father expended on her did not bring the cherished child to flower. Somewhere within, her intensities locked, and the tight bud stayed closed."

Nehru had to return to India soon after Kamala's death. He invited Indira to choose between going to school in the United States or in England to complete her rather fitful education. The fact that Nehru even suggested the United States was unusual, because there was hardly any precedent in those days for Indian students to venture beyond Britain for studies. Indira opted for Badminton School, a progressive institution near Bristol, whose headmistress was a woman named Beatrice Baker. Miss Baker was a Quaker, an ardent socialist, and a supporter of the League of Nations, and there is some reason to believe that Indira was influenced by her views concerning socialism.

It is tempting to wonder, however, how differently Prime Minister Indira Gandhi would have viewed Washington had she decided to study in America. Years later, President Lyndon B. Johnson—whose view of Indira Gandhi was far from charitable—said privately that he wished some American university had offered Indira Nehru a scholarship. Johnson was a great believer in the theory that one of the best ways to spread international goodwill was to invite Third World students to spend their formative years at U.S. educational institutions.*

The 1930s were stirring times for India and the world. Insightful observers like Jawaharlal Nehru knew that great upheavals were coming in Europe, and that this would affect the British position in India. On the Subcontinent, too, these were dramatic times. The Indian independence movement was gathering momentum. In its vortex was the Nehru family. Scarcely a day passed by without some significant incident taking place. For Indira, traveling between Europe and India in these teenage years, this undoubtedly would have been a period in which many of her political attitudes were shaped. Although distracted by the tragedy of her mother, Indira's growing political consciousness was deeply affected by the struggles of the time. Later, she was once to refer to herself as a "child of the thirties—a daughter of the twin fights against Fascism abroad and colonialism at home, and a by-product of the Great Depression."†

---

* The source for this information was L. K. Jha, the former Indian ambassador to the United States.

† Quotation provided by Professor Ralph Buultjens.

8

Lovers' Wedding

The damp, gloomy climate of Britain did not exactly make Indira feel at home. Kamala's death was still vivid in her tender mind, and Indira was severely depressed. Still, she found a great deal of cheer in the fact that Feroze Gandhi was in England at the same time, attending the London School of Economics.* For a young girl who had just lost her mother, and whose father was far away in India, Feroze's attention and solicitousness was very heady and flattering. Indira became fond of Feroze, an attachment that was to result in their ill-fated marriage some six years later.

Iris Murdoch, the celebrated British novelist, was among those who studied with Indira at Badminton. She still recalls the young Indian's early days in Britain. "Indira was regarded by us as a sort of princess with a destiny," the novelist says. "Badminton was a very left-wing school. Its academic courses were excellent, but it also generated an idealism amongst all of us. We all thought that we must fight for social justice. It was socialism of a sort, but a very liberal variety of socialism."

This is how Miss Murdoch remembers Indira Nehru:

> She was extraordinarily beautiful but also very frail. At times it was almost as if she would be carried away by the wind. She was a very dignified and aloof girl, but it was obvious to all of us that she was

* The London School of Economics, known widely by its acronym LSE, was especially popular with Indians wishing to study in Britain, not least because of its left-leaning

185

very unhappy and couldn't wait to get back to her country. She didn't like the school very much, and who can blame her. For a young girl brought up in India, it must have been awful to be confined to an English girls' boarding school, however progressive. She was not the only one in that situation. There were lots of other children of many nationalities, and a number of Jewish refugee children. We knew that Indira had just lost her mother and that her father was being permanently locked up by the British in India. As a result everyone looked after her and even spoilt her, but it didn't work. She wanted to go back. We were later together at Somerville, but she didn't stay there long either.*

At first, at least, Indira was pleased to be at Somerville College, Oxford.† She cut a striking figure because of her colorful saris and the North Indian–style salwar-kameez—long shirt over baggy pantaloons—which brightened the otherwise drab English environment. On some occasions, Indira even wore chic Western-style dresses. One relative recalls a visit to London and being met by Indira at a train station. The young Miss Nehru wore an elegant skirt and jacket, with a gauzy black veil over her hat. "She looked as though she had just stepped out of a high-class fashion house in Paris," the relative later said.

At Oxford, Indira would walk around a great deal, eschewing the bicycles favored by most students.‡ She also joined the Left Book Club, which promoted socialist literature. She concentrated on studying history, political science, and economics. Indira also enrolled in a course about the development of human thought. One would have assumed that such courses would be seen by Indira as an ideal follow-up to the erudite letters that her father had sent her from prison when she was a child, but academic work was clearly not Indira's forte. There were too many distractions—Feroze Gandhi certainly being one, as well as other Indians in Britain who urged Indira to become involved in local activities aimed at gathering support for the Indian independence movement.

On one occasion, Indira was asked by Jawaharlal Nehru's friend V. K. Krishna Menon to read out a message sent by Jawaharlal at a public

faculty which included Harold Laski, the well-known political scientist. In those days, a degree from the LSE was considered more prestigious in high Indian circles than a comparable degree from a major American university.
* Quoted by Professor Anand Mohan to author.
† Indira Gandhi was the first Somerville College student who became prime minister of her country. The second was Margaret Thatcher.
‡ Indira Gandhi once told Dom Moraes that she found it difficult to ride a bicycle while wearing a sari.

meeting organized by the Labor Party.* When she got there she was told she had to say a few words on her own as well. The thought terrified her so much that she could not utter a word. A wag in the audience shouted: "She does not speak, she squeaks!" Indira did not even dare to squeak: she abandoned her speech and left the room, humiliated and in tears. She was never able to accept criticism, and she certainly could never reconcile herself to ridicule of any sort.[†]

Still, Indira would later say that she did not fully savor Oxford: "I didn't think that I got out of Oxford as much as I might have. Only a part of me was there. All the time I kept thinking, 'When can I get back and do something in India?' " Many years later, Betty Friedan, the American feminist author, asked Indira to recall the "particular moment" in her life when she decided to enter politics. Indira chose not to refer to her days at Oxford when she was frightened to speak at public gatherings. Instead, she told Friedan that her decision was made at a public rally during the early 1950s when Prime Minister Nehru was unable to campaign on behalf of a woman candidate for a local election. "I found that I had the capacity to make people listen to me," Indira Gandhi said. "The good Indian would say it was just not in my stars to be that little Indian housewife."

Her friendship with Feroze Gandhi blossomed in Britain. He was a familiar face from home, and Indira never forgot how very dedicated Feroze had been toward her mother during her last months. It was Feroze who introduced Indira to a variety of Indians—Krishna Menon, the novelist Iqbal Singh, and K. S. Shelvankar.[‡] "One reason for choosing Oxford was that Feroze was in England," Indira Gandhi said years later. "I considered him more as a friend; it was a link with the family and India." He was always sweet, ever willing to help Indira with her studies. She would frequently travel by train from Oxford to London and dine with Feroze, Krishna Menon, and others at Indian restaurants. Indira also became associated with an organization that solicited volunteers for the International Brigade. The Brigade fought on behalf of the Republicans in the Spanish Civil War, and Indira was clearly entranced by that

---

* V. K. Krishna Menon was a close associate of Jawaharlal Nehru. He would serve as Nehru's defense minister after Independence. Menon was notorious for his long-winded speeches, and once delivered an address lasting several hours at the United Nations General Assembly—a record that stands.

[†]Ridiculing public speakers is a time-honored tradition at Britain's best universities, particularly Oxford and Cambridge. The practice carries over into Parliament, where debates are acidic and acerbic.

[‡]Years later, Indira Gandhi would appoint Shelvankar as India's ambassador to North Vietnam.

war. Shanta Gandhi—no relative of Indira or Feroze Gandhi, but a schoolmate of Indira's from their Poona days—recalls that Indira often helped her organize fund-raising events for the London-based Aid Spain Committee. Shanta Gandhi would perform Indian classical dances at some of these events. On one occasion, according to her, Indira impulsively offered her dainty meenakari bracelet for an auction. The filigree bracelet fetched fifty pounds, an impressive sum in those days.

Indira stayed in close touch with her father, mainly through correspondence. Bored at Somerville College, she was determined to join him in Spain in mid-1938. Jawaharlal was scheduled to travel to Spain to observe firsthand the Spanish Civil War, after a train journey through Italy and Czechoslovakia. His trip was to end in Cairo. Harold Laski, the eminence grise of British socialism, thought it a bad idea for Indira to "tag along" with her father; men like Laski had come to take a paternal interest in Indira during her English stay. Laski fancied himself an intellectual mentor for young and impressionable Indians who were studying in England at the time. Indeed, he had even given Indira an autographed copy of his celebrated book *The Grammar of Politics.*

"Look, you're just developing your personality, and if you tag along with your father, you'll just become an appendage," Laski told Indira. "So you'd better not go with him. You must now strike out on your own."*

Recalling the episode, Indira Gandhi said years later: "I listened very attentively, but of course I went along with my father! And Laski was very angry. He complained he had given a lot of time to me and that I just didn't take his advice."

The trip that Jawaharlal and Indira took through Europe proved exciting and educational for Indira, and enabled her to develop a cosmopolitan outlook which stayed with her all her life. There were "instant history" lessons as well. She was able to see for herself the confusion, contradictions, and tensions of prewar Europe. Like Jawaharlal, Indira was upset by Neville Chamberlain's appeasement of Adolf Hitler at Munich. In Spain, Indira witnessed the Civil War. The trip also exposed Indira to the fact that her father was mentally preparing himself for the day when India would become independent. Indeed, he often discussed the question of India's freedom with Europeans he met on the trip. After they arrived in Cairo, Jawaharlal suggested to Indira that she accompany him to India—an invitation that she accepted eagerly. But the two-week journey by sea turned out to be disastrous as far as relations between father and daughter were concerned. Jawaharlal and Indira had severe disagreements over her romance with Feroze Gandhi, with Nehru urging

* Anand Mohan, *Indira Gandhi* (New York: Hawthorn Books, 1967).

his daughter to delay marriage until she had completed her education. By the time their ship had docked in Bombay, Indira was not even on speaking terms with her father. She also subjected him to a stony silence during the long train trip from Bombay to Allahabad. In later life, Indira was to perfect the art of subjecting those with whom she had arguments—or those she did not like—to contemptuous silence, leaving them often to twist in the wind.

Indira spent the winter of 1938–39 in India, visiting with her paternal grandmother, Swarup Rani, for the most part. By this time, Indira had become an avid reader—Jawaharlal Nehru's exhortations had finally paid off—and she would eagerly delve into the 6,000-book library of the Allahabad house. Indira was also fascinated by the fact that Motilal Nehru's widow had become a revolutionary in her waning years, frequently attending anti-British rallies and even encountering lathi charges from the police. During one such attack, she was pummeled to the ground by a policeman and suffered a severe concussion. Indira shared many hours of memories with the old woman, sometimes joking with her about the time when Swarup Rani had wanted Indira to be wed through an arranged marriage. Swarup Rani died not long after Indira's visit to Allahabad in 1938, and Indira was to say later that she was glad she spent time with her grandmother during her last days.

Indira also spent time with Congress Party workers. In November 1938, she turned twenty-one and immediately qualified to become a full-fledged member of her father's Indian National Congress. The membership was promptly bestowed on her. In formal terms, at least, this was when Indira's political career started. Upon her return to England, Indira resumed her relatively busy social schedule, meeting luminaries such as George Bernard Shaw and Albert Einstein. But she became increasingly uncomfortable at being abroad. Her health could not adjust well to the bitter English winters; she often told friends that she hated the cold weather. Indira's friends—such as Krishna Menon—let it be known that she had decided to return to India because of an illness. She was relieved to leave, although Jawaharlal was upset that his daughter had decided to abandon her formal studies. Indira often told friends that she wished to be with her father who was accelerating his campaign against the British.

While it was true that Indira had developed a malingering case of pleurisy, "illness" was a polite way of explaining why Indira left Oxford. In truth, Indira was asked by the university authorities to leave the university. The officials were distressed at her failure to pass her Latin exam even at the second attempt. Clair Hollingworth, the well-known British writer and journalist and a contemporary of Indira's, describes the event as follows: "Indira was sent down from university. There was no question of her being allowed to stay on.'"* Even family members such as Vijaya Lakshmi Pandit, who did not particularly like Indira, maintained publicly that it was Indira's poor health that forced her to abandon Oxford.

Although Indira failed to get a degree, she learned a great deal in England about world affairs. Through Agatha Harrison, a disciple of Mahatma Gandhi, and Krishna Menon, the cantankerous South Indian lawyer who headed the London-based India League, she met eminent people such as Harold Laski; Stafford Cripps, the politician; and Edward Thompson, the poet and critic.† She listened to them intently and tried to imbibe wisdom from them. Few of these Britons later wrote recollections of their meetings with Indira, so it is fair to assume that she did not make a particularly strong impression on them. Her stay abroad widened Indira's interest in geopolitics, however, and certainly taught her a certain degree of self-reliance. She made political contacts among socialists that were to prove useful during her career as a world leader. "I was especially privileged that my father was friendly to and known and loved by such a wide variety of people—scientists, artists, literary people—in many countries abroad," Indira Gandhi later told Professor Anand Mohan, the historian. "Because of him, I was able to meet them and know them also."

Among those whom Indira also met, sometimes repeatedly, were such prominent Laborites as Aneurin Bevan and his wife, Jennie Lee; James Strachey, the well-known intellectual who had translated some of Freud's books; Ellen Wilkinson; Reginald Sorensen; and Herbert Morrison, who later became foreign secretary. Indira also spent time with Paul Robeson, the black left-wing American singer who was in London frequently in those days. Their friendship continued for many years until Robeson's death nearly thirty years after he and Indira first met. During this time, Indira became especially fond of Ernst Toller, the German-Jewish poet, and his wife, Christianne, who had fled Nazi Germany. Indira frequently dined with them, and the Tollers wrote glowing letters about her to

---

*The fiction of Indira's decision to leave Oxford voluntarily was maintained publicly for a long time. It was not until the late Dhiren Bhagat, a Bombay-based writer, dug up Indira's academic records and published them in *The Illustrated Weekly of India* in the early 1980s that the secret was out.

†There were persistent rumors that Krishna Menon and Indira became romantically close in Britain. Some have suggested that they retained a relationship even years later, especially after Feroze Gandhi had died. Other sources say that there was never any question of such a relationship because Menon, who never married, was a homosexual. However, Menon reportedly enjoyed a long affair with the wife of a junior Indian diplomat who later became a foreign secretary. The diplomat's career

Jawaharlal. In one such letter, Ernst Toller said: ". . . she is so beautiful, but so pure which makes one feel very happy. . . . She seemed to me like a little flower which the wind might blow away so easily, but I think she is not afraid of the wind." Indira surely enjoyed the Tollers' company not least because Christianne fed her well.

Feroze Gandhi and Indira Priyadarshini Nehru returned to India by ship in the late fall of 1940.* Because of the war—which had been declared on September 3, 1939—the ship could not use the Suez Canal and was forced to take the much longer route to India by way of South Africa. It halted for a week at Durban. The Indian community there decided to hold a reception for Jawaharlal Nehru's daughter. She accepted on the conditions that she would not have to speak, the memories of her last attempt in England still fresh. Yet she surprised everyone when she burst into a tirade against apartheid, the horrors of which Feroze and she had seen for themselves while driving through the city. She rebuked not only the South African regime but the Indian business community for being indifferent to the sufferings of the exploited blacks. In effect, Indira called the Indian traders two-faced—hypocrites who gave money to their fellow Indians but who made that money by dealing with the white regime. This sort of rhetoric, and attitude, certainly represented a change in Indira—she seemed transformed from being a shy, reserved young girl who was afraid to speak to someone who was beginning to be assertive and unafraid to voice her opinions.

Indira's affection for Feroze was now being openly demonstrated by her—the couple could be seen occasionally holding hands, even sneaking kisses surreptitiously. This, too, marked a change in Indira's behavior. In England, even those people with whom she spent a lot of time—such as Shanta Gandhi—had not expected that the relationship between Indira and Feroze would really expand into a full-blown romance. Indeed, Indira's maternal aunt Sheela Kaul sometimes met the couple in London but came away with the feeling that Feroze acted more like the watchdog than a suitor.

Jawaharlal, however, sensed that Indira was serious about marrying Feroze Gandhi. He hoped, however, that things would change when the

---

was promoted by Menon. Indira told a close friend that "Krishna Menon had one of the most evil countenances" she had ever seen.

* Feroze Gandhi had by now obtained a bachelor's degree from the London School of Economics.

couple returned to India. Jawaharlal felt that she had fallen for the first man who had come along, and he urged her to bide her time. She had confided to her friends that "I don't like Feroze, but I love him." Feroze and Indira were opposites in most ways, so it was no great surprise that there was this mutual attraction. She was slightly built, frail, and beautiful; he was stout and square. Indira gave the aura of being haughty, though she was actually shy—at least then. On the other hand, people warmed up to Feroze because of his warm, funny, and affectionate manner. Professor Anand Mohan writes: "Indira's own attitude toward Feroze had matured considerably. The more she observed him the more she grew to admire some of his qualities—his devotion to loved ones, his humane concern for all the world's oppressed, his personal involvement in impersonal causes, his great gusto for all the good things of life, and above all his urbanity of manner and spontaneity of wit. She fell deeply and indubitably in love with him."*

Indira and Feroze may not have perceived it as such, but to many Indians it was clear that they were divided by the "class" barrier that shaped social behavior and customs.† Indira belonged to an aristocratic family, whereas Feroze came from a conventional lower-middle-class family that owned a general store. Say this for Feroze: He never pretended to be anything else nor was he ashamed of his origins. As Nayantara Sahgal—Indira's first cousin—points out, Indira's choice to marry Feroze was probably influenced by her mother's fondness for the young man who had nursed her so devotedly during her declining days in Bhowali and Lausanne. To Indira, Feroze represented the known, comfortable, and familiar.

Jawaharlal Nehru's reaction to Indira's decision to marry Feroze was far from favorable. What worried him as well was that Feroze would not be able to give her the comforts that she was used to, a concern that Feroze's sister Tehmina also shared. Jawaharlal, in expressing his reservations about Feroze Gandhi, was being remarkably prescient. The union between Indira and Feroze would prove an unhappy one. Nehru was grateful for the solicitous manner in which Feroze had looked after Kamala in Bhowali and Allahabad, to be sure, but he clearly did not care much

---

*Mohan, *Indira Gandhi*, pp. 138–39.
†A distinction should be drawn between "class" and "caste." The former term applies primarily to economic status. The latter is a function of birth among Hindus. There are four principal castes—Brahmans, the highest born, who originally consisted of the priestly and intellectual sects; Kshatriyas, or warriors and administrators; Vaishnavas, or merchants and traders; and Sudras, the lowest born, or manual laborers. In today's India, of course, while caste origins are socially significant, professional qualifications generally matter more as class hierarchies acquire greater importance.

for Feroze's pursuit of Indira. On one occasion, Feroze wrote to him jubilantly describing photographs that he had taken of Indira in Switzerland. Nehru replied: "*If* you have taken these photographs, I must congratulate you." That was a rare instance of pettiness on Nehru's part; he was generally far more gracious to Feroze and everybody else, but it was becoming increasingly clear that he did not want Indira to plunge into matrimony right away.

Some scholars have suggested that Nehru's disapproval of Feroze stemmed from the fact that he was a Parsi, but that would be an incorrect assumption. Nehru, in fact, was a thorough liberal and completely secularist-minded. After all, both his sisters had married outside of the Kashmiri Brahman community to which the Nehrus belonged. Indeed, when his youngest sister Krishna married Gunottam "Raja" Hutheesing, Jawaharlal wrote to Mahatma Gandhi defending her right to marry a non-Brahman. A number of orthodox Hindus—but not Gandhi—had criticized Krishna's decision. Nehru felt that he had to respond, and he did so in a letter to the Mahatma that was made public quickly by the latter's aides: "I would welcome as wide a breach of custom as possible. The Kashmiri community—there are exceptions, of course, in it—disgusts me. It is the very epitome of petit-bourgeois vices, which I detest. I am not particularly interested in a person being a Brahman or a non-Brahman or anything else. As a matter of fact, I fail to see the relevance of all this; one marries an individual, not a community."

If Jawaharlal's reaction to Indira's decision to marry Feroze was less than enthusiastic, there were far more spirited objections from nearly everyone else when they heard that Indira was going to marry him. Ironically, Indira's own aunts, who had spiritedly both married out of the Kashmiri Brahman caste, were also aghast. The match seemed unsuitable to them perhaps because of the fact that Feroze Gandhi did not belong to a socially acceptable and wealthy family. Vijaya Lakshmi Pandit urged Indira not to flout family tradition—an ironic bit of advice, considering that she herself had once wanted to marry a Muslim and that her Maharashtrian husband, Ranjit Pandit, was from outside the Kashmiri Pandit clan. Krishna Hutheesing—whose husband was from the Gujarati community—also advised against the marriage, but relented when Indira insisted that she was truly in love with Feroze.

When Jawaharlal himself hinted that perhaps she would not be able to do without money, Indira was indignant. She did not want to be influenced by her father when it came to love and marriage. She argued with her father that the shortage of money did not matter and that the political activities that she and Feroze were committed to would sustain them. At one point, Indira even rudely reminded her father that, having neglected his own wife throughout their marriage, he was hardly in a position to give his daughter lessons concerning matrimony.

Nehru asked Mahatma Gandhi to intervene—for the second time in his personal life, the first being when Motilal Nehru had wanted to send Indira Priyadarshini to a school not of Jawaharlal's choice. The Mahatma, on seeing that Indira's mind was already made up, extracted a promise from Feroze and Indira that they would not get married without Jawaharlal's formal consent. The Mahatma took Feroze for a walk to discuss the matter, and later wrote to Jawaharlal that Feroze "would not think of marrying Indu without your consent and blessings."

Jawaharlal did not persist in his argument, and yielded to Indira. As Inder Malhotra says in his biography of Indira Gandhi: "A man of reason and an overwhelmingly affectionate father, Nehru gave in. In the first contest of wills between father and daughter, the daughter had won hands down."[*]

In late February 1942, the news of Indira's decision to marry Feroze appeared as a small front-page item in the *Pioneer*, a progovernment newspaper published in Lucknow.[†] That news item touched off a nationwide controversy. Hindu bigots condemned Jawaharlal for acquiescing to the marriage. Many Hindus were already enraged that, two years prior to Indira's proposed marriage, Indian Muslims had formally issued a call for a partition under which a new Islamic state called Pakistan would be created. In the minds of many of these Hindus, the very idea that a daughter of a prominent Hindu family such as the Nehrus would marry outside her faith was sacrilegious, and marriage between a Hindu and a Parsi seemed inconceivable. "The whole world seemed opposed to my marriage," Indira later recalled. On hearing the sort of talk that was spreading, Nehru rushed to his daughter's defense.[‡]

"A marriage is a personal and domestic matter, affecting chiefly the two parties concerned and partly their families," Jawaharlal wrote in a statement that was widely published in India.

> Yet I recognize that in view of my association with public affairs, I should take my many friends and colleagues and the public generally

---

[*] Malhotra, *Indira Gandhi*, p. 49.

[†] A news item also ran in *The Leader*, an Allahabad newspaper, on February 21, 1942, about the forthcoming wedding.

[‡] Nehru, in fact, left a dinner that he was hosting at Shantiniketan in Calcutta in honor of Mr. and Mrs. Chiang Kai-shek, and sped to Allahabad to be with the distressed Indira. The Chiangs had come to India to seek Indian support for the Chinese war effort against Japan, and in turn to express their backing of India's

into my confidence. I have long held the view that though parents may and should advise in the matter, the choice and ultimate decision must be with the two parties concerned. The decision, if arrived at after mature deliberation, must be given effect to. And it is no business of parents or others to come in the way. When I was assured that Indira and Feroze wanted to marry one another, I accepted willingly their decision and I told them that it had my blessing. Mahatma Gandhi, whose opinion I value not only in public affairs but in private matters also, gave his blessings to the proposal.

Indeed, so widespread was the hue and cry over the marriage of Indira Nehru and Feroze Gandhi that the Mahatma decided to make a public statement of his own. Gandhi's support of the marriage had resulted in his receiving several abusive letters. He now wrote an open letter to his critics, a missive that was published in his weekly newspaper *Harijan*:

> His [Feroze's] only crime in their estimation is that he happens to be a Parsi. I have been, and am still, a strong opponent of either party changing religion for the sake of marriage. . . . In the present case, there is no question of change of religion. The public knows my connection with the Nehrus. I also had talks with both parties. . . . It would have been cruelty to refuse consent to their engagement. As time advances, such unions are bound to multiply with benefit to the society. At present we have not even reached the stage of mutual toleration. . . . Feroze Gandhi has been for years an intimate of the Nehru family. He nursed Kamala Nehru in her sickness. He was like a son to her. A natural intimacy grew up between them [Indira and Feroze]. The friendship has been perfectly honorable. It has ripened into mutual attraction. But neither party would think of marrying without the consent and blessing of Jawaharlal Nehru. This was given only after he was satisfied that the attraction had a solid basis. . . .

Gandhi continued: "I invite the writers of abusive letters to shed your wrath and bless the forthcoming marriage. Their letters betray ignorance, intolerance, and prejudice—a species of untouchability, dangerous because not easily so classified."

Mahatma Gandhi's open letter did not sway those who felt that mixed marriages should not take place.* Feroze Gandhi's family members were

---

freedom struggle. Nehru had taken the Chiangs to Shantiniketan because it was the first educational institution in India to establish a department of Chinese Studies.
* Mahatma Gandhi's exhortations notwithstanding, the question of communally mixed marriages remains a sensitive one in India. While more and more young

also among those who tried to dissuade him. His sister, Tehmina, and his older brother Faredun, were adamantly opposed to the marriage. Their opposition reflected conservative attitudes of the Parsis who, like the conservative Kashmiri Pandit clan to which Indira Nehru belonged, did not endorse mixed marriages.* Moreover, Faredun Gandhi thought his brother to be a "vagabond," a man unlikely to be a responsible husband. Jawaharlal met with Faredun and Tehmina. He assured Tehmina, in particular, that the Nehrus were a secular-minded family and that, indeed, they welcomed Feroze. He told Tehmina that he had watched the growth and development of Feroze and that "whatever he does, I am sure he will always land on his feet."

Despite the opposition, however, Indira was determined to marry Feroze Gandhi. It was a memorable year in which to get married. "In the history of India's freedom movement, 1942 was the year that saw the fiercest and bloodiest conflict between the Congress Party and the British Government," writes Krishan Bhatia.[†] Mahatma Gandhi had formally launched his Quit-India Movement, and that year more than 50,000 Indians would be jailed. Scores of people were killed in clashes between Indian nationalists and the police.[‡] Leaders such as Mahatma Gandhi and Jawaharlal echoed the widespread frustration of Indians that while Britain was battling the Axis Powers in the name of freedom, India—Britain's biggest colony—should be deprived of it. British authorities, for their part, were angered that Indians were not fully supportive of the war effort.[§] They viewed the Indian demand for constitutional change and freedom as dangerous and distracting. And it did not help matters when Winston Churchill, the feisty new British prime minister, declared that he had not become His Majesty's head of government "to preside over the liquidation of the British Empire."

The wedding of Indira Priyadarshini Nehru and Feroze Gandhi took place on March 26, 1942, at Anand Bhavan in Allahabad. Indira and Feroze

---

people chose to marry outside their caste or religion, their numbers are tiny compared to the arranged marriages that take place within specific communities.

* Despite their conservatism, Parsi shopkeepers specialized in selling liquor. To this day, many of the shops that sell liquor all across India are run by Parsis. This is an intriguing phenomenon because prohibition was in force in India until not long ago, and liquor consumption was widely regarded as a liberal practice, one that was frowned upon by traditional segments of society.

[†] Krishan Bhatia, *Indira* (New York: Praeger, 1974), p. 100.

[‡] To this day, there has not been an accurate tally of fatalities.

[§] There were Indians who exulted over the initial traumas suffered by the British at

had wanted a very small affair, but Mahatma Gandhi convinced the couple that because their case had become a *cause célèbre*, there ought to be a national celebration marking their marriage. And so, in addition to close relatives and friends, hundreds of local nationalist leaders and Congress workers were invited. As happens whenever there is a wedding in India, huge crowds gathered out of curiosity. People climbed the banyan, neem, and peepul trees surrounding Anand Bhavan to catch a glimpse of the couple, who were married in a colorful tent that Indians call a shamiana. Two foreigners also witnessed some of the festivities—Sir Stafford Cripps and Eve Curie, a journalist and the daughter of the French scientist Marie Curie. Miss Curie had arrived at Anand Bhavan shortly before the wedding and was fascinated by all the elaborate preparations that went into a Hindu marriage. In particular, she was mesmerized by the Hindu tradition of choosing bangles for the bride. "To the bride of tomorrow a merchant had brought a basket full of translucent bracelets of glass, in all the colors of the rainbow," she wrote. "Indira took pleasure in making her choice at length. She picked carefully the bracelets that would exactly match her saris."[*]

The day of the wedding was sunny and cool. Anand Bhavan was gaily decorated with marigolds. Many rooms were filled with presents that had been sent by people all over India—silverware, saris, ornaments, fruits, and china. It was also an auspicious day, according to Hindu astrologers—Ram Navmi, the birth anniversary of Lord Rama, the mythological king of the great Indian epic the *Ramayana*. Though Indira and Feroze were not at all religious, both of them refused to renounce their religions as was required at the time under the Civil Marriage Law.[†] Their refusal meant that a civil ceremony could not be legitimately held, and neither could an orthodox religious one because there was no precedent for a ceremony involving a Hindu and a Parsi. A Hindu scholar from Delhi, Lachmi Dhar Shastri, came to the rescue. He suggested some Vedic hymns that would constitute, in effect, a secular ceremony but one that

---

the hands of the Nazis. Some Indians even wanted India to side with the Germans. Neither Mahatma Gandhi nor Jawaharlal Nehru supported such a move.

[*] Quoted by Miss Curie to Professor Ralph Buultjens.

[†] When Indira's aunt Krishna married Gunottam "Raja" Hutheesing in a civil marriage ceremony, they both formally renounced their religion. This was required under the terms of the Special Marriage Act of 1871. The Act was amended after Independence in 1947, and now allows marriage between members of different communities without the couple having to renounce their respective faiths. Years later, after the death of Indira Gandhi's younger son, Sanjay, there was a legal dispute over the distribution of Sanjay Gandhi's estate. The distribution would be decided according to the legal category of his parents' marriage. The Delhi courts held that Indira's marriage to Feroze Gandhi was performed according to Hindu specifications.

invoked the Universal Divine Spirit. So a semiorthodox Vedic ceremony suitable for this kind of a marriage was performed.* Shastri argued that there was no need for the couple to renounce their faiths because Hindu hymns were, in essence, secular, and therefore could be applied to marriage ceremonies regardless of participants' creeds. Some elders of the local Parsi community had wanted to demonstrate against the marriage, but Jawaharlal Nehru persuaded Feroze's mother, Rattimai, to talk them out of such action. Indeed, some of these Parsis even attended the wedding, along with an impressive array of distinguished Indians: Maulana Abul Kalam Azad, a Muslim who was president of the Indian National Congress; Dr. Rajendra Prasad, who would one day become Independent India's first constitutional president; and Sarojini Naidu, the poet who had first seen Indira as a newborn babe.

The assembled guests applauded when Feroze made his appearance. He wore an achkan—a long closed-collar coat that was made out of khadi—and tight trousers called churidaars. He had a baby face, with bright eyes and a high forehead, and he looked dashing, even taller than he really was. He smiled happily, nodding to guests he knew, waving at times. But Indira was the cynosure. She wore a simple pink cotton sari spun by her father during his recent term in jail.† She declined to wear jewelry, preferring fresh flowers instead.‡ Around her wrists, Indira draped fragrant motia blossoms that, in North India, usually signaled the start of summer. At nine o'clock in the morning, Jawaharlal Nehru escorted her to the mandap, the enclosure where the traditional holy fire had been built from twigs. The fire, as is required by Hindu custom, was fed clarified butter and incense by Brahman priests. Jawaharlal led Indira to a silk cushion that had been placed on the floor. Feroze sat next to her, Jawaharlal on the opposite side of the fire. A vacant cushion next to

---

*There was a precedent for this type of semi-Vedic ceremony. One of Indira's relatives, B. K. Nehru—who later became the Indian ambassador to the United States—married a Hungarian woman, Magdalena Friedman, who was Jewish, in a similar ceremony. It was the same Lachmi Dhar Shastri who drew up the Vedic hymns for their marriage and indeed even officiated at the ceremony. Before the wedding, however, the groom's family consulted with Sir Tej Bahadur Sapru, a distinguished lawyer who was also a friend of Motilal Nehru. He argued that Shastri's wedding rituals would not be validated in a court of law on the grounds that there was no precedent. The Nehrus, however, approved the ceremony anyway.

†Jawaharlal had been released from jail only three months before Indira's wedding. Four months after the wedding, he was back in jail. In all, Nehru would serve more than ten years behind bars between 1921 and 1945.

‡Indira had inherited some valuable jewelry from her mother. She would have inherited even more, but much of the jewelry had been sold by the Nehrus to pay for Kamala's huge medical bills during her illness.

Jawaharlal symbolized the place where Kamala Nehru would have sat. The hymns suggested by Lachmi Dhar Shastri were recited in Sanskrit—which neither Indira nor Feroze understood—but Jawaharlal had arranged for a printed translation into English, which was distributed to guests in a red folder. *

This is how Krishan Bhatia described the marriage ceremony:

> The opening hymn paid the young couple's homage to "the law of righteousness." As butter was poured over the flames, Indira and Feroze "resolved to dedicate" their lives "in the service of that light which leads humanity onwards" and prayed that their "hearts be possessed with love for all." The priest explained to them that clarified butter symbolized thought in the ceremony, the spoon with which it was poured represented thought translated into action, and the fire "the universal spirit in the life of man." The next part of the ceremony was devoted to "man's love of freedom and his determination to preserve it." According to one of the verses chanted during this part of the traditional ceremony, the bride was supposed to say, "If there are any people in the four quarters of the earth who venture to deprive us of our freedom, Lord, here I am, sword in hand, prepared to resist them to the last. I pray for the spreading light of freedom. May it envelop us from all sides."
>
> The ceremony also charged the bride and the bridegroom with the responsibility of preserving inviolate the "sovereignty of the people." This was followed by the most formal and important part of the ceremony, the kanyadan, or the giving away of the bride. The bridegroom was enjoined to deal with the bride in matters relating to dharma (spiritual and moral life), aratha (financial and economic matters), and kama (aesthetic pursuits) "with deference and self-control and in harmony with her wishes." The bridegroom was further called upon not to neglect her.
>
> With the chanting of hymns over, Jawaharlal placed Indira's hand in Feroze's. Together, their hands clasped and with a corner of the bride's sari tied to the bridegroom's achkan, they took seven steps around the fire, binding themselves into the eternal, irrevocable union.† Relations and friends then gathered around Indira and showered rose petals on her while chanting hymns urging her to

---

* Because the British had instituted strict laws against circulating any nonofficial printed material, the folder was stamped with the words "For private circulation only."

† It was ironic that the ceremony involved circumambulating a fire. The Zoroastrian religion is centered on fire worship, and the fact that Feroze and Indira walked

preserve the tradition of dignity and honor established by Indian womanhood.*

Strangely enough, both Indira and Feroze seemed subdued. Perhaps it was the realization that they had overcome formidable odds to get to this moment that sobered them. Indira's aunt Krishna Hutheesing wrote this about Indira's deportment on her wedding day:

> Frail and almost ethereal, she laughed and talked to those around her, but sometimes her big black eyes would darken and hold a distant and sorrowful look. What dark cloud could mar the joy of this happy day? Was it due to a longing for the young mother who was no more, by whose absence a void had been created which even on this day remained unfulfilled? Or was it the thought of parting from the father, a father whose very life she had been. She was leaving him now to a life that would be lonelier for him than it had ever been before. Maybe it was the breaking of all the old ties and the starting of a new life which brought a passing look of sadness to the young bride's eyes, for who could foretell what the future held in store for her—happiness? sorrow? fulfillment? disillusionment?[†]

Perceptive, and prophetic, words indeed. Reflecting on this period, Professor Ralph Buultjens makes two observations. "With the advantage of hindsight, it is now clear how mismatched Indira and Feroze were," he says. "In almost every area, except intelligence, the gap was too large to bridge. Second, a contemporary view of their marriage is an index of how substantially social mores have changed. The importance of the public controversy preceding the marriage will be difficult for young people to understand today—and now has an air of irrelevancy about it. It is inconceivable that such a controversy could arise in modern-day Indian society. Yet, in that period, this contretemps was so cacophonous that it surely must have had a lasting and unhappy impact on the marriage itself."[‡]

---

around a fire during their marriage ceremony was an unintended irony that did not escape some of the guests.
* Krishan Bhatia, *Indira*, pp. 104–5.
[†] Krishna Hutheesing, *Dear to Behold* (New York: Macmillan, 1969).
[‡] Interview with the author, New York City, December 1990.

9

Marriage by Fire

Indira and Feroze Gandhi went to Kashmir for their honeymoon. It was Indira who decided on Kashmir, for she had always loved mountains. Twenty-six years earlier, Jawaharlal and Kamala Nehru had gone to Kashmir on their honeymoon, too. For Indira, the trip also represented a symbolic return to her ancestral roots at a time when opposition in India to the marriage had still not quite abated. It had been a frenetic time before and during the wedding, and Kashmir offered respite and relaxation. Indira seemed delighted to be able to guide her new husband around this exquisite place from where, a very long time ago, Raj Kaul had set out for the dusty plains of Delhi. Indira and Feroze went on long treks in the hills, with Indira often leaving an out-of-breath Feroze far behind on narrow trails that wound up steep inclines. Motilal Nehru had once said, after witnessing his young granddaughter clamber up a hill in Kashmir during a family holiday, that she must have been a mountain goat in a previous reincarnation. *

There were lots of things for a newly married couple to do in lovely Kashmir, where spring was in full flower. Indira and Feroze frequented the sprawling gardens in Srinagar—Kashmir's main city—that had been built by Mughal rulers. They went for rides in shikaras, the slender boats

---

*Many years later, when Indira Gandhi was facing a particularly difficult political problem, she recalled this quote for Ralph Buultjens. She also told him that Motilal Nehru had said that Indira was the kind of person who would always take the most difficult route up a mountain, never the easy one.

that glide gently across Kashmir's myriad lakes. They went for walks along the banks of the Jhelum River. They went fishing for trout. They picked apples. And occasionally they even made love in fields, or in orchards—a terribly daring thing to do in conservative Kashmir. After a few days in the resort town of Gulmarg, the couple sent Jawaharlal a telegram: "Wish we could send you some cool breeze from here." Nehru riposted: "Thanks, but you have no mangoes." His reference was to the mango season, which was in full swing in the plains.* Indira loved mangoes, especially the Alphonso variety, and her father knew that she would be salivating at the very thought that mangoes were plentifully available in Allahabad's bazaars. These fruits were apparently not readily available in Kashmir. In a subsequent telegram, Jawaharlal said to the couple: "Don't hurry back. Live in beauty while you may."

Jawaharlal Nehru had always been enamored of Kashmir; perhaps it was an atavistic feeling that drew him to that lovely valley nestled in the high Himalayas. Long before Indira's marriage, he had written her a letter about a visit to Kashmir: "The loveliness of the land enthralled me and cast an enchantment all about me. I wandered about like one possessed and drunk with beauty, and the intoxication of it filled my mind. Like some supremely beautiful woman, whose beauty is almost impersonal and above human desire, such was Kashmir in all its feminine beauty of river and valley and lake and graceful trees. And then another aspect of this magic beauty would come to view, a masculine one, of hard mountains and precipices, and snow-capped peaks and glaciers, and cruel and fierce torrents rushing down to the valleys below."

But the honeymoon did not last beyond July, and in a startling way it presaged what would be a doomed relationship between Indira and Feroze. Relations between the Congress and the British authorities were heating up again, and Indira became increasingly distracted in Kashmir. She felt that she should be at Jawaharlal's side. Perhaps there was guilt on her part that she was enjoying the beauty of Kashmir while her father was struggling hundreds of miles away against the British oppressors. She knew that Jawaharlal, a widower since 1936, needed a woman to look after him—even though he was incarcerated most of the time by the British. Moreover, Feroze Gandhi was also somewhat anxious to get back into the fray—into the arena against the British—although it would be some time before he began participating in demonstrations.

---

* Every Indian is supposed to be a lover of mangoes, luscious, juicy fruits whose flesh is peachlike but far sweeter. The Allahabad area produces a special variety of especially sweet mangoes during the season, which extends from April through the end of May.

Feroze rented a small two-room apartment in the old section of Allah-abad. * He did not want to live in Anand Bhavan with his in-laws, but Indira did not agree with him because the Nehru family home clearly offered comfort and familiarity. Moreover, Anand Bhavan was where the political action was, and Indira was determined to join the Congress struggle against the British. Feroze wondered aloud to friends whether "Indira would become a Gandhi or whether I would be expected to become a Nehru." Indira may not have ever said so, but everybody did indeed expect Feroze Gandhi to "become a Nehru." He had married into a legendary family, one whose personal history was very much part of the national consciousness, and there was no way that Feroze could expect to carve out a completely independent identity. In his own naïve way, of course, he had thought that he could, but tragically Feroze was to be proven wrong.

Almost from the day that Feroze and Indira returned to Allahabad, Indira started participating in Congress activities.† It was a time of in-creasing tumult in India. Sir Stafford Cripps had been sent by the British war cabinet to propose dominion status for India, but he failed in his mission to persuade Indians to accept a constitution for self-governing. The Muslim League's demand for a separate Islamic state also proved too much for Sir Stafford to handle. It was clear that the British had no wish to transfer power to India while World War II was going on, and the impatient Indians did not wish to wait. Sir Stafford was sympathetic to the Indians' demands, but his prime minister, Winston Churchill, was in no mood to compromise. At this time, the British approach was that Indian independence was a secondary priority to their fight against Fascism. In these early days of the war, the British saw the need for defusing rising protests in India. Yet what they offered were mild pallia-tives sufficient only to further inflame the freedom movement. When protests increased, the British answered with repression.

Mahatma Gandhi declared that the Cripps-Churchill offer was "a post-dated check on a failing bank." The leader of the Muslim League, Mohammed Ali Jinnah, also rejected the offer.‡

"If that is all you had to offer, why have you come so far?" a deeply anguished Mahatma Gandhi asked Sir Stafford.

The Mahatma then initiated a "Quit India" agitation, calling for the British to leave India at once. Feroze and Indira attended a special two-

---

* This neighborhood was outside the Civil Lines, where Britons and the Indian affluent lived.
† Rallies and marches were declared illegal by the British authorities.
‡ Mohammed Ali Jinnah, a lawyer, became known as the father of modern Pakistan.

day meeting of the Indian National Congress in Bombay on August 7, 1942, at which Jawaharlal Nehru made a memorable speech. Indians, he said, did not wish to be treated as "a benighted backward people," and he accused Britain of having made Indians into "miserable, poverty-stricken wrecks of humanity." Nehru urged Indians to renew their struggle to drive the British out of India. Late that evening, he was arrested by the police, as were Mahatma Gandhi and every member of the Congress Working Committee. The British clearly did not want the Congress's call for civil disobedience to spread at a time when they were preoccupied with confronting the Axis, and the way to ensure that was to imprison the entire leadership of the Congress. Mahatma Gandhi and most of the Congress Working Committee members were taken to a facility in Poona, near Bombay. Jawaharlal Nehru, however, was incarcerated in a huge sixteenth-century fort in Ahmadnagar, some 200 miles southeast of Bombay. There he began his last and longest prison term under British rule—1,040 days.*

Bereft of its leadership, the Congress Party at first seemed to flounder. But soon, thousands of students took to the streets. They abandoned Mahatma Gandhi's strategy of nonviolence, and started burning police stations and government buildings. They blew up railway tracks. They cut telephone and telegraph lines. The police retaliated with great brutality, often firing tear gas—and even live ammunition—into protesting crowds. The British army was called in to suppress demonstrators.† Whatever goodwill there still was for Britain among Indians certainly vanished with such a show of overwhelming force. "Britain's Field Marshal Viceroy Lord Wavell . . . understood . . . that the Raj was doomed, for all the ranks of their Army that held [British administration together] were fast 'turning soft,' " says Professor Stanley Wolpert. "Britain's final two postwar years were a holding action designed to maintain some 'illusion of permanence,' while the newly elected Labor Government desperately searched for a formula to make the imminent transfer of power to Indian hands as peaceful as possible."‡

During this period, in the early 1940s, Indira was in frequent contact with the Congress "underground," men and women who had agitated

---

*Jawaharlal Nehru was released from prison on June 15, 1945. So determined were the British to prevent any contact between Nehru and the Congress that Indira was not even permitted the standard fortnightly visit granted to family members.
†To this day, there has been no reliable tally of casualties during this phase of India's freedom struggle. Some estimates put the death figure at more than 2,000.
‡Stanley Wolpert, *India* (Berkeley: University of California Press, 1991), p. 68.

violently against the British and who were sought by the police. She attended illicit meetings in and around Allahabad, and began organizing resistance cells around the country. Indira had, for all practical purposes, moved into Anand Bhavan; she and Feroze would meet occasionally when Indira took time off from her Congress Party work. Feroze, meanwhile, indulged his interest in horticulture by tending to the garden in Anand Bhavan. The estate had been largely neglected over the years, and Feroze decided that he would come to the rescue.

Along with Ram Avatar, the longtime gardener, he looked after the dahlias, roses, and narcissi. Anand Bhavan's garden soon became radiant and colorful, and even drew visitors who came to admire Feroze's flowers. Feroze became extremely popular with the help at Anand Bhavan, talking to them in their local dialects and sharing their meals. Years later, Ram Avatar would say that Feroze never behaved as though he was the privileged son-in-law of the Nehru household. "He was a simple man who never threw his weight about," the gardener said. * Jobs were difficult to come by in those days, especially because most available jobs were either with government agencies or connected to the war effort. Neither sector was particularly appealing to Feroze, and so he started selling insurance. He also began writing free-lance articles based on his experiences as a student in Europe, often drawing inspiration from the wonderful collection of photographs of Jawaharlal, Indira, and Kamala that he had taken himself.

Jawaharlal Nehru wrote often to Indira from jail, and it was clear that he was lonely and depressed. "The thought of you haunts me," he said in one letter. Everything he wrote was censored, and some of his letters did not even reach her. Similarly, her notes to him were scrutinized by the authorities, who also withheld some of them from Jawaharlal. Indira often felt like telling her father about the "games" she and her Congress colleagues would play with British authorities in Allahabad, but she wisely desisted. One such game involved hiding prominent Congress functionaries—those who were still out of jail—from the police. She personally looked after Lal Bahadur Shastri, assigning him an upstairs room in Anand Bhavan and making sure that he did not venture out of the premises. Anand Bhavan was carefully monitored by the police in those days, and Shastri would be surely recognized and arrested. † Indira hid Shastri's identity from even family members, who were simply told

---

* A conversation between Ram Avatar and Dom Moraes. See Moraes, *Mrs. Gandhi.*
† Shastri did venture out one day and was arrested by the authorities. This was the same Shastri who would one day succeed Jawaharlal Nehru as India's prime minister, and who would himself be succeeded in that post by Indira Gandhi.

that the room was occupied by an ailing family friend. She would carry
Shastri's meals to him personally three or four times a day.

Feroze was now drawn into the Congress struggle, not least because he
saw that Indira was now the lone Nehru family member in Allahabad
fighting against the British. Her aunt Vijaya Lakshmi Pandit had also
been taken to jail, and Feroze felt that Indira needed his support. He
took to his task with a vengeance, organizing local Congress cadres,
carrying messages surreptitiously from one Congress hideout to another.
He even grew a mustache to disguise himself because he knew that the
police had his photograph. Indira passed on to Feroze money and Congress Party literature that he, in turn, distributed to party workers. Both
Indira and Feroze knew, however, that the police were on to them and
that it was only a matter of time before they, too, were arrested. That
day turned out to be September 11, 1942, when Indira addressed a
public meeting. A police sergeant menacingly pointed a revolver at her,
whereupon Feroze—who had been watching the scene from a discreet
distance—rushed to his wife's rescue. Husband and wife were taken into
custody and driven to Naini Prison. All her life Indira had watched her
parents and aunts and family friends going to jail, and now she, too, was
part of the tradition. "I do not know of any other family which was so
involved in the freedom struggle and its hardships," Indira said later.
About her actual arrest, she would write: "There was no firing though
rifle butts were used and many were hurt. . . . The ride to the jail was
rather an extraordinary one, for [the policemen] in my van were apparently so moved by my talking to them that they apologized, put their
turbans at my feet, and wept their sorrow because of what their job
compelled them to do."*

   Indira would later describe her stay in jail as not being very memorable,
and indeed even degrading.† "No one who has not been in prison for any
length of time can even visualize the numbness of spirit that can creep
over one when, as Oscar Wilde writes, 'each day is like a year, a year
whose days are long,' and when day after day is wrapped up in sameness
and in spite and deliberate humiliation. Lord Pethick-Lawrence‡ has said
that the 'essential fact in the life of the prisoner is that he takes on a

* These police constables, of course, were Indians. Their superiors, however, were
usually Britons.
† Indira Gandhi was released from jail unconditionally on May 13, 1943.
‡ Lord Pethick-Lawrence was a British Labor Party leader who played an important
role in the negotiations that resulted in India's independence.

subhuman status.' Herded together like animals, devoid of dignity or privacy, he is debarred not only from outside company or news but from all beauty and color, softness, and grace."

In later life, Indira Gandhi would occasionally dramatize her prison stay, telling listeners that she had been abused and mistreated. "I was regarded as so dangerous that I wasn't even given normal prison facilities," she said. "I was determined to bear all privations and insults smilingly." In contrast to Indira's assertion, however, her aunt Vijaya Lakshmi Pandit—who was in the same Naini Prison from August 1942 to May 1943—has said in a published diary that "the treatment given to me and those who shared the barrack with me was according to prison standards, very lenient."* According to Mrs. Pandit's account, her daughter, Chandralekha—known as Lekha—and her niece Indira would read, and also devise silly games: The kerosene lantern was named "Lucifer"; a bottle of hair oil, whose cap had been misplaced, was called "Rupert, the headless Earl"; the jail cat was named "Mehitabel"—the cat produced four kittens while Indira was in jail, and constantly raided the women's supply of milk. They would practice their French. They each gave a special name to their corner of the barracks. Indira called hers Chimborazo; Chandralekha's corner was called Bien Venue; and Vijaya Lakshmi called her wall Wall View. They would frequently cook delicious meals from their rations and throw parties for themselves in the Blue Drawing Room, a section of the barracks so named because it featured an old blue rug that Mrs. Pandit had brought with her from Anand Bhavan.

A favorite subject of discussion was whether the menu should be written in French or English. According to Mrs. Pandit, at least, Indira's nine-month tenure in prison was spent with considerable levity and gaiety. There was even a party thrown to celebrate Indira's twenty-fifth birthday on November 19, 1942. One irritation, however, seemed to be that the prison authorities confiscated most of the foodstuffs that Jawaharlal and others sent to the women. In particular, Indira was upset that a consignment of Alphonso mangoes that Nehru had ordered for her was actually consumed by the prison superintendent; it turned out that the official had believed that Indira was not entitled to "special privileges" such as mango shipments.

Indira got to see Feroze periodically. He had been kept in the men's wing of Naini Prison, where he pursued his gardening hobby along with Mrs. Pandit's husband, Ranjit. There was little news that the prisoners

---

* Vijaya Lakshmi Pandit, *Prison Days* (Calcutta: Signet Press, 1945).

received about the momentous happenings outside—the war, India's freedom struggle. They had to rely on the occasional gossip that seeped through the prison walls, tidbits brought by friendly jailers. Feroze then arranged to get newspapers from an old man who came into the prison regularly to provide the institution with supplies. The newspapers would be rolled into a hollow niche in the old man's staff. The men would eagerly read these newspapers, then pass them over to the women's wing, where Indira and her companions awaited them with equal eagerness.

When Indira was finally released after 243 days in prison, says historian Anand Mohan, freedom came to her "somewhat as a shock."[*] Indira herself was to say later: "My unexpected release was like coming suddenly out of a dark passage. I was dazzled with the rush of life, the many hues and textures, the scale of sounds, and the range of ideas. Just to touch and listen was a disturbing experience, and it took awhile to get adjusted to normal living."

Not long after Indira's release from Naini Prison, Feroze Gandhi was also freed. Unlike Indira—who had never been formally tried—Feroze had been sentenced to one year of rigorous imprisonment. He had also been fined 200 rupees, a formidable sum in those days. Feroze joined Indira at Anand Bhavan. It was a particularly bleak time to be in the huge house. Its rooms and corridors echoed the voices of departed Nehrus, like Motilal and Kamala, and absent ones, such as Jawaharlal. The Congress Party seemed demoralized, with its top leaders still in jail, although popular feeling against the British presence continued to run high.

In 1943 the eastern state of Bengal suffered a great famine, the worst in India's recorded history. Some 3.5 million people died, not only because of a shortage of food but also because India's transportation system—which could have been speedily mobilized—was being used mainly for the war effort.[†] Vijaya Lakshmi Pandit would later write: "The famine in Bengal was man-made. . . . The most shocking aspect of the famine was not the catastrophe in terms of human life, horrendous though this was, but the fact that starvation existed side by side with plenty. In

---

[*] Jawaharlal Nehru spent some 3,262 days in prison. Incarceration is never a pleasant ordeal, but scholars note that Jawaharlal's father, Motilal Nehru, was treated with much greater deference when he was put in prison. Motilal was permitted letters, books, and newspapers. Since the lieutenant-governor of the state (then known as United Provinces, now as Uttar Pradesh) was a longtime friend, Motilal even occasionally received bottles of champagne and fine wines.

[†] One reason for the food shortage was that India traditionally received large shipments of rice from neighboring Burma. But the Japanese had overrun Burma, and this source of food was now cut off. Bengal, in particular, was hard hit.

Calcutta the rich—foreigners and Indians alike—continued to live in a state of affluence surrounded by every conceivable luxury while people outside their gates died of hunger and despair. The corruption was such that fortunes were made during this period, and every death was balanced by enormous gains for food speculators and others."[*] As part of a nationwide famine-relief drive, Indira organized a series of concerts featuring Uday Shankar, the virtuoso Indian classical dancer.[†] More than forty years later, the dancer's younger brother, sitar player Ravi Shankar, was to recall Indira's diligence: "Her energy was monumental, so monumental that my brother later told me he wondered how he could possibly keep up with all the programs Indiraji was suggesting."[‡]

Just as Indira and Feroze were settling down in Anand Bhavan, rediscovering each other again, there was a death in the family. Vijaya Lakshmi Pandit's husband, Ranjit, died unexpectedly in Lucknow Hospital on the morning of January 14, 1944.[§] He had not been well for quite some time, and Feroze had helped to look after him the previous year when they were both in Naini Prison.[**] But his death was a shock, and even though Indira had never liked Mrs. Pandit the two women drew closer now, however briefly.

It was at this time that Indira was determined to have children; like her father, she always had a soft spot for children, and once she even told Shanta Gandhi, her friend from London days, "I'll have lots and lots of children. What's the point of your marrying if you don't want children?"[††]

When Indira found out that she was pregnant, she moved to Bombay to live with her aunt Krishna Nehru Hutheesing; Anand Bhavan no longer had any women to whom Indira could turn to for comfort and counsel.[‡‡] Krishna was more than delighted to host Indira. Feroze stayed

---

[*] Pandit, *The Scope of Happiness*, pp. 172–73.
[†] Artists, film stars, and celebrities are still highly sought after on the fund-raising circuit in India. Indians seem to always respond mightily to calls for money to alleviate the impact of natural or man-made disasters. They are less responsive in normal times.
[‡] Conversation with the author, Bombay, February 1985.
[§] Mrs. Pandit had taken him there after Ranjit fell ill at their mountain retreat in Khali.
[**] Ranjit Pandit was later transferred from Naini Prison to Bareilly Central Jail, where his health deteriorated. He suffered a mild heart attack while behind bars. He was a prolific writer, translating old Indian epics into English from the original Sanskrit.
[††] Anecdote quoted by Professor Anand Mohan.
[‡‡] Vijaya Lakshmi Pandit had gone off to the United States, where her two daughters, Chandralekha and Nayantara, were enrolled at Wellesley College.

behind in Allahabad but visited Indira frequently. It was in Bombay, on August 20, 1944, that Indira and Feroze Gandhi's first son, Rajiv, was born. Prior to his birth, Indira had maintained a strict regimen of diet and exercise, guided by her aunt and by Dr. V. N. Shirodkar, a famous Bombay-based obstetrician.* Rajiv was an easy delivery. Indira recalled that she had just ordered a piece of toast. "As I was eating, Rajiv came out," she recalled later. "I was so sorry I couldn't finish my toast." She said later that "to bring a new being into this world, to see its tiny perfection and to dream of its future greatness is the most moving of all experiences and fills one with wonder and exaltation."

Indira was thrilled with the "tiny perfection" that was Rajiv Gandhi, and breast-fed him for several months. Jawaharlal Nehru was still in jail and did not get to see his first grandchild until Rajiv was almost a year old. In a letter to his sister Krishna, he displayed a concern with astrology—a surprising concern, given Nehru's well-known aversion to Indian-style spirituality and what he would often decry as astrological mumbo-jumbo. He told Krishna that he had urged Indira to "get a proper horoscope made by a competent person. Such permanent records of the date and time of birth are desirable."

Rajiv's parents returned to Allahabad with the newest member of the Nehru clan. While Indira and Feroze were tending to their first-born—Rajiv was described by everyone who saw him as a plump and happy child—major world events were occurring elsewhere. The Allies were moving swiftly against the Axis Powers. Churchill, Roosevelt, and Stalin had met at Yalta to give shape to a postwar world order. In Britain the Labor Party would soon be voted into office, and Prime Minister Clement Atlee—who was sympathetic to the idea of Indian independence—would order the release of Mahatma Gandhi from prison. Nehru himself was freed not long after that, and he promptly decided to revive *The National Herald*, the newspaper that he had started in Lucknow in late 1937, as a counterweight to *The Pioneer*, a newspaper that unashamedly supported the government. Nehru's paper had suspended publication when he and top Congress leaders were packed off to jail, mainly because there was no one to guide it and because its staff did not wish to submit to the strict censorship that the British were imposing at the time.†

---

*Dr. Shirodkar's hospital still flourishes in Bombay.
†In protest against prior British censorship, editors at the *Herald* often chose to leave columns, even pages, blank. By the time the newspaper closed down in 1942—when Mahatma Gandhi launched his Quit India movement—the publication was being

The father-in-law decided that his son-in-law should help reactivate *The National Herald*, and Feroze dutifully moved his young family to Lucknow. He told some relatives that journalism offered a wonderful opportunity to serve the nation—there was little doubt by now that Britain would give up its prize colony, and that India's independence was simply a matter of time. Some friends of Feroze saw in his acceptance of Nehru's offer a sign that the Nehrus could decide what Feroze ought to do and that he had to comply. Jawaharlal Nehru—who loved to write—could not direct the newspaper himself because he had been named president of the Congress Party and did not have the time.* Although the newspaper was indeed a vehicle for expressing the party line, Nehru did not want to invite personal criticism by running the enterprise himself.

At *The National Herald*, Feroze got along famously with the staff. His easygoing nature acted as an emollient in the uncertain atmosphere prevailing at the newspaper, for no one knew whether the enterprise would survive, let alone succeed. Feroze was considerate to the workers in the press room, and also to his editorial colleagues; they were impressed with his humor and concern for everybody's welfare. "He was a man with the common touch," recalled Chalapathi Rau, a senior editor who was Feroze's right-hand man. "He often worked in the press day and night. He loved machines, he did not mind the ink and the soot. This endeared him to the workers. They carried great influence with him. He could not think of taking disciplinary action against anybody, even in moments of great irritation." Rau and Feroze nursed *The National Herald* through to editorial strength and financial health—to the point where Feroze even planned a Delhi edition.†

Feroze rented a small bungalow in the Huzratganj neighborhood of Lucknow, a city not unlike Allahabad in that it had an Old World, genteel culture.‡ Indira joined him there, although she frequently com-

---

severely harassed by the authorities to the point where its daily editions were more symbolic than anything else.
* Nehru would soon be named as head of the interim government that oversaw the transition to freedom.
† Feroze had ordered European machinery for the Delhi edition but was forced to sell it when the Congress Party could not come up with funds to make final payments.
‡ Both Allahabad and Lucknow had, and continue to have, sizable Muslim populations. The sophisticates of both cities pride themselves on their cuisine and culture. Lucknow was founded by the Nawab of Oudh, and contained stately homes and palaces. Until the British took it over, it was even considered a decadent city where pleasures of the flesh were amply available. Courtesans maintained elegant establishments to which mothers of even aristocratic families sent their daughters to be educated in the art of conversation and social graces—with an ever-present

muted between Lucknow and Delhi, where Jawaharlal stayed in a small house at 17 York Road.* Try as Feroze and Indira would to fashion a reasonably normal family life, there was always something to divert the couple. The momentum toward independence was irreversible, and Indira was caught up in the excitement. She was, however, deeply troubled by the communal problems between India's majority Hindus and minority Muslims. Like her father, Indira was committed to secularism. She believed that the new nation of India would be home for people of all religions and creeds. However, other national leaders such as Jinnah felt otherwise.† Jinnah, head of the militant Muslim League, thought that he had been encouraged by the then viceroy, Lord Wavell, to seek partition of India into two states—India and Pakistan.‡ Such partition was opposed by the Congress Party, and Indira—along with her father and Mahatma Gandhi—felt that there would be enormous bloodshed if India were to be divided. Their fears were to be borne out eventually.

In Delhi, on December 14, 1946, Indira gave birth to her second son, Sanjay.§ Feroze became a particularly indulgent father. He would spend a lot of time with the boys, taking them to the zoo in Lucknow, and to museums. He made toys for them, too. And Feroze taught the boys a bit about gardening. He also taught them how to assemble models of cars, airplanes, trains, and engines. He bought them Meccano sets, and in time both Rajiv and Sanjay became quite proficient at using their hands for mechanical work.** Despite her commuting to Delhi, Indira made it

---

chaperone, of course. Satyajit Ray, the noted Indian director, captured the essence of Lucknow life in a wonderful film entitled *The Chess Players*.
* York Road was one of those streets that went through a name change after Independence. Its new name is Motilal Nehru Marg. "Marg" means road in Hindustani.
† Jinnah was suffering from cancer, which made him all the more determined to realize his dream of an Islamic Pakistan as soon as possible. He became Pakistan's first governor-general in 1947 and died the following year.
‡ Lord Wavell was eventually replaced by Earl Louis Mountbatten, who worked to keep India undivided after independence. But the pressures for partition proved too much, and India was ultimately divided in August 1947.
§ Sanjay, which means "victory" in Sanskrit, was born prematurely. Earlier on the day of his birth, Indira had accompanied Lady Cripps on a strenuous shopping spree in Delhi. Lady Cripps had wanted to buy a Kashmiri shawl and told Indira that only she, with her refined taste, could select the proper one for her.
** Years later, both Rajiv and Sanjay would say that their lifelong fascination with cars, planes, and mechanical things stemmed from the time they spent with their father.

a point to look after her sons personally rather than entrusting them to the care of servants, as upper-class Indians generally tend to do. Perhaps Indira's own lonely childhood, spent in the company of maids and nannies, was on her mind when she decided that her children would not be left in the care of nannies and ayahs.

She wrote in a widely distributed article entitled "On Being a Mother" that "when Rajiv and Sanjay were babies, I did not like the idea of anyone else attending to their needs and tried to do as much for them as I could. Later when they began school, I took care to have my engagements during school hours so as to be free when the boys returned home." She often narrated an anecdote about how a nursery school friend of Sanjay's came to visit with his society mother. When the lady remarked that Indira could not be having much time to spend with her sons, an offended Sanjay came to his mother's rescue with the words "My mother does lots of important work yet she plays with me more than you do with your little boy." Indira frequently went to the boys' school to discuss their progress with teachers, and at one point even volunteered to teach kindergarten classes. But Indira also took the boys with her to Delhi whenever she commuted, which meant that their early education in Lucknow was constantly being disrupted.

James W. Michaels, who reported on India for United Press during this period, offers this recollection of the years just prior to Independence:

> At this time Mahatma Gandhi and his protégé Jawaharlal Nehru were agitating furiously for Indian independence from British colonial rule. Like many Americans at the time I was ambivalent about Indian nationalism. It was bred into Americans that one nation ought not rule another and the arrogant discrimination against brown skins was irritating and stupid to most of us. But there was another side to British imperialism, at least in those twilight days. The unfairness, the irrationality of one nation ruling over another was tempered by the British sense of fair play and respect for law. From a political point of view such rule is no longer acceptable. But say this for it: Respect for individual and human rights in British India was of a far higher order than respect for individual rights is today in many so-called Islamic and Marxist-Leninist states.
>
> Individual rights were not the main issue in India then. Political freedom was. In the middle of World War II, when both the Western powers and the Soviet Union were in mortal battle against an evil

enemy, the Indian National Congress declared that independence came before cooperation in the war against Hitler. Without a firm promise of freedom Indians would not only not support the war effort, they would impede it. And impede it many of them did. But with few exceptions, there was no sympathy for the Axis powers: It was America's—Roosevelt's—call for freedom that Indians in general resonated to, not to Japanese propaganda about Asian solidarity. When the British finally conceded Indian independence, there was, therefore, surprisingly little bitterness in spite of the sometimes brutal history of British rule.*

Meanwhile, Jawaharlal Nehru began to make increasing demands on his daughter's time. Independence came on August 15, 1947, but it turned out to be less joyous for Jawaharlal than he had hoped. That was because Hindus and Muslims were engaging in the greatest communal carnage the Subcontinent had ever known.† Dom Moraes has written vividly about the tragedy of Partition:

> When Mountbatten‡ decided to pull out in August 1947, the country was totally unprepared for the transition, much less for the partition. Jinnah had wanted a huge tract of the Subcontinent, situated mainly in the northwest, to be Pakistan. What was eventually agreed to between the British, the Congress leaders, and Jinnah (who *was*, basically, the Muslim League) was that a certain tract of land from the borders of Kashmir in the northwest to roughly halfway down the western coast, plus the whole of Eastern Bengal (all of these were areas in which Muslims predominated) would be components of the new country. Jinnah described this arrangement as a "moth-

---

*Conversation with the author in New York City, 1985.

†Scholars are still in disagreement over how many casualties there were during the Partition. There could have been as many as a million Sikhs, Hindus, and Muslims killed between 1946 and 1948 when India and Pakistan were being formally divided. Professor Stanley Wolpert says that 10 million refugees crossed lines that were hastily drawn by the British on maps through the Punjab and Bengal, "which overnight became 'international borders,' leaving all Hindus and Sikhs on one side vulnerable to Muslim attack, and all Muslims on the other just as vulnerable to Sikh and Hindu attack."

‡Mountbatten's wife, Lady Edwina, reportedly had a long affair with Jawaharlal. Mountbatten was said to be aware of this relationship and, according to some Indian scholars, even privately condoned it. Although Mountbatten had fathered two daughters with Edwina, he was rumored to be a homosexual. In the British navy, some of his contemporaries caricatured him as "Mount Bottom."

eaten and truncated Pakistan." This may have been true: what was even more true was that there were large numbers of Hindus and some Sikhs left in these areas, and large numbers of Muslims left in areas of what was to be India. With the Muslim League shrieking on one side, and [extremist Hindus] on the other, it was unsurprising that riots broke out all over the land. Enormous numbers of non-Muslims flocked into India from Pakistan: the trains on which they traveled were stopped, the men castrated and killed, the women raped, and their breasts cut off and their genitals gouged out, left to die, the children bayoneted. Hindus and Muslims alike in places such as Calcutta shared the same fate, butchered in the slums, their deaths made a humiliation as well as a finality. *

Mahatma Gandhi asked Indira to tour the riot-ravaged neighborhoods of Delhi; Indira persuaded a group of doctors to accompany her. † "I trust you to see this work through," the Mahatma said to Indira. "I have asked several others and they have replied 'Yes, Bapu,'‡ but I know they are still hesitating." Indira concentrated her efforts on beleaguered Muslim neighborhoods, where residents were too frightened to seek medical assistance for fear that if they ventured out, they would be set upon by Hindus and Sikhs thirsting for revenge. § Cholera had broken out in some of these impoverished neighborhoods, and Indira took many risks moving about in those troubled times. Later she would tell friends how frustrated she felt when she saw Hindus unwilling to help Muslims. "I was determined that we were going to create a new nation where one's ethnic background and religion did not matter," she said to one family friend, L. K. Jha. * *

James Michaels has recorded India's birth especially poignantly:

> The two nations were born, India and Pakistan, amidst terrible bloodshed—bloodshed directed not toward the departing colonialists but

---

* Moraes, *Mrs. Gandhi*, p. 88.
† The Mahatma had opposed Partition. In fact, he was so dismayed that he refused to participate in the Independence celebrations.
‡ "Bapu" was an honorific that Indians used when addressing Mahatma Gandhi. The word means "big father."
§ Before Independence, one of the most prosperous provinces of India had been the Punjab. It contained Hindus, Muslims, and Sikhs. The British divided the Punjab almost neatly into two parts; that is why Hindus on the Pakistani side fled to India, and many Muslims on the Indian side of the Punjab opted to go to what was now Pakistan.
* * Anecdote provided by L. K. Jha in a meeting with the author in New York, 1984.

inwardly, Indian slaughtering Indian. For the Indian revolution took a strange turn. Not only did the colonial power leave of his own will, he actually sent one of his most influential and charming personalities, Lord Louis Mountbatten, to make sure that independence did not get delayed by bickering among the endless shades and gradations of Indian nationalism. Had the British suddenly seen the error of their old ways? It wasn't just that. They had lost the will to empire and had a war-battered economy to rebuild—and did not want to get caught in the middle as the various factions struggled for the prize of power that was now sure to fall. The British may not have left willingly but they left gracefully. In scenes unparalleled elsewhere at a time when colonialism was unraveling throughout the world, the last viceroy, Lord Louis, drew cheers from the Indian crowds almost rivalling those for Jawaharlal Nehru. The British left India, not with the lion's tail between his legs, but proudly and with general good feeling. Unfortunately, independence did not come peacefully. Deflected from resentment of the former oppressors, revolutionary ardor turned inward; Muslims and Hindus did some settling of ancient scores. Millions were uprooted from ancestral homes and literally hundreds of thousands died in cruel, senseless mutual slaughter. Pakistan, which was first conceived as little more than a bargaining chip in a grab for power by the brilliant and enigmatic Mohammed Ali Jinnah, was torn from India to hasten the independence timetable; it was as if the mothers in the King Solomon tale had agreed to settle their differences by putting the baby to the knife. Jinnah, the father of Pakistan, was not even a good Muslim; he smoked, drank, ate pork, and emulated the English gentleman. Never mind that he didn't really represent Muslim India . . . ; he understood power, understood that he could capitalize on Britain's desire to get out and on the nationalist mainstream's desire for democracy. Pakistan made no sense geographically, historically, or economically but there it was and there it is.[*]

Independence was a time of great emotion for most Indians, but especially for Indira. Her entire life had been played out to the soundtrack of the freedom struggle. "I was so excited and proud, I really thought I would burst," she told Professor Anand Mohan. "The absolutely overshadowing idea, of course, at that time was freedom for India and to do

[*] James W. Michaels, "From Mahatma Gandhi to Rajiv Gandhi," foreword to *Vengeance*, by Pranay Gupte, pp. 15–16.

whatever was necessary for it. And since at that time one somehow didn't believe it would come in one's lifetime, it meant it would be a lifetime of hardship. And you may have heard that my own . . . heroine . . . at that time was Joan of Arc. She died at the stake. This was the significant thing that I envisaged—an end like that for myself."[*]

Mahatma Gandhi was particularly pleased with Indira's work in trying to bring about communal harmony.[†] "Now I know your education and your years abroad have not been wasted!" he told her. The Mahatma had become a visibly broken man because of the communal riots. In a last-ditch effort to restore peace among Hindus and Muslims, he read out from the Koran, the *Bhagavad Gita,* and the Bible every evening at prayer meetings. On January 29, 1948, Indira took little Rajiv to meet the great man. He was staying at Birla House, not far from where he was scheduled to hold a huge prayer meeting the next day.[‡] Indira was accompanied by her aunt Krishna Hutheesing and by Vijaya Lakshmi Pandit's daughter Chandralekha.

"Hello! Have all these three princesses come to see *me?*" the Mahatma said to the group, teasingly. He was wearing a tiny Bengali straw hat for protection against the winter sun. When Indira made a complimentary remark about the hat, the Mahatma said, laughing, "An elegant Burmese hat is on its way. Shall I not look very handsome in that hat?" The Mahatma gave Rajiv an orange, then played with him.

Little Rajiv had brought some flowers for the Mahatma. He placed them at Gandhi's feet. Indira immediately chided her son. "We only place flowers at the feet of those who are dead," she said.[§] Her words carried a terrible prescience, as did what the Mahatma said to Rajiv: "It's good you came to see me today, because the next time you see me, it will be in a crowd." The next day, January 30, Mahatma Gandhi was

---

[*]Mohan, *Indira Gandhi.*

[†]The brutality that marked the Partition stemmed at least partly from the hard feelings Muslims and Hindus bore toward one another. Hindus carried long racial memories of the violent conquest of India by Muslims, and their brutality. The Partition, therefore, was a time of settling scores—even scores from a distant past.

[‡]The house was owned by G. D. Birla, a leading Indian industrialist who contributed vast sums to the Congress Party. After Independence, the Birlas became even more powerful—not least because of their close contact with Nehru and the Congress hierarchy. Choice commercial and industrial contracts frequently came their way—and continue to do so.

[§]Hindus traditionally garland people with flowers as a sign of welcome or respect. But flowers are only placed at the feet of deities in temples, or near the feet of corpses prior to cremation. Indeed, it is considered inauspicious to put flowers near the feet of the living.

dead, killed by a Hindu fanatic named Nathuram Godse who had publicly called the Mahatma "India's worst enemy."* Godse fired a revolver at the Mahatma as he was headed toward a prayer meeting. The "crowd" that Gandhi spoke of was to be the huge funeral procession in Delhi on January 31, 1948.†

"Little did we guess that we would never see his wide toothless smile again, nor feel the glow of his protection," Indira said later. The day of the assassination, Prime Minister Jawaharlal Nehru made an eloquent radio broadcast to the nation. "The light has gone out of our lives and there is darkness everywhere," he said. "The light has gone out, I said, and yet I was wrong. For the light that shone in this country was no ordinary light. The light that has illumined this country for these many years will illumine this country for many more years—and a thousand years later, that light will still be seen in this country and the world will see it and it will give solace to innumerable hearts."‡

Mahatma Gandhi still lives on in the minds and hearts of Indians. But his ideas are hardly followed by India's political leaders today. Of course, the Mahatma remains a political and spiritual icon in India, and his picture is obligatory on the walls of political organizations. Occasionally, politicians on the campaign trail even dust off quotations from Gandhi's writings. But he is a distant political memory nevertheless. Some years after the assassination, Dom Moraes interviewed Jawaharlal Nehru in New Delhi, and Nehru said: "I do not think any of the Mahatma's ideas are applicable today."§ At least, Nehru had the honesty to admit this.

Indira Priyadarshini Nehru Gandhi was now Jawaharlal Nehru's official hostess at the prime minister's residence at Three Teen Murti Marg. It was a role that she would play for the next seventeen years until Nehru's death of a heart attack in 1964—a role that came to be increasingly

* Godse, a right-wing Hindu and a social misfit, went to the gallows with two of his accomplices. His hatred of Mahatma Gandhi was shared by many Hindu extremists. They called the Mahatma "Mohammed Gandhi," often accusing him of being a "Muslim lover." Unfortunately, hatred of Muslims persists among some extremist sectors of the Hindu community to this day. There are many Hindus who argue that India should be formally declared a Hindu state since 82 percent of the population is Hindu. For a detailed study of the conspiracy behind Mahatma Gandhi's assassination, see *The Men Who Killed Gandhi*, by Manohar Malgaonkar (Delhi: Macmillan, 1978).
† The funeral has been marvelously depicted in the award-winning film *Gandhi*.
‡ Broadcast to the nation by Jawaharlal Nehru on All-India Radio, January 30, 1948.
§ Quoted by Dom Moraes in *Mrs. Gandhi*.

resented by her husband and one that contributed heavily to the destruction of her marriage. Jawaharlal had been a widower since 1936. His sisters had helped keep house for him but now they, too, had gone away to their own homes.* Indira was very worried about his health: The strain of India's freedom struggle had caught up with Nehru and he was visibly exhausted. Yet new and formidable challenges lay ahead—the task of building a new nation, the task of alleviating widespread poverty, the task of infusing Indians with a renewed spirit of nationalism. Now more than ever he needed someone to look after him. "It was sad to see him so lonesome," Indira once said to Professor Ralph Buultjens. "I felt that it was my duty to help him. It was also so important for the country that someone look after him. And there was no one else but me."[†]

She had to commute constantly between Lucknow, where her husband and sons lived, and New Delhi, where her father resided. Indira described herself as "a traveling salesman." Soon she started staying in Delhi for longer periods, with a few weekends spent in Lucknow with her husband. Naturally, the children had to be moved to Delhi as well. Thus the relationship between Indira and Feroze became strained. Deprived of the company of his wife and children, Feroze became extremely intolerant of Indira and his father-in-law. This led to a break between them that never really healed. Indira's priority remained being with her father; Feroze, with a career and personality of his own, could not be absorbed into it. He was not the least bit surprised by this, nor did he try to stop her. The doubts he had expressed in London at the time of their marriage—that is, whether Indira would become a Gandhi or whether he, Feroze Gandhi, would he expected to become a Nehru—were now being sadly revived.

The Pakistani writer Tariq Ali, who interviewed Indira Gandhi on several occasions for various British publications, says that Indira did not put her father ahead of her husband.[‡] It was just a question of deciding who was the more crucial political figure. The thought of her father alone, dependent on servants, without any family life, seemed unbearable to her. After moving to Delhi, Indira regularly took the children to Lucknow to see their father. But she began to feel that it would be easier if Feroze would come to Delhi to meet them. Feroze did indeed start doing so, but his trips began to become irregular as his relationship with

* Vijaya Lakshmi Pandit represented India at the United Nations. Krishna Hutheesing lived in Bombay.
[†] From notes maintained by Professor Ralph Buultjens.
[‡] Tariq Ali, *An Indian Dynasty* (New York: G. P. Putnam's Sons, 1985).

his wife and father-in-law deteriorated. The Gandhi marriage had started unraveling.

"At first, it was only a question of setting up a home for my father in New Delhi and coping with the social obligations of the prime minister's house," Indira recalled years later. "But gradually circumstances and my own intense interest in the path which the country was trying to follow drew me deeper into public affairs." One of her first acts after moving in with Jawaharlal was to redecorate her father's sixteen-room house, which belonged to the British commander-in-chief during the Raj. "I came over to look at it and was at once plunged in gloom," Indira recalled. The house was filled with huge oil portraits of stern and bemedaled British generals. "I felt they were watching my every movement, criticizing every unspoken thought," Indira said. "I could not be at ease until they were all taken down and hurriedly dispatched to the defense ministry." That is exactly what was done. Many of those portraits still remain in a New Delhi warehouse.

Feroze always felt like an outsider at the prime minister's official residence, where Indira, Rajiv, and Sanjay now lived. Even though Jawaharlal was always correct with Feroze, there was unspoken tension between them. Feroze would never relax in the older man's company. He found the atmosphere stifling, and his visits became more infrequent. On one occasion, Feroze's normal quarters in Nehru's house were being occupied by guests, and he was asked to spend the night in a tent in the compound.

Jawaharlal's domestic style was based on the English life-style which he had imbibed during his student days in Britain.* He had exquisite manners. Ever the patrician, Jawaharlal did not believe in talking much at the table. Feroze, in contrast, was loud and boisterous. He would heartily enjoy his meals, sometimes burping and belching—much to the embarrassment of his father-in-law—and frequently spinning out off-color jokes and ribald tales of the peccadilloes of Indian politicians. Nehru often ignored Feroze at his home, and sometimes even in public. Feroze, for his part, could not shoot back publicly at his legendary father-in-law, and so he often vented his spleen in private—at Indira, who was put in the awkward position of having to defend her father against her husband's wrath. Sometimes the two men would not speak to each other even when they were in the same room, and used Indira as the interlocutor. Indira seemed caught in the cross fire. Her close friend Pupul Jayakar

---

* Indira Gandhi once said that after a visit to Buckingham Palace, Nehru decided that henceforth the staff at Teen Murti Bhavan would pour milk and serve the sugar before the coffee. Apparently that was the custom of the British royal family.

told Dom Moraes that when she and her husband moved to New Delhi from their Bombay home in 1948, they would often invite Indira and Feroze for dinner. "Feroze seldom came," Mrs. Jayakar said. "When he did, he used to take me out on to the balcony and launch into a tirade about his family life."[*]

This was probably the moment when Indira Gandhi's marriage to Feroze reached an irreconcilable point. In the next decade, although various temporary truces and patch-ups were arranged, it was increasingly clear that the two had drifted so far apart that they would never live together again as husband and wife. Feroze himself was reported to have a growing number of liaisons with attractive and available women in the political circles of Delhi.[†] These rumors evidently upset Indira from time to time. She remained basically very fond of Feroze, who visited her and the children frequently at the palatial prime minister's residence. But his informal style and freewheeling political activities built unbreachable barriers between himself and Indira. Indira, more and more her father's political confidante, was taking the road that would eventually lead to national leadership. Feroze, without any serious focus in his life, was drifting into a kind of wayward existence of which Indira disapproved.

---

[*] Moraes, *Mrs. Gandhi*, p. 96.

[†] One of those reportedly linked with Feroze Gandhi was an attractive Congress leader named Tarkeshwari Sinha. There is a story told of how Indira dropped in to see Feroze one day at his bungalow and found a sari that he had bought. It was not the sort of sari that she wore, and so Indira immediately suspected that her husband had purchased it for someone else. She tore up the sari in a rage.

III

The Middle Years

10

The Apprenticeship

While Feroze Gandhi was growing more and more unhappy about the disintegration of his family life, his wife had already begun to subtly chart out a political career for herself. The conventional view of most Congress Party leaders in those days was that Indira was merely being a good daughter in the highest traditions of Hindu culture—looking after her widowed father in his time of need. No one could have suspected that Indira not only relished being in the inner circle of power, but had started yearning for power herself. In 1946 Govind Vallabh Pant, a senior Congress leader, had suggested to Indira that she run for Parliament. Pant felt that Indira had the ability to organize the masses and that, despite her seeming shyness, she knew how to communicate with political audiences. Pant and Jawaharlal Nehru were to become very close, especially in the mid 1950s. In the late 1940s, Pant was chief minister of Uttar Pradesh, India's most populous state and politically its most powerful. * Throughout his life, Jawaharlal seemed to need a mentor, or at least someone to turn to for political counsel. First it was his father, Motilal; then it was Mahatma Gandhi, followed by Vallabhbhai Patel, Rafi Ahmad Kidwai, Maulana Abul Kalam Azad, and finally, Pant. When Pant died in 1961, Nehru pretty much lost the last of the freedom-

* Uttar Pradesh has given India seven prime ministers: Jawaharlal Nehru, Lal Bahadur Shastri, Indira Gandhi, Charan Singh, Rajiv Gandhi, Vishwanath Pratap Singh, and Chandra Shekhar. Morarji R. Desai hailed from Gujarat State. P. V. Narasimha Rao, who became prime minister in June 1991, is from Andhra Pradesh.

struggle contemporaries whom he intimately trusted. From 1961 until his death in 1964, Nehru relied for political advice mostly on Indira Gandhi.

Pant's invitation was tempting, but Indira declined on the grounds that her father and family needed her far more than India's legislature. Still, Indira was certainly impressed by the glamour of being the prime minister's daughter. Publicly, at least, Indira maintained disinterest in pursuing a political career. She told Khwaja Ahmad Abbas, a well-known Indian writer: "I would have liked to be a writer. I would have liked to do research in history, or perhaps in anthropology, for that interests me even more than history. . . . If I wanted to have an easy life, I could have become an interior decorator—I am really interested in the subject. I could even have become a dancer, for I learned Manipuri [a classical Indian dance] in Shantiniketan."

The political apprenticeship of Indira Gandhi, in fact, began well before she assumed the role of her father's official hostess. Indira had been receiving political education by osmosis since birth in Allahabad. It did not matter, therefore, that she had not obtained academic qualifications, or impressive degrees attesting to her formal knowledge of politics. Even though she did not graduate from any university, Indira Gandhi was to collect an impressive number of honorary doctorates from educational institutions all around the world. According to her aides, she was awarded more than fifty such honors. Neither of her two sons, Rajiv and Sanjay, received bachelor's degrees either. * She would say often during her years as prime minister: "One's education is not judged by what one knows but what one becomes."† Politics was bred into her, and Indira's political education was dramatically accelerated when Jawaharlal moved into Teen Murti Bhavan and invited his daughter to be at his side during most of his meetings and nearly all of his travels during his long tenure as prime minister. Indeed, so conspicuous was her presence during Nehru's public appearances that there were wags who called Indira "Miss Prime Minister."‡ Others were not even so charitable.

When not with Jawaharlal at public meetings, Indira engaged in exten-

---

* Rajiv Gandhi studied at Imperial College in London; Sanjay learned automobile engineering at the Rolls-Royce factory in Crewe, England.
† Conversation with Professor Ralph Buultjens in New York City, 1983.
‡ Among these critics were some of Jawaharlal Nehru's colleagues from the independence struggle, men mostly, whose perception of Indira was that of a haughty and distant woman, someone not given to listening to another point of view. Other critics opined that Jawaharlal was being selfish in denying Indira and Feroze a proper family life of their own.

sive social work. Such work offered a timely opportunity to be visible, and to gather political IOUs that Indira would cash in much later in life. The country had been torn by religious frenzy during the Partition.* Although the ensuing riots and refugee movements were abating, there was still a great deal of tension between Hindus and Muslims all over the country. Thousands of Hindus who had fled from what was declared Pakistan were still encamped in refugee camps in Delhi and across northern India. Indira would go to the refugee camps and organize medical care, educational facilities, and employment. Years later, Raj Dhawan, a young accountant who had escaped from Lahore with his family, recalled Indira's presence at the refugee camp. "There was this slim young woman, who appeared a little bewildered by our stories," he said. "But she had the ability to listen carefully to us. Unlike other officials who came to those camps, Mrs. Gandhi took action—whether it was making sure we got enough food, or clothes for the children, or blankets."†

Indira's compassion for refugees seemed greater than her concern for her husband, who continued to live in Lucknow. Even though Indira suggested at one point that Feroze move in with her at Teen Murti Bhavan, he detested the very thought. People had already started addressing him as "the nation's son-in-law," and Feroze did not want his identity subsumed by the Nehrus. Had she truly desired it, Indira could have moved in with her husband and still acted as her father's official hostess, but she continued to stay with her father. It was a decision that had an adverse effect on the children as well. Years later, Sanjay Gandhi confided to friends that he sorely missed his father. Sanjay's older brother, Rajiv, shared this feeling. Jawaharlal and Indira set up a zoo at Teen Murti Bhavan for the boys, and the menagerie became so impressive—with dogs, red Himalayan pandas, parrots, and tiger cubs—that visiting statesmen often insisted on spending time with the animals. To facilitate the boys' education, Indira summoned Anna Ornsholt, a Danish governess, who had taught Vijaya Lakshmi Pandit's daughters. Miss Ornsholt had returned to Denmark after the Pandit girls had gone to college in the United States, but now she eagerly came back to India at Indira's invitation.

Since Feroze and Indira continued to live separately, rumors spread about the rift in their marriage. Some years after Feroze Gandhi's death—they never divorced—Indira Gandhi told Betty Friedan:

---

* Pakistan was "born" on August 14, 1947, a day before India's independence day.
† Mr. Dhawan established a flourishing business in Delhi. Of course, he also never hesitated to contribute to the Congress Party when asked.

I hear these stories that my marriage collapsed and I left my husband or that we were separated and it's not true. It wasn't an ideally happy marriage; we were very happy at times. It was partly because both of us were so headstrong and partly circumstances. I wouldn't have gone into public life if he had said no. But I am so intense in whatever I do that he must have been frightened to have it all concentrated on him. He wanted me occupied. He was very occupied with his own career. But when I went into public life he liked it, yet didn't like it. Other people—friends and relatives—were the worst. They would say "How does it feel being so and so's husband?" He would get upset and it would take me weeks to win him over. To hurt the male ego is the biggest sin in marriage. . . . Towards the end we were somehow getting over all this and becoming very close. *

Feroze Gandhi's newspaper, meanwhile, was flourishing in Lucknow. He was becoming increasingly fascinated with power politics as it evolved in independent India. Feroze felt that he had exhausted his prospects at *The National Herald.* Despite its name, the newspaper was really a provincial publication and little more than a mouthpiece for the Congress Party. Now he decided that he would run as a candidate for the Lok Sabha from the Rae Bareilly constituency near Lucknow in the 1952 elections.[†] Indira went to campaign for him; Jawaharlal went, too, but he in no uncertain terms showed his disapproval of Feroze for having dragged his wife out to the largely underdeveloped countryside. Feroze was very angry at Jawaharlal for raising this issue at all. But, as usual, he did not complain.

Feroze need not have bothered to invite his wife and father-in-law to campaign for him, because from the very start of his campaign it was apparent that the million-plus constituents of Rae Bareilly would chose him as their representative in Parliament. Feroze was elected by a very large majority. His popularity in Rae Bareilly increased with the years. He was reelected to a second term in 1957. He would visit his constituency frequently, speaking to local citizens in their native dialects. He often condemned fellow members of Parliament for their failure to "leave their air-conditioned comfort in Delhi." In those days, travel in Rae Bareilly was particularly difficult because there were few paved roads, and almost

---

* Friedan, "How Mrs. Gandhi Shattered the Feminine Mystique."
[†] This was the constituency from which Indira Gandhi herself ran so successfully much later. In the 1952 general elections, more than 173 million Indians were eligible to vote for nearly 4,000 parliamentary and state legislative representatives.

no public transportation. Feroze, in his open Jeep, became a familiar sight in the area's hundreds of hamlets and villages. He resigned from his post as managing director of *The National Herald* and moved to Delhi, where he was given a government house.*

Feroze was a man who enjoyed being surrounded by beautiful objects of art. His one-bedroom house on Queen Victoria Road contained exquisite lacquer work. He had designed his own furniture in Lucknow, and brought it along to Delhi. He also had a passion for roses and gladioli. In particular, Feroze's roses drew visitors galore to his garden. Not all visitors came to applaud his green thumb, however. Feroze quickly became the leader of a small group of legislators who were alarmed at the influence of big business in national life.[†] Perhaps it was his journalistic experience that had made Feroze a very meticulous man when it came to digging for information. He exposed the misdeeds of a business organization—the Bharat Insurance Company—which was headed by the enormously wealthy Dalmia family, particularly the gross misuse of insurance funds at the family's disposal.[‡] At first, Jawaharlal Nehru's cabinet ridiculed Feroze's efforts.[§] But as the evidence mounted, the government was forced to nationalize all insurance companies. Top executives of the Dalmia group were prosecuted and imprisoned, as was Ramakrishna Dalmia, the head of the Dalmia group. In 1958 Feroze excavated information that led to the indictment of the huge state-owned Life Insurance Corporation of India. Feroze's reputation as a parliamentarian and investigator rose when Nehru's trusted finance minister, T. T. Krishnamachari, resigned in the wake of his disclosures. Other top officials lost their

---

* All members of Parliament, as well as top civil servants, are given free housing in New Delhi. They are also given generous allowance for food, staff expenses, and travel. And there is a nice pension at the end of it all. When Feroze first moved from Lucknow to Delhi, he lived briefly with Indira at Teen Murti Bhavan. But the arrangement proved difficult for Feroze, and he shifted to his parliamentarian's bungalow.

† It is still highly unusual for parliamentarians to expose corruption in India. That may be because most legislators are deeply beholden to big business, or to other financial interests, whose money funded their election campaigns. Parliamentarians are also not beyond accepting bribes to change their vote or to facilitate the desires of their supporters.

‡ The Dalmia family saw this matter only as a temporary setback. The group continues to do well in India, and is favorably viewed by the Congress Party and even the Opposition.

§ Besides muckraking, Feroze Gandhi also authored several pieces of social legislation. Perhaps because of his journalistic background, he was especially concerned with the question of free speech. He successfully promoted a bill that gave the press immunity against being cited for contempt of Parliament.

jobs as well. Jawaharlal had considered Krishnamachari a personal friend, and did not bother to hide his irritation over Feroze's investigations.* The episode certainly did not bring Feroze any closer to Jawaharlal; even Indira felt that her husband was being excessively zealous in uncovering corruption.† A parliamentary colleague said that Feroze was a "gentle breeze that quickly developed into a storm."‡

Indira Gandhi always denied rumors that her marriage to Feroze was unhappy, even though Feroze confided the truth to his friends. She probably wanted to live with her delusion, and any suggestion of there being problems was totally ignored, at least publicly. But it was apparent to everybody in Delhi that relations between husband and wife were worsening steadily.§ Guests invited to dinner at the prime minister's house were frequently embarrassed to be in the company of Indira and Feroze. One evening, after an especially frosty dinner, one guest reported that a sour Feroze had eaten his meal without uttering a single word. This sort of tension was evident not only on the home front. When Jawaharlal Nehru openly showed displeasure that some Congress Party officials brought along their families to an official ceremony, Feroze Gandhi said, "I did *not* bring my wife along." Indira, who was sitting next to her father, was clearly uncomfortable. On another occasion, Feroze was unhappy with his seat at an official function because he had been relegated to the press section, not the section reserved for members of Parliament. He asked Tara Ali Baig, then chief of protocol, to change his seat.** But Mrs. Baig told him that only Indira could make the change since it was Indira who had made the arrangements in the first place. Feroze, of course, refused to petition his wife.

To some observers in Delhi at the time, such incidents seemed to

---

*Needless to say, Feroze made a growing number of enemies within the Congress Party and among India's businessmen. One former chief of protocol told Dom Moraes: "Feroze was an oaf. All he wanted to do was flail out, to hit people and hurt them. Nothing he did was in any way constructive."

†Indira Gandhi was never one to pursue corruption too diligently. After all, the big business houses of India—which shamelessly engaged in corrupt practices—were also heavy contributors to Congress Party coffers.

‡Bhatia, *Indira*, p. 113.

§Feroze had also returned to journalism, in a manner of speaking, by joining the *Indian Express*. This large newspaper gave him a national forum for his investigations beyond what Parliament offered.

**Tara Ali Baig was the wife of Rashid Baig, a diplomat. She later enjoyed a distinguished career as a writer and social worker. Mrs. Baig died in 1990.

underscore Feroze's male-ego problems—the husband not being able to adjust to his wife being a famous and important person. Although Indira herself did not believe in acknowledging the fact that she was having severe marital problems, she confided to her friend Dorothy Norman, an American author more than ten years her senior, that all was not well with her marriage. Indira and Dorothy Norman corresponded regularly from 1950 until Indira's death in 1984. The letters contained self-analyzing truths which Indira did not believe in revealing to anybody else while she was alive. The letters were only published a year after Indira's death, and until then their very existence was known only to Dorothy Norman. In 1954 Indira wrote to Miss Norman that she was in the middle of a domestic crisis and that she was deeply unhappy. "Now the hurt and unpleasantness does not matter that much," she said. "I am sorry, though, to have missed the most wonderful thing in life—having a complete and perfect relationship with another human being." In another letter, written after Dorothy Norman had sent Indira some recordings of Beethoven, she wrote: "The Nehrus were very unmusical people. It was Feroze who introduced us to the joys of Western classical music."

Feroze had begun to drink and smoke heavily. He put on a lot of weight, which smothered his good looks, and his health markedly deteriorated. He suffered his first heart attack in September 1958, and never quite overcame his coronary problems after that. Inder Malhotra, the eminent Indian journalist and editor, was with Feroze when he suffered the attack. They were in New Delhi and had gone out to dinner, and during the meal Feroze was stricken. Malhotra writes: "I remember that sad evening very well. It was warm and sticky. But Feroze insisted on being driven ten miles to dine at a café, started as a cooperative by waiters and other workers retrenched by the Indian Coffee Board after the closure of its coffee houses. . . . Feroze was in high spirits and seemed to be enjoying his food when the iron crab struck him."[*]

Indira was on her way to neighboring Bhutan with her father when Feroze was stricken.[†] A wireless message was sent to her but it took several days for the communication to reach Indira. By the time Indira returned to Delhi, Feroze was out of intensive care. She looked after him for several weeks, after which she herself had to undergo surgery to

---

[*] Malhotra, *Indira Gandhi*, p. 69.
[†] Bhutan was so inaccessible in those days that Indira and Nehru had to ride on horseback through Tibet's Chumbi Valley to get to the tiny Himalayan kingdom. Today, Bhutan is still quite primitive, although it is possible to fly to its capital, Thimpu.

remove a kidney stone. Feroze nursed her with great affection, perhaps hoping that they might be able to salvage what was left of their marriage. After Indira recovered from her surgery, the couple even went to Kashmir on a holiday with Rajiv and Sanjay. But the breach between Feroze and Indira seemed to widen. Nayantara Sahgal says: "It was an impossible situation, and no marriage in the world could have withstood its strain." To fight what he perceived as his utter isolation from his family, Feroze took to working excessively hard. His reputation as a muckraker grew, but at great personal cost. In early 1959, Feroze told Inder Malhotra: "Look here, before you hear a doctored version of it, let me tell you that I have stopped going to the Prime Minister's House completely."[*]

Feroze suffered a second heart attack on September 7, 1960, while he was attending a session of Parliament.[†] He refused to let anyone drive him to Willingdon Nursing Home, insisting instead on taking the wheel of his tiny Fiat.[‡] Indira was in Kerala at the time. Feroze kept asking doctors and nurses when Indira would come to his bedside. By the time she arrived at the hospital, Feroze was practically gone, and died before fully recovering consciousness early on the morning of September 8—four days short of his forty-eighth birthday. There are conflicting versions of whether Indira and Feroze actually got to exchange words when she got to the hospital. One version, authored by Inder Malhotra, has her sitting by Feroze's bedside, holding his hand tightly until he died the following morning. Another account, attributed to Krishan Bhatia, has her arriving at the hospital after Feroze died.

Indira seemed totally shattered, although there were those who wondered how she was able to summon such monumental sorrow in view of her estrangement from Feroze. She had neglected her husband, and taken their relationship for granted—always assuming that of the two men in her life, her father needed her more. She had hoped that later in life she would be able to mend her deteriorating relationship with Feroze—a naïve hope at best, and certainly not one in tune with reality. She was to recall the day of Feroze's death with acute pain: "I was actually physically ill. It upset my whole being for years, which is strange, because after all he was very ill and I should have expected that he would die. However, it was not just a mental shock, but it was as though somebody had cut me in two."[§]

[*] Malhotra, *Indira Gandhi*, p. 70.
[†] A few days before being stricken in Parliament, Feroze had experienced severe chest pains. His physician, Dr. H. L. Khosla, advised him to take a complete rest.
[‡] Dr. Khosla said later that he had ordered Feroze to stay put at Parliament House. He told Feroze that he would collect him there.
[§] Conversation with Professor Ralph Buultjens.

Thousands of people turned out for Feroze's funeral. "I didn't know Feroze had built up such a great following for himself," Jawaharlal said, as the funeral procession moved from Teen Murti Bhavan to Nigambodh Ghat. That remark revealed how increasingly out of touch Nehru was with ordinary people in his declining days—or, perhaps, he had simply convinced himself that his daughter's husband had not truly constructed a creditable career for himself away from the looming banyan tree that was Jawaharlal Nehru. It was little Rajiv who lit the funeral pyre of Feroze Gandhi, as Brahman priests chanted Vedic hymns. Twenty-four years later, Rajiv would participate in a similar ceremony for his mother.*

Years later Indira herself was to say this about her marriage to Feroze: "I did not have less love. I think my husband gave very deeply to me and I to him. I think giving is what makes for happiness. . . . I do not think he would have been the person he was if he had been married to the sweet little woman in an Indian movie. He would have been just an ordinary husband. I think this conflict helped him to grow also. Conflict and unhappiness are not the worst things that can happen. It is all the experience one has that makes one what one is—the wider the experience, the stronger one's personality."†

Indira Gandhi played a major role at the prime minister's house. Teen Murti Bhavan was a huge sprawling estate, much larger than Anand Bhavan in Allahabad where Indira grew up. She had to supervise every aspect of housekeeping; servants' wages, feeding and caring of animals in the private zoo, guest lists for dinners, and menus. She had to keep track of various culinary taboos of Indians—Hindus not eating beef, Muslims not eating pork, meat-eaters who were vegetarians on certain days of the week, and vegetarians who would not eat at all if meat or fish were served at the same table.‡ Her father would pick up new recipes from various countries and insist that these be prepared in his kitchen. Indira would ensure that Jawaharlal's wishes were carried out without too much moan-

---

*Feroze Gandhi was cremated in Hindu style even though he was a Parsi. Indira consigned some of Feroze's ashes to the confluence of three holy rivers near Allahabad. Some of the ashes were buried, according to Parsi rites, at the Allahabad Parsi cemetery, and the rest in Feroze's ancestral cemetery in Surat, a town in western India.

†Conversation quoted by Krishan Bhatia.

‡On one occasion, Indira had ordered a special meal for a Buddhist guest who was supposed to have been a strict vegetarian. An hour before he turned up, however, his aide sent word that the guest was looking forward to a "nice Kashmiri-style nonvegetarian dinner."

ing and groaning by the chefs. Jawaharlal's concerns about his role as India's prime minister clearly went beyond matters of state; they extended into his household. He had always believed in living elegantly, and his aristocratic upbringing certainly had bred into him certain expectations for the good life. Her job, Indira Gandhi told Professor Anand Mohan, "was like walking on a tightrope to adhere close enough to the formal side of protocol so as not to offend even the most particular of dignitaries and yet manage not to stifle the human element."*

Indira was not only chatelaine to her father, but increasingly began assuming the part of confidante as well, traveling all over the world with him. Wags would start calling her, among other thing, the "First Lady" of India.† In October 1948, Indira accompanied her father to the meeting of the Commonwealth heads of government in London. When Jawaharlal and Indira met Sir Winston Churchill, Churchill expressed some surprise that Nehru seemed to harbor no ill will toward him. Churchill, after all, had long resisted India's claims to independence.

"Is it not strange that we should be talking as friends when we hated each other such a short while ago?" Churchill asked Nehru.

"Sir Winston, we never hated you personally," Indira said.

"But I did, I did!" Churchill said.‡

From London, Jawaharlal and Indira went to Paris, where Nehru addressed a special session of the UN General Assembly on India's foreign policy on November 3, 1948. The speech is considered historic because Nehru enunciated the basic directions of India's foreign policy—in effect articulating what would later be codified as the principles of nonalignment. Nehru urged delegates to "take note of resurgent Asia's aspiration for political freedom, social well-being, human dignity, and the climate of peace," as Professor Anand Mohan puts it.

In October 1949, father and daughter made their first trip to the United States. Jawaharlal had been invited by President Harry Truman. Though Indira did not attend all the official functions that her father was invited to, she did get to go to the theater.§ Nevertheless, Professor

---

* Indira Gandhi once told Professor Anand Mohan that she would personally inspect light bulbs in Teen Murti Bhavan's guest rooms, and also the linen, to ensure that everything was just right for visiting dignitaries.

† Technically, an Indian prime minister's wife or companion cannot be called the country's "First Lady." That designation belongs to the wife of the president, who is the country's constitutional head of state. However, Indians rarely refer to the president's wife as "First Lady."

‡ Churchill was out of office at the time, of course, and Nehru also met with then-prime minister Clement Atlee.

§ Indira Gandhi was very fond of the theater, especially Broadway productions.

Anand Mohan says that their visit was largely disappointing for both Jawaharlal and Indira. Nehru's sensibility was offended by what he perceived as Washington's insistence on political reciprocity—India's request for food aid was held up for several months because of a feeling on Capitol Hill that New Delhi was not quite with the United States in its gathering global battle against Communism. Says Professor Mohan: "Nehru had acquired, as a student in England, much of the conventional British bias against the United States. He was by temperament an aristocrat, and shared with the British aristocracy a certain contempt for the Americans as the *nouveaux riches*. He was by intellectual inclination a Marxist, and shared with the British Left a deep-rooted suspicion of the Mecca of capitalism. He was by birth a Brahman, and had inherited an innate antipathy for the crassness of the world's leading acquisitive society."*

This first trip to the United States, and her father's reaction to Americans, undoubtedly left an imprint on Indira's mind. She never warmed up to official Washington during her political career, even though she was to visit the United States nine times before becoming India's prime minister—a great pity, because India and the United States shared values such as democracy and the free press, and the two countries would have made good political and economic allies.† Indira later told friends that she was overwhelmed by the "abundance and luxury which must be seen to be believed." Jawaharlal left with strongly negative feelings: He felt that American officials had been patronizing to him, and that even the titans of business with whom he lunched seemed to be condescending. However, several American newspapers—*The New York Times* among them—opined that it was Nehru who seemed patronizing when dealing with his American hosts.

Arthur M. Schlesinger, Jr., the historian who was special assistant to President John F. Kennedy, was to recall that during an official visit by Nehru and Indira to the United States in November 1961, the Indian prime minister was generally quite grumpy and unresponsive—despite Kennedy's charm and effusiveness.‡ Schlesinger also says that during a White House dinner that Kennedy hosted for the visitors, "Indira Gandhi assailed the President about American policy, praised Krishna Menon,

---

During her visits to New York and London, she made time to see shows, although sometimes such engagements had to be canceled on account of matters of state.
* Mohan, *Indira Gandhi*, p. 199.
† Indira Gandhi, of course, made many friends in the United States, such as Dorothy Norman. But her warm personal relations with Americans did not translate into lasting political ties.
‡ Arthur M. Schlesinger, Jr., *A Thousand Days* (New York: Greenwich House, 1983).

the professional anti-American of New Delhi, and otherwise elevated the mood of the evening." Kennedy, always the witty and urbane man, remained unperturbed. When it was time to propose a toast, the President said: "We all want to take this opportunity to welcome you to America, Mr. Prime Minister, though I doubt whether any words of mine can embellish the welcome already extended to you by Larry Spivak." Lawrence Spivak was then the gruff host of NBC's "Meet the Press," and only days earlier had subjected Nehru to a "sharp and unceremonious inquisition" on his television program, according to Schlesinger.

In 1953 Indira went again to England for the coronation of Queen Elizabeth II. She thought that all the pomp and pageantry of the coronation was a bit "outlandish," as she told Professor Ralph Buultjens. On the way back to India, Indira made a private trip to the Soviet Union, visiting, among other places, Tashkent. It was Indira's first visit to the Soviet Union, and the first of more than a dozen. In contrast to her American hosts, the Soviets fawned over Indira, which seemed to impress her. Escorted by Indian ambassador K. P. S. Menon and his wife, Indira visited Soviet Georgia, then various health resorts on the Black Sea. In Matsesta she took a dip in the sulphur springs—a dip that she later said cured her dandruff.* So thrilled were the Soviets over her presence that Ambassador Menon later reported that dozens of Russian girls who were born that year were named Indira.

The next year, Indira accompanied her father to China, where the Communist government entertained the Indian delegation lavishly. Nevertheless, Indira felt somewhat uneasy about Sino-Indian relations.† Publicly, however, she joined her father in acknowledging China's "historical claims" over Tibet, where Beijing had crushed a rebellion and caused an exodus of refugees that later included Tibet's spiritual leader, the Dalai Lama. In April 1955, father and daughter went to the Afro-Asian Conference held in Bandung, Indonesia, where Jawaharlal Nehru was one of the central figures. Nehru enunciated the fundamental premises of Indian foreign policy: nonalignment, peaceful coexistence, and the "neutralization" of Asia in the East-West Cold War. He tried to bring China into the community with the hope of ameliorating Chinese radicalism through the mechanism of better international relations. Nehru's critics saw craven cowardice in his attempts to justify China's takeover of Tibet. When

---

* Matsesta's sulphur springs have been renowned for their curative value since the time of the Romans.

† Her reservations about her father's espousal of "*Hindi-Chini bhai-bhai*"—"Indians and Chinese are brothers"—were borne out when China occupied Indian territory in 1962.

Prime Minister Sir John Kotelawala of Ceylon—now Sri Lanka—denounced the "neoimperialism" of Communist powers, Nehru stormed out of the session. The Ceylonese leader was supported by Pakistan's prime minister, Mohammed Ali Bogra, which also irked Nehru. Jawaharlal felt that Pakistan was echoing an effort by Washington to have the Communist bloc condemned at this conference. John Foster Dulles, the U.S. Secretary of State, had already termed Nehru's refusal to support Washington's campaign against Moscow as "immoral." Both Nehru and Indira felt that big powers blatantly manipulated small powers for their own gain in the East-West struggle.

It was Indira who stayed cool and urged her father to control his temper after the Ceylonese prime minister had introduced his resolution. She rushed to Sir John and pleaded: "Please don't upset my father. You know how easily irritated he can get. He will be all right in a little while."

Exposure to these events—and to the leaders who strode the world stage at the time—proved invaluable to Indira. Such education could not have been obtained anywhere other than at her father's side. Because of her father's position, Indira was also able to play host to many foreign dignitaries who were attracted by Nehru's work for Indian independence and his concern for international amity. They came to India by the planeload—Nikita Khrushchev, Marshal Nikolai Bulganin, Gamal Abdul Nasser, Chou-En-lai, Eleanor Roosevelt. Because Jawaharlal enjoyed the company of writers and artists, celebrities such as the poet W. H. Auden were also invited to Teen Murti Bhavan. The writer Dom Moraes, who studied under Auden at Oxford, recounts the story of the poet's visit to Teen Murti Bhavan. Indira had arranged an Indian dance performance, but had failed to provide alcoholic beverages for the guests since liquor was not served at the prime minister's house. Auden left grumpily, and Indira seemed peeved that the poet should chose to walk out in the middle of the dance performance.

Indira got the opportunity to make the personal acquaintance of eminent people from all over the world and to keep up with major global developments. She acquired first-name familiarity with foreign heads of state and government, and received a unique education in the art of diplomacy. On one occasion, Martha Graham, the American danseuse, was giving a performance at the prime minister's home. Indira had arranged the show, along with Lady Edwina Mountbatten, who was a frequent visitor. For some reason, Nehru was rather grumpy that evening. Indira and Lady Edwina had to push Nehru to the dais to make a speech thanking Martha Graham. Indira was to learn that even prime ministers needed to make such gestures in the interest of good public relations. At the same time, according to Professor Ralph Buultjens, Indira embarked on an accelerated program of reading books on history, diplomacy, and political science.

On the face of it, her role during Nehru's talks with world leaders was to see that tea was served correctly. Indira would usually sit by silently while Jawaharlal discussed weighty international issues with his peers. But she, too, started acquiring knowledge and skills about statecraft—and soon became accomplished enough to participate in diplomatic discussions. During Nehru's first official visit to the Soviet Union in June 1955, for example, an important item on his agenda was to ask the Soviets for assistance in developing heavy and basic industry in India. But Nehru seemed unable to bring up the subject. Indira knew that it was her father's pride that came in the way of his asking the Soviets for help; she knew that Jawaharlal did not want to appear a supplicant. Indira quietly let it be known that India needed aid. The Soviets obliged. The Soviet Union was to become a major aid-giver to India, especially in the industrial sector. The Soviets helped set up huge steel plants not long after Nehru's visit. The Soviets also became the leading sellers and suppliers of military equipment to India—more than a billion dollars' worth annually, at one point.

In 1952, the first general election under the new constitution was held in India. Indira campaigned frequently with her father, including stops in Rae Bareilly for her husband, Feroze. She traveled all over the country, and began to notice that she could move crowds with her oratory. Her Hindi became more colloquial; her English became more felicitous. She even managed to speak occasionally in local languages such as Gujarati, Punjabi, and Marathi. Experiences like these gave her confidence a big boost. In her capacity as mistress of the prime minister's house, Indira had to "protect" her father from the persistent demands of Congress factotums or other leaders who wished to meet him. She then began talking to them, listening to their complaints. "Being in the know," Indira was in a position to advise her father. She was even asked to substitute for her father at some Congress Party meetings. Since Nehru's dominating personality terrified most of his colleagues, they frequently approached Indira with petitions for political favors. She would relay these requests to her father, in the process collecting more IOUs that would be useful later when she became a full-fledged political figure in her own right. By the same token, Indira was also able to act as a moderating influence on her father, who had the tendency to be sometimes excessively swayed by counsel from such longtime friends as Krishna Menon. "Perspective and context" were what Indira often offered to her father.

In 1955, Indira was approached by U. N. Dhebar, a savvy Congress strategist who had become party president after Jawaharlal Nehru, and by Lal Bahadur Shastri, whom Indira had known from her Allahabad days. They wanted her to accept a nomination to the Congress Working Committee. The Working Committee was the highest policy-making body of the organization. Indira chose to contest an election for a seat on the Working Committee and was elected by a large margin. Krishan Bhatia notes that Indira could have opted to accept a nonelective nomination to the Congress Working Committee. Dhebar would have gladly put her name in nomination. But Indira chose the rough-and-tumble of elective politics instead. "She had placed her foot on the bottom rung of the ladder of political authority," Bhatia says in his book *Indira Gandhi*. But Indira's initial forays into party politics were low-keyed. At party conventions, for instance, she rarely demanded a seat on the dais—preferring, instead, to sit in the audience. This diffidence may not have stemmed from her modesty as much as from a desire on Indira's part to get a feel for crowds, for what the hoi-polloi of the Congress were saying and thinking. Indira also became active within the Women's Department of the Congress Party. In 1957 she was elected to the party's Central Election Committee, a body that evaluated applications from prospective Congress parliamentary and state legislative candidates. And in 1958 she was elected to the Congress Parliamentary Board which decided on party nomination for Parliament. [*]

Finally, in 1959, she was elected unopposed as president of the Congress Party after Dhebar relinquished the position. Indira's ascension to the presidency was made possible by Dhebar's strong recommendation to party elders, who included Govind Vallabh Pant. The walrus-visage Pant had not been a supporter of Indira initially, but was brought around by Dhebar, who believed that by supporting Indira the party's elders could find renewed favor with Nehru, with whom several had had some disagreements. [†] In the event, Pant agreed to go along with Dhebar's suggestion. Like other party leaders, he assumed that Indira would be pliable. Everybody was to be surprised later when Indira used the party presidency to push through much-needed organizational reforms and other changes that the hierarchy had long resisted. [‡] Rumors were rife then—and

[*] The Congress Parliamentary Board is the equivalent of the Politburo in Communist countries.
[†] Nehru had dropped strong hints that he wanted Indira to become Congress Party president. Khwaja Ahmed Abbas, the author, said later that it was apparent "that this daughter of the Indian revolution was all along being groomed as the heiress-apparent to her father's king-sized position in the country."
[‡] Many years later, the Congress Party bosses known as "the Syndicate" would be

later—of Jawaharlal Nehru's Machiavellian plans to groom his daughter as his successor. Nehru told a prenomination press conference: "Normally speaking, it is not a good idea for my daughter to come in as Congress president when I am prime minister." Yet he did not stop the Congress members from nominating her. Morarji Desai, a veteran of the freedom struggle who had automatically assumed that he would be prime minister after Nehru, insisted that Jawaharlal had pulled strings behind the scene to obtain the coveted Congress presidency for Indira. Morarji Desai was never fond of either Nehru or Indira, and he was correct in assuming that Jawaharlal did not want him to become India's prime minister. He was a man of excessive rectitude who, during his stormy tenure as chief minister of what was then Bombay State, introduced the disastrous policy of prohibition. Desai was later made finance minister in the national government by Nehru. Desai was reported to be close to big business, and there were numerous allegations about the financial dealings of his relatives. Desai's personal life, however, was beyond reproach. He was a teetotaler, did not believe in getting inoculations or vaccinations, and consumed only nuts—and Swiss chocolates. In 1977 Desai led an Opposition party, the Janata, to victory over Indira Gandhi's beleaguered Congress Party. Desai became India's fourth prime minister, but his tenure lasted less than two years because of bickering within the Janata Party. Desai gained some notoriety after a "60 Minutes" interview with CBS's Dan Rather in which he said that he drank his own urine every morning for therapeutic reasons. Desai was named by Seymour Hersh as a CIA agent in a controversial book that the American Pulitzer Prize–winning journalist wrote about Henry A. Kissinger.* Many people believed that Hersh had made an egregious mistake, and Desai even sued Hersh for libel in a Chicago court. Hersh won the case, and Desai appealed.†

For her part, Indira countered that she had been bullied into accepting the post by Govind Vallabh Pant and would have retracted her acceptance but for the fact that the media were already saying that she could not do the job.

"I must consult my father before I decide," Indira said to Pant.

"It has nothing to do with your father," Pant said. "It is for you to decide."

---

similarly surprised when Indira—compliant at first—swung into action against them and caused their downfall. In short, Indira often deliberately allowed people to underestimate her, but in the end got exactly what she wanted.

* Seymour M. Hersh, *The Price of Power: Kissinger in the Nixon White House* (New York: Summit Books, 1983), p. 450.

† The case was still pending in July 1991.

Indira later recalled: "I was terrified. I was really ⟨...⟩ sure that my father did not like the idea of my taking ⟨...⟩ role in party affairs."[*] She later said:

> This was a most important event in my political li⟨...⟩ were asked at that time by political observers: had ⟨...⟩ ately groomed me as his political heir? Or was he ⟨...⟩ Did he compromise my independence of thought ⟨...⟩ ⟨...⟩uld I remain in the public eye without attracting adverse comment? Was I able to stand for myself in Indian politics without compromising my independence as a woman? Finally, would my role have been easier if I had been my father's son rather than his daughter? These questions are not really for me to answer. All I can say is how I tried to fulfill what I considered to be my task.[†]

After Indira had been "elected" unopposed to the job, Jawaharlal paid a rare public tribute to her at a Congress Party meeting: "It is superfluous for me to say that Indira is my daughter and that I have love for her. I am proud of her good nature, proud of her energy and work, and proud of her integrity and truthfulness. What she has inherited from me, I do not know. Maybe she has inherited these qualities from her mother!" Indira herself made an impassioned speech. Then she quoted from a popular Hindi film song:

> We are the women of India
> Don't imagine us as flower-maidens,
> We are the sparks in the fire.[‡]

Though Indira was elected for a two-year term, she gave up the post after one year. She attributed her resignation partly to poor health. Indira also acknowledged privately that she was troubled by the fact that the Congress Party had transformed itself from a dynamic agent of change during the freedom struggle into "an election machine and little else." Nevertheless, Indira's tenure as Congress president was memorable. It was dominated by two major events. One concerned a decision taken by her father in 1957 when the map of the country was redrawn along linguistic lines. From the 1920s until 1945, the Congress Party had called

[*] Conversation with Professor Ralph Buultjens.
[†] Indira Gandhi, *My Truth* (Delhi: Vikas, 1981).
[‡] Translation from Hindustani.

ormation of linguistic provinces.* The provincial branches of
arty had been reorganized in 1921 on a linguistic basis, with units
eated for what are today the states of Andhra Pradesh, Kerala, and
Maharashtra. After Independence the Dar Commission was appointed
to advise the Constituent Assembly—the forerunner of Modern India's
Parliament—on its deliberations on demands for linguistic states. The
commission's report was submitted at the end of 1948, and it warned
with prescience that linguistically homogeneous states would have a
"subnational bias"—that their creation would threaten national unity.
Some Congress leaders were disappointed at the report, and appointed
Jawaharlal Nehru, Vallabhbhai Patel, and Pattabhi Sitaramayya—then
the Congress Party president—"to examine the question in the light of
the decisions taken by the Congress in the past and the requirements of
the existing situation." That group, known as "The JVP Committee"—for Jawaharlal, Vallabhbhai, and Pattabhi—supported the Dar
Commission. Linguistic division of India, the Committee said, "would
unmistakably retard the process of consolidation [and] let loose, while
we are still in a formative stage, forces of disruption and disintegration."†
The Committee acknowledged, however, that a "strong case" could be
made for the formation of Andhra Pradesh from the Telugu-speaking
areas of Madras State. If public sentiment proved "insistent and overwhelming," then other cases could also be considered. "This was the
opening wedge for the bitter struggle over States Reorganization which
was to dominate Indian politics from 1953 to 1956," says Michael
Brecher.‡

Ultimately, Jawaharlal Nehru did agree to the establishment of states
along linguistic lines.§ There were two notable exceptions made, however.** One was in Punjab where the demands of the Sikhs for a Punjabi

---

* The sources for a portion of the background on linguistic controversies in India are
Professor Robert L. Hardgrave, Jr., of the University of Texas at Austin, and
Professor Stanley A. Kochanek of Pennsylvania State University. Their excellent
book, *India: Government and Politics in a Developing Nation* (San Diego: Harcourt
Brace Jovanovich, 1986), is recommended reading for anyone who wants to under-
stand the evolving Indian state.

† Quoted by Joan V. Bondurant in *Regionalism Versus Provincialism: A Study in Problems of Indian National Unity* (Berkeley: University of California Press, 1958).

‡ Michael Brecher, *Nehru: A Political Biography* (London: Oxford University Press, 1959).

§ The States Reorganization Act, as it was finally passed by the Indian Parliament in
November 1956, called for fourteen states and six union territories. The boundaries
of each state were to be drawn so that they would conform with the region of a
dominant language, according to Professors Hardgrave and Kochanek.

** Other demands for statehood that were bypassed at the time included the tribal

Kamala Nehru with her one-year-old daughter, Indira, 1918. (Courtesy Nehru Memorial Museum and Library)

Jawaharlal Nehru in a family portrait (1927). Standing, from left to right, are Jawaharlal Nehru, Vijaya Lakshmi Pandit, Krishna Nehru, Indira Nehru, and Ranjit Pandit. Sitting, from left to right, are Swarup Rani Nehru, Motilal Nehru, and Kamala Nehru. (Courtesy Nehru Memorial Museum and Library)

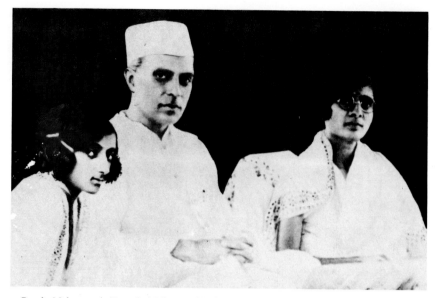

Pandit Nehru with Kamala Nehru and Indira Nehru (left) in 1931. (Courtesy Nehru Memorial Museum and Library)

A portrait of Nehru, June 1931. (Courtesy Nehru Memorial Museum and Library)

Indira Nehru during her visit to Singapore in 1937. (Courtesy Nehru Memorial Museum and Library)

Indira Nehru seated with her father during her marriage ceremony in Allahabad, March 1942. (Courtesy Nehru Memorial Museum and Library)

Prime Minister Nehru with Dr. Albert Einstein at his home in Princeton, New Jersey, 1949. At left is Mrs. Indira Gandhi; at right is Mrs. Pandit. (Courtesy Nehru Memorial Museum and Library)

Prime Minister Nehru with Indira Gandhi in 1951 in Kashmir. (Courtesy Nehru Memorial Museum and Library)

Prime Minister Nehru with Mrs. Gandhi, 1964. (Courtesy Nehru Memorial Museum and Library)

Mrs. Gandhi with President Lyndon Johnson on a visit to the United States in 1966.
Janki Ganju is at left. (Courtesy Janki Ganju)

Prime Minister Indira Gandhi with President Richard Nixon.
(Courtesy Indian Consulate)

Prime Minister Indira Gandhi with Javier Perez de Cuellar, secretary-general of the United Nations. (Courtesy Indian Consulate)

The Prime Minister addressing the Nonaligned Movement (NAM), 1980. (Courtesy Indian Consulate)

Indira Gandhi received by Leonid Brezhnev and other dignitaries on her arrival at Moscow Airport, September 20, 1982. (Courtesy Indian Consulate)

Indira Gandhi with Leonid Brezhnev just before the Soviet-Indian official talks. (Courtesy Indian Consulate)

Leonid Brezhnev, president of the U.S.S.R., and Indira Gandhi at Soviet-Indian official talks at the Kremlin Palace, Moscow, September 20, 1982. (Courtesy Indian Consulate)

Indira Gandhi and Leonid Brezhnev after signing a joint declaration between India and the Soviet Union on September 21, 1982. (Courtesy Indian Consulate)

speaking state were turned down on the grounds that the people spoke both Punjabi and Hindi. The States Reorganization Commission said that the formation of a Punjabi-speaking state would not solve language and communal problems, and "far from removing internal tension, which exists between communal and not linguistic and regional groups, it might further exacerbate the existing feelings."* The other exception that Nehru made concerned the commercially flourishing city of Bombay, which was part of what was then the bilingual Bombay State. The claims of Gujarati and Marathi language states were denied by Jawaharlal because, as Krishan Bhatia puts it, "the protagonists could not agree to which of them the metropolis of Bombay should belong." Though geographically a part of the putative state of Maharashtra, Bombay had massive investments by the traditionally commercial Gujarati community. The Gujaratis hailed from the northern region of Bombay State —what was soon to be Gujarat State.† Indira persuaded her father and the other Congress leaders to revoke the old decision under which Nehru had stuck to the concept of a bilingual Bombay state. Under that proposal, the city of Bombay was to be administered as a separate entity. Indira was alarmed over the fact that Bombay—a city ordinarily known for its hectic pace but easygoing nature—was experiencing ethnic rioting between Maharashtrians and Gujaratis, both of whom claimed Bombay as their own. There was widespread arson and looting. Two broadly based language front organizations had been formed: the Samyukta Maharashtra Samiti—to press the cause of Maharashtra state—and the Mahagujarat Janata Parishad, to advance the cause of a new Gujarat state.

---

areas of Jharkhand and Nagaland. Jharkhand was to be carved out of the Chota-Nagpur region of southern Bihar and the contiguous tribal districts of neighboring Orissa. Nagaland was to be formed out of a hilly area along the Assam-Burma border. Naga tribes—many of them converted to Christianity by American Baptist missionaries—sought help from international sources and from the United Nations to achieve independence from India. There was much agitation, some of it quite violent. Eventually, in 1963, the Nagas got their own state—but within the Indian union.

* It was Prime Minister Indira Gandhi who agreed to the creation of separate Punjab and Haryana states in March 1966. Hindi-speaking areas of the old bilingual Punjab states were now transferred to the new Haryana State. Both Punjab—where 56 percent of the people spoke Punjabi—and Haryana shared the same capital, Chandigarh, a modern city designed by Le Corbusier, the French architect. The dispute over Chandigarh still continues, however. Rajiv Gandhi's administration had renewed earlier promises that Haryana would get its own capital, but nothing came of this pledge.

† To this day, Maharashtrians and Gujaratis dominate Bombay. The trading and merchant communities in Bombay are overwhelmingly Gujarati.

"As Congress President, Indira realized that the party's opponents were exploiting the issue to alienate the public and that the next general election might cause its defeat," Krishan Bhatia writes.

> Indira also saw the pointlessness of preserving an arrangement that neither of the two constituents liked. The bilingual state's Chief Minister at the time, Yeshwantrao B. Chavan, too, saw the wisdom of undoing the enforced unity. Chavan was a swarthy politician from the Maratha clan, a genial but shrewd man who could be quite ruthless with his opponents. He made a name for himself not only as a politician but also a patron of the arts: Chavan often attended literary gatherings, and was a habitué of the Marathi theater. He was also a man who had a glad eye, and there were numerous stories about his dalliances in Bombay. Between them, Indira and Chavan persuaded a reluctant Jawaharlal to reverse what until then he had regarded as an irrevocable decision.[*]

On May 1, 1960, the two "new" states were inaugurated—Maharashtra and Gujarat.[†] Indira received kudos for her job from politicians of all persuasions, even though by now she was no longer the titular head of the Congress Party.[‡]

The second event of great consequence during Indira Gandhi's tenure as Congress Party president occurred in the southern state of Kerala. In the Third World, Kerala had become a metaphor for literacy and excellent health care. By 1955, when most states of the Third World were still backward, miserable places and still under their colonial yoke, Kerala already had achieved the highest literacy rate of any region in the developing world, an astonishing 95 percent. The Christian missionaries who had arrived in the eighteenth and nineteenth centuries had established English-language schools. Kerala's two princely states, Travancore and

---

[*]Bhatia, *Indira*, pp. 150–59.

[†]Professor Stanley Wolpert notes that one other new state "was born through the fires of regional revolt" during Nehru's era, the remote and forested homeland of India's former headhunting Naga tribe. The Nagas won statehood—they had been part of the eastern state of Assam earlier—on December 1, 1963. Nagaland became India's sixteenth state; India now has twenty-five states and seven Union Territories, or federally administered areas.

[‡]The bifurcation of Bombay state into Maharashtra and Gujarat has worked out remarkably well. Bombay is Maharashtra's capital, but Gujaratis continue to be a dominant commercial presence here. There has been virtually no ethnic rioting between Maharashtrians and Gujaratis since those ugly days in the late 1950s.

Cochin, were traditionally governed by rulers who promoted literacy, especially among women. The Hindu Nayyar and the Namboodiripad communities also vigorously pushed for education. Because Kerala had no industries until well into the 1960s, government service was the most sought-after career for the young. So they studied hard for the competitive entrance examinations, and the competition among Kerala's people in turn helped push ever upward the quality of education. * The state decreed that all education through high school would be free; moreover, even the salaries of teachers in many private schools were paid by the state from tax revenues. In addition, health services were free. The first public clinics for administering the smallpox vaccine were established in Travancore and Cochin.

Kerala was unusual in other ways, too. In the rest of India, women were largely confined to home and hearth, but in this state they were encouraged to study and to get jobs. The high status of women was mostly because much of Kerala's majority Hindu society was matriarchal. But Kerala also became a metaphor for something besides high literacy and good health care. It was the first state in the world where the Communist Party obtained power through legitimately held elections. That occurred in 1957. As literacy spread, Keralites started to harbor higher and higher economic expectations. But the system could not deliver. Because of the nature of the terrain, virtually all economic activity was confined to land cultivation or fishing. Yet each year the schools and colleges were turning out thousands of graduates. Unemployment rose beyond 15 percent, and soon there were violent demonstrations against the ruling Congress Party of Jawaharlal Nehru. A local Communist leader named E. M. S. Namboodiripad accused the Congress of "class exploitation." At rally after rally, he equated the Congress rule with British imperialism. Namboodiripad's rhetoric, combined with the growing unemployment and the rising expectations of Keralites, helped put the Communists into power.

Prime Minister Nehru actually seemed to be proud of the development. He told Krishan Bhatia of *The Hindustan Times* that perhaps now Communists all over the world would realize that they could attain power through the ballot box and become more tolerant of democratic political processes. Dom Moraes, in his biography of Indira Gandhi, recalls that the Fabian Socialist in Nehru even seemed delighted that a leftist government had come into being through democratic means. Nehru, according to

---

* Kerala's population of about 20 million in the late 1950s consisted of 50 percent Hindus, 25 percent Muslims, and 25 percent Christians. There was also a small Jewish community in Cochin.

Moraes, hoped that Kerala could be the precursor of other democratically elected Communist governments all over the world.

These developments in Kerala coincided with Indira Gandhi's desire to revitalize the aging Congress Party. She did not subscribe to her father's live-and-let-live attitude toward Opposition parties, much less applaud the takeover—however democratic—of an Indian state by the Communist Party. In 1958 she advised the Kerala unit of the Congress Party to prepare for a nasty battle with Namboodiripad's government. The Congress threw in its lot with the Nayyars and the Christians of the state, who had felt discriminated against by the Communist government; Namboodiripad's party had instituted radical land reforms, pushed out many influential and established Nayyars and Christians from the bureaucracy, and tried to bring about structural changes in the educational system over which the Nayyars and Christians had long held sway. The Communist government even tried to take over the parochial schools operated by the Christians and Nayyars.

Rioting now occurred. There were Congress-sponsored demonstrations all over Kerala. Police fired tear-gas shells at mobs. Then orders were given to shoot demonstrators who had become uncontrollably violent. Several civilians died in melees. It was clear to many observers at the time that Mrs. Gandhi was calibrating the demonstrations from Delhi so as to ensure that the law-and-order situation deteriorated rapidly. She could then persuade her father, the prime minister, to dismiss the Kerala state government on the ground that it was unable to check the spreading lawlessness. That is exactly what Mrs. Gandhi did, and Nehru accepted her recommendation. On July 31, 1959, the Namboodiripad government was deposed under a presidential order.*

But the lawlessness continued, this time fueled by the disaffected Communists. The Nehru-Gandhi axis ordered elections six months later. But in order to win the poll, Mrs. Gandhi had to make alliances with the Socialists and with the Muslim League. This was the same Muslim League that less than two decades earlier had agitated so fiercely for the partition of Greater India into India and Pakistan. Mrs. Gandhi's political marriage of convenience with the Muslim League distressed many of her supporters within and outside the Congress Party. The Congress now formed a coalition government with the League and the Socialists. The

---

*Although only the Indian president can technically issue a directive dismissing a state government, he invariably acts at the behest of the executive head of government—the prime minister. In other word, what a prime minister wishes, he usually gets.

Communist Party subsequently split into a wing favoring the Maoist version of Marxism—called the CPI-M—and another wing that leaned toward Moscow—the CPI. (The split had more to do with the estrangement between Moscow and Beijing, rather than developments in Kerala; but it further weakened the previously monolithic Communist movement in Kerala.) Over the next twenty years, both Communist wings held power as members of various coalition governments—but the supremacy that Namboodiripad enjoyed between 1957 and 1959 was never quite replicated again. It would not be incorrect to say that Indira Gandhi ushered in an era of coalition governments in Kerala; since 1960, in fact, the Congress and the Marxists have had to woo smaller regional and communal parties in order to form coalition governments. Fragility, not stability, has usually been the main characteristic of these administrations.

The Communist Party's earlier victory in the southern state had been a milestone in Indian politics. The Congress monopoly over the states ended; other parties showed that they could win elections.* There was widespread concern in India's leftist press about Kerala being to India what Yenan was to China (Yenan being the region from which Communism had spread all over China). There was general mistrust of two legitimately progressive reform bills in the local legislature. One was an Agrarian Reform Bill giving protection to farmers; the second proposal was for an Education Bill aimed at controlling private-run schools and colleges. The Kerala Congress was backing the right-wing agitation, which was designed to defeat these bills. Goaded by Indira, Nehru favored a policy of persuading the Communist ministry of Kerala to accept voluntarily the challenge of its opponents to put the two controversial bills to the test of a fresh vote by the people. The Kerala chief minister, Namboodripad, refused to accept this. Indira took a very tough stand. She challenged the credentials of these Communists by making statements that they were agents of China, which was attempting war against India. She defended the Kerala Congress's alliance with the Muslim League and the Christian Church. Indira believed that if the Congress did not participate in the anti-Communist agitation, the party would be finished in the state.

Though Nehru was not necessarily in favor of the method of siding with the right in order to get rid of the left, he did nothing to prevent his daughter from doing precisely that. Indeed, Communist leaders pub-

*Until that point, the Congress—the only true national party in the country—had swept practically every state where elections were held.

lished an "open letter" to Indira Gandhi in which they asked whether "the policy of isolating and annihilating the Communist Party was the aim of Congress throughout India?" The letter concluded by saying: "We hope that you will seriously consider the repercussions such an agitation, challenging a law passed by the legislature, by a section of the people affected by the law, will have throughout India. For it will mean that any sectional interest can challenge and try to defeat any progressive legislative measure by unlawful, threatening methods."

It was ironical indeed that the Communist Party would be lecturing Indira Gandhi on public morality. The concession to communal politics in Kerala gave the go-ahead signal to Congress workers throughout the country to compromise their long-cherished tradition of not engaging in such politics. Had Nehru stopped Indira at that point, he would have ended her maneuvers. Had Nehru lived longer he would have regretted the day he made this concession. Indira's role in Kerala offered a startling glimpse of things to come in the future. The Congress Party—controlled by Indira—had the Communists overthrown not because they were incapable of governing, but because the legally elected provincial government was not a Congress government.* Indira realized that the defeat of the CPI was very crucial; and she was so desperate to "win" in Kerala that she even formed an alliance with the Muslim League—even though the Congress Parliamentary Board denounced these intrigues. This meeting, held on August 2, 1959, was notable because Feroze Gandhi spoke out forcefully against the Congress adventure in Kerala. He denounced his party—and, by implication, his own wife—for signing up with right-wing forces in Kerala. Nehru later told friends that he found Feroze's remarks unforgivable.

Krishan Bhatia has summarized the Kerala imbroglio astutely: "The Congress Party, always proud of its secularism and averse to associating itself with sectarian elements, let its principles be subordinated to its political interests, and joined the Catholics and the Nayyars in denouncing the Communist administration. In the furor that the joint agitation created, the state government was accused of sins it had not committed, its motives were distorted, its political selfishness was exaggerated, and the good it had sought to do was completely overlooked."[†]

Ironically, Indira received maximum criticism from the quarter she

---

*This is exactly what Prime Minister Indira Gandhi would do many years later in the Punjab—when a legitimately elected Opposition government was dismissed by her for no other reason than the fact that her own Congress Party was not in power.
[†]Bhatia, *Indira*, p. 149.

least expected—Feroze Gandhi. Her husband believed that this kind of unjustified action would erode the Congress Party's democratic credentials, and even encourage authoritarian tendencies in the future.* They both had leftist leanings, but now he was surprised to see Indira bear down so harshly on Communists. On the other hand, Indira was sore that her husband, rather than backing her, had fought her as her bitterest foe. In a letter to Dorothy Norman, Indira complained about Feroze: "On the domestic front, Feroze has always resented my very existence, but since I have become the President [of the Congress Party] he exudes such hostility that it seems to poison the air. Unfortunately, he and his friends are friendly with some of our ministers, and an impossible situation is being created. The Kerala situation is worsening. . . ."†

Jawaharlal Nehru's assessment of his daughter's political development was one of private delight. In an interview he gave to Russi K. Karanjia, editor of the left-wing weekly newspaper *Blitz*, Jawaharlal said: "It is well known that I did not groom her or help her in any way to become the Congress Party President—but she did; and I am told even by people who do not like me or my policies that she made a very good president. Sometimes she chose a line of her own against my way of thinking, which was the right thing to do. . . . we worked more like political colleagues than a father-and-daughter combination. We agreed on some things. We differed on some others. Indira has a strong independent mind of her own, as she should have."‡

---

* Some historians believe that Feroze opposed Indira out of spite. But others, such as Inder Malhotra, say that Feroze was genuinely disturbed that Indira was acting in an undemocratic manner, that she was reneging on her liberalism.
† Letter dated July 21, 1959, from Indira Gandhi to Dorothy Norman.
‡ Quoted by K. A. Abbas in *That Woman* (Delhi: Indian Book Company, 1973).

II

Into Her Own

The Kerala episode of 1959 highlighted the fact that Indira Gandhi was capable of putting party above all—that she had a keenness for going for the jugular, and that she was tougher than most people had assumed. Indira did not have her father's soaring intellect but did possess something far more valuable to a politician—quickness of mind, and the ability to grasp the complexities of power politics. Indira also learned early on that she had the ability to manipulate people. Unlike Jawaharlal Nehru, who was almost touchingly naïve about other people's motives and intentions, Indira's instinct was not to trust people too readily. She saw how most favor-seekers who approached her father tried to be ingratiating and cloying, and she quickly figured out how to string people along.* Indira believed in relying on the counsel of only a few associates, whom she authorized to be her eyes and ears. But Indira had little hesitation in jettisoning those aides whose usefulness had ended—or who had demonstrated even the slightest disloyalty. Jawaharlal was a forgiving person; Indira was not.

During her years as her father's apprentice, her friends and allies included M. O. Mathai, Nehru's special assistant, and Krishna Menon, the prime minister's chief adviser on foreign policy. Both Mathai and Menon fell out with Indira later; both men hailed from Kerala, and both

*Some Indian psychologists contend that it is a marked cultural characteristic in India to be ingratiating. Indians generally seem anxious to please their superiors, but can be rude to their subordinates or to those whom they see as their social inferiors.

251

were ugly. Both were romantically linked with Indira, at least by the occupants of Delhi's society salons.* Mathai endeared himself to Indira by looking after young Rajiv and Sanjay.† He was a charming man from Kerala State who appeared one fine morning at Nehru's doorstep, and offered his services in exchange for room and board. In those days, it was still possible for ordinary Indians to walk straight up to the prime minister. Security was virtually nonexistent. (These days, of course, it takes a superhuman effort to get anywhere near the prime minister's aides, let alone the prime minister himself. As could be expected, security was strengthened after Indira's assassination.) With Mathai's cunning ability he built a formidable power apparatus around himself. The Nehrus and Gandhis have always been susceptible to the manipulations of advisers such as Mathai. Indira Gandhi had her own Mathais at different levels. These included Yashpal Kapoor and R. K. Dhawan, Dinesh Singh, and P. N. Haksar. Rajiv had Captain Satish Sharma, and later Mani Shankar Aiyar. These gentlemen were arguably even more powerful than the prime ministers they served because they controlled access to the prime minister and offered advice that was usually taken—advice concerning promotions and demotions, hirings and firings, the granting of coveted commercial and industrial licenses, and dealings with the media. Cabinet-rank ministers and top officials would approach them if they wished any favor from the prime minister.

As was perhaps inevitable, Mathai's name was romantically linked with Indira's; Mathai was a bachelor, and he lived under the prime minister's roof. Mathai himself encouraged such gossip. It was clear to most of Delhi that he was only too happy to be linked with the prime minister's pretty daughter. Years later, Mathai would say quite openly that he and Indira had slept together, that he even possessed films showing them making love.‡ As can be expected, Feroze did not like these rumors one bit. He was determined to teach Mathai a lesson. He found

---

*Inder Malhotra, in his 1989 biography of Indira Gandhi, states categorically that "not even a whiff of scandal attached to Indira's friendly relations with Krishna Menon though, like Mathai, he was a bachelor and, whenever in Delhi, lived at the Prime Minister's House." Notwithstanding Malhotra's assertion, there was no shortage of speculation concerning Indira's ties with Krishna Menon. In the Bombay parliamentary constituency that Krishna Menon represented, there was always gossip about his link to Indira.

†Indira Gandhi had a soft spot for people who got along well with her sons. Some of Sanjay Gandhi's thuggish friends even became her political instruments.

‡Despite such boasts, Mathai never produced the "evidence." His claims were dismissed by most observers as being publicity stunts, or the fevered ranting of a man who had fallen out of favor with the powerful.

out that Mathai had started a trust in his mother's memory and was soliciting large contributions, particularly from businessmen who sought special dispensation from Nehru. Feroze also found out that Mathai had purchased an orchard from an industrialist at what Inder Malhotra says was a "ridiculously low price." Malhotra, who knew Feroze Gandhi well, adds: "Feroze collected the evidence of Mathai's wrongdoing with the thoroughness he was famous for. But, uncharacteristically, he did not raise this matter in Parliament himself. This task he left to friendly MPs who were exceedingly well briefed."* Mathai had no option but to resign.†

The late 1950s and early 1960s were not an especially auspicious time for either Indira or her father. Feroze Gandhi had died after several years of declining health. Nehru himself seemed extraordinarily tired and worn out; in 1958, he had even volunteered to step down from the premiership but rescinded his offer after a national hue and cry. Indians, it seemed, could not imagine anyone else being prime minister other than Jawaharlal Nehru. Some observers suspected that Nehru's offer to resign was a political ploy to draw attention to the fact that he was beloved by ordinary Indians—and therefore indispensable. And then came the China debacle.

Officials at India's Ministry of External Affairs had noticed that the Chinese were showing chunks of Indian territory as theirs in maps distributed by the Chinese Foreign Ministry. The Chinese refused to revise these maps. At first, the Beijing government told Nehru that these maps dated back to the Kuomintang regime and that the Communist government—which won power in 1949—had not had the time to revise the cartography. Jawaharlal seemed reassured by this. He was soon to be deeply humiliated when the Chinese began to insist publicly that there was nothing wrong with the old maps. They soon started occupying the

---

* Inder Malhotra, *Indira Gandhi*, pp. 73–74.
†Nehru accepted Mathai's resignation on January 18, 1959. Mathai disappeared from the public arena for almost two decades. He surfaced in the late 1970s as the author of scurrilous books in which he made unsubstantiated innuendos about his romance with Indira Gandhi. These were so patently false that Mathai's books only earned him the discredit that was his due. In his critically acclaimed biography of Nehru (*Nehru: The Making of India* [New York: Viking, 1989]), M. J. Akbar says that although Mathai was exonerated of all charges, the real accusation—never made public at the time—was that Mathai was a CIA agent. Nehru's official biographer, Dr. S. Gopal, says that Cabinet Secretary Vishnu Sahay was privately convinced that Mathai had given American intelligence virtually every major Indian government file. It was on Sahay's recommendation that Nehru ultimately fired Mathai, according to Gopal.

territory that they claimed for themselves.* The Chinese even built a major highway linking Tibet to Sinkiang through the Indian section of the Aksai Chin region of Ladakh province. Tension between India and China heightened when the Dalai Lama, the spiritual and temporal head of Tibet, fled his homeland in 1959.† He was granted asylum in India.‡ Nehru tried to resolve the crisis diplomatically but failed. Nehru fervently believed that nations and their leaders could be persuaded to act rationally through the instruments of diplomacy. Indeed, Nehru felt that the key to Asian unity was Sino-Indian amity. India and China had concluded a treaty of friendship and trade in April 1954 in which they had also spelled out five principles of coexistence, known as "Panchshila." These five principles were: mutual respect for each other's territorial integrity and sovereignty; nonaggression; noninterference in each other's internal affairs; equality and mutual benefit; and peaceful coexistence. Nehru held that the Chinese would abide by this treaty of friendship and cooperation.

The Chinese had never accepted the McMahon Line, which the British colonial rulers had drawn arbitrarily in 1914 on the principle of the "highest watershed" dividing the two Asian countries. The division was authored by Sir Arthur Henry McMahon, a stern British civil servant. The border was never ratified by China, however. Nehru even invited Chinese Premier Chou En-lai to Delhi in 1960 to try to settle the dispute. But, as Professor Stanley Wolpert writes, "the 2,640-mile border dividing the two nations was so difficult to survey and the maps relied upon by each leader so different that nothing could be resolved."§ Misled by Defense Minister Krishna Menon and others who acted as though they wanted to appease the Chinese, Nehru even underestimated the significance of border skirmishes. Some advisers told Nehru that China would not do anything dreadful—such as invading India. Indira, however, was certain that Chinese intentions were far from benign.

Indira had long been disturbed by the border clashes between Chinese and Indian forces, and by increasing intrusions by the Chinese. In the winter of 1955, for instance, Chinese troops crossed into Uttar Pradesh's Garhwal district; the troops withdrew after Nehru protested. The Chinese built the Tibet-Sinkiang road in 1957—but India did not even discover

---

* According to Professor Stanley Wolpert, the Chinese occupied 52,000 square miles of Indian territory.

† The Dalai Lama is considered by Tibetans as a reincarnation of the Buddha.

‡ The Dalai Lama has spoken out eloquently over the years against Chinese tyranny. He was awarded the Nobel Peace Prize in 1989. He lives mostly in the Indian mountain town of Dharamsala, along with thousands of Tibetan refugees.

§ Stanley Wolpert, *A New History of India* (New York: Oxford University Press, 1977).

its existence until two years later. In October 1959, several Indian soldiers were killed by the Chinese in Ladakh. There were also fights between Chinese and Indian soldiers in Longju, a remote border outpost in the Northeast Frontier Agency (NEFA) area. Indira was alarmed by the increasing frequency of border skirmishes between the massive Chinese forces and the poorly equipped Indian units in the mountainous waste-lands.* What Professor Stanley Wolpert has called the "cartographic war" continued until September 1962, when Nehru ordered Indian forces to recapture "all our territories." Subsequent inquiries showed that De-fense Minister Krishna Menon had misled Nehru all along about the strength of the Indian Army. Not only was the army poorly equipped in the mountain regions, it was also poor in morale and leadership. Indira felt that the Chinese would respond with more aggression. It is still unclear whether Indira told her father that the Indian forces were simply no match for the Chinese, and that the Chinese would probably invade anyway. The chances are that Nehru, who was heavily influenced in defense matters by Krishna Menon, was probably not likely to listen to Indira.

Indira's fears were borne out when, in October 1962, the Chinese launched a major attack. They came into Assam and Kashmir, overrun-ning the Indian Army. The Indian Army was no match at all for the Chinese; there was a very real possibility that the Chinese would capture the Assamese capital of Gauhati. Indira flew on an Indian Air Force plane to Tezpur in eastern India. There she met with the army commander of the sector, Lieutenant-General B. M. Kaul, and later toured military hospitals and other facilities.† News reports that appeared in the national and international media praised Indira fulsomely for her visits to the front.‡ Nehru, in a temporary abandonment of his nonalignment, pleaded with Washington for assistance. The United States and Britain gave India weapons and ammunition. After their initial successes in the battlefield, however, the Chinese suddenly withdrew from Assam. The Chinese never explained their withdrawal. Dom Moraes believes that by invading India, Beijing underscored two things: one, that the Chinese no longer felt fraternal about India; and two, that China enjoyed military superior-ity over India. The idea, says Moraes, was to humiliate India—and in this the Chinese certainly succeeded.

* The Chinese had already occupied more than 14,000 square miles of Indian territory in Kashmir; they continue to hold on to this real estate.
† General Kaul was to write a controversial book later in which he gave dismaying details about how the political establishment had failed India's military.
‡ One headline read "Indira's Back to Front." (It was meant to be complimentary.)

This entire episode proved a military catastrophe for India, and a political disaster for Nehru personally. Never before had Indians reviled him, or even railed against him, and now Nehru seemed to be everybody's favorite target. Even President Sarvepalli Radhakrishnan chided Nehru for negligence.* The Indian press was scathingly critical of Nehru, too—an unprecedented development. Krishna Menon and several top brass resigned in disgrace. Nehru never really recovered from the trauma of the Sino-Indian War. He was a broken man; he had never thought that Premier Chou—whom he considered a friend—would be party to such a betrayal as the Chinese invasion. Nehru now grew to be even more reliant on Indira and consulted her for virtually everything having to do with matters of state. Despite Nehru's evident physical decline, he found time to rejuvenate the Congress Party and also trim the sails of men he felt were jockeying in an unseemly fashion for his job. This was done in late 1963 through the so-called Kamaraj Plan, named after the cagey Chief Minister of Tamil Nadu State, Kumaraswamy Kamaraj, who was also then the president of the Congress Party.

Nehru was concerned that the Congress, which had always prided itself on being a grass-roots organization, was losing contact—and popularity—with India's masses. He was also concerned that party bosses were condoning—even indulging in—corruption. Under the Kamaraj Plan, six cabinet ministers and six regional chief ministers were asked to resign in order to devote their energies more fully to strengthening the Congress Party at the grass roots. Kamaraj himself resigned. The men who resigned from Nehru's cabinet included Morarji Desai; Lal Bahadur Shastri; Jagjivan Ram, a leader of India's Harijans; and S. K. Patil, the Congress boss in Bombay. Four months later, however, Nehru brought Shastri back into the cabinet. Morarji Desai later complained bitterly that the Kamaraj Plan was a ploy on Nehru's part to "clear the decks" for Indira Gandhi.

Trevor Drieberg, who was then a news editor at the *Indian Express* in Delhi, has written movingly about Nehru's decline: "To Nehru, now 73, Beijing's perfidy was a mortal blow. It shattered his dreams of building an area of peace and economic cooperation in which the developing nations would get their fair share of material goods and play an independent role in world affairs. Overnight, he changed into a weary, disillusioned old man. He walked with a stoop, as though in pain, his face was somber and lined deeply, his elan was irretrievably lost."[†]

---

*Nehru was stung by Radhakrishnan's remarks. He had long considered the Tamil scholar a friend. Their relationship grew frosty after the Sino-Indian War of 1962.
[†]Trevor Drieberg, *Indira Gandhi: A Profile in Courage* (Delhi: Vikas, 1972), p. 46.

Although publicly the Congress Party's leadership said that Nehru would be around for a long time, it was clear that he was in failing mental and physical health. Despite his proclaimed agnosticism and rationalism, arcane Hindu rituals were undertaken by his household and some associates to restore his vitality. Meanwhile, colleagues such as Morarji Desai —Nehru's erstwhile finance minister—had already started to position themselves to win the premiership in a post-Nehru India. In January 1964, Jawaharlal suffered a stroke while attending a session of the Congress Party in Bhubaneshwar, capital of the eastern coastal state of Orissa; he returned to Delhi in a wheelchair. Yet Nehru did not give up the reigns of government. Indira now not only nursed her father, she closely monitored the functioning of Nehru's administration, and was virtually his only source of news. The press labeled her "the power behind the throne."* This meant that all events in the outside world, and everything to do with the governing of India, had to be filtered through her. Government bureaucrats took orders from Indira, always assuming that she was the prime minister's mouthpiece. Even Lal Bahadur Shastri, the senior minister in Nehru's cabinet, often had to wait his turn in a corridor outside Nehru's room. The fact that Indira was virtually running the government—albeit quietly and behind the scenes—did not sit well with the men who had hoped to succeed Nehru. They had already started spinning schemes concerning succession. Morarji Desai was one man who felt that when Nehru went—and this, Desai was convinced, was only a matter of months—the prime minister's job ought to be his.† At a news conference just five days before his death, Jawaharlal, when asked about the succession issue, replied: "My life is not going to end so soon."

After that news conference, Jawaharlal and Indira went off for a quiet holiday to Dehra Dun, a hill station not very far from Delhi. They returned to the capital late in the afternoon of May 26. On that evening, Jawaharlal Nehru seemed particularly wan and tired. Ever since his stroke earlier that year, he had withered. On this evening, he said to Indira: "I have finished my work." He then retired to bed. At a little after six o'clock the next morning, Jawaharlal woke up in pain. Physicians who were summoned to Teen Murti Bhavan found that his abdominal aorta had ruptured. Nehru lapsed into a coma. He was declared dead at around two o'clock that afternoon. When Indira looked around his bedroom

---

* The phrase was originally used by Inder Malhotra in a confidential memo to his editors.
† Morarji Desai always disliked Indira. He believed that she had poisoned her father's ear about him. Inder Malhotra says that Desai "opposed and harried her because of his firm belief that she had taken away the job which should, by right, have been his."

later that day, she saw that her father had written out a verse from Robert Frost:

> For I have promises to keep
> And miles to go before I sleep.

Trevor Drieberg has recalled with great eloquence his own feelings about Nehru's death; he echoed the sentiments of an entire nation. Drieberg had a busy day at the *Indian Express* following the announcement of Nehru's death. "It was only around midnight, when all the loose ends had been tied, that I sat back and breathed freely for the first time since the ill tidings had come. It was only then that the full impact of what had happened dawned on me. Nehru is dead, I repeated to myself. I shall never see Nehru again. It seemed unbelievable. Nehru was India. Nehru was universal. He represented all the basic decencies of human life. What now? And I thought of all the rats who were busy right at that moment sharpening their claws and preening their whiskers for the great race that would now begin."* Nehru's erstwhile friend and colleague Krishna Menon said: "The moment his [Nehru's] last breath was drawn, the issue [of succession] arose. None of these people who professed loyalty to him, who came from his state, in whose interests he sometimes disregarded people like me just to keep the peace—none of them had the decency to keep their mouths shut until he was cremated."†

Jawaharlal Nehru's funeral had to be delayed by a day as dignitaries from all over the world flew in. Inder Malhotra tells of a poignant vignette on the day of the funeral. Indira spotted several members of the staff household sitting around in extreme distress. They had refused to go home to bathe or change. She directed them to do just that, and then return to Teen Murti Bhavan for the funeral preparations. "My father always liked neatness," Indira told them. "There will be no slovenliness around him today." Never before had there been such huge crowds at a funeral—not even when Mahatma Gandhi died. The cremation ceremony occurred at Rajghat, not far from the spot where the Mahatma's funeral took place. Helicopters showered rose petals. "Indira Gandhi was serene and composed," M. J. Akbar wrote in his acclaimed biography of Nehru. "She went up the steps of the pyre, sprinkled holy water and gently placed a piece of sandalwood at her father's feet. She stood there, alone, silent, for nearly eight minutes. Then she took one last glance at

---

* Drieberg, *Indira Gandhi: A Profile in Courage*, p. 48.
† Ali, *An Indian Dynasty*, pp. 145–46.

her Papu's face and walked down."[*] Young Sanjay Gandhi lit the funeral pyre of his grandfather.

On June 12, after the traditional thirteen days of mourning, Indira scattered some of Nehru's ashes over Pahalgam, a valley in Kashmir. Ashes were also scattered in other parts of the country from Indian Air Force planes. And ashes were immersed in the Ganges at Allahabad. Nehru had always been an agnostic. He had indicated in his will that he wanted no religious rites performed at his funeral, but that his ashes be scattered over the Himalayas and also immersed in the Ganges "to be carried to the great ocean that washed India's shore." Nevertheless, the ubiquitous Brahman priests chanted their Vedic hymns, and Nehru was cremated in the traditional Hindu custom. In India it would be inconceivable that a high-born man like Nehru would not be given a traditional funeral—no matter what the man's personal preference.

There was immediate speculation in media and political circles that, with Nehru gone, Indira had bleak political prospects. Indeed, Indira even told Professor Ralph Buultjens that she longed to have an extended stay abroad, perhaps even at an English or American university.[†] Then she would settle somewhere in the Himalayan foothills, in a small bungalow, and write. But, of course, this was not how it would be. As Hindus would say, something entirely different was written in Indira's stars. She was destined for public life.

Jawaharlal Nehru never formally named a successor. Privately, Nehru wondered whether Indira would be fully acceptable to the Congress Party's old guard—the party chieftains who had been his associates in the freedom struggle, some of whom saw Indira more as a niece to be tolerated and perhaps even indulged rather than a national leader from whom to take orders. Some of these chieftains were certainly male chauvinists, and the very idea of being ordered around by a woman in a traditional society such as India was unbearable—especially if that woman was a widow who occupies a subordinate position according to orthodox Hindu custom. Publicly, Nehru declared: "The thought of dynastic succession is altogether foreign to a parliamentary democracy like ours, besides being repulsive to my own mind."[‡] He also said that

[*] Akbar, *Nehru: The Making of India*, pp. 581–82.
[†] Conversation between Indira Gandhi and Professor Ralph Buultjens in New Delhi, 1977.
[‡] Under India's Westminster-style parliamentary system, the leader of the majority

he had enough confidence in his colleagues from whom, presumably, a successor would be selected. Nehru, of course, was as vain about his immortality as anyone else; other than educating Indira by example and osmosis, he had never groomed any Congress Party leader for eventual leadership of the country.

The main contenders for the job were Lal Bahadur Shastri and Morarji R. Desai, who believed himself to be the natural successor to Nehru. In the event, Desai was outsmarted and outmaneuvered by Shastri, who had the support of the group of powerful Congress bosses known as the Syndicate.* This group of king-makers consisted of Atulya Ghosh from West Bengal, Sanjiva Reddy from Andhra Pradesh, S. Nijalingappa from Karnataka, S. K. Patil from Bombay, and Kumaraswamy Kamaraj, chief minister of Tamil Nadu.† Jawaharlal Nehru had approved of Shastri and thought him to be a good conciliator. Several Indian political analysts—like Professor Ashis Nandy—believe that the Kamaraj Plan was intended to clear the way for Shastri to take over when Nehru left the scene. It was Shastri who insisted on resigning from the cabinet when the Kamaraj Plan was put into effect; but there was tacit understanding between him and Nehru that Shastri would return to government whenever summoned by the prime minister. The Kamaraj Plan was really a scheme to disable Morarji Desai and to derail his ambitions of succeeding Nehru. The Syndicate promoted Shastri all the more because they were determined to prevent Morarji Desai from succeeding Nehru.‡ Though Desai was a seasoned administrator, he was unpopular because of his inflexible and intolerable nature. Even while Nehru was alive it was obvious that he did not particularly care for Desai. After his stroke in January 1964, Nehru invited Shastri to rejoin his cabinet as a minister without a portfolio. Desai was deeply disturbed by this move as he saw it not as a move to pave the way for Shastri but for Indira.

---

party in Parliament generally gets invited by the country's constitutional president to become prime minister.

* The Syndicate was supposedly formed at an informal meeting in the Hindu religious town of Tirupathi in Andhra Pradesh in October 1963, when some of the top Congress Party bosses met informally between devotional sessions at Tirupathi's shrines. Inder Malhotra, the eminent writer and editor, is generally credited with having first used "Syndicate" with reference to the old-guard Congress Party bosses.

† With the possible exception of Kamaraj, Congress bosses had a reputation for corruption. Virtually all top party officials accumulated great wealth, and bought a great deal of property in India and abroad.

‡ Krishan Bhatia says that since all of these Syndicate bosses hailed from non–Hindi-speaking areas—which constituted the majority of India's population, and therefore had the most representation in Parliament—none had a realistic chance of becoming prime minister himself.

At a session of the Congress Working Committee on June 2, 1964, in New Delhi, the acting prime minister, Gulzari Lal Nanda, put Shastri's name in nomination for party leader.* Earlier, Kamaraj had conducted a straw poll of party leaders and workers and found that Desai was not acceptable to many. After Kamaraj spoke to Desai in private, the latter agreed to withdraw his name from contention; indeed, Desai even graciously seconded Nanda's nomination of Shastri. As leader of the Congress Party, Lal Bahadur Shastri automatically became independent India's second prime minister. Throughout this drama, Indira refused to acknowledge that she had any political ambitions at all. In her letters to Dorothy Norman, Indira had been writing about feelings of "intense fatigue, dark despair" and a need for "privacy and anonymity."† Both her sons were in England: Rajiv was attending Imperial College in London, and Sanjay, having dropped out of school and being interested in cars, was receiving training at a Rolls-Royce factory in Crewe. (Sanjay Gandhi would later put this training to use when he launched a project to assemble the Maruti-Suzuki "people's car" in India. His project became a national scandal. It was well after his death that the Maruti car finally hit India's roads.) Her greatest desire, Indira told Dorothy Norman, was to be away from petty jealousies and malice in India. When Lal Bahadur Shastri invited her to join his cabinet she accepted very reluctantly, opting for the information and broadcasting portfolio.

According to Janki Ganju, Indira had traveled to London on a private visit when her aunt, Vijaya Lakshmi Pandit, phoned her there to say that the new prime minister would be offering her the portfolio.

"Why are you making this call?" Indira snapped at Mrs. Pandit. "Couldn't Shastri have called me himself?"‡

Shastri had been urged by Indira's supporters to make her India's minister of external affairs. They argued that with her familiarity with international issues—and leaders—she would be ideal for this job. Inder Malhotra recounts an incident in London in July 1964, when he met with Indira. She and Finance Minister T. T. Krishnamachari had traveled to London for the Commonwealth Prime Ministers' Conference—which Shastri could not attend because of an illness—and she was spending a few days in England after the meeting. The morning newspapers carried

---

* Gulzari Lal Nanda would again become acting prime minister in January 1966 when Shastri died of a heart attack in the Soviet Union.

† Welles Hangen wrote about a year before Nehru's death that Indira was universally assumed to be in the running to succeed her father. "No public figure in India disclaims political ambition so insistently, and none is more disbelieved," Hangen wrote in *After Nehru Who?*

‡ Recounted by Janki Ganju in a conversation with author, April 1991.

accounts of Shastri's newest cabinet member, Swaran Singh, who had been given the external affairs portfolio. "Should he not have consulted me and Krishnamachari?" Indira said to Malhotra. "I do not want that job. But surely I should have been consulted." Not quite a month had passed since Indira had joined Shastri's cabinet, but already she was beginning to feel slighted by Shastri.

Shastri realized that having Nehru's daughter in his cabinet would give it more power—and also satisfy Nehru's supporters. Shastri yielded to Indira's request that she not formally join the cabinet until the traditional month of mourning had passed. When he paid a call on her, the new prime minister—ever the modest man—said that Indira should have succeeded her father. Political analysts believe that had Indira really wanted the prime minister's job at the time, Shastri would have probably supported her. But, as Krishan Bhatia says, Indira lacked the political base in 1964 to successfully oppose Morarji Desai, who would undoubtedly have challenged her for the leadership. Lal Bahadur Shastri, despite his pleasant demeanor, was a wily politician. He did not want to give Indira a power base, and certainly did not want her to dominate his cabinet. Though an honest politician and essentially a good man at heart, Shastri also knew that he had to safeguard his own interests. He did not allow Indira any say in policy-making though he did appoint her to the cabinet's major committees. *

Indira, initially at least, took up her new job with enthusiasm—but it was the enthusiasm of the uninitiated, and soon she became fidgety. She lacked ingenuity. It was also clear that, even though her portfolio dealt with the media, she had little love for the press. Murray Fromson, then a correspondent for CBS News, told the author about his dealings with Indira in New Delhi. Fromson was covering the Indo-Pakistan War of 1965, and had obtained an exclusive visit to the battlefront in Kashmir. When he returned to the capital, however, the CBS film—those were the days when all field shooting was done on film, not videotape—was confiscated by the government on Mrs. Gandhi's orders. CBS, Mrs. Gandhi said, could not show any of the film until her censors had scrutinized every inch of it. Days went by, and Fromson heard nothing from either Mrs. Gandhi or her office. When he went to her office, he found her aides snipping away at the film, trying to remove pictures of insignia on Indian officers' uniforms! Finally, Mrs. Gandhi relented, and Fromson was able to get his film back. Nothing of what he had shot

---

* Cabinet committees in India rarely enjoy any great power, so Indira's membership did not necessarily enable her to wield much influence.

would have affected Indian security; the novelty of the CBS film lay in the mere fact that Fromson and his crew were the only media people who had obtained access to that particular battle zone.

Indira authored no great piece of legislation during her cabinet tenure. In fact, it seemed that Indira was often paying more attention to politics in general than to her ministry.* She also set out to establish her own constituency, and she did so by adopting a populist measure that had won great praise for her father. During his tenure as prime minister, Nehru had made it a practice to see people from all walks of life between eight and nine o'clock every morning.† Indira had been given a government bungalow at One Safdarjung Road, a modest accommodation compared to Teen Murti Bhavan.‡ She encouraged people to come and see her every morning, and they came in large numbers from all over the country with their accolades, their complaints, their hopes, their dreams.§

Shastri did not like to travel overseas** and sent Indira not only to represent India at the Commonwealth Prime Ministers' Conference in London but also on trips to France, Yugoslavia, Canada, Mongolia, and Burma. She was also sent to Moscow and met Leonid I. Brezhnev, the Russian who had deposed Nikita Khrushchev. From Brezhnev and others, Indira received assurances that Soviet policies toward India would not change. She went again to Russia in 1965 to assure the Russians that India still espoused nonalignment—in what was to become a regular pilgrimage to the Kremlin to consult with India's best friends among the

---

* Indira had been made fourth most senior member of the cabinet by Prime Minister Shastri, a rare honor for a newcomer to government. The Ministry of Information and Broadcasting actually is quite powerful since it controls the government-owned radio and television networks.

†This custom of meeting with ordinary people who were not required to make appointments dates back to the Mughal period.

‡Shastri did not want to move into Teen Murti Bhavan, where Nehru had lived since Independence. The new prime minister received a letter from Nehru's sister, Krishna Hutheesing, in which she discouraged Shastri from moving into a mansion that had been graced by Nehru for so long. At any rate, Shastri had decided that Teen Murti Bhavan should become a memorial to Nehru, and so it was that the estate was converted into a museum. To this day, Teen Murti Bhavan remains a star attraction on Delhi's tourist trail.

§Indira continued this practice even after she became prime minister. As Sikh terrorism increased in India, her security guards became more and more concerned about her welfare.

**Shastri had suffered a mild heart attack barely a month after he became prime minister. Moreover, he also felt ill at ease with foreign leaders. His English was not very good, and he was always conscious of his diminutive physical stature, the butt of jokes in India.

superpowers. All these foreign visits added to her self-confidence, and also gave her a fresh perspective on foreign leaders and their views concerning India. This perspective was to prove enormously useful when Indira Gandhi became prime minister and strode the world stage quite conspicuously in her own right as India's leader, and not as an epistle bearer for someone else.

During this period, there were times when Indira's actions seemed to suggest that she was already planning to become India's prime minister. She traveled extensively within India, meeting with Congress Party leaders and grass-roots workers. In January 1965, there were agitations in several states in the south over the question of India's national language. During Nehru's time, southern states had been assured that English would remain as their official language. But now Hindi zealots in the Hindi-speaking states of the north were pushing to impose Hindi all over India. *

"The first vigorous agitation for a 'linguistic province' emerged in the Telugu-speaking region of northern Madras, which wanted a state of its own, to be called Andhra, after the ancient Deccan Empire," says Professor Stanley Wolpert. "Nehru was less supportive of the linguistic provinces movement than Gandhi had been, and he succumbed to its popular pressure only after Potti Sriramalu, the saintly father of the Andhra movement, fasted to death in December 1952, leading to the creation of Andhra on October 1, 1953."† The princely state of Hyderabad was integrated into the new Andhra, as were the Telangana region that was part of the Madras Presidency, a section of the Bombay Presidency,‡ and parts of a state called Madhya Pradesh. The moment it was announced that a new state was being created along linguistic lines, scores of provincial leaders all across India began clamoring for states that would reflect their own language and ethnicity. Riots broke out. Property damage was in the hundreds of millions of dollars.

At that time, Jawaharlal Nehru did what heads of government do when they do not want to make a snap decision—he appointed a commission to study the nationwide agitation for linguistic states. That body was called the States Reorganization Commission, and it included three highly respected Indian public servants: Saiyid Fazl Ali, H. N. Hunzru, and K. M. Panikkar. The commission members spent two years reviewing mountains of memoranda, interviewing thousands of individuals all over

* The Hindi belt consists of Uttar Pradesh, Bihar, Himachal Pradesh, Haryana, Rajasthan, and Madhya Pradesh.
†Wolpert, *A New History of India*, p. 368.
‡Presidencies were the administrative regions created by the British.

India, and reflecting on the possible repercussions of slicing up India into linguistic units. They were not at all sure that such linguistic division would be good for the country. But pressures for linguistic states were building up dramatically, and in December 1955 the commission made the recommendations which led to the eventual creation of twenty-five states.

The basis for creating linguistic states was not just the demand for establishing formally the supremacy of various languages in their respective regions. It was also an acknowledgement of a basic fact of life in an ethnically diverse democracy: that politics in such a state is always the politics of the majority. Thus the Telugu-speaking minority in the old Madras Presidency—where Tamil was the language of the majority community—felt it was being left out of the political process and therefore out of economic progress. When Kerala State was created in 1956, to cite another example, the Malabar region—which was part of the Madras Presidency as well—was grouped together with the princely territories of Travancore and Cochin because, like them, it, too, was heavily Malayalam-speaking. Regional culture in India is strongly linked to language. Indeed, language, more than ideology or religion or even caste, is the main unifying factor in the country.

Whether the creation of linguistic states was good or not is a topic still under discussion in India.* And people still talk as much about how Nehru mollified various state renegades as they do about the granting of their demands. The chief example always cited in such discussions is that of Madras. In that southern region, well-organized Tamils had banded together in a political party called the Dravida Munnetra Kazhagam, widely known as the DMK. The DMK was overtly secessionist, much more so than any Sikh political group in the Punjab has been in recent years. Its leaders, such as C. N. Annadurai, asserted that the Tamils of the south needed their own nation to fully realize their potential; the message was that the Tamils resented efforts by the Delhi government to impose Hindi—a language spoken by 42 percent of the country's population, but mainly in the northern states—all across the country.

The DMK, because it was secessionist, was barred from contesting state elections in Madras—not because Nehru said so, but because Article 19 of the Indian constitution prohibited any secessionist party from participating in an election. In 1962, while Tamil agitation was in full swing, Chinese armies invaded northeast India. The DMK's leadership,

---

*The Indian press occasionally refers to the country's fissiparous tendencies. Indeed, Nehru years ago had established the Commission on Fissiparous Tendencies. No one I have met in India can remember what happened to that commission.

although in jail then, issued public statements supporting the Indian military's resistance to Chinese claims to barren, mountainous wastelands. After the cease-fire, Prime Minister Nehru did not forget the DMK's gesture. He quietly authorized his law minister to present in parliament an amendment that eased the strictures of Article 19. The DMK could now contest state elections in Madras. It did so and won a large victory. As the ruling party, it could hardly now agitate for secession. In more than two decades of DMK-dominated rule in Madras —whose name was changed to Tamil Nadu, or Land of the Tamils—no call to secession has been heard.

Nehru could have been obstinate: He could have kept the DMK leaders in jail, and he could have kept Madras state indefinitely under army rule. But he was convinced that when regional leaders shrieked for secession, they did not necessarily mean it—it was often an expression of regional frustrations, a desire to assert their local cultural identity. Nehru increasingly felt that the extraordinary ethnic and cultural diversity of India's regions must be allowed to bloom and blossom. He was aware that few regions in India—including the Punjab—could survive as independent countries; few Indian states were totally self-reliant in food and industrial requirements. In short, hardly any region could break away from the Indian Union and expect to thrive economically. Nehru knew that a concession here and there might be construed as a giveaway on his part, but that interpretation would be far outweighed by the good his action did in the long run for the country.

Now, in January 1965, there was fresh violence in the south.* In typical style, Shastri did nothing; he waited for the situation to simmer down. Even Kamaraj, who hailed from Tamil Nadu, decided to stay behind in New Delhi and not risk a trip to Madras, where irate mobs were burning buses and trains, and destroying government property. Indira Gandhi, however, decided to fly down to Madras to quell the trouble—without telling the prime minister about her trip. Shastri was not amused by this brash act, and still less pleased later when Indira received universal acclaim for calming Tamil mobs through her intervention. The Tamils seemed to be reassured by Indira's quiet approach, and by the fact that she held extensive discussions with local leaders. It did not matter that Indira herself hailed from the Hindi-speaking north; she came across as a national figure. Prime Minister Shastri later told his aides that he resented the fact that his minister of information and

---

*The scheduled date for the changeover from English to Hindi as India's national language was January 26. The southern states had formally agreed to this, but the masses clearly were opposed to the imposition of Hindi.

broadcasting had "jumped over my head." When journalist Inder Malhotra discussed this matter with Indira, she did not act contrite. "Do you think that this government can survive if I resign today?" Indira said to Malhotra. "I am telling you it won't. Yes, I have jumped over the prime minister's head, and I would do it again whenever the need arises."* This episode clearly established Indira Gandhi's reputation as a politician who could exercise strong leadership in a crisis.

Not long after the Madras crisis, Indira became involved in another situation, this one concerning India's security. In August 1965, there were reports that Pakistani troops in the guise of civilian volunteers had entered Kashmir. Their aim was to forment a pro-Pakistan movement in the valley, which was dominated by its Muslim population.†

Indira Gandhi took a special interest in Kashmir. She was, after all, a Kashmiri Brahman, a descendant of the scholarly, shrewd, and sturdy Hindus who flourished in a mountainous state that was overwhelmingly Muslim. Her ancestors had, of course, left Kashmir long before her birth to settle in Allahabad, a city on the banks of the River Ganges. Still, in Indira Gandhi's heart home was always Kashmir. Among the few people she was close to in her adult life were several Kashmiris. Indira had always been enamored of the snow-helmeted Pir Panjal Range that loomed over Kashmir. She would often tell friends how the crenellated peaks shimmered in the clear winter sunlight. To the west were the rich, alluvial plains of Pakistan; to the east lay the mountainous wastelands of Tibet, and beyond Tibet, China. Indira also painted graphic word pictures of the mighty Banihal Pass, through which invaders over the centuries had entered Kashmir.

Kashmir, Indira knew, was long known as "the Switzerland of India." With 85,000 square miles of choice real estate, over which India and Pakistan had fought costly wars to establish proprietorship since Independence, Kashmir was more than 80 percent Muslim, but ruled traditionally

---

*Malhotra, *Indira Gandhi*, p. 84.

†Hostilities between Indian and Pakistani military units had actually started early in 1965 in the Rann of Kutch, a marshy area in the western region where the two countries have a 200-mile-long border. Pakistani Patton tanks rolled more than ten miles into Indian territory and withdrew only after a cease-fire on June 30. India and Pakistan agreed to a joint commission—under United Nations auspices—to demarcate the border. Professor Stanley Wolpert notes: "Pakistan seemed the winner of Round One, though India had not committed its major forces to the Rann. In August-September, the center of conflict and scene of confrontation shifted north to Kashmir and the Punjab."

by a Hindu clan whose scions squandered their fortune on sex and soft living, while their subjects starved. Jawaharlal Nehru once said about this state: "Kashmir, even more than the rest of India, is a land of contrasts. In this land, overladen with natural beauty and rich nature's gifts, stark poverty reigns and humanity is continually struggling for the barest of subsistence. The men and women of Kashmir are good to look at and pleasant to talk to. They are intelligent and clever with their hands. They have a rich and lovely country to live in. Why then should they be so terribly poor?"

Indira had traveled to Kashmir for a brief holiday when she received news about the Pakistani infiltration. On the road from the airport, she could see massive camouflaged military bunkers in the shadow of which nestled knots of wooden houses.* At first sight, these houses resembled those marvelous toy homes that reminded Indira of those in the Swiss countryside, with A-shaped roofs and long beams supporting the ceilings. But instead of neat gardens and well-turfed yards, there were open sewers and dusty spaces in front of these houses. Men and women walked forlornly, with kangris, or coal stoves, under their robes; the kangris made everyone look heavily pregnant, men and women alike, but in a state where subzero temperatures are not unusual during the winter and where there is no such thing as central heating, the kangris serve as portable heaters. During political rallies, kangris serve as deadly weapons.

The road into the city from the Srinagar airport is edged with poplar, walnut, and chinar trees. Indira passed apple and cherry orchards and saffron fields. The road rolled over many culverts and streams; handsome children frolicked by these streams, but their clothes were frayed and often torn. There was a rundown appearance to these houses, an impression that was sustained all along the route into Srinagar. There was nothing beckoning, or even welcoming, about this capital city of 2 million people.

About 75 percent of Kashmir's 6 million people lived in the Srinagar Valley, the rest in Jammu. Mostly Muslims lived in Kashmir, and Hindus in Jammu. Kashmiris had long felt that the Delhi government neglected their economic development, despite the strategic importance of the state, which has borders with Pakistan and China. Indira Gandhi had long suspected—as did a few of her father's key advisers—that some of these Muslims did not want to continue to be a part of India, that they either preferred to join Pakistan or to create their own separate nation. That suspicion continued, and it lay at the heart of India's "Kashmir crisis."

---

*India had kept more than 100,000 troops in Kashmir since 1947.

268

Indira Gandhi knew that to understand the crisis, one had to go back to the nineteenth century. Kashmir until then had been ruled by a succession of Muslim rulers, mostly descendants of the Mughals or of various invaders who came from Afghanistan and Central Asia. In the early part of the last century, Kashmir was absorbed into the empire of Ranjit Singh, the Sikh maharajah who had braved the British and built a kingdom whose power was unchallenged at the time. One of his ablest generals was a man named Gulab Singh Dogra, a Hindu of the western Indian Rajput clan. Gulab Singh had performed well in battle, and Ranjit Singh rewarded him with suzerainty over Jammu, a territory that was situated south of Kashmir.

Ranjit Singh died on June 27, 1839, and almost immediately the British began freshly plotting to seize the Sikh empire. They began secret negotiations with Gulab Singh Dogra. He gave British troops "safe passage" through Jammu on their way to fight the First Afghan War in 1841. They were trounced in that war's critical battle, at the Khyber Pass in January 1842, but Gulab Singh was seen as a friend because of his assistance. Four years later, Gulab Singh displayed his friendship again, this time by refusing to assist his patrons, the Sikhs, in the First Anglo-Sikh War of February 1846. The Sikhs lost that war, and Gulab Singh was widely accused of being a traitor. But he came out ahead.

A month after the Anglo-Sikh War, the British "allowed" him to buy from them the territories of Jammu and Kashmir, which they had seized as a result of their victory over the Sikhs. Gulab Singh Dogra paid a nominal sum of seventy-five lakh rupees, or the equivalent of $75,000 at the time. Gulab Singh and his heirs were forever indebted to the British after the "purchase" of Kashmir. They showed gratitude by sending Kashmiri troops to help the British further defeat the Sikhs, then sent troops again to overwhelm the Afghan tribes, and helped in British military campaigns in the two great wars of this century. The Dogras were not benevolent rulers of their mostly Muslim subjects. They were profligate, they were corrupt, they were depraved. Maharaja Hari Singh, who was Kashmir's ruler when India became independent in 1947, paid a heavy price for his licentiousness. Some years earlier, he was the central figure in a major scandal in London, where blackmailers were prosecuted for attempting to extort large sums of money from him. Apparently, they had observed Hari Singh frolicking with British prostitutes whom they had supplied and then used to entrap him. *

---

* Hari Singh's sexual activities were no different than those of many of India's maharajahs. Wine, women, and song—indulgence in these pleasures characterized much of Indian royalty.

At the time of Independence, the rulers of the princely territories of India were given the choice of joining India or Pakistan. Pakistan's leaders cast covetous looks at Kashmir. The understanding was that states with heavily Muslim populations would associate themselves with the new Islamic nation of Pakistan, particularly if they were contiguous to it. Kashmir met both criteria. But Hari Singh dithered.* Local Muslims, led by the spectacularly popular Sheikh Mohammed Abdullah—widely known as Sher-E-Kashmir, or "the Lion of Kashmir"—did not seem especially thrilled with the idea of being part of Pakistan. Sheikh Abdullah, who had started a political party known as the National Conference, was a great secularist and was influenced in his beliefs by his close friend Jawaharlal Nehru.† Abdullah insisted that Hari Singh had no right to make any decision concerning the status of Kashmir—only the people could decide this, Abdullah said at rally after rally across the state, and not some degenerate feudal ruler.

The maharajah finally did accede his state to India. But only after Pakistani-sponsored tribesmen had launched an attack on Kashmir. Sheikh Abdullah and other Muslim leaders sought India's military help. Nehru, who had become prime minister of independent India, wanted to make sure that he could legally send his troops to counter the Pakistani-inspired attack on Kashmir.‡ He first wanted Hari Singh to agree to let Kashmir join India. Hari Singh, however, had packed up his jewels, Persian rugs, and paintings, gathered his family and his concubines, and fled to Jammu. He was traced there by Nehru's trusted aide V. P. Menon, who got the maharajah to sign a document of accession.§ Kashmir was now formally part of India. Accession to India was thus done under pressure, even though there was no opposition to it at the time from Kashmir's leading politicians, including Sheikh Abdullah. Nehru pledged that the accession would be validated by a popular referendum under international auspices, perhaps the United Nations.** Sheikh Abdullah

---

*On the eve of India's partition in August 1947, all except three princely states of British India—Kashmir, Hyderabad, and Junagadh—had chosen to join either India or Pakistan.

†There were rumors that Sheikh Abdullah was a bastard son of Motilal Nehru.

‡Nehru and Lord Louis Mountbatten finally ordered aircraft carrying the First Sikh Battalion into Kashmir.

§V. P. Menon was not related to Krishna Menon. He was an important civil servant who coordinated the integration of princely states into the Union of India in the late 1940s.

**The United Nations was the scene of several furious exchanges between the Indians and Pakistanis over Kashmir. Every United Nations attempt to arrange an internationally supervised plebiscite was rejected by India. Jawaharlal Nehru repeatedly

himself said: "Kashmir has linked itself to India, not because it has been lured by any material gain but because it is at one with her in the Gandhian ideals of justice, equality, and humanity. A progressive state could join hands only with another progressive one and not with a feudal state like Pakistan. Our decision to accede to India is based on the fact that our program and policy are akin to those followed by India. New Kashmir and Pakistan can never meet. Pakistan is a haven of exploiters. India is pledged to the principle of secular democracy in her policy and we are in pursuit of the same objective." The Lion of Kashmir became the state's chief executive.* But some of Nehru's key aides in Delhi whispered in his ears that the sheikh was secretly "soft" on Pakistan or that, worse, he wished to break away from India. The sheikh early on insisted that India should hold a referendum, as indeed Nehru had promised; there was little doubt in the years immediately after Independence that Kashmiris would have voted overwhelmingly to stay with India.

But Sheikh Abdullah and Jawaharlal Nehru had a falling out over the referendum issue—which Nehru aides saw as a code for Kashmiri secession from India—and over the next twenty years the sheikh spent more time inside Indian jails than outside them. No referendum was ever held in Kashmir. India and Pakistan were to go to war three times.[†] Countless debates were held at the United Nations over Kashmir. Pakistan continued holding on to a bite-sized bit of Kashmiri territory in the northwest of the state, and in the northeast China illegally held on to mountainous territory.[‡] Even though Sheikh Abdullah was incarcerated for a long time by the Indian government under the National Security Act, his supporters continued to agitate for a plebiscite.[§] Complicating this situation was the question of Pakistan's interference in Kashmir's internal affairs. Because Pakistan had joined John Foster Dulles's Western bloc "chain" of military alliances to contain Communism,

---

said that he would agree to such a referendum only after Pakistan first vacated the section of Kashmir it had "illegally occupied." Pakistan averred that it would do so only after Indian troops had left the larger portion of Kashmir that they controlled.

* Throughout his life, until his death on September 8, 1982, Sheikh Abdullah swore allegiance to India.

[†] In 1947, 1965, and 1971.

[‡] The Pakistani-held section of Kashmir, about one-third of the entire Kashmiri territory, was called Azad Kashmir, which means Free Kashmir. Access to Azad Kashmir was controlled by Pakistan.

[§] It was only on February 24, 1975, that Sheikh Abdullah and his associates agreed to disband their movement for a plebiscite.

it received massive military and economic aid from Washington.* This emboldened then–Pakistani dictator Field Marshal Mohammed Ayub Khan to become belligerent with India over Kashmir. Nehru had refused to consider any statewide plebiscite in Kashmir until, as he put it, Pakistan "totally vacated its aggression" from the part of Kashmir it had occupied since 1947.†

When Indira visited with ordinary Kashmiris this August of 1965, she found that the secessionist movement was being fueled by Pakistani propaganda. She knew that Ayub had massed large divisions on the border, and that Pakistan was obtaining military advice from both the United States and China. Indira visited with Indian security forces and boosted their morale. She traveled to the front, much to the nervousness of the generals. Indira also walked through Kashmiri neighborhoods where there was pro-Pakistan sentiment. She spoke about her own family's affection for Kashmir, and about the Nehrus' traditional ties to the region. Kashmir's future, Indira told crowds, lay with India. These public appearances softened the hostility that Kashmiris were increasingly showing toward the Indian government. In the event, Pakistan's reported plan to annex Kashmir through guerrilla infiltration did not succeed. When Indira returned to New Delhi, Shastri publicly praised her courage and skill at public relations.

Pakistan's Field Marshal Ayub, however, had military plans to take over Kashmir. UN observers reported that the number of cease-fire violations in Kashmir during the first half of 1965 had climbed beyond 2,000.‡ On August 14, Foreign Minister Zulfikar Ali Bhutto of Pakistan officially denied his country's involvement in the "uprising against tyranny" in Kashmir. He was, of course, referring to civilian unrest that was being encouraged by Pakistani infiltrators. On August 30, India sent troops across the cease-fire line at Uri to chase Pakistani raiders. On September 1, Pakistani army units crossed the cease-fire line near Chhamb. The Second Indo-Pakistan War was on. Field Marshal Ayub called the war Operation Grand Slam; the Sandhurst-trained Pathan personally directed Pakistan's military moves.

---

*Pakistan was a member of CENTO, the Central Treaty Organization; and of SEATO, the South East Asia Treaty Organization. Washington gave Pakistan an average of nearly $1 billion annually in aid.

†The Indians have argued that the state elections in Kashmir have served, in effect, as a sort of plebiscite.

‡UN peacekeeping teams had been in Kashmir since the Partition in 1947. Their presence is more symbolic than anything else, and they have not been able to control conflict on the borders. In fact, these teams are largely confined to reporting functions.

The war ended on September 23, when both countries accepted a cease-fire worked out by the United Nations. Indian troops had moved within three miles of one of Pakistan's biggest cities, Lahore. The Pakistani air force had performed creditably against the Indians. * Kashmir was still part of India. Prime Minister Shastri, who had long been the butt of Indian humor, overnight rose to heroic stature. In Pakistan, however, the 1965 war weakened Field Marshal Ayub, who was replaced in March 1969 by another military leader, General Aga Muhammad Yahya Khan.

As Shastri's fortunes rose, Indira felt increasingly sidelined. She was no longer being considered important or given attention by the prime minister, who increasingly relied on a handful of associates. Indira now contemplated resigning from the cabinet, and going off to London to join her two sons. Shastri was reportedly planning to appoint Indira as India's high commissioner to Great Britain.† With the end of the India-Pakistan War, Shastri finally came into his own. His impressive handling of the war gave him newfound confidence. With this great success, Lal Bahadur Shastri finally was able to shake off the shadow of his illustrious predecessor. Indira, by contrast, could only stew in frustration.

---

* A number of U.S. military officials later opined that the Pakistan air force acquitted itself better than its Indian counterpart.
† This is a full ambassadorial post. All ambassadorial posts to Commonwealth countries are called high commissioner.

12

Toward the Top

Although Indira Gandhi had politically come into her own in 1965, she was aware that her prospects for upward mobility in public life were hardly assured. India's "victory" in the 1965 war with Pakistan had been, militarily speaking, not especially impressive.[*] Still, Lal Bahadur Shastri had won new popularity, and Indians were beginning to see in him heretofore unsuspected qualities of strong leadership. This certainly meant that the Congress Party was not likely to turn to Indira Gandhi in the foreseeable future. Professor Stanley Wolpert writes: "For India, as for Pakistan, war—however brief—helped divert popular attention from growing internal conflicts and problems, uniting the nation as nothing but the nationalist movement had done before. India's negative position on a Kashmir plebiscite hardened as a result of her martial successes."[†] Relations between Indira and Shastri had never been entirely warm, and now she felt that the prime minister—notwithstanding his popularity—definitely viewed her as a potential rival.[‡]

In the wake of the cease-fire, there were many matters that needed to

---

[*] India's army, whose strength in Kashmir had risen to more than 150,000 men, seized Uri, which was just across the cease-fire line. (The total of troops at India's command more than 900,000 at the time, according to the International Institute for Strategic Studies in London.) More than 450 Pakistani tanks—mostly American-made ones—were reported destroyed. But India had taken just about 500 square miles of Pakistani territory, while Pakistan claimed 1,500 square miles of Indian real estate, including 340 square miles in Indian-held Kashmir.

[†] Wolpert, *A New History of India*, p. 375.

[‡] When Nehru was alive, Shastri treated Indira with great deference. After Nehru

275

be resolved between India and Pakistan, such as the return of prisoners of war. The Soviet Union stepped in as an interlocutor at this point. By late 1965, India had become a major military customer of the Soviet Union, with annual weapons purchases in the hundreds of millions of dollars. Premier Alexei Kosygin of the Soviet Union was intent on increasing Soviet influence in South Asia, and he saw himself as a peacemaker as well. So he invited Shastri and Ayub to Tashkent for a summit meeting. Shastri saw in this meeting a unique opportunity to bring about lasting peace to the Subcontinent. At the opening session of the summit, on January 4, 1966, Shastri said to Ayub: "Our objective at this meeting should be not recrimination over the past, but a new look towards the future. . . . Heavy responsibility lies on our shoulders. Instead of fighting each other, let us start fighting poverty, disease, and ignorance."* A week later, Shastri and Ayub had hammered out an agreement under which India and Pakistan agreed to withdraw their forces by February 25 to positions they held prior to August 5, 1965. With the normally phlegmatic Kosygin beaming proudly, the Tashkent Accord was signed on January 10 by the two leaders. It represented the most comprehensive agreement to date between India and Pakistan. It called for the restoration of trade and communications, and for new cultural exchanges. It also urged that disputes be settled "through peaceful means."

Lal Bahadur Shastri was pleased with his work in Tashkent, and he looked forward to his triumphant return home. But hours after signing the historic accord, he suffered a major heart attack and died. Indians were shocked. When Nehru had died, barely twenty months earlier, his colleagues—privately at least—suspected that his health was on the decline. But no one expected Shastri to die—least of all The Syndicate. Its powerful bosses had succeeded in deflecting Morarji Desai's ambition; they had played a major role in making Shastri prime minister, prompting Desai to charge that an undemocratic "caucus" had engaged in king-making. Now Morarji Desai felt that his day had at last come. He was confident that he would become India's third prime minister because he enjoyed considerable support within the Congress Party.† In what was widely seen as insensitive timing, Morarji Desai let it be publicly known

---

suffered his stroke in January 1964, it was Indira who persuaded her father to invite Shastri back into the cabinet. Durga Das, a distinguished editor and writer, says that after Shastri became prime minister, he even avoided seeing Indira. At one point, according to Das, Shastri told Indira that he felt "inferior" in her presence.
*Wolpert, *A New History of India*, p. 376.
†Technically, the party's parliamentary leader is chosen by the Congress Parliamentary Party (CPP), which consists of partymen elected to parliament.

within forty-eight hours of Shastri's death that he fully expected to be tapped for the dead man's job.

But the Syndicate's members did not relish the prospect of seeing Morarji Desai becoming India's next head of government. One of the party bosses, S. K. Patil of Bombay, even urged Kamaraj—who was party president—to take on the job. But Kamaraj declined, primarily because he was from Tamil-speaking Madras.* The Syndicate bosses were determined to stop Morarji Desai at all costs. They feared his independence, and rightly suspected that, once in power, he would eliminate their influence entirely. Morarji Desai had told associates about his concern over some of the bosses' profligate life-styles. For his part, Kamaraj expressed concern over how a post-Nehru and post-Shastri Congress might fare in the next general election, which was scheduled to be held in about thirteen months.† Morarji Desai had not bothered to build bridges with these party bosses, preferring instead to heap scorn and public ridicule on them. In politics, such insults are rarely forgiven or forgotten.

Indira Gandhi displayed remarkable restraint during this period. She had received word of Shastri's death at three o'clock on the morning of January 11. She summoned a few close political associates to map out a strategy. She cautioned them against aggressive or overt campaigning on her behalf. An open campaign, Indira said, would invite not only the wrath of Morarji Desai; it would also be seen as unseemly by the general public.‡ Indira also knew that in addition to Desai, there would be other contenders, including Gulzari Lal Nanda, the home minister, who was now acting prime minister for the second time in two years, and Yeshwantrao B. Chavan, the former chief minister of Maharashtra, who had been asked by Nehru to become defense minister after Krishna Menon's dismissal in the wake of the disastrous Sino-Indian War of 1962. Chavan, a canny politician, was discreet in his attempts to canvass support; but Nanda went all out and even pleaded with Indira to take herself out of contention.§ So low-key had Indira been in her "campaign" that media pundits had not even mentioned her prominently as a contender. But Nanda, Desai, and Chavan were certainly aware that behind Indira's apparent disinterest and decorousness was an ambition to get the top job.

---

*Patil had been backed by some party leaders but he, too, had many skeletons in his closet. He was a notorious womanizer, and also had reportedly accumulated great wealth in India and abroad. When he approached Kamaraj about the latter becoming prime minister, the Tamil-speaking leader said: "No English, no Hindi. How?"
†This election would be the first one after the death of Jawaharlal Nehru in 1964.
‡An excellent account of Indira's maneuvers is given by Bhatia in *Indira*.
§Neither man really stood a chance. Chavan had little appeal beyond his native Maharashtra; Nanda, a slightly comical figure, had no appeal anywhere.

Indira's plan was to act coy, to publicly deny that she was interested in becoming prime minister, and not to engage in active politicking.

It was Dwarka Prasad Mishra, the powerful chief minister of Madhya Pradesh, who formally suggested the name of Indira Gandhi for prime minister. Many suggest that Mishra acted in collusion with her.* Along with eight other chief ministers from states where the Congress was in power, Mishra issued a statement urging the election of Indira Gandhi. The chief ministers said that Indira would serve the interests of the country very well indeed—and the interests of the Congress Party would be best served by Indira Gandhi becoming India's prime minister. Kamaraj and the Syndicate bosses now lined up behind Indira. They were sure that they could keep tabs on her, and that she would be so grateful to them for having made her prime minister that she would faithfully follow all their directives.

The bosses asked Morarji Desai to withdraw from the race, but Desai refused. Jagjivan Ram, the veteran freedom-struggle warrior, had the support of fellow Harijan parliamentarians, and, to some Congress officials who liked neither Indira nor Morarji Desai, there appeared some possibility that he would emerge as a dark horse. Ram had earlier aligned his group behind Desai. But after the Syndicate offered him a senior cabinet post, he decided to throw in his lot with Indira.† Indira's crusty aunt, Mrs. Pandit, had supported Morarji Desai at first. But Indira went to see her, and Mrs. Pandit subsequently changed her mind. "It is a certainty that Mrs. Indira Gandhi will be India's next prime minister," Mrs. Pandit said after meeting with her niece. "We Nehrus are very proud of our family. When a Nehru is chosen as prime minister the people will rejoice. Mrs. Gandhi has the qualities. Now she needs experience. With a little experience she will make as fine a prime minister as we could wish for."‡

---

* There were reports at the time that Mishra recommended Indira at the suggestion of Kamaraj. It seemed that Kamaraj did not want to openly oppose Morarji Desai, and that getting Mishra to "sponsor" Indira was a way of putting up a trial balloon. Mishra was to become an Indira loyalist for many years until a falling-out with her. Mishra himself told friends that it was Indira who telephoned him at his residence in Bhopal—the capital of Madhya Pradesh—and urged him to come to Delhi and help her. That would have been in the hours immediately after Shastri's death. He complied. Later, Mishra and Indira rode together in a car to the airport to await the arrival of Shastri's body from Tashkent.

†Many years later, Jagjivan Ram would serve as defense minister in a Janata Party government headed by Morarji Desai.

‡The rapprochement between Vijaya Lakshmi Pandit and Indira Gandhi would not last long. Mrs. Pandit became a bitter political foe, and even supported Opposition parties against Indira.

And so it was that, on January 19, 1966, 526 members of Parliament belonging to the Congress Party gathered in the domed Central Hall of the circular, columned sandstone Parliament Building to elect their next leader.* It took them nearly four hours to cast their ballots. Outside, huge crowds waited in suspense. Finally, Satya Narain Sinha, the chief whip of the Congress Party, appeared outside the building. "It's a girl!" he shouted. There was thunderous applause.†

Indira Gandhi had won 355 votes to Morarji Desai's 169. Two ballots had been declared invalid.

When Indira appeared herself outside Parliament House, the crowds roared with delight. *"Indira Gandhi zindabad!"* they shouted. "Long live Indira Gandhi!" They also shouted: *"Lal gulaab zindabad!"* "Long live the red rose!"‡

Inder Malhotra, who was an eyewitness to much of the story on that extraordinary day when India got its first woman prime minister, has written vividly of his impressions. He stood in a corner of a veranda at One Safdarjung Road when Indira returned home after visiting President Radhakrishnan at Rashtrapati Bhavan, the old palace of British viceroys that was now the residence of India's head of state:

"Her fine, chiselled features bore just a trace of fatigue," Malhotra wrote.

> Her large, dark eyes wandered from one side to the other as she surveyed the exuberant scene. For the first time I realized the meaning of the expression "lonely in a crowd." For at the greatest moment of her life, surrounded by countless supporters and admirers, Indira seemed as lonely as she must have been during her childhood at Anand Bhavan.
>
> Both her sons were away in England. No other member of the family was around. Even her devoted personal staff and domestic retainers had merged with the happy, humming throng.

---

*The 526 Congress legislators were from both houses of Parliament, the Lok Sabha—the lower house—and the Rajya Sabha, the upper house.
†In all of India's recorded history, only one previous woman ruled a large area in her own right—Sultana Razia of the Muslim Slave Dynasty. In 1236, the founder of that dynasty, Shamsuddin Iltutmish, selected his daughter Razia to succeed him. Shamsuddin averred that Razia was a "better man" than his sons. She ruled well but was murdered three years later by her guards. A number of princely states in India, of course, had queens—like the courageous Rani of Jhansi, who participated in the Great Mutiny of 1857 and was killed in battle against the British. But between Sultana Razia and Indira Gandhi there had been no national female ruler.
‡Indira's father, Jawaharlal Nehru, always wore a red rose in his buttonhole. The

Somewhat helplessly and in a faint voice, she said: "Will someone, please, give me a glass of water?"[*]

In a letter that Indira wrote to Rajiv Gandhi three days later, she quoted from a poem by Robert Frost.[†] She told Rajiv that even as she was being acclaimed by the large Delhi crowds after her election as India's prime minister, these words kept swirling in her head:

> How hard it is to keep from being king
> When it is in you and in the situation.

They had wanted someone whom they could push around. They tried to think of someone who could oppose Morarji Desai yet be kept in check by them. Finally, they all agreed that Indira was such a person. For them, she was the perfect candidate. She possessed a pedigree; her family name was legendary; she cut an elegant figure; crowds responded well to her speeches; the fact that she was a woman went across well in a country where over 50 percent of the electorate was female; she was personally acquainted with many of the world's top leaders. She would be good for India's image, they thought. Indira's moment of glory had finally arrived, but only because of them. How wrong they were to be about her! In nominating her to be their handmaiden, they had signed their own pink slips as politicians of influence. They did not know it at the time, but from the hour that Indira Gandhi was elected prime minister, the Syndicate's days were numbered. Indira told friends such as Professor Ralph Buultjens that she was privately amused by the Syndicate's arrogance. Some party bosses referred to her as "Chokri"—the Hindustani word for little girl. She felt patronized by them, and Indira had resolved early on to trim their sails as soon as she was able to get a grip on her office, and on the Congress Party. Indira's conversations with close friends suggest that she skillfully went along with the Syndicate's wishes early on because she knew that only by pleasing them—or appearing to do so—could she have secured the backing of the Congress Party. But all along, Indira was scheming to get rid of these bosses partly because they would have restricted her freedom of

---

crowd was clearly hailing the coronation of another member of the Nehru political dynasty.
[*] Malhotra, *Indira Gandhi*, p. 89.
[†] Both Indira and Jawaharlal Nehru frequently read Robert Frost.

action, and partly because she considered them reactionary and ideo..
cally incompatible.

In assuming that Indira would be malleable, the Syndicate bosses
may have been guided by Indira's lackluster performance as minister
of information and broadcasting under Shastri. Her performance as a
parliamentarian had also been very poor. She had been tongue-tied, and
terrified of answering questions during legislative sessions. The party
bosses felt that Indira, the political novice, would be completely dependent on them for advice and assistance. What they underestimated was
that she was, after all, her father's daughter and had his spunk—and his
mass appeal—which sustained her during dark moments in those initial
months in power. The Syndicate did not appreciate fully that Indira was
popular not only with the liberals but also with the minorities such as
the Muslims and the Harijans. This meant that she could privately draw
on wide-ranging sources of counsel and support. At forty-eight, she was
ten years younger than her father had been when he became prime
minister in 1947, and her success was heartening to a new generation of
Indians who had matured in the first two decades after Independence.
"She was *our* kind of politician—cultivated, yet capable of reaching out
to the common people," said Shyam Benegal, one of India's leading film
directors. [*]

Indira Gandhi was sworn in as India's third prime minister on January
24, 1966. Two days later, on what is celebrated annually as India's
Republic Day, she delivered a radio address in which her speechwriters
seemed to have stitched together every cliché they could find. Mrs.
Gandhi pledged to continue her father's policies of secularism and socialism. She also promised administrative reforms. She thanked the United
States for its "sympathetic understanding and prompt help" in sending
grain to avert a famine. She praised the departed Lal Bahadur Shastri—a
little too effusively, given what her relationship with him merited. "My
own approach to the vast problems which confront us is one of humility,"
the new prime minister said in her broadcast. "The tradition left by
Gandhiji and my father, however, and my own unbounded faith in the
people of India, give me strength and confidence."[†] She would need
both.

While it was not generally considered to be an issue, the fact that
Indira Gandhi was India's first woman prime minister—and the second

---

[*]Conversation with the author, Bombay, September 1990.
[†]Broadcast to the nation by Prime Minister Indira Gandhi on All-India Radio,
January 26, 1966.

after Prime Minister Sirimavo Bandaranaike of Sri
l the media. * When Indira was asked at her first news
it felt to be a woman prime minister, she said: "I don't
a woman. I regard myself as a person with a job . . . I
ed nor nervous. This is just another job I have to do."

Mohan says that Indira's statement contained both an
inner truth and an oversimplification. "Her father had brought her up
just as he might have brought up his son had he lived," Professor Mohan
says. "The stigma of being a woman was never attached to her as it was
to thousands of middle-class women in India, and she grew up free from
that painful consciousness."[†]

In a conversation with Professor Mohan, Uma Shankar Dikshit, the
veteran Congress leader, told of the time when Indira discussed child-
bearing with him and two other men in a matter-of-fact manner.

> As we men listened dumbfounded, she explained to us all there is
> about childbirth, just as if it were one other natural function—like
> breathing or blowing your nose, for instance, which of course it might
> well be. As a man I wouldn't know. But that isn't how Indian women
> or even men regard it. . . . I have met hundreds of thousands of
> women in India—not all kinds of women but only the kind that was
> politically involved in the freedom movement. They claimed they
> were advanced and liberated and progressive. But I always detected
> in them some little complex or inhibition or squeamishness. Not so
> with Mrs. Gandhi. She talked freely and frankly on any subject. In
> fact, it is the men who would be embarrassed in her presence.[‡]

It was not a particularly good time to inherit Jawaharlal Nehru's mantle. The country had been through two debilitating wars, and two changes
in leadership, in four years. The annual rains—which Indians call monsoons—had failed for two successive years, and several areas of India
were faced with the specter of famine. Prices were shooting sky-high,

---

* Mrs. Bandaranaike and Indira Gandhi became good friends. They were dubbed
"Asia's socialist sisters." Uncharitable critics called them "wretched widows." Mrs.
Bandaranaike's husband, Solomon W. R. D. Bandaranaike, became prime minister
of Sri Lanka—then known as Ceylon—in 1956. He was assassinated in September
1959 by a Buddhist monk. Mrs. Bandaranaike, who succeeded him as leader of the
Sri Lanka Freedom Party (SLFP), became prime minister in 1960, and was prominent
in her country's politics for two decades.
[†] Mohan, *Indira Gandhi.*
[‡] *Ibid.*

and there was general economic hardship and discontentment. In the strategic northeast, Naga and Mizo tribes were rising up in arms in areas bordering China.* The Sikh demand for a Punjabi state along linguistic lines was growing more shrill. Leftist groups were agitating in West Bengal against food shortages. When she was merely a cabinet minister, Indira was only required to make recommendations to the prime minister; now she *was* the prime minister, and it was she who had to deal with the problems. She thought that she had received from her father an extraordinary education about prime-ministerial functioning. But it was one thing to be her father's daughter, and something entirely different to now occupy his seat.[†]

Indira Gandhi's debut as prime minister was somewhat less than brilliant. She seemed bewildered at first, groping in the dark for clues as to how to handle herself in office. Says Khwaja Ahmed Abbas, the well-known Indian writer: "Overwhelmed by the enormity and the profusion of the problems piling up on her desk, she set herself to do whatever little she could do, immediately. But she was neither a miracle-worker nor a dictator. She was the prime minister of a democracy run by a slow-thinking, slow-moving bureaucracy, and she felt hamstrung by the rules and the red tape of the Establishment. She could only make gestures, provide some earnest [expression] of her intentions, a token of action that must follow."[‡]

Meanwhile, the Congress parliamentarians who had voted for Morarji Desai became clamorous in their criticism. Some of her opponents believed that being a woman was her major handicap, and that the Indian masses would not accept her as a prime minister for too long. As it turned out, being a woman was not a handicap at all for Indira. Despite being a traditional and conservative people, Indians were accustomed to women taking a prominent role in national affairs since the days of the freedom struggle. India had women as parliamentarians, ambassadors, judges, lawyers, journalists, and diplomats. Professor Anand Mohan notes that Indian women did not have to fight for voting rights—it was assumed without question that they had the same rights as men when India became

---

* The Indian Army had exchanged fire with the Naga tribesmen.

[†] Echoing the sentiments of many Indians, the *Economic and Political Weekly* said: "A woman ruler is under a social handicap until she has been able to consolidate her position. In the beginning, every group leader wants to advise and control her, and so faction fights start among them. Either the ruler is able to satisfy everyone that she is not close to anyone in particular, as Queen Elizabeth I did, and enjoy a long tenure of office; or fails to survive the initial period of uncertainty. . . ."

[‡] K. A. Abbas, *That Woman* (Delhi: Indian Book Co., 1973).

independent. One political analyst also said that Indira was the "only man in a cabinet of women." Still, some Congress men and Opposition members continued to ridicule her. One of her most consistent critics was the Socialist leader, Ram Manohar Lohia. He seemed unable to accept the idea that India was being led by a woman. In one typical speech, for example, Lohia urged that Indira be defeated in the next election so that "this pretty woman does not have to suffer pain and trouble beyond her endurance." Lohia recognized, of course, that elections were still some time away. "We will have a pretty face for a time and she will be burdened with the weight of her father's and Mr. Shastri's misdeeds. To that we can safely add the burdens of her own misdeeds."

In the face of such hostility, Indira decided to spend some time out of Delhi and see for herself what was happening around India. She wanted to become a hands-on manager, she told her associates, and what better way than to go to the grass roots where the people were? She went first to the southern city of Trivandrum, capital of Kerala State. Instead of a warm welcome, however, Indira got a fiery reception from E. M. S. Namboodiripad's supporters; the Communists had not forgotten how, as Congress president some years earlier, she had destabilized their government. Prime Minister Indira Gandhi told Keralites that this time she had not come to their state as an antagonist. Kerala was experiencing an acute rice shortage; cultural habits being what they were in India, Keralites were refusing to switch to other food grains. Indira made public appeals to neighboring states such as Andhra Pradesh to release food stocks. In one speech before a crowd of more than 300,000 people, Indira pledged not to consume rice until the Kerala crisis was resolved.* A similar rice shortage had afflicted West Bengal, and Indira went there, too, to meet with leftist leaders who had led popular demonstrations for more food supplies.

Not long after her forays into Kerala and West Bengal, Indira attended her first session, as India's prime minister, of the All India Congress Committee. The party convention was held in Jaipur, a charming old city of forts and palaces and teeming bazaars situated in the western desert state of Rajasthan. Having served as party president in the 1950s, Indira

---

* The rice crisis was a largely artificial one. It resulted from the fact that, in order to ensure that food grains were distributed equitably, India had been divided since Independence into "food zones." Each zone had states with food surplus and a couple of states with chronic shortages. The government permitted food grains to be transported within each zone, but not from one zone to another. The idea was to prevent hoarding and price gouging—although this system had the reverse effect, for the most part.

was hardly unfamiliar with these party meetings, but in Jaipur she acted like a rank neophyte. She stumbled her way through several speeches and projected the image of a leader who was both nervous and distracted. She barely succeeded in getting the Tashkent Accord endorsed.* Indira also could not handle the food grain issue: she had earlier supported a move to scrap the food zones, but found herself befuddled during the debate on the question. Finally, she promised to review the government's entire food policy.

Indira's performance in Parliament during those early months as prime minister was equally dismal. She was not very articulate, and unable to think on her feet. The Opposition heckled her, and Indira seemed terribly flustered. Ram Manohar Lohia, the shrewd Socialist parliamentarian and longtime Nehru-baiter, nicknamed her "Goongi Gudiya," or "the Dumb Doll." This epithet was to stick for several years. Indira came to loathe proceedings in Parliament; she thought that Indian legislators—including some from her own party—were not capable of maintaining decorum and civility.† She started to skip sessions. Perhaps it was the memory of these early humiliations that made Indira so skeptical of Parliament in later years, even when she became—like her father—an accomplished debater. She once called Parliament a "zoo." On another occasion, she referred to legislators as "clowns in a circus." Judging from the abysmal caliber of men and women that Indians elect as their representatives, it is not hard to understand why Indira would feel so discouraged by what went on in Parliament. Rahul Singh, the distinguished Indian editor and columnist, says that Indira's uncertainty and lackluster performance during these early months as prime minister were attributable to the fact that she had no family anchor. "When Indira was Congress president in the 1950s, her performance was quite assertive," Singh says. "Her father was alive then, and she drew strength from that fact. Now there was no one she could turn to for guidance."

And as if her tentativeness were not enough, Indira also seemed to make a mess over the formation of her cabinet. She tried to remove Gulzari Lal Nanda from the Home Ministry; Indira felt that Nanda, a well-meaning but somewhat comical man, had undermined his public credibility by associating too closely with astrologers and holy men. She was also still pouting over the fact that he had tried to talk her into

---

* As could be expected, opponents of the accord felt that India was giving away hard-won gains from the Indo-Pakistan War.
† One parliamentarian who relished taking potshots at Indira was a man called Raj Narain. His remarks were sometimes so vulgar that he was chided by the Speaker.

yielding to his claims for the prime minister's post. Neither did Indira wish to award Jagjivan Ram with a high cabinet position, as the Syndicate had wanted. She was privately disturbed by persistent whispers concerning corruption close to the Harijan leader. But both Nanda and Ram complained bitterly to Kamaraj that the new prime minister was being imperious, and Indira was subsequently forced to give them cabinet posts.

Gulzari Lal Nanda was dismissed on November 8, 1966. What precipitated his dismissal was a nationwide agitation by Hindu conservatives for a total ban on cow slaughter. These conservatives organized a huge procession featuring fakirs and swamis who descended on Parliament and caused much pandemonium. The Hindus had thought that Nanda, who was then home minister, would be sympathetic to their cause because he was generally enamored of mystics. Many of these protesters were killed in a clash with the police outside Parliament House. Indira asked for Nanda's resignation. She told him that in her view, his association with swamis had "hampered" him in carrying out his duties. Nanda's dismissal did not endear Indira to the Syndicate, which by now was becoming concerned about the prime minister's occasional assertiveness. Indira's back-pedaling created the impression of a vacillating leader at a time that Indians were looking for greater firmness. Moreover, Indira also sustained the impression that the Syndicate was calling the shots.

Indira now started to rely on a group of advisers who had gathered around her during the Shastri era. The media quickly gave her group a name: the "Kitchen Cabinet." One of its prominent members was Dinesh Singh, scion of minor royalty and member of a zamindar, or landowning, family that had been close to the Nehrus. As was perhaps inevitable, the handsome Singh was soon romantically linked with Indira. Singh did not discourage such speculation, nor did he discourage talk that he was indispensable to Indira.* The "Kitchen Cabinet" had no fixed membership; Indira's inner circle expanded and contracted with her moods and needs. But the early—and most conspicuous—members of this informal group included Dwarka Prasad Mishra; Uma Shankar Dikshit; Inder Gujral, a scholarly politician; Asoka Mehta, a sour-faced socialist who became a kind of in-house economic guru to Indira; and Nandini Sat-

---

* Dinesh Singh rose to become foreign minister under Indira in 1969, but then was unceremoniously dropped by her. This was a familiar pattern of behavior for Indira: People who got too big for their breeches would be taught a lesson or two. She never liked people to publicly flaunt their good standing with her.

pathi, a parliamentarian from Orissa. These men and women served not only as advisers to Indira, but also as her eyes and ears in the political arenas of India. The group's members were ideologically diverse—from the socialist Mehta and Satpathi to the right-wing Mishra.* At this juncture, Indira did not see herself as doctrinaire, preferring instead to call herself a pragmatist. But in a revealing conversation with some editors, she said that she believed in socialism, "but not in a dogmatic way." Indira added: "I believe in the people's right to a better life—not only materially but also mentally and spiritually. I have been lucky to have had a rich life of the mind, and it hurts me to see people steeped in such poverty that they are rendered incapable of appreciating culture and the arts. I would like conditions to be created where all the people would be able to enjoy and appreciate these finer values of life."[†]

Many of those who had hoped that Indira would be a breath of fresh air in the stodgy environment of Indian politics were sorely disappointed by her early performance. First there was her inability to stand up to the Syndicate over the cabinet formation issue. Then it was her inability to lift the restrictions on food-grain movement. And finally, Indira disillusioned many backers when she would not lift the "Emergency" that had been imposed during the war with China in 1962.[‡] The Opposition—as well as liberal members of the Congress Party—were trying to get Indira to lift the Emergency now that the situation was stable. The chief ministers of various states, however, were reluctant to part with the sweeping powers that they had acquired during Emergency. Indira herself was reluctant to do away with it: Why should any politician cede away her power? Some civil libertarians saw in her reluctance early signs of the fondness for authoritarianism that Indira would exhibit later in her career.[§]

Indira realized that although she had reached the apex of India's political structure, the situation on the ground was far from sanguine. Much of central India was already in the grip of a severe famine. The population had surged beyond 475 million, and India's GNP was barely $31.4 bil-

* The pretty Nandini Satpathi was once a card-carrying member of the Communist Party. The fringe press in India had a field day with her, frequently running suggestive stories about her private life.

[†] Drieberg, *Indira Gandhi*, p. 71.

[‡] Technically, all civil liberties were suspended under the Emergency. The measure also gave the government draconian powers of arrest without trial.

[§] In 1975 Indira would impose another Emergency, suspending the constitution, in the face of growing political unrest. The Emergency would last two years, until her defeat in the 1977 election.

lion.* The 1966 harvest was expected to fall to 76 million tons—12 million tons lower than the previous year.† Indira's first budget, which had to be submitted to Parliament within a few months of her ascendancy to the prime ministership, would reflect the shrinking of resources for domestic development. Aid from the United States had been suspended during the Indo-Pakistan War of 1965, and Indira knew that in order to jump-start the economy, India would need fresh infusions of economic assistance from the rich donor countries. India was seeking 12 million tons of wheat and $435 million in loans and credits from the United States. India also needed loans and credits from multilateral organizations but was encountering resistance from agencies such as the International Monetary Fund (IMF) and the World Bank. These agencies were in a position to bail out India by offering short-term loans. But, under pressure from the United States—which influenced them heavily—they were laying down stiff conditions before agreeing to restore aid.

The most significant of these conditions was a substantial devaluation of the Indian rupee. The rupee's value, which the IMF felt did not adequately reflect its weakness, was 4.76 to the U.S. dollar. In June 1966, Mrs. Gandhi devalued the rupee to 7.50 to the U.S. dollar.‡ She insisted that devaluation was necessary to increase India's exports in order to earn more foreign exchange. (Devaluation of a nation's currency typically makes it cheaper for foreign buyers to purchase its goods; it also makes imports more expensive for that nation.) As could be expected, Indira's critics pounced on her for devaluating the currency. They accused her of "capitulation to American pressure." Professor Stanley Wolpert notes that all Opposition parties also interpreted the devaluation as an official confession of the failure of Indian economic planning. Almost since Independence, India's economic goals were spelled out in five-year plans.

With India in dire economic straits, Indira decided to visit the United States, which, she felt, was the only country that could quickly come to the rescue.§ Indira had been flattered to hear that Vice President Hubert Humphrey, after a brief visit to India, had publicly praised Indira as "quite a politician—in fact, a politician of great magnitude."** Indira

---

*Government of India statistics.
†Wolpert, *A New History of India*.
‡In July 1991, the Indian government devalued the rupee twice, for a total of nearly 20 percent. The exchange rate then was about thirty to the dollar.
§Even though the Soviets had become major military suppliers to India, Moscow was not in a position to give the sort of hard-currency assistance that India required.
**Quotation provided by staff of Mr. Humphrey in 1978 to author.

knew that this trip—coming as it did just ten weeks after she had become prime minister—must be handled delicately. The previous year, Prime Minister Shastri had been scheduled to visit Washington. But President Lyndon Johnson had rescinded his invitation to Shastri because India had criticized the American bombing of North Vietnam.* Now Johnson reissued the invitation, and Indira saw in it a timely opportunity to make a pitch for financial aid and for grain. Publicly, of course, Indira insisted that this was only a goodwill visit.

On the way to Washington, Indira had wanted to stop off in London —but decided against it—to indicate her displeasure over British Prime Minister Harold Wilson's pro-Pakistan tilt during the Indo-Pakistan War in 1965. She summoned her sons, Rajiv and Sanjay, to Paris. There they met with Charles de Gaulle, with whom Indira had several long conversations in fluent French.† Indira then flew to Washington, where she received a grand welcome from Lyndon Johnson. Johnson, in the words of Krishan Bhatia, "overwhelmed Indira with his display of courtesy and warmth toward her and his consideration for India.‡ Janki Ganju, India's lobbyist in Washington, recalls that after one working session with Indira and the Indian delegation at the White House, President Johnson walked her to Blair House, where she was staying. It was an unscheduled walk and the traffic on Pennsylvania Avenue was thrown into confusion.

Ganju was also witness to another spontaneous episode that highlighted how much Lyndon Johnson had been charmed by Indira Gandhi.

B. K. Nehru, India's ambassador in Washington, had arranged for a formal dinner at his residence. Prime Minister Gandhi and Vice President Humphrey were the guests of honor. As the predinner cocktail hour unfolded, there was a sudden flurry of activity at the door. Robert S. McNamara, who was then Secretary of Defense, nudged Ambassador Nehru's wife and whispered into her ear: "Foree—the President is here!" Mrs. Nehru—who was generally known by her nickname, Foree, rather than her real first name, Shobha—was stunned by the unexpected arrival. There was Lyndon Baines Johnson, larger than life, striding through the

---

* Washington was always sensitive to India's stance on international issues because of the influence New Delhi wielded in the Nonaligned Movement.

† Indira's French had always been very good, dating back to her school days in Switzerland. De Gaulle later told aides that of all the foreign leaders he had met, Mrs. Gandhi impressed him the most with her fluency in French and with her knowledge of world affairs. This was quite a compliment from a man who was not in the habit of giving out many.

‡ Krishan Bhatia was then writing for *The Hindustan Times*.

Nehrus' door, uninvited, unannounced—and in defiance of all established protocol.

"Mr. President, I hope you will stay for dinner," Mrs. Nehru later said to Johnson.

"My dear lady, what do you think I have come here for?" Johnson said.

"Ah, I knew it!" exclaimed Vice President Humphrey. "My President will never allow me to sit next to two pretty ladies!"

Mrs. Nehru scurried about trying to redo the seating arrangements. But there was no extra chair available for the extra place. What does one do when the President of the United States invites himself for dinner? The ambassador's predicament was solved by P. N. Haksar, who was then India's Deputy High Commissioner to Britain and who was part of Indira's entourage.* Haksar offered to skip the dinner, thereby making certain that President Johnson got to dine with the Prime Minister of India. At that dinner, Johnson announced—much to the surprise of the guests—that he would see that "no harm comes to this girl." In an expansive toast, the President told Indira that her country should expect "everlasting friendship and understanding" from the United States. Johnson later told Chester Bowles, who was serving his second stint as U.S. ambassador to India, that he found Indira "politically astute."

"The visit was a smashing success," recalled Krishan Bhatia.

> In welcoming her at the White House, he called her "a good and gracious friend." Knowing her deep attachment to her late father, Johnson praised him extravagantly and added that Americans liked to think that Nehru "belonged to us, too." Guests at the White House dinner for the Prime Minister were struck by the animation the two leaders showed. Mrs. Gandhi, radiant in purple silk heavily embroidered in gold, her dark hair with its dramatic white streak smartly coiffed, smiled up at an attentive President Johnson as he took her on his arm and beamed down at her. It was clear that the two were pleased with the occasion and with one another.[†]

Gone was the tongue-tied and hesitant Indira of the early days of her prime ministership. Here was a self-confident leader who was able to hold

---

* Haksar was later appointed by Indira Gandhi to head the prime minister's Secretariat in New Delhi. It was a powerful job, and Haksar became one of the most influential bureaucrats of his time. The appointment of Haksar—whose leftist tendencies had been acquired during his student days in Britain in the 1930s—pleased the left wing of the Congress Party. The left wing had been distressed by Mrs. Gandhi's original chief of the Secretariat, L. K. Jha, who was considered a rightist.

[†] Bhatia, *Indira*, p. 192.

her own with the head of state of the world's most powerful nation. Inc. Gandhi received fulsome praise from many top American newspapers anu news magazines. Indira did a "million-dollar public relations job," said one paper. Another publication said that "Indira Gandhi intended to remain . . . a moderate-minded, un-doctrinaire leader of India—not in our pocket, of course, but also not at our national throat."

Lyndon Johnson promised Indira Gandhi 3.5 million tons of grain and $900 million in project aid. Part of Johnson's response to Indira Gandhi was due to his warm Texan nature.* But he was also pleased because he had succeeded in getting from the prime minister what Washington had long wanted from India: Indira agreed to the establishment of an Indo-American Education Foundation, which would channel money into research, among other things. Both Jawaharlal Nehru and Lal Bahadur Shastri had rejected this proposal; they felt that such a "foundation" would give the Americans an undue influence on higher education and research in India. The U.S. plan was to use the rupees that had accumulated in India through the importing of American wheat under Public Law 480, for which payment was made in local currency.† The equivalent of hundreds of millions of dollars had been earned by Washington in Indian rupees; the United States had hoped to use this money for funding the new foundation. When Indira agreed to the creation of this new foundation, she could not have anticipated the furor that the news triggered back in India. Even educators who were not left-leaning opined that it was a bad idea—that because of the vast amounts that the Americans planned to spend, they would have enormous control over India's educational system.‡ The leftists saw in her acquiescence to Johnson a disturbing departure from nonalignment. Critics, engaging in typical Indian hyperbole, said that Indira had "sold out" to Western pressures. Krishna Menon—ever the opportunistic leftist—bitterly denounced the Indo-American Education Foundation as "an intrusion into the cultural and intellectual life of the Indian people."§ The proposal was later shelved.**

Time magazine said that "Johnson found her a fiercely independent ruler with a determination equal to his own."

†Under the terms of the Indo-American understanding over PL-480 imports, the revenues would not be repatriated. The Indian rupee was then—and still is—a nonconvertible currency.

‡The new foundation was reported to have an endowment of $300 million.

§Indira Gandhi would later accuse Krishna Menon of "rank misrepresentation and distortion of facts."

**This disappointed Lyndon Johnson, who, at one point, said he wished he could personally scold "these ungrateful Indians."

ed in this visit to a country that she had not especially
only had Lyndon Johnson showered her with attention
fts—the aid to India, plus a government yacht once used
an.[†] It felt good to be away from the clangor and confusion
acclaimed by audiences who displayed great goodwill
to receive overwhelmingly positive media coverage. She
met with leading members of the media, and with top businessmen,
emphasizing that—despite its large-scale poverty—India was on the
move. She pointed out that in 1965, 2 million kilowatt-hours of power
had been added to the national grid through expanded hydroelectric
projects; that new high-yield seeds were being tested in several regions
of India; and that nearly 70 million Indian children now attended school.
There was unprecedented economic and social transformation in the
country, Indira said. She spoke with eloquence and passion, surprising
even some of her closest aides with her clear and crisp presentations.

She told the National Press Club in Washington: "India, like the
United States, is wedded to the democratic ideal. . . . Today democracy
inescapably implies social welfare, equality of opportunity, reasonable
living standards, and dignity of individual. Man does not live by bread
alone. But equally, he needs bread to enjoy liberty."[‡] She very nearly
canceled her speech when she learned that the National Press Club did
not have a single female member, according to Janki Ganju. On March
30, Indira met a number of leading bankers, financiers, and industrialists
in New York City. "The aid which we have received hitherto has been
on a generous scale in absolute terms. But relative to other countries, it
has been somewhere at the end of the list on a per capita basis."[§] She
urged capitalists of the West to "open up your markets" much more than
they had been prepared to do. "In the last century, you tamed the Wild
West," Indira Gandhi said. "My appeal to you today is that in the next
few decades you should allow yourselves to be tamed by the developing

---

[*] However much Indira enjoyed herself, she was aware that as a female prime minister
she had to maintain a certain decorum. When Lyndon Johnson asked her to dance
with him during the White House banquet, she smilingly declined at first. "My
countrymen would not approve if they heard I had been dancing," Indira said. But
Janki Ganju swears that, at one point during the evening, Lyndon Johnson asked
her again for a dance—and Indira quietly and surreptitiously obliged.

[†] The yacht was converted by India into a vessel for oceanic research.

[‡] Jawaharlal Nehru, Indira Gandhi, and Rajiv Gandhi were frequently invited to
address the National Press Club and enjoyed the opportunity.

[§] Ironically, India's neighbor, tiny Sri Lanka, received more aid per capita than any
other country in Asia.

East." They were extraordinarily prescient words: the "Four Tigers" of Asia—Singapore, Taiwan, South Korea, and Hong Kong—and, of course, Japan, would make huge inroads in the U.S. market over the next twenty years. These inroads spawned protectionist sentiments in the American Congress—something that Indira, however indirectly, seemed to be anticipating and alluding to in her speech on that fine spring day in New York.

But perhaps her most significant political speech of the trip was given the next day at a banquet, also in New York, before an audience of more than a thousand Indian expatriates and others. In that audience also sat Secretary-General U Thant of the United Nations.* In the speech, Indira spelled out the basic tenets of India's foreign policy, saying that democratic and progressive countries such as India needed to be supported by other free nations. She asked the United States not to be "irritated by misunderstandings or diverted by difficulties." Then, obviously with the United Nations secretary-general in mind, Indira spelled out India's current position regarding the intractable Kashmir issue:

> Indo-Pakistani relations all too often are equated with Kashmir. Now Kashmir is not the cause but rather a consequence of Indo-Pakistani differences. There was no Kashmir problem on August 15, 1947, when India and Pakistan became independent. The problem, as it is called, arose some months later with the invasion of the state of Jammu and Kashmir by Pakistan. This is the United Nations finding and the basic fact. India agreed to, and indeed suggested, a plebiscite at the time, but on condition that the state was first cleared of the invader and peace returned. The United Nations endorsed this condition. Since this basic condition was never fulfilled by Pakistan, there could be no question of a plebiscite, which was categorically defined as the very last stage of a clearly defined sequence of events.
>
> It is now too late to talk of a plebiscite. The second invasion of Kashmir by Pakistan last autumn [September 1965] has destroyed whatever marginal or academic value the old United Nations resolutions might have had. Kashmir is also vital now to the defense of India in Ladakh against China. Any plebiscite now would definitely amount to questioning the integrity of India. It would raise the issue of secession—an issue on which the United States fought a civil war not so very long ago. We cannot and will not tolerate a second

---

*U Thant was from Burma. He was the first Asian secretary-general of the United Nations.

partition of India on religious grounds. It would destroy the very basis of the Indian state.*

Finally, in that speech, Indira Gandhi dealt with the question of China's expansionist policies. "China is taking great care to avoid direct military involvement in Vietnam," she said. "But China's shadow does fall across Southeast Asia. The real threat from China is, however, less military than political. But Chinese influence will be diminished if its neighbors in Asia and nations of the developing world can build around popular and forward-looking nationalist governments dedicated to fulfilling the aspirations of their people. They would also be greatly strengthened in this purpose were they to see a strong and viable alternative model to Beijing." That model, of course, was democratic India.

Indira was mindful that India had criticized the American involvement in Vietnam; such criticism had even become a major irritant in Indo-American relations. On this visit, however, not a word of such criticism came from her. Had she expressed publicly her thoughts about the Vietnam question, it was unlikely that Lyndon Johnson would have felt as openly warm about the Indian prime minister.† India needed American aid, and Indira was quite prepared to put national interest before anything else at this particular time.‡ Indeed, Indira even told President Johnson that "India understood America's agony over Vietnam." Many Indians were horrified at this statement. Even Gamal Abdel Nasser of Egypt and Marshal Tito of Yugoslavia expressed shock.§ Her polite reference to Vietnam would have surely enraged Jawaharlal Nehru, with whom Indira had traveled not long before this visit to meet President Kennedy.**

On her way back to India, Indira Gandhi stopped over in Moscow to meet Prime Minister Alexei Kosygin. He assured her that—notwith-

---

*Indira Gandhi's remarkable references to Kashmir still stand as a definitive expression of Indian policy.

†Indira felt that the U.S. presence in Vietnam was wrong. She associated Western intrusion in Asia with neocolonialism. Johnson's war was becoming increasingly unpopular in the United States and would later result in his declining to run for a second term in 1968.

‡Indira later told her critics that acceptance of foreign aid did not mean "acceptance of foreign domination." She added: "Even Lenin had taken American aid after the Russian revolution."

§Nasser and Tito, of course, could be expected to criticize the United States in a knee-jerk fashion. Neither man was especially liked in Washington as a result.

**As Kennedy's Vice President, Johnson had visited India. He embarrassed diplomats when, while touring the Taj Mahal in Agra, he emitted an old-fashioned Texas yell to test the Mughal mausoleum's echo chamber.

standing the thaw in relations between Washington and New Delhi—
there would be no change in Russia's policy of friendship with India.
Then they got down to discussing the Vietnam War. The Soviets, of
course, had played a two-faced game all along: They railed against U.S.
involvement in South Vietnam, yet Moscow supplied weapons to the
Communist regime of North Vietnam. Kosygin told Indira that there
had been concern in the Kremlin about her dealings with Lyndon Johnson. The Soviets, Kosygin said, felt that she spoke to Johnson about
Vietnam not in critical tones—as might be expected of a prime minister
of India—but in language that seemed to suggest softening of the long-
standing Indian disapproval of the American presence in Southeast Asia.
The United States, said Kosygin, simply had to withdraw from Vietnam. *

"How can you expect the Americans to pull out of Vietnam until they
can find a way to save face?" Indira said.

"How many Asian lives will be lost while the Americans are thinking
up a way to save face?" Kosygin replied.

Things did not go well for Indira after she returned to India. The devaluation of the rupee—which pleased India's creditors at the IMF and the
World Bank—proved highly unpopular.† Even Kamaraj, the Syndicate
boss, criticized her—although his pique seemed to be more over the fact
that Indira had not fully consulted him before devaluing the currency by
57 percent.‡ Morarji Desai also condemned the move. In an address that
was broadcast to the nation on June 10, Indira denied that the rupee had
been devalued under foreign pressure.§ She asked Indians to tighten

---

* American forces left Vietnam in 1975. The North Vietnamese swept into the
South and unified the two Vietnams.

† Of course, devaluation is rarely popular. The IMF has been widely accused in the
Third World of recommending drastic steps such as devaluation and suspension of
food subsidies without concern for the social and political consequences. Riots and
coups have occurred in the wake of governments instituting draconian measures
suggested by the IMF in the interest of economic reform.

‡ So furious was Kamaraj that he engineered the unprecedented approval of a resolution by the Congress Working Committee condemning the devaluation. Kamaraj
also flew off to Moscow to assure the Soviets that, notwithstanding Indira's warm
contacts with Lyndon Johnson, India was not about to abandon its traditional
nonalignment. Kamaraj was reported in those days to be quite willing to entertain
the deposing of Indira. He would have surely done so had it not been for the fact
that the general elections were to be held early in 1967.

§ Indira soon became convinced that she had been misled by her advisers about
devaluation. The measure did not obtain the intended results. This made her increas-

their belts. * Adding to Indira's problems was the fact that the Johnson administration was inexplicably dragging its feet over dispatching the promised grain.[†]

Gravely disappointed in Johnson, Indira became publicly critical of U.S. policies in Southeast Asia. In July 1966, Indira broke her long silence over Vietnam. She condemned the American decision to bomb Hanoi, the capital of North Vietnam, and Haiphong, its largest port. She also withdrew her support of the Indo-American Education Foundation. Indira then appealed to Britain and the Soviet Union to reconvene the Geneva Conference of 1954 in order to assess the impact of the American bombing of Vietnam.[‡] "It is necessary to secure the withdrawal of all foreign forces from Vietnam and to insulate that unhappy country from every foreign interference—so that the people of Vietnam determine their own future free of external pressures," Indira said.

She floated a seven-point proposal for ending the Vietnam War. This proposal—which was immediately condemned by Washington—called for a cease-fire. India, as chairman of the International Commission for Supervision and Control, would safeguard "standstill arrangements" after the cease-fire.[§] Indira's plan called for a major international effort to rehabilitate and develop the three war-ravaged states of Indochina —Vietnam, Laos, and Cambodia. Indira had consulted Krishna Menon before drafting her Vietnam plan, and Menon—delighted to be given an opportunity to wriggle back in favor—contributed some strong anti-American language to the prime minister's proposal. Peace, Indira said,

---

ingly suspicious of accepting advice too easily—and also wary of the motives of those who offered counsel.

* One cartoonist depicted Indira making a speech about belt-tightening to a large audience, and someone in the crowd yelling back: "Send us the belts first!"

[†] Ambassador Chester Bowles was instructed by Washington to tell Indira's government to streamline its agriculture program. But Bowles refused to convey the message to the agriculture minister on the grounds that Washington's language was "extraordinarily insensitive."

[‡] The Geneva Conference of 1954 resulted in a peace settlement in Indochina after the defeat of the French forces by the Vietnamese at Dien Bien Phu.

[§] The other members of the International Commission for Supervision and Control were Canada and Poland. The commission had been created as part of the Geneva Agreements of 1954 to monitor observance of the accords by all parties. India, a neutral power, was supposed to be the referee; Poland, a Communist state, would be balanced by Canada, a democracy. By 1963, however, the commission had long ceased to perform any useful function, according to Neil Sheehan, the Pulitzer Prize–winning author and journalist. But the commission continued to maintain offices in Hanoi and Saigon, and its staff members enjoyed diplomatic privileges in both cities.

was the "special responsibility of nonaligned countries." She pledged to work with Nasser and Tito to find a "just solution" to the "bitter and bloody" war—a solution that would satisfy "the legitimate rights and hopes of the people of Vietnam.""

Indira Gandhi made another trip to the Soviet Union in 1966, during which she signed a joint communiqué that labeled the U.S. action in Vietnam "imperialist aggression." Indira also publicly urged the United States to stop its bombing of North Vietnam.[†] Washington was quick to react. Lyndon Johnson sharply reduced the flow of aid into India, thus confirming Indira's belief that the United States only provided aid with strings attached. Never again would Indira warm up to the United States.[‡] This visit also offered Indira an opportunity to strengthen ties with Moscow at a time when India was worried about the Soviet desire to improve relations with Pakistan.

Indira went to Moscow because it was expedient for her to do so. The widespread notion in the United States—and throughout the West—in the Cold War years that India was a "client" state of the Soviet Union was fundamentally wrong. It missed the reality of India's geopolitical interests, its colonial history, its place in the Third World after independence, and the influence of socialism on India's founding fathers who guided successive Indian governments. They designed a foreign policy of nonalignment that was tilted toward the Soviet Union. Even in Cold War years India and the Soviet Union were as dissimilar in their economic and political systems as were perhaps Britain and the Soviet Union, or Sweden and the Soviet Union. Unlike the Soviet Union, India has always had a basically capitalist—that is, market—economy, a free press, and an elective, multiparty democracy. Indeed, barring the pro-Soviet Communist Party, no other party—not even the Congress, which as the ruling party was mainly responsible for building close ties with Moscow—ever showed any great predilection for the Soviet model of political and economic development. Indeed, on occasions Indira Gandhi publicly chided Indian Communists for blindly praising the Soviet Union without examining the pitfalls of its system.

It is true that in the early years of his rule Jawaharlal Nehru spoke

---

[*] Wolpert, *A New History of India*, p. 379.

[†] Ambassador Chester Bowles told a White House official that Indira Gandhi was hardly alone in calling for a halt to such bombing. The pope and UN Secretary-General U Thant had also urged such a step. To which the White House official said to Bowles: "Yes, but the pope and U Thant don't need our wheat."

[‡] Indira Gandhi continued her criticism of Washington over Vietnam. She even sent Ho Chi Minh an effusive telegram on his seventy-seventh birthday in 1967.

highly of Soviet economic planning—but never to the extent of advocating the dismantling of private enterprise. His writings and speeches were replete with denunciations of dogmatism in Communist thinking and practice.* India supported the Soviet Union because it was in turn supported by the Soviet Union in international, regional, and bilateral matters. There are well-known examples of such support: the Kashmir issue; the Bangladesh war in 1971; the Indo-Soviet Treaty for Security and Cooperation signed in 1971; and the rupee trade between the two countries.† Indira knew that Moscow's political backing was always essential to India to counter Washington's long-standing support of Pakistan. Besides, as she found out from her experience with Lyndon Johnson, the Americans were capable of dealing quite firmly with Third World states—even countries as demographically big and geopolitically important as India. In those days, the Soviets were far more astute in their relationships with the emerging nations of the developing world.

The balancing of India's economic and political interests through a carefully calibrated and calculated relationship with the superpowers became an early priority of Indira Gandhi. This meant enhanced political relations with the Soviet Union, and significant economic relations with the Western powers. Indira eventually ensured that the Soviets became the chief suppliers of military hardware for India—including such items as the MiG-29, the highly sophisticated fighter plane that Moscow has offered to almost no other Third World nation.‡ But since the Soviets could not give India "breakthrough technology," Indira turned to the West, and to Japan, for technical and economic assistance. Because its relationship with the United States was largely based on economics, it became easier for Indira to condemn or criticize Washington politically at forums such as the United Nations. And precisely because India relied so heavily on the Soviet Union for military assistance, it proved virtually impossible for Indira to condemn forthrightly such matters as the Soviet invasions of Hungary in 1956, of Czechoslovakia in 1968, and of Afghanistan in 1979. Ironically, though, the interests of the two superpowers converged during India's 1962 border war with China, when Washington

---

* Indeed, one can sense a lot of Nehru's thinking in President Mikhail S. Gorbachev's criticisms and appraisals of the Soviet record.

† The rupee trade meant that, for the most part, Indians did not have to pay in hard currency for their weapons and other purchases from the Soviet Union. For the Soviets, too, this arrangement was quite convenient because they were not exactly flush with hard currencies such as the U.S. dollar.

‡ The Soviets also permitted India to manufacture Soviet-designed tanks and airplanes.

and Moscow both helped Delhi substantially by providing military and political support.* Both powers thus proved a bulwark against China at a time when Beijing was hostile toward the Soviets as well as toward the Americans.

In her first few months as prime minister, Indira thus became more of a specialist in foreign than domestic policy. A strong commitment to international institutions such as the United Nations was also renewed. Indira saw these institutions as important mechanisms for settling world disputes and preventing infringement by outside powers on her own areas of geopolitical interest. In Indira's early years in power, India enjoyed significant influence in such international forums, and frequently set the agenda and tone for debates at the United Nations.† Both Jawaharlal Nehru and Indira Gandhi had a wide-ranging worldview that moved them to give much more attention to foreign affairs than most Third World leaders. "Foreign affairs" was not only a major part of these prime ministers' duties of state, the subject was a key element of their personal intellectual interests. What we have here were examples of how the sheer force of personality, cerebral orientation, and international activity could affect their own role and status. Involvement in "foreign affairs" heightened Indira's stature at home. Indians savored the notion of Indira Gandhi being consulted by the mandarins of the international community.‡

But why did other nations, particularly in the Third World, look to India for some strong element of leadership? Professor Ralph Buultjens says: "After all, to most of us from the Third World, 'India' means more than just India alone. She stands for all those values and cultural traditions that sustain societies from which we come. And so, India's leadership is not only a matter of size and skill, but also a sentimental and civilizational mix which exerts such a strong pull on people who belong to once-colonized societies. No one recognized this more than Indira Gandhi."§

---

* Historians have argued that the Chinese abruptly pulled out of the land they occupied in Assam during the 1962 Sino-Indian War after reports that the United States was flying weapons and supplies into Calcutta.

† India also succeeded in obtaining scores of top-level bureaucratic jobs for Indians within the United Nations. Indians also gained access to lucrative middle-level jobs. Today, Indians constitute one of the biggest nationalities at the United Nations.

‡ Indeed, Rajiv Gandhi kept up this practice of traveling overseas to meet with world leaders even after his election defeat in 1989. This often embarrassed the men who followed him as prime minister, because it often appeared as though India had two prime ministers—one for domestic affairs, and another, Gandhi, for foreign affairs.

§ Conversation with the author, New York City, 1987.

I3

The Perils of Power

Indira felt wonderful being on the international stage in her own right, and throughout her prime ministership she would always savor her celebrity status. Her name raced across the front pages of newspapers all over the world, and foreign television reporters clamored for interviews with her. By now, Indira was starting to become more comfortable with the news media. She was also careful in her choice of words when being interviewed. Indira had felt deeply embarrassed when, at a news conference, she had said that India was being plagued by "inflation and rising prices." Indira's proposal to end the Vietnam War did not lead anywhere, to be sure, but it certainly got her wide publicity—as did her calls for an end to the American bombing of Vietnam. The left, in particular, seemed relieved that India was renewing her nonaligned credentials. But however enthusiastic Indira was about foreign relations, domestic affairs demanded her immediate attention. The economy was sputtering. There were sporadic food riots. And in the strategic border state of Punjab, militant Sikhs continued agitating for a Punjabi suba, or state, frequently battling with their Hindu neighbors.

The "Punjab story" would open and conclude Indira Gandhi's stewardship as prime minister: it was one of her first major crises after she became prime minister in 1966, and eighteen years later the Punjab would be the last great—and tragic—episode of her life. The Punjab was a rich agricultural state; at its eastern border was the federal capital of Delhi, and to the west was Pakistan. Today's Punjab, with 2 percent of India's total population, supplies some 15 percent of India's food grains. It is

301

primarily wheat that is grown in the Punjab, which has always had an excess for shipment to the rest of India. Since well before the traumatic days of Partition, Punjab was "a region of unresolved bilingual as well as communal conflict," as Professor Stanley Wolpert puts it. * Originally, the Punjab embraced an area that included Punjabi- and Hindi-speaking regions. Language was primarily at the heart of the conflict in 1966: Punjab's Sikhs were demanding statehood—this state would include the predominantly Sikh, Punjabi-speaking northwestern half of Punjab. The overwhelmingly Hindu portion of the Punjab was in the Hindi-speaking southeastern region of Haryana. The Sikh-Hindu polarization dated back to the last century, when India's British rulers successfully sowed the seeds of mutual suspicion among members of the two communities. It was quite an achievement for the British, and one that was the harbinger of what was to be repeated: divide and rule. The British proved adept at pitting community against community, region against region, rajah against rajah—thereby giving themselves the opportunity to settle quarrels they themselves had spawned and thus consolidate their own position.

The differences the British generated among Sikhs and Hindus were especially noteworthy because Sikhism was born out of Hinduism in the sixteenth century. Unlike Hinduism, which evolved over the centuries out of the hymns and naturalistic beliefs of the pastoral Aryans who came to India from Central Asia, Sikhism is a revealed religion.[†] Its founder, Guru Nanak (1469–1539), claimed to have had mystic experiences. God appeared to him and said, according to Nanak himself: "Nanak, I am with thee. Through thee will My Name be magnified. Go into the world and teach mankind how to pray. Be not sullied by the ways of the world. Let your life be one of praise of the word (Naam), charity (Daan), ablution (Ishnaan), service (Sewa), and prayer (Simran)." Nanak was a simple, gentle soul whose sensibilities were outraged by the mistreatment of the lower classes by upper-caste Hindus, and by the abuses perpetrated by the country's Muslim rulers of the time.

Khushwant Singh, the eminent Sikh historian and writer, says that it is still unclear whether Guru Nanak intended to reform Hinduism, or form a new sect, or bring Hindus and Muslims together. "It would appear that in his early career he tried to bring the two communities closer to

---

* Wolpert, *A New History of India.*
[†] The source for much of the historical background to this chapter is Khushwant Singh's *A History of the Sikhs* (Princeton: Princeton University Press, 1965), generally acknowledged to be the definitive work on the subject.

each other," Singh says. "Being himself a Hindu he was at the same time equally concerned with reforming Hinduism. But as the years went by and his message caught on among the masses, he decided to give his teachings permanency through a sect of his own." Guru Nanak's disciples were called Sikhs—the word means "disciple." They did not chant Sanskrit hymns to stone idols, as Hindus did, but sang devotional songs that Nanak had composed himself in his native language, Punjabi. Sikhs also broke down existing caste barriers and encouraged communal dining in the guru's kitchen, a ceremony known as Guru ka Langar. Inder Malhotra notes that Guru Nanak's message combined the best of both Hinduism and Islam while rejecting their dogma and bigotry. Nanak's chief disciple, Angad, devised a new script, Gurmukhi; Guru Nanak had bypassed his own sons and named Angad his successor. Several decades later, Arjun, one of Sikhism's ten main gurus, built the Golden Temple in Amritsar.*

It was Arjun's son, Hargovind—Sikhism's sixth guru—who fashioned a militant role for the Sikhs. He urged his followers to arm themselves. He appointed himself both spiritual and temporal head of the Sikh community. The Sikhs were seen as the militant arm of Hinduism. In fact, Tegh Bahadur—Sikhism's ninth guru—appeared before the ruling Mughal court as a representative of the Hindus of northern India to resist forcible conversion to Islam. He was beheaded. Tegh Bahadur's son, Gobind Singh—the tenth and last guru—completed the transformation of the Sikhs into a martial community. He directed his male followers not to cut their hair and beards, to append the name "Singh"—which means "lion"—to their first names, and to always carry a kirpan, or sword. The Sikhs continued to be the defenders of India's Hindus against Muslim tyranny: They fought not only the Mughals but also Afghan and Pathan invaders. Most of these invaders came into India from Central Asia by traversing the mountains of the northwest. They inevitably first did battle in the Punjab, which lay in the rich alluvial plains below these mountains.

Sikh monarchs like Ranjit Singh (1780–1839) worshiped in Hindu temples and made the slaughter of the Hindus' sacred cow a criminal offense punishable by death. By 1849—ten years after Ranjit Singh's death—there were several Anglo-Sikh wars, and the British had annexed the Punjab, where in 1799 Ranjit Singh had established his formidable empire, the first and only Sikh kingdom in Indian history. The Muslim rulers of India, the Mughals, had also by now been reduced to figureheads; the surviving Mughal emperor, Bahadur Shah, was a British pensioner

---

* Amritsar sits on the Indian side of the border between India and Pakistan.

in Delhi. It was the British who sowed the seeds of Hindu-Sikh separatism during the Great Mutiny of 1857. Sikhs could have joined other Indians in driving the British out of India, but chose instead to rally around the foreigners. Sikhs were apparently still resentful that during the annexation of the Punjab by the East India Company, most of the troops had been purbiyas, or Indian foot soldiers recruited by the British from India's eastern provinces. The British rewarded loyal Sikh princes with land; they inducted Sikhs into the British army in large numbers, and they used Sikh troops to keep rebellious Hindu chieftains under control. Even while this was happening, a Hindu revivalist wave washed across northern India. For example, Hindu leaders of the Arya Samaj proselytized against Sikhism and tried to bring Sikhs back into the Hindu fold. * This raised the Sikhs' hackles and suspicions concerning Hinduism's attempt to re-absorb Sikhism.

The Akali movement of the 1920s to wrest control of the Sikh gurdwaras, or temples, from the Hindu-influenced priests who managed them also aggravated Hindu-Sikh relations. The Akali movement found expression in the creation of the Akali Dal, which was formed as the militant wing of the Shiromani Gurudwara Prabandhak Committee (SGPC). † The Committee was formed as a result of the passage of the Gurudwara Act of 1925 which "institutionalized Sikh communal separatism," according to historian Rajiv Kapur. ‡ The SGPC eventually took over the supervision of Sikh temples, and became "something of a Sikh parliament," as Inder Malhotra puts it. The SGPC came to be controlled by the Akali Dal, which to this day remains the dominating force in Sikh politics. Akali Dal leaders, however, seemed adept at miscalculating what actions would be in their interests. While the Indian National Congress was agitating for India's freedom from the British, the Akalis continued to collaborate with the latter. Many Akali leaders held that the Congress was actually a Hindu movement, and expressed alarm that Hinduism would swallow Sikhism if the Congress ever came into power.

---

* The Arya Samaj was founded by Dayananda Saraswati in Bombay in 1875. It was initially created as an organization for Hindu revival and Vedic proselytizing. After 1905, the Arya Samaj proved important in the development of nationalist political activism in the Punjab. Its most famous leaders were Lala Rajpat Rai and Pandit Madan Mohan Malaviya. The Arya Samaj's activities later in the 1900s—in tandem with right-wing Hindu political groups—included the reconversion of Muslims to Hinduism. This would occasionally touch off communal riots.

† The idea here was also to cleanse the Sikh community of the corrupting influence of the mahants, the priests and caretakers of Sikh gurudwaras who took in money from worshipers.

‡ See Rajiv Kapur, *Sikh Separatism* (London: Allen & Unwin, 1986).

During World War II, the Akalis enthusiastically supported the British war effort; the Congress abstained. It was at a huge Sikh rally in Amritsar on August 20, 1944, that Master Tara Singh, a cagey old Sikh leader who had been in the forefront of Akali Dal activities since 1935, first issued a formal call for a sovereign Sikh nation called Sikhistan (which later came to be called Khalistan). His colleagues were plainly amused; Tara Singh had formed an alliance with the maharajah of Patiala—one of India's leading princely states, which also happened to be in the Punjab—and this gave the Sikh leader access to considerable resources. *

By this time, India's Muslims had started agitating for their own state, Pakistan. Sikhs correctly saw the rising Muslim communalism as a threat to their own well-being, just as it was to that of the Hindus. When Partition came in 1947 and Pakistan was carved out of India, the Sikhs of the Punjab were the worst losers. They had hoped for a separate Sikh state; but neither the British nor Indian leaders such as Jawaharlal Nehru took these hopes seriously. The general feeling among officials who were carving up India into India and Pakistan was that there simply were not enough Sikhs to warrant a full-fledged Sikh state.[†] "Sikhs discovered to their dismay that they were being left high and dry," says Inder Malhotra. The choicest farmland of the Punjab was in its western region, which was given to Pakistan. Thirteen of the Punjab's twenty-nine districts went to India, and just 38 percent of the land area—mostly scrubland or meadows with poor topsoil—with very little of the vast irrigation network that the British had helped build. Two million Sikhs, terrified of being locked into the new Muslim state, migrated eastward to India, leaving behind their hereditary homes and possessions. They also left behind 150 Sikh shrines. Their migration, and that of another 2 million Hindus from Pakistan to India, coincided with a reverse flow of traffic of 4 million Muslims who left the eastern Punjab and northern India to relocate to Pakistan. They clashed. A bloodbath ensued. Nearly 2.2 million men, women, and children died, many of them Sikhs.[‡] This tragedy perhaps explains why Sikhs—who form 10 percent of India's

---

* The maharajah of Patiala, of course, was hardly the embodiment of the good Sikh. He was fond of alcohol, which he termed "nectar prescribed by my religion"; he also hosted huge orgies, invitations to which were cherished by other royalty in India.
[†] For more about the hopes of Sikhs for a separate state see *Sikh Separatism*, by Rajiv Kapur, and *Indira Gandhi*, by Inder Malhotra,
[‡] The tragedy of the Partition has been vividly captured by Khushwant Singh in his novel *Train to Pakistan* and by Sir Richard Attenborough in his Oscar-winning film, *Gandhi*. An extraordinary Hindi novel about the Partition is *Tamas*, by Bhisham Sahni (New Delhi: Penguin Books, 1988). *Tamas* was made into a moving TV film by Govind Nihalani.

military forces of 1.2 million—fought especially ferociously in the three wars between India and Pakistan following independence in 1947. But considering the historical Sikh animosity toward Muslims, it is especially puzzling how proponents of Khalistan have proclaimed Pakistan as an ally in their attempt to set up a new nation in the Punjab.* In the two decades after independence, Punjab's Sikhs worked especially hard to make their state India's success story. The central government in Delhi, under Prime Minister Nehru, encouraged economic development and poured billions of rupees into projects for building canals and dams in the Punjab. Sikhs also prospered elsewhere in the country: They gained a virtual monopoly over the road-transportation industry, for instance, and they obtained important positions in the government bureaucracy.

The notion of an autonomous Sikh state took on new life after Nehru's announcement in 1956 that new Indian states would be fashioned along linguistic lines. Nehru's decision was shaped by a lengthy and violent agitation in the Telangana region of south-central India—in the area that is now Andhra Pradesh state—for a Telugu linguistic state. Thirteen of India's fourteen major languages would thus find a formal home within the boundaries of a new state. But Punjabi was the only language not thus represented.† Sikhs resented this, and the Akali Dal launched a Punjabi suba—or "linguistic state"—movement in April 1960. Master Tara Singh termed the Nehru government's decision a "decree of Sikh annihilation."‡ The Punjab's Hindus suspected that in demanding a Punjabi-speaking state what the Sikhs were really after was a Sikh majority state; these suspicions were shared by Prime Minister Nehru. When census commissioners came around, Punjab's Hindus claimed their chief language was Hindi—not Punjabi, which was actually their prime lingua franca. "The battle over language in effect became a confrontation between Punjabi Hindus and Punjabi Sikhs," Khushwant Singh says. The Congress government in the Punjab was headed by Pratap Singh Kairon,

---

*When the original Punjab province was divided at Partition in 1947, its capital, Lahore, went to Pakistan. In maps published by Sikh militants, the putative state of Khalistan shows large tracts of Pakistani Punjab as being part of the new Sikh theocratic state.
†The Punjabis were especially angered when the old Bombay State was divided into Marathi and Gujarati-speaking areas—the new states of Maharashtra and Gujarat.
‡Master Tara Singh was actually referring to the verdict of the Nehru-appointed States Reorganization Commission (SRC), which ruled against a Punjabi-speaking state. The SRC submitted its report to Nehru in October 1955, but the prime minister did not implement its recommendations for another year. In 1956, India was reapportioned into fourteen states and six centrally administered "Union territories."

who was not especially keen about involving himself in agitation over a Punjabi suba. Inder Malhotra and another highly respected Indian journalist, Nikhil Chakravarty, tell of an encounter between Nehru and Ajoy Ghosh, a leader of the Communist Party of India. Ghosh had pleaded with the prime minister that the statehood demands of the Akalis be accepted.

"I envy you, Ajoy," Nehru said to Ghosh. "You do not have to run the country. It is my responsibility to do so. Sikhs are fine people but they are led by separatists and fanatics. I cannot hand over a state to them on the border with Pakistan. But such things are not permanent. As national integration proceeds, we will surely have a Punjabi-speaking state."

It was Nehru's daughter who eventually made the decision in 1966 to split the Punjab. * She had just become prime minister, and felt that the statehood question had gone on long enough. There would now be three states: Haryana, with 16,835 square miles and 7.5 million people, of whom barely 5 percent were Sikhs; Himachal Pradesh, with 10,215 square miles and 1.2 million people, barely 2 percent of them Sikhs; and Punjab, with 20,254 square miles and a population of 12 million people, about 52 percent of them Sikhs. The Sikhs got their Punjabi-speaking state, but its land area now covered just nine districts, not the Punjab's original thirteen. In what was one of those monumental absurdities that could only occur in India, Punjab and Haryana were to have the same capital—Chandigarh, the "City of Silver," which had been designed by the great French architect Le Corbusier in the 1950s. The two states would share buildings and government facilities in Chandigarh until such a time when Haryana built its own capital. Haryana has not been able to build its own capital because of a cash crunch. Although Punjab's partition went into effect on November 1, 1966, it was not until prominent Sikh leader Darshan Singh Pheruman's fast unto death in October 1969—a troubling event that was soon followed by Sant Fateh Singh's threat to set himself on fire—that Indira promised Chandigarh exclusively to Punjab. Her pledge, made in early 1970, has yet to be fulfilled.

On November 1, 1966, Indira Gandhi presided over the latest partition of the Punjab. The concession to the Akalis had actually been made in March that year. But the partition was not universally welcomed, even though some government officials characterized the partition as a gift to

---

* Soon after Independence in 1947, Punjab had been zoned into two administrative units—Patiala and the East Punjab States Union, better known by the acronym PEPSU.

the Sikhs for their valor during the Indo-Pakistan War of 1965. Critics within the Congress Party shrieked that Indira had acted precipitously. Some Congress leaders felt that "acceptance of the Sikh demand would create at India's sensitive border with Pakistan a small state inhabited by a community whose religious sentiments might be exploited by Pakistan to generate political turmoil."* Still others opined that a Punjabi-speaking state would soon lead to a Sikh demand for secession from India—prescient fears indeed. Even though Congress Party boss Kamaraj had supported Indira on the Punjab question, there were some Congress men who felt that Indira should not have yielded to the demand for a Hindi-speaking Haryana. Indira seemed to have conceded to this demand after a particularly tragic outburst of communal riots in Delhi. The riots were allegedly fueled by the Jan Sangh, a right-wing Hindu revivalist party whose appeal had been growing in northern Hindi-speaking states.[†] Three hapless members of the Congress Party had been burned alive in those riots, prompting an angry Indira to declare at a rally: "There are no tears in my eyes. There is anger in my heart. . . . Is it for all this that so many freedom fighters and martyrs have sacrificed their lives? How would I hold my head high and say India is a great country and meet foreign dignitaries—when violence and discord have fouled the atmosphere? The political parties who are instigating this violence are doing India great harm. They are not true Indians."[‡]

Indira was beginning to unveil a tactic that was to characterize her political style—the questioning of her political opponents' patriotism. Although her action concerning the Punjab question was widely praised by Sikhs at the time, the thorny issue of Sikh autonomy was to be transformed into something terribly intractable and sad over the next two decades. Thousands of innocent Hindus as well as Sikhs would be killed by Khalistan terrorists. And Indira herself would become the most prominent victim of the Punjab tragedy in 1984. "It was in Punjab . . . that the real test of Indira's leadership and statesmanship lay," says Inder Malhotra, "and it cannot be said that she withstood it with any degree of credit. On the contrary, by design, default, or drift, she allowed the crisis to deteriorate until the military assault on the Golden Temple [on June 5 and 6, 1984] became unavoidable. And once Operation Blue Star—as the military action at the shrine was code-named—took place,

---

*Bhatia, *Indira Gandhi*, p. 187.

[†]The Jan Sangh was later folded into the Bharatiya Janata Party (BJP), which, during the 1980s came to political prominence on, among other things, the platform of Hindu fundamentalism.

[‡]Indira spoke at a public rally where she was welcoming a visiting Yugoslavian delegation.

other grim and gory events unfolded themselves as inexorably as in a Greek tragedy."[*]

That tragedy not only resulted in the assassination of Indira Gandhi; it has also meant perhaps a permanent alienation between Hindus and Sikhs in the Punjab. The fact is, however, that the Punjab's Hindus and Sikhs lived mostly in amity for four centuries. There had been periodic agitation since the 1930s for a separate Sikh nation—which at first was called Sikhistan—but a hard-core separatist movement did not get going until the late 1970s. By then, Sikh leaders had realized that the arithmetic of population in the Punjab, as elsewhere in India, increasingly favored the country's Hindu majority, which was breeding at the rate of nearly 3 percent a year, or twice the rate of the Sikhs. That translated into diminishing power for the Sikhs, these leaders said.

In a perceptive report prepared for the U.S. Congressional Research Service in August 1984, Richard P. Cronin said that the Sikh-Hindu crisis was rooted in a long-term assertion of a Sikh communal identity. Cronin, an expert on Asian affairs, said that in addition to this assertion, four specific developments helped exacerbate the Punjab problem:

- The return to power of Prime Minister Gandhi's Congress Party in the January 1980 national parliamentary elections, and her subsequent dismissal of the opposition Akali Dal and Janata coalition that had governed the Punjab State since 1977. Mrs. Gandhi had lost the 1977 parliamentary election to the opposition Janata Party, following two years of draconian emergency rule. Indira had feared that the national agitation sparked by her political foes would not only create chaos in India but also topple her government. The agitation had followed a judge's ruling in the Allahabad Court that Mrs. Gandhi had engaged in questionable electioneering practices.
- The victory of the Congress Party in the June 1980 state elections in the Punjab. The elections were widely assumed to have been rigged, and the Akalis were especially resentful.
- The growing economic discontent among Sikhs and other Punjabis over agricultural pricing and industrial licensing policies of the Gandhi government.
- The emergence of Sant Jarnail Singh Bhindranwale, a militant Sikh fundamentalist, as a dominant force in the Sikh heartland.

Richard Cronin, whose research resulted in a remarkably clear analysis of the Punjab situation, said that the accelerating tempo of the Sikh

[*]Malhotra, *Indira Gandhi*, p. 287.

agitation for a homeland and the violence in the Punjab may be dated
from the brief arrest of Bhindranwale in connection with the assassination
of a Hindu Punjabi newspaper editor, Lala Jagat Narain, in September 1981.

"The government's ineffective attempts to deal with Bhindranwale led
him from one political triumph after another until he met his death in
the June 5–6 [1984] army attack on his headquarters in the Golden
Temple in Amritsar," Cronin wrote in his report, which was published
two months before the assassination of Mrs. Gandhi.

> Wherever blame may lie for the failure to find a peaceful settlement,
> an early end to the confrontation is unlikely. Although the Gandhi
> government had earlier conceded most of the specifically religious
> demands, it is still not clear whether an accommodation can be
> reached on the more contentious economic and territorial demands,
> whether Prime Minister Gandhi will deal with the "moderate" Akali
> Dal leaders now under arrest, or whether she will seek to bargain
> with other representatives of the Sikhs. It is too early to tell whether
> the storming of the Golden Temple has been a net gain for stability
> by eliminating Bhindranwale and his extremist supporters, or a net
> loss due to the radicalization of previously uncommitted Sikhs.
>
> It also remains to be seen what the long-term impact will be on
> the stability of this vital grain-producing state. Although Hindus
> predominate in the cities and towns, the Sikhs constitute a strong
> majority in most of the countryside. Punjabi Hindu traders and busi-
> nessmen in rural villages are especially vulnerable to local Sikh major-
> ities. Even before the Golden Temple incident, terror and communal
> killings had spread to border villages north and south of Amritsar,
> causing anxious Hindu Punjabis to flee. The Hindu majority in
> Punjab's cities and towns also resorted to violence. A continuation
> of this violent polarization would be a major setback for India and
> could presage a wider breakdown of civility between ethnic, religious,
> and linguistic groups that live side-by-side in many parts of India.

The Punjab had thrived economically, largely because of the "green
revolution." Because of a new canal system financed by the central
government and high-yield seeds that were distributed by Delhi in the
1950s, crop production in the Punjab has risen six-fold since 1951. More
than 60 percent of the state's population of some 12 million was engaged
in agricultural production—production that accounted for more than 62
percent of the Punjab's annual income. The high-yield grain developed

at the Rockefeller Institute in the United States and at Ludhiana State University in the Punjab by Norman E. Borlaug—an American scientist who was later awarded the Nobel Prize—resulted in rice production increasing from 892 kilograms per hectare in 1950 to 3,000 kilograms by 1981, wheat production grew from 901 kilograms per hectare to 3,100 kilograms during the same period. As the state prospered, Sikhs started to look for new ventures in which to invest their wealth, for a better yield on their crops to pay for the rising costs of fertilizers and mechanization. Richard Cronin says in his congressional report: "Many Sikhs came to see the Indian government's policy of controlling all industrial licensing from New Delhi and steering investment to poorer but more populous and vote-rich provinces in the Hindi heartland as an obstacle to these aspirations. Some frequently quoted figures include the claim that 70 percent of the state's cotton and 60 percent of its molasses are 'exported' for processing to other states due to the refusal of New Delhi to approve licenses for plant construction. The Delhi government was also judged slow to create adequate price incentives for Punjabi wheat and rice."*

Revolutions have a way of levelling out, and the Punjab's "green revolution" and the economic progress associated with it reached a plateau in the early 1970s. Punjabi farmers found themselves not as well off as they had been a decade earlier. Around this time, Sikhism's elders discovered to their dismay that the religion's hold over the young was loosening as Western life-styles were imported into the state. Indeed, the "green revolution" that Norman Borlaug and others spawned in the Punjab generated many spinoffs. The number of primary schools in the state rose from 7,183 in 1967 to 12,400 by 1982; in 1967, there were just 700 high schools in the state, but by 1982 the figures had climbed beyond 2,200. In 1967, there were seventy-one colleges in the Punjab; by 1980 there were 200. In 1967, the Punjab had no medical colleges; by 1982, there were nine, including two in Amritsar.† Sikhs also went abroad in increasing numbers to work—to Western Europe, North America, and to the oil-rich countries of the Gulf—and they repatriated to their relatives in the Punjab the equivalent of hundreds of millions of dollars annually. This money stimulated consumerism.

But as the Punjab's schools and colleges began turning out more and more graduates, there was not enough expansion in the nonagricultural economy to provide jobs for them. Indeed, unemployment was now on

---

* Richard Cronin, *Report on the Punjab* (Washington, D.C.: Congressional Research Service, 1984).
† *Educational Statistics* (New Delhi: Government of India Press, 1983).

the rise because other than agriculture there were no major industries in the state. As families grew bigger, land holdings became smaller. The annual influx of more than 200,000 low-caste Hindu workers from Uttar Pradesh and Bihar states, who were hired to work on Punjab farms, also created some social tensions. Many of these migrant workers would stay on and enroll as voters, thus fattening the percentage of Hindus in the state. Sikh clergymen felt that their religion was under siege. More specifically, they felt that Sikhs and the Punjab were being Hinduized.

Even as the proportion of Sikhs in the Punjab was declining, Mrs. Gandhi's ruling Congress Party in Delhi accelerated its interference in socioreligious politics in the state. Mrs. Gandhi seemed determined to prevent the political ascendancy of the Akali Dal. The Akalis stepped up their demands for the readjustment of state boundaries to include in the Punjab the Punjabi-speaking areas of neighboring Haryana, Rajasthan, and Himachal Pradesh. The Akalis also wanted Chandigarh to be the exclusive capital of the Punjab, and they demanded a fairer allocation to the Punjab of the waters of the Rivers Ravi, Sutlej, and Beas. Akali leaders formed a committee of eminent Sikhs and asked them to compile a list of their "legitimate demands."

On October 16, 1973, the Akali Dal Working Committee approved a document of those demands. That document came to be known as the Anandpur Sahib Resolution, which not only included these demands but also referred in vague language to a "separate Sikh nation." Actually, the word used in the resolution was "quam," which in Punjabi meant anything from a community to a nation. That resolution was interpreted by Mrs. Gandhi and her advisers as a call for a separate state. Indira was also upset over a section in the Anandpur Resolution that called for restricting the central government's "interference" in defense, foreign relations, currency, and general communications. "No prime minister, let alone one with as firm a conviction as Mrs. Gandhi that India needed a strong central government, could ever accept those terms," say Mark Tully and Satish Jacob of the BBC. "To concede that demand would have meant threatening the unity of India. It could well have destroyed the whole economy because each state would have been able to set up tariff barriers impeding the free movement of goods within the country."* What was also unacceptable to a number of Mrs. Gandhi's advisers was the demand in the Anandpur Sahib Resolution for "the complete nationalization of the trade in food grains." And the Akalis urged that "all key industries should be brought under the public sector." Akali

* *Amritsar: Mrs. Gandhi's Last Battle*, p. 46.

leaders were to acknowledge openly that one of the ideas behind the Anandpur Sahib Resolution was to crack open the capitalist hold on the Punjab's economy.

The Anandpur Sahib resolution was passed at a meeting the Akali Dal held in the historic Punjab town of Anandpur, where the head of the ninth Sikh guru, Tegh Bahadur—who was decapitated by the Mughal emperor, Aurangzeb, on November 11, 1675—was cremated by his son and successor, Guru Gobind Singh. (Anandpur is the site of one of Sikhism's five major gurudwaras [temples]; the other four structures are the Golden Temple in Amritsar; Dam Dama Sahib in Ropar; Patna Sahib in Bihar; and Hazoor Sahib in Maharashtra's Nanded district). The Akalis said in their resolution that the central government in Delhi should restrict its functions in the Punjab to defense, foreign affairs, communications, and currency. The resolution advanced the proposition that the Sikh religion was "not safe without sovereignty." Khushwant Singh has said that this could be interpreted "as leading to Khalistan."

A separate state was never formally called for by the Akalis, but Punjab's Sikh fundamentalists thought it a worthwhile idea, one whose time had come. The purity of Sikhism, they said, could only be preserved in an independent Sikh nation. Their fervor was fueled and financed by wealthy Sikhs living abroad. Preachers in Sikh temples throughout America, from New York's Queens County to the West Coast, railed against the Indian government; some of them urged worshipers to contribute to "the cause." There was never any doubt as to what that "cause" was. Money that was thus raised eventually was spent on weapons purchases. Many Sikhs living in the United States, Canada, and Western Europe deny that their contributions financed the Khalistan terrorists. But weapons do cost money, and the Punjab militants have had access to sophisticated firepower.

Jagjit Singh Chohan, a London-based Sikh physician who had once served as finance minister in several Punjab governments, became a cheerleader—indeed, even a father figure—for an incipient Khalistan movement. He called himself "President of the Republic of Khalistan," and quickly established lobbying organizations for Khalistan in Western capitals, including Washington. Chohan's representatives, such as Gurmit Singh Aulakh, buttonholed congressmen in Washington and testified at hearings about Indian "atrocities" in the Punjab. Aulakh, who started the Council of Khalistan in Washington—and was registered with the Department of Justice as a lobbyist—became highly popular with right-wing legislators who had a reputation for India-baiting. In California's San Joachim Valley, Sikh settlers were organized by wealthy fruit farmers such as Didar Singh Bains of Yuba City to speak out about the "Sikh nation." These farmers not only opened their hearts and minds to Chohan's clarion calls for a Sikh homeland, they also opened their thick wallets. Also in Washington was Ganga Singh Dhillon, who headed the World Sikh Organization, and spoke out forcefully against the Indian government's alleged mistreatment of Sikhs. "I am a Sikh first, then an Indian," Dhillon, who came to the United States in 1962, said. "Sikhs are a nation by any definition—and a nation must have a home. Whether you call it Khalistan, an independent Punjab, a sovereign state—whatever. I am asking for a Sikh homeland—where I may become master of my own destiny, where we could protect our women and children, where my children are raised according to the Sikh tradition, where my religious shrines are not allowed to be run over by army tanks."*

While Jagjit Singh Chohan—whom Ganga Singh Dhillon calls "a great man"—worked furiously overseas to gather political and financial support for Khalistan, Sikh fundamentalists were also hard at work in the Punjab. In the late 1970s, these fundamentalists rallied around a fiery leader, Sant Jarnail Singh Bhindranwale. He hailed from a Sikh Jat family that had been in farming for several generations. Jats dominated the Sikh community, and it is the tradition among them to send their sons either into the military or to coopt them into agriculture. Even though Bhindranwale's father, Joginder Singh, was a relatively poor farmer, he saw to it that all his seven sons—of whom Jarnail Singh was the youngest—went to school and also learned the Sikh scriptures. Joginder Singh employed six of his sons on the family farm, and dispatched Jarnail Singh to the Damdami Taksal, a Sikh seminary founded some 200 years ago by Baba Deep Singh, a Sikh hero who defended the Golden Temple against the Afghan invader, Ahmad Shah Abdali.† At the theological school, Jarnail Singh quickly rose to prominence with his steely commitment to Sikh orthodoxy, his oratorical ability, and his friendship with the seminary's head, Kartar Singh. Indeed, so fanatical was Jarnail Singh that he refused to allow doctors to cut Kartar Singh's hair after he had been severely injured in an automobile accident; the physicians wanted to operate on his skull. Kartar Singh subsequently died of his injuries, but he had already anointed Jarnail Singh as his

---

*Interview with author, June 1985.
†Baba Deep Singh's fight against the Afghans was valiant but ultimately unsuccessful. Legend has it that the Afghans cut off his head but that the brave Baba Deep Singh continued to fight with his head in one hand and a sword in the other. In Sikh schools, homes, and temples, one can see illustrations of a decapitated Baba Deep Singh defending the Golden Temple.

successor—bypassing his own son, Amrik Singh. Amrik Singh later became head of the radical All-India Sikh Students Federation, whose members launched many terrorist activities in the Punjab and beyond in the cause of Sikh separatism. As head of the Damdami Taksal, Jarnail Singh was invested with the title of Sant, or holy man. He also took on the last name, Bhindranwale—Bhindran was actually the name of the village from where many heads of the Damdami Taksal had hailed; "wale" meant "hailing from."

By the time Sant Jarnail Singh Bhindranwale became head of the Damdami Taksal, Indira Gandhi had already imposed her notorious Emergency—and subsequently lost the 1977 election to the Janata Party. Her greatest political foe, Morarji Desai, had led the Janata to victory in a campaign whose moral spearhead was the freedom-struggle veteran, Jayaprakash Narayan. Desai was now prime minister. In the Punjab, Desai's Janata Party formed an uneasy coalition with the Akali Dal; some Akali leaders were wary of the Janata because its predominant wing comprised of the erstwhile Hindu-oriented Jan Sangh.* Akalis had still not overcome their suspicions that India was headed toward a Hindu Raj in which Sikhism would be absorbed.

Even while Indira was fretting during her post-1977 political exile, she entrusted her younger son, Sanjay Gandhi, with the task of exploiting weaknesses in the Janata-Akali coalition. Sanjay, an astute if amoral man, believed that the only way to dislodge the coalition from power was through political skulduggery. He sought the help of Zail Singh, a Sikh politician who had been chief minister of Punjab's Congress government from 1972 until 1977, when the Janata-Akali coalition came to power. Zail Singh, behind his bonhomie and humor, was a canny political operative. Zail Singh suggested to Sanjay that they should try to break up the Janata-Akali coalition. The Akali Dal at that time was dominated by three men: Parkash Singh Badal, a wealthy farmer who had become chief minister; Sant Harchand Singh Longowal, a religious preacher who had organized spirited opposition to Indira Gandhi's Emergency; and Gurcharan Singh Tohra, a Communist sympathizer who headed the Shiromani Gurudwara Prabandhak Committee. Zail Singh and Sanjay Gandhi schemed to throw the Akali leadership into disarray. "At first, Sanjay thought of playing these three against each other," say Mark Tully and Satish Jacob of the BBC. "But Zail Singh, with his deep knowledge of the complexities of Sikh politics, realized that displacing

---

* In 1967 and 1969, the Akali Dal had formed the government in the Punjab through alliances with the Jan Sangh.

one of the Akali Trinity would only lead to a strong alliance of the other two. He recommended Sanjay to look for a new religious leader to discredit the traditional Akali Dal leadership."*

That religious leader would be Sant Jarnail Singh Bhindranwale, a man right out of central casting for the role of agent provocateur. He accepted the Sanjay Gandhi–Zail Singh invitation only too eagerly. The assignment, after all, offered the prospect of making Bhindranwale a national figure—if only the right political issues could be found. Until now, Bhindranwale had only been railing against such "evils" as shaving off beards and cutting long hair and against the consumption by Sikhs of alcohol and drugs. Sanjay Gandhi could have hardly cared less whether Sikhs cut their hair or not. Moreover, Bhindranwale's concerns about maintaining the purity of Sikhism were shared by scores of other Sikh preachers. What fascinated Sanjay about Bhindranwale, however, seemed to be a certain blazing fire in his eyes—and his willingness to do Sanjay's bidding, even if those directives veered toward the instigation of violence. The initial targets of that violence were the Nirankaris, a Sikh revivalist sect founded in the nineteenth century. The sect's founder, Baba Dayal Das, warned against the increasing tendency of Sikhs to engage in such traditional Hindu practices as idol worship, and pilgrimages to holy sites along the Ganges. "Nirankari" means "formless," and the sect gained great popularity throughout the Punjab. The high priests of the Golden Temple even issued a religious edict condemning the Nirankaris as heretics. There were several riots between Nirankaris and orthodox Sikhs—and now, encouraged by Zail Singh and Sanjay Gandhi, Sant Jarnail Singh Bhindranwale methodically sought to exploit these communal tensions.

In April 1978, the Akali government of the Punjab announced that—notwithstanding the orthodox Akalis' disapproval of the heretical sect—the Nirankaris would be allowed to hold a convention in Amritsar on the thirteenth of that month. On the day of the convention, Bhindranwale happened to be attending a meeting at the Golden Temple where Jeevan Singh Umranangal—who was revenue minister in the Akali government—spoke about why the Punjab government could not prevent the convention from taking place. He was interrupted by Bhindranwale.

"We will not allow this Nirankari convention to take place!" the Sant shouted. "We are going to march there and cut them to pieces!"†

---

*Tully and Jacob, *Amritsar: Mrs. Gandhi's Last Battle*, p. 57.
†This anecdote is mentioned in Tully and Jacob, *Amritsar: Mrs. Gandhi's Last Battle*.

The march ended in violence. Bhindranwale stormed into the Nirankari headquarters, where Fauja Singh, one of his associates—who was actually an agricultural inspector in the Punjab government—flourished a sword and tried to slice open the neck of Baba Gurbachan Singh, the Nirankari guru. A gun battle ensued. Twelve of Bhindranwale's followers and three Nirankaris were killed. Sanjay Gandhi and Zail had succeeded, through the charismatic Bhindranwale, in setting the stage for the Punjab's destabilization.

And what destabilization it proved to be. Bhindranwale and his Sikh fanatics mounted a wave of attacks on Nirankaris and other "disbelievers" all across the Punjab. In New Delhi, there was a spate of demonstrations organized by groups claiming to be defenders of the Sikh faith but sponsored by Indira Gandhi's Congress Party. These demonstrations contributed to an already tense situation in the capital, where Morarji Desai's Janata Party government was being riven by internal dissent and rivalries. Meanwhile, Zail Singh had covertly helped Bhindranwale to form a new political party, the Dal Khalsa—the Party of the Pure—whose aims included not only the harassment of the Akalis but also the creation of Khalistan. Indeed, BBC correspondents Mark Tully and Satish Jacob quote a government of India "white paper" on the 1984 army action in the Golden Temple where there is a reference to the Dal Khalsa. "The Dal Khalsa was originally established with the avowed object of demanding an independent sovereign Sikh state," the White Paper said. Bhindranwale was shrewd enough not to be openly associated with the Dal Khalsa on the grounds that he was a religious figure, not a politician. But the Dal Khalsa, say Mark Tully and Satish Jacob, was always known as Bhindranwale's party. They note that Zail Singh would frequently telephone editors of newspapers based in Chandigarh and urge them to give extra prominence to "positive" news about the Dal Khalsa. *

At the behest of Zail Singh and Sanjay Gandhi, Bhindranwale now tried to capture control of the 140-member Shiromani Gurudwara Prabandhak Committee. In the 1979 elections to the SGPC, Bhindranwale's candidates were able to win only four seats. The Akalis still retained overwhelming control of the SGPC—which meant that they continued to have access to the SGPC's formidable financial support and were also able to call on the organization's gurudwara network for political support. This was a politically critical year for India—and Indira. The Janata Party was unraveling, and Morarji Desai was replaced in the prime minister's post by his associate Charan Singh. Indira Gandhi knew that it

* Tully and Jacob, *Amritsar: Mrs. Gandhi's Last Battle*, p. 60.

would be only a matter of months before new general elections were held. She also intuited that the Congress Party would be voted back into power and that she would become prime minister once again.

Once the Janata government had collapsed in Delhi in late 1979—not the least because Indira worked covertly to encourage Charan Singh to depose Morarji Desai from the prime minister's seat—and the election campaign was rolling, Indira Gandhi had to determine the best way to use Bhindranwale. She and Sanjay now thought that Bhindranwale should drum up votes for the Congress. He had become a celebrity in the Punjab; he had become a thorn in the side of the Akali Dal. Most of all, Bhindranwale was *their* man, thought Indira and Sanjay. The Sikh preacher, despite his earlier insistence about not being a politician, plunged zestfully into politicking. He actively participated in the campaigns of three Congress candidates, among them the president of the Punjab Congress Party, R. L. Bhatia. Indeed, Bhatia even distributed posters that said: "Bhindranwale supports me." Bhindranwale also made several campaign swings through the Gurdaspur constituency—a hotbed of pro-Khalistan sentiment—where, the Janata Party candidate later alleged, Mrs. Gandhi herself once had appeared on the same dais as Bhindranwale during the election campaign. Indira denied this but, in an interview with BBC's "Panorama" program, she said: "Mr. Bhindranwale did go and speak for one of our candidates in the elections. I don't know which candidate it was. I don't know whether he know him personally or he was annoyed with the local Akalis."[*]

Indira Gandhi and her Congress Party won the January 1980 national elections handsomely. Zail Singh now became Home Minister in Indira's cabinet, which gave him control of the Delhi police and of the national intelligence agencies. Later in 1980, the Congress won power in the Punjab, too, after state elections were held in that turbulent state. But if Zail Singh entertained any hope that one of his handpicked candidates would become chief minister, he was to be sorely disappointed. Indira clearly did not want Zail Singh—or any other Congress chieftain—to become too powerful in his own home state. To offset what Indira perceived to be Zail Singh's self-confidence that he was indeed the master of Punjabi politics, she appointed Zail Singh's bitterest rival, Darbara Singh, as chief minister. Although a Sikh, Darbara Singh prided himself as a secularist, and he was less disposed than Zail Singh—who had been trained as a preacher at the Sikh Missionary College in Amritsar—to arrive at any accommodation with the Sikh fundamentalists in the Pun-

[*]Tully and Jacob, *Amritsar: Mrs. Gandhi's Last Battle*, p. 62.

jab. His cabinet reflected Darbara Singh's preference for like-minded secularists. The new chief minister also "adopted a hard-line policy on both Sikh and Hindu extremists," according to Mark Tully and Satish Jacob. Zail Singh, meanwhile, could only gnash his teeth in Delhi. But Zail Singh was not one for sweating silently. He enlisted Bhindranwale's help in undermining Darbara Singh.

That year—1980—turned out to be inauspicious for Indira Gandhi as far as the Punjab was concerned, despite the fact that her Congress Party was once again in the saddle and the Akali Dal seemed to be in disarray. The Punjab situation would steadily deteriorate; events would career out of Indira's control—not least because of the transformation of Sant Jarnail Singh Bhindranwale from "holy man" of the Punjab into what the media liked to call "Sant Monster," as in Doctor Frankenstein's Monster. "Frankenstein" in this case, of course, was a composite of Indira Gandhi, Zail Singh, and Sanjay Gandhi. They created him, and now they were faced with the consequences of their creation. On April 24, 1980, the Nirankari guru, Baba Gurbachan Singh, was shot and killed by assailants in his Delhi home. Bhindranwale, who had kept up his campaign against the Nirankaris, was immediately suspected of masterminding the murder; he sought refuge in a hostel within the compound of the Golden Temple. To the surprise of many people, Zail Singh rose up in Parliament and told that august body that Bhindranwale had nothing to do with the killing of Baba Gurbachan Singh. On September 9, there was another murder—this time of Lala Jagat Narain. Narain, a Hindu, owned a number of newspapers, including one that had supported the Nirankaris and criticized Bhindranwale, the Punjab Kesari. Bhindranwale had hated Narain. For his part, Narain had proven adept at hyperbole, warning in editorial after editorial that the Khalistan movement had gripped virtually every Sikh in the Punjab—and that Hindus had better watch out.

Bhindranwale made a number of incendiary recordings in which he urged his followers to escalate the campaign against those whom he called disbelievers. The Sant, in fact, was enamored of the tape recorder; he always insisted that his sermons and public speeches be preserved on tape. Shortly after the murders of Baba Gurbachan Singh and Lala Jagat Narain, Bhindranwale said, in a recording that was reportedly distributed widely in the Punjab: "Whoever performed these great feats deserve to be honored by the Akal Takht, the highest seat of the Sikhs. . . . If their killers came to me, I would weigh them in gold."

If police suspicions were correct, the Sant would have had to weigh himself in gold; he was said to have planned both murders. Four days after the killing of Lala Jagat Narain—who was shot as he was traveling from Patiala to Jalandhar—All-India Radio (AIR), the government-owned national radio network, announced that there was a warrant out for Bhindranwale's arrest. At that time, the Sant was reported to be in the Haryana community of Chando Kalan. No arrest was made, however. The BBC's Satish Jacob was later told by a senior Haryana police officer that the Haryana chief minister, Bhajan Lal, had personally ordered an official car to transport Bhindranwale from Chando Kalan to his own gurudwara in the Punjab. The Sant was driven 200 miles in that car to the safety of his own shrine at Mehta Chowk, near Amritsar. Kuldip Nayar, the veteran Indian editor and author, says that Chief Minister Bhajan Lal was telephoned by Zail Singh and told not to arrest Bhindranwale. * Chief Minister Darbara Singh of the Punjab told Inder Malhotra that the home minister was "protecting him still"—meaning that the relationship between Zail Singh and Bhindranwale was close.† According to the official version of the episode, when the Punjab police arrived in Chando Kalan they found that Bhindranwale had already left. The police account is at variance with eyewitness testimony of villagers, who claimed that the officials deliberately set fire to a couple of vans containing Bhindranwale's posters and propaganda; the police said that "there was subsequent violence when some followers of . . . Bhindranwale fired upon the police party. There was an exchange of fire and incidents of arson occurred." Those "incidents" enraged Bhindranwale because his tapes and transcripts were destroyed in the inferno. In subsequent homilies, the Sant would say to his audiences: "What would you do if someone killed your nearest and dearest? They have insulted my guru by burning my papers." A number of highly regarded political analysts and journalists—including Mark Tully and Satish Jacob—believe that it was the burning of his papers that represented a critical turning point in Bhindranwale's relations with Zail Singh and Indira Gandhi.

* Kuldip Nayar grew increasingly critical of the Congress Party over the subsequent years. In 1990, he was made India's high commissioner to Britain by Prime Minister V. P. Singh—a job that Nayar resigned from, following the toppling of Singh by Chandra Shekhar.

† Bhajan Lal headed a Janata Party government in Haryana at the time that Mrs. Gandhi returned to power in Delhi in January 1980. Lal at once transferred his loyalty to the Congress. Mark Tully and Satish Jacob suggest that Lal was very anxious to please Mrs. Gandhi and that he would have surely arrested Bhindranwale since there was a warrant out for him. Tully and Jacob say that for Bhajan Lal not to have arrested Bhindranwale but instead given him an official car to escape pointed clearly to the fact that "he had instructions from the central government to do so." Those instructions, says Kuldip Nayar, came in a telephone call to Lal from Zail Singh.

On September 20, Sant Jarnail Singh Bhindranwale decided that he would allow himself to be arrested by the Punjab police. Chief Minister Darbara Singh was determined to take the Sant into custody; the gurudwara at Mehta Chowk was surrounded by heavily armed police. However, the police inexplicably permitted the preacher to address a large congregation before he was taken away to jail, and in his speech Bhindranwale predictably sallied forth against the Darbara Singh government. That speech could well have been written by Zail Singh, so virulently anti-Darbara Singh it was. No wonder that minutes after Bhindranwale was driven away by the police, his supporters opened fire on the constables who remained at the site. In the gun battle that followed, seventeen of Bhindranwale's men were killed and at least a dozen policemen were injured.

As if on cue, Punjab was shaken by a series of terrorist acts after Bhindranwale's arrest. On the day of the arrest itself, three Sikhs on motorcycles fired on Hindus in Jalandhar, killing four and injuring twelve. The next day, another Hindu man was killed in Taran, near Amritsar, and thirteen others were seriously hurt in a similar sort of attack. Then a freight train was derailed not far from Amritsar. On September 29, an Indian Airlines plane was hijacked to the Pakistani city of Lahore. Hindus were pulled out of buses by Sikh gunmen, who then shot and killed them at point-blank range. Banks were held up. Policemen were followed home and then murdered. Not all victims were Hindus, of course. Sikhs who had expressed some concern for the deteriorating law-and-order situation in the Punjab were gunned down. It was apparent that the perpetrators of this violence were the bearded young men recruited by Bhindranwale—men who shared his firebrand fundamentalism and who responded unthinkingly to his charisma. At this point, the Akalis submitted a new list of demands to Indira Gandhi; at the top of their list was a demand for the "immediate and unconditional" release of Sant Jarnail Singh Bhindranwale from Ferozepur Jail. *

On October 14, 1980, Zail Singh appeared in Parliament to announce that Bhindranwale had nothing to do with the murder of Lala Jagat Narain. To widespread disbelief, the Sant was released from jail. It is inconceivable that Zail Singh could have acted without the approval of Prime Minister Indira Gandhi; she had already been approached by Delhi Sikhs close to the Congress urging the freeing of Bhindranwale. Zail Singh still sought to undermine Darbara Singh, and Bhindranwale, of

---

* Bhindranwale insisted that his guards be only Sikhs who wore long, unkempt beards in the traditional style. The government agreed to this.

course, could be very much useful to him—or so Zail Singh continued to believe. The release of Bhindranwale from jail "was a Himalayan blunder," writes Inder Malhotra. "It was also a major turning point in Bhindranwale's career and Punjab's history. His supremacy in Sikh politics was now complete and unshakable."[*] Bhindranwale moved into the Golden Temple complex in Amritsar, and began directing a new wave of murder and intimidation of Hindus and political opponents across the Punjab and even in Delhi. He even came triumphantly to Delhi and participated in a procession that wound up at the Bangla Sahib Gurudwara, not far from Parliament House. The Sant's supporters brandished rifles and semiautomatic pistols in open defiance of the policemen who kept crowds at bay: The police were technically under the control of the Home Ministry, whose head was Zail Singh. The minister could have easily issued an order for the arrest of Bhindranwale's supporters for illegal possession and display of firearms. But, of course, the militants were allowed to roam free that day.

Not surprisingly, Bhindranwale became a media star. Journalists from all over the world came to interview him. It is disputable whether it was Bhindranwale's status as a media star rivaling Mrs. Gandhi or his role as a terrorist leader that roused the prime minister's choler. Mrs. Gandhi was reported to be upset that Bhindranwale was being given enormous media coverage. According to at least one highly placed aide, she complained to a group of newspaper owners about this. By now, Bhindranwale had convinced himself that he did not need the support of either Zail Singh or Indira Gandhi. He would scornfully refer to the prime minister as "that Brahman woman"—a reference, of course, to the fact that Indira Gandhi was born a Hindu. Bhindranwale knew that Mrs. Gandhi's credibility was eroding nationally over the Punjab question; her government was perceived to be unable to check terrorism. In December 1982, for example, Bhindranwale was told that Rajiv Gandhi—who was clearly being groomed by Indira for political stewardship—had recommended that the government expel the Sant from the Golden Temple. "Tell him to come and try," Bhindranwale said. "I am not afraid of him or his mother. Who is she anyway? A pandit's daughter. Tell her to come here if she wants to talk with me."

The talks between the Gandhi government and the Akalis had not amounted to much. Indira saw that the violence in the Punjab was escalating sharply, and on October 6, 1983, the Indian government dismissed the Darbara Singh administration and imposed President's

[*]Malhotra, *Indira Gandhi*, p. 258.

Rule. After dithering for months over whether she should send her troops to flush Bhindranwale out of his sanctuary in the Golden Temple, Mrs. Gandhi finally authorized a military operation for June 5 and 6, 1984. Not only was Bhindranwale killed during that operation; so were hundreds of men, women, and children who had come as pilgrims to the shrine. Sikhs around the world were outraged; some swore vengeance.

Janki Ganju, the Washington lobbyist for India, recalls meeting Indira on August 14, 1984.* There was mounting concern among her aides about reports that assassination plots were being hatched against her. Some of her aides were insistent that she skip the traditional Independence Day address from the ramparts of the Red Fort on August 15.

"Tell me, Ganju, how many of your presidents have been killed?" Indira said to Ganju. The reference was to U.S. Presidents, of course; even though Janki Ganju was an Indian citizen and indeed worked on behalf of the Indian government in Washington, Indira would always tease him by calling him "American."

Ganju started reciting the number of American Presidents who had been killed. Indira interrupted him.

"I know my history," she said. "The point I'm trying to make is that if someone wants to get you, they can always succeed."

She paused, then added: "I'm going to give my speech tomorrow."

That Independence Day address was to be Indira Gandhi's last one from the Red Fort. On the morning of Wednesday, October 31, 1984, Indira Gandhi was murdered.

Because Indira's political life was so intertwined with that of the Punjab, I traveled to Amritsar within a day or so after her death to see for myself the impact of her murder on Punjabis. I went at the invitation of Inder Mohan Khosla, who was then the manager of the local branch of the Standard Chartered Bank.† On the evening of the day I flew in from New Delhi, Khosla—whom I had met through relatives—took me to the home of Kusum and Satish Chander Mahajan. The Mahajans had lived in this city for several generations, and had prospered in business. Both Satish and Kusum, an elegant Hindu middle-aged couple, seemed pained at the chasm that now separated Amritsar's Sikhs and Hindus.

"There's a total divide between Sikhs and Hindus," Kusum Mahajan

---

*Conversation with author, April 1991.
†Khosla retired from the Standard Chartered Bank in 1990 and now lives in Bombay, where he is a financial consultant.

said, in her book-lined living room. "They no longer come to our homes, and we are seldom invited to theirs."

How long had it been since the Mahajans visited the Golden Temple?

"The temple doesn't have any longer the aura the Vatican does," Mrs. Mahajan said, with surprising acidity in her voice. "It's become the hotbed of Sikh politics. Sikhs and Hindus are being increasingly separated—but the separation of the Sikh religion and Sikh politics is no longer there."

The next day, I wanted to walk into the Golden Temple by myself. After all, Hindus had been visiting it for hundreds of years. But Inder Singh Monga, a Sikh I had met at Khosla's bank, suggested that I wait a bit.

"There's a meeting on at the temple," Monga, who worships daily at the temple, said. "All the high priests are there today. They're deciding what to do about the killing of Sikhs that is going on in Delhi. You might want to wait until tomorrow."

The five high priests of Sikhism ordinarily met at the Akal Takht, Sikhism's Vatican. It is an impressive three-story building with marble walls, domes with gold leaves, and balconies that offer an unimpeded view of the Harimandir, the main "Golden Temple," which sits in the middle of a pond that Sikhs consider sacred. It is from the Akal Takht that the high priests periodically issue hukamnamas, or encyclicals, and tankhaiyas, or formal condemnations of irreligious conduct. The priests usually met without fanfare and worked quietly. Few of India's 14 million Sikhs had heard of these five men; fewer still knew their names.

"Most of us Sikhs don't even know who these five men are," Noni Chawla, a young man who was then the marketing director of the ITC-Sheraton hotel chain, had told me in Delhi. * "Sikhism is a religion that doesn't demand too much attention to its hierarchy."

But Mrs. Gandhi had jailed the political leaders of the Sikh community. Officials of the Akali Dal and the Shiromani Gurudwara Prabandhak Committee—the 140-member organization that oversees most of India's Sikh temples, with an annual budget of $10 million raised mainly from individual donations—had been incarcerated ever since October 6, 1983, when Indira Gandhi put the Punjab under direct control of the Delhi government. Bhindranwale, who had become a de facto leader of the Sikhs, was dead. A political vacuum now existed among Sikhs. So the five head priests of the Akal Takht found themselves in a unaccustomed and uneasy role as high-visibility Sikh spokesmen. This role required

---

* Noni Chawla is now based in Bombay as a top executive for ITC Limited.

them to span the long-standing divide between their religion and politics. And the head priests quickly made a mess of things. Their spokesman, Giani Kirpal Singh, issued a condolence statement following the murder of Mrs. Gandhi. Within a day, he withdrew it. "We are neither happy with her death nor do we condemn it," Kirpal Singh was quoted as saying. The remarks did not please Amritsar's Hindus.

The day I turned up in Amritsar, the head priests were reported to have urged Sikh members of Mrs. Gandhi's ruling Congress Party to immediately resign. The following day, they rescinded that directive. In Hindu homes, and even among some Sikhs I met in Amritsar, the five priests were coming under increasing criticism for not issuing a strong call for religious harmony and asking Sikhs not to retaliate for the attacks against them in Delhi and northern India. Their silence was construed as suggesting timorousness or as an implied threat that left open the possibility of a Sikh counter assault. Some weeks before the Gandhi assassination, the high priests had written a note to then President Zail Singh. The government, the priests said, was courting trouble. Zail Singh, who was widely and correctly perceived as a stooge of Mrs. Gandhi—who had selected him to be India's constitutional president —visited the Golden Temple on September 26, 1984.* That visit took place not long after the Delhi government had repaired some of the damage to the Golden Temple incurred during the military assault in June. Giani Kirpal Singh, the first among equals of the five head priests, hectored him publicly.

"If the government continues its anti-Sikh attitude and treats us like second-class citizens, it will not only endanger the unity of the country, but also cause communal disharmony," Kirpal Singh said. He then listed the things the high priests wanted done immediately:

- The revocation of the Delhi government's ban on the All-India Sikh Students Federation. Many members of this organization had been imprisoned on charges of terrorism.
- The unconditional release from prison of all Akali Dal leaders as well as activists of the Sikh students' federation. These leaders, and also top officials of the Shiromani Gurudwara Prabandhak Committee, had been locked up to prevent them from further stirring up Sikhs.
- Adequate compensation to the families of the people who were killed

---

*When asked by a newspaper reporter about his selection by Mrs. Gandhi for the Indian presidency, Zail Singh replied: "If my leader had said that I should pick up a broom and be a sweeper, I would have done that. She chose me to be president."

or injured during the army's assault on the Golden Temple. The government had not released the names of the terrorists who were killed during the army operation, nor the names of pilgrims who were trapped in the Golden Temple and died in the crossfire between the troops and the terrorists.

• An end to the random arrests of Sikh youths in the Punjab. The authorities periodically rounded up youths suspected of sympathizing with terrorists.

The hectoring and scolding were deliberate. The high priests had earlier excommunicated Zail Singh by issuing a tankaiya against him: He was accused of religious misconduct. Why such a strong step? Because the president of India is technically the commander-in-chief of the country's armed forces, and since the military had assaulted the Golden Temple the president should be held accountable for the action. Zail Singh was almost reverentially subdued when he visited the high priests in Amritsar.

"I ask for sincere forgiveness from the gurus for the unfortunate incidents," he said. That was at once interpreted by the priests as an apology from the Gandhi government for the military assault. The tankaiya against Zail Singh was lifted. He was a Sikh again.

For almost three years prior to her death, Mrs. Gandhi had been negotiating with the Sikhs. The Akalis had submitted a list of forty-five demands to the Delhi government in September 1981. These demands—which were virtually identical to the ones enumerated in the Anandpur Sahib Resolution—were grouped into religious, political, and economic categories. Manmohan Singh was among those involved in the negotiations, some of which were held in secret.* Singh, a pleasant man of about sixty, was chairman of Frick India, a flourishing engineering company. A Sikh, he headed such organizations as the Delhi Chamber of Commerce. The secret talks started in October 1981, Manmohan Singh told me, but they progressed only fitfully, floundering often over the issues of Chandigarh, the capital that the Punjab shared with neighboring Haryana and which the Akalis wanted turned over to their state immediately. There was also disagreement over the critical question of the sharing of river waters. In mid-February 1983, Mrs. Gandhi announced

* Subhash Kirpekar of *The Times of India*, who has covered the Punjab extensively for a decade, says that in addition to the known meetings there were eight secret ones in New Delhi and Chandigarh between Punjab leaders and representatives of the central government. These secret meetings, held between 1981 and 1984, included one that was convened at the Chandigarh Airport lounge. Kirpekar says that Rajiv Gandhi was a participant at some of these meetings.

the partial acceptance of some Sikh religious demands: Instead of the original Akali demand for a radio station, for example, she agreed to allow the broadcast of religious services from the Golden Temple on All-India Radio. The government also agreed to the Akali demand that Sikhs be allowed to carry the kirpan—the traditional knife that all Sikhs are asked by the religion to always carry—on all domestic flights of Indian Airlines; the specification was that the kirpan not be longer than six inches. But the Akalis dismissed these concessions as being fraudulent. They stepped up their agitation against Mrs. Gandhi. Manmohan Singh was one of those who urged everyone to cool down. But the prime minister was in no mood to listen to anyone. Singh recalled to me a conversation he had with Dr. P. C. Alexander, Mrs. Gandhi's principal private secretary and her key adviser on the Punjab.*

"The PM never listens—either she demands an explanation, or she gives you a lecture," Singh quoted Dr. Alexander as saying.

In fact, Mrs. Gandhi declined to meet personally with the Akalis, passing on the task instead to top aides such as Dr. Alexander. Her son and heir-apparent, Rajiv Gandhi, also occasionally met with the Sikhs. Manmohan Singh told me that the Akali Dal's president, the late Harchand Singh Longowal, expressed to him his dismay over Mrs. Gandhi's refusal to meet with him or the rest of the Akali leadership.

"She's said to oppose the Anandpur Sahib resolution," Longowal said to Manmohan Singh. "But why don't you tell her for me that she can delete anything from it she wants—and we will agree!"

Singh said that when he relayed Longowal's request to Dr. Alexander, the latter said: "The Anandpur Sahib resolution is not even an issue in all this."

The Akalis and other familiar with the on-again-off-again negotiations suspected that Mrs. Gandhi was being recalcitrant because she had an ulterior motive. She let the Punjab crisis drag on, they suspected, in order to rally the state's Hindus behind her and in order to unify the Hindu majority of the north Indian states, all of whom were concerned about the growing shrillness of the Sikhs' agitation.† By stonewalling the Sikhs, Mrs. Gandhi was consolidating her position with the Hindu

---

*Dr. P. C. Alexander was later named by Prime Minister Rajiv Gandhi as India's high commissioner to Britain. After a stint there as ambassador, he served as governor of the southern state of Tamil Nadu. He continues to be consulted by Indian leaders, even though he no longer holds a government post.

†It was ironic that Rajiv Gandhi would use the same divisive tactics as his mother in the Punjab. In the campaign for the November 1989 election, the appeal to Hindu chauvinism was unconcealed and shameless.

majority of North India, whose support she deemed especially critical in the national elections that were to be held by January 1985. As the Akalis's dealings with Mrs. Gandhi faltered, the strength of the Bhindranwale extremists rose. More than 500 Hindus and moderate Sikhs were killed by the terrorists. On April 25, 1984, a senior Punjab police official named A. S. Atwal was shot to death at the entrance of the Golden Temple. The assailants were seen running into the temple, and the widespread assumption was that they were Bhindranwale's men.

But Bhindranwale told Manmohan Singh that his group had nothing to do with the Atwal murder.

"I can prove to you that it was the Indira Congress people in Punjab who killed Atwal," the thirty-seven-year-old preacher told Singh. "Why does the government accuse me of being a murderer? In my whole life I haven't even killed a sparrow."

Bhindranwale's sentiments to Manmohan Singh ran counter to his other pronouncements, however. His homilies were always fiery and filled with threats against Hindus. He promised that if the Sikhs did not get their own nation, "rivers of blood will flow" in the Punjab. He drew crowds the like of which had never been seen before in the Golden Temple.

Manmohan Singh told me that the mobs that attacked Sikh homes in Delhi after the murder of Indira Gandhi often shouted the name of Bhindranwale—they were taking revenge for the murders Bhindranwale and his men committed. He himself had to flee his home in New Friends Colony, hidden in the trunk of his car.

"Even in the darkest days of the Partition, I walked upright across the border from Pakistan," Manmohan Singh said to me. "Even then I didn't have to hide. At my age, I cannot forget this humiliation. It will never be the same for me again."

His twenty-two-year-old son, Gurmohan Singh, had said to him: "Dad, at your age isn't it simply better to stay at home and fight the mobs with your gun—rather than hide like this in your car?"

And Manmohan Singh had replied: "No, at my age, discretion is the better part of valor."

As he was being driven away from his home, Manmohan Singh thought of how, only a few weeks ago, he had led a delegation of Indian businessmen to the United States. He had told Americans in speech after speech how proud he was to be an Indian.

"I would never have dreamed that in my own country I would have to run away from a mob like this," Manmohan Singh said to me, tears in his eyes.

14

Party Times

As 1966 came to a close, Indira found herself besieged with requests from foreign journalists—especially television correspondents—for interviews. It seemed that the world was expecting a major famine in India, and a lot of Western reporters flew in to cover the expected tragedy for the audiences back in the affluent industrialized countries. Indira's father had enjoyed give-and-take with the media; Nehru met with the press at least once a month, in addition to giving interviews—both on the record and off—to newsmen he particularly liked. Indira, in contrast, always gave the impression of having to suffer through media sessions, even though her self-confidence increased noticeably. Between 1966 and 1969, for example, she held only three formal news conferences. Assessing Indira's relations with the press, Frank Moraes, one of India's most respected editors, had this to say: "Nehru talked a great deal in an interview. You started him off, and off he went. She [Indira] is not forthcoming. She's rather like a convent schoolgirl, tongue-tied. Nehru didn't care what the newspapers said about him. With her, if there's an article, editorial, or cartoon she doesn't like, one of her entourage lets her disapproval be known."* Years later, Rajinder Puri—whose acid pen has been the bane of Indian politicians—put it this way: "Indira, in fact, does not have a style which she may call her own. And because the style is phony, the words ring false, with a jarring clatter against the manner she perhaps

*Quoted by Nayantara Sahgal in *Indira Gandhi: Her Road to Power* (New York: Ungar, 1982), p. 39.

329

seeks to emulate—that of her father. Her every gesture, every mannerism, seems to be modelled on that of the late Jawaharlal Nehru. The hurried, almost running walk, the rambling informality, the simulated anger with an uncomprehending public—it is all there, a trifle parodied, a little grotesque, as it evokes nostalgic memories of the original. . . ."*
On January 1, 1969, Indira ended her news conference with these words: "I hope it will be a year of better reporting."

She tended to pay a bit more attention to the foreign press in those early years in power than to the domestic media. Indira was concerned about her image overseas, and she felt that through interviews she could make appeals directly to foreign constituencies that influenced policymakers—particularly in the rich donor nations of the West. Famine was averted in 1966 because of assistance from United Nations agencies and the government's own efforts to better distribute food grains. Her media appearances were becoming smoother. Indira, the political neophyte, was also becoming more sophisticated in her understanding of power politics: She worked diligently to anticipate the moves of her opponents within the Congress Party and outside it. Her informants had told her that some members of the Syndicate were plotting to remove her from office.† She did not need spies, of course, to sense that there was increasing resistance to her among the party bosses who, only a few months back, had lavishly praised her and installed her as prime minister.

The party bosses were belatedly discovering that Jawaharlal Nehru's daughter was no dumb doll, that she had ideas of her own about how the country should be run, and that she did not especially relish being controlled by men who, she felt, were increasingly out of touch with the times. When she set out to dismiss Gulzari Lal Nanda as home minister, Kamaraj and others opposed the move; Indira later won the day, however. But when she expressed the desire to fire Finance Minister Sachin Chaudhuri and Foreign Trade Minister Manubhai Shah from her cabinet, the Syndicate said no. Indira thought that Chaudhuri and Shah were incompetent, and that they seemed to rely on the Syndicate's advice far more than on her directives as prime minister.

All of this would ordinarily constitute the sort of political gamesmanship that goes on in most democracies. But Indira—quite correctly—viewed these developments as a matter of political life and death. The February 1967 general elections were on the horizon. Opposition

---

*Rajinder Puri, India: The Wasted Years (New Delhi: Chetana Publications, 1975).
†S. K. Patil once told the author that he though Indira was "disastrous" for the country. Patil was too shrewd a politician to oppose Indira openly, but he did consult with some industrialists about the possibility of toppling Indira in a party coup. The idea was to buy off Congress parliamentarians.

leaders such as Ram Manohar Lohia were already urging Indians to "throw the rascals out"—meaning, of course, the Congress. The party was being depicted in sections of the media as moribund, corrupt, and without fresh ideas for recharging India's economic development. Like Opposition parties, the Congress Party was now selecting its candidates for the elections. Naturally, Indira was anxious that as many of her allies as possible got nominations to run. Indira knew full well that her future as party leader depended on whether Congress parliamentarians selected her after the elections. Assuming the Congress secured a majority, it was inevitable that she would become India's prime minister. But the Syndicate was determined to put the squeeze on her. Knowing that she and Krishna Menon were once again close—at least politically—the party bosses turned down Krishna Menon's request for a ticket from Bombay. Indira was appalled. But there was little she could do openly to annul the Syndicate's action. Krishna Menon, furious over being denied a ticket by the Congress Party, resigned from the organization. He ran in the election as an independent candidate from the North Bombay constituency—for which he had sought the Congress Party ticket—but was defeated.

So she swallowed this insult and bade her time. Within the Syndicate, there now were ever stronger sentiments to replace her after the election. Several aspirants to Congress tickets were denied the privilege for no other reason than the fact that they were Indira's supporters. On December 25, 1966, Indira gave an interview to *The Times of India*. She discussed the Congress Party's prospects for the elections and expressed confidence that she would lead her party back into power. Then, in what was a clear allusion to the Syndicate, Indira said: "Here is a question of whom the party wants and whom the people want. My position among the people is uncontested."* This was as clear a signal as Indira could send to the Syndicate that she could face them confidently.

That self-confidence was hard-won. Indira had already set about campaigning seriously, traveling long distances to attend rallies in dusty villages and crowded townships. Winter had gripped northern India, and Indira's diminutive figure, with a shawl draped around her slender shoulders, became a familiar, indeed even welcome, sight in rural India—where Indira knew the votes were. In January and February 1967, Indira traveled more than 35,000 miles, crisscrossing India with extraordinary energy.† As her reputation for being a good campaigner spread, Indira was deluged with invitations from party organizations from Assam

---

*Interview published in *The Times of India*, December 26, 1966.
†Congress Party estimate put her at nearly 200 rallies during this period.

to Gujarat, from Kashmir to Kerala, to put in appearances on behalf of local candidates. She adopted her father's style of going right into a crowd to speak to people individually. Some of her speeches were even based on those of her father's. While her delivery of a written speech could be flat, Indira seemed to be most effective when speaking spontaneously in Hindi and English. Critics noted that Indira's written speeches in those early years in power tended to be dull. With time and experience, her formal speeches improved considerably. However, to the end, Indira remained a much better impromptu speaker than when using a formal text.

At one rally in Jaipur, capital of Rajasthan, Indira was heckled by a large crowd sympathetic to the Maharani of Jaipur, a local dowager who supported the right-wing Swatantra Party. *

"Go and ask the maharajahs how many wells they dug for the people in their states when they ruled them, how many roads they constructed, what they did to fight the slavery of the British," Indira said. "If you look for an account of their achievements before we became independent, all you will find is a great big zero!"

Indira quickly acquired a feisty style that was appreciated by the crowds, largely the peasantry. She used metaphors from everyday life which they could easily understand. She spoke simply, giving an easy-to-digest definition of socialism which they could comprehend. "Poverty should be eradicated, disparities between the rich and poor should be reduced," Indira proclaimed in speech after speech. "The backward classes, be they Harijans or hill people, should have an equal share of the natural resources." Every speech would end with a shout of "*Jai Hind*"—"Long live India!"—and the crowds would respond resoundingly. Occasionally, however, Indira encountered hostility from her audiences. During a rally in Bhubaneshwar, for instance, someone hurled a stone at her, hitting Indira's nose. She began to bleed profusely. But Indira insisted on continuing her speech. When she returned to Delhi, she had to have an operation on her nose—it had been fractured.†

During these appearances, Indira discovered that her audiences responded warmly to references to her father, and to the Nehru family's

---

*Indira Gandhi did not especially like the Maharani. Years later, the Maharani—Gayatri Devi—was to be jailed by the Indira government during the Emergency of 1975–77.

†Indira Gandhi had always been sensitive about the size and shape of her nose. Inder Malhotra says that when Indira was about to be operated on after the Bhubaneshwar incident, she asked her surgeons "to treat the accident as an opportunity for much-needed plastic surgery on her nose." The surgeons, however, merely repaired her fracture and did not perform plastic surgery on Indira's nose.

links with India's freedom struggle. Indira began to be perceived as a genuinely national leader; in contrast, the Syndicate bosses were seen as petty and parochial figures. None of them enjoyed the kind of national recognition—even affection—that Indira did. Indira rarely attacked the Syndicate in public; she seldom even referred to them. She knew that she had become a political figure in her own right, a woman with a future—if only this next election could be won.

Not all public appearances had to do exclusively with the election campaign, however. Indira, carrying on her father's practice of meeting with students, traveled to the southern city of Bangalore on January 8, 1967, to deliver a convocation address at the university there. "Amidst the din and dust of electioneering, I have this welcome opportunity of meeting young men and women," the prime minister said. "Not without reason are you the bridge between today and tomorrow, between continuity and change, between tradition and modernity. I am not a political person in the narrow sense in which politics is generally understood. It is the occupational hazard of politicians and administrators to be obsessed with 'now.' Yet the present moment and its problems can be understood only in the context of the flow and direction of history. The present is the road between the past and the future. To pinpoint this and to give a correct perspective should be one of the functions of universities."

Then, in what seemed to be an allusion to Syndicate bosses—although it was unclear whether any of them bothered to take notice at the time—Indira said: "The conflict in India is not primarily one of ideology as such, but a clash between those who cling to old ways of thought and those who want India to understand the changes which are occurring all over the world and to adapt herself to the needs of the second half of the twentieth century. The resistance offered by old modes of thought to the force of the new explains much that is happening around us. Change and modernity do not necessarily mean breaking with national experience. What is needed is a correct understanding of the meaning of tradition." What Indira seemed to be implying was that she represented the forces of change, yet she was rooted in the highest—and purest—traditions of the freedom struggle, the movement that her own family had been so much a part of.

It was during this 1967 election campaign that Bharat Mata—Mother India—established herself firmly on the Indian political map. Indira articulated the themes of poverty alleviation and social equality—themes that she would sharpen in subsequent campaigns. Appearing at a rally in her Rae Bareilly constituency, Indira said: "My family is not confined to a few individuals. It consists of scores of people. Your burdens are comparatively light, because your families are limited and viable. But my burden is manifold, because scores of my family members are poverty-stricken—and I have to look after them. Since they belong to different castes and creeds, they sometimes fight among themselves, and I have to intervene—especially to look after the weaker members of my family, so that the stronger ones do not take advantage of them." The Pakistani-born writer Tariq Ali has an interesting interpretation of Indira's speeches during this time: "The merit of [her] approach was two-fold. It avoided explaining why the country was in such a mess and why poverty was increasing, and it simultaneously projected her as a leader above parties. They [the masses] were her family, her responsibilities. The Congress Party was not mentioned very often."[*]

Indira began to believe that the warm reception she got at rallies around the country would translate into votes when Indians went to the polling booths in February 1967. It was a naïve belief, however, for Indira misread the mood of the electorate. Notwithstanding Indira's growing appeal, the Congress Party lost ground around the country because of a strong perception that it had not delivered fully on its promises of economic and social improvement for the masses, most of whom still lived in poverty. Indira learned that drawing crowds was one thing; getting people to vote for you was another. The Indian novelist Shashi Tharoor likes to tell the story of a Congress candidate in the Madurai constituency in southern India. Indira had agreed to address a rally on his behalf. It was the biggest gathering ever to be held in Madurai—nearly a million people, by one estimate. When the election results came in, however, the Congress candidate lost so badly that even his deposit was lost. The Congress's majority fell from more than 200 seats to a bare working majority of twenty. The party was able to capture only 40 percent of the vote—which meant that in the 520 seats contested for the Lok Sabha, the Congress had been able to secure only 283 seats.[†] The left-wing parties did quite well, as did the Jan Sangh.[‡] In state legislatures, the Congress did even more poorly. It was able to hold on to only 1,661 out of 3,453 seats. Non-Congress governments—established by Opposition coalitions—came to power in Bihar, West Bengal, Madras—later known

[*] Ali, *An Indian Dynasty*, p. 161.
[†] In the previous election, the Congress had obtained 361 seats. It captured about 45 percent of the overall vote.
[‡] The two Communist parties won forty-two seats; their tally in the previous election had been twenty-nine. The right-wing Jan Sangh won thirty-five, up from fourteen; and the Swatantra Party, which was funded mostly by big business, increased its representation from eighteen to forty-four seats.

as Tamil Nadu—Orissa, Kerala, and the Punjab.* The elections were interpreted variously as a swing to the right and as a swing to the left. In fact, the pattern of Congress defeats was highly idiosyncratic, related to the peculiarities of each state, with no consistency in the direction of opposition sentiments.† "The reason for the Congress drubbing was not far to seek," writes Trevor Drieberg.

> It was not due to the failure of the Nehru magic embodied in his daughter to work on the electorate. A combination of events after the 1962 elections turned the tide of popular opinion against the Congress. The most important of them were the humiliation of the Chinese invasion in 1962; Nehru's death when the bewildered, frustrated nation needed his comfort and guidance most; the incidents in the Rann of Kutch and the subsequent large-scale India-Pakistan war, in which many people suspected India had not done as well as Congress and government spokesmen claimed; a widespread monsoon failure which brought with it privation and suffering to millions, and the threat of famine; and finally, the rise in living costs resulting from the ham-handed manner in which devaluation of the rupee was undertaken. . . . More and more, the Congress was coming to be identified in the minds of the urban and rural poor and middle classes with privilege and inequality and unshamed self-interest.‡

Indira, like most Congress leaders, was stunned by the voters' verdict. She had not expected that the Congress would take such a dive.§ But her shock was softened somewhat by the fact that Syndicate bosses such as S. K. Patil and Atulya Ghosh lost their races in the elections.** Even Kamaraj, the Congress president, was defeated—by a student leader.

---

*In April 1967, the Congress coalition government in Uttar Pradesh fell. And in Rajasthan, the Congress-dominated government proved to be so unstable that President's Rule was imposed by Indira.
†Hardgrave and Kochanek, *India: Government and Politics in a Developing Nation.*
‡Drieberg, *Indira Gandhi,* pp. 74–75.
§Professors Robert Hardgrave and Stanley Kochanek write: "Results of the 1967 elections revealed the breakdown of the Congress system of reconciliation and consensus. The elections radically changed the political map of India, marking the end of one-party dominance and the emergence of a new political era. In the decade from 1967 to 1977, the Congress, at one time or another, lost control of nearly half the state governments. It was torn by schism and emerged, reincarnated, under Prime Minister Indira Gandhi's increasingly centralized and personalized authority."
**The only two members of the Syndicate who won their parliamentary races were Neelam Sanjiva Reddy in Andhra Pradesh, and S. Nijalingappa in Karnataka.

Nine members of Indira's cabinet also lost their races. "Overall, it was a bad result for the Congress, but a good one for Indira Gandhi," says Tariq Ali.[*] One would have thought that, with such a disastrous showing, the Congress would attempt to achieve greater party unity. Although many in the party realized that the election results would have been much worse without Indira, internecine party squabbles continued. Morarji Desai was once again bent upon staking his own claim for the prime minister's job. He had won by a large majority in his own election and this, he reasoned, had placed him in a stronger position personally than before. That was only his opinion, of course. While Morarji Desai had indeed won a thumping victory in Gujarat, his coattails were not long enough to assure a victory for the Congress in the state. While it was true that Desai enjoyed wider name recognition than, say, Yeshwantrao B. Chavan or Jagjivan Ram, that did not necessarily mean that Congress parliamentarians were prepared to forsake Indira and turn to Desai. Kamaraj, in fact, undertook a thorough head count of these parliamentarians and found that Indira was preferred by them by a very large margin. He publicly called her "an incompetent amateur" and "unfit for office." Indira did not respond openly to Desai's criticisms. Her style was to score quietly, then hit back only when she was sure of not just stinging her opponents but destroying them. Desai set about marshaling his forces for what everybody knew would be a rough fight with Indira. But that fight never quite materialized because of Kamaraj's intervention, and sustained mediation by a group of senior Congress leaders including Dwarka Prasad Mishra, the chief minister of Madhya Pradesh and Mrs. Gandhi's ally, and C. B. Gupta, chief minister of Uttar Pradesh and a man considered sympathetic to Morarji Desai.

Kamaraj, the old warhorse, recognized that the already-bruised Congress Party could not survive another divisive battle over the leadership question. Moreover, the Syndicate was hardly in a position to impose its will on Indira or even the party. Some of his Syndicate colleagues might have entertained the notion of deposing Indira, but Kamaraj was certainly being realistic. Krishan Bhatia writes: "Much of the Syndicate's influence within the Party and the government was the result of the shrewdness of its members in backing the winning horse. It could ill afford to make a mistake or even take a chance on a doubtful entry at a time when it lay battered and bruised. Kamaraj, therefore, gave Desai no indication of his willingness to switch sides."[†]

[*] Ali, *An Indian Dynasty*, p. 162.
[†] Bhatia, *Indira*, p. 201.

Kamaraj told Indira that, in the interests of party unity, she should invite Desai to become deputy prime minister. She should share power with him.

"He wants the Home Ministry," Kamaraj said to Indira. "He also wants the authority of being the senior-most minister in the cabinet."

"No," Indira said. "There cannot be two captains of the team."

Finally, but reluctantly, Indira agreed to offer the deputy prime minister's post to Desai, who was seventy-one years old at the time. The last time that the title of "deputy prime minister" had been conferred on anyone was back in 1947. Jawaharlal Nehru had made Vallabhbhai Patel his deputy prime minister—and also Home Minister—a position that Patel held until his death in 1950. Both Patel and Morarji Desai hailed from Gujarat, and Desai often called himself a disciple of the right-oriented Patel. Indira told the media that she had invited her longtime adversary into her cabinet "in the interest of party unity." But he would not be given the powerful Home Ministry. The Home Ministry was given to Yeshwantrao B. Chavan, who already had held it in Indira's previous government. Because the Home Ministry controlled a number of key police and intelligence agencies, Indira seemed somewhat reluctant to give the post to Desai who, she felt, would surely use his power to undercut her. Instead, Desai was given the finance portfolio, the same ministry he supervised when Jawaharlal Nehru had asked him to resign in 1963 under the Kamaraj Plan. When asked why he was joining the government of a woman whom he had long ridiculed, Desai replied: "My friends wanted me to do so." By now, Morarji Desai had made his peace with the Syndicate. After the formal swearing-in ceremonies for Indira, Desai could not resist another gratuitous crack: "We are placing on her head a crown of thorns."

Indira noted these comments, maintaining her own record of offensive remarks that Desai continued to make about her. Indira told friends that she could have easily rejected Kamaraj's advice and refused Desai a cabinet post; her own political situation was strong enough at the time to weather the resulting storm, should one have occurred. But, she told these friends, she did not especially want to take on a new fight at this stage. Besides, she was already planning to render Desai politically impotent. In coming weeks, Indira managed to isolate him completely by not including even one of his supporters in her cabinet. She also excluded Neelam Sanjiva Reddy, a member of the Syndicate, making him instead the Speaker of the Lok Sabha.* Even though Morarji Desai

* The job of Speaker in the Indian Parliament is not as powerful as that of the

was the deputy prime minister, and Indira did indeed consult him on key economic issues and parliamentary tactics, the compromise between them was clearly of a cosmetic nature. Indira used Desai to enhance her own understanding of administration and parliamentary politics, knowing all along that the day would not be far away when she would have no use for him.

Indira would soon also have little use for the Congress Party's "old guard." These leaders had initially read the 1967 election results some-what differently from Indira, averring that it was the Congress Party's organizational failure that brought about its debacle. They had felt that the Congress needed a strongman at the head of government, not dainty and diminutive Indira Gandhi. The bosses seemed to be least concerned with public perceptions of the corruption within the top echelons of the Congress; after all, the bosses benefited most from the accouterments of power. The opulent life-styles of these leaders surely did not stem from an honest day's work. The bosses were concerned with maintaining their links to grass-roots party organizations, of course, but mainly to local factotums who would do their bidding. For most of the Congress bosses, it had been a while since they hitched up their trousers or dhotis and trudged through the muddy roads of India's villages.

Indira, however, did things differently at this stage. She had traveled widely during the election campaign—far more widely, in fact, than any of the Syndicate bosses—and seen for herself how badly off most Indians still were. "The word 'poverty' means nothing until you have walked into a village hut, or an urban slum," Indira told Janki Ganju, the old Nehru family friend. The important thing was not only how Indira reacted to poverty, but how the poor people of India perceived her. And the poor masses saw her as a leader, as someone who was sympathetic to their plight, as a woman who would feel their anguish as acutely as themselves. Most of all, they seemed to believe in her—that Indira Gandhi would act after she had made her rousing speeches before them.

At this point in her career, Indira Gandhi was demonstrating the beginnings of a technique that would serve her well in the future. When-ever she had political problems with the barons of her party—and this occurred from time to time in her career—Indira went over their heads to the people. Indira had grasped early on a seminal truth of Indian politics: Mass support was much more important than purely organiza-

---

Speaker of the U.S. House of Representatives. The Indian Speaker is essentially entrusted with keeping order during parliamentary sessions. Sanjiva Reddy later became president of India.

tional support—a fact which many of her political opponents never seemed to understand.

"Although the conventional perception is that the years 1966 and 1967 marked the political seasoning of Indira and were a turning point in her political approach, this was not really so," says Professor Ralph Buultjens. *

> In this period, she was simply putting into effect techniques, strategies, and concepts which were already very clear in her mind. Also at this time, Indira began to realize how deeply senior party leaders really resented her. But to her mind, there was nothing new in this, because she felt they had always constricted the more liberal and progressive side of her father's policies. While Nehru had tried to accommodate the innate conservatism of many Congress leaders, Indira was determined to prevent their brake on her efforts. Her determination flowed from both her strong belief in progressive politics and her understanding that her mass-oriented programs could be politically advantageous.

Those who knew Prime Minister Gandhi well—such as Professor Buultjens—say that although she successfully confronted the Syndicate over the question of forming her cabinet after the 1967 election, Indira's first truly decisive battle with her political adversaries involved another matter. It was over the choice of nominating the new president of the country that Indira fought openly with the Syndicate. The nomination was an occasion for confrontation, to be sure, but it ultimately involved a far more serious question than even the political development of Indira Gandhi. That question had to do with India's commitment to secularism, and whether a country with an overwhelming Hindu majority was at least prepared to accept as its head of state a man from a minority community. The post of president was, of course, largely a ceremonial one.† There was not much to do for the president other than hosting

---

*Conversation with the author, March 1991.

†Professor Stanley A. Wolpert notes that the president and vice president have powers in keeping with their roles as ceremonial heads of state, republican rather than royal, except for one "emergency" clause. This clause, borrowed from the constitution of the Weimar Republic, allowed India's head of state to suspend the constitution for six months at a time in the interests of national security. But the president rarely acts without advice from the prime minister. As the country's constitutional head, the president has status but no executive power.

state banquets, making goodwill visits abroad, and turning up at ribbon-cutting ceremonies. A large estate—the old Viceregal palace in New Delhi, now known as Rashtrapati Bhavan—came with the job, as did innumerable perks.

Since Independence in 1947, there had been two presidents. The first was Dr. Rajendra Prasad, a distinguished lawyer who had presided over the national Constituent Assembly, which had been indirectly elected in 1946 by provincial assemblies; he became president of India on January 26, 1950, when India's new constitution went in effect and the country formally became a republic.* Dr. Prasad was reelected president in 1952, under the provisions of the new constitution. In 1962 Dr. Sarvepalli Radhakrishnan, a Vedantic philosopher of international repute, succeeded Prasad; he had served as vice president for ten years. The seventy-nine-year-old Dr. Radhakrishnan was virtually blind, and generally in ill health. Some Congress chieftains privately wanted Dr. Radhakrishnan to serve a second five-year term, and Radhakrishnan himself was reportedly keen to carry in Rashtrapati Bhavan. Some of these bosses felt that, in view of the divisions within the party, a new candidate—such as Dr. Zakir Husain, the vice president (1897–1969)—might not get votes in a Presidential election. The president was technically chosen by an electoral college consisting of members of Parliament and of state legislators.

But Indira's choice for president was not Dr. Radhakrishnan but Dr. Husain. She had not forgiven the president for criticizing her father in the wake of the Sino-Indian War of 1962. Dr. Radhakrishnan had also behaved in a somewhat patronizing manner toward Indira in the early days of her stewardship. Moreover, Indira felt that the choice of Husain would be especially welcomed by India's sizable Muslim minority: Zakir Husain was a Muslim and a widely respected scholar. Indira held that the ascension of Dr. Radhakrishnan to the presidency after serving as Dr. Rajendra Prasad's vice president had set a precedent. Born in Hyderabad, Husain had obtained a doctorate in philosophy from the University of Berlin. He had joined Mahatma Gandhi in the freedom struggle. Husain later served as vice chancellor of Aligarh Muslim University for eight years following India's independence. He had also started the Jamia Milia Islamia in Delhi, an educational institution for Muslims but where non-Muslims were also welcome. Jawaharlal Nehru had appointed Husain as governor of Bihar; on one occasion, Husain publicly reminded the Con-

* January 26 is a national holiday in India, marking Republic Day. A grand parade is held in New Delhi, and each year a foreign dignitary is invited to be an honored guest.

gress Party of its secular heritage. Husain quoted at some length from Jawaharlal Nehru's concept of a secular state: "What it [the secular state] means is that it is a state which honors all faiths equally and gives them equal opportunities; that, as a state, it does not allow itself to be attached to one faith or religion, which then becomes the state religion. . . . In a country like India, no real nationalism can be built up except on the basis of secularity. Narrow religious nationalisms are relics of a past age and are no longer relevant today."

When it became known that Indira wanted Dr. Husain to succeed to the presidency, Hindu right-wing groups such as the Jan Sangh criticized her fiercely. It was apparent that they were not prepared to accept a Muslim in such a high post. But Indira was determined that India—whose secularism was enshrined in the Constitution—should elect a Muslim as its president. "When people want to know why Zakir Sahib was bypassed, what answer will you give?" Indira would say to those who objected to the possibility of a Muslim being awarded the highest public job in India. "To me, Muslims and Hindus are Indians first and foremost." Indira was reaffirming her own secularism here, for in her mind there was never the slightest prejudice concerning Muslims. Like her father, she always believed that religion and caste should not matter. But in India in those days—and even more so these days—that sort of belief would be severely challenged by bigots.

"Religion has an important place in our culture, our society, and our personal beliefs and values," Indira Gandhi said to Professor Ralph Buultjens. "It has no special place in our state framework and no place in our politics. Our secularism never means opposition or indifference to religion. It means that all religions will receive equal recognition and respect, and that no one religion will have exceptional privilege or will influence government policy. The idea of an established religion or a government authorized by religion is abhorrent."*

But for an overwhelming number of India's majority of Hindus, Muslims remained the ancient enemy. There was little forgiveness toward Muslims because of real or perceived historical wrongs, much less the kind of trust and tolerance that Jawaharlal Nehru and Indira Gandhi had urged.

If this sounds too dramatic, consider the following: Of the 4,000 officers of the elite Indian Administrative Service in the early 1970s, only 120 were Muslims. In the 2,000-member Indian Police Service, there were only fifty Muslims. India had about 5,000 judges, but only

---

* Statement made to Professor Ralph Buultjens by Indira Gandhi in New Delhi.

300 of them were Muslims. There were nearly 120,000 officers in the country's fourteen nationalized banks, but only 2,500 of them were Muslims. M. J. Akbar, in his *India: The Siege Within*,* refers to a survey of some of India's top private-sector companies in the early 1980s. The survey found, for example, that at Pond's India Limited, only one of the corporation's 115 senior executives was a Muslim; at DCM, the figure was two out of 987; at Brooke Bond, fourteen out of 673; at ITC, seventeen out of 966; at J. K. Synthetics, five out of 536; at Ambalal Sarabhai, only five out of 628 executives were Muslims. In 1985, when I visited Aligarh, once a flourishing city for Islamic culture and still the seat of the Aligarh Muslim University—where Dr. Zakir Husain was once the vice chancellor—I was told that the city's renowned locksmith industry had collapsed. Once the products of individual locksmiths from this Uttar Pradesh city used to be exported to the Middle East and to Europe. But these Muslim locksmiths could not overcome competition from the big lock factories that mushroomed in India in the 1950s and 1960s. Now there are few independent locksmiths left in Aligarh. And the government had made no efforts to assist those whose businesses collapsed when the machine age arrived: Few of the old locksmiths were hired by the new factories. "The ordinary Muslim has been left out of India's economic and political mainstream," George Fernandes, one of India's leading labor leaders and a former member of the cabinet, told me. "And he faces a bleak future. Muslims don't get ordinary jobs so easily. The Muslim is not wanted in the armed forces because he is always suspect—whether we want to admit it or not, most Indians consider Muslims as a fifth column for Pakistan. The private sector distrusts him. A situation has been created in which the Muslim, for all practical purposes, is India's new untouchable."†

Indira Gandhi knew that the economic plight of India's Muslims had been dramatically exacerbated since independence—but it did not begin when British rule ended in 1947. Jawaharlal Nehru, in *The Discovery of India*, said that historical causes blocked up avenues of development and prevented the release of talent. He identified these causes as the delay in the development of a new industrial middle class, and the "excessively feudal background" of the Muslims. Indeed, it can be argued that the Muslim ethos in India started shredding when the Mughal Empire collapsed in the late eighteenth century. I met people in India who contended that the country's "Muslim question" would never be resolved

*Harmondsworth, U.K.: Penguin Books, 1985.
†Conversation with the author in New York City, 1985.

until the "Pakistan question" was settled once and for all. Since Independence, India's relationship with Pakistan has been disturbed and distrusting. Pakistan, after all, was an invented country, carved out of India's body because of the insistence of Hindu-haters like Mohammed Ali Jinnah. Jinnah was a British-educated lawyer who felt that Muslims would never enjoy first-class citizenship in a Hindu-dominated independent India. He was proven substantially right—even though two of India's constitutional presidents have been Muslims, and Muslims have served in the national cabinet. A number of national organizations, but particularly the Hindu-based Rashtriya Swayamsevak Sangh (which is more popularly known by its acronym, RSS) have engaged in Muslim-baiting over the years. Their virulent propaganda: The Muslim may be an Indian citizen, but his sympathies lie with Pakistan.

Hindu chauvinists have long expressed public alarm over the Muslims' proclivity for procreation. Their argument is that the Muslim hordes could again overrun India—as they did starting in the tenth century, when Muslim invaders came pouring in over the Khyber Pass and defeated squabbling Hindu rulers. The Hindu's racial memory is long and strong, and these days it is constantly pricked by irresponsible communalist organizations that have sprung up in many parts of the country. The leaders of these groups tell the Hindu that he must neither forget nor forgive the butchery and bloodshed that the Muslim conquerors brought wherever they went. In the western Indian state of Gujarat, for example, they tell horror stories of Mahmud of Ghazni, a Muslim tyrant who plundered the fabulous Hindu temple of Somnath, and also destroyed 10,000 other Hindu shrines in the province of Kanauj. Mahmud's armies wept through the area in A.D. 1025. So passive and pacific were the Hindus that they simply stood by while Mahmud's men ravaged the temples, slaughtered Hindu males, and raped and carried away Hindu women. The pillage of Hindu temples was especially favored by Muslim invaders because these temples were rich with the offerings of their devotees; and the rape of Hindu women was an attractive proposition, too, because they were beautiful and submissive. The Muslim plundering of India continued vigorously through much of the next 600 years: Nearly six centuries after Mahmud of Ghazni's raid of Somnath and Kanauj, the Mughal emperor Aurangzeb would ruthlessly put to the sword Hindus who refused to be converted to Islam.

During my travels through India, I have often come across many fellow Hindus who said that such historical wrongs had to be corrected. "But what fault is it of today's Muslims—the majority of whom were born after Independence?" I said one afternoon in Hyderabad to a local Hindu civic leader. "Why should majority Hindus now hold Muslims accountable for this terrible past? The Muslims of today want to live in peace."

"I agree it's not their fault," he said. "But sons have to pay for the sins of their fathers." These are attitudes you cannot easily hope to overcome. Organizations such as the RSS and the Shiv Sena in Bombay flourish because of strong anti-Muslim ideology. Now even the Congress Party seems to have come around to occasionally embracing naked communalism. The votes, after all, are with the majority Hindus—this was quite clear in the December 1984 national elections.

As economic opportunities declined for ordinary Muslims, they were faced with three choices: to emigrate to Pakistan; to join the underworld in India; or to take up jobs in the oil-rich states of the Arabian Peninsula, which were then just starting to launch ambitious development plans for their backward societies. Indira knew that even though Muslims were a minority in India—about 10 percent of the population—India contained a larger Muslim population than any country except Indonesia and Pakistan.* In other words, Muslims really constituted a state within a state. If Zakir Husain were to be named president, it would not only mean a reaffirmation of India's secularism. The elevation of Husain could translate into continued political gratitude from India's Muslims—indeed, Muslims generally preferred the Congress Party to the Opposition groups.

The question of whether Zakir Husain, a Muslim, should become president of India brought to the forefront an issue that had long been festering under the surface of public life in India: Were Muslims truly full-fledged citizens with equal opportunities, or were they second-class citizens? That question has still not been resolved and most likely never will. After all, how majority Hindus relate to minority Muslims has a lot to do with historical and atavistic feelings about Islam and Muslim conquerors. Not long after Indira's assassination, I went to Hyderabad, one of India's leading centers of Muslim culture, to see for myself how the "Muslim Question" had been played out in a bellwether region. Of the area's 6 million people, about 600,000 are Muslims. The percentage of Muslims, in fact, is about the same as the national figure, 10 percent. The Muslims of Hyderabad, with a few exceptions, are not a happy people. Here too, their sentiments mirror the national scene. Muslims, I found, were a

---

*Bangladesh was yet to be born in 1967. Its traumatic birth, after a war between India and Pakistan, took place in December 1971. Bangladesh had formerly been known as East Pakistan.

troubled, unhappy minority in India. Trevor Fishlock, formerly Delhi correspondent for the London *Times*, wrote an insightful book titled *India File* in which he characterized the country's Muslims as follows: "They are the rather unhappy remnant of a once powerful and conquering people whose forts, mosques, and domes dot the landscape and remain among the most distinctive of Indian images."* Historical animosities between Muslims and Hindus have survived in the country, and are particularly evident here in Hyderabad. No less a person than former chief minister Nandamuri Taraka Rama Rao told me: "We have to have special protection for our Muslim minorities here." Some protection. Majority Hindus periodically start riots against Muslims here, and the latter respond. Shops are burned and property is looted.

Not long after Indira Gandhi's assassination, I went to meet Mehboob Khan, a scion of an old-line nawabi family that had long been admirers of the Nehrus. Indira Gandhi had visited the Khans occasionally. His ancestors were Muslim noblemen who were given property and prominence by Hyderabad's early nizams some 300 years ago. Khan's father, Shah Alam Khan, owned a large tobacco company. The family, consisting of Khan's parents, and his six brothers and their wives and children, along with his own spouse and five children, lived in a sprawling mansion. The house and its lawns were an oasis of sorts, for outside the high walls was one of the most congested sections of Hyderabad. Khan had invited me for what Indians call "high tea." Laid out on a long mahogany table was a spread so immense that I could have feasted for a week. There were a dozen varieties of sandwiches; kebabs; mutton chops; fried turnovers filled with curried shrimp; custard pastries; assorted biscuits; and mangoes, oranges, grapes, apples, and bananas. And there was tea—rich, aromatic, sweet, milky tea. It was, Mehboob Khan said softly, only an ordinary "high tea," and could I please forgive him. For a moment I thought Khan was joking. But he was being perfectly serious. The exquisite rituals of hospitality among Hyderabad's Muslim nobility require such apologies. I had been introduced to Khan by my father-in-law, Anand Mohan Lal, who had cautioned me to be patient with such rituals. Khan explained how each item on his table was prepared. And he did not eat anything until I had finished.

I thanked him profusely for the wonderful collation.

"It was nothing," Khan said, "it was nothing at all."

He was a huge man, so huge that when he stood up he had to be careful not to bang his head against the chandelier that was fixed to the

---

* Trevor Fishlock, *India File* (London: John Murray, 1983).

high ceiling of his living room. I had come to see him because of his connections in Hyderabad's Muslim community. Soon after I had finished the "high tea," a group of men walked in. Each wore a long sherwani, a gold-brocaded jacket that reached to the knees, and the typically Muslim peaked cap of lambs wool. Each man also wore white pantaloons. They bowed to Khan, then quietly sat down.

Mehboob Khan had invited them to tell me about how Hyderabad's Muslims felt about their condition in modern-day India. Hyderabad, Khan told me, was an ethnic microcosm. What I would hear and learn here would be mirrored elsewhere in India, too. His guests were apprehensive about what might happen to Muslims after the death of Indira Gandhi. They were alarmed at the riots against the Sikhs in northern India. (There had not been such attacks against Sikhs in southern India, whose states were controlled by Opposition parties.)

"We are apprehensive because when one minority is subjected to this kind of brutality, how can other minority communities feel safe?" said Sulaiman Sikander, a local Muslim civic leader. "We thought for a long time that the Congress was a protector of the minorities. But in recent years we became disillusioned. And this episode concerning the Sikhs does not reassure us at all."

"Such riots aren't communal," Mehboob Khan said. "They are political. That's what is so troubling. Minorities are being made a hostage for political considerations—to get votes from the majority."

A man named Abdul Aziz spoke about the September 1984 Hindu-Muslim riots in Hyderabad. More than 150 Muslims died then, he said, and dozens of shops owned by Muslims along Abid Road were burned down. Indira Gandhi flew to Hyderabad for a political function, but she did not visit the affected areas. Despite an estimated property loss of more than $10 million, the Delhi government sanctioned only the equivalent of $10,000 in damage reparations.

"And worse, no one was arrested, no one was punished for the attacks against us Muslims," Aziz said, in Urdu. "How can you create confidence among minorities with a situation like this? There have been riots against Muslims in Ahmedabad, Meerut, Assam, and Muradabad—and no arrests there either, and very little by way of compensation to those who lost so much."

It occurred to me that Abdul Aziz could well have been speaking on behalf of the Sikhs who had been attacked in northern India. Few culprits had been arrested for rioting against them, too. I reminded the group that the Nehru family had always been known for its commitment to secularism. Should not Rajiv Gandhi be given a chance to demonstrate his own commitment?

"Of course," said Mehboob Khan. "But the question is, will Rajiv be able to break away from the communalist hold over the Congress Party? We used to vote for the Congress because we felt that the other political parties had become polluted with communalism. Now look what has happened."

I asked the group if they considered themselves Indians. They seemed stunned.

Mehboob Khan finally said: "This continuing suspicion of Muslims in India must stop. What have we done that is antinational? How many Muslims have been involved in espionage? Is there really a basis for suspicion? Did we not fully support the government when there were wars? Did we not contribute to the national defense fund? Did we not send our men to fight for our homeland? So why are we still suspect? What more do we need to do to establish our bonafides?"

In the presidential election of 1967, Opposition parties decided to unite behind one candidate. They knew that the overall Congress majority in Parliament and the state legislatures was just about 2 percent, so that a small shift in voting could easily ensure the election of an Opposition-backed presidential candidate. Opposition leaders enticed Chief Justice Koka Subba Rao of the Supreme Court into resigning from the bench. Subba Rao was due to retire in about a year's time, but he seemed to have been persuaded that his prospects of becoming India's next president were strong.

Indira thought that Subba Row's action was questionable; judges were traditionally nonpartisan, and the very fact that the chief judge of the country's highest court should align himself with political parties was highly inappropriate. But Indira was not beyond deal-making: At one point, she even suggested to the Opposition that Subba Rao be nominated as vice president, with Husain as president, so that the election could be unanimous. Some Opposition leaders appeared receptive to such a deal, but Kamaraj scotched it.

Indira prevailed on the Congress Parliamentary Board, which endorsed Zakir Husain's candidacy by a vote of five to four. In the presidential election itself, Husain won by more than 108,000 votes, or about 7 percent of the total number of ballots cast by parliamentary and state legislators. The victorious Congress candidate for vice president was Varahagiri Venkata Giri, a former labor organizer who had served as minister of labor in the central government, and earlier also as general secretary of the All-India Railwaymen's Federation. Indira now knew that she had the Syndicate on the ropes. What she did not fully appreciate was that the old party bosses were hardly about to cede their power without more intrigue and chicanery. What the bosses did not seem to realize was that their special era of power and privilege was rapidly drawing to a close—and that Indira Gandhi was determined to ensure that in her India there would be only one wielder of real political power.

IV

Triumph and Twilight

15

Taking on Titans

In the battle to ensure Zakir Husain's nomination for president, Indira Gandhi had shown that she could marshal key votes within the organizational structure of the Congress on issues that mattered to her. Muslims were pleased with Zakir Husain's election to the presidency; Indira received encomiums from the world media as well for supporting so determinedly—and skillfully—a man from a minority community for India's highest public office. During this period, Indira was also beginning to establish a modus vivendi with Morarji Desai, who still did not like her much but who had started to curtail his criticisms—no doubt in the worthy cause of self-interest. Desai even supported her choice of Husain. More than the Congress Party bosses, Desai understood the arithmetic of the presidential election—that Indira's choice would be supported by the Communists and independent legislators. In other words, once Indira had resolved that Zakir Husain would be India's next president, she went all out to campaign for him, creating an irreversible momentum in his favor.

The truce between Indira and Desai turned out to be temporary. It began unraveling over the question of relations between the central government and state governments. That question was to assume even greater significance during the latter part of Indira's career as prime minister. Morarji Desai now started telling associates that he felt Indira was not "stern enough" in dealing with ministries in various states that were controlled by Opposition parties. In particular, Desai—whose own politics were definitely right of center—felt that Indira was being excessively tolerant of Communist leaders in West Bengal and Kerala. He knew how hard Indira had worked in the late 1950s, when she was Congress president, to topple the Communist government in Kerala. And now the same Indira suddenly seemed quite willing to live and let live. Krishan Bhatia writes: "What shaped her attitude toward the non-Congress state governments was the conviction that in a federal system of government, the center must learn to live with states ruled by rival parties. Like Desai, she would have preferred to have her own party rule all the states, but she did not feel inclined to embark on a vendetta against those who had succeeded in defeating the Congress by legitimate, constitutional means. While she saw the wisdom at that stage in avoiding confrontation with the non-Congress state governments—if she could get along with them by giving them a long rope—Desai, still an unbending disciplinarian, saw in that stance unpardonable weakness and a vindication of his original claim that she was unfit to be the leader."[*]

Indira knew full well that the Indian constitution provided for a federal system with certain unitary features and also a formal bias in favor of the central government. But she also knew that in a vast country such as India, whose states were primarily predicated on linguistic divisions, regional forces had to be given adequate play. Since the reorganization of India's states along linguistic lines in 1956, there had been a gradual devolution of power to the states. The politics of universal adult franchise—the fact that every Indian above the age of twenty-one could vote—also began to strengthen the federal base of the Indian polity.[†] Professors Robert L. Hardgrave, Jr., and Stanley A. Kochanek note that although there are numerous special features of the Indian constitution that give it a highly centralized form, the two most important are the distribution of powers between the central government and the states, and the financial provisions affecting the distribution of revenues.[‡] During the first twenty-five years after independence, say Professors Hard-

---

[*] Bhatia, *Indira Gandhi*, p. 217.
[†] Hardgrave and Kochanek, *India: Government and Politics in a Developing Nation.*
[‡] In India, states do not have their own separate constitutions in addition to the federal constitution, as they do in, say, the United States. Centralizing features of the Indian constitution include a single integrated hierarchical judicial system; all-India administrative services that provide officers at the national, state, and district levels; a national police force; and a national election commission that supervises all national and state elections. The Indian constitution defines the powers of both the center and the states, and provides for the governmental structures of each. For an understanding of the Indian constitution, the author wishes to acknowledge the work of Professors Hardgrave and Kochanek.

grave and Kochanek, several factors combined to impart to the Indian political system an explicitly federal character that could be characterized as "cooperative federalism." These factors included the restraint exercised by the central government in trying to impose its will on the states. The political and administrative dependence of the central government on the states in critical policy areas resulted in a cooperative federalism based on a bargaining process between the center and the states. "The essentially federal character of the Congress Party, with its strong party bosses," according to Professors Hardgrave and Kochanek, "provided the political base for this bargaining process—a process that took place within the Congress 'family' so long as the party retained power both at the center and within the states. It was a politics of accommodation, but one weighted toward the center."

It was this politics of accommodation that Jawaharlal Nehru understood very well, and that Indira Gandhi appreciated—at least during the first years of her prime ministership. Indira was keen to establish cordial relationships with various state chief ministers, including ones belonging to Opposition parties. Now, in 1967, the amity that Indira had fashioned with state barons—especially those of the South—was suddenly jeopardized by the issue of India's national language. She and Morarji Desai severely disagreed over the replacement of English by Hindi as the national official language. Under the Indian constitution, Hindi was to become the official national language by the year 1965.* Some of India's southern states—where Hindi is not predominantly spoken—agitated fiercely, claiming that the heavily Hindi-speaking North wanted to engage in a form of cultural imperialism. In 1959, Jawaharlal Nehru had said that, notwithstanding the constitutional provision for the replacement of English by Hindi as the national language, English would continue as an "associate official language as long as any part of India may want it." Indeed, Indira herself had endorsed her father's statement when she traveled to Madras in early 1965 to ameliorate the linguistic passions that had burst out in violent demonstrations against the imposition of Hindi.† More than sixty people were killed in police firings in and around Madras, and some media estimates put the death toll at 300. Hindi books were

* Article 343 of the Indian constitution stipulates that "the official language of the Union shall be Hindi in the Devnagari script."
† In accordance with constitutional requirements, Hindi became the official Indian language on January 26, 1965, exactly fifteen years after the constitution went into effect.

burned. All colleges and schools in Tamil Nadu were closed. Two young men poured gasoline on themselves and then set themselves on fire.* In 1961 the National Integration Council—which had been formed during Nehru's time to strengthen secularism in the country—had recommended the adoption of a three-language formula under which all schools in India would be required to teach in three languages; the regional language; English; and Hindi for the non-Hindi states, and another Indian language for the Hindi-speaking states. Indira concurred with this formula, and in 1967—despite pro-Hindi demonstrations in the North, including her own Uttar Pradesh State—the government came forth with a constitutional amendment that seemed to pacify the non–Hindi-speaking states. "Someone has to bell that cat sometime," Indira said, referring to the divisive language issue. Now the non–Hindi-speaking states did not have to automatically or immediately adopt Hindi as their sole administrative language.

Morarji Desai, however, viewed Indira's concession not as an act of statesmanship and national accommodation but as a sign of weakness. In keeping with his own inflexible nature, Desai said publicly that since the constitution had clearly established that Hindi should be the national language, there was no room for any accommodation on this issue. Indira suspected that Desai was trying to undermine her in Uttar Pradesh—the biggest of the Hindi-speaking states—where there had been pro-Hindi agitation. Indira, of course, also had in mind that English was an international language and that without it, Indians would be at a disadvantage in the global community. Desai, in turn, held that Indira's stand concerning accommodating the linguistic concerns of the non–Hindi-speaking states was meant to weaken the position of the leader of the Uttar Pradesh Congress Party, C. B. Gupta. Gupta had been a supporter of Desai's claims for becoming prime minister; he had also been a prominent advocate of imposing Hindi as the sole administrative language all across India.

Indira and Desai would eventually come to a permanent parting of ways. The language question contributed to their mutual distrust. So did Desai's trip to the United States within months of becoming deputy prime minister. Johnson administration officials were impressed with Desai's right-of-center positions on economic and geopolitical issues; Desai—who held the finance portfolio—expressed the view that the

---

* For more on the linguistic problems of India, please see Robert L. Hardgrave, Jr., "The Riots in Tamilnad: Problems and Prospects of India's Language Crisis," *Asian Survey*, August 5, 1965.

Indian economy needed to be liberalized, and that there were far too many bureaucratic regulations concerning economic activity. He was also privately critical of New Delhi's increasingly warm relationship with Moscow, and this scored him points in Washington, too. Indira felt that Washington was sending signals to pro-American elements in Indian politics to "rally around" Desai and perhaps build him as a viable alternative to her leadership, according to Krishan Bhatia. By this time, Indira's earlier warm relationship with President Johnson had cooled. There was little doubt that Washington would have preferred Desai as prime minister. Years later, when Desai became India's prime minister after defeating Indira's Congress Party in the 1977 elections, American officials would rejoice: There would be a feeling that Desai would bring Delhi closer to the United States. But, of course, Desai would find out that a nation's foreign policy cannot be changed or calibrated that quickly.

Indira, not one to take her own suspicions and resentments lightly, hit back at Desai in 1968 when he presented his budget before Parliament. The annual budget is one of the most widely anticipated documents in India. It is the finance minister who unveils it in the Lok Sabha, and for days preceding the event there is much speculation over new taxes and excise duties. In the 1968 budget, Desai had proposed a small indirect tax on prosperous Indian farmers. Agricultural income, for the most part, is not taxed in India as part of a government policy to encourage what is still India's biggest economic sector. When word got out that Desai was proposing such a tax, there was an uproar in the powerful agriculture lobby. Farmers protested bitterly, organizing marches in New Delhi. Indira sought to mollify them. Eventually, Desai's tax proposal was abandoned, and Desai felt—rightly, of course—that Indira had personally humiliated him. Meanwhile, Indira had also started to give tacit support to a group of rebels within the Congress Party known as the "Young Turks."* The Young Turks wanted the Congress to revert to the socialistic programs that the party had promised to institute during Nehru's heyday. They argued that only through economic leftism could the Congress Party hope to recapture grass-roots support among India's deprived

---

* The group was named by the Indian media after the "Young Turks" of Turkey who, during the early part of the century, promoted social and political reform in what had become a moribund society. Those reforms were intended to Westernize Turkey and, in effect, disestablish Islam. The most famous of these "Young Turks" was Mustafa Kemal Ataturk (1881–1938) who took part in the 1908 Young Turk movement, and went on to become the first president of Turkey (1923–1938). Ataturk, who started the Turkish Nationalist Party, is generally known as the founder of modern Turkey.

millions. One of the Young Turks, Chandra Shekhar, accused Morarji Desai in Parliament of collaborating with his son, Kantilal, in peddling influence to big business.* Desai told friends that he was convinced Indira was behind Chandra Shekhar's attacks against his integrity. The Congress bosses asked Indira to reprimand Chandra Shekhar, but Indira did not do so. The Young Turks, quietly assisted by Indira, stepped up their attacks against bosses like Kamaraj, Siddavvanshalli Nijalingappa, S. K. Patil, and Atulya Ghosh. They accused these old-guard leaders of having sold out to big business; on some occasions, the Young Turks even implied that the bosses of the Syndicate were in the pay of the CIA, which Indian politicians frequently accuse of sabotaging everything in India—from the economy to the monsoons. So shrill were these attacks that Siddavvanshalli Nijalingappa—then the Congress President—characterized the Young Turks as "noisy radicals."

The tactics of these noisy radicals suited Indira just fine. She had made up her mind to engage in a thorough housecleaning of the Congress Party, even if that meant a formal split between her and the Syndicate. She had also learned that the Syndicate was once again trying to get rid of her from the prime minister's post. Siddavvanshalli Nijalingappa himself wrote in his diary on March 12, 1969: "I am not sure if she deserves to continue as prime minister. Possibly soon there may be a showdown."[†] A few weeks later, Nijalingappa and Morarji Desai met to discuss what the former called "the necessity of the PM [prime minister] being removed." Nijalingappa had not been a political foe of Indira, but in time she was to see him as working hand in glove with the Syndicate. Indira heard that the Syndicate had made a secret deal with Desai under which he would become prime minister after the general election in 1972. Indira therefore quietly encouraged Chandra Shekhar and the Young Turks to escalate their attacks on the old guard. Some of the Young Turks circulated stories of the alleged sexual excesses of Syndicate bosses—particularly S. K. Patil, who was notorious for his glad eye and reportedly maintained many mistresses. In the struggle for domination of the Congress Party, Patil had upped the ante himself by criticizing Mrs. Gandhi —although not by name—and urging those Congress members who did not conform to party traditions—meaning, of course, toe the Syndicate's

---

*Chandra Shekhar and Indira Gandhi later had a falling out. He was one of the leaders of the Janata Party that defeated Mrs. Gandhi's Congress Party in the 1977 elections. In November 1990, Chandra Shekhar himself became prime minister after he engineered the collapse of Prime Minister V. P. Singh's government.

†Contents of the Nijalingappa diaries were disclosed by the veteran Indian journalist Kuldip Nayar.

line—to get out of the organization. Indira knew that despite this fire and brimstone, Patil did not have the support of a majority of Congress parliamentarians, while she did.

The radicals also mounted a campaign for the nationalization of banks and other measures that they felt would cleanse India's economic system. * Since 1950 there had been demands from left-wing politicians for the nationalization of banks. These politicians felt that the private-sector banks had simply not given enough credit to farmers and to fledgling businesses, especially in the backward regions of the country. The Young Turks accused India's commercial banks of favoring big business. However, even Nehru—notwithstanding his Fabian Socialist beliefs—had not been in favor of such nationalization. In the changing atmosphere of 1967, when Indira Gandhi was already moving to the left, the Young Turks again put a demand for outright nationalization of banks. Chandra Shekhar argued that bank nationalization would give Indira's government political control of the banking system, something that clearly appealed to the prime minister. Indeed, the All-India Congress Committee had adopted a Ten-Point Programme in June 1966 that called for a variety of "socialist measures," including land reform and bank nationalization.

Morarji Desai, of course, opposed the move to nationalize banks. He argued that it was enough for the government to exercise "social control" over banks, and thus force them to extend more credit to farmers and small businesses. This "social control" was to be imposed through a national credit council, and other committees, stacked with government officials and representatives of the powerful Reserve Bank of India, the country's central bank. For the moment, Indira sided with Desai; but she said that she did so with what she characterized as "instinctive misgivings." The Young Turks were disappointed, of course, that there would be no outright bank nationalization; but there clearly seemed to be an understanding between them and Indira that when the time was more propitious, she would act boldly on the banking question. As Trevor Drieberg puts it, the bank nationalization and related moves to introduce more state control of the economy were India's equivalent of the Cultural Revolution in neighboring China, which was being convulsed by internal

---

* The issue of bank nationalization gathered significance after the adoption by the Congress Working Committee in May 1967 of the so-called Ten-Point Programme. This resolution, which was discussed only superficially at the time, called not only for bank nationalization. It included such items as removal of private-sector monopolies, nationalization of general insurance, curbs on property, state control over exports and food grains, and the abolition of privy purses and privileges of India's erstwhile royalty.

357

social and political conflicts stemming from Mao Zedong's call to young Communists to purge the system of those he viewed as conservatives. The Cultural Revolution was, of course, an attempt on Mao's part to consolidate his own political position—as was Indira Gandhi's effort to nationalize India's banks.

It was to be another two years before Indira acted on the bank nationalization issue. She used the intervening months to coopt leftists in the Congress Party and to strengthen her position in the event of a showdown with the Syndicate. Indira saw such a showdown as being inevitable. And in order to secure her own position among party members—and the public at large—Indira had to demonstrate that her economic policies were left of center. Her speeches and private conversations increasingly began to contain references to socialism. In April 1969, Indira came out in the open as a standard-bearer of socialism. This occurred at a meeting of the Congress Party in Faridabad, some twenty miles outside Delhi. Party president Nijalingappa had openly challenged the efficiency of India's public-sector enterprises, calling them criminally wasteful. He was right, of course. But Indira countered that such criticisms of state participation in industrial growth constituted a central challenge to the very principles of planned development in India. She said that the public sector had to be encouraged because India's capitalists did not want to tie up their money in long-term projects that yielded few returns immediately. Moreover, Indira said, in a poor country like India it was simply unadvisable to leave key industries—the so-called commanding heights of the economy—in the hands of individuals or private-sector cartels.

Indira Gandhi was clearly signaling to the Syndicate at the Faridabad meeting that, in addition to her political disagreements with the bosses, she also had different economic views. These bosses dismissed those signals as signs of emotional overdrive on Indira's part. But on July 19, 1969, Indira Gandhi nationalized fourteen leading commercial banks, stunning the Syndicate. She obtained a presidential ordinance nationalizing these banks. Besides being an economic move to the liking of leftists, the bank nationalization was also a move to isolate her political opponents. As the Preamble to the Banking Companies Act of 1970 would later put it, the main objective of nationalization was "to meet progressively, and serve better, the needs of development of the economy in conformity with the national policy and objectives." As Indira saw it, India's national policy would be socialism—not the rigorous kind that characterized the nations of Eastern Europe, but a more gentler one that did not necessitate the establishment of a police state to supervise the people's welfare. After Indira's broadcast to the nation that evening during which she announced the nationalization, thousands of people began to gather outside her house. They represented a cross section of the masses: low-wage government employees, auto rickshaw and taxi drivers, and the educated unemployed. They shouted slogans in support of the prime minister. Some even loudly denounced Morarji Desai, who had resigned only three days earlier after Indira told him that she would dismiss him. Nayantara Sahgal, Indira's cousin, was among those who viewed these public demonstrations somewhat skeptically: "The use of money and transport to bring workers to meetings, along with government's control of radio, had always given the ruling party an edge over others. But this was the first time street demonstrations had been staged by a prime minister. Their size and regularity, and the expertise now in evidence, had the gloss of preparation and planning, and of the Communist genius for efficient organization. Also a recognizable Communist technique was Mrs. Gandhi's vocabulary of class war and the cry that all who were not with her were against her."*

Indira, however, explained the public support as a sure sign that she was succeeding in removing "the stigma that the Congress was a party of the elite, the political wing of the Establishment which had taken over from the British and which treated the country as though it was its private property—to be run for the profit of a microscopic section of the nation."†
Indira was also hailed in Parliament, where she delivered an impassioned speech justifying the nationalization. The show of positive public sentiment really seemed to surprise the Syndicate bosses. They had not anticipated that Indira's socialist maneuver would find such resonance among the masses. For her part, Indira discovered that Indians responded enthusiastically to any political move that promised economic emancipation—no matter that the bank nationalization would, in time, prove an unmitigated disaster and hurt, rather than help, the Indian economy. The important thing for Indira was that ordinary people *perceived* her to be their champion—to be on their side—while the greedy old bosses of the Syndicate luxuriated in their dubious dens of power, accumulating great wealth and consorting with women young enough to be their granddaughters. In February 1970, the Supreme Court invalidated Indira's action as being unconstitutional, but the prime minister later enacted laws that answered the court's objections. In the event, the banks stayed nationalized—and Indira and the Young Turks had won a major victory.

*Sahgal, *Indira Gandhi: Her Road to Power*, p. 46.
†Drieberg, *Indira Gandhi: A Profile in Courage*, pp. 110–11.

Not only were the leading commercial banks—with their enormous resources—under government control, but Indira's nemesis, Morarji Desai,
was out of the cabinet.

Desai's exit had been rancorous. When he heard about Indira's decision
to nationalize the banks, he thundered: "As long as I am finance minister,
this cannot be implemented. If the prime minister wants to do it, she
will have to change her finance minister."

That was exactly what Indira proceeded to do.

"You are quite welcome to stay on as deputy prime minister, however,"
Indira told Desai, after first telling him that she would relieve him of the
prestigious finance portfolio.

Desai responded that he could hardly be expected to continue in
Indira's administration if the ministry he had so valued was taken away
from him. He tendered his resignation. Indira, however, deferred formal
acceptance of Desai's resignation until the day she would announce the
bank nationalization. In an exchange of letters during this period with
C. B. Gupta, the chief minister of Uttar Pradesh, Indira said that some
party leaders were "conspiring" against her. Although Indira did not
name Desai explicitly, he was convinced that her reference was clearly
to him. He accused her of paranoia. Indeed, whenever it suited her
during her long career, Indira leveled charges of conspiracy against colleagues—as a way of getting rid of them politically from her circle.

On August 28, Indira made a speech before the Bankers Club of New
Delhi. Everyone expected her to be defensive about the nationalization
in front of an audience that was certain to be resentful and hostile. But
the Indira who turned up at the meeting was relaxed and even jovial.

"I think it was a bit of a challenge for me to come to your meeting
this evening—because this is one group of people with whom I am not
too popular at the moment," she said.

The standing-room-only audience laughed nervously at her attempt to
lighten the somber mood of the event. Indira went on to proclaim the
virtues of bank nationalization, gently scolding the august bankers for
what she said were gross abuses. She had shown India's capitalist establishment how she could wield power. From the time of the nationalization
until her death, the titans of industry and commerce usually went out of
their way to please her—even when she was briefly in the political
wilderness between 1977 and 1979.

President Zakir Husain died of a heart attack on May 3, 1969, some
months before the bank nationalization episode. In the short time that
he had occupied Rashtrapati Bhavan, Husain strengthened the universal

perception of him as a secularist. "To him secularism was more than a moral conviction or an intellectual principle," Trevor Drieberg wrote of Husain. "It was part of his personality, arising spontaneously from his refinement and humanism. His election as president was both a recognition of his invaluable services to his country—and the vindication of India's belief in tolerance and a multi-religious society."[*] Zakir Husain's death represented a major blow to Indira Gandhi at a time when she was just starting to erect her leadership stanchions in the political soil of India—and the Congress Party. There was a predictable dispute once again in the Congress Party over who should become president of India. Vice President V. V. Giri became acting president, and Indira wanted him to get the job in his own right. He was a genial man, given to wide smiles and heavy meals. The Syndicate, which had already resolved to do away with Indira, began to prepare for a showdown. Under no circumstances were they going to allow her to choose the presidential candidate. "In the unexpected vacancy at the top and the need to fill it, the Syndicate saw an opportunity to humiliate Indira publicly, to demonstrate to her and the country the extent of its own power, and to create circumstances in which she could be eliminated when necessary," says Krishan Bhatia. "Indira was acutely conscious of the threat to her future, and in the following months fought them hard—sometimes with her back to the wall."[†]

Congress Party president Siddavvanshalli Nijalingappa went over to see Morarji Desai to inquire if Desai would be interested in becoming president of India. Desai was still in Indira's cabinet at this point; his bitter resignation would come later in the year over the bank nationalization issue.

"I must stay on in the cabinet," Desai said to Nijalingappa. "Otherwise that woman will sell the country to the Communists."

When it became clear to her that Vice President Giri would not be endorsed by the Congress Working Committee, Indira toyed with the idea of proposing Jagjivan Ram, the Harijan leader, for the presidency. A Ram candidacy would be certainly popular with India's minorities. But Ram had his weaknesses. Indira was told by her intelligence operatives that Ram had failed to pay his income taxes for almost a decade. Indira also learned that Ram indulged extravagantly in sexual activities that included sleeping with one of his daughters-in-law.[‡] Kamaraj and his

---

[*] *Ibid.*

[†] Bhatia, *Indira*, p. 221.

[‡] Jagjivan Ram's son was to be later involved in a scandal featuring photographs that were taken of him making love to a woman who was not his wife. The pictures were

fellow Syndicate bosses wanted Neelam Sanjiva Reddy, fifty-six, for the post. Reddy was Speaker of the Lok Sabha, and had also been president of the Congress Party between 1960 and 1962. He had been a member of Indira's cabinet, but she unceremoniously dumped him after the 1967 elections. The choice of president was important to both sides. The president could, on the advice of the prime minister, dissolve Parliament and order fresh elections. In fact, Indira Gandhi was to become adept at massaging the president into signing virtually whatever ordinance she wanted. Those in opposition to Mrs. Gandhi believed that this would be the main hold she would have on Congress parliamentarians. On the other hand, the situation could well go against her, too, if enough Congress parliamentarians expressed no confidence in her.

The real issue in the presidential election was clearly Indira Gandhi's political future. It was clear that the Congress Party, which had been all things to all men, was tottering; it was in danger of imploding on account of these conflicts between the old guard—as represented by the Syndicate—and the supporters of Indira Gandhi. The 1967 general election had shown that the old Congress system of reconciliation and consensus had nearly collapsed. Writing in the *Indian Express* at the time, Trevor Drieberg said: "In spite of the wishes of its leaders, the party itself is being polarized under the pressure of external forces which the leaders cannot suppress. The time has come when Young Turk and Old Gandhian can no longer hang together—even if the alternative is hanging separately. If they refuse to polarize, as they should, they face a much worse fate—total atomization." The Syndicate did not want to let go of its hold, such as it was, on the party organization.

It was obvious that there were intractable problems between the old guard and supporters of Indira Gandhi. The *Indian Express* captured the sentiment of many observers when it editorialized: "If the Congress breaks up, it will be calamitous for the country. . . . Mrs. Gandhi is at times prone to ruffle her colleagues by her speech. More often she is apt to startle them by studied silence. . . . This habit of mind and approach does not make for happy individual relations, or for the smooth conduct of public affairs. . . . Collective cabinet responsibility is the cornerstone of our constitution. Lapses from the principle account for much of the misunderstandings and controversies generated in recent weeks. . . . A close understanding between the Congress Party president and the prime minister is long overdue."[*]

---

published in a magazine called *Surya* during the early 1980s. The magazine was edited by Indira Gandhi's daughter-in-law Maneka Gandhi.
[*] *Indian Express*, March 19, 1969.

But no such "understanding" would be forthcoming. The party's president, Nijalingappa, stood firmly behind the Syndicate's choice, Neelam Sanjiva Reddy. The Congress Parliamentary Board, after a lopsided vote in favor of the Syndicate's candidate, named Reddy as their official choice for the position. Indira, whose candidate in the Board vote had been Jagjivan Ram, after all, was furious. She was so enraged, in fact, that she went against the advice of some of her closest associates and encouraged Vice President Giri, who was seventy-five years old, to publicly state that he would contest the election as an independent if the Congress named Reddy as its candidate. Giri was backed by the left parties in Parliament. Indira Gandhi then made a crucial decision. As was customary for a prime minister, Indira refused to call on the Congress representatives to vote for Reddy. Indeed, Nijalingappa had instructed Indira to exhort Congress parliamentarians to support Reddy. Instead, Indira called for a "vote according to conscience."

"A free vote will rejuvenate the party, restore confidence, and strengthen unity," Indira said.

In a subsequent note to Nijalingappa, Indira warned against disciplinary action against her or any parliamentarians who might vote against the official Congress candidate. "I feel that the issues involved go beyond the presidential poll. The result of the election, one way or the other, will not resolve the differences over the manner in which our basic policies of democracy, secularism, socialism, and nonalignment, are implemented." The battle reached its peak with the Syndicate approaching the right-wing Jan Sangh and Swatantra parties to support Reddy. This infuriated Indira, and she denounced the Congress leaders for the breach of an important principle—of secularism. Indira herself denounced Nijalingappa for "perfidious activities"—such as these meetings with Opposition leaders. She contacted the chief ministers of all states, including those where non-Congress governments were in power. Indira brushed off the irony of these contacts with Opposition parties.

At 10:30 P.M. on August 20, 1969, the results of the presidential election were announced in New Delhi. Vice President V. V. Giri had won the presidency, although narrowly—420,077 votes to 405,527 votes. Indira's tactics of courting the Opposition had paid off: Although nearly two-thirds of the Congress parliamentarians and state legislators voted for their party's candidate, Reddy, V. V. Giri was elected because of support from the Communists, right-wing Akalis, some Socialists, Independents, and the DMK of Tamil Nadu. The people who had thought that she was just a docile woman whom they could push around were proven wrong again. The "Goongi Gudiya"—the Dumb Doll—had outsmarted them all. Professor Stanley Wolpert has put it well: "The electoral victory of V. V. Giri confirmed that Prime Minister Indira Gandhi had emerged stronger and far more popular than the party machine that had put her in power just three and a half years earlier. The interlude of collective leadership was over; so was the era of united Congress Party rule; that of Indira Raj had begun."*

Indira Gandhi always relished jousting with the bosses of Indian politics. A political high-roller, she played brinkmanship in a manner that sometimes made her opponents gasp. For the most part, Indira emerged victorious from her battles—against the corrupt bosses of the Syndicate, for example. But there were times during her prime ministership that Indira met her match.

One such match was a man who began his public career not as a politician but as an actor, one who played the role of a god in many guises. Not long after Indira's death, I went to see him in the southern state of Andhra Pradesh.

The capital of Andhra Pradesh is a 400-year-old city called Hyderabad. It has one of the most modern airports in India, and one that works remarkably well in spite of the heavy traffic. The city is situated some 1,800 feet above sea level on what is called the Deccan plateau. Hyderabad and its twin city, the much younger Secunderabad, together have a population of nearly 6 million.[†] Hyderabad, with its crumbling forts, old monuments, its silver bazaars, and its filigree markets, has long been a tourist attraction. The climate is agreeable through most of the year. A number of the nation's top military officials have built retirement homes in the area; Hyderabad and Secunderabad have large cantonments, and retired military personnel presumably find the atmosphere congenial. Hyderabad used to be the seat of the old Deccani Muslim nawabs, or noblemen, and also of the Nizam of Hyderabad State, once believed to be the wealthiest man in the world.[‡] The noblemen of Hyderabad developed a highly literate and sophisticated culture. The Old World manners and graciousness of the nawabs still survive in some measure in Hyderabad. Old Hyderabadi families still serve up heavenly meals in high style. But the grand old palaces and mansions of Hyderabad

---

*Wolpert, A *New History of India*, p. 382.

[†] Secunderabad is pronounced Sikh-under-abaad. It was initially a contonment during the British Raj, but later expanded into a flourishing city.

[‡] The Nizam's heirs are still wealthy. Their riches include properties in Europe, the United States, and Australia. The huge estate in Hyderabad where the Nizam lived also belongs to them.

are being torn down at an alarming rate, to make way for modern high-rise apartment blocks or commercial buildings. Progress has come to Hyderabad in a big way. The old farmsteads around the city have been gobbled up by electronic factories and textile mills and glass industries. The air here, once considered the most salubrious of all of India's medium-sized cities, is steadily becoming sour. The plane trees are dying, and the meadows get browner every year.

At the time of independence, the Nizam of Hyderabad dithered over joining India—even though his state had a majority Hindu population. The Nizam wanted nationhood for Hyderabad; he was said to have hired Pakistani fighter planes to "attack" India in order to achieve his goal. But the Nizam was tamed by the strong-willed Vallabhbhai Patel, then India's home minister: Patel dispatched two divisions of the army's Southern Command to "convince" the Nizam that joining India was in his best interests. Hyderabad acceded to India.

Andhra Pradesh had become a key Congress Party stronghold in the South. Its politicians prospered, its bureaucrats became corrupt. Indira Gandhi would decide in Delhi who served as Andhra's chief minister, and ministerial selections appeared to be based solely on one criterion: loyalty to the prime minister. She picked a succession of incompetent men to head Andhra's state administration. None of these men was likely to pose a challenge to Mrs. Gandhi, regionally or nationally. Indira did not pay much attention to whether these chief ministers possessed the ability to build a local base of political support for her Congress Party. Because of this centralization, state Congress governments started to disintegrate. There were increased mass protests over such issues as food-grain shortages, corruption, and nepotism. As these protests grew violent, the central government would dispatch paramilitary units to quell demonstrations. Mrs. Gandhi's increasingly authoritarian style had transformed center-state relations from one of political bargaining to one akin to feudal tutelage, according to W. H. Morris-Jones.* Professors Robert Hardgrave and Stanley Kochanek assert that under Indira Gandhi the politics of manipulation displaced the politics of accommodation. The centralization of power centralized problems. In other words, the central government increasingly had to deal with such issues as law and order in the states, when state governments should have been the ones to attend to them. Increasingly, too, Indira would act arbitrarily concerning the sending of paramilitary units to states without fully soliciting the counsel

* W. H. Morris-Jones, "India—More Questions Than Answers," *Asian Survey*, August 14, 1984.

of her state chief ministers. The inability of personally appointed retainers to cope with local problems created a range of new and increasingly dangerous headaches for the central government. At the same time, Mrs. Gandhi's intransigence or insensitivity in handling these disputes resulted in a deepening crisis for the Congress Party and the nation. *

In Andhra the state's economy languished because of weak local leadership. Law and order broke down. Even the police would riot for raises. But the Congress flourished because no opposition party could raise the money needed to develop a strong grass-roots organization in this overwhelmingly rural state of 60 million people. Salvation, as it were, came in the form of a wealthy movie star who had specialized in roles depicting mythological Hindu gods. The actor's name was Nandamuri Taraka Rama Rao—known popularly as NTR—and he decided to switch from the world of make-believe to make-belief. He had starred in 300 films over thirty-five years, and had become the most popular star in the history of Telugu-language movies. Political commentators began calling him the "Ronald Reagan of India." Like Reagan, who had successfully made the transition from celluloid to real-life politics, NTR wanted to shape the political beliefs of his people. In 1982 he formed a new party, called the Telugu Desam, or the Telugu State Party. The party was populist in orientation, but its *raison d'être* was the issue of greater state autonomy.†
NTR's ambition was simple: to gain power.

NTR made the corrupt local Congress chieftains his main targets. More important, he said that regional creativity and aspirations were being stifled because Andhra was being ruled not from Hyderabad but from Delhi. He touched a raw nerve among everyday people, whose living conditions had been daily deteriorating. He capitalized on his stardom by appearing at public rallies in saffron robes, which recalled the roles of mythological gods and holy men that he often played in Telugu movies. The simple rural folk in the countryside showered him with rose petals; the city folk lavished rupees on the Telugu Desam Party. In New Delhi, Mrs. Gandhi grew concerned over NTR's growing popularity. She sensed that her Congress Party was about to take a drubbing in the forthcoming election.

Indira was right. When the January 1983 election results were announced, NTR had won power. His Telugu Desam obtained nearly 150 seats in the 295-member Andhra Pradesh Assembly. This was a clear majority for him. In addition, about thirty independents pledged support

* Hardgrave and Kochanek, *India: Government and Politics in a Developing Nation.*
† *Ibid.*

to NTR's party in the state legislature. As chief minister, the former film star moved quickly to establish his own particular style. Road signs and bulletins in government offices now were required to be not only in English but also in Telugu. NTR made virtually all his public addresses in Telugu, too. He started a free midday meal program in state schools. He authorized state subsidies for rice, an Andhra staple. The government's Anti-Corruption Bureau doubled its annual investigations to 2,000 during NTR's first year in office. Shrewd leaders make use of their popularity by sometimes ramming through unpopular measures while they can. NTR trimmed the state government's bloated bureaucracy of 30,000 employees by lowering the retirement age from fifty-eight to fifty-five years. The state budget was streamlined, but more money was channeled into promoting cultural activities such as the Kuchipuri dance native to Andhra, the theater, and the work of local poets, essayists, and novelists. As Andhra chief minister, NTR joined other non-Congress Chief Ministers of Tamil Nadu, Pondicherry, and Karnataka in forming a Southern Council to establish what he called "a new balance" in center-state relations.

Back in Delhi, Indira Gandhi was alarmed. Despite the spirit of accommodation toward states that she had displayed early in her prime-ministerial career, by now Indira had become a great centralizer. She was not swayed by the contentions of supporters of greater states' rights that their demands were fair. Indeed, Indira felt that such demands would encourage secession and certainly jeopardize national integrity. Indira's suspicions were supported by key aides, and by the military brass. Indian elites seemed to favor a strong central government. "The increased level of caste, language, religious, and regional conflicts raised new fears of fissiparous tendencies and political separatism," say Professors Hardgrave and Kochanek. "These fears, combined with the slow and erratic pace of economic development, led these elites to demand a stronger and more forceful central government. Prime Minister Indira Gandhi capitalized on these fears. . . . She believed in a strong central government, and the concentration of power in party and government in her hands."

Moreover, NTR had become a media star: Foreign journalists and television crews started paying him a great deal of attention. Her aides warned Mrs. Gandhi that he would soon export his political and cultural revolution to other parts of the country. And if he became a national figure, NTR would be a direct threat to Mrs. Gandhi, whose own nationwide popularity was declining. In those dog days of August 1984, it seemed that the Opposition stood a good chance of coming back into power in the forthcoming elections. There were also widespread rumors that Indira Gandhi would amend the constitution and postpone elections until a time when her Congress Party was better placed to win.* In July the chief ministers of various states met with Indira in New Delhi under the auspices of the National Development Council. The Council was an advisory body consisting of chief executives of all twenty-five states and members of the Planning Commission. The meeting had been called to discuss economic issues. Instead, NTR got up and read out a statement on behalf of the non-Congress chief ministers protesting against the dismissal, earlier that month, of Chief Minister Farooq Abdullah of Kashmir.†

"I would urge you to stop making political statements at this meeting," Mrs. Gandhi said to NTR. "This is not a political meeting."

The Andhra chief minister ignored her and continued reading. Whereupon Mrs. Gandhi asked that NTR's statement be struck off the Council's record. At that point, NTR and other non-Congress chief ministers walked out of the chamber. Indira seemed determined to assert her authority. She then ordered all non-Congress officials—who were not chief ministers and who had stayed on in the room as they were supposed to do—to get out. After these second-echelon factotums had left, chief ministers belonging to the Congress Party successfully urged Indira Gandhi to allow them to pass a resolution condemning the behavior of their non-Congress counterparts who had walked out earlier. There was much uproar over this incident. The media widely interpreted Mrs. Gandhi's behavior as imperial, intolerant, and insensitive.

Indira Gandhi now set into motion a plan to get rid of Nandamuri Taraka Rama Rao, whom she could not stand. She thought that he was a hypocrite and a charlatan who capitalized on his film career to make political hay. Rajiv Gandhi, who by now had been made a general secretary of the Congress, was persuaded to become a party to the plot. Of course, all top Congress officials, including Mrs. Gandhi, later denied any complicity. The Gandhis were still heady from the recent "victories" in Kashmir, where Chief Minister Farooq Abdullah had been toppled in July 1984, and in the border state of Sikkim, where a majority Opposition government had been peremptorily dismissed. In Andhra, as in Kashmir and Sikkim, the instrument of Mrs. Gandhi's manipulation was the Delhi-appointed state governor. The Andhra governor was a man named Ram Lal, a former chief minister of Himachal Pradesh, against whom charges of misuse of power were still pending in that northern state.

---

*Under the constitution's requirements, the next general election was to be held by January 1985 at the latest.
†Please see Chapter 16.

On August 16, 1984, Governor Lal suddenly announced that NTR had lost his majority in the Andhra State Assembly and that he had dismissed NTR from the chief minister's job. In India governors are appointed by the president upon the recommendation of the prime minister. Governorships are very comfortable sinecures; governors do exactly as they are told by Delhi. NTR had only been back a day from the United States when the governor's announcement was made. He had just gone through triple coronary bypass surgery in America. He learned that he was being replaced by a man he had named to his own Telugu Desam cabinet, Nadendla Bhaskara Rao. Governor Lal had dispensed with normal procedures in announcing the new government; ordinarily, no chief minister can be dismissed and someone else asked to form a new government unless there is a show of strength on the floor of the state legislature. Bhaskara Rao never had to prove that he now commanded a majority in the assembly through defections that he had engineered from NTR's party.

NTR was appalled. So were most Andhra-ites. So was the nation. Indira claimed that she had no prior knowledge about Governor Lal's intentions to dismiss the chief minister. Lal defended himself by declaring that he had consulted with New Delhi before firing NTR. It turned out that Lal had talked on the telephone with Arun Nehru—a relative of Mrs. Gandhi—who was widely believed to be the "big bully" of the Congress Party. Nehru presumably gave Lal the green light. At any rate, it is unlikely that Nehru would have acted against the wishes of his aunt Indira. NTR claimed that he had documented evidence of the allegiance of 161 of the assembly's 295 members—enough to ensure a comfortable majority. He now did something so dramatic that the media were beside themselves with joy because of the opportunity that NTR's actions afforded them for a strong, continuing story: NTR rented a train and escorted the 161 legislators to meet President Zail Singh in Delhi. There was simply no question that NTR had ever lost his majority. The 161 legislators happily posed for photographs on the steps of Rashtrapati Bhavan, the Indian president's sandstone palace. They waved affidavits of allegiance to NTR. Accompanied by NTR—who was so weak he had to be propped up in a wheelchair—the legislators spoke at rallies in Delhi. But even then Bhaskara Rao continued in office in Hyderabad. NTR now sequestered his legislators in hotel rooms in two neighboring states to make certain that none of them was bribed into defecting to Bhaskara Rao's party. Legislators were being offered the equivalent of $300,000 each to leave NTR's fold. Popular protests against Mrs. Gandhi mounted all over Andhra. There was violence.

Finally, in a face-saving gesture, Indira removed Ram Lal as governor and replaced him with Shankar Dayal Sharma, another Congress Party hack.* Congress Party officials quietly spread the word that it was all Ram Lal's fault, that the governor, not Mrs. Gandhi, had illegally deposed NTR! The new governor's arithmetic was better than that of his predecessor. He could count how many Andhra legislators supported Nandamuri Taraka Rama Rao. NTR was eventually reinstated. He was now more popular than ever before. Indira Gandhi had fought what was to be the last political battle of her life, and she had lost.

By 1988 NTR accelerated his nationwide appearances. The Opposition parties had banded together in an effort to oust Rajiv Gandhi, forming the Janata Dal—the seven-party National Front—and NTR constituted part of the leading edge of this campaign. Whether the Opposition would continue to stay together and win the next election was arguable; perhaps NTR could invoke his mantras to ensure that the coalition did not come unglued, as Opposition alliances had in the past. He continued to wear his saffron robes in public. In private—especially at night—he reportedly wore saris. There were whispers that an astrologer had warned him that NTR's life and political career were in danger unless he garbed himself in such female attire. Danger? It did not take an astrologer to know that NTR had made powerful enemies in Andhra Pradesh. They revealed to local newspapers that, despite all his talk of rectitude, NTR had not been beyond looking the other way when close relatives made millions in questionable deals.

There were other problems, too. His administration was finding it difficult to sustain its rice-subsidy program, under which 9.6 million Andhra Pradesh families received rice at two rupees a kilogram. (The families, in order to qualify, had to have a monthly income of no more than 500 rupees.) When the program was launched, amidst much fanfare, these low-income families were eligible to receive twenty-five kilograms of rice per month, but now that figure was lowered to fifteen kilograms. Why? Well, said NTR, because Rajiv Gandhi's government was not allocating enough rice to the state. Gandhi's Congress Party, NTR said, "has mortgaged the interests of the people." Some NTR critics saw things differently. They suggested that bureaucratic mismanagement in NTR's state administration had brought about the rice crisis. Indeed, one of the banes of the Third World has long been the inability of local governments to ensure proper distribution of food grains. When drought struck Africa's

---

* Sharma became India's vice president in 1988.

Sahel region, local leaders implored the West to provide emergency food relief; Mother Nature was vilified as being the cause of the famine. These politicians were unwilling to admit that, as much as the drought, it was their own bureaucratic ineptness that ensured poor distribution of existing food supplies.

In Andhra Pradesh, I thought, one thing was certain. NTR would surely exploit this crisis to his political advantage—even if, in the short run, the situation highlighted his own administration's management failures. After all, the rice program was essentially an antipoverty program, and such programs are always the staple of politicians' rhetoric in India, especially during elections. I was convinced that as the national election approached in 1989, NTR would miraculously—in the manner of his movie roles—produce additional rice for the poor of Andhra Pradesh. Rice had a way of translating into votes. In the event, NTR did not seem to have enough rice. His party was resoundingly defeated by the Congress in 1989; NTR himself lost in one of the two constituencies where he contested elections.* His influence greatly diminished, NTR now began to think more about his political survival than issues such as center-state relations. He had started out as a populist organizer for the poor, but the trappings and perks of power became too tempting for NTR in the end. He and those around him wound up pulling the wool over everyone's eyes, yet insisting all the while that they were acting in the public good.

That public—the people of Andhra Pradesh—in time came to see through the Telugu Desam, and its leader NTR. It was unlikely that he would soon be embraced by them in the fashion of the early 1980s. From her niche in Nirvana, Indira Gandhi must have surely smiled when NTR lost—and smiled hugely.

---

* The Congress victory in Andhra Pradesh was in keeping with its success in the South. In the North, however, the Congress lost heavily—and, as a result, V. P. Singh and the Janata Dal were able to form the new national government.

16

Indira Raj

The election of V. V. Giri as president of India in mid-1969 represented more than a major victory for Indira Gandhi and the Young Turks. It hastened the formal split of the Indian National Congress into the pro-Indira wing, and the pro–right wing loyal to Morarji Desai and the Syndicate. And it signaled the personalization of power by Indira Gandhi in a manner that no Indian leader, not even her father, had displayed. Alarmed at the prospect of a breakup of the Congress following Giri's election, the Syndicate tacitly backed Home Minister Yeshwantrao B. Chavan's efforts to bring the Congress factions together. Chavan, who had supported Neelam Sanjiva Reddy's candidacy in the presidential race, drafted a "unity resolution" that he unveiled at party headquarters at 7 Jantar Mantar Road on August 25. Indira did not show up for the meeting, but her minions did. They hooted and jeered some of the Syndicate bosses as they elbowed their way through pro-Indira crowds to enter the premises. Chavan was trying to ensure his own political survival as much as he was attempting to keep his party together. Chavan's resolution was approved at the meeting, but it was obvious that the fissures within the Congress were too wide and deep to be bridged effectively. Although Chavan himself tried to weasel his way back into Indira's confidence, he would never fully regain her trust. Some years later, Chavan would desert Indira again to join the Janata Party. He would become deputy prime minister. And when Indira returned to power in 1980, Chavan would again try to return to her camp.

No one knew better than Indira Gandhi that the Congress was about to break up for good. As 1969 unfolded, dissension within the party increased rapidly. Indira had dismissed Morarji Desai, gone ahead and nationalized the banks, moved to abolish the privy purses of the princely states, had not supported the party's choice for the president of India, and instead called for a "vote according to conscience." After Giri's victory, some sixty Congress parliamentarians—those supporting the Syndicate, of course—demanded that Indira be disciplined by the party for having planned the defeat of the party's presidential candidate, Reddy. But the Syndicate bosses decided to drop their idea of disciplinary action against Indira. To Indira, it simply did not matter at this stage what the Syndicate did. For her it was now war, and she was determined to do away with the aged bosses permanently. At the core of Indira's thinking was this: By eliminating the party bosses, she would be doing more than getting rid of what she perceived to be their malevolent influence. She would be asserting the primacy of the Congress Party's parliamentary wing. It had been traditional for the party leaders—who were not necessarily members of Parliament—to dictate party policy to legislators at the center as well as in the states. As long as the parliamentary leader of the ruling party—meaning the prime minister—was in consonance with the Congress bosses, the overall arrangement worked just fine. But when the disputes between Indira and the Syndicate began, the whole question of party supremacy in legislative matters came dramatically to the fore.

Indira began a signature drive for an early session of the All-India Congress Committee to elect a new party president, even though Nijalin-gappa's term was not yet over. What was emerging here was a tactic that Indira would use frequently during her career—hit your opponents when they are down. That was not particularly original of her as far as the practice of politics goes, but in the Indian context such hardball was seen by many observers as unseemly for a woman. Nijalingappa wrote her a bitter letter on October 28 in which he accused her of promoting a personality cult. "You seem to have made personal loyalty to you the test of loyalty to the Congress and the country," Nijalingappa said.* On November 1, two meetings of the Congress Working Committee were held—one at Indira's house, which was attended by ten Committee members loyal to her; and another at party headquarters on Jantar Mantar Road, where another ten Congress members loyal to the Syndicate showed up. The one neutral member, K. C. Abraham, shuttled between both meetings.

On November 8, Indira wrote an "open letter" to Congress members

---

*Text of letter made public by the Congress Party.

in which she defined the conflict as being one not merely as a clash of personalities or for a fight for power. The essence of the dispute lay in the conflict of ideologies, of attitudes, Indira said. "It is a conflict between two outlooks and attitudes in regard to the objectives of the Congress, and the methods in which the Congress itself should function," she wrote. "The Congress was molded by Mahatma Gandhi and my father to be the prime instrument of social change. . . . In his last years, my father was greatly concerned that there were people inside the Congress who were offering resistance to change. My own experience even before the fourth general election [in 1967] was that the forces of status quo, with close links with powerful economic interests, were ranged against me."[*] For sheer hypocrisy, Indira's language was stunning; after all, no one in the country was more courted by capitalists and better supported financially by them than the prime minister of India. These "powerful economic interests" may have made for handy villains, but Indira was hardly their hapless victim.

On November 12, 1969, the Syndicate bosses decided that they had had enough of Indira Gandhi. They expelled her from the Congress Party; it was Nijalingappa who, as party president, was entrusted the task of formally informing Indira of her expulsion.[†] The bosses then instructed the party to elect a new leader who, naturally, would be the new prime minister as well. Only sixty-five Congress parliamentarians went along with the Syndicate; 226 voted for Indira. This meant, of course, that Indira lost her majority in the 525-seat Lok Sabha. So she formed her own Congress Party, the Congress (R); the (R) was for Requisitionist, but eventually Indira's party came to be known as Congress (I). The (I) stood for—what else?—Indira. The Syndicate's Congress was called Congress (O), the (O) denoting Organization. Indira had the support of the masses, who believed that all this happened because she was fighting for them. In an emergency session of the All-India Congress Committee, 446 out of 705 delegates voted with Indira. The split of the Congress led to a changed political atmosphere. In a six-page letter that she sent to members of the Committee, Indira wrote:

Outside the narrow confines of our party, great and turbulent changes are taking place in the minds and hearts of our people. There are

[*] Text of letter made available by the All-India Congress Committee.
[†] The party's head could technically expel any member, as long as he was supported by a majority of the organization's upper echelon. No vote was ever taken about Indira's expulsion; at any rate, the expulsion became an irrelevant matter because

new trends of thought. There are new aspirations. And there are new tensions apart from other older tensions. Political consciousness has matured and deepened among the masses, and in this process many ideas, some old and some new, are being canvassed, and a kind of crystallization has been steadily taking place. Faced with this change in the national political environment, our party has been in danger of losing its orientation—it has been trying to cope with the situation by a ritualistic repetition of the formal positions of the past without making fresh assessment of the needs of the present and the future in accordance with its own living revolutionary tradition. . . . In this situation, it is necessary for the Congress to recognize frankly that it no longer commands in full the loyalty and emotions of the nation as it did in the past. It must also recognize that it cannot discharge the role of leadership unless it redefines its position sharply in relation to the competing points of view in the country—and it can serve as an effective instrument of the national purpose only if it revitalizes its membership and its methods of functioning. *

In this new reincarnation, Indira Gandhi showed a shrewdness and historical understanding that had not been apparent earlier. "She had become something ruthless and new," says Nayantara Sahgal. "She had astonished people with her flair for cool assessment, shrewd timing, and the telling theatrical gesture, above all, with her capacity for a fight to the finish, even to bringing the eighty-four-year-old party of liberation to rupture. She had made use of realpolitik, suiting the action to the moment's need, undeterred by any backlog of sentiment or ethics. Her own emergence from an image of extreme withdrawal and reserve was now complete."†

Indira now had an opportunity to start afresh. She was still the prime minister of the country, but not beholden to party bosses. From now on, cabinet members, party presidents, and various chief ministers would get their jobs and stay in them entirely on the basis of their loyalty to Indira. She would also periodically reshuffle her cabinet so as to keep any possible rivals off balance. From 1969 to 1977, notes Professor Stanley A. Kochanek, the Congress had five presidents, the turnover apparently designed to prevent institutional consolidation of power by any potential political

---

an overwhelming number of Congress parliamentarians sided with Indira and joined her reincarnated Congress.
* Text of letter made available by the All-India Congress Committee, November 1969.
† Sahgal, *Indira Gandhi: Her Road to Power*, p. 53.

challenger.* From the time that the Congress split in 1969, Indira sought to centralize what had been fundamentally a federal party since independence, Professor Kochanek says. "Despite the party split, the new Congress was still under an umbrella of highly disparate interests," he writes.

> The ideological polarization so many had foreseen never took place. In state after state, Mrs. Gandhi's nominees were challenged by dissident factions and forced to resign. As weak and ineffective governments struggled to survive, internal factionalism was joined by mounting popular discontent. Mrs. Gandhi, increasingly intolerant of dissent, came to rely more heavily on coercion. She viewed criticism from within Congress as traitorous, and criticism from the Opposition as anti-national, fascist or foreign-inspired. She took attacks on inept and often corrupt state governments as personal affronts—and so more and more they came to be.[†]

On the economic front, Indira promised the private sector that she would not tilt totally towards the left, even though her government stayed in power because of Indira's alliance with the Communists and left-leaning Independents. A thinly veiled no-confidence motion sponsored by the Congress (O) over the question of why the government had sent an uninvited representative to the Islamic Conference in Rabat, Morocco, the previous September did not carry in Parliament. Had there been a full vote on a no-confidence motion, and had the minority government lost, Indira would have had no choice but to call a general election prematurely. Meanwhile, her popularity with ordinary Indians kept increasing. Huge processions marched through the wide boulevards of New Delhi, chanting slogans in support of Indira. The Syndicate stayed muted. There was little the bosses could do to deter Indira at this stage. "Considerably more significant than the disrepute into which the Syndicate had fallen was the change in the country's temper," says Krishan Bhatia. "The leadership that had emerged as a result of the independence movement had grown old and lost its appeal. That a particular leader had spent many years in a British prison or had worked under Mahatma Gandhi, had . . . ceased to be important. The country was ready for a new generation of leaders, and in Indira's challenge to the old guard it saw the change whose time had come."[‡]

---

* Stanley A. Kochanek, "Modern Indian," in *Indira Gandhi's India: A Political System Reappraised*, edited by Henry C. Hart (Boulder: Westview Press, 1976).
[†] Hardgrave and Kochanek, *India: Government and Politics in a Developing Nation.*
[‡] Bhatia, *Indira*, p. 231.

Socialism was clearly the ideology of this new order. Indira set up a Monopolies and Restricted Trade Practices Commission to regulate expansion of private trade and industry. She also gathered more bureaucratic power around the prime minister's secretariat. The Intelligence Bureau had been under the powerful Home Ministry, but Indira had it brought directly under the control of the prime minister. She detached the bureau's External Wing, which gathered intelligence overseas, and affiliated it to the newly formed Research and Analysis Wing (RAW). Indira increased the annual budget of this new intelligence unit from the equivalent of $5 million to $20 million. Indira had no compunctions about using RAW to provide her with incriminating information about Union and state ministers. Some of them led very colorful lives, and Indira—and later, her sons Sanjay and Rajiv—frequently asked for dossiers on real or perceived opponents that were filled with juicy stories, real or fictional. She reshuffled her cabinet, and dropped a number of junior ministers who she thought were still close to the Syndicate. Dinesh Singh, Indira's onetime favorite, was also let go after a series of demotions. Indira said that she was concerned about his "hobnobbing" with the Opposition, and with the Syndicate.

In 1969, the centenary year of Mahatma Gandhi's birth, Indira Gandhi had emerged as a truly national standard bearer of the Mahatma's Congress Party. But in the process of this emergence, Indira had pretty much demolished the genteel, slow-moving organization that Mahatma Gandhi had bequeathed to India. Indira's Congress would move fast, and move furiously. As she told Professor Ralph Buultjens, "There was no time to lose. We had to get India moving again."* During this period, the Indira government approved plans for a new "people's car," which was to be called the Maruti, after the monkey god of the epic *Ramayana*. The idea was to make a cheap car that would be affordable to India's growing middle class. All sorts of people were asked to apply for the appropriate licenses; the government said that there would be an "open choice" for the contract award. However, the license for this prestigious project was given to a young man named Sanjay Gandhi. He had no experience at all as an industrialist. But he happened to be the younger son of the prime minister. Indira Gandhi had started to practice the very nepotism which she had so condemned in the bosses of the Syndicate. In the event, it would be many years before the Maruti project got off the ground; it would be characterized by corruption and incompetent management. And whenever there was criticism of the project, Indira would

* Conversation with Professor Ralph Buultjens, New Delhi, 1977.

take it personally—after all, she would say, attacks against her son, Sanjay, were really attacks against her.

In a country like India, with widespread economic inequalities and deprivation, anyone who lives well is easily conspicuous. Among the most flamboyant of India's citizens were the former rulers of the princely states. At the time of independence, the rulers had an average of eleven titles; 5.8 wives; 12.6 children; 9.2 elephants; 2.8 private railway cars; 3.4 Rolls-Royces; and 22.9 tigers killed.* While most of these princes lived extravagantly, a few of them were so poor that their revenue did not exceed the income of a shepherd. The princes were sovereign in their territory before independence. They would exploit and plunder their subjects. But they were required to stay within the limits put down by the British, and for this the British had set up officers to keep an eye on them—indeed, the British had been responsible for the creation of some of the princely states. This arrangement came to be known as the Subsidiary Alliance. After independence, however, most of these states joined the Indian entity. The maharajahs were allowed to keep their titles, personal flags, and car number plates. They were also entitled to gun salutes on big occasions. This arrangement of the Indian government began to attract criticism over the years, particularly from left-wing politicians who felt that an egalitarian India should not encourage such elitism. The Congress Party's disposition toward the princes changed dramatically after several of them joined—and funded—the right-wing Swatantra Party. In the 1967 general election, quite a few of the princes won seats in Parliaments and local legislatures. This strengthened Indira's resolve to trim the royals' sails. She knew there was growing national resentment over the fact that the privy purses—which ranged from the equivalent of a few hundred dollars annually to several million dollars—were exempt from taxes. The profligate and debauched life-styles of some of the rulers also drew attention—and headlines. Indian royals, Indira told friends, were an anachronism.

The princes had been guaranteed their privileges under the Indian constitution. Indira realized that if she was to do away with those privileges, she would have to change the constitution itself. Thus Indira introduced a bill that would amend the constitution for the twenty-fourth

---

*Larry Collins and Dominique Lapierre, *Freedom at Midnight* (New York: Simon and Schuster, 1975). These statistics pertained to the situation in 1947, although afterward many princes continued to enjoy a luxurious life-style.

time since November 26, 1949, when that great document was approved by the Constituent Assembly. The amendment would derecognize the rights of Indian royalty. The bill would also abolish the privy purses. When a vote was taken in the Lok Sabha, the bill got the two-thirds majority that was needed for approval—but by exactly eight votes. The Opposition was able to prove that six votes were invalid: five votes had been cast twice and one had been placed "accidentally" for an absent member. The Speaker of the Lok Sabha agreed to hold an inquiry, but declared that the majority had not been affected. But in the upper house of Parliament, the Rajya Sabha, Indira's bill failed by one vote. That was when Indira asked President V. V. Giri to issue an order withdrawing the special status that the maharajahs had been given under the constitution. Several princes went to the Supreme Court to file a protest, and the court upheld them. It said that the president's move had been unconstitutional. That was when Indira Gandhi asked President Giri to dissolve Parliament and order a snap poll to be held in February 1971.

This election, Indira felt, would enable her government to seek a fresh mandate "to effectively implement its socialist and secular programs and policies." In a radio address to the nation on the evening of December 27, Indira said: "There comes a time in the life of a nation when the government of the day has to take an unusual step to cut through difficulties in order to solve the pressing problems with which the country is beset. The present is such a time."

From January 1971 to March of that year, Indira traveled far and wide through the country. She addressed more than 400 rallies that were attended by over 20 million people. Indira spent forty-one of the fifty-two days between January 13 and March 5 on the campaign trail, covering 30,000 miles by plane and helicopter, and 3,000 miles by car, Jeep, and train. Not one meeting or rally was canceled by her. On one day in mid-February, Indira turned up at fourteen rallies in four states. Not even Jawaharlal Nehru had campaigned with such maniacal energy. Her slogan through the campaign was "*Garibi hatao*"—"Let's get rid of poverty." Her campaign had aroused the expectations of the people. Astrologers, news reporters, and political pundits seemed as busy as the prime minister; the former all seemed to agree on two things: Never had there been such a hectic political campaign in India, and the Congress would barely get a majority in the next Parliament.

More than 150 million Indians—out of 272.7 million registered voters—cast their ballots in the elections, which were held between March 1 and 10.* When the election results came in, Indira had won 352 out

* Because of India's sheer size, polls are nearly always staggered. Since voting is by

of a total of 518 seats contested. The opposition had been routed. The Congress (O) won only sixteen seats. The era of the Syndicate was truly over. With a two-thirds majority in Parliament, Indira was now in a position to get any legislation she wanted passed. Indira Gandhi was now indisputably the most powerful politician in India, and possibly the most powerful woman in the world.

Her power gradually shaped Indira Gandhi's outlook—no dissent would be allowed, no criticism tolerated. Everything, everyone, was judged on the single overarching criterion of loyalty to Indira—that, and how useful they were to sustain Indira's own power. As a result, virtually every region in India began to have its fires: Kashmir in the north, another strategic border state like Punjab, where local Muslims were believed by Indira to be "soft" on Pakistan and desired independence from India; Assam in the east, where local tribes massacred Muslim refugees; Andhra Pradesh in the south, where a regional ethnic party clamored for greater state rights; Tamil Nadu, whose local leaders had supported the Tamil insurgency in Sri Lanka; and Maharashtra in the west, where Hindus and Muslims had murdered one another.

One winter evening in 1984, I went to see Romesh Thapar in Delhi. A tall, silver-maned man, with a rich, resonant voice and the assured ease of an aristocrat, Thapar was one of India's best political analysts. He and his wife, Raj, published a magazine called *Seminar*, which for nearly three decades had been the country's most important intellectual monthly. Along with their friend Professor Rajni Kothari of the Center for the Study of Developing Societies, the Thapars had become Delhi's most sought-after sources for local writers and visiting journalists. They were very congenial, and seekers of insight were rarely turned away by them, no matter what the hour, or the visitors' ideology. Because they rarely hesitated to question the Delhi government's policies and express their reservations about many of Mrs. Gandhi's actions, the Thapars and Professor Kothari had not endeared themselves to the prime minister's aides and associates. Romesh Thapar had once been a close adviser to Indira Gandhi but had a falling-out over what he charged were her authoritarian tendencies. *

Thapar received me in his art-filled house on Kautilya Marg, and Raj

---

paper ballots, such staggering gives the Election Commission more time to properly supervise the polls.

* Raj Thapar's memoirs were published posthumously in India in 1991. They caused a great uproar because of her pungent comments about India public figures, including Indira Gandhi.

promptly offered tea and toast. The collation warmed me up; the Delhi winter had frozen my blood. The conversation quickly turned to Indira Gandhi's legacy. What had she left behind, I asked? "When she died, she left nothing behind," Romesh Thapar said. "She left nothing behind of any redeeming value. She tried to destroy our parliament, our judiciary, our press, and she tried to undermine the states—particularly states that were governed by opposition parties. Look how she tried to destabilize the Punjab. And look what she did in Kashmir."

"Those who maintain that an India without Indira is a land without a leader should think again," Thapar said. "Indira Gandhi left behind a sterile political landscape. The infrastructure, designed by her father to buttress healthy federal functioning and to cultivate those autonomies without which no democratic system can be sensitive and effective, civilized and respected—that infrastructure had been made impotent. The basis of a genuine secular policy is not to integrate various ethnic communities but to create mutual respect between the majority and the minorities—this was lacking under Indira. Assam and the tribes of the northeast took the first onslaught of 'imperial' Delhi's aberrations."*

"Punjab was massively mishandled," Thapar continued,

and even the monster of terrorism was nurtured to divide and rule the assertive but stupidly advised and led Sikh community. Kashmir followed, a crude example of authoritarian intervention, endangering another strategic area. And then, Andhra. Only a popular revolt in that state, from village to village, revived Chief Minister N. T. Rama Rao, who had been illegally unseated, and made Indira Gandhi retreat. These events, punctuated by the storming of the Golden Temple which had been fortified almost as if with the blessings of Indira Gandhi's minions, and the incredible partisan handling of the

---

* In the eastern state of Assam, which produces much of the crude oil that is making India nearly self-sufficient in petroleum, local tribes were angry over the influx of Muslim refugees from neighboring Bangladesh, whose increasing presence, they feared, would confer on indigenous tribes the status of minority groups. Bloodshed occurred periodically, with the biggest massacre taking place in May 1983, when thousands of tribes people, armed with bows and arrows and spears, killed thousands more of the Muslim émigrés. Mrs. Gandhi's government was astonishingly tardy in clamping down on the tribes people, whose electoral support her ruling Congress Party had sought: she pushed through local elections that were blatantly rigged by her party. The situation deteriorated so rapidly that Assam and the Punjab were the only two Indian states where the December 1984 national parliamentary poll was not held: In both cases, the political situation was deemed too unstable, with a high potential for violence.

traumatic aftermath, took on the dimensions of a classical tragedy as she was gunned down in vengeance by her own security guards. And what happened then? The lumpen leaders she had cultivated in her Congress Party sparked a holocaust against the Sikh community stretching from Delhi to Bengal. The corrupt police system looked on. The government sat paralyzed.

I told the Thapars that I planned to travel around India to see for myself what impact Mrs. Gandhi's politics and policies had on the lives of everyday people. I thought that India seemed to be awash with chaos. Were there any signs of a new social order? Or was India unraveling?

"If you looked at the scene even before the assassination, you could see that Indian states were highly disturbed over the concentration of power in Delhi," Thapar said.

But then came October 31 and the assassination. The public was terrified. There was a total breakdown of law and order. There was a shock wave across the country, and Rajiv Gandhi capitalized on it. He raised the specter of disintegration. People thought, "Let's support and strengthen the national government at this time of crisis." But well before Indira's death, the crisis of political and economic man-agement in India had already expressed itself in many parts of the country—in Punjab and Kashmir, for instance. As the states were alienated, you saw the Congress base becoming restricted to the Hindi-speaking heartland in the north. Thus, Rajiv and his Congress had to mobilize Hindu opinion, rather than fashion the kind of national secular consensus that his grandfather, Jawaharlal Nehru, put together. Rajiv won the election largely because of this undis-guised appeal to the majority of Hindus, because of nationwide sympa-thy over the murder of his mother, and because of the 500 crores of rupees [then the equivalent of $500 million] that the Congress Party spent on slick advertising and electioneering.

I knew I was keeping Romesh and Raj Thapar from their dinner engagement. But even as I looked at my watch, Romesh Thapar signaled me to stay on.

"The question now is, will the trauma of 1984 continue into 1985?" Thapar said. "How will Rajiv Gandhi manage relations between the center and the states? If there is to be a new social order, it will have to spring at the level of our states. The corrective measures in our subconti-nent have to come from the states—because it is in the states that you implement policy and affect the everyday life of people. Any alternatives to the current national political mess, any new social order, must come at the state level. So if you are traveling through India's states, I wish you God-speed!"

That was the last time I saw Raj Thapar; she died several years later after a long battle with cancer. Romesh Thapar died of a heart attack not long afterward.

Nehru, Shastri, Indira—there evolved over the years a gradual suspicion among everyday people about the Indian state itself. During the latter part of Indira's reign, the state dropped all notions of benevolence. And people's suspicion about the state, which kept accumulating wide-ranging police powers, was coupled with the disgust people felt over the growing corruption and criminalization in public life. Then you had situations like Punjab and Kashmir, where Mrs. Gandhi constantly employed cost-calculating approaches instead of instituting measures that would lead to lasting solutions to thorny problems. She let thorny problems become thornier.

The speaker was Ashis Nandy of Delhi's Center for the Study of Developing Societies. Professor Nandy and I were talking in his musty, book-filled, and generally untidy office at the center's building on Rajpur Road in Old Delhi. Squirrels played on the well-kept lawn outside his office. Bougainvillea and magnolia trees offered plentiful color to the scene. Nandy, a prolific writer and academician, was urging me to start my fresh round of travels in Kashmir. By the time I met Nandy, I had already been to the Punjab where I had seen for myself the impact of Indira Gandhi's handling of a sensitive communal issue in a strategic border state. Now I was eager to go to Kashmir, where Indira had won the last political battle of her life.

I found it useful to meet with people like Romesh Thapar and Rajni Kothari and Ashis Nandy. They gave me their valuable time, asking nothing in exchange except my attention; they offered insights into the Indian scene; they provided pointers to what was happening in different parts of the country; and, without unduly imposing their own assumptions and opinions, they helped me make the connections between what I saw and heard and felt and the broader currents that coursed through India at this particular point in time.

As I flew to Kashmir, I thought about what Ashis Nandy had said about Indira Gandhi's "cost-calculating" approach to the management of power. She had, in fact, gone home again to Kashmir to whip it into line. I looked out of the window of the Indian Airlines airbus, and I gasped at the view. The plane was cruising over the snow-helmeted Pir Panjal Range. The crenellated peaks shimmered in the clear winter sunlight. To the west were the rich, alluvial plains of Pakistan; to the east lay the mountainous wastelands of Tibet, and beyond Tibet, China. Soon we were over the mighty Banihal Pass, through which invaders over the centuries had entered Kashmir. It was ironic, I thought, that the most recent invader had been a hometown girl. I checked in at the Hotel Broadway, a modern Scandinavian-type building with comfortable rooms and a polite staff. In the lobby were several electric stoves. Large men wearing thick sweaters and peaked lamb's-wool caps lounged on sofas, consuming liquor. I was immediately beset by carpet salesmen, and purveyors of shawls. To decline such offers was to offend, and the sales-men sulked away. But I wanted to read up on tourist literature, which I had picked up at Srinagar's airport. I was also waiting for my friend Rahul Singh, who was driving up to Srinagar from the state's winter capital of Jammu, which lay south of the massif I had flown over on the way to Kashmir's elevated valley. Rahul Singh was then the editor of the Chandigarh edition of the *Indian Express*, and he was coming to Kashmir to get a reading on the election campaign that was on in full fury here. We had agreed to link up in Srinagar, a place neither of us had visited for years.

The tourist brochures were shabby. The photographs were poorly re-produced. Kashmir did not seem inviting in this literature. And, indeed, tourism—the mainstay of the state's economy—was sharply falling off. I had been told in Delhi that in the first eleven months of 1984, Kashmir attracted 275,000 domestic tourists and about 45,000 foreigners; the previous year, the figures had been 400,000 Indians and 44,000 foreign-ers; and in 1982, more than 600,000 Indian tourists and 50,000 foreigners were estimated by the authorities to have skied, toured, trekked, played golf and tennis, fished, hiked, camped, or climbed mountains in Kashmir. State officials attributed the decline in tourism to poor publicity about Kashmir, and the poor publicity to the fact that since 1983 the state had been experiencing a political upheaval. Moreover, tourists who traveled by land seemed deterred by the fact that virtually all major roads into Kashmir led up from a troubled neighboring state, the Punjab.

Tourists were also deterred by reports of growing unemployment in Kashmir. This, to be sure, was a classical case of the chicken-or-egg theory, because with fewer tourists coming to Kashmir, the state's tourism industries and such tourist-predicated businesses as carpet manufacturing and shawl making slid into the doldrums. About 75 percent of Kashmir's 6 million people live in the Srinagar Valley, the rest in Jammu. In the valley alone, there were said to be more than 200,000 unemployed adults by December 1984. Kashmiris have long felt that the Delhi government has neglected their economic development, despite the strategic importance of the state, which has borders with Pakistan and China. This sentiment was highlighted by Sonam Gyalsan, a lean, compact lawyer from the remote Kashmiri province of Ladakh. I was introduced to Gyalsan by C. B. Kaul, Srinagar correspondent for the *Indian Express*.

Kaul had brought Gyalsan to my hotel so that he could meet Rahul Singh, but since Singh was late in getting here from Jammu I served as a stand-in. Gyalsan, whose family members in Ladakh are still pastoral tribesmen, is a member of the Kashmir state assembly, and he invited Singh and me for breakfast the next morning. He cooked a Ladakhi breakfast for us in his small suite in Srinagar's hostel for legislators. There was no heat in the suite, or gas, or electricity. Gyalsan lit up a kerosene stove and swiftly concocted a thick soup called snamthuk. In it were chunks of mutton, bits of goat cheese, barley, flour, ginger, and rich local butter. The snamthuk was very filling, yet it was followed by boiled eggs, outsize apricots that Gyalsan had brought from Leh—Ladakh's capital—boiled cauliflower, and milky tea that was so sweet that my teeth vibrated as I consumed it. The meal made me drowsy, but I perked up when Gyalsan started to talk.

> We tribespeople are the modern-day "untouchables" of Kashmir. There are still 140,000 of us in Ladakh's two districts, Leh and Khargol. But look how we are forced to live—in caravans, in shacks made out of sheepskin, in degrading poverty. I have tried to impress on the powers-that-be in Delhi and in Srinagar that Ladakh should be developed in the national interest. After all, we, more than any other Indians, directly face two enemies—Pakistan and China. We are in the front line. Ours is the first blood to be shed whenever there are wars, or even minor skirmishes. And what do we get in return? Nothing. No jobs, little investment in economic development. Even the Indian Army people are sometimes arrogant in their dealings with us. Indira Gandhi said she cared for all of India's border peoples. Not much evidence of her caring in our area. I hope Rajiv Gandhi is more attentive.

Sonam Gyalsan's life story is a sort of Indian Horatio Alger tale. He was born in 1940 in a caravan near Nurla Village in Ladakh, the youngest of five brothers and a sister. His parents were nomadic traders in wool, and they frequently wandered into neighboring Tibet. Gyalsan traveled with them as they traversed mountain roads that rose as high as 18,000 feet. Winters were harsh, but at these heights it was bitterly cold even during the summers. His parents would stop at tiny hamlets to bargain for Shartush shawls, made out of the fine hair that grows under the necks of the spiral-horned wild mountain goats known as Tsos. (These shawls now can cost the equivalent of $7,000.) When he was sixteen years old, his parents arranged his marriage to Tsering Dolkar, a fourteen-year-old girl. (They now have four children.) As Gyalsan learned to read and write in his parents' caravan, it struck him that there were not too many people he would encounter who enjoyed literacy. And the people of Ladakh, whose native language was Tibetan, simply could not communicate with traders and visiting politicians from the Kashmir Valley; the outsiders spoke Kashmiri and Hindi and Urdu, but seldom Tibetan.

"As a child I was inspired by biographies of Nehru and Mahatma Gandhi," Gyalsan said. "These books instilled in me a strong drive to uplift myself. I studied very hard and obtained admission to a high school in Srinagar, and then won a scholarship to Ram Jas College in Delhi. It was on a visit home one day that I learned there was not a single lawyer in Leh. Feuds and disputes were still being settled the old-fashioned way—with fists, or knives, or abusive language! I decided to become a lawyer."

He received a law degree from Delhi University and returned home to Ladakh to set up his practice. He started civic organizations to inculcate in Ladakhis notions of hygiene; he coaxed friends in Delhi to underwrite visits by physicians to attend to Ladakhi children's illnesses (the infant mortality rate in this remote northeast province of Kashmir was well over 300 per every live 1,000 births;); he persuaded the Srinagar administration to build several primary schools. Gyalsan even founded a chapter of the Lions Club in Leh—at 12,000 feet above sea level, the Leh chapter is believed to be the highest Lions Club in the world.

It was only a matter of time before he entered politics. Gyalsan headed several delegations that went to Delhi to ask Mrs. Gandhi to formally declare Ladakh a backward area so that it could receive special development funds from the central government. The prime minister was not especially receptive. No special funds were allocated for the development of Ladakh, although vacation bungalows for government officials were erected near Leh. A hydroelectric project called Stakna was delayed so much by the government that the initial budget of $5 million now ballooned five times, with Delhi giving the money only grudgingly. Kashmir state officials in Srinagar did not seem particularly inclined to assist the 140,000 people of Ladakh, most of whom were Buddhists.

So Sonam Gyalsan ran for the state assembly elections and won a seat. In the legislature, he has been vocal and insistent about obtaining a better deal for Ladakh.

"I see myself as a link between my backward society and the rapidly progressing modern-day India," Gyalsan said to me. "I am a Buddhist —and Buddhism asks each of us to go outside of ourselves and look for the larger good. I don't especially subscribe to political rhetoric. I say to the big shots in Delhi: 'Don't just tell us how much Ladakh means for the security of the nation—show us.' Delhi has been allowed by people like us to get away with neglect and inattention. Well, our time has come. We won't stay silent any longer. We want everything that other Indians want—better schools, better homes, better health care, more jobs, cheaper food, good roads. We want to be part of the Indian dream, and not just dream that dream."

I thought that Sonam Gyalsan was exceptionally articulate about his objectives for the people of Ladakh, a people who have not profited by their association with India. But they are not alone. In states like West Bengal, Bihar, Orissa, Andhra Pradesh, and Maharashtra, you often come across backward tribes whose life has not improved in the four decades years since Independence. Such tribal communities as the Adivasis and Bhils still live in primitive conditions, foraging through forests for food, occasionally slaughtering a goat, sometimes raiding farms in the night. At least Gyalsan's Ladakhis could be represented in a legislature, at least Sonam Gyalsan could relay their yearnings and long-ings to a wider audience. The aborigines of most of India have little such representation, few special allowances. Indira Gandhi often spoke eloquently about the economic and social needs of these backward areas, but development in those areas was slow and government funds slower still.

Gyalsan had spoken about his people's dreams. Different people dream different things. The mostly Buddhist people of Ladakh are, after all, a minority community in a state whose population is overwhelmingly Mus-lim. Indira Gandhi had long suspected—as did a few of her father's key advisers—that some of these Muslims did not want to continue to be a part of India, that they either preferred to join Pakistan, or that they wanted their own separate nation.

Accession to India was thus done under pressure, even though there was no opposition to it at the time from Kashmir's leading politicians, such as Sheikh Abdullah. Nehru pledged that the accession would be validated by a popular referendum under international auspices, perhaps the United Nations. Sheikh Abdullah himself said:

> Kashmir has linked itself to India, not because it has been lured by any material gain but because it is at one with her in the Gandhian ideals of justice, equality, and humanity. A progressive state could join hands only with another progressive one and not with a feudal state like Pakistan. Our decision to accede to India is based on the fact that our program and policy are akin to those followed by India. Now Kashmir and Pakistan can never meet. Pakistan is a haven of exploiters. India is pledged to the principle of secular democracy in her policy and we are in pursuit of the same objective.

Sheikh Abdullah, the "Lion of Kashmir," became the state's chief executive. Throughout his life and until his death on September 8, 1982, he always publicly swore allegiance to India.

It was only on February 24, 1975, that the sheikh and his supporters agreed to disband their movement for a plebiscite. Their agreement was formalized in the six-point Kashmir Accord, which was sculpted by Prime Minister Indira Gandhi's trusted foreign-policy adviser G. Parthasarathy. The accord resulted not only in the abandonment of the plebiscite movement; it pledged Sheikh Abdullah to honor Article 370 of the Indian Constitution, which gave Kashmir special status within the Indian union. And the accord specifically emphasized that Kashmir was a constituent unit of India. The accord cleared the way for a triumphant return to power by the sheikh, who was duly made Kashmir's chief minister on February 25, 1975. He was to serve in that office until his death of a heart attack seven years later, at the age of seventy-seven. Whatever his political appeal, the sheikh's administrative helmsmanship had not been especially distinguished: Corruption rocketed under the sheikh, the state's development plans went astray, and the budget ran amok.

Dynastic politics is perhaps a special characteristic of Kashmiris. Sheikh Mohammed Abdullah's anointed heir-apparent, his flamboyant son Farooq, was sworn in as Kashmir's chief minister. Farooq Abdullah had trained to be a physician and, indeed, had practiced medicine for several years in Britain. He married an Irishwoman. He loved fast cars and motorbikes. He was so fond of Mrs. Gandhi that he called her "Mummy."

But "Mummy" was less than appreciative of two things: one, the fact that however supportive Farooq Abdullah was of her as a national leader, Kashmir still was governed not by her Congress Party but by the National Conference, which was technically at least an opposition party: and two, the fact that Farooq Abdullah had joined with chief ministers of other opposition-ruled states in starting a forum to reform Center-state relations. Mrs. Gandhi felt that implicit in the formation of this forum was the hope that India's squabbling opposition parties would fashion a common front against her ruling Congress Party in the next parliamentary elections, which were widely expected to be held by January 1985. (They were, of course, held in December 1984.) Farooq Abdullah, perhaps out of political naïveté and inexperience, may not have realized that his very presence on a public platform with opposition politicians would be viewed dimly indeed by Indira Gandhi. "Mummy" set into motion a plan to unseat him, initiating first a sinister whispering campaign against the physician-turned-politician. Suggestions were floated that Farooq Abdullah was sympathetic toward Sikh separatists. Then a rumor circulated in Delhi that Abdullah had made a secret deal with Pakistan's military dictator, Mohammed Zia ul-Haq, under which the National Conference would act as a fifth column in India on behalf of Pakistan. Some Gandhi associates openly joked about Abdullah's sexual preferences and questioned his loyalty to his wife.

The eminent Indian writer M. J. Akbar, in his best-selling book, *India: The Siege Within*, has a particularly astute passage that assesses this period in Farooq Abdullah's star-crossed tenure as Kashmir's chief minister:

> The Abdullahs were always conscious that, no matter how many times they protested otherwise, they would forever be vulnerable to the charge of being "soft" toward Pakistan, and in quiet league with secessionists. They knew that each time Delhi wanted them to kneel, it would always resurrect this allegation and, if necessary, even use such an excuse to dismiss the government. Sheikh Abdullah had spent his life listening to accusations of treachery; his only answer lay in his personal faith and self-confidence, and in the end he was vindicated. Farooq Abdullah now knew that it was only a matter of time before the many hostile forces started such a smear campaign against him. He decided to meet the problem head-on. One of the mistakes which the Sheikh had made, in his son's view, was that he had kept himself confined, by and large, to his own state. Farooq Abdullah decided that he would build personal and political bridges across the country. He would convince India, and not just Mrs. Gandhi, about his commitment to the country. If he could clear the minds of the people and the political parties in the rest of the country, he would be much less dependent on the goodwill of just one party, the Congress. If, therefore, he was ever called secessionist, he hoped

that there would be more than one powerful voice in India saying that the accusation was a partisan fraud designed to cover up an unethical power game.

The game was much more unethical than Farooq Abdullah had bargained for. Mrs. Gandhi coaxed his brother-in-law, G. M. Shah, who hated his wife's brother with a passion, to form a cabinet with the help of "defectors" from Abdullah's National Conference. The men and women who now affiliated themselves with Shah were all promised—and subsequently given—cabinet positions. Farooq Abdullah seemed unaware that these moves were being plotted in his own backyard. On the afternoon of the evening he was deposed, the tall, handsome chief minister was gamboling with Shabana Azmi, the film actress, who had turned up in Kashmir to shoot a Hindi movie. Srinagar's masses rioted when they heard the news of Abdullah's overthrow. Mrs. Gandhi sent in troops to restore law and order. Opposition leaders around the country roared their disapproval. No amount of protests helped. Farooq Abdullah was out, G. M. Shah was there to stay, and Indira Gandhi had won in July 1984 what would be her last political victory. Indira Gandhi may have succeeded in dethroning Farooq Abdullah in July 1984, but by the end of the year he had humiliated her Congress Party in the Kashmir Valley. (And, indeed, by 1987 Abdullah—having made his peace with Rajiv Gandhi—was back in the saddle, only to lose his job when the state government was dismissed again and Kashmir put under President's Rule because of the deteriorating law-and-order situation.)

Not long after the assassination of the prime minister, it was announced by her son that national parliamentary elections would be held across India on December 24 and 27. Astrologers consulted by Congress Party chieftains said that those were the most auspicious dates for a poll, and so it was decided that the election would be held in some states on the first date and in the rest of the country on the latter date. In the event, Rajiv Gandhi's Congress won an unprecedented 401 out of 508 seats contested in all of India's twenty-five states other than Assam and Punjab (where the poll was postponed on account of unstable political conditions). The 107 seats the Congress did not win included all three in Kashmir. Farooq Abdullah's National Conference steamrollered candidates put up by Abdullah's brother-in-law, Chief Minister G. M. Shah. The losers, who were backed by the Gandhi Congress, included Shah's own son. The winners included Farooq's mother, Begum Akbar Jehan Abdullah.

It is not only Kashmir's indigenous politicians, such as the Abdullahs, who have long been suspected by Delhi of harboring secessionist, or pro-Pakistan, sentiments. The Abdullahs have had to prove themselves as being more "kosher," more "Indian," than political leaders in other Indian states. But even ordinary Kashmiris are generally perceived by ordinary Indians elsewhere as not quite emotionally "with" India. The feeling among many top government officials in Delhi is that the Kashmiri Muslim has yet to completely reconcile his state's formal affiliation with India, and that among these Muslims India is still viewed as an alien country. These officials point to surveys that have showed that the most popular radio and television programs in the Kashmir Valley are not those broadcast by India's government networks but by those of Pakistan.*

What Kashmiris call "Delhi's handiwork" has involved a continuing effort to discredit the state's political leaders, especially those not belonging to the Congress Party. For example, Mrs. Gandhi's henchmen spread the word that Farooq Abdullah accumulated a personal fortune of $50 million during his twenty-two months as Kashmir's chief minister, and that among other things he maintained a fleet of twenty expensive foreign-made cars. His father, Sheikh Mohammed Abdullah, amassed even greater wealth, according to the propaganda spread by the Abdullahs's opponents. But whenever Farooq Abdullah referred to reports that some of Indira Gandhi's factotums were charging million of rupees in fees just to provide access to her or to ensure that a valued industrial license was approved, he was at once accused of being unpatriotic, or of lying.

The whispering campaign concerning Kashmiris's "patriotism" had been also extended to the state's Muslim religious leaders and organizations. Here the critics and questioners have probably been on firmer ground—for the theological leaders of this overwhelmingly Muslim state have frequently flip flopped over their allegiance. The Jamaat-E-Islami, a religious organization with considerable support among peasants, had been openly pro-Pakistan. It was only when neighboring Pakistan's military dictatorship started establishing a cruel, intolerant theocracy that the popularity of the Jamaat-E-Islami began to wane in Kashmir. The Muslims of Kashmir may be religious, but they have never been known to be Hindu-haters or Hindu-baiters. Kashmiri Muslims like the idea of free speech, and their leaders have seldom advocated clamping down on political or even theological dissent. I think General Zia ul-Haq—the late Pakistani dictator—did India a great service: He showed Kashmiri Muslims how intolerant and intolerable life could be in his Islamic

---

*That may well be because Pakistan's broadcasts, although heavily religious in nature, are generally much better produced that the Indian ones.

state—and this in turn seems to have convinced many Kashmiri Muslims that they would be guaranteed far more liberties under Delhi's continued Raj than under Islamabad's iron rule.

The passage of time, however, has worked to enhance the appeal of Kashmiri nationalism. In times of tension, moderate forces have had a declining appeal as younger zealots appear to have gained a stronger position in Kashmiri politics. The Indian government's response has tended to be repressive—a policy that, in turn, has helped to fuel greater resentment among the masses. By the end of 1991, a kind of standoff prevailed—with large segments of Kashmiri territory out of government control by night and heavily policed by Indian troops by daylight. Increasingly, Kashmiri nationalism draws encouragement from ethnic separatism from other parts of the world. In addition, Kashmir continues to be a pawn in the continuing conflict between India and Pakistan. The confluence of all these forces gives little hope for any peaceful settlement in Kashmir in the immediate future.

"In some ways, Kashmir today is part of Indira Gandhi's legacy," says Professor Ralph Buultjens. "Her attitude to Kashmir was a mixture of sentimental attachment to the land of her ancestors with her determination not to yield an inch of Indian territory. Her belief in strong central government continues to influence New Delhi's policy on Kashmir. To Indira Gandhi, it was inconceivable that anyone who lived within the Indian Union would want to disrupt the unity of the nation. This heritage has helped to shape the larger Indian attitude to Kashmir, and still prevails."

17

Empress of India

There were four defining events during Indira Gandhi's tenure in power. One was her dispatching of Indian troops to the Golden Temple in Amritsar in June 1984. Another significant event was her imposition of the Emergency in 1975 under which the constitution was suspended; that action led to her fall from power two years later in an election that witnessed the parliamentary victory of an Opposition group. A third defining event was her demolition of the Syndicate, and her creation of a new Congress Party in 1969.

The fourth defining event of Indira Gandhi's stewardship of India was the 1971 Indo-Pakistan War, which resulted in the creation of Bangladesh from what was then East Pakistan. To understand this tumultuous event, which consolidated Indira's power in India and made her a genuine world figure—and prompted some observers, such as Henry Kissinger, to call her "Empress of India"—it is necessary to examine the roots of the hostility between India and Pakistan. *

Pakistan was the bitter fruit of the British Raj. Its national ethos was shaped by the Hindu-Muslim fratricide in India that was the basis for its being. Pakistan was to be the first Islamic state of the postwar, postcolonial era—but the jubilation over independence was quickly canceled out by the cataclysmic violence of displacement. At least 14 million refugees—no one knows the precise number—moved between India

* The *Economist* of London is widely credited with popularizing the term "Empress of India." The last real empress, of course, was Queen Victoria. Indira's critics used the term frequently—and not charitably, of course.

and Pakistan in the most wrenching two-way migration of this century, crossing into what they had always known as a nearby neighborhood but was now suddenly a new home in an alien nation. So there was not any allowance, nor any time, for political growing pains, no luxury of developing national mechanisms that would expedite entry into the modern world. Pakistan came of age as a nation instantly and bloodily, an entity superimposed on a subcontinent where religious tensions had long been subsumed by the dream of driving out colonialism. And as if communal bloodshed were not baptism enough, Pakistan's political adulthood was branded by a border war with India in 1947, the first of three conflicts that widened the chasm between two nations that sprang from the same womb—two nations with the same culture, the same cuisine, some of the same languages, the same racial memories, and the same history.

That common background, however, did not yield the same economic development strategies for the two nations that had simultaneously won their "freedom at the midnight hour"—Jawaharlal Nehru's famous phrase. India, from the very beginning, seemed to know what social, political, and economic goals it wanted to pursue. Its leaders, proclaiming secularism and socialism, had an expansive vision of the future: the alleviation of poverty, the promotion of democracy and nonalignment, the dismantling of a debilitating caste system. Because of India's sheer size, of course, and because of its ethnic diversity, administering the country would always be a messy, untidy, and disputatious affair. But there was never an ongoing search for identity, no constant asking: "What are we?" India's leaders were homespun—"sons of the soil," in the phrase of Professor Ralph Buultjens—and after independence they stayed home to shape the national agenda. But Pakistan's postindependence leaders were transplants—born mostly in British India and infused with secular instincts and a Western sensibility rather than the Islamic ethic they formally embraced. Unlike Jawaharlal Nehru and his associates, who were the fountainheads of virtually all political activity in India, they had no master plan for development. It was as if, having achieved their once improbable ideal of nationhood, the Pakistanis were at a loss for a new goal. Moreover, the new nation's leaders were widely resented by indigenous landowners and segments of the middle classes whom they were suddenly governing. During their political lifetimes, they would always be known as mohajirs—refugees.

"That legacy has continued to haunt Pakistan to this day," says Shahid Javed Burki, a well-known Pakistani author and economist.[*] Instead of

---

[*] Interview with author, Washington, D.C., 1988.

being able to get down to the task of building a new, independent nation, Pakistan tried to relive the past and justify its existence. And because of this, the country has not been able to develop the political institutions that are essential for robust social and economic development. The country has followed different and often contradictory paths in trying to achieve national objectives that were also being constantly redefined. "No matter who its leaders have been, Pakistan has been in the throes of a continual identity crisis," says Burki.

That identity crisis surfaced dramatically in 1971. Field Marshal Mohammed Ayub Khan's war with India in 1965 had ended not only in a defeat for Pakistan but also in a fall from grace—and office—for him. In March 1969, Ayub was deposed in a *coup d'état* carried out by his protégé, General Agha Muhammad Yahya Khan. Yahya promised to hold elections and to restore such institutions as a free press; the Pakistani press had been muzzled since 1958. Yahya knew that the state, primarily a military one, had begun to weaken. There had been a spate of demonstrations by students. These protests had gathered enough momentum to prompt foreign reporters to say that Pakistan, at long last, seemed to have a prodemocracy movement. There were marches against the military regime in both West Pakistan and East Pakistan, and sometimes students from Karachi and Lahore—cities in West Pakistan—protested side by side with students from Dacca and Chittagong, the two major urban centers of East Pakistan. When Pakistan was created, more than a thousand miles of Indian territory separated West Pakistan from East Pakistan. All that bound the two regions was the fact that their inhabitants were overwhelmingly Muslims. But the Muslims of East Pakistan increasingly came to resent the fact that the reins of government were overwhelmingly in the hands of Punjabis from West Pakistan.

These Punjabis held the East Pakistan Bengalis in utter contempt. They viewed the mostly puny Bengalis as physically inferior; they even thought that Bengali culture was inferior to that of the Punjabis. * Though the population of East Pakistan was primarily Bengali, the top positions in the civil service were held by Punjabi Muslims. The Pakistani military, too, was dominated by men from West Pakistan. The situation worsened

---

* The Punjabis prided themselves on hailing from pure Aryan stock—descendants of the Central Europeans who invaded and settled northern India 3,000 years ago. The Bengalis were considered hybrids, descendants of darker and shorter indigenous people.

because of the language problem. Urdu was declared the official language of the state. This irked the Bengali Muslims, for whom no language compared to their own beautiful and mellifluous one. Large numbers of Bengali students were killed in anti-Urdu riots. These students began to be revered as martyrs in East Pakistan.

When Yahya Khan promised to allow free elections to be held in December 1970, he did not anticipate that the Awami League—the dominant party in East Pakistan—would not only capture 160 out of the 162 seats allocated to East Pakistan but would even manage to secure a majority in the Pakistan National Assembly, even though the League had not contested any seat in West Pakistan. The League had demanded autonomy for East Pakistan within a federal Pakistan. Indeed, the League's leader, a charismatic man named Sheikh Mujibur Rahman, even expected to be named by Yahya Khan as head of the national government in the wake of the election results. After all, his majority in the National Assembly entitled him to be the prime minister of the whole of Pakistan. Sheikh Mujibur also demanded that there be an equal number of Bengalis in the army. Sheikh Mujibur was to become the "Father of Bangladesh," and its first head of government. A dreamy and thoroughly incompetent man—notwithstanding his good intentions —he allowed corruption and nepotism to flourish. Eventually, Sheikh Mujibur was murdered by people he had trusted, but not before he had firmly placed Bangladesh on the road to financial and administrative ruin. Some Bangladeshis, claiming to be relatives of Sheikh Mujibur, opened fancy curry restaurants in New York City; others dabbled in business, and even were suspected by American authorities of consorting with underworld figures.

Complicating the picture for Yahya Khan was the fact that a populist party called the Pakistan People's Party (PPP) won hands down in West Pakistan—eighty-one of the 139 National Assembly seats allotted to West Pakistan. The PPP's leader was a youthful demagogue named Zulfikar Ali Bhutto. He was the scion of a wealthy landowning family from the Sind Province of West Pakistan, and a product of Western education. Bhutto, who had served as Ayub Khan's foreign minister, was also a political liberal who was perceived by his supporters as a man who was going to liberate Pakistan from the grip of the military and the mullahs, the Muslim clergy. He promised "*Roti, kapda aur makaan*"— "Food, clothing and shelter."

At first Yahya Khan—a man excessively fond of alcohol and sex—seemed nonplussed about what to do about the election results. He had figured that no party would get a majority and that he, Yahya, would emerge as an "arbiter among a gaggle of squabbling politicians," as Inder Malhotra has put it. * When Henry Kissinger—then the national security adviser to President Richard Nixon—visited Islamabad during this period, a half-inebriated Yahya asked him during a state banquet: "Do you think that I am a dictator?"

"Mr. President, for a dictator you run a lousy general election," Kissinger reportedly replied. Like other top officials in U.S. administrations since the end of World War II, Kissinger subscribed to the position that Pakistan should be a bulwark against Soviet expansionism in Asia. Since the 1950s, Washington had been giving considerable economic and military assistance to Islamabad. This aid continued even during the early months of 1971, when American and Western reporters wrote about the atrocities perpetrated by West Pakistani troops in East Pakistan—and there was strong sentiment in Congress to suspend American assistance. Many U.S. congressmen felt that Yahya Khan should abide by the results of the elections and allow Sheikh Mujibur to form a government.

But Yahya Khan was hardly about to turn over the day-to-day management of his government to an administration headed by Sheikh Mujibur. That would have been highly unpopular with Yahya's military—and almost certainly would have resulted in his overthrow.† Yahya developed an alliance with Bhutto, whose party had won in the Punjab, traditionally considered the heart of Pakistan. Bhutto's relations with the army then were better than those of Sheikh Mujibur, who was thoroughly distrusted by the generals. When the National Assembly was about to convene in Dhaka, the capital of East Pakistan, Bhutto announced that he would boycott the session until he and Sheikh Mujibur could hammer out an understanding about "a new power structure" in Pakistan. It was, of course, clear to everybody that Bhutto had no intention of cooperating with the Awami League leader, let alone sharing power with him. Yahya Khan now postponed indefinitely the opening of the National Assembly, touching off a wave of protests all across East Pakistan. Crowds were massacred by Yahya's troops; rape was commonplace. Young Punjabi soldiers from West Pakistan openly declared that they intended to impregnate Bengali women and thus improve the genes of the next generation of Bengalis.

On March 25, 1971—two weeks after Indira Gandhi won her over-

---

* Malhotra, *Indira Gandhi*, p. 132.
† In the event, Yahya was overthrown by his own generals in December 1971, after Pakistan had lost the 1971 war with India and East Pakistan became Bangladesh. The generals named Bhutto to head the government.

whelming victory in the Indian general election, and a week after she formed a new government—Yahya Khan ordered a full-scale military crackdown on East Pakistan. He thus put into motion what was to become a murderous civil war, one that widened into a conflict between Pakistan and India, and ultimately resulted in the birth of the new nation of Bangladesh. Students, teachers, and intellectuals were especially the target of Yahya's troops and police. A particularly ruthless commander named Lieutenant-General Tikka Khan—who soon came to be called by the media as the "Butcher of Bangladesh"—was entrusted with the task of controlling the agitated Bengalis. Tikka Khan had earlier won his spurs in Baluchistan, the rugged province in West Pakistan, where he brutally put down a rebellion among hill tribes. Sheikh Mujibur was arrested and taken to West Pakistan. Forty-eight hours after Yahya's crackdown, Major Zia-Ur Rahman—later to become president of Bangladesh in a coup, and still later to be assassinated—declared East Pakistan as Independent Bangladesh. There was little else that the desperate Bengalis could do other than declare themselves a putative nation: The violence being inflicted on them by the West Pakistan–led military was so heavy that the people of East Pakistan were permanently alienated from their supposed brethren from the West. "Genocide" was a term used by foreign newspapers and television networks to characterize the horrors being visited upon East Pakistan.

Indira's—and India's—sympathies clearly lay with the people of East Pakistan, now Bangladesh—both Muslims and Hindus. Indira told Krishan Bhatia that "India had no part in the internal development of Pakistan—West or East," but she also expressed to him her concern over the "battle that Pakistan was waging against its own citizens."* Yahya Khan had held "mock negotiations" with Sheikh Mujibur, but it was never his intention to allow the East Pakistani to become Pakistan's prime minister.† Thousands of Bengalis started fleeing their land. The initial attacks by the West Pakistani troops had been against local Hindus, and so the first wave of refugees consisted of these Hindus who had stayed behind in East Pakistan after the Partition of 1947. The troops then turned against anyone suspected of being sympathetic to the Awami League. No one knows to this day how many people were killed in 1971; the figure most frequently used in the India and Western media is 3 million dead, and 10 million who became refugees. India became con-

---

* Bhatia, *Indira*, p. 238.
† The Indian and international media played up these "mock negotiations," but Yahya never seemed to realize that the whole world had seen through his moves.

cerned because these refugees had begun to filter into West Bengal. Yahya Khan's regime made it clear that the refugees would not be allowed to return to their original homes. Indeed, rabid Muslim leaders even began advocating the distribution of Bangladeshi Hindus' assets among the Muslims who had stayed behind—something that was reminiscent of the tragedy of the 1947 Partition when the property of fleeing Hindus was seized by the Muslims of West Pakistan.

The Awami League was allowed to set up a government in exile in Calcutta. Indira Gandhi was faced with a dilemma: If she did not inter-vene and let the situation take its own course then there was a chance that East Pakistan could tilt toward Communism. This was not very acceptable because there was then a possibility that East Pakistan would unite West Bengal in a common cause. It would also mean that the Awami League, which had often been likened by political writers to the Indian National Congress, would be sidelined. If Indira intervened, then it would definitely lead to another war with Pakistan. It would also mean risking the wrath of the United States, which had already started aligning itself toward Pakistan, as well as that of China, which was now supplying weapons and military aid to Pakistan. Months later, in an essay for *Foreign Affairs*, Indira Gandhi wrote: "We would normally have welcomed the attainment of freedom by any victim of colonial oppression but usually it would have little direct impact on us. Bangladesh, however, was a part of our Subcontinent. How could we ignore a conflict which took place on our very border and overflowed into our own territory?"

As the atrocities increased, so did the pressure on Mrs. Gandhi to intervene. Right-wing Hindu organizations protested vigorously against the slaughter of their Bangladeshi brethren by Muslim soldiers.* Some influential political commentators started calling for an Indian campaign to cut Pakistan down to size. Mrs. Gandhi took stock of the situation, though she did resist the pressure from her people for quite a few months. She called on Indians to be calm as the situation was one of "watch and wait." Indira was anxious that no matter what action she took concerning Bangladesh, there be a national consensus behind it. Close associates say that she had determined as early as June 1971 that India would have no choice but to go to war with Pakistan over Bangladesh. According to General Sam Manekshaw—now Field Marshal Manekshaw—Indira had issued orders in April 1971 to prepare for war with Pakistan. Manekshaw,

---

* Right-wing Hindu leaders said that the fact that West Pakistani troops were forcing Bangladeshi Hindus into India suggested that they were intent on fully Islamicizing East Pakistan.

who hailed from the small Parsi community, was then the army chief. He later said that he was struck by the "clarity of the briefing issued to me by my political command." Indira had set a deadline of about ten months for a peaceful solution to the Bangladesh problem. If there were to be a war, Indira told Manekshaw, it could not last more than three weeks. Any conflict that went beyond that time frame was certain to become internationalized—and highly costly to India in terms of casualties and matériel.

Indira was deeply worried about the refugees who were pouring in continuously from East Pakistan. The burden of caring for this extraordinary cohort was too much for a poor country like India, which could barely cope with its own impoverished millions. India was spending the equivalent of 6 or 7 million dollars each day in looking after this tide of involuntary immigrants. The prime minister had to impose special taxes—including postal surcharges—to raise funds for the care and upkeep of these refugees. Mrs. Gandhi appealed to the world community to speed up a political settlement in Pakistan, so that the refugees could be sent back. She told several foreign correspondents, including Sydney Schanberg of *The New York Times*: "The world is not doing its moral duty toward Bangladesh. Instead of condemning Pakistan for the callous, inhuman, and intemperate butchery that its military has organized in Bangladesh, most countries have taken the safe path of praising India for its relief efforts, or offering some assistance for the refugees."

"We have no intention of absorbing these people here—no matter what," Mrs. Gandhi subsequently told the BBC. "I am absolutely determined about it."* Addressing a group of West European journalists, she said: "Conditions must be created in East Pakistan, Bangladesh as it is called, in which there is not military terror but normal democratic functioning of the people's will, so that refugees are enabled to return to their homes and their safety is guaranteed. The rulers of Pakistan must be made to see that there is no other way. It is the duty of every country which has any influence with Pakistan to impress the truth upon them."

At a news conference in New Delhi on October 19, 1971, Indira was asked by an Indian journalist whether she would be prepared to hold talks with Yahya Khan. Indeed, the Pakistani dictator had urged that there be bilateral talks between India and Pakistan over the situation in Bangladesh.

"What is there to discuss between India and Pakistan?" Indira said

---

*Interview given by Indira Gandhi to the British Broadcasting Corporation in October 1971.

tartly. "The problem is not an Indo-Pakistan problem. The problem is between the military regime of West Pakistan, and the people and . . . elected representatives of the people of Bangladesh. Any solution which is found must satisfy the people of Bangladesh and . . . the people whom they elected not too long ago to represent them."

The very fact that Indira had started using "Bangladesh" when referring to East Pakistan suggested that she had accepted the notion of a new entity there. She thought that Yahya Khan was a crude man. In August 1971, in fact, Yahya had told an interviewer from *Le Figaro*, the French publication: "Mrs. Gandhi is neither a woman nor a head of state by wanting to be both at once."

What would he say to Indira if there were to be a meeting between the two leaders, the interviewer asked?

"I would say: 'Shut up, woman—leave me alone and let my refugees back'" was Yahya's reply.

Yahya had increasingly begun to accuse India of not allowing Bangladeshi refugees to return to East Pakistan. The absurdity of his position was obvious: Yahya was saying, in effect, that India deliberately held on to the 10 million Bangladeshi refugees in order to embarrass Pakistan—no matter that this was a major financial strain on India. A number of right-wing congressmen joined Nixon administration officials in accepting Yahya's position. Indira saw to it that the refugees were well cared for, and given food and clothing. Great care was taken that no epidemics—especially cholera—broke out. The refugees were housed in camps, but isolated from the local population on the Indian side of the border with Bangladesh. Meanwhile, the Mukti Bahini, or Liberation Army, that was formed by the people of Bangladesh was given sanctuary in India. These guerrillas were trained by the Border Security Force of India. Yahya shrieked that Indira had all along planned to dismember Pakistan, an accusation that found resonance in some foreign capitals. This prompted Indira to make a strong speech in Parliament on May 26, 1971.

"We have heard much talk of democracy," she said.

The Allies claimed that the Second World War was fought to save democracy. But when democracy is so flagrantly and so brutally being destroyed, we do not hear much comment, nor do we see the sort of spontaneous strong responses which the situation warrants. Could there be a greater or a clearer expression of democracy than the one we witnessed in the elections in Pakistan? . . . We are told by some countries that while they may disapprove of what is being done by the military rulers, they cannot be a party to the disintegration of

Pakistan. Is it suggested that we wish the disintegration of Pakistan? Have we not . . . at every step tried not only for propriety in our relationship but also for friendship? If there is a struggle between the two parts of Pakistan, it is certainly not of our making but of the rulers of Pakistan. Is it anybody's contention that the methods being used today can achieve any integration or stability worth the name now or in the future.

Mrs. Gandhi then addressed Yahya Khan's charge—which he had leveled against India during several sessions with visiting foreign reporters—that New Delhi was encouraging secession in East Pakistan. "The question of secession is also being raised," Indira said.

This is a distortion of facts. It is conveniently forgotten that the majority of Pakistan's people live in the eastern region. In a democratic system, the majority does have certain rights. They cannot be accused of secession if they assert those rights. However, if today there is such strong feeling amongst our people, it is not merely because the democratic rights and liberties of 75 million people are being crushed but because of the damaging effect which this cruel tragedy is having on our entire country economically, politically, and socially.

It is a problem created by calculated genocide that is resulting not only in the murder of tens of thousands of men, women, and children, but also forcing many more to seek refuge and shelter in India. It is a problem that threatens the peace and security of India and, indeed, of Southeast Asia. The world must intervene to see that peace and security are reestablished and maintained.

But, of course, the world community did not intervene. Many countries cited the clause in the United Nations Charter that forbids member-states from interference in the "internal affairs" of a member country of the world organization.* The Nixon administration, in fact, tilted toward Pakistan, arguing that it was India's meddling in Pakistan's internal affairs

---

*When it suited member-states, of course, this clause was ignored. The noninterference clause was most dramatically ignored after Iraq invaded Kuwait in August 1990, and the United Nations Security Council voted to institute sanctions against the Baghdad regime, and to support military intervention. Subsequently, the United Nations also acted to come to the rescue of Iraq's Kurds, who were terrorized by Saddam Hussein.

that was causing many of East Pakistan's problems. In July 1971, Henry Kissinger visited India at the suggestion of President Nixon. He left no illusion in Mrs. Gandhi's mind where Washington's sympathies lay. Moreover, Kissinger made it clear to Indira that should China intervene on Islamabad's side in the event of an Indo-Pakistan war, India should expect no help from the United States. Indira knew that Kissinger was trying to promote better relations between Washington and Beijing; he would make a secret visit later that month to China, and the Pakistanis would be instrumental in arranging that trip—Kissinger, in fact, took off for China from a Pakistani military airfield. Memories of India's disastrous war with China in 1962 were still fresh in most Indians' minds. Beijing's leaders were now openly siding with Yahya Khan, accusing India of helping secessionist Bangladeshis. Mrs. Gandhi felt that it was time to muster international support. She felt that India needed some sort of shield. That was when she decided to visit Moscow to finalize the Indo-Soviet Treaty of Peace, Friendship and Cooperation. That treaty was signed in New Delhi by the two nations amidst great fanfare on August 9, 1971.* It would not come up for renegotiation for another twenty years.

Indira felt that this treaty took care of any threat that China may have posed without compromising India's position in the Nonaligned Movement. But many Americans and Europeans did not see it that way. Krishan Bhatia offers insight into the circumstances of the treaty, which had been initially discussed by India and the Soviet Union in 1969:

> [In 1969] the Soviet leadership was beginning to shed some of its suspicions about Indira's ideological moorings originally fostered by her swift move to devalue Indian currency in 1966 under seeming World Bank pressure, and by the warm welcome that President Johnson had accorded Mrs. Gandhi during her visit to Washington soon after she became Prime Minister. Not only had Brezhnev and Kosygin seen indications of India's moving closer to the United States under Indira's leadership, but Indira in her turn had her own reasons to be wary of Soviet intentions. It was about that time that Moscow endeavored to adopt a nonaligned posture in the affairs of the Subcontinent, and started for the first time supplying arms to Pakistan in the hope of gaining certain political leverage with its military rulers. The quantities of arms given to Pakistan were limited, but they were enough to distress India. Also, during a visit to New Delhi in the beginning of 1968, Kosygin offered Indira advice about affairs in

* This treaty was renewed in 1991.

Kashmir, and management of various Soviet-collaboration industrial projects that to Indira's sensitive ears sounded not like friendly counsel but unwarranted interference. By the middle of 1969, however, both sides had overcome much of their suspicion and realized the fruitlessness of drifting apart. Indira's confrontation with the Congress Party Old Guard and her close association with the Communist Party of India—the Moscow-affiliated section of Indian Communists—in her temporary tacit coalition government [just before the 1971 election] brightened her image in Brezhnev's eyes.*

Indira was aware that in Western capitals such as Washington and London, the Indo-Soviet Treaty would be seen as a sellout by India, an abandoning of its long-held nonalignment. She did not want India to be perceived as a client state of the Soviet Union; nor did Indira want the treaty to be seen as a defense pact between the two countries, a kind of NATO arrangement. Therefore, the treaty called for "consultation" between the two countries in the event of either one being militarily attacked. At that time, the Soviets were highly concerned about China's Communist regime—which had had a falling out with Moscow in the 1950s—and an alliance with India offered the Soviets a strategic political—and possibly military—presence on China's southern flank. The alliance with the Soviets suited Indira just fine, coming as it did at a highly delicate time for India during its contretemps with Pakistan over Bangladesh. This was the first time that India had concluded a treaty with a big power, and Indira privately told friends such as Professor Ralph Buultjens that she had misgivings about the formal alliance with Moscow. No matter what gloss New Delhi put over it, Indira felt, India's nonalignment would henceforth always be characterized as left-leaning.

Mrs. Gandhi tried to appeal to the world community on behalf of Sheikh Mujibur Rahman. After his arrest, the sheikh had been taken to West Pakistan and subjected to a secret trial. He was held incommunicado in a jail, which gave rise to reports that the "Father of Bangladesh" was being tortured. Indira decided that she would travel to Western Europe and the United States to solicit support for the Bangladesh refugees, and perhaps trigger international action against Pakistan. She went on a twenty-two-day tour that took her to Austria, Belgium, Britain, France, West Germany, and the United States. In all the countries except the

* Bhatia, *Indira*, pp. 244–45.

United States, she received an encouraging response—in the form of new aid commitments—and sympathy for the plight of the people of Bangladesh. Nevertheless, she was advised to show restraint and try to settle the problem with Pakistan amicably, rather than having a military showdown. In fact, everywhere, the politicians she met—as well as editors and political pundits—kept telling her to "show restraint."

When Indira met Sir Alec Douglas-Home, the British foreign secretary, he said to her: "Our fear is that there would be war."

"We won't start it," Indira said to him.*

On another occasion, an interviewer from the BBC asked if India was demonstrating sufficient "restraint" in its dealings with Pakistan.

"When Hitler was on the rampage, why didn't you say, 'Let's keep quiet and let's have peace with Germany and let the Jews die'?" Indira said.

During this trip overseas, Indira tried to make world leaders understand that the dispute was to be settled between Yahya Khan and the Awami League. India was just trying to protect her own interests as the refugee problem was drawing her into the court.

During the course of her stay in England, Mrs. Gandhi met with the Indian community. "I am sitting on top of a volcano—and I honestly don't know when it is going to erupt," she told a group convened by the India League. Mrs. Gandhi's visit to the United States, however, was not much of a success. President Nixon and Mrs. Gandhi did not agree on any policy matters. "Nixon and Mrs. Gandhi just did not like each other," says Janki Ganju, the India lobbyist in Washington. "She thought that it was appalling that Nixon sided with Pakistan—the very same Pakistan whose troops had killed more than 3 million Bangladeshis. She felt very strongly about this. She also felt that Nixon had read India wrong. She thought that he did not understand that India would never give in to pressure from Washington or anywhere else. Mrs. Gandhi was skeptical that she would ever bring Nixon around to India's point of view about Bangladesh."†

Indira was right about this, of course. Richard Nixon had had a long-standing relationship with Pakistan. When he was Dwight Eisenhower's Vice President, Nixon had been instrumental in getting Pakistan military aid from Washington, and also in inducting the Islamabad regime into a military pact with the United States. He had vigorously supported John Foster Dulles's policy of containing Communism. Indira was well aware

---

*Encounter mentioned by Inder Malhotra in his news dispatches and in *Indira Gandhi*.
†Conversation with author, March 1991.

that Washington's attention to South Asia had been inconsistent. Not-withstanding Nixon's personal warmth toward Pakistan, Washington had traditionally considered Turkey far more central to American concerns about the southern flank of the Soviet Union.* Strategically, Turkey was viewed as being more significant than Pakistan: Over the years, in fact, Washington's support of Pakistan was guarded. In the 1965 and 1971 wars between India and Pakistan, U.S. administrations failed to give Pakistan the full military support it demanded, and this was to result in a general decline in U.S.-Pakistan relations through the late 1970s.† It was only with the Soviet invasion of Afghanistan in December 1979 that Washington reassessed its relations with Pakistan and found reasons to reverse the trend of a lukewarm relationship. Suddenly, Pakistan became a "front-line state" against Soviet expansionism, and has received $3 billion in military and economic aid since 1980 (with another $4 billion package subsequently).

As Indira flew to Washington, she thought about how the basic prem-ises of U.S. policy in South Asia had centered on the notion that this region was generally prone to socialist economic thrusts such as those articulated by the late Jawaharlal Nehru; that Pakistan vaguely repre-sented a barrier against Soviet expansion in Asia but was strategically of secondary value to American defense interests; that India—whose politi-cal and military ties with Moscow had been warm and strong—was virtually adversarial to American security interests; that the Indian Ocean could be freely used by American naval forces and that the flag could be shown when necessary; that the perceived growing Soviet influence in the area had to be blocked through economic and military aid to recep-tive nations. Indira had been informed by Janki Ganju that the Nixon administration was indeed planning to accelerate military assistance to Islamabad—this despite public assurances by American legislators that new military aid would not be forthcoming until the Bangladesh crisis was resolved. In April 1971, under pressure from Congress, the Nixon administration had suspended the processing of a special $80 million arms sale to Pakistan, according to Krishan Bhatia; Nixon had committed the United States to this sale despite strong protests by India. Ganju found out that even though Secretary of State William P. Rogers had assured New Delhi that no American arms were being supplied to Yahya Khan,

---

* The United States, in fact, has maintained military bases in Turkey since the early 1950s.
† President Nixon had been prepared, however, to offer Pakistan limited nuclear capability in the event that the 1971 Indo-Pakistan War dragged on.

a deal to provide spare parts for military equipment was actually in the works.

Indira was determined not to be cowed down by the President of the world's most powerful country. She especially sought out American legislators who were becoming critical of Nixon's tilt toward Pakistan, and urged them to influence public opinion in the United States. A number of these legislators, such as Senators Edward M. Kennedy and William Saxbe, had traveled to India to see for themselves the plight of the Bangladeshi refugees.

Meanwhile, the brutality of the Pakistani army kept intensifying. The Mukti Bahini, the Bangladesh liberation army, were fighting very bravely. Public opinion in India against the Pakistani atrocities was reaching a high. Ordinary Indians and Opposition members were demanding that something be done. Mrs. Gandhi was still holding back, reluctant to make the first move. On December 3, 1971, Yahya Khan, having become cocky and impatient, launched an air attack against eight Indian bases. It was a very foolish move. The attack achieved nothing, but succeeded only in putting the onus of starting the war on Pakistan. Had Yahya Khan waited one more day, India would have been held responsible for the war: Indian generals had decided to take advantage of the full moon and strike the following day. Yahya Khan had been led to believe that either China or the United States, or both, would intervene on Pakistan's behalf.

Indira Gandhi was in Calcutta addressing a meeting when the news was conveyed to her. She flew back to New Delhi at once, where the cabinet members and the Opposition had assembled for an emergency meeting. The general consensus was to formally declare war. A state of emergency was declared within the country, and the Indian Army crossed into East Pakistan to fight side by side with the Mukti Bahini. Mrs. Gandhi was kept informed of every move of the Indian troops. The United States cut off economic and military aid to India while continuing to send supplies to Pakistan. The Pakistani troops tried to enter Kashmir but were held back by the Indian Army. On December 9, the United States sent its Seventh Fleet toward Dhaka in an effort to intimidate India. Before the U.S.S. *Enterprise* could reach anywhere near Indian waters, Moscow dispatched its own fleet for the same region. On December 12, a senior Soviet minister arrived in India to monitor the events.

On December 13, General Sam Manekshaw sent an ultimatum to the Pakistani troops. They were surrounded and were asked to surrender within three days. On December 16, the Pakistani troops surrendered. More than 92,000 soldiers were captured and incarcerated in prisoner-of-war camps in India. In Pakistan the military was totally deflated, Yahya Khan was forced to resign, and Zulfikar Ali Bhutto was handed the reins of what was left of Pakistan. The people of India were jubilant. The victory of 1971 was a catharsis for a nation that had been humiliated at the hands of the Chinese in 1962. The media all over the world agreed that Mrs. Gandhi's role in this had been very commendable. "Mrs. Gandhi's handling of this period of crisis and danger, during the tense months preceding the war, and the war itself, illustrated that, when reality had to be faced, when it could not be obscured by rhetoric or enveloped by the slide and slither of innuendo, she could come to grips with it," says Nayantara Sahgal. "The unilateral ceasefire she declared immediately on Pakistan's collapse in East Bengal was an act of states-manship."*

The people of India were disgusted with the treatment of Bengali Muslims, and this was the first time since 1947 that there was little sympathy for Pakistan from the Indian Muslim minority. People in India hailed Indira Gandhi as Durga, the invincible goddess of war who rode on a tiger. Villagers began worshiping her as Shakti. The president of India awarded her the Bharat Ratna, the highest honor that the country conferred on an individual. The 10 million Bangladeshi refugees were sent back. Mrs. Gandhi was given a heroine's welcome when she visited Dacca. The Simla summit of 1972 between Mrs. Gandhi and Zulfikar Ali Bhutto was a success. Pakistan was given back all its prisoners of war. The summit resulted in Pakistan's recognition of Bangladesh.

"There are moments in history when brooding tragedy and its dark shadows can be lightened by recalling great moments of the past," Indira wrote to President Nixon after the Bangladesh war.

> One such great moment which has inspired millions of people to die for liberty was the Declaration of Independence by the United States of America. That declaration stated that whenever any form of government becomes destructive of man's inalienable rights to life, liberty, and the pursuit of happiness, it was the right of the people to alter or abolish it. . . .
>
> This tragic war . . . could have been averted if, during the nine months prior to Pakistan's attack on us on December 3, 1971, the great leaders of the world had paid some attention to the fact of revolt, tried to see the reality of the situation and searched for a genuine basis for reconciliation. . . . War also could have been

---

*Sahgal, *Indira Gandhi: Her Road to Power*, p. 85.

avoided if the power, influence, and authority of all the states, and above all of the United States, had got Sheikh Mujibur Rahman released. Instead, we were told that a civilian administration was being installed [in East Pakistan]. Everyone knows that this civilian administration was a farce; today, the farce has turned into a tragedy. . . .

The fact of the matter is that the rulers of West Pakistan got away with the impression that they could do what they liked because no one, not even the United States, would choose to take a public position that while Pakistan's integrity was certainly sacrosanct, human rights and liberty were no less so—and that there was a necessary interconnection between the inviolability of states and the contentment of their people.

Indira Gandhi ended her dramatic letter to Richard Nixon with these words: "Will Pakistan give up its ceaseless and yet pointless agitation . . . over Kashmir? are they willing to give up their hate campaign and posture of perpetual hostility toward India?"

Heavy questions, those, and ones that Indians still ask.

Nations, like people, finally must come to terms with themselves. Pakistan is no longer a young nation; it was born more than forty years ago, at the same time as India. If Pakistan's fundamental problem remains its undefined identity, then its curse has been militarism. And that curse has captured Pakistan's political system and stoked the politics of repression. Pakistan's leaders—national and local alike—have been largely indigenous for at least two decades; but they continued to be imposed on the body politics. And with their special brand of cynicism, they have often used Islam as an overriding ideology to reinforce the ethos of authoritarianism. This has created what Professor Ralph Buultjens calls "an artificial leadership which draws its sanctions from God and the gun."[*]

The Bangladesh crisis of 1971 highlighted that how Pakistan deals with the question of developing democratic leadership and viable political institutions will be the most fundamental long-term test for the country. This test has been made all the more serious because of the continuing violence inside the country, the continued friction with India, the continued turbulence on its western border with Afghanistan, and the sim-

[*] Interview with author, New York City, 1989.

mering tensions of regionalism. This means that the common people must be given the chance to freely choose their leaders. This means lasting democracy, however home-bred and divergent from the Westminster or Washington models.

"People must be allowed to take power on the basis of the imperatives of statecraft," says Shahid Javed Burki. And what are the imperatives of statecraft? Internal stability, accommodation with neighbors, and economic development. In other words, a new national ethos. Mohammed Ali Jinnah, Pakistan's founding father, had said to his countrymen: "You may belong to any religion or caste or creed—that has nothing to do with the business of state. . . . We start with the fundamental principle that we are all citizens, and equal citizens of one state. We should keep that as our ideal. And in the course of time we would cease to be Hindus and Muslims—not in the religious sense, because that is the personal faith of each individual—but in the political sense as citizens of the state."* Jinnah is long gone, and he spoke at a time when Pakistan was young and raw and impressionable. But his message, broadcast more than four tumultuous decades ago, is still very much valid. A more open and tolerant system need not imply abandoning Islam as the state philosophy. For ordinary Pakistanis, hope lies in the notion that nations are always capable of self-renewal. Hope lies in the possibility of change.

Because Indira Gandhi had signed a twenty-year treaty with the Soviet Union in August 1971, there soon developed a perception in the international community that India publicly endorsed everything the Soviets did in the global sphere. Indira's critics were to point to her hesitation in criticizing the Soviets after their invasion of Afghanistan in December 1979. Indeed, had it not been for the Pakistan factor, India would certainly have been far more vocal and critical of the Soviet action in Afghanistan. In all the United Nations deliberations and resolutions condemning the Soviet invasion, India abstained from voting rather than voting against the resolutions. India's consistent stand was that the Soviets should withdraw from Afghanistan but, simultaneously, other powers—meaning, of course, the United States—should stop their interference in the internal affairs of Afghanistan.

It should also be noted here that Afghanistan, because of its own historical feud with Pakistan, has been India's closest—if rather ineffectual—ally in the Subcontinent. This also explains why India was rather sympathetic to the People's Democratic Party of Afghanistan (PDPA) rather than to its fundamentalist rivals, whose victory could have had a

---

* Speech reported in the Pakistan media, 1948.

negative fallout on the domestic communal situation in India. But Indira Gandhi was deeply offended when the Soviets took India's support for granted on the Afghanistan issue. She was peeved that India was not informed in advance about the Soviet military action in Afghanistan in December 1979—so much so that she made her anger known by refusing to see the Soviet foreign minister when he came to Delhi later to meet with Indian officials.

Two main factors—one domestic and the other related to foreign policy—influenced Indira Gandhi's cool and mildly hostile relationship with the United States. It must be remembered that quite early in her prime-ministerial career she had to face formidable opposition from her seniors—the Syndicate bosses—within her own party who were trying to restrict her powers or, if they could, even replace her with someone from among their own ranks. And the Syndicate happened to be right-wing in domestic socioeconomic issues, and pro-U.S. in their foreign policy preferences. Since it was a matter of survival for Indira, and since the populist path she chose required her to show that she was wedded to socialism, her instincts turned against the United States. On the external front, a high-water mark of Indira's prime-ministership was her role in the liberation of Bangladesh. And in this war, the Nixon administration chose to support Pakistan to the hilt. It even sent an aircraft carrier from the U.S. Seventh Fleet to the Bay of Bengal.

Following India's smashing victory in the Bangladesh war, there was no doubt that Indira wanted—and actively worked for—India to emerge as a strong regional military-political-economic power. When *Time* magazine featured India as "the mini-superpower" a few years ago, it was an India that was, to a large measure, a product of Indira's leadership and policies. She was not very sensitive to the concerns of the other neighboring countries of the region—Pakistan, Bangladesh, and Sri Lanka. The most striking example is Bangladesh, in whose liberation she played such a crucial role, but which soon developed a fairly negative, even hostile, relationship with India. While the question of sharing river waters ostensibly explained the falling-out between India and Bangladesh, the more fundamental cause was Bangladesh's suspicion of India's regional ambitions. The Pokhran nuclear experiment in 1974—when India exploded what Indira said was a "peaceful" nuclear device—served to create legitimate suspicions in neighboring capitals about India's hegemonistic aspirations.

But it should also be emphasized that at least two of the major neighbors—Pakistan and Sri Lanka—did not quite go along with India's legitimate stand on the demilitarization of the Indian Ocean and, specifically, on Diego Garcia, where the United States maintained a military base. Clearly, India's concerns and global outlook were different from those of Pakistan, Bangladesh, and Sri Lanka—and this, in turn, led Indira Gandhi to fashion a least accommodative regional foreign policy. India did not have any major problems with Nepal in Indira's time, except that she was always wary about China trying to increase its presence and influence in that mountainous nation. Indira's emphasis on building a strong blue-water navy has today resulted in India having a naval presence in the surrounding seas which is being noticed with some concern even by faraway countries like Malaysia and Australia.

The Indo-Pakistan military conflicts—all of which were won by India—have resulted in a situation where India and Pakistan pump huge sums of money into defense: Pakistan spends nearly $2 billion a year on defense (its gross national product is roughly $31 billion); India, whose GNP is nearly $180 billion, is estimated by the London-based International Institute for Strategic Studies to spend $6.3 billion on defense. Neither country can afford such expenditures. Two-thirds of Pakistan's 500,000-man military is positioned along the border with India. India has stationed several crack divisions of its 1.2 million-strong armed forces on its side of the border. Since 1958 Pakistan has been almost continuously under military rule. An elected democratic administration was brutally squashed in 1977 by General Mohammed Zia ul-Haq, who took over as the head of government. General Zia did not block the "trial" and subsequent execution of his civilian predecessor, Zulfikar Ali Bhutto. Not that Bhutto was ever a friend of India, but it was generally felt by Indian policymakers that a civilian leader in Pakistan was more likely to arrive at a political accommodation with India than a military figure. Indian leaders, to be sure, like to portray Pakistan as the continuing villain in the great drama of the Subcontinent. But it might be recalled that when the then–military dictator Marshal Ayub Khan proposed a no-war pact with India in the late 1950s, Nehru's aides ridiculed Ayub. Similarly, when Zia brought up the subject again during Mrs. Gandhi's last years, the Pakistanis were also ridiculed. And Zia continued to be regarded with suspicion by Prime Minister Rajiv Gandhi until the Pakistani leader's death in a mysterious air crash in August 1988.

Indian leaders point to the current rearmament of Pakistan by its main Western ally, the United States. Washington is reported to give Islamabad more than a billion dollars of arms each year, allegedly to strengthen Pakistan against expansionism by the Soviet Union, which had invaded and occupied Afghanistan, Pakistan's northwestern neighbor, in December 1979. But policymakers in Delhi have no doubts that

414

these arms will be used eventually by Pakistan against India. India, for its part, is also accelerating the arms race by buying more weapons not only from its traditional supplier, the Soviet Union, but also from France, Germany, and Britain. Both India and Pakistan are developing nuclear weapons as well, although the leaders of both countries strenuously deny this. "The fact remains that militarily Pakistan is no match for India," George Fernandes, the Indian labor leader, told me. "But Pakistan serves as a convenient scapegoat, an excuse for more arms deals which produce massive commissions for Congress Party agents who negotiate the deals with foreign suppliers."

On August 17, 1988, a momentous event occurred that shook Pakistan to its foundations. At 3:47 P.M. an American-made C-130 Hercules transport plane of the Pakistan air force took off from a small military airport at Bahawalpur. It was a bright, sunny afternoon, with barely a cloud in the sky. On board were nearly twenty senior Pakistani military officers. Also on board was President Zia ul-Haq of Pakistan; Arnold L. Raphel, the U.S. ambassador to Pakistan; and Brigadier General Herbert M. Wassom, an American military adviser. They were headed for Islamabad, Pakistan's capital, a 330-mile flight that would ordinarily have taken less than an hour. In Bahawalpur, Zia and his brass had watched a demonstration of the prowess of the M1A1 Abrams, one of the most sophisticated tanks in the world. The manufacturer of the tank, General Dynamics Inc., was so keen to make a sale that the American company had trimmed the overall price of a package deal by $500,000 to $3 million per tank. Indeed, Zia seemed so impressed by the tank's awesome capabilities that the General Dynamics executives at the scene were certain that the deal would be clinched.

Zia left the demonstration in his usual cheerful mood, pausing to chat with several local security personnel and others before he boarded the C-130. The plane took off with a roar, but in less than four minutes, while it was at an altitude of 4,000 feet and still climbing, the aircraft lost radio contact with the control tower. The plane crashed at 3:51 P.M. There were no survivors.

Pakistanis were stunned. They immediately suspected sabotage. At the top of their list were the Soviet Union and Afghanistan. Indeed, many Pakistanis recalled that just two weeks before the crash, their foreign minister, Sahabzada Yaqub Khan, had met in Moscow with his Soviet counterpart, Eduard A. Shevardnadze. During their meeting, the Soviet minister had warned the Pakistani that Pakistan's support of the Afghan mujahadeen guerrillas would "not go unpunished." There had lately been several Afghan and Soviet raids across the Pakistan border. India also came naturally under suspicion. But Indian commentators were quick to point out that it did not make sense for their country to get rid of Zia. He had, after all, attempted a rapprochement with India in recent times, despite the occasional saber-rattling that he engaged in to satisfy the more extreme segments of his domestic constituency. To be sure, Prime Minister Rajiv Gandhi and his key associates suspected Zia of sponsoring terrorism in the Punjab. But by and large, relations between the two countries had not deteriorated to a point where yet another war was inevitable. Moreover, Gandhi was privately known to be respectful of Zia's skill in holding together his ethnically diverse nation and in resisting the clamorous calls of Baluchis and Pathans and others for more regional autonomy, if not independence. There was a growing realization in New Delhi that Zia was probably the least thorny leader that India could expect in Pakistan at the present time.

Exactly two months after the crash, Pakistani investigators issued a 365-page report that attributed the accident to sabotage. It ruled out mechanical failure as a cause. An earlier report, prepared by a team of American experts, had suggested that mechanical malfunction had probably been the cause of the crash, although the investigators also said that the malfunction could have been the result of sabotage. The Pakistani report said that phosphorus had been found on mango seeds in the wreckage. A crate of mangoes had apparently been loaded on to Zia's plane as a gift for the dictator. The implication of the phosphorus finding was that a bomb had been planted in the mango crate. The truth will perhaps never be known.

Zia's death left a huge political vacuum in Pakistan because no other military figure had the stature to take his place: In fact, all the important military men who might immediately have picked up power from the ruins of Zia's aircraft also perished on board. Soon afterwards, Acting President Ghulam Ishaq Khan, a civilian, announced that in November 1988 elections would be held for 217 members of the 237-seat Pakistan National Assembly (the remaining twenty seats are reserved for women and minorities, who are elected indirectly by National Assembly members). Zia had dissolved the Assembly in May 1988, ostensibly because he claimed it had grown corrupt. The real reason, his critics suggested, was that he became alarmed over the Assembly's growing assertiveness; some key legislators had begun to challenge Zia's personal authoritarianism and his style of administration. A few legislators even hinted that his associates had permitted and participated in a flourishing heroin trade.

Zia also sacked in the same month Prime Minister Mohammed Khan Junejo on the grounds that he had become ineffective. Junejo, installed as a puppet executive by Zia, had begun to acquire stature and nascent popularity that suggested a possible political alternative to Zia in the future. President Khan announced that in November 1988 elections would also be held for Pakistan's four provincial assemblies. The new National Assembly, and these regional legislative bodies, would then together choose a president. The president, in turn, would name a prime minister, who constitutionally runs the government but whose power does not exceed that of the president. The Pakistani president appoints the chiefs of the armed forces and the judiciary, thus giving him an authority which enables him to impose his will on the body politic and control virtually all centers of political power.

The main political groupings vying for power in Pakistan were Benazir Bhutto's Pakistan People's Party, whose inspiration remains the memory and the policies of the late Prime Minister Zulfikar Ali Bhutto—Benazir's father, whom Zia overthrew in 1977 and hanged in 1979 following a kangaroo-court verdict of malfeasance and abuse of office. Another grouping was called the Islamic Democratic Alliance, a melange of right-wing and religious factions with a lot of support in the Punjab province. And there was the Pakistani Awami Itehad, which consisted of parties spearheaded by former prime minister Junejo. The latter two groupings contained remnants of the once all-powerful Muslim League, the political arm of Zia's system. Finally, there were smaller groups of regional forces concentrated in specific cities or areas.

The election campaign was also marred by confrontations between Benazir Bhutto's followers and her opponents. The violence raised key questions: Had Pakistan achieved sufficient political maturity to elect a woman to its national leadership? If elected would she be able to govern effectively in a system so heavily weighted against the active political participation of women? And would the slightest perceived civilian lapse in governance provoke the intervention of the military?

The fundamental reality of Pakistan was unlikely to be changed in the short run, demonstrating an old political truth: Those who use authoritarian methods as a self-proclaimed argument for stability leave a legacy far more volatile than the condition they seek to cure. After all, the military would still be waiting and watching in the wings, and there would always be lingering doubts that contemporary Pakistan could be effectively governed by any other authority. The sad legacy of Zia was that in holding his contentious nation together by the strength of his personality and the sinews of militarism, he ensured that civilian institutions which could

417

lay the foundations of genuine grass-roots democracy never fully developed. And there was another part to his legacy that I am not so sure will serve Pakistan well in the long term. For reasons of political expediency—having to satisfy domestic fundamentalists and also foreign donors such as the fanatically Muslim Saudis—Zia took Pakistan so far down the road of Islamization that it may well be irreversible. He introduced the Islamic shariat law, which restricts many personal freedoms and institutes brutal punishments. Zia initiated the barbaric practices of lashing and chopping limbs for criminals. And he presided over an era that witnessed the dramatic deterioration of women's rights. All these measures upset and undermined Pakistan's growing middle classes. In the emerging countries of the Third World, it is the middle classes that are most often the well-springs of national development and, indeed, of a nation's moral and political fiber. In imposing social and political restrictions of this nature, Zia further eroded a potential source of stability in nation-building. Where he could have engendered invaluable alliances, he ignited unnecessary alienation.

The November election certainly established Benazir Bhutto as the single most important political figure in Pakistan, and at the politically tender age of thirty-five. (Several political stalwarts, including former prime minister Junejo, lost in the election.) Benazir Bhutto acquired the mantle of national leadership, but the political inheritance that she and her generation assumed was a difficult one, compounded by the unclear mandate which the election provided. By 1990, Benazir was out—the victim of a civilian coup.

The violent death of President Mohammed Zia ul-Haq dramatically changed the political topography of his native Pakistan. To his friends abroad, especially in Britain and the United States, it seemed that Zia shrewdly maintained stability in his clangorous Muslim state of 103 million people. But it was the stability of the gun rather than the stability that flows from the establishment of democratic institutions. As Professor Ralph Buultjens puts it, "Zia's internal legacy, for all his accent on order, is ultimately one of confusion and uncertainty in Pakistan's political system."

This legacy doubtlessly will have profound implications as the leadership sweepstakes continue in Pakistan. But politics in all of South Asia has also been profoundly affected by Zia's death. Policymakers in Western chancelleries now have a unique opportunity to rethink conventional wisdom about the area. On the chessboard of global politics, South Asia occupies an important corner, a strategic niche where the diplomatic, economic, and geopolitical interests of the world's great powers intersect.

For Washington the stakes are especially high because of Soviet troop withdrawal from Afghanistan. Several new political openings and economic opportunities could be developed out of the general uncertainty in a part of the world which, with very few exceptions, has not been especially noted for a pro-U.S. stance. Indeed, at the postcolonial birth of these nations, no foreign nation was held in higher esteem than the United States because of President Franklin Roosevelt's long-standing support of their yearning for freedom from the British Raj.

The nine nations of the region—Afghanistan, Bangladesh, Bhutan, Myanmar, India, Maldives, Nepal, Pakistan, and Sri Lanka—possess a fifth of the world's 5.4 billion people. They are undergoing an unprecedented period of demographic transformation and political transition. More than 50 percent of people in this region are below twenty years of age. This cohort is now coming of political age. Western policymakers must recognize that the economic and political aspirations of these young people, if not met adequately and with alacrity, might well produce a new surge of radicalism. Such radicalism has already been foreshadowed by riots in Myanmar and by accelerated agitation in Sri Lanka by the Marxist Janatha Vimukhti Peramuna (JVP) and the Tamil Tigers, who have fought for a separate ethnic state. In the region's behemoth, India, there is a discernible weakening of the long-dominant Congress Party. There are growing doubts whether militarism as a political force can last not only in Pakistan but also its former province, Bangladesh. There are also questions about the viability of the feudal monarchies of Nepal and Bhutan. Myanmar is undergoing political spasms and no one knows how the current unrest is going to play itself out. And in Sri Lanka, long considered by the West as a model of democracy and development, Tamil separatists still have not accepted the bold peace treaty signed in July 1987 between India and the administration of President J. R. Jayewardene.

The rapidly changing political, economic, and social contexts of the region are now eroding many long-held premises. The erosion has already resulted in a reassessment of Washington's relations with India; indeed, the notion of India being a Soviet satellite state seems to have given way to the view that there could well be a relationship that would satisfy American strategic interests. Such a relationship would be predicated on a mutual understanding of each other's problems, or at least a recognition that Indian leaders, for domestic political reasons, would need to maintain India's "nonalignment," however left-leaning. The emphasis in this new relationship would be on what President Ronald Reagan called "the pragmatic"—substantial commerce and technology transfers. (Already, the United States buys $3 billion worth of Indian goods annually, making it India's biggest trading partner after the Soviet Union.) That would also mean encouraging American investment in joint ventures. Prime Minister Rajiv Gandhi, like President Jayewardene in Sri Lanka and President H. M. Ershad of Bangladesh, undertook economic reforms that were conducive to foreign investment. With rising literacy and the spread of mass communication—especially television—the people of South Asia are increasingly aware of the benefits of the market economy. They are not going to blindly accept the old and discredited shibboleths of socialism as a panacea for economic ills or a prescription for economic progress.

The most immediate—and fundamental—contribution that Washington and its Western allies could make in the region, however, is through the promotion of democracy. Unless more genuine democracy is developed, the longer-term political stability that is required for meaningful development is unlikely to be sustained. The culture of militarism that is a creeping menace in many Third World countries could be superficially attractive in the short term but, as in Pakistan, leaves major problems in its wake. The authoritarian caudillo is an attractive bet for the super-powers, but these dictators are really short-term political animals—they are sprinters, rather than long-distance runners who could sustain the long-term dynamic of development. The concentration of power in one person is far more dangerous than the messy, diffused, and untidy processes of an open political system. Western policymakers must be mindful that the countries of South Asia have never been so internally fissiparous. All sorts of regional forces are being strengthened at the expense of the center. Since these countries achieved independence, the often artificially constructed central government has held sway for the most part. Now, with provincialism ascending in such countries as India, Myanmar, and Pakistan, it is unlikely that these countries can continue to be governed in the old centralist way. And it is precisely here that they could draw lessons in governance and administration from the American federal system. The U.S. historical experience may have considerable validity as a framework of government in South Asia. (Indeed, Sri Lanka's constitution draws heavily on the American model.)

The West must also freshly attend to the area's new grouping, South Asian Association for Regional Cooperation (SAARC). The very formation of this organization, which was patterned after ASEAN, suggests that South Asian countries are moving toward some sort of regional common market. While their markets may currently be largely closed to foreign goods (because of these countries' foreign-exchange shortages and their import-substitution policies), the opportunities surely exist for

American companies to participate in developing the consumer-goods sector through the joint ventures that are being sought. Moreover, countries like India, Nepal, and Sri Lanka are extremely anxious to crack down on the drug traffic that is worsening in the region. They urgently need help from Western—specifically British and American—law-enforcement agencies. Such help could be channeled through SAARC.

Finally, Western policymakers (and their counterparts in South Asian countries) must be mindful of one terribly important point: This may well be the last generation in the Third World on whom repression can be used as an instrument of government policy. More and more, local governments will have to cajole, persuade, and negotiate with their domestic opponents. And this is where the British and American system of discourse and debate could serve Western policymakers well in dealing with the resurgent nations of South Asia. Although Third World leaders and citizens may not often openly acknowledge it because of domestic political constraints, the time-tested values of democracy and dissent inherent in the British and American systems have always elicited their admiration. The promotion of multiparty democracy and development will be the West's greatest gift to South Asia, the wakening giant of the Third World.

According to Professor Ralph Buultjens, Indira Gandhi would have seen it somewhat differently. "Mrs. Gandhi felt that there was little that the outside world needed to instruct South Asia about democracy," he says. "It was her view that democracy must spring from indigenous roots. Only then would it have some meaning for the people of South Asia. She saw a strong linkage between development and democracy, and was prepared to accept and acknowledge the contribution that the outside world had to make toward economic progress. But politics had to evolve from within the region and was not an ethos that Washington or London should seek to shape."

Indira Gandhi's view may have been pertinent in her time, but more recent events have demonstrated that democracy can be best encouraged with international support—a fact of political life as true for South Asia as for many other regions.

18

Friends, Neighbors, and Enemies

The Bangladesh crisis of 1971 convinced Indira Gandhi that Pakistan would always be an implacable foe, but one with whom India would somehow have to work out a modus vivendi. "The efficient conduct of the Indo-Pakistan War of 1971 was both balm and stimulant to a nation humiliated by the Chinese in 1962 and, in the hope of peace, persuaded into an indeterminate conclusion with Pakistan in the war of 1965," says Nayantara Sahgal, the novelist and biographer. "Mrs. Gandhi's handling of this period of crisis and danger, during the tense months preceding the war, and the war itself, illustrated that, when reality had to be faced, when it could not be obscured by rhetoric or enveloped by the slide and slither of innuendo, she could come to grips with it."[*]

In July 1972, Indira met with President Zulfikar Ali Bhutto at the Indian hill resort of Simla to discuss bilateral relations between their countries. That meeting was not altogether a cordial one. Indira told friends and colleagues that she did not trust Bhutto; his reputation as an arrogant and vain man had preceded him, and Indira seemed reluctant to even shake hands with Bhutto when they met in Simla. Bhutto fancied himself as a ladies' man, and initially acted very smooth with Indira—something that she found a bit comical. Bhutto actually was trying to be chivalrous, Pakistani delegates insisted, but some Indian officials saw in his courtesies and flourishes more than a hint of exaggeration. Prior to the meeting, Bhutto had said on numerous occasions that

[*] Sahgal, *Indira Gandhi: Her Road to Power,* p. 85.

423

he did not think that Indira was a particularly bright woman and that she had merely traded on her family name.

The meeting resulted in the "Simla Agreement," which led to an exchange of prisoners-of-war, and to the recognition of Bangladesh by Pakistan. After the summit with Indira, of course, Bhutto was fulsome in his praise for the Indian prime minister. The Pakistani President was accompanied by his daughter, Benazir, who would become prime minister of her country in one day.

"Believe me, we are interested in peace," Bhutto said to Indira. "We want to turn the corner. We want to make a new beginning. We are dealing with a difficult situation with many past prejudices. We should forget the past bitterness and hostility, and strive to achieve peace with honor." Indira later said to some Indian journalists that she was intrigued to hear those words emanating from Bhutto, the very man who, only a few months before the Simla Summit, had threatened a "thousand-year war" with India.

The summit went badly at first. The Pakistani delegation insisted that the Indians would have to agree to hold a plebiscite in Kashmir; the Indians demanded that Pakistan should recognize Bangladesh. While top officials of both sides argued in committee rooms, Indira fretted in private, and Bhutto spent most of his time watching Hindustani movies. Some of the foreign correspondents who gathered in Simla started filing reports that the Indo-Pakistan talks were about to collapse. Indeed, the suspense over whether the summit would result in anything at all was maintained until the final formal banquet that President Bhutto hosted on the evening of Sunday, July 2, 1972, at the state governor's residence, which was called Himachal Bhavan. The late Piloo Mody, a member of the Indian Parliament and a friend of Bhutto, described the scene just prior to the banquet:

> Very soon the atmosphere became overcharged with energy, with consultations back and forth suddenly taking place between Bhutto and his party in the Reception Room and Mrs. Gandhi and her party in the Billiard Room. The two leaders would meet, and then go back for further consultations, and then meet again. Meanwhile, the press corps had descended on Himachal Bhavan and forced [its] way into the halls and living room. As this hectic activity was going on, doors leading into the Reception Room and the Billiard Room were continuously being opened and shut. At the moment when the door to the Billiard Room opened, it revealed an unforgettable sight. Despite a score of photographers and cameramen being present, they

failed to take this immortal picture: As the door to the Billiard Room opened, we saw Jagjivan Ram sitting on the Billiard Table, Mrs. Gandhi leaning over the green, frantically scratching away—obviously at the draft treaty—with Yeshwantrao B. Chavan and Fakhruddin Ali Ahmed poring over the table, with a host of bureaucrats surrounding them. It was a great shot that will have to be kept in memory![*]

That same billiards table served as a podium when Indira and Bhutto finally convened to sign the Indo-Pakistan agreement, which held out the promise of a political settlement in Kashmir and an end to other border disputes between the two countries. But it would be another year before an agreement was reached between India and Pakistan for the mutual repatriation of prisoners of war, and the exchange of Bangladeshi nationals in Pakistan for a large number of Pakistanis in Bangladesh. And it would not be until 1974 that Pakistan would formally recognize Bangladesh; following that recognition, a tripartite agreement was signed between India, Pakistan and Bangladesh under which, among other things, Bangladesh agreed not to put on trial 195 Pakistani POWs who were still held for "war crimes." It was only in 1976 that India and Pakistan renewed full diplomatic relations, and reopened railway links that had been cut off since the 1965 war.

Not long after the signing of the Simla Agreement in July 1972, Indira spoke in the Lok Sabha about relations between India and Pakistan. "The very first remark I made to Mr. Bhutto was that we have to decide—Pakistan and India have to decide—whether the interests of these two countries are complementary or are they now, or are they always going to be, conflicting," Indira said. "If we think that our interests conflict, then you can have one agreement or a hundred agreements—and you will not have peace. But we believe . . . that our interests are largely the same, that the major problems we face are the problems of the poverty of our peoples, of the economic backwardness of our countries and the incessant effort of foreign powers to pressurize us. . . . When this is the state of affairs, do we permit it, or should we say 'Enough. We have had enough of the traps of others. Today we must realize what is in our real interests'? There is no doubt that the real interests of this country, as of Pakistan, lie in peace between the two countries."[†]

[*] Piloo Mody, *Zulfi, My Friend* (Bombay: Orient Paperbacks, 1973).
[†] Remarks from a statement in the Lok Sabha, July 31, 1972.

Indira knew that the question of peace between the two countries would be determined by how Pakistan dealt with the question of developing democratic leadership and viable political institutions.* This meant that the common people had to be given the chance to choose their leaders freely—this meant democracy, however homebred and divergent from the Westminster or Washington models.

General Zia's very presence in office kept Indira Gandhi on her toes—at least as far as Pakistan's geopolitical intentions were concerned. Just as she had never warmed up to Zulfikar Ali Bhutto, Indira had mainly negative feelings about Zia. The Pakistani dictator had told associates that when Indira returned to power in the 1979 election, it came as a "big shock" to him. Indira and Zia met for the first time in April 1980 in Harare, where many world leaders had gathered to celebrate Zimbabwe's independence. On the day of their meeting, recalls Inder Malhotra, the local newspapers had published unfavorable comments that Zia had made earlier about Indira.

"Madam, please do not believe everything you read in the newspapers," Zia said to Indira, when they met.

"Of course not," Indira said. "After all, aren't they calling you a democrat and me a dictator?"†

Zia made the foolish mistake of presenting Indira with a coffee-table book on Pakistan that showed all of Kashmir, and three principalities in the western Indian state of Gujarat, as part of Pakistan. During their Harare encounter, Zia also kept referring to the good relationship he had ostensibly established with Morarji Desai, when Desai had been India's prime minister. Finally, according to H. Y. Sharada Prasad, who had accompanied Indira to Zimbabwe as her spokesman, Indira said to Zia: "You do not seem to realize that Mr. Desai is no longer in charge of our government."

Not long before her death in October 1984, Indira Gandhi told Professor Ralph Buultjens that she did not believe that the United States would stop promoting Pakistan as a counterweight to India on the Subcontinent. She realized—perhaps too late in the day—that Pakistan had developed much better political relationships in Washington than the

---

* Since Indira's time, this fundamental test has been made all the more serious because of the continuing violence inside Pakistan, the continued friction with India, the continued turbulence on its western border with Afghanistan, and the simmering tensions of regionalism.

† Anecdote quoted by H. Y. Sharada Prasad to Inder Malhotra.

Indians had. Indira was aware that the Pakistani foreign service had skillfully cultivated contacts on Capitol Hill and in the White House. India's representatives in Washington, for the most part, seemed sluggish—time-servers mired in endless paperwork and usually out of touch with the political realities of Congress, the administration, and even of general American public opinion. Janki Ganju, the longtime India lobbyist in Washington, had often urged Indira to expand India's public-relations operations in the United States. "Because the Americans may seem to write off India, India cannot write off the United States," Ganju frequently said to Indira. But Ganju faced the behemoth of the Indian bureaucracy in New Delhi, a creature so unable to see the value of his work that it repeatedly stymied his efforts to streamline India's image in America. Ganju felt that the relatively "good image" of Pakistan in the United States translated into American financial support and military assistance for Pakistan—assistance that, in turn, meant that Pakistan was likely to remain India's principal security concern for a long time, not so much because of the military threat that Pakistan posed, but because of the insecurities that led Pakistan to look beyond the region for help and alliances.

In contrast to many chauvinistic Hindu politicians—some of whom belonged to the Congress Party—Indira was aware of the need to coopt India's Muslims into the great drama of development. With a population that constituted 10 percent of the overall Indian population, no national leader could afford to write off India's Islamic cohort. But in reaching out to Muslims, Indira often fashioned alliances with figures of dubious reputation. One of them was Haji Mastaan, who had prospered by becoming an underworld kingpin. His life story inspired a film producer to make a box-office hit. Mastaan lived as a boy in a packing crate on the Bombay docks. He joined a street gang, following the example of many Muslim youths from destitute families; he quickly rose to become its leader, then entered the lucrative world of gold smuggling. In the movie there is a scene based on a real-life confrontation Mastaan had with a top government official who had threatened to have him arrested. The rising young gangster says to the official: "For the record, I don't know what smuggling is. Between you and me, I've always been a smuggler. I am a smuggler. And I will always be a smuggler. Let's see what you can do about it, big shot! Do you think you can put me in jail? Do you think you can have me hanged? Let's see if you can find the proof. The only way you can stop me is if three or four of you guys get together and decide to pump a few bullets into my body. But you won't, will you? You guys don't have the guts."

Mastaan eventually gave up his life of crime—but only after he had made millions. He now devotes his time to philanthropy and social work in Bombay. But there are those who suspect that once a smuggler, always a smuggler.

The question of Muslim support was also important to Indira because of India's political position concerning the Middle East. Tens of thousands of Indians had left for the oil-rich sheikdoms of Arabia to make a living. Their remittances fetched India valuable foreign-exchange—some $2 billion-plus annually. Moreover, Indian construction companies obtained major contracts in the Middle East—not the least because India, especially under Indira, was perceived to be a supporter of the Arab cause. India's support was largely predicated on the belief that the Arab nations would, when push came to shove, take India's side in the dispute with Pakistan over Kashmir.

Indira Gandhi felt, especially in the early 1970s, that the long-festering problems concerning Palestine, the Occupied Territories, Lebanon, the Gulf, and regional economic development seemed nowhere near any equitable solutions. Nor did there appear to be any serious effort aimed at getting the peace process to advance meaningfully. She felt that there had been a persistent lack of political will to support necessary political action. And the overall situation had been worsened by mutual distrust and suspicion between the advocates of various sorts of action. Fundamentalist radicals of different faiths carried on subversive agitation that could only erode the authority and sovereignty of nation-states in the region, and even beyond. "In order to lift the situation out of its current quagmire, there must be recognition that the region requires both economic and political initiatives that would be workable," she told Professor Ralph Buultjens. "However, everyone dealing with this part of the world seems obsessed with procedural matters. The Middle East situation has become a surrealistic minuet."

Indira believed that for the peace process to be successful both Israel and the Palestine Liberation Organization must offer their respective people practical options. The most appropriate vehicle for the achievement of such a settlement was an international conference under the auspices of the United Nations. Indira felt that the world community could hardly afford to wait until the Arabs and Israelis made suitable compromises that would bring them to the negotiating table. She was particularly fascinated by the Middle East because it has always been a remarkable mosaic of peoples and cultures, largely bound together under the rubric of Islam, yet enjoying a remarkable diversity of faiths: Judaism, Christianity, Zoroastrianism, Sikhism, and Hinduism. This mosaic has provided for the welfare and well-being of the majority and minority alike. Cultural congeniality, to be sure, plays an important role in the national tapestry of any country. But in the Middle East, in particular, Indira felt that you could not talk of promoting peace and harmony— politically or sociologically—unless there was a congenial environment. But the environment remained freighted with violence and malevolence. There was no resolution in sight for the endemic and seemingly perennial problems in Palestine, Lebanon, and the Gulf (since the Iran-Iraq War started in 1980). Indira would have been pleased that a Mideast parley finally took place in October–November 1991 in Madrid.

Indira also felt—quite strongly, in fact—that historically, Israel's attitude toward the Palestinians had been one of denial. Since Israel refused to recognize the existence of a distinct "Palestine problem," how could it possibly accept responsibility for its resolution? Through semantic reduction, the inhabitants of the land that encompassed Israel in 1948 became "refugees." Never mind that they were there to begin with. Indira felt that Israel deflected attention from critical issues by first quibbling over the number of refugees and accusing the Arabs of exaggeration, and later by rewriting historical geography. Israeli Prime Minister Golda Meir even said: "Palestine did not exist; therefore there were no Palestinian people; and thus, there is no problem." Indira's response was: "We cannot deny to the people of Palestine their inalienable right to the homeland from which they were exiled."* This "denial of reality," Indira told associates, was exemplified by Mrs. Meir's assertion that Palestine was "Southern Syria."†

An assessment of Indira's Middle East policies suggests that her political investment in the Arab cause obtained little return—at least as far as Kashmir was concerned. Not only did several Arab states openly support Pakistan during the 1965 and 1971 wars, but some of them sent weapons, ammunition, and even military advisers.

---

*Speech by Indira Gandhi at the Third Nonaligned Summit, Lusaka, Zambia, September 9, 1970.
†Indian diplomats argue that this "denial" persists as more recent Israeli prime ministers have attempted to banish the term "Palestine" from history, geography, and politics.

19

Transforming Democracy

Early on the morning of June 12, 1975, Neivulne Krishna Iyer Seshan kept flouncing from one teletype machine to another in his small office in a New Delhi bungalow.* He was waiting for what could be ominous news and, as could be expected under the circumstances, Seshan was nervous.

Seshan was senior private secretary to Prime Minister Indira Gandhi, and the news he awaited concerned a court judgment in Allahabad, Mrs. Gandhi's hometown. There a high court justice by the name of Jag Mohan Lal Sinha was scheduled to deliver his verdict on a petition by a small-time politician named Raj Narain, who had lost to Indira Gandhi by more than 100,000 votes in a parliamentary race in 1971. Charging that Mrs. Gandhi had illegally used government officials and apparatus in her campaign, Narain sought to have the results overturned. The hearings had taken four years, and now the denouement was approaching. No one knew how Justice Sinha would act. A number of Congress Party officials had offered him large amounts of money if he ruled in favor of Indira, but Sinha had scornfully rejected these bribes.† Mrs. Gandhi's

---

*Indian prime ministers seem to consistently select South Indian men to be their private secretaries. Jawaharlal Nehru had M. O. Mathai; Indira had Seshan; Rajiv Gandhi employed Vincent George. The answer may lie in the fact that South Indians are generally considered more diligent workers than other Indians.
†The source for this information was Romesh Thapar, the writer and editor. He told the author that some Congress officials had offered Justice Sinha up to the equivalent of $50,000 in bribes, and an assurance that he would be appointed to the Indian Supreme Court.

aides had also enlisted the assistance of Intelligence Bureau operatives to tap Justice Sinha's phones. Also tapped were the phones of Sinha's stenographer—to whom the judge would have presumably dictated his imminent decision. Some intelligence agents were even assigned to cup their ears to the outer walls of Sinha's garden in order to catch fragments of conversations he might have within the precincts of his home. At the suggestion of local Congress factotums, a swami had been positioned in front of the justice's home, and this mendicant had assured Congress officials that "all would be well." Indira Gandhi, who had increasingly become enamored of astrology and mysticism, seemed reassured by this prediction.* Since the court hearings ended on May 25, 1975, Justice Sinha had not left his modest Allahabad home. Despite the efforts of the Intelligence Bureau, nobody knew how the judge would decide in the Indira Gandhi case.

It was not just Seshan, of course, who waited with anxiety. So did Indira's sons, Rajiv and Sanjay. Rajiv—then a pilot with Indian Airlines—was present in the prime minister's bungalow that morning, and Sanjay Gandhi was at his Maruti automobile complex a few miles outside the capital. The nation waited, too, for this could be history in the making. It was generally a tense time for Indira, not only because of the imminent judgment concerning fifty-two counts of campaign malpractice. The years since the Bangladesh war had not gone as well as she had hoped. Looking after the Bangladesh refugees had meant that India's granaries were virtually empty. The economy was not growing rapidly, and popular distress—and unrest—was spreading. The energy crisis following the Arab-Israeli War of 1973, when oil prices rocketed, had resulted in the quadrupling of India's oil import bill. By 1974 India's budgetary deficit had soared to $2 billion, or twice the amount that the country received annually in foreign aid. The underground nuclear explosion on May 18, 1974, in the Rajasthan desert, which Indira insisted was for peaceful purposes, attracted a great deal of criticism from the West, including Washington. Indira dismissed such criticism as irrelevant: "India has not ever been an easy country to understand. Perhaps it is too deep, contradictory and diverse, and few people in the contemporary world have the time or inclination to look beyond the obvious, especially because in our country we have the greatest scope for free expression of opinion—and all differences are constantly being debated."

---

* A Hindu charlatan named Dhirendra Brahmachari seemed to have excessive access to Indira Gandhi. This swami, whom many Indians called Indira's Rasputin, spent a great deal of time with the prime minister. He was reputed to be corrupt, and a sexual debauch.

Within India itself, Indira and the Congress were coming under increasing attacks. In Bihar and Gujarat states, thousands of students and workers took out marches to protest against spiraling inflation and against Congress corruption. Several Congress officials were accused of accepting questionable cash and other gifts—from such donors as Haji Mastaan. *
Jayaprakash Narayan, a veteran of the freedom struggle, led a popular movement in Bihar against the Congress. "India needs nothing less than a total revolution," declared the man known widely as "JP." Narayan had once been an ally of Jawaharlal Nehru, but had resigned from the Congress in 1936 over policy disagreements. He then founded India's Socialist Party, and later became a member of Parliament. Indira had always thought of Narayan as a somewhat naïve figure—he had once expressed admiration for Pakistan's erstwhile dictator, Ayub Khan—but now Narayan seemed to be capturing the popular imagination with his campaign against Congress corruption and inflation. Says writer Tariq Ali: "Narayan believed that only a return to the village as the central unit of political and economic life would take India forward. His program was simple. He wanted a voluntary federation of village republics based on sarvodaya, or welfare of the community. The means to be used to gain this end would be nonviolent mass resistance as popularized by Mahatma Gandhi. In normal circumstances, this attempt to [replicate] history would have ended in farce, but the particular circumstances in India at the time were such that people were waiting for a lead."† Narayan teamed up with Morarji Desai to form the Janata Morcha, or People's Front, a grand alliance of non-Congress parties that included such radical groups as the Maoist Communists and Left-Socialists; the right-wing Swatantra Party; the extreme right-wing Anand Marg, a group prone to violence; and the Jan Sangh, a Hindu militant party.

The Janata Morcha's criticisms of Indira found resonance all over India. Almost daily there were huge demonstrations against the Congress in some part of the country or the other. Meanwhile, labor strikes had also begun to intensify: in Bombay—India's humming industrial capital—there were nearly 13,000 such strikes between October 1973 and June 1974. By mid-1974, a million railway workers went on strike to protest against the arrest of their union leader, George Fernandes, and other labor doyens. Indira told her ministers that she was determined to crush the railway union, and soon paramilitary forces were deployed

---

* Indira's main accomplice in extorting cash from underworld bosses and industrialists was L. N. Mishra, the railways minister. Mishra was reputed to be extremely corrupt, a man who lived luxuriously and decadently. In January 1975, he was blown up with his railway carriage. The murder was never solved.
† Ali, *An Indian Dynasty: The Story of the Nehru-Gandhi Family.*

against the strikers. More than 60,000 were arrested. The railway system—which had some 50,000 miles of track laid mostly during the British Raj—was paralyzed. The secretary of the National Railway Workers Union, C. Radhakrishnan, described Mrs. Gandhi's persecution of his colleagues as follows: "The government tried everything. We were hunted like criminals and they literally tried to starve us into submission. During the strike, short of using the air force to bomb the railway colonies [housing complexes], they used every method to terrorize us and break the strike. The army and navy were both called out. They were used to guard all railway installations against sabotage, to operate signals and telecommunications, to run trains under the protection of armed guards, and generally to keep order."[*] The railway strike lasted twenty-two days, and in the end Indira prevailed through the show of force. There were those who began to fear that by calling upon police and troops to run essential services such as the railways, Indira was putting into place a mechanism to usurp democracy and install authoritarianism. Perhaps Indira had no choice in light of the widespread political chaos in India.

There was general agreement among Indians that Indira's promises to eradicate poverty had turned out to be just that—promises. Her government by now had started to assume greater control of India's economy—far greater control, in fact, than even in Nehru's heyday. A series of radical land reforms was undertaken; a number of industries, including coal mines, were nationalized in 1973; corporate and individual taxes were increased. Indira told an interviewer from the Bombay-based magazine *Blitz*: "If anybody tries to say that poverty can go in my lifetime or during my tenure as prime minister, it just cannot. It has very deep roots."[†] Political opponents had started to shrilly taunt Indira about her 1971 campaign pledge, "*Garibi hatao*," pointing out that getting rid of poverty was simply beyond the capability of the prime minister. In Gujarat State, Morarji Desai undertook a fast unto death to bring down the corrupt Congress government of Chimanbhai Patel. Desai's fast resulted in the dismissal of the Patel administration and imposition of President's Rule in February 1974. Under President's Rule, the state would be administered by New Delhi, and so Desai went on another fast to demand fresh elections. "The pressure on Indira was building—and we were all curious as to how she would deal with it," recalls Gerson da Cunha, a social commentator who was then a top corporate executive. "We soon found out."[‡]

[*] *Race Today* (London), April 1975.
[†] Interview with R. K. Karanjia, *Blitz*, April 1973.
[‡] Conversation with author, New Delhi, September 1990.

British Prime Minister Margaret Thatcher with Indira Gandhi during her brief stopover in the capital on September 29, 1982. (News Bureau)

Prime Minister Indira Gandhi on a visit to the United States in 1982. With her is Janki Ganju. (Courtesy Janki Ganju)

Prime Minister Indira Gandhi with President Ronald Reagan in 1982.
(Courtesy Janki Ganju)

Queen Elizabeth II of Great Britain with the heads of government of the Commonwealth
countries in New Delhi on November 23, 1983. (Courtesy Indian Consulate)

Queen Elizabeth with Prime Minister Indira Gandhi during the Royal Tour of India in 1983. (Courtesy Globe Photos)

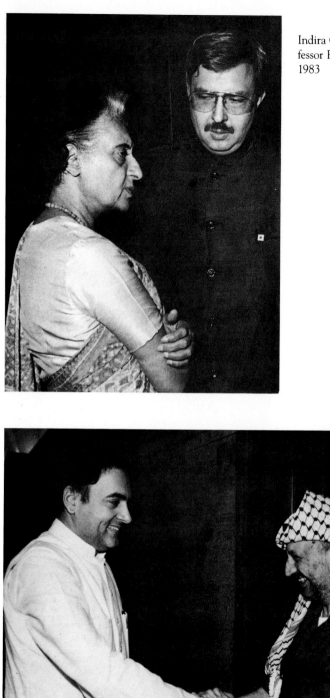

Indira Gandhi with Professor Ralph Buultjens, 1983

Prime Minister Rajiv Gandhi receiving Yasser Arafat, chairman of the Palestine Liberation Organization (PLO), in New Delhi, April 18, 1985. (Courtesy Indian Consulate)

Prime Minister Rajiv Gandhi addressing a joint session of the U.S. Congress, Washington, D.C., June 13, 1985. Vice President George Bush (left) and Speaker of the House Thomas P. O'Neill, Jr., are shown applauding. (Courtesy Indian Consulate).

Mrs. Gandhi with sons Rajiv (left) and Sanjay (right). (Courtesy Nehru Memorial Museum and Library)

Feroze Gandhi, husband of Indira. (Courtesy Nehru Memorial Museum and Library)

Prime Minister Indira Gandhi. (Courtesy Indian Consulate)

Prime Minister Indira Gandhi with sons Sanjay (left) and Rajiv (right). (Courtesy Indian Consulate)

Mrs. Gandhi with her family. Left to right: Rajiv, Sonia (Rajiv's wife), and Sanjay. (Courtesy Indian Consulate)

Funeral of Indira Gandhi, November 3, 1984. Son Rajiv Gandhi stands second from left. (Courtesy Globe Photos)

Funeral of Rajiv Gandhi, May 24, 1991. Rahul performs the last rites for his father. (Courtesy Globe Photos)

*   *   *

At 9:55 A.M. on June 12, 1975, Justice Jag Mohan Lal Sinha walked into Room 24 of the Allahabad High Court, a dilapidated building dating back to the days of the Raj.* The courtroom was crowded. After the lean, fifty-five-year-old judge had seated himself, a court aide shouted to the audience: "Listen, gentlemen, no clapping when the Judge Sahib announces judgment on the poll petition of Raj Narain."

Justice Sinha had before him a 258-page document—his decision on the case. He said: "I shall read out only my findings on the various issues involved in the case."

He paused, then said: "The petition is allowed."

There was a gasp from the audience, and then applause. Reporters dashed out of the room to contact their editors.

Hundreds of miles away in New Delhi, Neivulne Krishna Iyer Seshan paled when he saw the United News of India teleprinter clack away a dreaded flash: "Mrs. Gandhi Unseated." He tore off the paper from the machine and rushed toward a room where Indira was waiting. Seshan saw Rajiv Gandhi outside the room, and gave him the UNI message. It was Rajiv who broke the news to his mother, who seemed to take it stoically at first. Over the next thirty minutes, more wire-service copy was handed to her, spelling out Justice Sinha's verdict.

The judge held Indira Gandhi guilty of two corruption charges. One was that she illegally used the services of a government official named Yashpal Kapoor—who was attached to the prime minister's secretariat—to "further her election prospects." Kapoor's presence on the government payroll was in itself a boondoggle: He was among those who planned the Congress Party's "dirty tricks," and Indira had found a way to get Indian taxpayers to pay for Kapoor's services. Justice Sinha said that although Kapoor had started campaigning for Mrs. Gandhi on January 7, 1971, and resigned from the prime minister's secretariat on January 13, he remained on the government payroll until January 25 that year. The judge noted that Mrs. Gandhi had declared herself a candidate for the 1971 election on December 29, 1970, and so the placement of Kapoor on the public payroll was clearly a violation of the law.

Justice Sinha also found Indira Gandhi guilty of Raj Narain's charges that she used officials attached to the Uttar Pradesh state government to construct rostrums from which she addressed election rallies. These officials had also illegally rented loudspeakers and other equipment with

* The author is grateful to Kuldip Nayar for supplying details of the courtroom drama surrounding Justice Sinha's decision.

government funds. "Raj Narain had lost by over 100,000 votes, and these improprieties would not have materially changed the outcome," says author and columnist Kuldip Nayar. "They were too thin to justify un-seating a prime minister. It was almost like unseating the prime minister for a traffic offense. But the law was the law, and it was quite clear that any assistance sought from a government servant 'for the furtherance of the prospects' of a candidate's election was a corrupt practice. Sinha himself said in the judgment that he was left with no choice. There was no special provision for the prime minister, and he could not have given any other verdict. Even the punishment for contravention of the law was fixed, and the judge was left with no discretion."*

Justice Sinha's decision meant a mandatory penalty that would bar Indira Gandhi from holding—or contesting—any elective office for a period of six years.

In her bungalow in New Delhi, Indira told Rajiv and others that she had no choice but to resign as prime minister. A number of Congress chieftains who had gathered at her home began to sob. But virtually everyone present urged Indira not to resign from office. "There will be chaos if you left your job," the twenty-eight-year-old Sanjay Gandhi said to his mother. His older brother agreed. Indira herself would publicly say only that she would appeal Justice Sinha's decision in the Supreme Court. But years later, she confided to writer Dom Moraes that there was never any question of resignation. "After my judgment in 1975, what could I have done except stay?" Indira said to Moraes. "You know the state that the country was in. What would have happened if there had been nobody to lead it? I was the only person who could, you know. It was my duty to the country to stay, though I didn't want to."† That assertion of indispensability was typical of Indira. In her mind, only she could run India. By now she had come to believe a phrase that the Congress president, Dev Kant Barooah, had coined: "Indira is India; India is Indira." *L'état, c'est moi?*

Jayaprakash Narayan's Janata Morcha, however, insisted that Indira Gandhi vacate her office at once. Mass protests were initiated by Nara-yan. The Congress Party reacted by organizing marches of its own, trans-porting tens of thousands of peasants and workers to New Delhi from outlying villages and towns to demonstrate in support of Indira Gandhi. Jayaprakash Narayan strongly urged President Fakhruddin Ali Ahmed to dismiss Indira from office. Many newspapers called for Indira's resigna-

---

*Kuldip Nayar, *The Judgment* (Delhi: Vikas, 1977), pp. 3–4.
†Moraes, *Mrs. Gandhi*, p. 220.

tion. By a remarkable coincidence, the results of the state elections in Gujarat were announced on June 13—the day after Justice Sinha's decision against Indira. The results showed that the party led by Narayan and Morarji Desai had won resoundingly. Nani A. Palkhivala, one of India's eminent constitutional lawyers, was summoned by Indira to give her advice. Palkhivala—who later became a vociferous critic of Mrs. Gandhi, and also served as India's ambassador to the United States—told the prime minister that she should immediately appeal Justice Sinha's decision, and that there was no need for her to resign pending a Supreme Court decision.

There were some dissidents in the Congress Party who wanted Indira to step down, perhaps in favor of a temporary prime minister until the Supreme Court decision. But Indira outmaneuvered them, averring that unless she was at the helm of the country there would be more chaos, and that the Congress itself would collapse. Indira appeared at a large progovernment rally in New Delhi on June 20; on the rostrum were Sanjay, Rajiv, and Rajiv's wife, Sonia. Indira told the cheering crowd that she would serve India "until my last breath—national service has been a family tradition." All 983 buses of the Delhi Transport Corporation were taken off their usual routes and put into service—at no cost to the Congress Party—to bring Congress supporters to the rally and later to the prime minister's house. On June 24, 1975, Justice V. R. Krishna Iyer, the Supreme Court judge who was on duty—the court itself was formally on vacation for the summer—ruled that Indira need not resign until the full court met in the fall, but that the prime minister could not vote in Parliament. Jayaprakash Narayan and the Janata Morcha at once vowed to keep protesting until Indira resigned. He asked the police and the army not to take orders from a "disqualified head of a discredited government." At a huge public meeting on the Ramlila festival grounds in New Delhi on the evening of June 25, Jayaprakash Narayan and Morarji Desai both denounced Indira Gandhi as "moving toward dictatorship and fascism."

Unbeknownst to Narayan and Desai, Indira Gandhi was planning to arrest them and all other major Opposition figures. She was also plotting to suspend India's cherished constitution. Egged on by Sanjay Gandhi, Indira drew up a list of newspapers that were to be either banned or whose circulation was to be severely curtailed. Another list contained the names of journalists who were to be put behind bars. Armored units were stealthily put on full alert by the government. What Indira had in mind was the declaration of a national "Emergency"—anyone could be arrested without habeas corpus. Shortly after ten o'clock on the evening of June 25, Indira and Siddhartha Shankar Ray—then the chief minister of West Bengal—drove to Rashtrapati Bhavan, the residence of President Ahmed. Indira told the president what she had in mind, and Ray hinted that since Indira had promoted Ahmed's candidacy for the presidency, it would be only appropriate if Ahmed went along with the prime minister's request for the president's signature on the document imposing the Emergency. Ahmed was actually quite anxious to please Indira. At 11:45 P.M., he cravenly signed a proclamation of a state of emergency. "A grave emergency exists whereby the security of India is threatened by internal disturbances," the proclamation said. President Ahmed authorized the government to impose media censorship, suspend court proceedings, and override the legislative and judicial branches of government, if necessary. By dawn the next day, Jayaprakash Narayan, Morarji Desai, and 676 other Opposition leaders had been arrested under the draconian Maintenance of Internal Security Act (MISA). At 2:00 A.M. on June 26, power to all major newspapers in New Delhi was cut off, thus imposing a news blackout on the capital. At 8:00 A.M., Indira addressed the nation on All-India Radio. "The president has proclaimed an emergency," she said. "This is nothing to panic about. I am sure you are conscious of the deep and widespread conspiracy which has been brewing ever since I began to introduce certain progressive measures of benefit to the common man and woman of India. In the name of democracy it has been sought to negate the very functioning of democracy. . . . Certain persons have gone to the length of inciting our armed forces to mutiny and our police to rebel. . . . Now we learn of new programs challenging law and order throughout the country. . . ."

On July 22, 1975, Indira appeared before the Rajya Sabha, the upper house of Parliament, and said: "The decision to have emergency was not one that could be taken lightly or easily. But there comes a time in the life of the nation when hard decisions have to be taken. When there is an atmosphere of violence [without] discipline, and one can visibly see the nation going down, then the time has come to stop this process." Self-serving words, of course, but words that highlighted Indira's belief that had she not acted, India would have exploded in a new orgy of violence. Thousands of students, journalists, and lawyers were herded into jails. Foreign newspapers reported that Indira's government had put nearly 50,000 people behind bars immediately after the Emergency was declared; in all, some 110,000 people were jailed during the twenty-one months of the Emergency. Government figures now available indicate that 34,988 persons were arrested under the Maintenance of Internal Security Act (MISA); and 75,818 persons were jailed under the Defence of India regulations. "Those who are in should be out—and those who are out should be in!" declared Piloo Mody, a member of the Swatantra Party, before he was hauled off to jail. On July 4, twenty-six Opposition parties and groups were formally banned; Indira also imposed strict censorship on the domestic and foreign press.

In Parliament—with most Opposition members either behind bars or abstaining—Indira won an indefinite extension of the Emergency. She also forced through two historic amendments to the constitution: One barred India's courts of law from hearing any challenges to the Emergency; the other amendment retroactively exonerated Indira Gandhi from any legal charges pending against her—as well as from "all possible future charges of criminal actions while she was in high office."[*] The amendments themselves were declared immune to Supreme Court review. India's hard-won democracy had been dramatically and suddenly transformed into a dictatorship, and Indira Gandhi had become a full-scale autocrat. Huge posters with Indira's face were festooned everywhere. The caption read: "She Stood Between Chaos and Order."

From his prison cell, Jayaprakash Narayan keenly followed Indira's machinations. He maintained a prison diary, and one of the entries said: "I had always believed that Mrs. Gandhi had no faith in democracy, that she was by inclination and conviction a dictator. . . ."[†]

For the next twenty-one months—until she was defeated in an election which brought Narayan's Janata Party into power—Indira ruled with an iron fist. "As regards the arrests after we declared emergency, there was a list of the main Opposition leaders, which I approved," she told Dom Moraes. "The rest of the arrests were left to the discretion of state governments and the police: The idea was to arrest anyone who was likely to exert a troublesome influence in the country or the area. We had spent so much time fighting all the chaos that we had no time to work for the country. If we could find time to breathe, we could find time for work. Emergency was necessary."[‡] Ordinary Indians respond well to authority, and even better to threats of severe punishment. Suddenly, trains began running on time, traffic in overcrowded cities became orderly, shoppers fell into neat lines at stores, there was almost no hoarding of food grains, consumer prices tumbled, and there was virtually no chaos at bus stops. In short, India functioned remarkably efficiently for twenty-one months. Today, with chaos widening in the country, many Indians recall the Emergency days with a strange sort of yearning.

It is now clear that Indira Gandhi exaggerated the perils faced by India

---

[*] Wolpert, *A New History of India*, p. 399.
[†] Jayaprakash Narayan, *Prison Diary* (Bombay: Popular Prakashan, 1977).
[‡] Moraes, *Mrs. Gandhi*, p. 222.

in mid-1975. The Commission on the Emergency headed by former Supreme Court Chief Justice J. C. Shah, collected voluminous evidence of wrongdoing on the part of the Gandhi administration during the Emergency. The Shah Commission's report said:

There is no evidence of any breakdown of law and order in any part of the country—nor of any apprehension in that behalf; the economic condition was well under control and had in no way deteriorated. There is not even a report of an apprehension of any serious breakdown of the law and order situation or deterioration of the economic condition from any public functionary. The public records of the times, secret, confidential or public, and publications in newspapers, speak with unanimity that there was no unusual event or even a tendency in that direction to justify the imposition of emergency. There was no threat to the well-being of the nation from sources external or internal. The conclusion appears in the absence of any evidence given by Indira Gandhi or anyone else, that the one and only motivating force for tendering the extraordinary advice to the president to declare an "internal emergency" was the intense political activity generated in the ruling party and the opposition, by the decision of the Allahabad High Court declaring the election of the prime minister of the day invalid on the grounds of corrupt election practices. There is no reason to think that if the democratic conventions were followed, the whole political upsurge would in the normal course have not subsided. But Madame Gandhi, in her anxiety to continue in power, brought about instead a situation which directly contributed to her continuance in power and also generated forces which sacrificed the interests of many to serve the ambitions of a few. Thousands were detained and a series of totally illegal and unwarranted actions followed involving untold human misery and suffering. *

Not long after the March 1977 elections in which she was defeated, Indira Gandhi assessed the Emergency in a conversation with her friend Professor Ralph Buultjens. "As soon as it was possible to do so, I called for elections," Indira said. "Many advised against it, but I felt that we had already postponed elections for a year and that we should seek a mandate. Taken as a whole, does this record reflect the actions of one who is opposed to democracy?"

"It was one of the most difficult periods of modern history," Indira

---

* *The Shah Commission Report* (New Delhi: Ministry of Information and Broadcasting, 1978).

440

continued. "Critical and often unfavorable developments affected the poorer nations, unprecedented readjustments were taking place in the international system. We were often struggling against these trends. I think that the eventual judgement will be that we did not do badly. . . ."[*]

If Indira was the architect of the Emergency, Sanjay Gandhi was the enforcer. A man of small stature whose reputation had been primarily that of a playboy, Sanjay seized the moment. He had never done much with his life until now, other than tinker around with cars. As an apprentice at the Rolls-Royce plant in Crewe, England, Sanjay was not thought of highly by his peers. In New Delhi, Sanjay gathered around him a group of young thugs who reorganized the wing of the Congress Party known as the Youth Congress. Many of Sanjay's colleagues, such as Jagdish Tytler, rose to political prominence in their own right when Rajiv Gandhi became prime minister in 1984 after the assassination of his mother.

"You see, Sanjay isn't a thinker—he's a doer," Indira told Dom Moraes. "I mean, cent per cent a doer. When he wants something done, he gets it done."

Sanjay Gandhi had wanted to develop a "people's car" for India. The automobile industry was dominated by a Calcutta-based branch of the Birla family, which had long funded the Congress Party; the Birlas' company, Hindustan Motors, produced the Ambassador, a behemoth whose technology had not been changed substantially since the 1950s. The other giant of the business was the Bombay-based Premier Automobiles Limited (PAL), which produced a version of Italy's Fiat. These two manufacturers monopolized the Indian market. Sanjay wanted to come out with a car that cost no more than the equivalent of $3,000, which he felt common people could afford; the models in the sellers' market cost several times that amount, and the waiting list was a decade long.

Sanjay Gandhi built a prototype of his "people's car," the Maruti, in a backyard garage in New Delhi. The prototype was widely criticized in the media, and in political and professional circles, as being a technical disaster: The car just did not work very well.[†] Nevertheless, Sanjay Gandhi's company, Maruti Limited, was granted a license in November 1970 to produce 50,000 cars annually. Chief Minister Bansi Lal of Haryana State evicted residents from the villages of Mahalada, Dhund-

---

[*] Conversation between Indira Gandhi and Ralph Buultjens, April 1977, New Delhi.
[†] A joke making the rounds in those days was as follows: Sanjay's Maruti car would solve India's gasoline problems as well as unemployment problems. Why? Because the engine would not accept any gas, and it would take fifteen Indians to push every Maruti.

era, and Kheterpur, compensating them shabbily for their property in order to build the Maruti plant. Bansi Lal would soon become one of Indira Gandhi's henchmen during the Emergency. Sanjay Gandhi, of course, was also able to persuade businessmen to invest in the company and had no trouble raising millions of dollars to get Maruti started. The project proved an economic and technical failure from the start. By the time the Emergency was declared in June 1975, no "people's car" was available to the people. Eventually, the company had to be bailed out by India's nationalized banks, and it was not until the early 1980s, after Sanjay's death, that the Maruti finally hit the Indian streets. The car that was finally produced was developed by Japan's Suzuki Motors. Today, of course, the Maruti Company is doing very well. But its retail price is five times what Sanjay Gandhi had envisioned in 1970. Sanjay Gandhi would never have received the Maruti commission had his last name not been Gandhi. Family connections work magic in India.[*]

Another thing that Sanjay Gandhi badly wanted to do was control India's runaway population growth. That goal was contained in a five-point program which he unveiled: "Limit families to only two children. Never accept dowries as a condition for marriage. Teach one illiterate person to read and write. Clear or upgrade slums. And plant one tree every year." These were highly desirable objectives, but Sanjay drew fire because of the excesses that accompanied their enactment: Boys under fourteen were reportedly sterilized forcibly, among other things. Although it later became the fashion among many Indians to attack Sanjay Gandhi for his zealousness concerning population control, the fact was that he had done his homework in demography. He had sought advice from several international agencies and from local family-planning officials. Experts at the United Nations Fund for Population Activities (UNFPA) had told him that the world's overall population was growing at an alarming rate. Between 1950 and 1980 the world doubled its population.[†] Why was the world's population growing so fast? Because more people were being born than were dying, and because each year more people entered the child-bearing stage. The 127 countries of the Third World added more than 1 million people every five days; the rich industrialized countries, only about 8 million annually. In the poor countries of the Third World, which could least afford galloping population growth rates, the burgeoning numbers of people were outpacing the

[*] For a full and fascinating account of the origins of the Maruti car, please see Kuldip Nayar's *The Judgment.*
[†] United Nations Population Fund is the source for these statistics.

ability of social and economic systems to provide adequate housing, fuel, and food. The sort of galloping population growth experienced by Third World countries such as India exacerbated the difficult choice between higher consumption now and the investment needed to invite higher consumption in the future.

Both Sanjay and Indira Gandhi knew that the Indian government had an uneven record on population control. In the early 1950s, India became the first Third World country to formally make family planning a matter of national policy. Its first five-year plan, which was unveiled in 1952, established a population planning committee. Subsequent five-year plans talked loftily about the need to press on in population control. According to the third five-year plan, in effect between 1961 and 1977: "Stabilization of growth in the population over a reasonable period is at the very center of planned development." The sixth five-year plan (1978–83) emphasized the need for population control in direct language. It called for the "promotion of policies for controlling the growth of population through voluntary acceptance of the small family norm, the protection and improvement of ecological and environmental assets, the encouragement of the active involvement of all sections in the development process through appropriate education, communication and institutional strategies." In the early years of the national family-planning programs, practitioners had access mostly to sterilization and condoms. In 1966 the nationwide use of the intrauterine device (IUD) was approved by the government. Over the years, the Indian government persuaded the United States, other Western donors, and the United Nations to pump more than $2 billion into population-control programs. And yet the population continued to grow annually at the rate of 2.1 percent. The largest number of babies were born where there already were the most people—the countryside, where 70 percent of India's population lived in abject poverty. Moreover, improved health care had lowered the death rate in many parts of the country; killer diseases such as smallpox had been eradicated. Infant mortality had been brought down. The life expectancy of Indians increased from thirty-two years at Independence in 1947 to fifty-five by 1975. With more people living longer, and with the population base expanding each year, India's "population problem" posed formidable challenges to Prime Minister Gandhi.

Sanjay Gandhi's grandfather Jawaharlal Nehru was a relatively late convert to the idea of family planning. Even though it was apparent at Independence that India's annual population-growth rate would soar, Nehru did not launch a national family-planning campaign until the early 1950s. His first minister of health and family planning was a spinster of great rectitude who privately endorsed Mahatma Gandhi's oft-quoted view that celibacy was the best contraceptive. Nehru's daughter herself dithered over family planning. It was not until the Emergency that the government acted decisively, under the direction of Sanjay Gandhi. Indira Gandhi's defeat in the 1977 election was at least partly attributable to public revulsion over excessive family-planning zeal during the Emergency.

It was hardly surprising, therefore, that when Indira Gandhi subsequently returned to power in 1980 she barely referred to population control or family planning in her early speeches. This meant that the Indian government's family-planning apparatus remained lethargic, although some individual states of the Indian federation—especially those in the southern region, which had remained untouched by the population controversy of the Emergency period—continued with their population-control programs. By February 1984, Indira Gandhi had felt sufficiently emboldened to start talking publicly once again about the great problem of overpopulation. Perhaps her self-confidence had been restored by the fact that the United Nations had earlier given her an award for her devotion to population issues. The United Nations was bitterly criticized by the far right in the United States for its selection of Indira Gandhi, and of the co-winner, the then Chinese minister of health, in sections of the American media. Werner Fornos—president of the Washington-based Population Institute—recalls that Mrs. Gandhi told participants at the Asian Forum of Parliamentarians on Population and Development in New Delhi that month that India was strongly committed to family planning and that her country did not lack the motivation, but only the financial capability, to decrease substantially its high rate of annual population growth.

"We will not be able to sustain the well-being of our population much longer without a major breakthrough in population control," Indira Gandhi told her audience, which had seemingly been ignorant of the fact that India had never lacked for resources for her myriad family-planning programs. Between the Indian government's own investment in population programs, and foreign assistance, more than $200 million was available each year for such projects; while India, of course, could use more money for population control, the amount that was available was by no means inadequate. In that speech to the Asian parliamentarians, Mrs. Gandhi went on to talk about the general population challenges facing the continent. "All over Asia the need to limit our population so that the impact of development can reach all sections is widely recognized," she said. "But schemes for smaller families can succeed only when

the general masses of the people participate actively in their implementation. Unfortunately, we do not have much time."

I cite this speech because Indira Gandhi spoke eloquently about the
general problem of overpopulation facing not only Asia but also the
entire Third World. I also cite her speech because Rajiv Gandhi had
talked ambitiously of doubling India's annual population expenditure to
some $500 million. But the fact remains that existing funds—both do-
mestic and foreign—cannot seem to be fully utilized for population projects. In the southern state of Karnataka, I was told recently by local
officials that nearly $100 million in money earmarked in their state for
population projects lay unused because an adequate infrastructure and
management to sustain good programs was not in place.

"Rapid expansion of population eroded the gains of development,"
Mrs. Gandhi said to the Asian parliamentarians assembled in New Delhi
in February 1984. "The burden falls on the poor and underprivileged,
increasing their problems and narrowing their range of choice. For many
of the affluent countries, prosperity itself worked as a contraceptive—but
we cannot leave things to be sorted out by such a long-drawn-out process
of fertility control. We just don't have the time. To achieve faster progress, we in Asia need a breakthrough in our population-control programs
in a limited time frame. The crucial stage is now, in the life cycle of the
present generation."

According to the World Health Organization (WHO), 150 million
children under the age of five in Third World countries were affected by
malnutrition in 1986 because of inadequate access to proper food; in
India, according to government estimates, nearly 40 percent of the population cannot afford to buy sufficient food to ensure adequate caloric and
nutritional intake.*

UN officials told Sanjay Gandhi that one of the dramatic consequences
of rapid population growth would be that between 1975 and the year
2000, a billion new jobs would have to be created to accommodate the
Third World's expanding labor force—more than what existed in the
entire industrialized world; in addition, job opportunities would have to
be created to satisfy some 400 million people who, according to the
United Nations, were already unemployed or underemployed in developing nations. And nowhere would the burden of providing for a growing
labor force be greater than in India.

Sanjay Gandhi frequently emphasized the following points, which were
drafted by the Washington-based Population Reference Bureau:

* *World Health Organization Annual Report,* 1988.

- Third World countries, which contained more than 75 percent of the global population of 5 billion, accounted for less than half of the world production of major food crops.
- The worldwide demand for food was expected to double by the year 2000 because of population growth in the Third World.
- The Third World's per capita food production of 260 kilograms in 1975 was only one-third of that of the industrialized states. A level of 180 kilograms—or around one pound of grain or cereal daily—is considered a subsistence threshold below which lies the malnutrition that stunts physical and mental growth. While North Americans and Europeans averaged a daily intake of 3,000 calories during the 1970s, the figure for almost sixty-five countries of the Third World actually declined to less than 2,100 calories daily during the same period; the average daily requirement is 2,400 calories. The average American consumed 3,658 calories per day; the average Indian took in barely 1,880 calories. Sanjay said that the annual consumption of pet food in France alone could adequately feed 12 million children in India!

The reductions in fertility are likely to have a major impact on the age structure of India's population. Like other Third World countries with moderate-to-high fertility, a relatively large percentage of India's population—more than 40 percent—is under fifteen years of age. The statistics work out as follows: In 1980, there were 267 million Indians under fifteen years of age; by 1991, this number would grow to 281 million if population-control goals are met. These Indians are yet to enter the child-bearing stage. Moreover, the number of job-seekers will keep increasing between now and the year 2000. In 1980, for instance, there were 380 million Indians between the ages of fifteen and sixty-four; by 2000, there will be more than 600 million Indians in this employable age group, an increase of almost 60 percent. By the year 2030, according to current projections, the labor force in India will have almost 900 million people, the size of the country's current population. Where are the jobs going to come from?

The possibility that India will succeed in dramatically reducing average family size to two children appears remote. In order to ensure that India's population does not surge beyond a billion by the year 2000, contraception prevalence must be extended to at least 60 percent of these married people. To put it another way, the number of couples using family-planning methods needs to rise by 144 percent, or from 27 million to 66 million between 1980 and 1990, and by 62 percent, or to 107 million between 1990 and 2000. Moreover, in order to properly educate the public about contraception and in order to ensure that the effective family-planning programs are in place in all of India's states, India will need to spend some $85 billion on family planning in the next fourteen years, according to the Population Institute, a development think tank in Washington. (India spent $141 million on population programs in 1980 and $275 million in 1985.)

Are the Indian authorities capable of extending family planning so dramatically? The present generation in India is far more receptive culturally as well as sociologically to the concept of population control than in most other states of the Third World. The government today need not worry much about religious or ethnic opposition to family planning. Even the Roman Catholic Church has not openly asked India's 12 million Catholics to protest against family planning—although, of course, the Church does not endorse artificial contraception, but supports "natural" family planning, which relies on the biological rhythm cycle of the female. There is no serious resistance from India's Hindus, who constitute some 80 percent of the population, nor from the country's Muslims.

If India does not act very soon, it may well be forced to adopt what many Americans believe are excessively rigid—and, to many Westerners, morally unacceptable—population-control policies that neighboring China has instituted. The Chinese government insists that there is no element of force or coercion in its program, under which the Chinese people are constitutionally required to keep family size to one child. But foreign reporters and writers have contended that abuses involving forced abortions and sterilizations are hardly uncommon in China, even though the government says it does not condone such violations of the law.

I do not think that India can afford to replicate the Chinese way of tackling overpopulation without seriously violating the issue of human rights and without undermining its painstakingly cultivated democratic system. That is why, I feel, any Indian prime minister has only to look over his shoulder toward Beijing to see a haunting, and troubling, scenario of what awaits his ancient land if his modernization programs do not give an urgent priority to population control now.

In March 1977, James Michaels, editor of *Forbes*, visited India. Almost alone among major Western editors, Michaels had publicly defended Indira Gandhi's imposition of the Emergency. Now he had come to India to observe the parliamentary elections that had been postponed by Indira since 1976.

"Thirty-two years had passed since I wheeled my bicycle through the crowds in Chandni Chowk on the morning after FDR's death," Michaels later wrote, recalling his stint in India as a correspondent for United Press during the 1940s.

447

Except for the grand old Imperial buildings and the still resplendent uniforms of the President's Guard, Paul Scott's India is gone. Delhi is no longer British and Mughal. It is all commerce and politics now, a sprawling industrial center as well as the capital. It is a Punjabi city now, its character transformed by the hundreds of thousands of Hindu and Sikh refugees who fled east after Pakistan was carved from India's flesh. I am dining at the home of old Indian friends. They have a visitor, another old friend who lives to the north in the hills above Almora. There he owns a small fruit orchard, employing about three dozen workers. The man from Almora is puzzled. All the polls, all the newspapers, are predicting that Indira Gandhi will win the general election, that her party will win in a landslide. The prime minister had been ruling under a State of Emergency which gave her government extraordinary powers to arrest, to censor, to punish, and to suspend civil liberties. By and large, these powers were used sparingly but there were certainly abuses. Indira's youngest son, Sanjay, had launched a powerful campaign to bring down India's birth rate. This was not a brutal dictatorship as we see it today in so-called Marxist-Leninist countries but neither was it the usual Indian state of live-and-let-live. India was flirting with totalitarianism. Just flirting, mind you. Stung by criticism of her use of the new powers Mrs. Gandhi had called the election, confident that the masses would be sufficiently pleased by her government's somewhat heavy-handed progress against crime, corruption and inflation that they would forgive the relatively minor infringements against personal liberty.

Which was why my friend from Almora was puzzled. "Everybody" thought Mrs. Gandhi would win. But the illiterate men who tended my friend's orchard told him privately that they intended to vote for the opposition. Why? Well, they said, they appreciated all Mrs. Gandhi had done for the country but they were disturbed that the police had come one recent night to a neighboring village and carted off the village schoolmaster, who had, apparently, been openly critical of Sanjay Gandhi's male sterilization campaign. My friends wondered: Could the polls and the experts be wrong? Could Mrs. Gandhi possibly lose? Lose she did and overwhelmingly. Indira Gandhi even lost her own seat in Parliament. Her party was swept from office. The experts were scarlet-faced. But would she accept defeat? Would she mount a coup? She went quietly from office. I later spoke to several fairly ordinary Indians. How did they feel about the election results? A significant number said the same thing: They had voted against her only to teach her a lesson; they did not want her to lose but they did not want her to win so strongly that it would go to her head and give and her son too free a hand.

So the 1977 elections showed clearly that India was no pushover for totalitarianism even when it was exercised in the name of the masses. The voters firmly rejected it. They were not about to follow anyone blindly, not even the tough daughter of Jawaharlal Nehru, hero of independence. There clearly would be no Khomeinis in India, no Castros, no Qaddafis. Indians had reacted to a power grab, no matter how moderate, pretty much as Western Europeans and Americans would. The opposition, now in power, made a terrible mess of things and Indira Gandhi was prime minister again in 1980. But she had learned a lesson: In her comeback period she ruled democratically, ruthless where she had to be, but always recognizing now the limitations to her ability to exercise power. In the end she was removed from power undemocratically—by traitors' bullets. Even this tragedy did not seriously damage democracy in India. After a brief outburst of brutality, the country regained its balance as surely as the United States did after the assassination of John Fitzgerald Kennedy. Mrs. Gandhi's successor, her older and sole surviving son, Rajiv, was confirmed overwhelmingly by the voters, and he, too, learned the limits of power in a democracy.

A strange kind of democracy you may say. One family has ruled for forty of the nearly 42 years since independence. Rajiv Gandhi succeeded his mother; Indira Gandhi, after a lapse of a couple of years succeeded her father, Jawaharlal Nehru, as prime minister; and Nehru reigned from independence until his death in 1964. Nehru's father, a wealthy Allahabad lawyer named Motilal Nehru, had been head of the nationalist party long before independence. And although Mohandas K. Gandhi, the Mahatma, had stirred and roused the masses to clamor for freedom, he never exercised real power, giving instead his blessing to Nehru. A royal family? Four generations of them. Maybe, but Westerners would do well to remember how close the United States came to making the Kennedys a royal family. We should remember, too, that even Nehru had to live with the constraints and frustrations that democracy and the rule of law imposes. *

The five years between 1975 and 1980 saw the rise, fall, and resurrection of Indira Gandhi. The first rise was through the assumption of dictatorial power. The second rise was through democratic power in 1980. It

---

* James W. Michaels, *From Mahatma Gandhi to Rajiv Gandhi*, pp. 16–19.

was almost like a Greek tragedy where hubris is followed by nemesis, and the redemption of suffering brings about a restoration. Actually, the years 1977 through 1980 saw Indira at her best. She was fighting three battles. One was against a government committed to destroying her politically. While her lawyers were fighting in the courts, she took the battle to the streets of India. The second battle was to win back the affection of the people. To do this, she had to counter a lot of opposition in her own party. And the third battle was with herself—whether to retire or fight on. She even refused several deals offered by the Janata Party. This period was a monument to her character, which was much greater in adversity than at any other time in her career. For the first and only time in her life, the Emergency clipped her political antennae. As Indira herself admitted later, she lost touch with her basic constituency—the poor and deprived masses. The disloyalties of many old comrades led her more and more to depend on Sanjay. In 1977 India saw for the first time a non-Congress government at the Center—and large numbers of Congress men abandoned their party. These included some of her closest associates, some of whom joined her opponents in an attempt to destroy Indira. The venality of Indian politics was exposed to its fullest—and Indira came through it looking much better than when she was in power. Character is far more visible in adversity than it is in prosperity, especially in politics.

While she was always a physically brave person, there was an emotional and psychological bravery that showed itself fully in those three difficult years. In the March 1977 elections, more than 200 million voters trekked to the polls in what was then the biggest exercise in adult franchise anywhere. Jayaprakash Narayan's Janata Party won 43 percent of the vote, and Indira's Congress obtained only 34 percent. For the first time since Independence, an Opposition party came into power. Morarji Desai, India's old adversary, became prime minister. Indira was indicted by a vengeful Janata Party, but despite being jailed for about a week, nothing much came of the charges. Sanjay Gandhi was also briefly interned, and Indira visited him in jail, urging him not to lose heart. "This, too, shall pass," she said to her son.

In defeat, many facets of Indira unfolded—she had time to engage in cultural activities. She wrote the text for a photo book on India. She read more than ever before. And she also had the time to talk more leisurely about the vagaries of life. Indira traveled overseas to Britain, at the invitation of the London-based industrialist Swraj Paul. The woman behind the mask of power was more evident now than at any other time. In those years, she was more Nehru's daughter in the fullest sense than at any other period of her life.

V

Beyond the Dynasty

20

Domestic Affairs

In the summer of 1979, Professor Ralph Buultjens went with Indira Gandhi on a political tour of the southern Indian state of Karnataka. She was out of office at the time, and had already started plotting to regain power. A passionate proponent of child-care and health programs, Mrs. Gandhi had invited Professor Buultjens to see for himself what she called "grass-roots India." To the dismay of her staff and the disarray of her campaign, she insisted on a long and dusty detour to visit a small orphanage which she had inaugurated a decade earlier. "These children have no votes," complained a political aide—encapsulating in this observation one of the primary reasons for child neglect in the Third World.*

At this child-care center, somewhere between Bangalore and Mysore, Mrs. Gandhi discussed what she termed "surrogate cannibalism." As infants cried and toddlers clutched at her colorful sari, Mrs. Gandhi said to Ralph Buultjens: "A large part of the world is overfed and on diets. In other places, thousands of infants die because they don't get any food. This is really a modern form of cannibalism because the overfed are indirectly eating these infants. What else can you call the selfish overconsumption of food that will sustain life if it is made available to dying children?"

At that time, Professor Buultjens thought this judgment rather severe. Now, as both the statistics of infant deaths and sales of diet products escalate, he wonders whether Mrs. Gandhi was correct. "Has not contem-

* Information provided by Professor Ralph Buultjens.

453

porary civilization evolved its own sophisticated mechanisms of cannibal-ism?" he asks. "Indira's concern for the fate of India's children was clear. These trips were not publicity stunts."* Throughout her political career, Indira Gandhi was always on the move. There was scarcely a week during which she was not out of Delhi. She always regarded these journeys as her conduit to the Indian masses. In many ways, she saw the power-broker elite of Delhi as an incestuous and self-serving circle whose viewpoints did not adequately reflect the conditions and attitudes of the bulk of India's people. Indira frequently made the point that only by being with the masses could you understand the masses—and the masses were not in Delhi. This approach made Indira probably the most domestically trav-eled leader that India has ever had. To be sure, these were not disinter-ested voyages of discovery. They brought her both publicity and visibility—but they also flowed from a genuine and almost matriarchal concern with "my people." Interestingly, on every one of these trips, Indira met first with local notables before she went out to be with the masses. That way, she was better briefed about parochial issues than any other prime minister of India.

But those who were in power following the 1977 elections saw in such trips—correctly, as it turned out—a renewed effort by Indira to reach out to the masses. The Janata Party, led by her old adversary Morarji Desai, was hounding Indira. She and her son Sanjay had already been briefly incarcerated. It was a humiliating time for Indira: The Congress Party, for the first time since Independence, now sat in the Opposition, and Indira Gandhi was not even a member of Parliament. Later, Indira would claim that the abuses attributed to her during the Emergency constituted Janata-inspired propaganda. But several judicial inquiries—including the Shah Commission—established that at least twenty-two political prisoners died in jail during the Emergency. George Fernandes, the Socialist leader, was tortured, as was his brother Lawrence. Snehlata Reddy, a pretty actress who was close to George Fernandes, was kept in such horrible conditions in jail that her asthma worsened and she died upon her release.[†] Sanjay Gandhi's minions showed such zeal in razing slums that even historic districts such as the Turkman Gate area in Old Delhi were demolished and residents—who were overwhelmingly Muslim—dispatched to live in new townships where they felt culturally alien. In other parts of North India, there were violent protests against Sanjay's population-control program. These incidents soon took on a

---

*Conversation with author, New York City, March 1991.
[†]See *The Shah Commission Report.*

mythology of their own, eventually contributing to Indira's defeat and downfall.

To this day, Indians debate why Indira decided to call the elections in March 1977. Nayantara Sahgal, the biographer and novelist, writes:

> The element of risk now seemed small, as far as a Congress win was concerned, for it had held the stage without competition. . . . During that period [of the Emergency] Mrs. Gandhi had disciplined the dissidents in her party through arrest or the threat of arrest. She had successfully introduced, and systematically pushed, the idea of dynastic rule, a thing she would have found difficult if not impossible to do in normal times. The Opposition was severely handicapped by nineteen months out of the public gaze, with no chance to make its views heard, while the government, with its monopoly of public meetings, demonstrations, and media control, had been able to keep up a steady barrage of accusations and condemnation in extreme language against it. Some Opposition leaders were crippled with illness in long confinement. . . . For the Opposition as a whole, the process of reassembling, collecting funds, and preparing for an election would be painful. The censored press—its independent editors dismissed or silenced—had daily assured Mrs. Gandhi of her popularity. It is certain she believed the election would be a formal affair renewing her mandate.
>
> There were other hopeful signs for a ruling party victory. The Emergency had benefitted by two good harvests when grain had been abundant and its price comparatively stable. With about 80 percent of the average Indian budget spent on food grains, inflation in the basic needs had been kept in check. High inflation in the West at this time had provided Indian exports with a noticeably improved market, and these had fetched better prices, adding substantially to India's foreign currency reserves, as had the government's belated measures against smuggling and tax evasion.[*]

Inder Malhotra, who had avidly followed Indira's career, says that she decided to hold the March 1977 elections because "she wanted to regain her credentials as a democratic leader which she had lost." He writes: "She was also concerned about her place in history. She did not want to be known to future generations as the leader who destroyed democracy in India, so lovingly nurtured by her own father. . . . she was prepared

---

[*] Sahgal, *Indira Gandhi: Her Road to Power*, pp. 176–77.

to lose the poll and power, if necessary, to bring democracy back."* In the election, the Congress secured 154 seats in Parliament, while the Janata coalition bagged 302 seats.

The trips that Indira Gandhi took to meet ordinary Indians became a kind of catharsis. During the first few months after her election defeat, Indira was given to spells of depression; occasionally she even cried in public. She was concerned about physical harm that might be done to Sanjay and to her. While she struggled with this despondency, the Janata government began to unravel. Coalitions rarely work in politics, and this first-time-ever Janata coalition in India seemed doomed from the start. Within four months, the price of major foods rose nearly 5 percent, and by the end of 1977 inflation had climbed to 11 percent. The Morarji Desai administration used up Indira Gandhi's unprecedented surplus of 18 million tons of food grain; and within twenty months, the Janata government had frittered away the $3 billion that it had inherited in foreign exchange reserves from Indira.† Just about a year after her defeat, Indira contested a parliamentary by-election in Karnataka's Chikmagalur constituency and won handsomely. She had launched herself on the road back to power.

Indira's return to power was facilitated by the discord within the Janata coalition. Morarji Desai had a falling out with his powerful home minister, Charan Singh. The latter had wanted to investigate Desai's son, Kanti, against whom all kinds of corruption charges were being leveled. Singh also bickered constantly with Jagjivan Ram, the Harijan leader, who served as Desai's defense minister. By the early summer of 1979, Desai had lost the backing of the Janata's left wing. Raj Narain—who had defeated Indira in the 1977 election—and George Fernandes resigned from Desai's cabinet. The defections were so heavy that the ruling party was eventually left without a working majority in Parliament. Morarji Desai resigned on July 19, 1979, on the eve of a no-confidence motion. President Neelam Sanjiva Reddy—who had succeeded the late Fakhruddin Ali Ahmed—then asked Charan Singh to form a government. The Singh government lasted just a few weeks, and President Reddy dissolved Parliament on August 22, 1979. He ordered new elections in January 1980.

"I could sense victory within our grasp," Indira told Professor Ralph

---

*Malhotra, *Indira Gandhi*, p. 192.
†From research by Professor Stanley A. Wolpert.

Buultjens, years later. "The Janata had made a mess of things, and I did not see how voters would bring them back into power."[*] Khushwant Singh, the author and historian, said: "The Janata people were clowns. They deserved their disgrace."[†] Indira's campaign slogan now was "Elect a government that works!" During the sixty-three-day campaign, Indira traveled 45,000 miles, visited 384 constituencies, and addressed more than 1,500 rallies.[‡] In January 1980, thirty-three months after her defeat, Indira Gandhi returned to power. "Everybody expected her to win," recalls Babulal Jain, a Delhi-based businessman, who was close to the Congress in those days. "People wanted her back. People wanted some stability."[§] Indira's Congress Party won 351 seats, a two-thirds majority in Parliament. The Janata Party obtained only thirty-one seats. Indira contested two constituencies: In Uttar Pradesh's Rae Bareilly, she won by 140,000 votes; in Andhra Pradesh's Medhak, she romped home by more than 219,000 votes over her opponent. Indira gave up her Rae Bareilly seat, and retained her Medhak constituency. In the Amethi constituency of Uttar Pradesh, Sanjay Gandhi also won handily. This constituency was to be inherited in 1981 by Rajiv Gandhi. Friends of Indira such as Professor Ralph Buultjens and Janki Ganju were convinced that Indira was grooming Sanjay to take over from her when the day came for her to pass the political baton of the Congress Party.

That day, of course, never arrived. On the morning of June 23, 1980, barely six months after the Congress's historic comeback to power, Sanjay Gandhi was killed. The thirty-three-year-old Sanjay was at the controls of a stunt plane that had been given to him as a gift by Dhirendra Brahmachari, the sinister swami who had weaseled his way into Indira's confidence.[**] There were suspicions that the American-made plane had been sabotaged—by the CIA, of course—but the fact was that Sanjay was a poor pilot who should never have been allowed to fly the sophisticated aerobatics plane. A few weeks before the tragedy, the director-general of civil aviation had said that Sanjay was violating safety regulations by flying the plane, and thus endangering not only his life but also those of others. But no one cautioned Sanjay about his love of flying, let alone

---

[*] Conversation recollected by Professor Ralph Buultjens to author.

[†] Conversation with author, New Delhi, January 1980.

[‡] Information provided by Professors Robert L. Hardgrave, Jr., and Stanley A. Kochanek.

[§] Conversation with author, New York City, May 1991.

[**] Indira, whose reliance on swamis and astrologers was noted earlier, had become highly superstitious by 1980. She summoned a dozen Hindu priests to her home at One Safdarjung Road to "purify" the residence.

asked him to stop flying the stunt plane. In India nobody dares to reproach those in power, and Sanjay was very much entrenched in power by now. When Sanjay Gandhi found out that the director-general had written this negative report, he arranged for the immediate removal of the official, Air Marshal J. Zaheer. The air marshal was replaced by his deputy, a meek man named G. R. Kathpalia, who agreed with Sanjay about everything.* Indira had given Sanjay free rein over her administration: It was Sanjay who ordered bureaucratic transfers, and who oversaw business licenses. As he had been during the Emergency, Sanjay Gandhi was again a much-feared man.

Indira Gandhi was shattered by her younger son's death. Only eighteen days earlier, Sanjay had been made general secretary of the All-India Congress Committee (AICC). His followers insisted on a huge state funeral for him, and she tamely acquiesced. Sanjay's body was cremated not far from the site of Jawaharlal Nehru's funeral ceremony. Dozens of statues of Sanjay were built across India, at taxpayers' expense. Schools, streets, and hospitals were named after him. Many of the new parliamentarians who had been elected under the Congress banner seemed especially distraught, and with reason. After all, their ticket to political glory was Sanjay. Of the 351 Congress parliamentarians, at least 234 had been personally selected by Sanjay, and of these some 150 were considered hard-core Sanjay followers. Most of them tended to be thuggish young men whose goals seemed only these: to serve Sanjay, and to make as much money as possible during their tenure in power. Those who knew Indira well—such as Professor Buultjens and Pupul Jayakar, the writer—say that she changed almost overnight after Sanjay's death. Mrs. Jayakar told Inder Malhotra that Indira's "face aged, the eyes became stark, the hair was pushed back carelessly, the footsteps heavy." In a letter to Pupul Jayakar, Indira wrote: "One can overcome hate, envy, greed and other such negative and self-destroying emotions. But sorrow is something else. It can be neither forgotten nor overcome. One has to learn to live with it, to absorb it into one's being, as a part of life."[†]

In 1984, not long after Indira's assassination, I visited Medhak to see for myself what her constituents had thought of her. I decided to assess the

---

*Kathpalia often accompanied Sanjay Gandhi to the general aviation airport where Sanjay would take off in his stunt plane. For a senior civil servant to be so obsequious was outrageous.
†Malhotra, *Indira Gandhi*, p. 223.

impact of Indira Gandhi's agricultural and rural policies. Medhak had been Mrs. Gandhi's last constituency. She was elected from there in 1980. For years she had contested parliamentary polls from the northern Indian state of Uttar Pradesh. But in 1980, she had moved to Medhak not only because it was considered a "safe seat" for her. She wanted to demonstrate that she was truly a national leader, that she could be elected from all parts of the country—that Indians anywhere would respond favorably to her. I was driven to Medhak by Pramila David. She was gracious enough to take time off from the Shilpa Clinic in Hyderabad, where she ran innovative family-planning programs for the poor. People who came to the clinic could also sign up for free vocational-training projects.

Dr. David was a legendary figure in Andhra Pradesh because she had helped thousands of destitute men and women in cities, towns, and villages to find jobs, and thus gain self-respect. She particularly assisted Harijans. India's Harijans constituted an important element of Indira's winning majorities over the years—and when the Harijans abandoned Indira in the March 1977 elections, she and her Congress Party lost. "The Harijans did not vote for Indira largely because of Sanjay Gandhi's slum-clearing projects," says Jagdish Aurangabadkar, a well-known Bombay photographer who hails from a Harijan background. "They felt that Indira was sacrificing their interests in the name of some vague campaign to streamline India's cities. But what are slums to outsiders are homes to people who live there."[*] During her years in the political wilderness, Indira vowed to win back the Harijans. She made a much-publicized visit to the remote hamlet of Belchi in Bihar, one of India's most backward—and violent—states. A number of Harijans had been butchered by upper-caste village people in Belchi, and Indira spoke emotionally about these outrages. In May 1980, two men were sentenced to death and fifteen others to life imprisonment in connection with the Belchi episode. In early 1981, after Indira had been in office for a year, she had to contend with violence in Gujarat state over the question of affirmative action. A student from an upper-class family had been denied admission to a medical college in Ahmedabad because the seat was reserved for a Harijan. More than 400 people were killed in protests. Harijans were attacked in Gujarat's cities; in turn, a militant group calling itself Dalit Panthers—"dalit" means downtrodden—terrorized upper-class Hindus in rural areas. Finally, Indira mollified Hindus by asking the state government to raise the stipend of medical students; she also authored a resolu-

[*] Conversation with author, Bombay, August 1989.

tion in Parliament reaffirming educational and employment quotas for Harijans and backward classes.*

"A shining secular image and a capacity to arouse hope and confidence in the minds of the minorities, the weak and the oppressed, had been among the more attractive qualities of Indira whether in power or out of it," says Inder Malhotra. This secularism was also echoed in both Sanjay and Rajiv Gandhi. There are more than 100 million of these Harijans in India today, an overwhelming number of them in southern states like Andhra Pradesh. Their numbers constitute a veritable nation by itself, and no national leader can afford to write off their numbers. The origins of untouchability lie in Hinduism's rigid and unrelenting caste system, according to historians like Romila Thapar.† This institutionalized intolerance, Thapar has said, was a result of the early Aryans' prejudice against the darker races they encountered during their conquest of northern India. The Chinese traveler Fa-Hsien, who came to India in the fifth century A.D., wrote that the persons who removed human excrement were considered untouchable by India's majority Hindus.‡

It was Mahatma Gandhi who started calling the untouchables Harijans, or "Children of God." As a young woman Indira had been exposed to the Mahatma's beliefs, and was deeply influenced by Gandhi's views on egalitarianism and a classless society. "The moment untouchability goes, the caste system itself will be purified," the Mahatma said. He invited hundreds of Harijans to accompany him during his travels around India. He ate with them. He took them along to political rallies, to temples, to the homes of Brahmans. And in the southern princely state of Travancore, Gandhi ran into resistance from the royal family and its Brahman allies in Travancore and virtually all of the Kerala region, of which Travancore was a part. So roughly did Travancore's royalty and Brahman hierarchy treat untouchables that they were required to carry bells to warn other pedestrians that they were coming. Whenever Hindus heard these bells, they scattered for cover. Beginning in late 1923, a campaign to aid the Harijans was launched in Vaikom, a community in Travancore. The campaign was led by a Tamil from the neighboring

---

*While Indira Gandhi successfully dealt with the question of affirmative action for minorities, at least one of her successors was not so fortunate. In late 1990, the government of Prime Minister V. P. Singh collapsed over the issue of affirmative action. Singh had revived an almost-forgotten report of the Mandal Commission, which called for accelerated action concerning more jobs and scholastic admissions for backward communities. Singh's commitment to the Commission's recommendation triggered widespread protests across India.
†Romila Thapar, *A History of India* (London: Perguin, 1966).
‡For a summary of Hindu castes, see page 192n.

Madras presidency, a man named E. V. Ramaswamy Naicker. Naicker, or EVR as he was widely known, agitated for better living conditions for the untouchables of Vaikom. Specifically, he wanted untouchables to be allowed to traverse the road in front of Vaikom's great Hindu temple. EVR's friend, the Maharaja of Travancore, became so upset over the agitation that he imprisoned Naicker. Mahatma Gandhi arrived in Vaikom to protest on behalf of the local untouchables. The maharaja's police put up barricades on the roads in front of the Hindu temple. Even Gandhi was not allowed access to the temple.

"My agitation here is nothing less than to rid Hinduism of its greatest blot," the Mahatma declared. "The curse of untouchability has disfigured Hinduism." He negotiated for months with the maharaja, who finally relented. Travancore's authorities now agreed to open up the roads on three sides of the temple to all people, including untouchables; the fourth side was barred to untouchables. It took another decade of agitation on Gandhi's part to ensure that Harijans could not only walk on the roads outside temples but also worship inside if they wished to. If Gandhi's efforts led to increased social acceptance of Harijans, it was the work of a man named Bhimrao Ramji Ambedkar that eventually resulted in positive economic and political gains for them. Ambedkar was a lawyer who had received his doctorate from Columbia University. In 1949 he helped draft India's constitution, which formally outlawed untouchability. He was also an untouchable. Ambedkar organized civic associations for the welfare of the Harijans. He influenced newspaper publishers to write editorials urging the end of discrimination against untouchables. Ambedkar rejected Hinduism, embraced Buddhism, and persuaded hundreds of thousands of Harijans to convert. He even formed the Republican Party of India to ensure that Harijans joined independent India's political mainstream.

Largely because of Ambedkar's work, the national government decreed that affirmative action be undertaken on behalf of Harijans. Special job slots were set aside for them in public-sector industries. Air India, the government-owned airline, was ordered to step up its hiring of Harijan stewards and stewardesses, a directive that caused considerable grumbling among the upper-class people who had traditionally joined the airline because of the glamour involved: Many of these non-Harijans felt that the new employees simply were not bright or beautiful enough.* Resistance to

* In a conversation with the author in June 1991, a senior Air India official was highly critical of employees from backward communities. They simply did not have class or couth, he said vehemently, and they had contributed to the decline in the airline's prestige. Unfortunately, his attitude toward Harijans and others is not the exception in contemporary India.

the emancipation of Harijans continued in many quarters. When Acharya Vinobha Bhave, a respected social activist and disciple of Mahatma Gandhi, tried to lead a group of Harijans into a Hindu temple in Deogarh, in Bihar State, Brahman priests physically attacked the frail Bhave. The incident shocked the nation. Prime Minister Nehru's administration immediately drafted a bill that made the practice of untouchability a criminal offense.

Discrimination against Harijans persists in contemporary India. Occasionally newspapers carry gory accounts of Harijans being beheaded in remote areas by high-caste Hindus, or the disfiguring of Harijan women. In Tamil Nadu and Andhra Pradesh, there have been incidents where entire rural neighborhoods of Harijans were set upon by Hindu hordes, who then burned down homes and killed residents. In some parts of the south, Harijans signed up with Muslim mullahs for conversion—out of frustration with the existing social order and on the assumption that the egalitarianism of Islam would somehow ensure a better economic life for them.* I do not know, however, whether changing one's faith in itself can bring about a change in one's social and economic status, or in the way others might perceive a person.

"Indira knew that India's social problems were those of the oppression of some groups by others," the social commentator Gerson da Cunha told me one day in Delhi. "Caste is probably the major factor in politics today—and Indira recognized that. She knew that by tending to the grievances of the dispossessed, she could win their votes. The backward classes, Harijans and others, responded to her. They did not doubt her sincerity—although, in truth, there was very little by way of affirmative action taken during the Indira years."†

It would be a very long time before the spirit of corrective legislation would be mirrored in broad social attitudes toward Harijans, Pramila David said to me as we drove toward Medhak in December 1985. The countryside seemed dry; it had not rained for months. Indeed, drought had affected twelve of Andhra's twenty-three districts, and the state's food production was expected to fall substantially short of the 1984–85 target of 1.25 million tonnes. Peanut, rice, sorghum, and millet yields

---

* The most publicized of these conversions took place in February 1981, when more than 1,000 Harijans in the village of Meenakshipuram in Tamil Nadu State became Muslims. This prompted rabid right-wing Hindu groups to launch campaigns to reconvert Harijans back to Hinduism.

† Interview with author, New Delhi, September 1990.

were not expected to equal the previous year's harvest. Many villages were running out of potable water. In the Telangana region of the state, villagers traditionally held an annual festival of flowers in honor of Bata-kamma, the local goddess of life. But, Dr. David told me, this year there had not even been enough water for the ritual bath given by priests to the goddess, who is supposed to usher in a year of abundant harvests. The lack of water was viewed by villagers as a bad omen. We arrived in a village called Brahmanpalli. We went to the home of a man named Krishna Reddy, whose family had once owned hundreds of acres of land here but whose property now had shrunk to eighty acres because of Andhra's land-ceiling regulations. Reddy was not home, but his Austra-lian-born wife, Joan, welcomed us to their ranch-style house. A group of local peasants had already assembled in anticipation of our visit (Pramila David had telephoned the Reddys the previous day). They sat on the stone floor of Joan Reddy's veranda, not exchanging a word with one another. The women sat separately from the men, at some distance.

I talked with Gajam Balaram, who belonged to the weaver community. He was a tall, thin man who wore a white dhoti, or sarong, a long white shirt, and thonged sandals. He had a cadaverous face, which appeared ghoulish because of white holy ash he had daubed on his forehead. He was extremely worried, Balaram said. The crops on his two-acre plot were failing because of the drought. Villagers did not have enough cash to spend on themselves, so his family's textile retail shop simply had no business these days. He had to abandon weaving because of competition from Hyderabad's textile mills. "Our life is no better than when I was a child," Balaram said in Telugu, which Pramila David translated for me. "In fact, my childhood was happier than the life I am able to give to my own children."

But had not this been Indira Gandhi's constituency, I asked. Surely she must have helped people here.

"Politicians!" Balaram said. "We can never believe any of their prom-ises. They say so much during election time, then they vanish." The acute need in the Brahmanpalli area, he said, was for better drinking water, for sewage pipes, and for a hospital. The 10,000 residents of the area had been clamoring for these for many years, Balaram said, but to no avail. "What good is it to us even if our representative was the prime minister of India?" said a man named Nandi Narasingrao. He had completed high school but could only find a job on a rice farm. He had recently gotten married, Narasingrao said, but now he was finding it difficult to feed his new bride. "What face do I have to show before my in-laws?" he said.

I asked a woman named Mutuah if Mrs. Gandhi was going to be missed in this area.

"Why should we miss her?" Mutuah, a Harijan, said. "Her death makes no difference to our daily lives. Our struggle to survive goes on regardless. Did Indira Gandhi truly care for us here?"

And it went on that way from village to village in Medhak. In Islampur, Paddalpalli, Topran—in community after community of mud and brick homes, dusty roads and dry, brown fields, I heard the same sentiments. The need was not only for improved health-care facilities and better schools; it was also for bank loans to develop farms and local businesses. The need was for jobs. The need was for someone to come and listen to these villagers, but Mrs. Gandhi had not been here for many months and now, of course, she was gone. Medhak was not her son's constituency, so it would be unlikely that this area would figure in Rajiv Gandhi's travel plans. For Indira Gandhi, India's rural poor were a valuable vote bank. She understood very well indeed that poor Indians worshiped her—she was Bharat Mata, Mother India, and often all she had to do was to just show up in rural localities for villagers to shower her with affection, even adoration. Her helicopters, her motorcades—all these glamorous trappings of powers simply dazzled the gullible peasants. By the time anyone bothered to analyze her speeches, there was no time to ask Indira questions for she had to move on to the next village for the next rally and the next address. Her charisma and her cunning always worked for her.

The casual visitor to India seldom gets to see how and where the majority of Indians live. Hyderabad and Bombay and Calcutta may seem congested, filthy, and overwhelming, but the country's cities and towns hold barely 30 percent of India's 900 million people. The rest of the population lives in 576,000 villages, fewer than half of which are electrified.

In Hyderabad I was urged by N. P. "Potla" Sen, a former chairman of Indian Airlines and of the Food Corporation of India, not to neglect traveling through India's countryside. Sen had worked closely with Indira Gandhi in promoting better food production.* India had a cultivated land area of nearly 150 million hectares, roughly the same as the United

---

* Potla Sen later joined the Commonwealth Secretariat in London as a top executive. After his assignment was over, he returned to India and became chairman of Clarion's, one of the country's largest advertising agencies. Sen remains a consultant to various government bodies.

States. But while only 4 million American families depended on agriculture for their livelihood, in India the figure was 70 million. There had been projected in the Western world an erroneous image of an India constantly hit by famine, Sen remarked. In reality, one of the most spectacular achievements of post-Independence India had been in agriculture, he said. Indeed, during the Africa famine of 1985–86, India was the biggest donor of food grain to the drought-ravaged continent, after the United States. When the British left the Subcontinent in 1947, annual food production in India was about 50 million tonnes. By December 1984, the figure had increased threefold.

The only serious famine since Independence occurred in the eastern state of Bihar in 1965 because of drought: That year, the national grain production fell to 76 million tonnes, a drop of 12 million tonnes from the previous year.* President Lyndon Johnson complied with a request from Indira Gandhi to make up this shortfall with an emergency shipment of 12 million tonnes of wheat. Widespread famine was averted, although hundreds of Biharis perished before the food grains could reach them. Now India maintained a buffer stock of 22 million tonnes, 7 million tonnes more than the minimum level established by the government, Sen said.

The danger to Indian grain production is less and less from drought because of new irrigation techniques; the danger is increasingly from rodents who often rule warehouses. It is estimated that more than 15 percent of India's annual grain production is destroyed by these rodents. And the danger now is that more and more of India's farmers are being driven toward the "poverty line" because of sharply increasing fertilizer costs and lagging grain prices. (A government-appointed Agricultural Prices Commission sets these prices on the basis of a complex and highly disputed formula.) In April 1973, Indira Gandhi decided to nationalize the wholesale trade in food grains. The government became the sole buyer of wheat and rice. Soon after the decision was announced, food stocks disappeared from shops and warehouses. There were widespread food riots. Eventually Indira rescinded her decision.

The leading spokesman for Indian farmers, Sharad Joshi, claims that despite impressive strides in agriculture, the Indian farmer is not a prosperous individual. He says that more than 25 percent of the farmers in the Punjab—considered India's showcase of agricultural development—now live below the poverty line. A study done by the Agricultural Prices Commission in 1979 showed that farmers owning up to 7.5 acres of land

---

* Data from Administrative Staff College, Hyderabad.

had neglible household savings each year; those owning between 7.5 acres and fifteen acres saved up to $250 annually; and those farmers owning between twenty-five acres and the national land ceiling of eighty acres per individual saved at the most $2,000 a year. Since 1979 fertilizer prices have risen by nearly 35 percent, so that the Indian farmer now pays the equivalent of almost seventy-five cents for a kilogram of nitrogenous fertilizer. Sharad Joshi says that while such costs have escalated, the wheat procurement price is now only $1.50 a kilogram—representing only a doubling since 1967. Farmers in India's most productive agricultural zone, the Punjab, have been especially hard hit. In the Punjab, which produces 60 percent of India's food grains, the consumption of fertilizers is particularly high—134 kilograms per acre, compared to the national average of 36 kilograms. Farmers are finding that they are no longer getting remunerative prices for their production. This has fueled a great deal of resentment. Joshi asked farmers to switch to non–food-grain production where they might obtain better revenues: forests for lumber, horticulture, and oilseeds. As a last resort, Joshi said, farmers could even leave some of their land fallow.

I found that farmers were increasingly being organized politically, a new development in post-Independence India. Their cry: We want a fairer shake. The farmers were first formally banded together in early 1984 in the southern state of Tamil Nadu under the aegis of the Bharatiya Kisan Union (BKU). So popular did the organization become—its name translates as the Union of Indian Farmers—that soon branches were started in other states. But it was not until Sharad Joshi emerged on the scene that Indian farmers got a truly national spokesman. Joshi, a slim, intense man, used to work for the United Nations. He had a brilliant academic career and joined India's elite civil service before being deputed to the United Nations. He decided, however, that he preferred being an activist to being a paper-pusher. He had always been concerned about such things as better health care for rural families and better economic development in the countryside. So he started a lobbying group called the Shetkari Sanghatana (which means Fraternity of Farmers). It was his nationwide agitation on behalf of farmers that forced the government to create a commission to investigate farmers' grievances. Increasingly, Indian politicians seem to take up cudgels on behalf of farmers. A coarse politician from the largely agricultural Haryana, a man named Devi Lal, rose to power in his state and later became deputy prime minister in the V. P. Singh government, on the platform of a better deal for farmers.*

* Devi Lal also helped to topple V. P. Singh in late 1990. In the May–June 1991

466

"What a farmer needs most is to be assured of his market and of his remunerative prices," Indira Gandhi once said. "As more and more small farmers grow salable products, they find that they are unable to get a reasonable return on their labor and investment. A small increase in output often causes a large drop in price. Conversely, small shortfalls in production lead to panic purchases by the well-to-do—thus disproportionately increasing prices to the consumer. Agricultural growth has to be coupled with stability of production, producer-oriented procurement, and consumer-oriented marketing."* Despite agriculture being India's biggest industry, it never became a major concern for Indira. She made speeches galore to and about farmers, but there was never a vigorous push to reform agriculture. Of course, Indira did encourage agricultural research: In 1966, after she became prime minister, Indira's government initiated a high-yielding-variety program in wheat, which led to the doubling of India's wheat production in six years. Although India achieved food self-sufficiency during Indira's time, malnutrition was still prevalent—not because there was no food in the market but because many Indians simply did not have the money in their pockets to buy that food. The central fact of Indian economic life remained the problem of poverty. And it is here that Indira failed to alleviate the wide misery of the masses.

Remuneration for food-grain production and the rising cost of fertilizers are not the only main issues that affect India's countryside. Land reform continues to be a controversial subject. As the British consolidated their colonial rule, India's traditionally self-sufficient village system began to disintegrate. In 1830 Sir Charles Metcalfe, one of the ablest British civil administrators of his time, wrote: "The village communities are little republics having nearly everything they want within themselves; and almost independent of foreign relations. They seem to last where nothing else lasts. This union of the village communities, each one forming a separate little state in itself, is in a high degree conducive to their happiness, and to the enjoyment of a great portion of freedom and independence."†

Within a few years, the village system about which Sir Charles wrote so astutely had changed dramatically. In *The Discovery of India*—probably the best literary history of the country—Jawaharlal Nehru writes: "The

---

elections, Devi Lal suffered a double humiliation when he lost races for both a Parliament seat and a seat in the Haryana State Assembly.
* From an address at the Fifteenth Regional Conference of the Food and Agricultural Organization (FAO), New Delhi, March 10, 1980.
† Burn, Sir Richard, ed., *Cambridge History of India* (Cambridge, U.K.: 1980).

destruction of village industries was a powerful blow to these communities. The balance between industry and agriculture was upset, the traditional division of labor was broken up, and numerous stray individuals could not be easily fitted into any group activity. A more direct blow came from the introduction of the landlord system, changing the whole conception of ownership of land."

"This conception had been one of communal ownership, not so much of the land as of the produce of the land," Nehru continues. "Possibly not fully appreciating this, but more probably taking the step deliberately for reasons of their own, the British governors—who themselves represented the English landlord class—introduced something resembling the English system in India."[*] The British at first appointed agents, known as revenue farmers, who collected land tax from peasants and delivered it to the government. These agents developed into landlords. The village community now was deprived of all control over the land and its produce, Nehru says, and "this led to the breakdown of the joint life and corporate character of the community; the co-operative system of services and functions began to disappear gradually." Big landowners were created by the British after their own English pattern, according to Nehru, chiefly because it was far easier to deal with a few individuals than with a vast peasantry. "The objective was to collect as much money in the shape of revenue, and as speedily, as possible," he writes. "It was also considered necessary to create a class whose interests were identified with the British." That class, the landlords, steadily gained in power and prestige. In Bengal they were called zamindars; elsewhere the word for them was malik. They exploited the peasantry. They accumulated vast fortunes. They were often cruel. But they were loyal to the British, and that was what mattered. During the British Raj, feudalism became a solid institution. The landlords did not wholeheartedly support the freedom movement—not the least because its leaders, such as Mahatma Gandhi and Nehru, were committed to instituting land reform once independence was achieved. The Congress Party had pledged to abolish absentee landlordism; the party's leaders assured peasants that they would secure for them permanency of tenureship and a fair share of the crop.

Krishan Bhatia noted in *The Ordeal of Nationhood* that in Nehru's home state of Uttar Pradesh, during the years that the Congress held limited local power before independence, it had enacted legislation for the abolition of the zamindari system. Bhatia, the former editor of *The Hindustan Times* and that Delhi newspaper's Washington correspondent

[*] Nehru, *The Discovery of India*.

468

for many years, wrote that the law protected the cultivator from the landlord's high-handedness by assuring him permanence of tenure as long as he paid a reasonable rent for the holding. The tiller was also given the option to own the land he worked on by paying moderate compensation to the absentee owner. Independence came, but years went by before there was any significant land and tenancy reform or meaningful land-ceiling legislation. In countries where there has been noteworthy land reform—such as Sri Lanka, Malaysia, and Thailand—the tiller was always given ownership so that he put in his best effort. It has been widely recognized that to maximize production you must make the tiller the owner of his land. But since the British took over India, the farmer has depended for his livelihood not just on the quality and quantity of his production but, more importantly, on the whims of the landed aristocracy. Moreover, antiquated social customs among India's peasants had resulted in fragmentation of land holdings where tillers had possession of property: Fathers would bequeath land to their sons, who would divide up the property into small and uneconomic plots. In the early years after independence, no sweeping land reforms were possible for a variety of reasons: Land records were poorly maintained, deeds were fudged, and it was difficult to accurately establish ownership; there was considerable absentee landlordship; there were fraudulent practices such as "gifting" land to peasants who were in truth the landlords' serfs. Landlords developed cozy relationships with India's new rulers; they started contributing heavily to the ruling Congress Party. Indira Gandhi did little to discourage such relationships when she came to power: Wealthy landlords, after all, could contribute generously to the coffers of her Congress Party.

Krishan Bhatia writes: "Before 1947 the Congress Party was a mass movement and not the Establishment. Its sense of social justice was strong and its concern for the underprivileged in the rural areas genuine. The landlords then stood by the British government."* The dividing line disappeared after independence, when the landlords joined hands with the Congress chieftains. For almost a decade after Independence, there was not even a new land-ceiling law in many Indian states. Land reform was always a subject to be handled by the state governments, unlike foreign affairs or defense or telecommunications, which were the prerogatives of the central government. It was only in 1957 that relevant legislation came into being in these states, but it was so lenient toward landlords that tenants and tillers actually suffered under its terms. Landlords were now allowed to select between thirty acres in some states and 200 acres

---

*Krishan Bhatia, *The Ordeal of Nationhood* (New York: Atheneum, 1971), p. 246.

in other states for personal cultivation; they could also parcel out property to family members. As a result, what was meant to be reform legislation resulted in a situation in which landlords actually could legalize large holdings in their own names and in the names of relatives; the landlord was also permitted to throw out existing tenants from the portions of his property he had chosen for "self-cultivation."

"Instead of bringing greater security to the real cultivators of land, the reforms only added to the numbers of landless peasants and sharecroppers," Krishan Bhatia said in his critically praised book. "Most state governments conveniently looked the other way while this process was occuring." By 1971, nationwide concern mounted over the question of land reform. In many states, absentee landlords controlled large chunks of land; their tenant-farmers languished. Regional newspapers, particularly those published in vernacular languages, highlighted abuses in areas such as eastern Uttar Pradesh and Bihar.

Even Indira Gandhi, who seldom believed anything that appeared in the media, was forced to acknowledge that landlords were exploiting the peasantry in some parts of India. Mrs. Gandhi had, by 1971, consolidated her personal authority within the Congress Party. She was aware that there was little a national government could do to push through land reforms; but since her Congress Party also controlled many of India's states, the prime minister could apply pressure on her local representatives. She did so in an imaginative manner. She issued the new rallying cry, "*Garibi hatao!*" The prime minister's public relations campaign glossed over the fact that the Congress Party's economic policies had exacerbated poverty since Independence; these policies had promoted the development of heavy industries at the expense of light and consumer-oriented industries, which create more jobs. With the exception of a much-publicized dam or hydroelectric project here and there, or some irrigation scheme, the Congress had also generally neglected rural economic development. Mrs. Gandhi's "*Garibi hatao!*" call could be seen as an indictment of her own policies, and, indeed, some of the prime minister's political opponents as well as some figures in the intellectual community were skeptical. But it was not taken that way by ordinary Indians. They were thrilled at this new theme the prime minister was sounding.

Implicit in the "*Garibi hatao!*" call was a promise of further land reform. With great fanfare, Mrs. Gandhi launched in 1974 India's fifth five-year plan. It envisioned the expenditure of $10 billion by 1979 on agriculture projects. The assumption seemed to be that if agriculture was formally highlighted in the government's economic program, then things like land reform would follow. India's five-year plans set production targets; they are also a statement of the government's broad economic and social policies. The documents are mostly unreadable. Some states acted on land reform; some states ignored the subject altogether. You can still visit regions like Bihar and come across landlords who control 200-acre properties. These landlords tend to be major contributors to political parties, and therefore get special dispensation when the politicians whom they support come to power. Indira Gandhi especially sought the support of such landlords in big farming states like Uttar Pradesh and Maharashtra.

One afternoon I met a farmer named Shivram Ghate outside of Lonavla, a town about ninety miles from Bombay. Lonavla is situated in the hills of the Sahyadri Range that hug the western coast of India; many affluent Bombayites have weekend homes here. The train ride to Lonavla is quite pleasant, with the route taking the traveler through two dozen tunnels and over scores of trestles. The motorist also finds the journey delightful because the two-lane highway from the coast winds through forests and valleys. My parents long ago had bought a small bungalow here, and as a child I would enjoy spending holidays in the cool heights of Lonavla. My memories of the place were of country roads cutting through verdant fields, and of hills across which ran thick woods that seemed inviting, not intimidating. I was never much of an explorer of woods, but my father often took me for long walks. We would stop and talk to peasants who chopped firewood, and we would occasionally visit local farms where maize and rice were cultivated. They were happy days. When I visited Lonavla this time, it was an altogether different place. I had not been here for more than a decade, largely because my trips to India from New York were always hurried. I was truly startled by the changes that had occurred in the intervening decade. Gone were the quiet streets of a small town; today's Lonavla had become an urban metropolis, a chaotic city of mushrooming housing developments, roads through which lurched fume-belching trucks and cars. There were rivers of people everywhere. Beggars thronged street corners; even the quaint railway station was filled with urchins who clutched travelers' sleeves and demanded money.

Perhaps the most startling change was how denuded of forests and greenery the whole place now seemed. Beyond the edge of the urban sprawl, during a walk through what remained of the countryside, I encountered Shivram Ghate, the farmer. He was furrowing the soil with a tractor. Ghate was a small, sinewy man, of about fifty; his skin was tanned deeply; his face was lean, and his teeth stained from a lifetime of chewing tobacco and paan, the betel leaf favored by Indians. Ghate wore a dhoti and a loose chemise; Hindi music played from a small cassette recorder that he had placed in a compartment below the dashboard of the tractor. Ghate seemed like a typical farmer from the area. He told me that his income was about 10,000 rupees a year—the equivalent then of about $500—and that he had inherited his acre of land from his father. I said that his income appeared much higher than that of most local farmers, but Ghate pointed out that the amount was considerably less than the average annual income of a clerical worker in the area. Because of rising costs of fertilizers, seeds, and farm equipment, he was getting to keep less and less of his income each year, Ghate said. Fortunately, he added, his three sons were grown up and worked as factory hands in Lonavla; they supplemented his income.

What was his most pressing worry other than inflation?

"Water," Ghate said in Marathi, the local language. "What farmers could once use freely now is channeled to these new houses that are rising here." It was a complaint one hears from farmers all over India. Because of the seasonal nature of India's rainfall, even areas of high rainfall have problems of water supply. Although the country has abundant resources in its river systems and groundwater supplies, these resources are likely to remain constant while demand increases with population growth, industrial expansion, and continued urbanization. The World Bank estimates that 80 percent of India's 562,000 villages are without safe and clean water supply, and only 50 percent of the country's urban population has ready access to potable water. Up until recently, the Bank notes, Indian water development has involved a disjointed, uncoordinated pursuit of several different goals by the central and state governments: development of industrial and municipal water-supply systems; hydroelectric power; flood control; irrigation; and water quality control. Pollution of water resources continues to be a major problem as well: Several British television documentaries in recent months have shown how the mighty Ganges River has been polluted heavily because of industrial and other wastes dumped into it in places such as the holy city of Benaras.* When farmers such as Shivram Ghate

---

* A massive cleanup program of the Ganges has been initiated, involving local and international agencies. But this is certainly going to be a daunting and long-term task. Indeed, says the World Bank, almost 80 percent of India's rivers are said to be polluted by sewage and industrial and agricultural wastes. In recognition of all this, Rajiv Gandhi's administration announced in September 1987 that it was initiating a "National Water Policy" to harmonize central and state government programs. Already, however, various experts have voiced doubts about the capacity of the national government to implement the policy.

talk about water problems, they usually also allude to wider problems having to do with land use and soil erosion. India is about two-fifths the size of the continental United States; about 70 percent of the country either has short crop growing seasons—less than 179 days—or inadequate growing seasons, or dry spells that generally last almost twelve months. Poor biomass cover, caused by long dry seasons that are followed by intense monsoon rains lasting two to four months, often cause severe soil erosion. This is exacerbated by poor farming practices. Moreover, says the Hyderabad-based Center for Energy, Environment and Technology, about a quarter of the 65 million hectares under irrigation suffer from waterlogging or salinization. *

I remarked to Shivram Ghate about the changes I had seen in the local natural scenery. Lonavla was no longer bucolic. "What can I tell you?" he said, shrugging. "Everybody wants to chop away our trees for fuel. Our local government people say we must use efficient electric stoves for cooking—but then the power supply here is unreliable. So people prefer to rely on their fuel wood." It is not just in Lonavla that India's forest cover is being depleted at an alarming rate. This is happening virtually everywhere in the country—even in the foothills of the great Himalayas. The reasons? Rapid population growth, lack of fuel for domestic cooking needs, and intensive cattle grazing in forest.† I asked Ghate about the government's much touted "social forestry" projects. He was not familiar with them, the farmer said. I explained that these projects—supported by various international donors, such as Britain, Canada, and Sweden—encourage farmers to plant trees on their own land;

---

* World Bank officials say that "wastelands" in India are increasing at an alarming rate. "Wastelands" are defined as unproductive land or areas producing crops substantially below their potential. More than 45 percent of India's potentially productive land area of 266 million hectares is now categorized as wastelands, with the figure edging upward. Why this increase in wastelands? Because of the burgeoning demand for fodder and fuelwood, overgrazing, lack of natural regeneration of land, soil erosion, salinity, and desertification. Indians often point to the wastelands of the Middle East or the Sahara as dramatic examples of how nature and man combine to alter the environment, transforming more and more areas into desert. But the process has intensified in India as well.

† India has only about 0.33 percent of the world's forests, but it has 16 percent of the world's population, 25 percent of the global cattle population, 50 percent of the buffalo population, and 20 percent of the globe's goats. While government statistics assert that India's total forest cover is more than 74 million hectares, surveys by international authorities suggest that the actual figure is half that amount. The World Bank says that most of the fuel-wood extraction in rural areas is illegal or unrecorded. And the problem with illegal chopping of trees is that no trees are planted to replace those that are destroyed. Such activity results in loss of wildlife habitats and in soil erosion, siltation, floods, and droughts.

villagers are urged to develop community woodlands and also to rehabilitate denuded forest. Ghate asked me how this program was working out,
and I said that I did not know. It was perhaps too early to tell, I said.
"But at least a beginning seems to have been made," the farmer said,
smiling, as he restarted his tractor. "In India, however, we start a lot of
things and often never carry on."

As I left him, it occurred to me that he could have been speaking
about Indira Gandhi's own oft-declared commitment to preserving the
environment and protecting India's natural resources. The prime minister
supported the notion of India's Ministry of Environment and Forest, and
pushed through several pieces of legislation calling for tough action
against those who damage the environment. But India is a vast country
and its governmental machinery simply cannot be the sole taskmaster.
In the final analysis, the cause of environmental protection must be
sustained by grass-roots efforts of community leaders, businessmen, and
peasants themselves. The cause calls for massive national cooperation,
not from the top down but the bottom up. And I am not so sure that
Indians are often inclined to galvanize themselves for causes whose re-
wards are not easily forthcoming.

During her years as prime minister, Indira Gandhi gathered around her
men and women who were involved in a number of pressing social issues
such as population and child welfare. One of these people was Rajni
Patel, a prominent Bombay lawyer, who headed the local unit of the
Congress Party. He and his wife, Bakul, undertook to rehabilitate a
huge slum in Bombay called Dharavi. After Indira's death, I traveled to
Dharavi at the invitation of Bakul Patel, who wanted me to tour one of
her projects involving the health care and education of poor children.
Mrs. Patel wanted to take me to Dharavi to see for myself one of the
world's fastest growing communities—a slum thickening at the rate of
nearly a thousand people a week. Already, the Dharavi population had
risen beyond 2 million, or nearly a fourth of the total number of people
who lived in Bombay, India's great commercial city. Dharavi now enjoyed
the dubious distinction of being the world's biggest slum. There were
dilapidated shanties and crumbling huts as far as I could see; there was
little open space, not much greenery. Many of the narrow streets were
unpaved, and even a bicycle could kick up a tornado of dust. Ditches
served as sewer canals. The stench of excrement was strong. Flies and
stray cats fought over mounds of refuse. Children, seeking relief from the
intense heat, played in ponds of muddy water. Here and there television

antennae shot up from huts. I could see a couple of shacks that served as video parlors, with garish movie posters advertising the entertainment. An occasional new structure—built out of bricks, rather than corrugated sheets which constituted the walls of many Dharavi homes—attested to the philanthropy of private donors, such as Mrs. Patel, who had pooled their resources and started kindergarten classes and health-care clinics. In one such building, children of preschool age were being read stories from India's great epic, the *Mahabharata*. I wondered whether the children understood what was being read to them, but the woman who was doing the reading in Marathi—her badge identified her as Sandhya Mangnekar—was so emotive and expressive that the children were rapt. Outside this building was a small playground, where swings and jungle-gym sets had been neatly arranged. Beyond the playground, of course, were more squat, ugly shanties.

What this slum really needed, I thought as I toured Dharavi, was to be demolished and replaced by modern housing. But I knew that, in an India of 900 million overwhelmingly poor people, such a possibility was nonexistent. And even if there were resources and the political will to replace India's slums, just how would you level a place such as Dharavi, which by itself contained more people than most Western cities? Where would you move the residents while the new housing was being constructed? The social tensions caused by such displacement would be frightening. "The conventional norms of urban renewal, those so fashionable in some American cities, may not apply to India," Indira Gandhi once said to Bakul Patel. "We are not in a position to level these slums. I am quite mindful of what happened during the Emergency."[*] She was referring to the Turkman Gate episode in Old Delhi, where associates of Sanjay Gandhi had razed an old Muslim community and forced thousands of residents to move to a new housing colony where they had problems adjusting.

Bakul Patel and I came across an especially sad sight in Dharavi. A local couple—Shantabai Kamblay and her husband, Gangaram—were crouched over their infant son. The baby's tiny body, swathed in a white sheet, had been placed on the mud floor of the Kamblays' home. Several relatives has assembled in the one-room shanty, which stood in a small dusty plot in Dharavi. Smoke from incense sticks swirled in the room; muted sunlight squeezed in through a small window whose shutters hung from rusty hinges. In this dim interior, the baby's body seemed to float

[*] Conversation quoted by Bakul Patel in an interview with author, Bombay, September 1990.

eerily just above the floor. The child was barely two months old, and he had just died. A Brahman priest from a neighborhood Hindu temple was chanting Sanskrit hymns, beseeching the deities to spare the deceased's atma, or soul, from another rebirth.

Soon there would be a funeral, a brief cremation ceremony in a field about a mile away. Few would be present other than the parents and relatives. Gangaram Kamblay, a thin man with a pockmarked, cadaverous face, had taken the morning off from his job as a laborer with a construction company in Bombay. After the funeral, he would return home for a ritual bath, as was required under Hindu custom. Shantabai had already collected water in metal pails from the community tap, since few homes in Dharavi had plumbing or running water. As in much of the Third World, women here are the hewers of wood and drawers of water. Kamblay would then board a bus to a commuter train station. The journey to his job would take two hours. At the end of this day, Kamblay's foreman would deduct twenty rupees, then the equivalent of about two dollars, from his daily salary of twenty-eight rupees, because Kamblay would miss more than half a day's work and because he had not called in to say that he would be absent; it did not count, of course, that there was not a telephone within miles of his home in Dharavi, nor did it matter that there wasn't a phone at the excavated site where he'd been assigned by his employer.

Shantabai Kamblay would not go to work at all on this day. Her job, as a cleaning woman in a municipal building about four miles from her home, fetched her some five rupees a day. She ordinarily walked to work. But on this cursed day she would stay at home to comfort her three surviving children and nurse her private grief over yet another death in the family. In the last seven years, the Kamblays had lost four children, each within the first year of birth. This child had died of respiratory complications. Or was it diphtheria? Gangaram Kamblay's uncle, a toothless old man who occasionally dabbled in the occult, said that evil spirits had paid the household a visit. Nobody ventured to challenge the uncle. The earlier deaths had resulted from diphtheria and diarrheal infections. The parents said that the child had suddenly developed a raging fever, that he did not respond to icepacks applied on the forehead and some herbal potions and balm, and that, within a day, he simply stopped breathing. A physician was sent for, but he arrived too late. There was, of course, nothing that the doctor could do, and there was no point in a postmortem. There was not even time for him to relay more than a word or two of sympathy to the bereaved parents. The doctor, an earnest young man who had recently graduated from medical school and was assigned to perform a year of community service in Dharavi and other slums near Bombay, had to move on to nearby homes.

"*Amchay mool gelay, amchay kharab bhagya ahay,*" Shantabai wailed in Marathi. "Our child has died, this is our bad fate."

I did not know what to say to the woman; she seemed inconsolable. The death of a child is a shattering event, whether the child is one's firstborn or twelfth. I had not planned on being present to bear witness to Shantabai's particular fate. It was sheer chance that led me to the Kamblay household. Shantabai Kamblay's "bad fate" was one the thirty-year-old woman shared that day with 2,500 other mothers all across India, and with 40,000 mothers all over the Third World. For 2,500 children die every day in India—the same number as all men, women, and children who died when poisonous fumes from a Union Carbide fertilizer plant smothered Bhopal in 1985. * Most of the victims lived in the shadow of the fertilizer plant in slums and squatter settlements.†

"In a big country like India, it's often taken for granted that the poor will always live in poverty," Bakul Patel said to me, as we drove out of Dharavi that morning. "How many of us stop and think about what 'poverty' really means to those who are actually in it? Poverty has many components—not having enough to eat, not having enough clothes or decent housing. For fathers and mothers it means not being able to care for your children properly. And for children it means having little hope of any improvement in their lives. Poverty also means, as you have seen in Dharavi, disease, death and sorrow."

Disease, death, and sorrow—the theme song of the Third World. Not far from Dharavi are modern factories, four-lane highways on which cruised sleek automobiles, and an airport where huge commercial jets

---

* United Nations Children's Fund (UNICEF).

† United Nations Population Fund, New York. All across India and the Third World, there are scores of such urban slums. The World Bank estimates that there are perhaps 1.2 billion people who live in extremely poor and unhealthy housing in Third World countries; of these, some 150 million sleep in the open. In the next twelve years, the Third World's squatter population is expected to swell by almost another billion. Back in 1950, urban dwellers in Third World areas numbered just under 300 million compared to 225 million in Europe. To put it another way, the growth rates of slums and squatter settlements in the Third World are at least twice the rate of overall urban growth in developing countries. According to Habitat, a United Nations agency, Third World cities continue to grow at a rate of more than 3.5 percent annually, or about 50 million people. By the year 2000, these cities will be expanding by some 80 million people a year, or more than 215,000 people a day. Africa's urban population is expected to rise by 440 percent between 1985 and 2025. By the year 2025, almost two-thirds of the Third World's population will be urban.

landed daily. The contrasts of modern India always seem startling to me. Since 1947 India has become the world's tenth biggest industrial power; the world's largest democracy, with 900 million people who enjoyed regular free elections; and a country that produces its own jet fighters, cars, locomotives, computers, and satellites. It even exports food grains to needy countries in Africa. And yet India could not eradicate its own urban poverty. "In India, we should like health services to go out to the home, instead of larger numbers of people gravitating toward centralized hospitals," Indira Gandhi once told Bakul Patel. "Services must begin where people are, and where problems arise."* Despite industrial prosperity and overall economic growth, more than 30 percent of the Third World population afflicted by high infant mortality and childhood disability lives in India.† Why could India not eradicate its own urban poverty or take proper care of its children?

"A lack of political will and commitment," said Bakul Patel. "That may seem to you a simplistic answer. But it's really as simple as that. Our politicians and government leaders talk about national defense and national economic growth and about nonalignment. But no one gives a damn for our poor children. The neglect of children will continue until children are made a hot political issue. That's when our politicians will wake up—because political issues translate into votes. And votes are what politicians seek, don't they? Indira Gandhi was no exception. She may have proclaimed '*Garibi hatao!*' but poverty is still with us."

Bakul Patel said that, despite Indira Gandhi's numerous promises there was no comprehensive national legislation to protect the rights of children in India. Child labor in India was no longer only a problem in traditionally agrarian areas. One had only to look into wealthy and even

---

*Quoted by Bakul Patel in a conversation with author, Bombay, September 1991.
†Habitat says that countries would have to double or even triple their shelter, infrastructure, and service capabilities just to maintain the status quo. The growth of urban populations has outpaced the growth of adequate employment and of proper government services to sustain urban centers. According to the United Nations Population Fund, some 40 percent of the populations of Nairobi, Lima, Manila, and San Salvador live in slum communities. One slum dweller in three had no access to clean water in 1983, and two out of three had no adequate sanitation facilities. Bombay attracts some 12,000 migrants every day from rural regions in search of jobs that simply aren't there. They bring their children with them—and they beget more children. According to the United Nations, 18 million babies are born in India every year—more than in the whole of Latin America, and almost as many as in Africa. And it is in slum communities such as Bombay's Dharavi that infant mortality rates are staggering. Since the environment is so devoid of hygienic living conditions, even children who survive often grow up into unhealthy adults.

middle-class homes to see how many children were employed as servants. What was needed desperately was a renewed politically directed national campaign to ensure that India's children got proper food, health care, and education. Not that India had stood still, of course. Since Independence India had eliminated smallpox; established 11,500 primary health care centers in India's states; trained 250,000 government paramedics and some 300,000 private sector midwives and nurses; and reduced India's annual mortality rate from twenty-seven per thousand to twelve.[*] Bakul Patel said she did not mean to scoff at this progress. Rather, she said, much more could have been done if federal and state politicians had worked more energetically and cooperatively on health care and child welfare issues. If only a fraction of the money that Indira and the Congress Party raised from wealthy Indian industrialists for political campaigns had been channeled into slum rehabilitation projects, millions of poor people would have been much better off.

But what about private, voluntary organizations such as hers? Couldn't their role be expanded?

"These organizations can barely touch the fringes of the problem," Mrs. Patel said. "We simply don't have enough financial resources. In any Third World country, there is no substitute for grass-roots programs run by local people themselves. Government can only do so much—what it can do, however, is to provide the money and political commitment that galvanize grass-roots community programs. And in India, it is especially important that our authorities fuel the 'fires' that are already being lit by local social workers in thousands upon thousands of poor communities. I cannot tell you how important such encouragement is—our constituency is so large that, at best, we of the private sector can only do a bit here and a bit there."

It seemed to me that, notwithstanding Bakul Patel's pessimism, her "bit here and a bit there" was still quite effective. These efforts, however minuscule when measured against the awesome scale of India's poverty, at least offered some tangible hope to overcome India's horrors. Mrs. Patel's involvement with child welfare and maternal care dated back more than two decades, when she married a man named Rajni Patel. He was one of India's best-known criminal lawyers and social activists, and a confidant of Jawaharlal Nehru and Indira Gandhi. It was her husband's passion for social service that influenced Bakul Patel; in fact, it was her husband who first brought Mrs. Patel to the slums of Dharavi. Rajni Patel died a few years ago, but Bakul Patel—who makes her living as a

[*]United Nations Population Fund, New York.

479

management consultant—continues to give much of her time and her own funds to slum improvement in Dharavi and other areas. Indira Gandhi was often moved by the plight of poor women and children, and Bakul Patel told me of several instances when tears came to Indira's eyes as she met with slum dwellers who pleaded with her for help and succor.

Later that morning we visited Mrs. Patel's nearby Harinagar Center. It was situated in a community called Jogeshwari, another sprawling suburb of Bombay. To reach the center, we drove through a maze of narrow lanes that were bordered by huts. Tall coconut trees swayed over this community, looking like sentinels. We reached a small bungalow which housed the Harinagar Center. The six-room edifice was surrounded on all four sides by a garden in which grew roses, daffodils, and tomatoes. The staff was clearly delighted by Mrs. Patel's unannounced visit, and one woman quickly fashioned a garland of marigolds and draped it around Bakul's neck in a form of traditional greeting.

We had come at a busy time. In one room, a dozen girls—who seemed between ten and fourteen years old—were being taught sewing. Their teacher was a woman named Ayesha Islam, twenty-five years old, who, even as she supervised the class, was nursing her own one-year-old daughter, Shebana.

What made her want to teach?

Her salary—the equivalent of about ten dollars a month—wasn't what brought her to the Harinagar Center. Ayesha told me that the income of her husband, Mohammed Islam, was enough to support her family, which also consisted of three other children. Mohammed was a taxi driver; in fact, said Ayesha, he owned two taxis and leased out one to a cousin. She herself owned a small seamstress business in a nearby neighborhood.

"I felt that I should teach girls from my community to do something with their lives," Ayesha Islam said, speaking in Hindi. "When they grow up and get married, they shouldn't have to depend on their husbands. Sewing is something they can do in their own homes, something that can bring them money. Remember that all of these girls come from poor families. Their parents try and marry them off at an early age because they don't want burdens. Then these girls become beasts of burden in their husbands' households. Why should any girl have to go through life like that? So I teach these girls to be able to stand on their own two feet."

A progressive view indeed, especially one coming from a Muslim woman who was herself raised in an orthodox home and married off when she was only fourteen years old. Her attitude toward education was one

I'd heard in dozens of Third World communities, reflecting a realization that literacy was a vital component of development. According to the World Bank, the numbers of children enrolled in primary and secondary schools in the Third World grew from 144 million in 1960 to 700 million in 1985. In contrast, the figures for Europe during this same period went from 100 to 123 million. The number of teachers in the Third World had risen in this period from 4.7 million to 26 million.*

In an adjoining room in the Harinagar Center, Meena Laxman Naik, a pretty eighteen-year-old nurse, was offering a course on health and hygiene. Her "class" consisted of local mothers, some of whom had brought their infants. Miss Naik was discussing such things as the importance of boiling drinking water. Hanging on the walls were posters about vaccination, monitoring the growth of children, and the virtues of reading. These were in Hindi, Marathi, and English. She offered her course once a week.

Supervising the Harinagar Center was a sprightly twenty-five-year-old woman named Vanita Patil. Miss Patil, it turned out, was not even a resident of Jogeshwari. She commuted daily from a distant neighborhood called Worli; the ride, which involved taking two buses, meant a ninety-minute commute each way. Her father was a schoolteacher, and he had greatly influenced her, Vanita Patil told me. She said that the Harinagar Center accommodated nearly 2,000 women and girls every year. In addition to the obvious—teaching participants about child care and hygiene, and preparing them for new vocations—there was something else that the Center achieved. What was that? "Communal harmony," Miss Patil, a Hindu, said, pointing out that the Center's students were both Hindus and Muslims; there were even some Christians. She was alluding to the fact that in recent years there had been some violent confrontations between multiethnic Bombay's Hindus and Muslims, mostly over petty politicians. These confrontations had especially upset Indira Gandhi, who personally issued appeals for communal harmony.

"But here at our center I tell people that we shouldn't be each other's enemies," Miss Patil said. "I tell them that Hindus and Muslims both have a common enemy—the real enemy is the poverty that is killing our children and ruining our lives. I ask these people to join hands."

With a degree in education from the University of Bombay she could have surely gotten a reasonably well-paying job at a local college or school, I said. Why was she toiling away at this small community center in an obscure neighborhood? Why this troublesome daily commute?

* *World Development Report*, World Bank, 1990.

"Because I believe in reaching out," Vanita Patil said.

One striking feature at the Harinagar Center is what Indian child welfare workers call the anganwadi system—quite literally, the "court-yard" system. This involves the coopting of local women who are familiar with their community and its social and cultural dynamics, and who are themselves known and trusted within that community. The anganwadi worker, who is required by the Indian authorities to be at least eighteen years old, is offered three months of training by municipal health officials. *

"What the anganwadi worker really does is to empower local mothers with the elemental knowledge necessary to raise healthy children," Bakul Patel said to me. "It's such knowledge, plus the supply of support services, that fortifies women in poor localities. It's important to put these women at ease and make them familiar with elementary things they can do in their daily lives to improve their own health and their children's."

Nargis Banu, twenty years old, was one anganwadi worker I met at the Harinagar Center. She was instructing a thirty-year-old woman, Shameen Ahmad, about the need to give added daily dosages of vitamin A to Shameen's three small children. The vitamin syrup was being provided free by the anganwadi. Nargis told me that she admired Indira Gandhi because the prime minister had drawn attention to the plight of poor women—especially to battered wives.

One of Shameen's children, a chubby girl named Shamshed, was

---

* The worker is expected to spend about five hours daily, five or six days a week, at the anganwadi, for which the state government gives her the equivalent of about twenty dollars a month. She teaches local mothers how to prevent and cope with common illnesses. She also educates mothers about monitoring the growth of their children, proper nutrition, and the value of vaccinations, breast-feeding, weaning, and proper birth spacing. The anganwadi worker discusses how family planning can contribute to better health in the community: close spacing of births—by less than two years apart—leads to higher mortality among infants and children because the mother's body has not had time to recover from the previous pregnancy. Moreover, the anganwadi workers tell local residents, pregnancies among women under twenty and over thirty-four are hazardous because there is a much higher incidence of low birth weight, congenital abnormalities and infant deaths, and maternal mortality—a real concern since the United Nations estimates that some 500,000 Third World women die each year from conditions arising out of pregnancy or childbirth and another 25 million become seriously ill after childbirth. The role of anganwadi workers in spreading knowledge about health and education has been found to be so effective that municipal health officials often organize family planning and inoculation campaigns in areas outside slum communities through them. Anganwadi centers such as Harinagar also offer preschool education and early mental stimulation activities for children under the age of six.

protesting the administering of the vitamin syrup. So Nargis surreptitiously extracted a lollipop from a cookie jar, poured some syrup on it, and invited the girl to take the candy. Shamshed snatched the lollipop and began licking it with relish. Nargis said that it was important that the anganwadi worker "not talk down" to local mothers. It was also important that these mothers and their children not become dependent on "outside solutions" to health problems. Thus, Nargis told me, she encouraged women to fill in growth-monitoring charts by themselves, to devise nutritious diets for their children that used plenty of vegetables and fruit, and to incorporate hygienic habits into daily domestic life. What Nargis said to me was another version of the old saying "Prevention is better than cure."

All across India there are now hundreds of workers such as Nargis Banu and scores of anganwadi centers. Are they really making a difference at the grass roots by "reaching out"? Not in a macro sense, to be sure, because the scale of the problem is so large in India. But in urban areas served by anganwadi centers, malnutrition among children under the age of seven is 60 percent below children in neglected regions. Moreover, the infant mortality rate in anganwadi areas has been brought below the national average of 91. Immunization and school enrollment rates are usually higher in anganwadi communities. And, just as important, women in these areas are starting to have fewer babies. With the increased availability of contraceptives and family planning education, Indian women are becoming converts to the notion that, in family size at least, "small is beautiful."

In addition to bearing and raising children, women among the poorest groups perform most of the work that sustains the family economically. "Population and health programs must increasingly—and urgently—focus on our women," Bakul Patel said. Later that day, Bakul Patel and I talked at some length about grass-roots development. With slums in the Third World growing so rapidly, was there a realistic prospect of improving life for the poor masses?

"The Third World's urban slums are growing because of distorted economic priorities and a lack of political commitment to upgrading slums," Mrs. Patel said.

> Take India's case. After more than forty years of independence, are we paying sufficient attention to what's been happening in our vast rural regions? It's fine to emphasize industrial growth, self-reliance in defense and computer technology. But we still haven't completed our irrigation network, and despite all kinds of platitudes from politicians,

there simply aren't enough incentives for farmers and not enough economic opportunities for rural people in their own environments. So what happens? Those deprived people trek to our already over-crowded cities for jobs. Bombay alone attracts some 12,000 newcomers a day. There's no housing for them so they drift into our slums. And these slums keep growing until they become cities in their own right. And it isn't just the physical expansion of these communities. Think of the growing number of unemployed or underemployed people who live in the slums—and of their growing tensions and frustrations. From the shacks of Dharavi to the favelas of Brazil, we have a very serious problem on our hands.

Could not the slums of India and Brazil and elsewhere be somehow razed and replaced by better housing?

"It's too late for that," Mrs. Patel said. "Upgrading the shantytowns of the Third World is the only realistic answer available to us now. The main thing is to make these places more inhabitable—and that means installing better drainage, water pipes, community lavatories, and electricity. There is so much local labor that can be used cheaply and readily for slum upgrading, and many grass-roots voluntary organizations who possess the motivation and manpower."

"The new self-confidence of local residents in these areas is tangible," Mrs. Patel said. "Development projects should be replicable—and development assistance should create a snowball effect."

Snowball effect? The General Assembly of the United Nations, in proclaiming 1987 the International Year of Shelter for the Homeless, noted that the population of slum and squatter settlements is increasing at twice the rate of cities and four times faster than the world population. By the year 2000, sixty cities will have populations of 5 million or more, of which forty-five will be in the developing countries.* Ten of these cities will be in India.

* United Nations Population Fund, New York. The goals of the international community, the General Assembly has declared, must be to improve the shelter and neighborhoods in the developing countries, and indeed to dramatically improve housing for all the poor and disadvantaged people of the Third World by the year 2000. An especially noteworthy housing project supported by the United Nations Development Programme was in Malawi—a project that, in 1987, was awarded a $15,000 prize by the Building and Social Housing Foundation of the United Kingdom, a nongovernmental organization. According to the United Nations, innovative features of this project included designs of simple houses based on the "house-that-grows" concept. This allowed the owner to enlarge a home as family size and income expanded. The houses were fashioned from indigenous building materials such as

"Institutional and political commitment, innovation, awareness and local economic requirements, and sensitivity to local culture—those are the keys to alleviating the depressing situation of the Third World," Bakul Patel said. "It's not enough for leaders such as Indira to say they want change. The key to change lies in the follow-through. And that's where Indira was not energetic. Her intentions were good. But she left behind a legacy of uncompleted programs and projects. And now the challenges facing India are much greater—because the scale of poverty is more vast."

Bakul Patel's view is shared by many Indians. There are others who feel, of course, that Indira did the best anyone could do in such a terribly difficult and complex situation. As Indira Gandhi became increasingly preoccupied with political survival during her last years, she unfortunately neglected social issues more and more. And so, while the long-winded speeches on poverty eradication and the plight of slum children continued, there was little by way of personal attention to policy-making concerning these topics, let alone administrative follow-up. Appearing in slums often became a matter of political expediency. The extraordinary thing was that India's poor continued to believe that Indira was indeed Mother India, and that she would somehow ease their pain. They waited for a very long time for this to happen.

---

sun-dried bricks, ventilation blocks, and roofing sheets. And the cost? No more than ninety dollars for materials for a four-room house. Both Indira Gandhi and Sanjay Gandhi had advocated such housing for Indian slums such as Dharavi.

21

The World According
to the Nehrus
and the Gandhis

The main hall of the United Nations General Assembly in New York City is massive. Whenever delegates assemble in the auditorium, the scene resembles some great international jamboree—which is exactly what General Assembly sessions often tend to be. The floor becomes a riot of color and costumes, and the vast chamber resonates with the twangs of a thousand tongues.* If there can be said to be a collective living room for the 160-plus nations of the world, then the General Assembly chamber is surely it. At one time or the other, virtually every major postwar world leader has come here to hold forth on topics ranging from the sublime to the bizarre. There are those who insist that the ghosts of some of these leaders still swirl in the Assembly hall—Charles de Gaulle, Nikita Khrushchev, John Fitzgerald Kennedy, Konrad Adenauer, Lester Pearson, Winston Churchill, Harold Macmillan, Jawaharlal Nehru, Kwame Nkrumah, Gamal Abdel Nasser—and, of course, Indira Gandhi and Rajiv Gandhi. During her tenure as India's prime minister, Indira focused heavily on the United Nations and on the Nonaligned Movement in an effort to fashion for India a distinct identity as leader of Third World nations. Rajiv continued that tradition.

To the casual outside observer, trips by Indian leaders to London or to Moscow or to Washington may mean little. But in the corridors and

---

*The General Assembly of the United Nations formally convenes each September, with the annual session lasting through December. But special sessions of the Assembly can be called at any other time, depending on the issue in question.

chancelleries of international power, where nuances of expression are delicately yet thoroughly analyzed, the shadings and substance of what India's leaders say do indeed count a great deal. After all, India is not only the most populous country in the world after China; it also enjoys unusually high prestige among those 127 countries that constitute the Third World. International politics—even in this age of *glasnost*—is as much a struggle for the hearts and minds of these emerging nations as it is a direct struggle for global supremacy for the big powers.

Rajiv Gandhi once said that his mother did not see her political constituency as being confined to India. "As prime minister of the world's largest democracy, she saw the whole world as her audience," he said, reflecting a view that others had of him as well when Rajiv was India's prime minister.* Some critics were less charitable than Rajiv Gandhi, asserting that India's concern about international issues meant less attention to domestic matters. "She performed better in the realm of foreign policy than on the domestic front," says Professor Bhabani Sen Gupta, the distinguished New Delhi–based political scientist and commentator. "As Nehru's daughter, Indira developed a worldview even in the first blush of her youth. From the long and informative letters she received from her father in prison, she got broad and often subtle glimpses of world history. If there was a running theme in those somewhat loosely composed pages, it was that of the imperialist and colonialist domination of the European powers of the great and once-glorious civilizations of the East. No doubt Indira Gandhi grew up with an ideological vision of the world."†

Indira understood that major nations counted their pluses and minuses on the world stage on the scorecard of geopolitical influence—and that here India ranked high. That is why India's foreign policy pronouncements are generally a matter of concern for the big powers such as the Soviet Union, the United States, and Britain; that is why those powers frequently solicit India's support on world issues; that is why Indira Gandhi was assiduously wooed by Moscow; and that is also why it is all the more astonishing that Washington pretty much wrote off Indira as a potential ally. "Indira Gandhi's foreign policy actually began in 1971—framed and knocked into shape on the crucible of the Bangladesh liberation war," Professor Sen Gupta says. "All that she wanted and lived for was to be recognized as the indisputable leader of an India that had

---

* Conversation with Rahul Singh in 1985, as quoted by Mr. Singh to author.
† Professor Bhabani Sen Gupta's comments were originally made in a symposium on the Indira era in early 1986. He subsequently spoke to the author at length during two meetings in New York in 1989 and 1990.

finally arrived as a power to be reckoned with. She believed that India's arrival was her principal achievement as a nation-builder."

Indira often turned to veteran Foreign Office types for policy assistance—types whom she seemed to prefer over political operatives for discourse on international affairs. These men included Romesh Bhandari, who was to become foreign secretary, and his brother-in-law, Kunwar Natwar Singh, an essayist and book reviewer. A major source of advice on international issues was Professor Ralph Buultjens, who assisted Indira with ideas for many of her major speeches. One speech still quoted in the international community two decades after it was first delivered was given by Indira at the UN Conference on the Human Environment in Stockholm, on June 14, 1972. "The inherent conflict" in man's emphasis on progress, Indira told the world parley, "is not between conservation and development, but between environment and reckless exploitation in the name of efficiency."

"It is clear that the environmental crisis which is confronting the world will profoundly alter the future destiny of our planet," Indira told the United Nations gathering.

No one among us, whatever his status, strength, or circumstance, can remain unaffected. The process of change challenges present international policies. Will the growing awareness of "one earth" and "one environment" guide us to the concept of "one humanity"? Will there be a more equitable sharing of environmental costs and greater international interest in the accelerated progress of the less developed world? Or will it confine itself to one narrow concern—that of exclusive self-sufficiency? . . . It is essential to grasp the full implications of technical advance and its impact on different sections and groups. We do not want to put the clock back or resign ourselves to a simplistic natural state. We want new directions in the wiser use of the knowledge and the tools with which science equips us. And this cannot be just one upsurge but a continuous search into cause and effect, an unending effort to match technology with higher levels of thinking. We must concern ourselves not only with the kind of world we want, but also with the kind of man who should inhabit it. Surely we do not desire a society divided into those who condition and those who are conditioned. We want thinking people, capable of spontaneous, self-directed activity, who are interested and interesting—and who are imbued with compassion and concern for others. *

* From "Man and His World," an address by Indira Gandhi on June 14, 1972, at the United Nations Conference on the Human Environment, Stockholm, Sweden.

Many years after Indira Gandhi had spoken thus, Maurice F. Strong, secretary-general of the conference, told me how moved he was by Indira's speech. "Mrs. Gandhi set out for all of us an agenda for the decades to come," Strong said.* (Maurice Strong has been appointed secretary-general of the 1992 United Nations Conference on Environment and Development [UNCED], scheduled to be held in June 1992 in Rio de Janeiro.)† The United Nations was organizing the 1992 Brazil Conference to fashion integrated strategies that would prevent further degradation of the global environment, and ultimate decline of the world's economy, and to rectify damage already done. The strategies would support efforts of individual countries to promote sustainable development in every region of the world.

Indira recognized, of course, that the question of Third World development that will support and sustain the environment is politically a highly sensitive one. There are sharply divergent views on issues and priorities, especially between the governments of Third World nations and those of the more developed countries. Developing countries maintain that their ability to deal with global environmental risks will increasingly depend on access to additional resources necessary to integrate considerations about the environment into development plans and projects. With a global recession and a "debt crisis" afflicting the world economy, many Third World leaders are gloomy about the prospects for more investment and concessional aid from the industrialized countries.‡ Their leaders contend that these developing societies must also have access to the latest, most efficient and competitive, environmentally sound technol-

---

*Conversation with author, Geneva, October 1990.

†The concept of development that is environmentally sustainable yet economically progressive was first raised in the 1972 United Nations Conference on the Human Environment held in Stockholm. However, from then until 1987 when *Our Common Future*, the report of the World Commission on Environment and Development, was published, little was done to integrate this dual concept in practical terms. The Brundtland report—named after Mrs. Gro Harlem Brundtland, prime minister of Norway, who chaired the Commission—stimulated debate on the need to translate the concept of sustainable development into practical measures for action. Among its recommendations was a proposal that regional and global meetings be held to promote the integration of environment and economic development. Following a directive from the United Nations General Assembly, a UNCED secretariat has been set up in Geneva where UNCED's secretary-general, Maurice Strong, and his staff were based. Two regional offices, one in New York and the other in Nairobi, were also set up to assist the Geneva headquarters staff.

‡According to the World Bank's 1991 *World Development Report*, the donor nations gave $50 billion in "Official Development Assistance" to Third World countries in 1990. These countries' overall external debt was around $1.3 trillion.

ogy. It would be safe to say that Indira Gandhi was the first world leader to articulate this position; her death, as Maurice Strong says, deprived the global community of one of its most vocal champions of the twinned causes of environment and development.

Since Independence, there has been a striking consistency in India's overall approach to the world. This approach was sharply defined by Indira Gandhi during her fifteen years in power, and it embraced a number of guiding themes:

- *A genuine belief in global nonalignment.* At the heart of these were several constructs: that nonalignment offered India an opportunity to act as a balance between the power blocs of the United States and the Western alliance on the one side, and the Soviet Union and its allies on the other; and a conviction that nonalignment offered a kind of special protection enabling India to refrain from taking sides on geopolitical issues of rivalry between the superpowers. Nonalignment was espoused by Indira as a worthy cause in itself to advance the political and economic interests of the "powerless" countries of the world. But nonalignment did not necessarily translate into India's silence on global issues. For example, Indira, perhaps much too reflexively, was quick to side with Arab states in their disputes with Israel. In 1982, when Israel's air force was bombing Beirut, Indira issued a strong condemnation—a statement that resulted in virtually every member of the Nonaligned Movement following suit. When the prime minister was later asked by journalists why she spoke out so forcefully against the Israelis, she said that she viewed the Palestine Liberation Organization and the Lebanese as brethen. "Those who suffer for a cause we truly believe in suffer for all of us—and we must stand with them whatever the cost," Indira said. [*]
- *The establishment of India's regional role and dominance in South Asia.* By its very size, its ancient culture, and its military strength, India's position in the region is very significant. Altaf Gauhar, the distinguished former editor of the London-based magazine *South*, characterizes India as the "big boy on the block." [†] Hence, the 1971 war of "liberation" that resulted in the creation of Bangladesh from East

---

[*] Source: Crown Prince Hassan bin Talal of Jordan, in an interview with author, Amman, January 1991.
[†] Conversation with author, Washington, D.C., 1989.

Pakistan; hence, the 1987 treaty with Sri Lanka aimed at ending the civil war between that island nation's minority Tamils and majority Sinhalese;* hence, the November 1988 dispatching of troops to the Maldives to crush an attempted coup there. There has long been a strong feeling in India's External Affairs Ministry that without a continuing role for India as the region's policeman, there would be considerable outside interference in South Asia. One of Indira Gandhi's fundamental concerns was to keep both the Soviet Union and the United States out of South Asia. She helped form the South Asian Association for Regional Cooperation (SAARC) during the Seventh Summit of the Nonaligned Movement in New Delhi in 1983. This grouping of seven nations was intended to promote collective self-reliance in nine fields: agriculture, rural development, planning, health, education, transport, telecommunications, sports, and culture.†

- *The balancing of India's economic and political interests through a carefully calibrated and calculated relationship with the superpowers.* This has meant enhanced political relations with the Soviet Union, and significant economic relations with the Western powers. The Soviets have been the chief suppliers of military hardware for India—including such items as the MiG-29, the highly sophisticated fighter plane that Moscow has offered to almost no other Third World nation. But since the Soviets cannot give India "breakthrough technology," Delhi has had to turn to the West, and to Japan, for technical and economic assistance. Because its relationship with the United States has been mainly one based on economics, it has been easier for India to condemn or criticize Washington politically at forums such as the United Nations. And precisely because India relies so heavily on the Soviet Union for military assistance, it has proven virtually impossible for Delhi to condemn such matters as the Soviet invasions of Hungary in 1956, of Czechoslovakia in 1968, and Afghanistan in 1979. Ironically, though, the interests of the two superpowers converged during India's 1962 border war with China, when Washington and Moscow both helped Delhi substantially by providing military and political support. Both powers thus proved a bulwark against China at a time when Beijing was hostile toward the Soviets as well as the Americans. During the 1975–77 Emergency, Indira Gandhi moved toward an improvement in relations

*The civil war continued well into 1991, with thousands of casualties. The most prominent fatality was Rajiv Gandhi.
†For more on the establishment of SAARC, see *South Asia in International Politics*, by Pramod K. Mishra (Delhi: UDH Publishers, 1984).

with China. In 1976, in fact, the countries exchanged ambassadors after a hiatus of fifteen years—much to the chagrin of Moscow. Where possible, Indira tried to take positions that did not publicly pit Washington against Moscow, a practice that subsequent prime ministers have maintained. India's success in getting the two superpowers to support India in its dispute with China represented an unusual achievement. More than two decades later, the United States and the Soviet Union were in agreement over the necessity of evicting Iraq from Kuwait. India supported the twelve UN Security Council resolutions that called for the removal of Iraqi troops from Kuwait.[*]

- *A strong commitment to international institutions such as the United Nations.* Indira viewed these international bodies as important mechanisms for settling world disputes and preventing infringement by outside powers on her own areas of geopolitical interest. India has had extraordinary influence in such international forums, and has frequently set the agenda and tone for debates at the United Nations. Moreover, Indians have traditionally held high positions and perhaps a disproportionate number of posts at international agencies within the UN family.[†]

In a speech at Columbia University in 1949, Jawaharlal Nehru stated the goals of Indian foreign policy as follows:

India is a very old country with a great past. But it is a new country also with new urges and desires. . . . Inevitably she had to consider her foreign policy in terms of enlightened self-interest, but at the same time she brought to it a touch of her idealism. Thus she has tried to combine idealism with national interest. The main objectives of that policy are: the pursuit of peace, not through alignment with any major power or group of powers, but through an independent approach to each controversial or disputed issue; the liberation of subject peoples; the maintenance of freedom both national and individual; and the elimination of want, disease, and ignorance, which afflict the greater part of the world's population.[‡]

---

[*] India's position concerning the Gulf Crisis, however, irked many Western countries. At first India seemed reluctant to criticize Saddam Hussein, who has been a long-standing friend of New Delhi. Later, then–Prime Minister Chandra Shekhar allowed American military planes to refuel in Bombay. But permission was withdrawn after commotion in the media and criticism by Rajiv Gandhi and the Congress Party.
[†] Indeed, Indians applying for jobs at various arms of the United Nations have been told lately that there already are far too many Indians in the system.
[‡] Quoted in William J. Barnds, *India, Pakistan and the Great Powers* (New York: Praeger, 1972), pp. 47–48.

Aside from India's historical strengths and geography, what explains the country's conspicuous role on the world stage? The answer to that is simple: Both Jawaharlal Nehru and Indira Gandhi had a wide-ranging worldview that moved them to give much more attention to foreign affairs than most Third World leaders. "Foreign affairs" was not only a major part of these prime ministers' duties-of-state, the subject was a key element of their personal intellectual interests. What we have here is an example of how the sheer force of Third World leaders' personality, their cerebral orientation, and international activity, can affect their own role and status—and that of their nations in international and domestic politics. Involvement in foreign affairs has heightened the stature of Indian leaders at home. Many Indians savor the notion of their leaders consulting with the mandarins of the international community and being consulted by them. Rajiv Gandhi kept up his practice of traveling overseas to meet with world leaders even after his election defeat in 1989. This often embarrassed the men who followed him as prime minister, because it often appeared as though India had two prime ministers—one for domestic affairs, Chandra Shekhar, and another for foreign affairs, Rajiv Gandhi. *

But why do other nations, particularly those of the Third World, look to India for some strong element of leadership? I posed this question recently to Professor Ralph Buultjens. He replied: "After all, to most of us from the Third World, 'India' means more than just India alone. She stands for all those values and cultural traditions that sustain societies from which we come. And so, India's leadership is not only a matter of size and skill, but also a sentimental and civilizational mix which exerts such a strong pull on people who belong to once-colonized societies."†

Rajiv Gandhi inherited the mantle of the Nonaligned Movement leadership from his mother. In 1986, during the twenty-fifth anniversary of NAM's founding, Rajiv Gandhi passed the three-year chairmanship to Prime Minister Robert Mugabe of Zimbabwe (Yugoslavia is the current chairman). NAM had the potential to be a major force in promoting Third World economic development and keeping such issues as the environment, population control, and child and maternal welfare on the

---

* Rajiv Gandhi made a last-minute—and ill-advised—attempt to prevent the allied forces from launching a war against Saddam Hussein. He flew to Moscow and Teheran on a unilateral peace mission, which, of course, failed.
† Conversation with author, New York, April 1991.

front burner of the global agenda. But the movement has never quite gotten itself organized, even though Indira Gandhi tried to get her fellow leaders to focus more sharply on social and humanitarian issues. "Her frustration was over a lack of an enforcing mechanism within NAM," says Professor Ralph Buultjens. The movement did not have a secretariat, nor any formal authority to get governments to adhere to the lofty goals they proclaimed at NAM summits.

Addressing foreign ministers from NAM nations in New Delhi in 1981, Mrs. Gandhi said:

> Of great concern to all of us are the wide inequalities and disequilibria in the economic and social structures of the world, and the glaring imbalance between demographic pressures on the one hand, and access to material and technological resources on the other. What should be invested in construction is being channeled into destruction. There is a global waste of talent and resources. The solution of today's critical international economic problems needs the total involvement of all nations. Global well-being will be illusory unless the aspirations of developing countries are reflected in the management of the international economy, and in the outcome of international negotiations. No less urgent is the ending of inequalities within our own societies.

Indira knew that the Nonaligned Movement's primary value had been its growing numerical strength, its role as a collective spokesman for Third World concerns, and its potential moral weight as a pressure group for global disarmament. By the time NAM's 101 member states met in New Delhi in 1986, it was clear that the movement suffered from fractiousness and from a lethal infusion of ideology administered by outgoing chairman Fidel Castro. Indeed, at no point during its troubled lifetime had the movement, whose members represent more than half of the world's population, been more afflicted with malaise, frustration, and even political impotency. There were deep divisions in the movement over ideology and tactics, and if there was agreement over anything it was that the movement had gone adrift in recent years, with no clear strategy for action, no sense of political direction. Among some of the movement's influential leaders, in fact, there was pained questioning whether the movement, as presently constituted, was really useful, and whether it should survive at all.

And yet, gloomy as the picture was, the Nonaligned Movement had an unusual and perhaps final opportunity to fashion a bold new technocratic agenda that would revive NAM, and bring development issues again into the forefront of the Third World's agenda. The movement had another chance to focus its and the industrialized world's attention on the problems of poverty, overpopulation, and infant mortality—and it had the opportunity to catalyze concerted worldwide action to alleviate these interlinked problems. Why? Because the sheer size of its global constituency meant that NAM could effect significant change in Third World countries' development and economic policies. Despite a poor track record of results, which would normally make it inconsequential in world affairs, NAM still was important as a forum for discussion and Third World opinion-making—and as a barometer of superpower influence in the global arena. Indira Gandhi knew that such change could only come if NAM was prepared to reexamine its relationship with the one nation whose technical assistance and expertise were badly needed to ensure further global development.* NAM's feisty attitude toward the United States had done a great deal to dilute Washington's enthusiasm for Third World politics. Yet, simultaneously, many of the states that constituted NAM had become the arenas for American-Soviet rivalry. India had long been a classic case of a country that both superpowers wooed. India's leaders, however, insisted that the country would take no sides. Nevertheless, on the basis of India's votes in such international bodies as the United Nations, many Americans perceived that India's "nonalignment" was invariably left-leaning.

"Indira tried to strengthen the center of the movement," Professor Sen Gupta says. "She wanted NAM to play a more effective role in fighting neocolonialist penetration of Third World economies, global militarization, and the renewed superpower nuclear arms race." But, of course, the New Delhi summit ended with little more than resolutions. The superpowers were not especially inclined to sit up and take notice of still more calls for a New International Economic Order, let alone an International Conference on Money and Finance for Development, a conference that Indira had herself proposed.† When Indira Gandhi visited the United Nations in 1983, she spoke eloquently of how the fundamental realities of international economic life were mirrored in NAM's efforts to change global economic structures. The nonaligned countries' basic

---

*Toward the end of her life, Indira Gandhi seemed to soften her hostility toward Washington, according to her associates. President Ronald Reagan's cordial and courteous attention to her may have at least partly explained this shift.
†Mrs. Gandhi renewed her call for such a global parley when she came to UN headquarters in New York in September 1963. Only twenty heads of government or their deputies turned up, a disappointment for Mrs. Gandhi.

contention concerning their economic situation has not changed greatly since the mid-1970s, when emotions ran high at the United Nations and other forums over the question of the New International Economic Order (NIEO). Simplistically perhaps, Third World nations invested much hope in the NIEO; this new world economic order was seen by many Third World leaders as an important way to alleviate long-standing problems such as slow economic growth and escalating poverty in developing countries. The NIEO was seen as a potential economic rainmaker!*

"Indira couldn't do much because the world had changed and NAM was no longer the force it used to be in the 1950s and 1960s," according to Professor Sen Gupta. "She was unable to persuade the Reagan administration to alter its hard-line ideological stand with regard to the Third World both in terms of institutional economic aid and military intervention in 'local wars' or conflicts."†

By the time NAM met in New Delhi for Indira Gandhi's summit, the movement was divided and disputatious, and its agenda appeared to have no priorities. Moreover, the United States had yet to come to terms with the fact that it could not maintain its highly charged ideological rhetoric and expect to win friends across the board among developing nations. It had to be perceived as muting its verbal pyrotechnics; it had to be seen as willing to push vigorously to completion its practical incentives to tackle the Third World's major problems like the debt crisis. NAM itself had been pretty much ineffective in alleviating this crisis or in getting the industrialized West to address itself to the underlying causes of the

---

* The NIEO was essentially a formalization of long-standing concerns and demands of the Third World states for a better economic deal. They wanted better trade arrangements with the industrialized West, a greater transfer of technology to pull their backward economies into a postindustrial age, and stepped-up development assistance. When NAM was founded, some of its leaders seemed to hold that political liberty meant automatic economic development and progress. But by the early 1970s, NAM leaders had learned a bitter lesson: that without a strong economic base, political strategies can collapse. Economics had moved to the center stage of world politics. The style and level of discourse between the West and the Third World have undergone shifts over the years.

†Many analysts feel that if American foreign policy is to achieve its objective of increasing Washington's global influence, a redefined relationship with NAM or some of its more moderate members should be a priority. The confluence of NAM's own crisis of purpose, the context of world politics today, and the economic uncertainties plaguing the Third World provide a unique opportunity for Washington to win friends and recapture its long-forgotten high standing in the Third World. Still, analysts feel that for both sides to take corrective action would be difficult, given the long history of suspicion and antagonism between Washington and the Third World.

debt situation. For more than a decade, nonaligned nations had used a body called the G77 (diplomatic shorthand for the Group of 77, which actually has 127 members, twenty-six of them—like China, for instance—not belonging to NAM) to raise matters of economic relevance. And perhaps the most dramatic Third World demand lay in the call more than a decade ago for the establishment of a "New International Economic Order" (NIEO).

What Indira Gandhi and other Third World leaders were proposing under NIEO was a fundamental restructuring of the world economy so as to benefit the poor countries. Poor countries argued that the existing international economic order was structured to their disadvantage. They maintained that because of the weighted voting structures of the International Monetary Fund and the World Bank, the Third World lacked appropriate influence in these institutions. They claimed that the prices of the primary products that constituted their largest exports had regularly fallen in relation to the prices of the manufactured goods they sought to import from the industrialized countries; the poor states of the Third World insisted that this was primarily due to the monopolistic position of multinational concerns that purchased their products.

"Developing countries generate 20 percent of the world's output, absorb 30 percent of the total exports of the developed countries, and, in the 1970s, had higher rates of investment—why should they be denied their rightful share in decision-making?" Mrs. Gandhi said. " 'Debt crises' are there because private international banking, alert and sensitive as it is to opportunities for profitable recycling, cannot perform the function which, by its very nature, can be undertaken only by suitably strengthened international organizations dealing with problems of money and finance for a developing world economy."[*]

During the mid-1970s, NAM was indeed able to achieve briefly a shift in global debate from an East-West focus to a North-South one, but it was unable to sustain the momentum largely because the movement simply could not draft a clear agenda for economic and sociopolitical action. While the poor countries vociferously argued that the terms of trade had gone against them, the rich states maintained that any price changes in imports and exports merely reflected market trends and consumer preferences. The West said that influence in institutions where important decisions were taken had to be related to responsibilities. And consequently, the states that had a major share in world trade and sup-

[*] From "Peace and Development," by Indira Gandhi (the Raul Prebisch Lecture, Belgrade, June 8, 1983).

plied the funds for development assistance should have a determining voice in the IMF and World Bank. And so, in the years following the hullabaloo over NIEO, the movement was unable to win any major economic concessions from the West's financial organizations in tackling the debt crisis. The World Bank says that capital-importing developing countries now owe more than $1.3 trillion to Western lending institutions, a fact that results in severely curtailing the availability of Western commercial funds for any meaningful internal development.

Further, the insecure nature of this debt imposes an air of uncertainty over international financial markets; the stability of many Western lending institutions has consequently become linked to the repayment capacities of many almost bankrupt developing countries. * Indira Gandhi and other leaders of developing countries wished not only that their basic economic interests be safeguarded and enhanced; they wanted through a new and just international economic order to assert their sovereign rights as members of the world community. The exports of about twelve major nonoil commodities account for more than 80 percent of the total import earnings of the developing countries. Sharp fluctuations in the world prices of raw commodities, coupled with increased expenditures for the import of manufactured goods from industrialized countries, plus the cost of servicing debt to Western financial institutions, have all but wiped out many Third World states' ability to channel meaningful monies into their own development. In 1974 the developing countries' debt amounted to $135 billion; by 1985 the figure was touching a trillion dollars; at the end of 1991, the debt figure was $1.3 trillion, according to the World Bank.† To this figure, Professor Ralph Buultjens adds $150 billion that the Soviet Union and various East-bloc countries owe to Western banks. On average, 60 percent of this new debt (and more than 80 percent in the case of Latin America) was loaned by commercial bankers, who saw marvelous credit opportunities in developing countries that wished to stride toward modernity. The bankers had billions of petrodollars at their command. Thus, between 1972 and 1979, the indebtedness of the so-called Less-Developed Countries (LDCs) increased at an average annual rate of 21.7 percent. And their indebtedness has kept increasing since then as well. Consider the case of China, which in 1981 had almost no external debt. By the end of 1987, it had piled up some $33 billion in

---

* In partial recognition of this, Citibank in effect wrote off $3 billion of its Third World loans in the spring of 1987, and other major Western lenders to developing countries soon followed suit in writing off some of their loans.
† World Bank, 1991 *World Development Report*.

foreign debt, making it the world's sixth biggest debtor. In 1986 about 60 percent of China's $3.3 billion foreign borrowing that year came from Western and Japanese banks.

"My mother recognized that India had to be at the forefront of critical international issues such as debt—that if India was quiet, then developing countries would not be heard as they needed to be heard on these issues," Rajiv Gandhi said.* Both Rajiv and Indira Gandhi traveled a great deal to hold forth at global forums on international issues. "Indira was one of those leaders—Kennedy, Nasser, Sukarno, and Willy Brandt may be cited as other examples—who find it easier and more congenial to shine in the realm of foreign policy and international relations than to make their mark by grappling with the more daunting and demanding internal problems," says Inder Malhotra. Indira loved to travel abroad, "at least partly because the elaborate and often effusive welcome in host countries impresses the people back home." Between 1980 and late 1984, Indira Gandhi went overseas no fewer than eighteen times, visiting nearly forty countries.† These trips meant that Air India had to refurbish one of its Boeing 707s specially for Indira's use; since the Air India fleet was relatively small, each trip of the prime minister's would disrupt the carrier's global schedule.

When Indira Gandhi referred to debt and trade issues at the March 1983 Nonaligned Nations summit in New Delhi, her remarks were well received. The seventh NAM summit was a glittering affair, and the Indian capital was especially spruced up for the occasion. When the time came for Indira to formally take over NAM's chairmanship from Fidel Castro, she extended her hand to him, but Castro, in a well-applauded show of affection for Indira, gave her a crushing bear hug instead. "My sister!" Fidel Castro said emotionally.

Coupled with the question of rising external debt of Third World countries is their mounting domestic debt. In India, for example, the 1988 figure was $125 billion. To be sure, many Western industrial nations have vastly larger long-term debts (the federal debt of the United States, for example, is edging past $2.4 trillion). But these Western debts are also secured by vastly richer domestic resources and better access to liquidity. From the back seat, then, Third World states have wanted to get into the driver's seat. Developing states were hard hit by the dramatic

* Interview with the author and Bernard Kalb, New Delhi, September 1990.
† Malhotra, *Indira Gandhi*, p. 263. Malhotra often traveled with the Gandhi entourage in his capacity as an editor and columnist.

decline in the role of the dollar in the early 1970s; the dollar had been central to the Bretton Woods system as the currency of international trade, and its convertibility into gold was a critical element. After all, nearly 80 percent of the world's trade was conducted in—or at least translated into—the American dollar. With the American trade deficit exceeding $10 billion by 1971, President Nixon suspended the convertibility of the dollar into gold, and the world's major currencies were forced to float against one another. (The U.S. deficit is now edging toward $200 billion.) Indira Gandhi simply did not pay sufficient attention to economic problems such as domestic budgetary deficits. She expected that her finance minister would take care of the matter. Besides, the government could always print bank notes!

When Indira Gandhi spoke at the United Nations not long before her assassination about the need for restructuring the global economy to help poor countries, there seemed to be a perception among some Western observers that she was calling for something radical. However, demands for a major change in the world's skewed economic system were first voiced at the Bandung Conference of Afro-Asian leaders in 1955. Every summit of the Nonaligned Movement has echoed such demands. At the United Nations, too, the Third World states have broadcast their concerns. But more than three decades after Bandung, few, if any, major changes have been instituted where it matters most to the Third World countries—in the trade and aid policies of the industrialized states, and in the global monetary and financial institutions such as the International Monetary Fund and the World Bank, where the wealthy industrialized powers retain a dominant controlling voice.

Indira Gandhi knew that NAM had been wholly unsuccessful in persuading the Western industrialized countries to agree to global negotiations that would correct economic imbalances between rich and poor nations. Indira understood that at the heart of the matter was the question of different perceptions of self-interest in the developing world. The evolution of economic development had moved some nations in different directions from others, giving, for example, newly industrializing states in the Third World different sets of concerns from the more traditional agricultural economies there. Shahid Javed Burki, a Pakistani and a senior official of the World Bank, says: "The NIEO was neither desirable nor achievable."* In a paper he delivered at a recent meeting in Beijing, Burki said that those associated with NIEO simply were not able to define their positions concerning agenda items.

Indira Gandhi also understood that the very concept of NIEO was a

---

* Interview with author, Washington, D.C., October 1988.

romanticized one, and therefore unworkable. It was also doomed to failure because the Third World, in exchange for a transfer of resources from the wealthy North, was not prepared to offer any significant concessions of its own. Since the NIEO concept was first floated more than a decade ago, the Third World has been unable to agree on specific approaches and responses for negotiations with the West; bickering and sharp dissension are rampant within G77. This economic coalition of Third World states tried to cut a deal: It supported OPEC's tactic of price hikes and the brandishing of the oil weapon in exchange for the oil cartel's "willingness to behave as the shock troops" of the NIEO.* Indeed, the industrialized West seemed somewhat affected by this tactic, which stemmed from perhaps an exaggerated perception on the part of the South of its own power.

In October 1981, Indira Gandhi traveled to the Mexican resort of Cancún for a North-South summit, where leaders of fourteen Third World countries and eight industrialized nations had gathered. The summit was intended "to break the deadlock between rich and poor nations over a new and just international economic order," says Inder Malhotra. However, nothing of note came out of the Cancún summit because the chasm between rich and poor nations was too wide. But Indira did score points with President Ronald Reagan over the question of allowing Cuba to attend the summit. Some Third World nations had insisted that Cuba be represented, since Fidel Castro was the chairman of the Nonaligned Movement at the time. But Indira persuaded Cuba's supporters not to persist in their position. She argued that if Cuba attended the summit, the United States was certain to boycott it. The "whole purpose of the exercise" would be defeated.[†] The Cancún episode illustrated how much clout Indira Gandhi carried among Third World leaders. Unfortunately, leaders of the industrialized countries tended to be far less impressed by her political objectives. It is arguable, of course, whether any Third World leader was in a position by the mid-1970s to exert much influence in the West: Developing nations were generally perceived by industrialized nations as beggars, and their leaders as supplicants holding out begging bowls. Indira resented this perception, to be sure, but there was little that she could do about it.

The Cancún summit, of course, was not the first North-South talkfest that Indira had backed. From 1975 to 1977, President Valéry Giscard

---

*Conversation with Jyoti Shankar Singh, a lawyer and economist, who works for the United Nations Population Fund.
[†]Malhotra, *Indira Gandhi*, p. 264.

d'Estaing of France convened in Paris the Conference on International Economic Cooperation, an enterprise that Indira Gandhi supported. The Indian delegation was large, and articulate about the Third World's needs. Indira personally monitored developments, even though she was preoccupied with the Emergency that she had by then imposed at home. Participants included industrialized states and a selection of Third World countries. The conference followed the format urged by G77; this format linked oil price discussions to broad proposals on trade, finance, aid, raw materials, and the transfer of technology from the North to the South. OPEC had insisted on the participation of developing countries at the conference. The West had not really wanted to discuss the North-South issue at the conference, which disturbed Mrs. Gandhi; the West had wanted initially to discuss the oil situation with OPEC, perhaps with a deal in mind for long-term price stability. But OPEC then brought in developing countries, largely as a means to gain legitimacy for its oil price hikes. In exchange for admission to the conference—and the resulting widening of the agenda to include North-South questions—the Third World would endow OPEC with its endorsement of the oil price rises. The Paris conference, however, was unable to produce any formula satisfactory to all participants and was subsequently overtaken by events. The West was able to absorb successfully the shock of the 1973–74 oil price rise, and the industrialized states embarked on a massive conservation program that enabled them to be less frightened of OPEC maneuvers.

Further, Third World leaders felt that their OPEC counterparts were not fully behind the South's set of demands for major restructuring of the world's financial system—a system that had worked well in recent years for OPEC members. OPEC's leverage—and, by extension, that of the developing countries—was diluted. OPEC sought its economic future in increased linkage with the West rather than underwriting a commitment to NIEO. Petrodollars ended up in London and New York, rather than in Bangladesh or Malawi or India. Then, in 1979, NAM leaders at the Havana summit called for fresh "global negotiations" between the North and South. Nothing happened here either: The call did not receive sufficient support to translate it into reality.

By 1981—a year after Indira Gandhi had returned to power—world oil prices were falling; the world was entering a terrible recession. And finally, there arrived the Reagan administration. This administration, in tandem with politically and fiscally conservative governments in Britain and West Germany, was unwilling to accommodate the demands of the Third World for new negotiations, preferring to rely on market forces rather than on some international planning mechanism to deal with global economic problems. In fact, the attitude of the Reagan administration was perceived by NAM and by G77 officials as being downright hostile to Third World interests. Earlier, especially during the Carter years, it had seemed to many in NAM that the United States—which had retreated into neoisolationism following the Vietnam debacle and which had sought détente with its adversary, the Soviet Union—was prepared to replace the Cold War with the NIEO as the central element of international life. But after the Soviet invasion of Afghanistan in 1979 and the election to the American Presidency the following year of Ronald Reagan, bipolar realities reasserted themselves. The Cold War and U.S.—Soviet Union relations became, once again, the crucial, preeminent issues of the age.

The Cold War is officially over now. But many NAM and G77 officials appear alarmed that under current conditions of reduced Third World political and economic strength, the industrialized countries will push efforts aimed at institutionalizing Western economic advantages. These leaders cite the undercutting by the Reagan and Bush administrations of multilateral mechanisms, including UN bodies that could conceivably play an active role in promoting Third World development, such as UNCTAD, the United Nations Conference on Trade and Development. Nonaligned states are discovering that protectionism is gaining converts in the United States and elsewhere in the West. They are also finding that multilateralism is under siege these days, with the Bush administration sidestepping cumbersome international bureaucracies in favor of regional or bilateral accords that are more susceptible to political calibration by Washington.

With George Bush, of course, the general disregard for Third World–oriented international organizations and movements such as NAM is unlikely to change, although the style may be less dismissive than Ronald Reagan's. Few Western industrialized countries seem to take the movement seriously; indeed, many officials of the politically conservative administrations of the United States, Britain, and West Germany, for example, speak scornfully of the movement. And Indira Gandhi's recent successors—Rajiv Gandhi, V. P. Singh, and Chandra Shekhar—were not as knowledgeable as she was on the intricacies of foreign policy. Consequently, their impact on international issues was not as great as hers.

The Nonaligned Movement was started to support the postwar struggle against colonialism; to encourage newly independent nations to be neutral in the face of escalating Cold War confrontation between the two superpowers, the United States and the Soviet Union; and to assist the impoverished countries of the Third World to develop their economies and achieve social progress. Implicit in its founding at the Belgrade summit of 1961, when twenty-five states signed NAM's first declaration of peace, disarmament, and cooperation, was the recognition that the United Nations had been unable to provide the collective security system promised by its Charter. The movement upheld the cardinal tenets of nonintervention and noninterference in a sovereign state's territory. The movement's founders intended NAM to provide a moral umbrella for poor nations that rushed toward modernity. For newly independent nations that wished to make a mark in the world community, NAM held out the possibility of a place in the sun.

But in the perception of the general Western community, at least, much of the promise of NAM has not been fulfilled. Among ordinary Americans, there is a widespread, and seemingly unshakable, suspicion that the movement, far from being neutral in the superpower competition, in fact consistently tilts toward the Soviet Union, which, in the words of Fidel Castro of Cuba—a former chairman of NAM—is viewed by many in the Third World as a "natural ally" of developing countries. Indeed, it has often seemed that the movement seized on the slightest American folly in international affairs, while its condemnation of the Soviets on such matters as the occupation of Afghanistan was relatively mild, if not muted. Indira maintained that the Soviet invasion of Afghanistan was not the source but the consequence of deepening superpower rivalry in the region. Under Indira, India's reaction to the Afghan crisis was shaped by a regional perspective and by the fear that South Asia would become an arena of great-power confrontation and international conflict. In this context, Indira viewed American military support for Pakistan as destabilizing.*

After Indira Gandhi had met with President Reagan at the White House in August 1982, she was asked by an American reporter: "Why does India always tilt toward the Soviet Union?"

"We don't tilt on either side," Indira said acidly. "We walk upright."†

Indira Gandhi felt especially possessive about the Nonaligned Move-

---

*Conversation with Professors Robert L. Hardgrave, Jr., and Stanley A. Kochanek.
†In an interview that the author and Bernard Kalb had with Rajiv Gandhi in New Delhi in September 1990, Rajiv said: "I had very good personal relations with Presidents Reagan and Bush—this is really what led to a lot of opening up between our two countries. We did have serious differences on issues, of course, but these personal relationships go a long way in international relations."

ment. It was like family for her—not the least because her father was responsible for the movement's creation. The movement was actually conceived fifteen years before the 1961 Belgrade summit, essentially in the mind of Jawaharlal Nehru. Back in September 1946, almost a year before India obtained its independence from Britain, Nehru delivered a radio address in which he said: "We propose as far as possible to keep away from power politics of groups aligned against one another which in the past have led to world wars and which may lead to disaster, on an even bigger scale, in the future."

Those were the seeds of the concept that eventually came to be called "nonalignment." Nehru's words were uttered at the start of the Cold War, when the two superpowers maintained, in the buzzword of the time, a "balance of terror." It was a bipolar world then, and in the emerging nations of Asia and Africa, particularly, there were fears about a nuclear holocaust, and there was also mounting concern about the application of the Truman Doctrine of containment of Communism—these new nations saw themselves being dragged willy-nilly into the superpower conflict. For the most part, these former colonial possessions did not wish to accept military alliances with the superpowers or with their former colonial masters. What Nehru advocated was the idea that the new nations could pursue vigorously the axioms of independence, development, and peaceful coexistence.

Implicit in what Nehru was saying was the notion of neutrality, which John Foster Dulles would later bitterly criticize as being "immoral." It was India that took it upon herself to develop the theme of nonalignment. In the early postwar years, India insisted that the United Nations should be—as Jagat S. Mehta, a former Indian foreign secretary, has put it—a "universal, nonideological" organization.* India lobbied for the admission to the United Nations of Communist China, a country at whose hands it was to suffer a humiliating defeat in the border war of 1962. India warned the West about the consequences of broadening the Korean War. India played a valuable, behind-the-scenes role in the 1954 Geneva Conference on Indochina. And India cautioned the newly decolonized states against taking sides in the superpower rivalry. Through such involvement, India managed not only to stake out world visibility in international affairs; it also set the stage for the eventual adoption of the nonalignment credo of assertive independent positions on world issues. Nehru saw the new nations of Asia and Africa as a "moral make-weight

* Jagat S. Mehta, "Nonaligned Principles and Nonaligned Movement," *Mainstream*, March 1983.

to restore the balance in the world," a phrase he used in a conversation in 1954 with Varindra Tarzie Vittachi, a Sri Lankan journalist and author.* Nehru had traveled to Colombo to attend the Colombo Powers Conference. This conference led to the 1955 Bandung Conference, the first summit-level meeting of twenty-nine African and Asian leaders. What happened at Bandung was to prove extremely useful to the figures who eventually were to establish NAM. A debate took place over the concept of "peaceful coexistence" between the socialist and capitalist systems; there were spirited discussions about the value of national security through external assistance; and, of course, there was a great deal of talk concerning the perceived threats of Communist expansionism. Conference participants opined that nations had the right to choose their sources for economic assistance. And they collectively called on the International Bank for Reconstruction and Development—better known as the World Bank—to offer assistance to the poor nations according to their development needs.

Six years later, in September 1961, Nehru and twenty-four other leaders who had met in Bandung were reunited in Belgrade for what came to be known as the First Conference of the Heads of Governments of Nonaligned Countries. The summit lasted for five days, there were merely five items on the agenda—items that dealt broadly with questions such as nonintervention and the sovereign rights of states—and there was also a "message" in the final declaration addressed to President Kennedy of the United States and to Prime Minister Khrushchev of the Soviet Union, urging both to start direct negotiations to remove the nuclear threat. Although the final communiqué made an impassioned plea for peace and disarmament, it contained not a word about the Soviet Union's thermonuclear explosion, which the Russians set off even while the Belgrade summit was on. This omission annoyed President Kennedy. Robert Shaplen of *The New Yorker* told of meeting a Yugoslav diplomat in New Delhi years later who recalled a conversation with Khrushchev just before the Belgrade summit. The diplomat quoted the Soviet leader as saying: "You tell Tito that I'm getting ready to build a wall in Berlin and that I'm going to set off a bomb during his conference. Ask him who, then, is more important—his nonaligned movement or the Soviet Union?"[†]

* Details recalled to author by Tarzie Vittachi in a conversation in New York, September 1990.
[†] Robert Shaplen was one of the very few American journalists who paid attention to the Nonaligned Movement. Most editors and reporters in the American press have tended to dismiss NAM as inconsequential and irrelevant.

The summit had its discordant notes. President Sukarno of Indonesia urged a confrontational stance toward the United States, which he repeatedly characterized as imperialistic and antagonistic toward developing countries. It was Nehru who held that confrontation with a superpower would do nothing to advance the cause of the nonaligned states, and what came to be adopted by the summiters was the Nehru view that the final communiqué should emphasize peace and cooperation. The summiters left Belgrade without planning to hold another summit. Nonalignment, in their view, was not meant to be an "anti-bloc." But there was to be a subsequent summit, three years later, in Cairo. It was held at a time of a continuing border dispute between China and India, an issue that was dodged by the participants at the Cairo summit, although it was the first clear-cut test of how NAM members would deal with the thorny question of what to do when a member state's territory was violated by force. And in evading this question, the nonaligned leaders established a precedent that has haunted the movement ever since—that unless blame could be fairly and squarely placed on "Western imperialism," intra–Third World disputes should be played down in the quest for consensus and unity.

It was to be six years before another summit would be held, this time in the Zambian capital of Lusaka. By this time, the membership of NAM had more than doubled, and the summiters resolved now to meet every three years. Already an institutionalization process was taking place, the very thing that the movement's founding fathers had wanted to avoid. In addition to the declarations, the summiters approved fourteen different resolutions—which were nonbinding and which few took seriously —ranging from issues such as development, disarmament, and peace to the question of setting up a "zone of peace" in the Indian Ocean, and to a suggestion for an international convention on the laws of the seas. At Lusaka, too, appeared the first hints of a Third World stand on the need for a North-South dialogue on economic issues. Economic issues were prominently bruited about at the next summit, held in Algiers in September 1973. The question of détente figured in these deliberations as well, but it was the issue of a Third World state's sovereign rights over its natural resources that generated a lot of debate. Outside of NAM precincts, OPEC had already begun to flex its muscles; the concept of oil as a weapon was well in place.

Indira Gandhi, like other leaders of nonaligned countries, hoped that somehow the use of the oil weapon by OPEC would also have simultaneous advantages for Third World countries that relied for valuable foreign exchange primarily on one-commodity exports. It was, in the event, a vain hope because the oil situation was not replicable for most other natural resources; moreover, the oil-producing states barely assisted the Third World countries, preferring instead to invest their surplus petrodollars in the industrial economies, through which the funds were often recycled at high interest rates to desperately poor nations. The Algerians put a special stamp on the Nonaligned Movement, which was that of greater shrillness in articulating economic issues. Their leadership of NAM signaled accelerated involvement of the Third World with development economics, but in the West this was viewed as a radicalization of the nonaligned movement. At the next summit, in Colombo in 1976, the moderate figures of the movement—including Indira Gandhi—tried to soften NAM rhetoric on economic issues, but the demands escalated nevertheless for the creation of a New International Economic Order (which by now had been approved by the General Assembly of the United Nations).

The "radicalization" of NAM reached its apogee at the 1979 summit in Havana, and it worried Indira Gandhi. Fidel Castro, the activist host, made no secret of his ambition to take NAM more toward the Soviet Union, which he characterized as the "natural ally" of developing countries. To be sure, he met with resistance—among other people from Marshal Tito of Yugoslavia, then in his declining days. In an acclaimed address, Tito called on the movement to "remain the conscience of mankind" and he warned against a partisan shift. Stronger protest came from Burma, a founding member of the movement: It announced its withdrawal from NAM. Castro was determined to push through a final communiqué that denounced the United States, but it was the last-minute intervention of Yugoslavia, India, and a few other Asian states that resulted in a muting of such language to a more even-tempered admonition against all forms of "hegemony and domination." The leaders of NAM may have resisted Fidel Castro's efforts to push their movement more squarely into the Soviet camp, but it is hardly disputable that the Soviet Union has higher esteem than the United States at NAM gatherings. At least a dozen NAM members—such as Afghanistan, Angola, and Ethiopia—have been openly aligned in political or military terms with the Soviets. More than a quarter of the member states are ruled by authoritarian governments, mainly of a leftist persuasion.

While both the United States and the Soviet Union amply supply arms to the Third World, Moscow often offers terms—such as barter for coffee from Ethiopia, fish from Mozambique—that are easier on the recipient countries in the short run. NAM and Indian leaders insist that the movement does not curry favor with the Soviets. They aver that if

NAM positions on issues such as decolonization, NIEO, and Palestine seem similar, that is because Moscow votes with the Third World, not the other way around. NAM leaders point out that the United States votes with the Third World majority at the United Nations some 80 percent of the time—that it is just when there are divergences of opinion and voting that Washington chooses to emphasize the different voting patterns between its allies and the Third World majority. There are significant differences between how Moscow and Washington court NAM. Leaders of the movement say that NAM often comes into voting forums at the United Nations with its position on specific issues already made up at earlier caucuses or small meetings.

But the United States is seen as not paying sufficiently close attention to such small meetings—and so, as Indira Gandhi herself once put it, "The United States gets slightly startled at the end of the race, and then gets bitter."* It is often a question of technique that has been neglected by the United States. The Soviets are generally far more vigilant about how NAM members stand on specific issues. While American diplomats are perceived generally as being neglectful or indifferent about these small but critical caucuses, Soviet representatives often seem far more energetic and attentive to the concerns of the Third World. For Washington, the game in Third World voting has often been lost because there simply has been no contest. The Soviets and their friends have used NAM differently: For example, Moscow dispatched a conspicuously large delegation to the New Delhi summit in 1983; the Russians produced thirty books on nonalignment, which were distributed free of charge to delegates. No comparable Western effort was evident. Indira Gandhi publicly expressed appreciation of the Soviet interest in NAM. In NAM circles, there is resentment that the popular and official definition of nonalignment in the United States is "equidistance" from the superpowers, keeping both the Soviets and the Americans in constant symmetrical distance. But in such important Third World states as India, nonalignment, dating back to Jawaharlal Nehru's time, is often defined as freedom to act independently in the pursuit of national self-interest, even if it means tilting to one superpower under a given set of circumstances.

Because Cuba's own political positions were at great variance with many of NAM's members, the movement slid into three years of near-paralysis. Cuba opposed any NAM attempt to condemn the Soviet invasion of Afghanistan in December 1979. It was not until the New Delhi summit of 1983 that the NAM leadership was able to undertake any

* Quotation provided by Professor Ralph Buultjens.

meaningful effort to bring the movement back on its rails. Criticism of the West was by no means abjured, but the rhetoric was less strident.

Indira Gandhi highlighted the question of development and of nuclear proliferation. She pointed out that it was important to trim global defense expenditures: She noted that a single nuclear aircraft carrier cost $4 billion—which was greater than the gross national product of half of NAM's members. "Peace is not merely the absence of war," Indira said. "It is not a passive concept, but a positive one. It is a feeling of well-being, of goodwill. . . . The high level of military expenditure in advanced economies has contributed greatly to the [global] economic crisis. It impinges on other elements like cost, supply, demand, rate of accumulation of the reproductive capital, claims on research capacity and human skills, and the entire scheme of national priorities. For every hundredfold rise in productive capacity, there seems to be a thousand-fold increase in destructive capacity. Some governments say 'Arm today, disarm tomorrow.' But today's arms can deny us our tomorrows."*

Indira Gandhi also renewed earlier NAM calls for a new international monetary conference to review and revise the Bretton Woods system on which the postwar global economic structure was constructed. It was a structure, she said, that increasingly discriminated against the developing countries.† Mrs. Gandhi's mostly moderate deportment was the most pleasing aspect of the lavish summit, but the most startling episode was a speech by Foreign Minister Sinnathamby Rajaratnam of Singapore. Rajaratnam did not actually deliver the speech but distributed copies to delegates. And with good reason, for had he spoken what he had written,

---

* According to the 1991 World Development Report of the World Bank, the global community spends $1 trillion annually on the military. Of this amount, nearly $800 billion is spent by the industrialized nations. These nations give barely $50 billion in aid—"Official Development Assistance," or ODA—to Third World countries each year. But the very fact that Third World nations spend $200 billion on arms annually hardly gives them the moral right to criticize the global arms race.

† However, few NAM leaders believe that there will be a dramatic turnabout concerning trade, aid, and development in the Bush administration. More and more, NAM and G77 officials are starting to accept the validity of Singapore's assertion that the way to make progress on such issues as trade and aid is not by passing meaningless resolutions seeking global negotiations. A better way, they assert, is by pursuing more market-oriented economic approaches. But Indira Gandhi was right in calling for a new Bretton Woods–type summit. Such a summit must be aimed not, as the original one did back in 1944, at restructuring the entire world financial system but at cogently addressing the critical issues of debt and development. India's unique development experience eminently qualifies it to take a strong leadership role in organizing such a summit. But will the West show up?

511

many summiters would have walked out on him. In retrospect, his was one of the most clearheaded, pithy, and unsentimental assessments of the nonaligned movement ever. It was also one of those rare times that a delegate had taken on the movement in a frontal assault and questioned NAM's integrity. *

Of the movement, Rajaratnam said that its "past is one of which we can be justly proud. Its present condition however does it no credit. And finally, if it persists in its present course, its future will be one of shameful oblivion." Rajaratnam—who belonged to the Tamil community that long ago migrated to Singapore from India—then went on to criticize the movement's "self-delusion." He said that Third World states had less to fear from a return of Western imperialism than from the military ambitions of their own neighbors. He said that pro-Soviet members had become the "true motor" of the movement. He accused both the United States and the Soviet Union, but especially the Russians, of using the ancient technique of proxy wars to gain control of the movement. "We are witnesses to our own slow-motion hijacking and if we do not wake up to this fact and do something to abort it then the ship of nonalignment and all those who sail in it may wake up one day to find that they have docked in a Soviet port," he said. †

Indira Gandhi was not especially appreciative of Rajaratnam's speech. Nor was she enthusiastic about Fidel Castro's persistent efforts to direct NAM toward Moscow because, Castro kept saying, "The Soviets are the developing world's natural allies." Indira pointedly said later: "We have neither natural allies nor natural adversaries. We have tried not to be openly critical or use a strident type of voice." Those words may have been self-serving, but in the perception of Indira's critics continued to be far less charitable. She was seen as a political leader who seized every opportunity to scold others—especially Washington. "There was a certain contradiction between Indira's efforts to improve relations with the United States and her repeated protests that inimical foreign forces were out to subvert and harm her country and herself," Inder Malhotra writes. "Of course, she never identified the U.S. by name in such denunciatory declarations, but those speaking on her behalf left no one in any doubt that the accusing finger pointed at least to the CIA, if not at the U.S. government." ‡

---

* In Third World diplomatic circles, it is considered impolite for one country to criticize another—let alone an entire grouping such as the Nonaligned Movement—in public forums.

† Speech circulated to delegates by the Singapore delegation.

‡ Malhotra, *Indira Gandhi*, p. 291.

Yet it must be remembered that Indira Gandhi's two decades in power coincided with a period of extraordinary tension and turmoil in world affairs. She understood the historic nature of the times and tried, in her own way, to provide leadership for the underprivileged in world politics. While the tone and themes of her approach were often strident and sometimes deeply partisan, she did make a case for justice for the Third World in international politics. If, at some future date, Third World countries are able to participate more fully in determining the destiny of our planet, much credit will have to be given to Indira Gandhi for having sustained a Third World position in a largely inhospitable environment in critical times past.

22

Power Plays

Nonalignment. Development. The alleviation of extreme poverty. These are all worthy principles and goals that have long formed an essential part of Indian foreign policy and domestic concerns, and repeatedly enunciated by Jawaharlal Nehru, Indira Gandhi, Rajiv Gandhi, and all their successors—V. P. Singh, Chandra Shekhar, and Pamulaparti Venkata Narasimha Rao.[*] But principles in political life, like rules in a public-school dormitory, do get breached from time to time. Jawaharlal Nehru symbolized rectitude and probity in public life; his daughter, however, looked in the other direction when her associates—such as L. N. Mishra—engaged in wholesale corruption. Indira's supporters argued that the money collected by Congress barons never went into her pocket; the funds were intended for use by the party. That, of course, was a handy explanation to justify all sorts of abuses. While Indian industrialists—especially those who sought licenses for expansion—were the prime targets of this extortion, the biggest profits were made by Congress officials in defense deals. The practice of siphoning commissions from such deals reached its zenith during the five years following Indira's assassination.

Picture this scene: January 1986. A crispy cool morning in New Delhi. Prime Minister Olof Palme of Sweden is walking in a heavily guarded garden with his friend and political soulmate Prime Minister Rajiv

[*] Rao, seventy years old, was sworn in as India's ninth prime minister on June 21, 1991. The Congress Party did not win a majority in the May–June 1991 election, but was invited by President R. Venkataraman to form the government.

Gandhi of India. Palme had also been a good friend of Indira Gandhi and had participated in the Six-Nation Appeal for Nuclear Sanity, issued on May 22, 1984. The Appeal, Indira's last major international initiative, called for an immediate freeze on the "testing, production, and deployment of nuclear weapons." Besides Indira Gandhi and Olof Palme, the sponsors included Presidents Raoul Alfonsin of Argentina, Julius K. Nyerere of Tanzania, and Miguel de la Madrid Hurtado of Mexico. Prime Minister George Papandreou of Greece was also a sponsor. The preparatory work for the Appeal took four years.

On this day, the talk between Olof Palme and Rajiv Gandhi turns to the bitter war between Iraq and Iran. The year is 1986, and the conflict has already dragged on for six years at a cost to the combatants of more than $100 billion, and a million lives. Palme is pessimistic that anything can be done by the superpowers to end the war, especially the United States—whose bombing of Hanoi he once likened to Nazi Germany's efforts to exterminate the Jews.* And yes, says Palme, there is another unresolved matter as well—one that directly concerns his country and India. Rajiv Gandhi, a fellow member of Palme's International Nuclear Disarmament Commission, knows perfectly well what Palme is referring to.† He listens carefully as Palme spells out how Sweden would sweeten a deal under which India would buy $1.3 billion worth of howitzers from a failing Swedish weapons manufacturer. To undercut an attractive offer from a French competitor, GIAT, India has been offered unprecedented state export credits, which Sweden had previously prohibited for arms deals. This would be neutral Sweden's biggest export order ever; the acquisition of the Bofors-made 155mm gun would enable India—in the event of a war—to shell Lahore, the second largest city in neighboring Pakistan, from within Indian territory. Sweden, says Palme, badly needs India's business. Its competitors—Austria, the United States, France, Britain, and even South Africa—have enough orders to sustain their domestic weapons industries for a long time. But the very survival of Sweden's armaments sector depends on Gandhi's decision. Olof Palme reminds Rajiv Gandhi of his long friendship with Indira, and of how Indira has always been highly regarded in Sweden.

What followed was a nod, maybe also a nudge and a wink, and most certainly a handshake. Within a month or so, India and Sweden signed the deal, and soon afterward Sweden started shipping Bofors howitzers

---

*This remark has been widely quoted, although Olof Palme maintained strenuously that he did not mean to accuse the United States of genocide.

†Olof Palme was highly sought after on the international circuit as a speaker and mediator. He had no difficulty finding funding for all sorts of schemes to further "peace."

at the monthly rate of fourteen. The order guaranteed employment for the company's 5,000 workers for at least another four years. On the day that the deal was signed, Bofors's chairman threw a champagne dinner for all employees and their families at the company's main plant in Karlskoga. There was also much jubilation in Bofors's parent company, Nobel Industries, founded by Alfred Nobel, inventor of dynamite and the man who instituted the Nobel Prizes. And the clincher for the Indian deal? Commissions worth more than $100 million had possibly as much as $200 million, according to various investigators. Until 1987, Bofors resolutely denied that large payments were made in the howitzer deal. But after energetic digging by Swedish journalists, including Bjorne Stenqvist and Bo G. Andersson of Stockholm's *Dagens Nyheter*, Bofors came clean—up to a point. It admitted it had paid about $60 million to its India agents. And for what services rendered was this amount paid? Nobel Industries President Anders Carlberg said in an interview in mid-1988 that the payments "weren't bribes or commissions but windup costs" paid to Bofors's agents responsible for the India territory. * The payments, Carlberg insisted, were necessitated by an earlier meeting in New York in October 1985 between Palme and Rajiv Gandhi during the fortieth anniversary celebrations of the United Nations. India's need for new howitzers was discussed. Gandhi, said Carlberg, demanded of Palme that there be no middlemen in any future weapons deals between Sweden and India. Palme then relayed the information to Carlberg. As a result, according to Carlberg, he had to wind up a long-standing deal with Bofors's Indian representatives.[†]

I asked Carlberg who received the $60 million. Each time I posed the question, the handsome Swede froze me with his cold steel-blue eyes and then shook his head. "I am not going to tell you," he said. Some Indian publications—most notably the Madras-based daily newspaper, *The Hindu*, and the Bombay-based *Imprint* magazine—have carried out impressive investigations strongly suggesting that Bofors's money went to Indian expatriates and to companies associated with these foreign-based businessmen.[‡] On November 4, 1988, then–Opposition leader V. P. Singh disclosed that he had evidence of payments by Bofors exceeding

---

* Interview with author, New York City.
[†] Present during this interview with the author was Lawrence Minard, then deputy managing editor (and now managing editor) of *Forbes* magazine. Minard seemed amazed that the Swede would insist on offering such a puny and implausible explanation.
[‡] *The Hindu* initiated an investigation that took its Geneva-based correspondent, Chitra Subramanium, all over Europe. The Bofors story was personally supervised by the newspaper's associate editor, N. Ram.

$15 million to Swiss bank accounts allegedly held by Indians. Singh, formerly Gandhi's finance and defense minister and later his deadly political adversary, implied that the bulk of this money was paid to accounts personally controlled by Rajiv Gandhi. The accusation raised another political furor in India. In late April 1988, India's Joint Parliamentary Committee ruled that Bofors need not reveal the identities of whoever received the questionable payments. This predictably touched off a political storm, with Opposition leaders charging that the Congress-dominated committee had performed a whitewash, and that Gandhi was shielding his friends and associates. The suspicions concerning Bofors haunted Rajiv until his assassination. A senior Indian government official who worked under both Rajiv and Indira told me: "It was not that Indira was beyond authorizing commission-taking. But she was smart enough never to let the finger of suspicion point directly at her. Rajiv wasn't as smart as his mother."[*]

The lesson of the Bofors story is that sometimes a combination of a nation's strategic needs and its leaders' greed force an unsavory modification of foreign policy. India is no exception to this. And the Bofors episode spilled over from being a "foreign" issue into a highly charged domestic controversy. Eventually, the Bofors issue brought down the Rajiv Gandhi administration in the election of December 1989. To put it another way, the harsh realities of Rajiv Gandhi's foreign policy dragged India's lofty moral principles into the mud. Indians legitimately asked whether there was any difference between the political and financial behavior of Rajiv Gandhi and his associates, and that of, say, Zaire's corrupt dictator, Mobutu Seko Sese, or the deposed Philippines despot, Ferdinand Marcos.[†]

For Rajiv Gandhi's well-wishers, it was tempting to term these accusations baseless political charges. But India's masses were becoming increasingly conscious of the need for probity in government, and they were not likely to take the same generous view of "windup costs." The Bofors case was a glaring example of how developing nations get enmeshed in economic commitments that arise partly because of superpower geopoli-

---

[*] Conversation with author, New York, June 1991. The speaker asked for anonymity.
[†] Both Mobutu and Marcos were alleged to have secreted away billions of dollars in foreign accounts. These dictators also reportedly bought choice real estate in many Western countries. While their avarice was not matched by some Indian politicians, the latter certainly did well by their access to power. Relatives and friends of several top Gandhi aides, for example, suddenly became entrepreneurs in America, or landlords. The source of their instant wealth was never disclosed, but it could hardly have been their own sweat or enterprise.

tics. It can be argued that if the United States had not armed Pakistan beyond its legitimate military requirements, India would not have accelerated the arms race on the Subcontinent. Of course, Pakistanis could well argue the same case the other way around—substituting the Soviet Union for the United States. The fact is that with an annual defense budget of $10 billion, the Indian government is in a position to award a lot of lucrative contracts to foreign suppliers. A middleman by any other name is still a middleman—and bribes by any other name are still bribes.

There have long been reports that Congress leaders have secreted vast amounts siphoned from big arms deals. These amounts, according to numerous allegations, are kept abroad and then channeled into India during election time to benefit candidates belonging to the ruling Congress Party. And foreign arms suppliers, ever anxious to develop new business in the Third World, are often only too willing to pay commissions demanded of them: In most cases, of course, these "commissions" paid to middlemen are factored into the overall amounts billed to the purchasers. The practice began during the long reign of Indira Gandhi and, some say, even during Jawaharlal Nehru's time. "Commissions have been paid for a long time—the middle man is ubiquitous in India," says Babulal Jain, a New Delhi businessman. * While Swedish law prohibits bribes for arms deals, authorities have long turned a blind eye to such practices, especially at a time when Sweden badly needs export orders and when the international arms bazaar has become a buyer's market.

Gandhi has denied that he or any of his associates received bribes from Bofors, although Swedish authorities belatedly began investigating charges that the money was transferred into Swiss bank accounts of three Indian companies. A month after meeting Gandhi in New Delhi, in February 1986, Palme was murdered as he left a Stockholm movie theater. † Not long afterward, Palme was posthumously awarded India's prestigious Jawaharlal Nehru Prize, which is given annually to individuals who promote world peace and nonviolence. It now turns out that the charismatic Swede was also a strenuous salesman for Swedish arms exports even as he traveled the world declaiming on disarmament. Indeed, when Palme headed a UN peace mission to Iran in 1979, not long before he became prime minister for the second time, he was setting the stage for oil and arms deals for Sweden.

Why this surreptitious salesmanship? A familiar story, although one

---

* Conversation with author, New York City, June 1991.
† A former psychiatric patient was convicted of the crime in July 1989, but the conviction was overturned a few months later.

that many self-righteous Swedes wish to play down. It underscores the fact that international leaders such as Olof Palme and Indira Gandhi, who did not hesitate to preach to the world about high morality in politics, also did not hesitate to act in their own self-interest when it suited them. It was important for Palme to save Sweden's arms industries from going under the double burden of declining domestic demand and the aftereffects of steel mill closures on regions traditionally housing defense producers like Karlskoga, where Bofors employs 80 percent of the labor force. Arms exports not only ensured the defense industry's survival; they also paid for important technological research in defense. As a lifelong socialist, Palme believed in full employment—as long as some-one else paid for it. And so he worked his charm, first on the Iranians, then on the Indians. It could hardly have been coincidence, there-fore, that in the three years after Palme took office in 1981, Sweden concluded oil deals with Iran amounting to nearly $200 million; oil purchases from Iraq, meanwhile, totaled barely $5.75 million, according to Swedish government estimates. Moreover, Iran heavily bought con-sumer goods from Sweden—more than $500 million worth in 1984 alone. Officially, at least, Sweden was supposed to be neutral in the Iraq-Iran war. And legally, Swedish companies were forbidden to export arms to areas where there was armed conflict or human-rights violations. Just around this time, the products of Swedish arms producers—mainly Bofors—were reportedly reaching Iran stealthily via Singapore.* The goods included nearly 1,000 RBS-70 antiaircraft missiles, which were routed to the Middle East—including Iran—through two Singapore com-

* According to Sweden's Bureau of Statistics, Singapore was Sweden's biggest weap-ons customer between 1977 and 1986, buying $1.40 billion worth of goods, or almost 11 percent of all Swedish arms exports during the period. This was not the first time that Swedish companies had acted in a questionable fashion in the Third World. Palme wasn't the only Swede connected with arms deals to die under mysterious circumstances: In January 1987, Carl-Fredrik Algernon, director of Sweden's arms export agency, fell in front of an incoming subway train at Stockholm's Central Station. He had emerged as a key figure in various investigations of Bofors. Witnesses said at first that the sixty-one-year-old Algernon was pushed in front of the train, but the testimony was later recanted. His death has been officially termed an accident and possibly a suicide. Most Swedes believe the "accident" to have been a murder. "Swedes take great pride in their social stability," says Dr. Ian Anthony, an arms expert based in Stockholm. "These mysterious, unresolved matters perplex them and cause much angst." Sweden's then–prime minister, Ingvar Carlsson, swore in late September 1987 that stricter rules would be drafted governing weapons exports. He also promised a crackdown on the foreign marketing operations of arms firms, and more rigid monitoring of preliminary contracts between arms producers and potential buyers.

panies, Allied Ordnance of Singapore (AOS), and Unicorn International. Both firms were partly owned by Sheng Li Holding Company, the Singapore Defense Ministry's investment company, or by Bofors.*

The Indians, who felt they got a good deal on the 400 Bofors howitzers, were not about to cancel the deal with Sweden, no matter what corruption charges were leveled against the Rajiv Gandhi administration. As for the alleged bribes, Bofors says that neither Prime Minister Gandhi nor his family were recipients. It will be quite a while before all the Swedish investigations are completed, and meanwhile Bofors was doing business.† For weapons suppliers, countries such as India are choice customers. And when local governments encourage commission-giving on the part of weapons suppliers, the potential for corruption is awesome. Governments are, after all, supposed to be the guardians of the public welfare. But when governments are in league with shady characters, who remains to protect the public interest? And are not commissions a theft of public money that might otherwise be spent on economic development for the masses? Whenever brash journalists tried to raise these points with Indira Gandhi, she would reply with steely looks. But because she did not answer these questions did not mean that they were not valid.

And no case symbolized the misuse of public money as much as that involving Sanjay Gandhi's Maruti car. The equivalent of millions of dollars from the treasury went into supporting Sanjay's venture between 1970 and 1975, and yet no "people's car" appeared on the streets of India. After Indira's election defeat in 1977, an investigation was carried out by a public commission headed by Justice A. C. Gupta of the Indian Supreme Court. Justice Gupta examined 712 affidavits and more than 2,000 government files; he questioned 268 witnesses and held 111 public sessions to obtain testimony. In a huge report issued on May 31, 1979, Justice Gupta said: "The affairs of the Maruti [companies] . . . appear to have brought about a decline in the integrity of public life and sullied the purity of administration. . . . From the interest taken in Maruti's progress by men from the Prime Minister's Secretariat and the way even matters connected with the country's defense were subordinated to the interest of Maruti Limited, and the prevailing sense of fear that prompted implicit obedience, one is left in no doubt as to the origin of the power that made such a state of affairs possible. Sanjay Gandhi exercised only

* This information was uncovered by the author during the course of an investigation for *Forbes* magazine.
† With the return to power of the Congress Party in June 1991, it was all but certain that the truth about Bofors would never be known. It would surely be in the interest of the culprits to destroy whatever evidence they could find in government files.

a derivative power; its source was the authority of the prime minister. . . ."*

When asked by reporters about Justice Gupta's report, Indira Gandhi scornfully dismissed it as "just plain trash."† After she returned to power in January 1980, Indira immediately nationalized the Maruti enterprise—thereby, in effect, canceling out its record and absolving her son of any past wrongdoing. This act on Indira's part was almost certainly the result of her gratitude to Sanjay for masterminding her victory. Biographer—and relative—Nayantara Sahgal writes:

> If [Indira] preferred to ignore the material available to her, it can only have been because she had set her heart on bequeathing power to her son. She treated the national controversy surrounding Sanjay's business dealings and his role in politics as quite simply a lie, the invention of her enemies. . . . Sanjay's conduct during the Emergency had contributed to his mother's defeat in 1977, yet he was more directly responsible for her triumphant return three years later—and Mrs. Gandhi believed she owed her political resurrection at least in part to Sanjay's advice and management. Much of her private torment and anxiety must have centered on the undisciplined young man, dangerously addicted to the short cut, who had to be shielded from the public consequences of his actions. . . . Guilt feelings are part of parenthood, and it is possible that Mrs. Gandhi labored under some degree of guilt toward the problem marriage that her sons felt had treated their father unfairly. . . .‡

After Sanjay Gandhi's death in 1980, there was considerable anxiety among members of Indira's coterie about access to Sanjay's private papers and files. Indira, in fact, surreptitiously tried to recover Sanjay's keychain and watch from the plane wreckage in New Delhi. This fueled speculation about just how much Sanjay had squirreled away. Indira's self-possession, says Nayantara Sahgal, was "widely remarked when she returned to recover Sanjay's keys and watch, both articles essential for access to his finances and documents, from his mangled body. This insured that control of these would be hers and not pass to Sanjay's widow, Maneka, and Maneka's family, with the unforeseen political implications this might involve." Maneka was twenty-three years old when Sanjay died.

* *Report of the Commission of Inquiry on Maruti Affairs* (New Delhi: Government of India Press, 1978).
† Quoted by Murli Deora to author.
‡ Sahgal, *Indira Gandhi: Her Road to Power*, pp. 216–17.

In the event, Indira and Maneka were to have a massive and public falling out. Indira was already determined to pull Rajiv, by then a pilot with Indian Airlines, into politics. "Maneka—young, ambitious and fiery—considered herself to be the rightful heir to [Sanjay's] mantle and was prepared to fight for what she believed to be her right," says Inder Malhotra. "In her view, Rajiv was not only a usurper but also unfit for the role expected of him. Sanjay's acolytes, anxious to preserve the positions of power and influence they had managed to occupy, would also have preferred Maneka to be their new mentor. But they were left in no doubt that the very idea was anathema to Indira. Not only was Maneka not a member of the Nehru-Gandhi clan, her marriage to Sanjay notwithstanding, she was also intensely disliked by her mother-in-law—who was extremely fond of Rajiv's wife, Sonia. Indira was deeply suspicious of Maneka's motives, affiliations and designs, and would give her no quarter."[*] Maneka felt increasingly isolated in Indira's household: She had continued to live there after Sanjay's death, not the least because Indira was very fond of Sanjay and Maneka's young son, Feroze Varun.[†]

Many Indian sociologists, including Gerson da Cunha, have pointed out that tensions between mothers-in-law and daughters-in-law are especially high in Indian joint families. This was indeed true of Indira and Maneka, especially after Sanjay's death. The two women screamed at each other frequently, with Indira insisting that Maneka not engage in any political activity that would be embarrassing to the family. Maneka had already started criticizing Rajiv in public, more than once calling him "lazy" and "indolent." Unlike the toughs with whom Sanjay associated, the young men around Rajiv Gandhi were part of the Westernized elite that enjoyed the good life in modern-day Delhi. They frequently traveled abroad; they especially enjoyed the company of American friends; they were at home in the swanky clubs, discotheques, and restaurants of London, Paris, and New York; and in their bachelor days many had foreign girlfriends. Maneka perceived, correctly, that it would be only a matter of time before the Rajiv coterie would displace the Sanjay coterie within the upper reaches of the Congress Party. Rajiv was asked by his mother to run for Parliament from Sanjay's constituency, Amethi, in Uttar Pradesh. In June 1981, Rajiv was elected by a landslide.

"Yes, I do feel excited about going into politics—but daunted, too," Rajiv told Trevor Fishlock, then a correspondent in India for *The Times* of London. To Ian Jack, who represented the London *Sunday Times*,

[*] Malhotra, *Indira Gandhi*, pp. 236–37.
[†] Feroze Varun was born in 1979.

Rajiv said: "I want to attract a new breed of person to politics—intelligent, Westernized young men with nonfeudal, noncriminal ideas, who want to make India prosper rather than merely themselves." Years later, of course, Rajiv's words would seem very hollow indeed—even dishonest—because the very men whom he had brought to power looted India as few had done before, not even the most venal of Indira Gandhi's aides.

Maneka now began to deliberately provoke Indira. She felt that Indira was drifting away from Maneka and her son under the influence of Rajiv and Sonia, and she sought to assert her presence through political visibility. She would criticize her mother-in-law—by implication, to be sure—at public meetings. She sold off *Surya*, the scurrilous magazine that Sanjay had launched for her, to political opponents of Indira. Finally, in late March 1982, Indira Gandhi threw her daughter-in-law out of her house. It was an ugly occasion, one where the servants were instructed to deposit Maneka's suitcases and belongings outside the prime minister's bungalow in New Delhi. Maneka, humiliated so publicly, left. She took her son with her and for a long time afterward Indira was denied the pleasure of seeing Feroze Varun Gandhi. In a letter that Indira wrote to Maneka, she said: "Although you came from a different background, we accepted you because of Sanjay. But now we see you cannot adjust." The episode tarnished Indira's image, and Maneka never reconciled with her mother-in-law. Maneka in large part blamed Rajiv and Sonia Gandhi for the rift with Indira. She felt that they were jealous of her and Sanjay in the years when Sanjay bravely faced political opposition and Rajiv and Sonia distanced themselves from the misfortunes of the family. Maneka's animosity toward Rajiv continued, and she opposed him in the December 1984 election from the Amethi constituency. Rajiv won handily. In 1989 Maneka got her own back, in a manner of speaking, when she was made a minister in the Opposition Janata Dal government. But such are the twists and turns of politics that in the May–June 1991 election Maneka lost her reelection bid for Parliament. But then, of course, Rajiv Gandhi was dead.

Notwithstanding India's spirited talk of nonalignment and economic self-sufficiency, Indira Gandhi knew that India needed sustained and good relations with the big powers. Consider the following figures: In 1983, nearly 10 percent of the country's total imports—mainly capital goods and machinery—of $13.5 billion came from the United States; 8.1 percent from Britain; 9.6 percent from West Germany; 12.7 percent from Japan; 5.3 percent from the Soviet Union; and 9.4 percent from other industrial countries.* And the exports from India? Of nearly $10 billion in gems, tea, coffee, leather, textiles, and other commodities, nearly 20 percent went to the United States; 14.9 percent to the Soviet Union; 10.7 percent to Japan; 10.6 percent to the Common Market countries; 5.9 percent to West Germany; and 5.9 percent to Britain.

Because the United States is India's biggest trading partner, one would expect relations between the two countries to be more affable. But the relationship has been, at best, ambiguous. At the heart of this has been India's attempt to prevent the extension of American power around the Third World—power that Indian officials see as being intimidating to small and medium-sized countries. Of course, there is also the historical resentment over Washington's selection of Pakistan as the cutting edge of its South Asia policy. Squaring off against this historical animus is the mounting Indian desire for American technology. And so, after Rajiv Gandhi became prime minister, Delhi was a bit more flexible toward Washington, even though the latter did not always reciprocate.

Two main factors—one domestic and the other related to foreign policy—influenced Indira Gandhi's cool and mildly hostile relationship with the United States. First, the internal factor: It must be remembered that quite early in her prime-ministerial career she had to face formidable opposition from the seniors—the Syndicate—within her own Congress Party who were trying to restrict her powers, even to the extent of plotting to replace her with someone from among their own ranks. The Syndicate happened to be right wing in domestic socioeconomic issues and pro–United States in their foreign policy preferences. Since it was a matter of survival for Indira, and since the populist path she chose required her to show that she was wedded to socialism, her instincts turned her against the United States. "Look, the big powers are all out for their own interests," Indira once told *Forbes* editor James Michaels and other American correspondents. "We are not under an illusion that anybody is going out of his way to help us."†

It took a right-wing American President, Ronald Reagan, to thaw the cool relations between the United States and India. During Indira Gandhi's 1982 visit to Washington, it was clear that Reagan was keen to court her.‡ And Indira seemed uncharacteristically responsive to his overtures. Asked by White House reporters about a new phase in bilateral

---

*Statistics provided by the government of India.
†Quoted by James Michaels to the author.
‡This was the first visit that Indira had made to the United States since 1971, just before the start of the Indo-Pakistan War of 1971.

relations between the United States and India, Indira replied: "We think that we should be friends—and we want to do everything we can for friendship. Of course, we cannot jettison our basic policies. . . ."*

Relations between the Soviets and India grew warm during Indira's years as prime minister. In 1980 Moscow and New Delhi announced that they had signed a deal under which the Soviets would supply India with $1.6 billion in arms over the next ten years. The Soviets also agreed to supply India with some 15 million barrels of oil annually at below-market prices. Thus the Soviet Union came to enjoy a status in New Delhi that it possessed in virtually no other major Third World country. Originally, tacit alliance with Moscow was seen by Indian policymakers as a balance against U.S. interests in the region. But the relationship became far more deep and complex than that. In 1971, for instance, the two countries signed a treaty of peace, friendship, and cooperation. Since then, the Soviet Union has been steadily importing more consumer goods from India, and India has been buying more military hardware from Moscow. Indeed Soviet aircraft, submarines, tanks, and other weapons systems have become the mainstay of India's armed forces.† Since Mikhail Gorbachev rose to power, he has already visited India several times. In late November 1988, for example, he announced in Delhi that the Soviet Union would extend to India about 3.2 billion rubles—or about $3 billion—in credit to cover the Soviet construction of two nuclear reactors to produce electricity for southern India, as well as several nonnuclear energy projects. With such gestures continually emanating from Moscow, together with large-scale cultural and educational exchange programs, it will be difficult to dislodge the Soviets from a very special place in the minds and hearts of Indian officials, if not necessarily everyday Indians. A cordial relationship with the Kremlin also helps Delhi to blunt threats from indigenous Communists. During Gorbachev's November 1988 visit to India, for instance, he did not meet with Indian Communist leaders, as he had done during his 1986 trip. With such gestures, Gorbachev seemed to be taking out political insurance that India's public reaction to Soviet adventures and misadventures in the international arena would be, at the worst, moderate.

If India's relationship with the Soviet Union has been remarkable, then perhaps even more extraordinary is India's nexus with Britain. This is a relationship between a former master and slave who now treat each

---

*Quoted by Janki Ganju in an interview with the author, May 1991.
†India has the world's fourth biggest military force—after the Soviet Union, the United States, and China.

other as fully equal members of the comity of nations. Despite occasional political hiccups, such as the question of immigrants to Britain, the relationship between India and Britain continues to be a model for former colonial bosses and subjects—a relationship that Indira Gandhi nurtured. Indeed, as time recedes, even the colonial relationship develops the glow of nostalgia which engenders a residual affection. This remains a relationship more lodged in friendship and affection than that between any other imperial and subjugated country. Amicable personal relations between successive leaders of the two countries partly explains this relationship: For instance, Indira Gandhi developed an unusual and unlikely friendship with the ideologically very different Mrs. Thatcher. And Rajiv Gandhi maintained a cordial connection with Number 10 Downing Street. When Mrs. Gandhi was assassinated, Prime Minister Thatcher flew to Delhi for the funeral, a gesture that was applauded and admired by tens of millions of Indians who did not seem as impressed by the other world dignitaries who had also flown to Delhi to pay their last respects to the "Empress of India."

A key aspect of the India-Britain relationship has been the fact that India has not nationalized substantial British investments, unlike many other newly independent Third World countries that appropriated British commercial assets after gaining freedom. Trade and financial relationships have prospered, moreover; perhaps Indian and British businessmen understand each other's commercial ways better than most other players in a two-way commercial traffic. Cricketing ties between the two countries also help. British cricket stars such as Ian Botham are as much household names in India as they are in Britain; similarly, Sunil Gavaskar—who holds the record for having scored the most number of runs in official, or "test," matches between countries—is as well-known in Britain as he is in India. Moreover, the million-strong Indian community in Britain has, for the most part, adapted well to its new home, and it has played an important though unobtrusive role in British society. As with Britain, India's relationships with Western European countries have a strong degree of warmth and an increasing element of economic benefit. Indira recognized that India was heavily dependent on external assistance for its domestic development needs. Since Independence India has received more than $35 billion in foreign aid: Of this amount, 79 percent has been in loans; 14 percent in commodity assistance, and 7 percent in outright grants. The United States accounted for more than 45 percent of all aid to India between 1947 and 1975.[*]

---

[*] Hardgrave and Kochanek, *India*, p. 360.

The relations between India and Western European countries were cemented when many construction and weapons contracts were awarded to European companies during Indira's tenure as prime minister. After Rajiv Gandhi took office in 1984, Sonia Gandhi's Italian heritage was an unstated but important factor in strengthening such ties, and Rajiv Gandhi never hesitated to refer to his "European connection" during his state visits to Europe. As Europe grows into closer union with the approach of 1992, it is likely that its relationship with India in the Common Market will grow because they will both represent medium-sized powers lodged between major superpower blocs of the world. *

There is no doubt that Indira wanted—and actively worked for—India to emerge as a strong regional military, political, and economic power. Indira was not very sensitive to the concerns of some of the other countries of the region—Pakistan, Bangladesh, and Sri Lanka. The most striking example is Bangladesh, in whose liberation Indira Gandhi played such a crucial role, but which soon developed a fairly negative, even hostile, relationship with India. The antagonism supposedly stemmed from a bilateral dispute over the sharing of river waters, but it really had to do with Bangladesh's resentment over the big-power role that India sought for itself in the region. Indira Gandhi's Pokhran nuclear experiment in 1974 served to create legitimate suspicions in neighboring capitals about India's hegemonistic aspirations. † According to Professors Robert Hardgrave, and Stanley Kochanek, perhaps the main factor in Indira's decision to develop a nuclear potential was India's isolation in the 1971 Indo-Pakistan War and its increasing dependency on the Soviet Union. They write: "India's entrance into the nuclear club served to underscore its preeminence in the South Asian subcontinent—but it also gave impetus to the possibility of a nuclear arms race in the subcontinent as Pakistan strives to achieve a comparable nuclear capability. . . . India has demonstrated nuclear capability, but it has thus far resisted arguments

---

* To supplement the $1.6 billion in Soviet arms that India agreed to buy at concessionary prices starting in 1980, Indira Gandhi also sealed a deal to buy $1.3 billion worth of French Mirage jets.

† A nuclear device was exploded by India in May 1974 in a desert in the western state of Rajasthan. Indian officials insisted that it had been a "peaceful" explosion, but there has been widespread suspicion that India was developing a nuclear weapons capability. India has long refused to sign the Nuclear Non-Proliferation Treaty. Indira Gandhi's position was that the treaty was discriminatory and that it was as important to control "vertical proliferation" as "horizontal proliferation," according to Professors Hardgrave and Kochanek. By detonating the nuclear device, India became the sixth member of the exclusive "nuclear club," previously consisting of the United States, China, the Soviet Union, Britain, and France.

by the 'pro-bomb' lobby within India for exercising the weapons option. Nuclear proliferation in South Asia is not inevitable, but it hangs in the balance of Indo-Pakistani relations and the perceptions each nation has of its own security requirements and deterrence capabilities."[*]

It should also be noted that at least two of the major neighbors—Pakistan and Sri Lanka—did not quite go along with India's legitimate stand on the demilitarization of the Indian Ocean and, specifically, on Diego Garcia. Clearly, India's concerns and global outlook were different from those of Pakistan, Bangladesh, and Sri Lanka. This, in turn, led Indira Gandhi to fashion a least accommodative regional foreign policy. With regards to Nepal, India did not have any major problems in Indira's time, but she was always wary about China trying to increase its presence and influence in that mountainous nation.[†] Indira's emphasis on building a strong blue-water navy has today resulted in India having a naval presence in the surrounding seas which is being noticed with some concern even by faraway countries like Malaysia, Australia, and Indonesia.

On balance, it is clear that India's consistency in foreign policy has paid important dividends—although not always to the liking of Western policymakers. To them, India's pronouncements on world affairs often seem self-righteous, moralistic, and preachy—a charge that has some validity, of course. You only have to sit through a committee session at the United Nations to be persuaded about the pompousness of many Indian officials. However, such loftiness must be perceived as an abrasive shield behind which an old culture seeks to hide some of its domestic failures and insecurities. India has no more of a monopoly on moral values than any other Third World country or industrialized nation, but Indian officials have yet to accept this fully. Still, the management of Indian foreign policy by successive prime ministers, starting with Jawaharlal Nehru, has contributed significantly to the country's enhanced esteem in world affairs. These consistencies, although fertilized by personal relationships of Indira Gandhi with foreign leaders, are likely to be maintained whatever the political complexion and creed of future Indian governments.

During Indira Gandhi's last years of life, a serious ethnic problem began to bubble in neighboring Sri Lanka. In May 1991, that ethnic crisis

---

[*] Hardgrave and Kochanek, *India*, pp. 359–60.
[†] Bilateral relations between India and Nepal became extremely shaky in 1989, however, when India imposed what was a virtual embargo on Nepal. The Indians were furious that the Nepalese had sought to acquire new weaponry from China.

would claim the life of Indira's son Rajiv. It could be argued that had it not been for the tacit—albeit indirect—support given to the guerrilla group the Liberation Tigers of Tamil Eelam (LTTE), by Indira's government, what started as a relatively minor ethnic conflagration in Sri Lanka would never have developed into a full-scale civil war that eventually was to pull India into its grip. The LTTE received sanctuary, weapons, and money from the Indian state of Tamil Nadu, whose chief minister, the former actor M. G. Ramachandran—MGR—was Indira's only main ally in the southern part of the country. While Indira claimed to be embarrassed by MGR's support of the LTTE at a time when her government was denouncing Pakistan for aiding Sikh terrorists in the Punjab, she clearly was able to restrain her disapproval.

Indira was privately reluctant to undercut the LTTE because the Tamil guerrillas had tremendous support in Tamil Nadu. Indira was facing the prospect of elections in 1984, and the Congress Party's chances were by no means assured. Indira needed the support of the South. Appeasement of the Tamils was seen by her as politically expedient. "I'll settle this whole thing after the election," Indira told several associates. Professor Ralph Buultjens says Indira was never happy with the support given by MGR to the LTTE.

A second reason why Indira did not restrain the LTTE was that the guerrilla group was the main thorn in the side of one of Indira's irritants in the region, Sri Lanka's septuagenarian president Junius Richard Jayewardene. President Jayewardene was Ronald Reagan's kind of Third World leader: He hated Communism, promoted free-enterprise, and was not afraid to call Americans the good guys and Marxists the bad ones. Indira disliked Jayewardene intensely—not the least because at an election rally he once asked Sri Lankans to defeat their prime minister, Sirimavo Bandaranaike, and her son, Anura, in the same way that the Indians had "thrown out their cow and calf" in the 1977 elections—Indira and Sanjay. He had, on several occasions, acted presumptuously toward India, deliberately tweaking India's nose on a number of issues such as his pro-Washington foreign policy. Indira knew that Jayewardene wanted Washington to develop better links with Sri Lanka: The pear-shaped island had the best deep-water harbor in the world in Trincomalee and was therefore considered a place of great strategic importance for American interests. With the Soviets expanding their military presence in the Indian Ocean, Washington—which already had ready access to Trincomalee—would be delighted to maintain some sort of staging post in Sri Lanka. Senior officials in Washington saw Sri Lanka as the sixth finger in the Asian "hand" of security, which also included South Korea,

Singapore, Indonesia, Malaysia, and Thailand, all countries favorably inclined to American interests.

But now this extraordinary bastion of Western-style democracy and friend of Washington was facing a clear and present danger, and Jayewardene sought active political and other assistance from Washington.* Tall, ascetic in his personal habits, and an authentic aristocrat, Jayewardene was too proud a man to openly ask for alms. At any event, more financial aid is not what he necessarily wanted, but additional American investment to develop his country's agricultural base and light industries. He felt that with Sri Lanka's high literacy rate and skilled labor force, American companies could quickly make healthy profits. An American economic presence, Jayewardene felt, would inevitably serve as a prophylactic against political sabotage. He felt he had already made the gestures and accommodations toward Washington: Jayewardene had permitted the Peace Corps to come in for the first time; he had said yes to the installing of the Voice of America's biggest transmitter, a 2.5-million-kilowatt facility that would beam propaganda from Iran to China. American naval ships used Sri Lankan ports at will. Jayewardene frequently derided India's adherence to socialism. He also made several disparaging comments about Jawaharlal Nehru.

All of this showed a great lack of prudence on Jayewardene's part, and it galled Indira Gandhi. She felt that Jayewardene had sold out to Washington and that Sri Lanka planned to create an American military presence on the soft underbelly of India. But Jayewardene claimed that there was a Marxist conspiracy to destabilize Sri Lanka and overthrow his freely elected government. Libya had been funneling arms to ethnic guerrillas who wanted to establish a separate Tamil state in the northern region; there was evidence that some of these guerrillas had been trained by the Palestine Liberation Organization in Lebanon. Jayewardene made two major miscalculations: one, that the United States and Western European powers would physically come to Sri Lanka's aid in the event of any conflict with India; and second, that he could talk to India as a coequal sovereign nation. Sovereign Sri Lanka and India certainly were coequal, but not in Indira's view.

At the heart of Sri Lanka's ethnic problem was a simple, central point: When a minority community perceived that economic and social development was passing it by, it would agitate. The Tamils of the

---

*The Reagan administration, which heaped praise on the free-market orientation of Jayewardene's development policies, gave Sri Lanka more economic assistance per person than to any other country in Asia.

northern and eastern regions charged that the Colombo government's economic policies had deprived their community of choice jobs and education. Sinhalese conservatives responded that for too long it was the Tamils who held the majority of bureaucratic and other choice positions and also dominated the universities; the Sinhalese said that it was time that such imbalances were corrected. And the implications of Sri Lanka's ethnic problem extended beyond this country's borders to other Asian and Third World states: Places like Malaysia, Indonesia, Bangladesh, Myanmar—once Burma—and India, which have large and traditionally disaffected minorities, could find themselves suffering from identical economic setbacks if the ethnic situation within their own borders worsened. And if Jayewardene, the Sinhalese establishment, and the Tamils were able to fashion some formula through which a lasting amity between the Sinhalese and the Tamils was achieved, then perhaps Sri Lanka's efforts could well serve as a model for other countries with ethnic conflicts.

According to government statistics, Sri Lanka had 7 million Sinhalese, 1.2 million "native" Tamils, 700,000 Muslims, 40,000 Malays and other minor ethnic community persons, and 625,000 Tamils of recent Tamil origin, the so-called stateless Indians, who worked primarily in the lush tea plantations of central Sri Lanka. The Sinhalese are overwhelmingly Buddhist, while the Tamils are mostly Hindus. The Sinhalese are believed to have migrated to what is now called Sri Lanka more than 2,500 years ago from regions that now are parts of Bihar and West Bengal states in India. Joining them in the journey across the forty-mile-wide Palk Strait separating India and Sri Lanka were the first Tamil migrants, who settled down in the northern part of the island around what is today the Jaffna Province. With the arrival of Buddhism from India around 240 B.C., Sinhalese civilization flowered and Buddhism spread rapidly, but the Tamils clung to their Hinduism. Settlers continued coming from India, bringing with them religious and cultural influences that have deeply affected the island. There were other visitors: Ptolemy called the island Taprobane, from "thambapanni," meaning copper-colored sand; Arab sailors called it Serendib, the root of the English word "serendipity." Marco Polo was another visitor. The Portuguese introduced Christianity, and later American missionaries established schools and colleges in the Jaffna area. The Dutch came, and were later thrown out by the British, who made Sri Lanka—Ceylon, as they called it—into a crown colony. It was the British who created a plantation economy based on tea, rubber, and coconuts. They opened roads and railways, they made English the official language, and they created an elite native class that strived to emulate its colonial rulers.

In 1948 Ceylon became independent, and postindependence politics have been pretty much dominated by two major parties—the leftist-oriented Sri Lanka Freedom Party and the United National Party of Jayewardene. A change in the country's constitution in 1972 saw Ceylon become Sri Lanka, the ancient Sinhalese name for the island. (Sri Lankan tea, so popular in the West, continues to be marketed as Ceylon tea in order to preserve consumer identification.) Jayewardene was convinced that the way to really develop his country's economy was through untrammeled free enterprise—a radical posture in the Third World, where many leaders favor state-directed socialism. Sri Lanka was long considered a model of political and economic development, one of the Third World's few authentic success stories. In less than a decade, Sri Lanka brought down its annual population growth rate from nearly 3 percent to less than 1.7 percent through an imaginative family-planning program fashioned by the government and by the United Nations Fund for Population Activities. By instituting a free, nationwide health-care project it lowered its infant mortality rate from 140 babies per 1,000 in 1945 to thirty-eight per 1,000 by 1980. A measure of such an achievement was the fact that Sri Lanka's infant mortality rate was one-third that of Africa's and less than half of the rest of Asia. Under successive leaders, Sri Lanka sustained such an achievement by accelerating the construction of schools and promoting free education, building clinics and hospitals, offering free health care, and embarking on a stepped-up program of training midwives and nurses.

By promoting rural development through such ambitious projects as the $6 billion Mahaweli program—under which dams and irrigation canals are being built—Sri Lanka kept its peasants on the farms and thus was able to check overcrowding in cities like Colombo, which actually declined in population during the 1980s. Sri Lankans lived longer than most Asians, ate better, seemed happier generally. The average Sri Lankan woman now had four children; in neighboring India, women averaged five births each; in Bangladesh, the figure was six children per woman, and seven in Pakistan. Because of a massive education drive, men and women were marrying later, and the concept of a two-child family seemed to be catching on. Jayewardene had steadily but firmly repudiated the socialist policies of his predecessor, Sirimavo Bandaranaike, under whom a massive and costly welfare system had been created, allocating scarce public money to subsidize everything from rice to kerosene. The socialists had restricted foreign travel, clamped down on imports, and imposed an artifically high value on the Sri Lankan rupee. But Jayewardene, by promoting a free-trade zone, among other things, where

Western, Japanese, and Hong Kong companies set up factories to produce shoes, clothes, and electronics, was able to pull down the unemployment rate from 30 percent to 15 percent by 1983.

I went to see President Jayewardene in 1983. Sri Lanka was like a picture postcard come alive—the bright smiles of the people; the miles of palms and fronds swaying in gentle Indian Ocean breezes that waft the fragrance of jasmine; the glistening beaches; the vast tea plantations climbing up gentle hills; the frothy seas. Even the sunlight seemed a rich green. It was the Vesak season when I arrived in Sri Lanka in mid-May, ordinarily a time for much fun and festivity, an occasion to observe the Buddha's birthday and to festoon homes and public buildings with gay lights; to decorate neighborhoods with pandoles, colorful exhibits high-lighting episodes from the Buddha's life; to exchange gifts and consume sweetmeats and generally to engage in a spree of merrymaking. It was a disturbing Vesak for the seventy-seven-year-old Jayewardene because two American civilians had just been kidnapped by Tamil separatists who were demanding $2.8 million in gold and the release of twenty suspected terrorists held in Sri Lankan jails. In the event, the Americans, Stanley and Mary Allen, were released unharmed after five days in captivity during which, the Allens said, they were never threatened with death and never once told about the ransom demands. Even their release was not a complete victory for Jayewardene—it was the intervention of Prime Minister Indira Gandhi, who issued personal appeals to the Tamil terror-ists, that was widely seen as bringing a nontragic end to the episode. Some hard-line Sinhalese in Jayewardene's cabinet had opined that any involvement by Mrs. Gandhi in the kidnapping incident would constitute a form of foreign interference in Sri Lanka's domestic matters.

Of the dozens of statesmen and world leaders I had personally inter-viewed in more than ten years of foreign reporting, I found Jayewardene especially engaging. He was a sound, solid man, a man of down-to-earth common sense, practicality, and sagacity. Jayewardene was about to embark on official visits to China and the United States—trips that were likely to annoy Mrs. Gandhi, whose own relations with Beijing and Washington were frosty, at best—and I thought this would be as good a time as any to elicit fresh views from Jayewardene on a number of matters. I had last interviewed him in late 1982, during an election campaign in which Sri Lankans overwhelmingly reelected him to another six-year term in the presidency. The Jayewardene of 1982 was sprightly, confi-dent, energetic. But in July 1983, devastating racial riots rocked Sri Lanka, bringing into the open the long-felt ethnic rivalry between the majority Sinhalese and minority Tamils of the country of 16 million people.

Now I was seeing a very different Jayewardene: moody, downcast, no longer ramrod straight, even smiling less brightly. He appeared sleepy, and not very vigorous. It was an unhappy Vesak for him because of the abduction of the Americans, an incident that attracted international media attention and which pretty much ensured that potential Western investors and many tourists would stay away, at least for the foreseeable future. This would doubtless undermine Jayewardene's ambitious plans to transform his country into an economic dynamo to rival neighboring Singapore. But I felt that there was something deeper gnawing at Jayewardene. As I watched him going through the motions of public conviviality, it occurred to me finally that here was a man who was becoming increasingly despondent because he would not, in the years remaining to him, be able to bring about a lasting peace among his people and also give them fully the better life he had promised.

Jayewardene was privately willing to concede to the northern Tamils some advanced form of regional autonomy under which the predominantly Tamil areas—around Jaffna and Trincomalee—would enjoy such things as powers of taxation and police and a greater say in local economic development. But for nationalist Sinhalese in Colombo, any such regional autonomy seemed like disguised separatism. These conservatives torpedoed Jayewardene's personal ideas about how to achieve rapprochement with Jaffna Tamils, and Sri Lanka seemed headed for another, possibly violent, phase of separatist agitation. The kidnapping of Stanley and Mary Allen appeared to escalate the tensions to the point of internationalizing what until now had been largely a domestic issue with domestic dramatis personae. Few people in Colombo thought this would be the last incident of its kind. And the more terrorism grew, the more the inclination of the Sinhalese-dominated government to put its hackles up and resist any rapprochement with the Tamils.

Jayewardene was also preoccupied with India and Indira Gandhi. There was a traditional suspicion of India among Sri Lankans which had to do with sheer size: big sister versus tiny brother. But Jayewardene felt that Indira Gandhi would be delighted to see him toppled. Of course she would. She would have preferred to see him replaced by former prime minister Sirimavo Bandaranaike; the two women were ideologically much closer than Indira and Jayewardene could possibly ever be. Some influential Sri Lankan officials contended that the Indian High Commission in Colombo had become a nest of spies and that its members worked surreptitiously to destabilize the Jayewardene government. While this may not have been wholly accurate, the very fact that such scuttlebutt was bruited about suggested a deepening distrust of Indian intentions and actions. Now that the Tamil Nadu state government had openly embraced some of the Tamil separatist leaders, Jayewardene was convinced that a specific Indian plot existed to move separatism along and divide up his small country. There was little doubt in Jayewardene's mind that the racial riots of July 1982—in which hundreds of people died and property loss was in the millions of dollars—were put into motion by agents of Indira Gandhi. *

"Much as I respect Indira Gandhi," Jayewardene told me, "the fact is that she remains uneasy about Sri Lanka. Why can't she accept the fact that we want to travel on our own independent road?" Jayewardene suggested that by deputing her trusted aide, an Indian Tamil named G. Parthasarthy, to engage in shuttle diplomacy between Delhi and Colombo, Indira was in effect meddling in Sri Lanka's sovereign internal affairs. Parthasarthy's sentiments clearly seemed to be with the Tamils. Jayewardene's protestations had no effect whatsoever on Indira. She was upset that he had brought in the Israeli Mossad to help train his forces in counterinsurgency. Indira was also upset over reports that Jayewardene had asked Pakistan's army to assist Sri Lankan troops.

"If any foreign troops were to be invited by Sri Lanka, India would consider that to be a serious matter," Indira told Jayewardene in a private telephone conversation. She also told him that if outside military assistance was indeed needed by Sri Lanka, then Indira should be consulted by Jayewardene. Indira also offered to send Indian troops, should Jayewardene want them to put down the Tamil insurgency. Eventually, those troops landed during Rajiv Gandhi's term as prime minister. Rajiv had resolved that his early achievements would include ending India's estrangement with neighboring Sri Lanka. And for a time, as with all his other initiatives, Gandhi's policy of reaching out appeared to work. That policy culminated in the announcement on July 29, 1987, of an accord under which India would help end the civil war. Indian troops—some 20,000 of them—were dispatched to police the pact. †

When I visited Sri Lanka again three months after the accord was announced, however, Sri Lanka's civil war was still raging. And this time its victims included not only innocent Sinhalese and Tamils but also members of the Indian peacekeeping force. ‡ As the United States learned in Vietnam and the Soviet Union in Afghanistan, India was discovering how quickly big powers can be pulled into the messy politics of small

---

* India, of course, denied any complicity.
† The Indian contingent was widely known by its acronym, IPKF—Indian Peace-Keeping Force.
‡ Eventually, more than 2,500 Indian soldiers died in Sri Lanka.

Third World states. In his hurry to rush through an accord with Sri Lanka, Gandhi seemed to overlook a key characteristic of militants from minority ethnic groups. People who are willing to die for an independent state are not so easily coaxed or subdued into accepting anything less. But why kill Indian peacekeepers, particularly troops from a country that once offered shelter to these separatists? Because the Gandhi administration was increasingly pressurizing the radicals to accept the terms of the accord—terms that guaranteed a form of semiautonomous regional identity for Tamils within a federated Sri Lanka. Tamil separatists, having lost more than 3,000 of their most committed guerrillas, found the accord's compromises indigestible. The most rabid of the militants wanted nothing less than an independent state—something that Indira Gandhi herself had opposed on the grounds that it would further destabilize the region. * They argued, moreover, that they were not consulted nor courted as they should have been in an arrangement intended to determine their future. Consequently, they now fought against their old foes, the Sinhalese-dominated Sri Lankan forces—and against India's army, which tried to disarm as well as pacify and win over reluctant radicals. The militants' strategy clearly was to keep up the violence long enough to generate extreme discomfort for Rajiv Gandhi in India, whose 55 million indigenous Tamils constituted a powerful lobby.

When Rajiv Gandhi became India's prime minister in 1984, he seemed determined to fashion better relations with India's smaller and highly wary neighbors. One of the principal thrusts of Gandhi's foreign policy was Sri Lanka. The 1987 peace accord was widely hailed as a major diplomatic triumph for Gandhi. † He and the pact's other political parent, President Jayewardene, complimented themselves on their perspicacity in preempting the establishment of a separate Tamil state. The accord was also supposed to have demonstrated that regional powers in the Third World could solve local problems without the intervention or active assistance of the superpowers.

The unraveling of the pact raised questions about the political longevity of President Jayewardene. A military coup in Sri Lanka was a distinct possibility because of growing frustration within the country's

---

* One fear that Indira had was that an independent Tamil nation carved out of Sri Lanka's northern and eastern territories would seek a federation with the southern Indian state of Tamil Nadu. Indira knew that the Tamils of Tamil Nadu had not forgotten their own secessionist struggle of the early 1950s.

† In retrospect, many critics of the pact argue that Rajiv Gandhi was seriously misled by some influential members of his foreign policy establishment. These critics assert that India should never have agreed to send troops into Sri Lanka in the first place.

now-sidelined armed forces. Perhaps mindful of this, Jayewardene canceled his plans to attend a Commonwealth summit in Vancouver. Jayewardene had shown great courage in agreeing to a political solution to
Sri Lanka's ethnic crisis at a time when the Tamil militants were said to
be militarily at their weakest. But he had not brought his own government
and various local political forces solidly behind the accord. He tolerated
the inflammatory rhetoric of his prime minister, Ranasinghe Premadasa,
who bitterly denounced the Indians before the UN General Assembly,
albeit by implication.* Many Sinhalese leaders were unwilling to make
much-needed political concessions to those whom they viewed as unreconstructed terrorists. These stormy protests among significant segments
of Sri Lanka's Sinhalese community, along with India's military intervention in the island-nation of 16 million people, created a volatile political
situation because existing political mechanisms were unable to contain
fresh outbursts of Sinhalese chauvinistic emotions.

Underlying the crisis were the intricacies of multiethnic politics. The
process of accommodation in a multiethnic polity like Sri Lanka demanded that the concerns of minorities be addressed in a compassionate
and continuing fashion—something that the Gandhi-Jayewardene pact
sought to establish. Otherwise, their resentments would inevitably be
passed on from generation to generation, gathering a separatist momentum and inducing a siege mentality. (To be sure, such accommodation
could sometimes breed charges of excessive concessions to Tamils, but
that may be less of a long-term cost than risking the wrath of this
determined community, and its expatriate brethren in Europe and North
America.)†

Action on the ground in the form of renewed terrorist activities by the
LTTE and other Tamil guerrilla groups quickly dashed the high hopes of

---

* Premadasa succeeded Jayewardene as Sri Lanka's president. He at once asked the
Indian peacekeeping troops to leave.
† President Jayewardene repeatedly told Indira Gandhi and Ronald Reagan that the
source of most of the money for Tamil separatist activities was from North America.
There were dozens of expatriate Tamil groups peppered around the United States
who raised hundreds of thousands of dollars from fellow Tamils and U.S. liberals
and sent the cash to their brethren back home. The Tamils in the United States and
elsewhere in the West hopped on the bandwagon of human rights: They dramatically
spread the "word" that Sri Lanka's majority Sinhalese were hounding and persecuting
its minority Tamils. Organizations like Amnesty International issued reports endors-
ing this viewpoint; even the Massachusetts legislature went along, passing a resolution condemning the persecution of minorities in Sri Lanka. Jayewardene
peremptorily dismissed the potency of these outside efforts to draw world attention
to what the Sinhalese were doing to the Tamils.

the July accord. With the failure of Tamil militants to surrender their weapons and be more responsive to Indian persuasion to conform to the pact's terms, the agreement began to come apart. By not making the Tamil militants a party to the agreement, Rajiv Gandhi and Junius Richard Jayewardene undercut their own hard efforts. India said that it was prepared to sustain the campaign against Tamil guerrillas until the last of them had been overpowered. Such a resolve may have been laudable, but it was unrealistic. Many Indians felt that New Delhi should unilaterally declare a cease-fire and invite the Tamil militants to a new round of talks. India's credibility and Gandhi's reputation were eroding rapidly. Many Gandhi critics thought that India, which continuously hectored other warring nations to cease hostilities, needed to heed its own prescription. Otherwise it would be vulnerable to the very charges of human rights violations against the Tamils that it once accused the Jayewardene government of fostering. On September 20, 1989, a couple of months before Rajiv Gandhi's Congress Party lost power in a national election, the young prime minister reached an agreement with the Sri Lankans that provided for the phasing out of the Indian troops. The first batch of troops left Sri Lanka's Amparai district before the election results were announced. The Tamil guerrillas accelerated their terrorist activities. *

It all deteriorated tragically for Sri Lanka and for the Indians. Events went beyond everybody's control, gathering a momentum of their own. Rajiv's assassination was widely considered a revenge killing by the LTTE: Its concern seemed to be that if the Congress Party won the May–June 1991 election and Rajiv once again became prime minister, India might very well launch a new and punitive campaign against the LTTE's presence in India—perhaps even send troops into Sri Lanka again. Who knows? The lesson of this is that very clever leaders sometimes outsmart themselves, that events cannot be calibrated with the precision of intellectual calculations. The cast of characters who fueled the Sri Lanka crisis—Indira, Rajiv, Jayewardene—are gone from the political scene, but the tragic play continues. This lovely island-nation seems to be in its death throes. The tragedy of Sri Lanka was part of Indira Gandhi's legacy not only to India but also Asia.

---

* The LTTE was suspected of arranging the murder in early 1991 of Ranjan Wijeratne, the Sri Lankan minister of state for defense. Among other victims of terrorists have been prominent Sri Lankan Tamils who did not agree with the LTTE.

23

India After Indira
and Rajiv

There was widespread hope that post-Indira India would unburden itself of its outmoded, unproductive state-guided "socialism" and liberalize its economy. In his first formal address as the new prime minister of India, Rajiv Gandhi talked about his determination to continue his assassinated mother's policies of nonalignment abroad and socialism at home. No one expected he would say otherwise, especially so soon after Indira Gandhi's assassination. But the forty-year-old Mr. Gandhi then slipped in a line about how India's private sector had "adequate scope to enhance the productive potential of the economy."

Those words had been inserted in Rajiv Gandhi's televised speech at the suggestion of the prime minister's inner circle of friends, a small coterie of young men infused with a Western sensibility. To the cognoscenti who were on the lookout for clues concerning what directions Rajiv Gandhi was likely to guide India, the very fact that the British-educated premier referred to the role of the private sector was encouragement enough that a further loosening of restrictive economic controls was likely. Gandhi was characterized by associates as "basically a free-enterpriser."*

The young men who were now Gandhi's closest advisers on policy matters were known to be impatient with the ponderous pace of economic development in India. Like Rajiv Gandhi, they were troubled by the

---

* It is now clear that Rajiv's grounding in economics was nonexistent. It is doubtful whether even some of his closest political associates truly understood how the market economy worked.

heavy overlay of bureaucratic controls that afflicted Indian industry and that had plagued productivity. Indeed, at a private dinner party in New Delhi not long before Indira Gandhi's assassination, Rajiv Gandhi quoted from an essay by former chancellor Ludwig Erhard of West Germany, a prime architect of his country's extraordinary economic recovery after World War II: "Let the men and the money loose, and the economy will prosper."*

Everybody agreed, however, that it would not be easy for Rajiv Gandhi to let the men and the money loose. Any shift in domestic economic policy by Rajiv would hinge on how quickly and effectively he was able to consolidate his personal political position with the ruling Congress Party. The party's corrupt satraps would not take too kindly to any dismantling of India's notorious License Raj, since it was their control of the economic controls that often provided lucre for party—and personal—coffers. Moreover, many of these entrenched Congress Party officials, who had been effectively "bought" by India's leading industrial families, were likely to resist the promotion of fresh competition in India's heavily protected domestic economy because such competition would undercut the hegemony of their patrons. And these party barons would not take too kindly to a cutting back of inefficient and wasteful state-run enterprises because this would mean a diminution of their own powers of political patronage and job creation.

There was wide euphoria, particularly among young Indians, that Rajiv Gandhi would inaugurate a new era of domestic prosperity. While I shared some of this euphoria, I felt that Rajiv was likely to proceed slowly and cautiously on any program to deregulate the economy and inject more competition in India's private sector. Rajiv was surely bound to run into resistance from the entrenched bureaucracy, and from Indian industrialists who did well by protection. When I mentioned my reservations to M. Narasimhan, one of India's most respected economists and then head of the Administrative Staff College in Hyderabad, he said: "But there is a lot of hope for the future. We are taking a hard and cold look at such things as stimulating external and internal competition, at using such things as interest rates and tariffs to calibrate the economy rather than merely rely on physical controls. There is no device or measure that we are not prepared to study."†

---

* Quotation supplied by journalist Rahul Singh.
† Narasimhan was appointed by Rajiv Gandhi to chair a committee to recommend changes in the system of industrial controls. His comments were made in an interview with the author in December 1984 in Hyderabad.

"We simply have to readjust our economic policies to make ourselves economically self-sufficient," Narasimhan continued. "We have to do such things as improve our trade prospects." This meant, among other things, persuading Indian industrialists to be export-conscious; these industrialists have traditionally concentrated on the huge Indian domestic market.* He pointed out that ever since Rajiv Gandhi's entrance into political life, the Indian economy had already moved in the direction of liberalization. Rajiv Gandhi was widely credited with getting his mother to rethink some of India's long-standing economic policies. Some import restrictions had already been lifted; foreign exchange controls were relaxed; industrial collaboration with Western investors had been encouraged; American firms were brought in for further oil exploration; the Japanese firms of Suzuki, Toyota, Nissan, Isuzu, and Honda were invited to produce Indian-assembled automobiles, motorcycles, and trucks.†

India also was raising more and more capital in commercial markets abroad, especially in Britain and the United States. This represented a significant departure from long-standing Indian policy which frowned on such borrowing as well as borrowing from multilateral financial institutions such as the World Bank and the International Monetary Fund. One benefit of this policy had been that India's annual debt-service rate stayed at just 13 percent, compared to four or five times more for most Third World states; a disadvantage was that foreign investment of all types, including commercial credit and bilateral aid, had been just about $1.5 billion annually, or around 2 percent of the gross domestic product—compared to an annual 12 percent for neighboring Pakistan, 19 percent for Sri Lanka, and 17 percent for Bangladesh. Alas, Rajiv Gandhi's government borrowed to such an extent that, by 1991, India became the developing world's biggest debtor after Brazil and Mexico. Its external debt rose to $80 billion.‡ In 1980, India's external debt was $20 billion. In the next ten years, over $60 billion was borrowed from abroad. Critics of the Gandhi administrations—particularly of Rajiv's government—pointed out that India had little to show for these massive borrowings. Cynics were asking how much had been stolen or recycled into Swiss bank accounts. Others claimed that mismanagement of foreign

---

*International trade accounts for only 15 percent of India's gross domestic product of $161 billion.

†In the early years after Independence, foreign collaboration was confined to "high-priority" sectors such as fertilizer plants, steel mills that were erected with foreign government support, and aeronautics factories.

‡In June 1991, India sold more than twenty tons of gold in order to obtain hard currency for badly needed imports and for debt service.

debt was no more than a reflection of similar mismanagement of the domestic economy.

Rajiv Gandhi was reported to be instrumental in convincing Indira Gandhi that India needed to diversify its weapons-acquisition program. Traditionally, the reliance here was heavily on the Soviet Union. With an annual defense expenditure of more than $8 billion, India was a key Third World market for the Soviets. Now India was buying fighter planes from France and Britain, and there were reports of a $3 billion deal in the works with the United States for military technology. If Rajiv Gandhi's predilections were any indication, India could well move toward further military hardware diversification and tap Western suppliers. That, of course, happened—largely because some of Rajiv's associates saw in such diversification a marvelous opportunity to generate kickbacks for themselves. Western arms suppliers were only too willing to offer these payments because of the inroads they were able to make into Indian defense purchases. The illegal commissions said to have been paid in the Bofors weapons deal are staggering by any standard.

The feeling among many informed observers in India in 1984 was that the young prime minister would soon have to undertake major reforms of the Indian economy if the country was to get moving. The annual economic growth rate fell in 1983 to just about 2.5 percent, or almost a third of the rate in the last two years of Indira Gandhi's rule, largely because of sluggish productivity—and despite bountiful agricultural harvests. "Time was running short for India by the time Rajiv came to office: More than 350 million of India's population were under fifteen years of age—which was to say that a population boom of horrendous proportions was in store for India as more and more people entered the child-bearing stage," recalls Dr. Lessel H. David, a demographer at the Administrative Staff College in Hyderabad. *

For these growing masses, "socialism" would not be a soothing shibboleth any longer—if it ever was. For any meaningful improvement in the daily lives of ordinary Indians, Rajiv Gandhi was going to have to shed his socialist heritage and boldly throw open India's doors for competition and enterprise.

Rajiv bungled it. Corruption and maladministration characterized his rule. In the end, the son of Indira Gandhi wasted away the opportunity of a lifetime. Rare is the ruler of any country who had such a free hand with policy as Rajiv Gandhi had from 1984 to 1989. With an overwhelming majority in Parliament, and an almost dictatorial control

---

* Conversation with author, New Delhi, September 1990.

over his party, Rajiv was in a unique position to restructure the economic and administrative system of India. Yet his haphazard approach to policy-making, his political inexperience, and the absence of any abiding ideological commitment or sense of direction produced only feeble and ineffective results. Rajiv's tolerance—if not involvement—in gigantic corruption seriously weakened his ability to govern with credibility. At the end of his tenure, Rajiv Gandhi was left mouthing empty slogans and defending what most observers considered a maladroit stewardship. In an interview in late 1990, Rajiv Gandhi acknowledged that many of his ambitions did not bear fruit. "Yes, we did start out with a major liberalization program," Rajiv said. "What we didn't start out with was an understanding of how the system worked."*

Not only was an understanding of the system missing in Rajiv Gandhi; he was also a poor judge of people. While it is natural for most political leaders to cobble together a coterie of trusted friends, Rajiv surrounded himself mostly with men who had little experience in politics but who saw in their newfound proximity to power a unique opportunity to quickly make vast sums of money. These aides became political barons in their own right—dictating national and international policy, and cavalierly dismissing bureaucrats and state officeholders whom they did not like. Not even during the most imperial periods of Indira Gandhi's rule had her own associates—nor even Indira herself—behaved so arrogantly.

In their quest for public office and the payoffs of power, venal politi-cians have inflamed communal passions and employed every cynical trick to promote personal gain. Without hesitation, or regard for the long-term consequences of their action, they have further divided India along caste, class, and regional lines. Even then–Prime Minister V. P. Singh, notwithstanding his pious pronouncements about national harmony, was not above exploiting communal and caste issues. He announced job quotas for lower castes at a time when it was politically expedient, and when it was unlikely that more jobs could be realistically created to satisfy that underprivileged cohort.† One consequence of his announcement was that middle-class students engaged in self-immolation, and urban

---

* Interview with the author and Bernard Kalb, New Delhi, September 1990.
† V. P. Singh dusted off a long-forgotten study called *The Mandal Commission Report* that called for affirmative-action quotas in education and employment for the very backward classes. While Singh insisted that he had only the welfare of poor people in mind, his detractors accused him of pandering to the poor in an effort to gather political support.

communities were outraged over the prospect of their educated children being denied jobs on account of their class or caste. Another consequence was that the Singh government fell as law and order collapsed. Singh, of course, cannot be singled out as the sole villain. Indian politicians have increasingly exploited and manipulated all the societal and structural weaknesses inherent in a developing society that is still not quite rid of the psychological baggage of colonialism.

In India's fifth decade of freedom from the British Raj, the secularism and nonviolence espoused by Mahatma Gandhi and Jawaharlal Nehru may well have been cremated by their recent successors. It is, of course, always convenient for today's politicians to resurrect the memories and mantras of Gandhi and Nehru at election time, because those names are now enshrined in Indian mythology. * But the leadership mantle of India's founding fathers has been bequeathed to unworthy mandarins. Today's politics has become the profit-making playground of the worst and dimmest men whose vision does not extend beyond their wallets. Look around New Delhi, India's capital, and see for yourself how politicians have been able to stretch their technically low salaries into massive real estate and other investments. To accommodate self-interest, politics has become pricey, and every politician has a price tag that rises with every political crisis. Political deal-making is no longer done in backrooms; trading is openly conducted on the very floor of Parliament. In Indian politics, there is clearly no such thing as recession: Commerce is lively and lucrative, and continuous. And payment often is demanded not in local coins but in hard currency abroad. For example, the reported going price for "defections" to Chandra Shekhar's rebel group in November 1990 was the equivalent of $300,000 per parliamentarian. † The venality of India's politicians is breeding the kind of unrest that requires repression. That means more dependency on the military and on paramilitary forces. The long-term implications of this are frightening.

What has brought about this desperate situation? Party structures have sought people who can buy or bully votes, rather than men of distinction. Large numbers of greedy misfits have been drawn to politics because political power has offered avenues for social mobility in a land still

---

*Needless to add, few people refer to Indira Gandhi during elections these days. Not even her son, Rajiv, publicly talked much about her life and career during the December 1989 and May 1991 election campaigns.

†This kind of money was reportedly being offered by some top industrialists, and by Indian businessmen based overseas. There was wide speculation in the Indian media that the bribes came most notably from businessmen who were being investigated by the Singh administration for financial irregularities.

layered with class and caste divisions. "The corruption of politics has led to the radical reactions that are making India increasingly ungovernable," says Professor Ralph Buultjens. "India needs statesmen, not politicians." India's slide into a sinkhole of violence, if unchecked, will surely send shock waves throughout a strategic zone extending from the Red Sea to the South China Sea. In the fevered atmosphere in which the country now finds itself, however, few policymakers are in a position to give serious thought to badly needed economic development and expansion.

Exacerbating the situation is the human tragedy of the Gulf Crisis: Hundreds of thousands of workers from the Subcontinent were forced to return home, thereby placing unwelcome pressures on the already fragile indigenous social fabric. India—and its neighbors—now faced a new employment crisis. A major flow of hard-currency revenues, Kuwait, suddenly dried up because of Iraq's invasion in August 1990. Professor Ralph Buultjens says: "What was once thought to be among the most promising areas of the Third World is collapsing into chaos. Religious, ethnic, and separatist struggles are destroying the cartography of Asia. The region appears unable to approach any problem without an outburst of violence." In Sri Lanka, the ethnic conflict between majority Sinhalese and minority Tamils continues to consume lives. Pakistan and Bangladesh remain mired in political uncertainty. Myanmar is governed by a straightforward dictatorship. In the Himalayan kingdoms of Nepal and Bhutan, embattled regimes struggle to survive challenges from incipient mass movements clamoring for civil liberties and human rights.

The unfortunate convergence of three overlapping conflicts explains the rapidly deteriorating political situation in India:

- *Militant Hindus versus pacifist Hindus.* There is a great debate going on among the country's 700 million Hindus about what sort of India they want—secular or sectarian? Irresponsible right-wing Hindu leaders have encouraged resentment long dormant among many Hindus. These leaders proclaim that in the pursuit of a genuine secular state, India's leaders have mollycoddled Muslims, often favoring them with special education and employment privileges. Leaders of parties advocating Hindu militancy argue that it is high time for India's majority to assert itself. Not long before his death in 1964, Jawaharlal Nehru said: "The danger to India, mark you, is not Communism. It is Hindu right-wing communalism." He was terribly prescient.
- *Militant Hindus versus militant Muslims.* A growing number of India's 100 million Muslims have been emboldened by the rise of fundamentalism in the Middle East. They do not share the secularist view of

political development in which modernization goes hand in hand with a liberal ethos. They are distressed by what they perceive to be encroaching Westernization in Indian society. These Muslims, newly assertive of their Islamic identity, do not allow the arithmetic of their minority status to deter head-on confrontation with militant Hindus.

- *Separatist movements in strategic border states.* Kashmir's Muslims seem to want nothing less than independence; in Punjab, Sikh militants are seeking to fashion the theocratic state of Khalistan; the eastern state of Assam is rife with ethnic and tribal terrorism. These upheavals breed cultural alienation, which in turns spawns violence that fans across the nation. In each case, the Indian government suspects foreign meddling—by Pakistan in Kashmir and Punjab, and by China in Assam. If this is indeed so, the violence will not soon abate.

A number of critical questions present themselves: Is the communal conflict in India unique or is it a bizarre echo of rising fundamentalism and micronationalism in the Islamic world? Is today's incendiary political situation a reaction of the lower middle classes and poorer people to rise of a more secular—and increasingly affluent—middle class? Has the political and administrative system crafted at Independence exhausted its capacity to deal with the problems of a new, more complex, and even more populated time? There can be little doubt that the rise of Hindu right-wing militancy is at least partly an expression of dissatisfaction with the slow pace and uneven patterns of economic development. A lot of poor Hindus feel—rightly or wrongly—that secularist policies have made them poorer than poor Muslims and other favored minorities.* Weak leadership at the federal level, combined with mounting assertiveness by regional leaders catering to parochial interests, has contributed to the acceleration of national problems. I feel that militant Hindus must come to terms with the truth that those who use communalism as a self-proclaimed argument for stability leave a legacy far more volatile than the condition they seek to cure. Civilian institutions which could lay the foundations of genuine grass-roots democracy can never be fully developed by pursuing the politics of parochialism.

These militants need not look beyond neighboring Pakistan to comprehend what happens when narrow-minded leaders engage in such politics. For reasons of political expediency—having to satisfy domestic funda-

---

*This viewpoint is certainly held by the militant Bharatiya Janata Party (BJP), which is being increasingly seen as the organization reflecting extremist Hindu beliefs.

mentalists and also foreign donors such as the Saudis—the late President Zia ul-Haq took Pakistan so far down the road of Islamization that it may well be irreversible. He introduced measures that restricted many personal freedoms, and instituted barbaric punishments such as death by stoning for adulterers. And he presided over an era that witnessed the dramatic deterioration of women's rights. All these measures upset and undermined Pakistan's growing middle classes. In the emerging countries of the Third World, it is these middle classes that are most often the wellsprings of national development and, indeed, of a nation's moral and political fiber. In imposing social and political restrictions of a draconian nature, Zia further eroded a source of stability in nation-building.

Hindu chauvinists argue, of course, that India could never go the way of Pakistan—if only because Hinduism is a far more tolerant religion than Islam. That "tolerance" may well shine in Hindu scriptures. But the ethnic violence and sectarian passions unleashed by Hindu storm troopers against hapless Muslims certainly don't suggest tolerance. India's traditional name may be Hindustan—Land of the Hindus—but India was always a land of many faiths. "India was always a land where everybody felt *included*, not excluded," says Shehbaz H. Safrani, a New York–based scholar of Islam and art history. "India coopted everybody. Muslim invaders, Christian missionaries, Zoroastrians—everybody stayed on and assimilated without losing their identities. That is the magic of India—you can be what you are, and you can also be an Indian at the same time." Indeed, the magic of India—its very nationhood, in fact—is substantially the product of Muslim contributions in art, architecture, literature, even politics. Muslims like Maulana Abul Kalam Azad struggled with Mahatma Gandhi and Jawaharlal Nehru to drive out the British colonialists, and were frequently jailed for their nationalist beliefs. That is why India's Muslims deserve to be honored, not vilified. In a secular state that has prided itself on its separation of temple and state, there should be no room for the practice—and passions—of communal politics. The real threat to India comes not from minority Muslims but from the vicious intolerance emanating from Hindus who have betrayed their faith.

With the prospects so bleak, is there any hope for some stability? What is a way out of the mess? The political and administrative system crafted at Independence almost five decades ago has exhausted its capacity to deal with the problems of a new, more complex, and more populous era. Weak leadership at the federal level, and mounting assertiveness by regional leaders catering to parochial interests, have contributed to the acceleration of national problems. One way to resuscitate the once buoyant hopes for economic, social, and political development in India would be the instituting of a presidential form of government that would be less of a hostage to parochial disputes and transient legislative alliances than the current Westminster parliamentary model. Presidential leadership has not exactly worked well in the neighborhood, to be sure—witness the political abuses in Pakistan and Bangladesh. Yet India's cultural diversity, size, and quest for statesmen of truly national stature make it a more appropriate vehicle for this system. A strong federal leader is needed to make the center hold in a multiethnic, polyglot country such as India.

There is also an urgent need for a resurgence of that spirit of selfless enthusiasm for public service and moral purpose that characterized the stirring days of India's struggle for independence. This would require a new national movement in which the media, grass-roots civic groups, perhaps even the judiciary can play a renewed role in the selection of national and local leaders, and in shaping national policy. To be sure, India is not short of men and women of distinction. But these members of the middle classes, perhaps rightly from their personal point of view, generally choose to find satisfaction in law, business, education, or the sciences. By their inaction, and their reluctance to fully participate in the political process, however, India's intelligentsia must share the blame for the emergence of a new ruling class of corrupt leaders whose self-interest overrides the national interest. I am encouraged, therefore, by the emergence of groups such as Ektaa, which was formed not long ago in Bombay by young professsionals to elicit accountability in public life. How effective they will be remains to be seen.

The true victims of today's deteriorating situation are everyday Indians who deserve better, and who continue to hope for a redemption of the pledge of equitable development that was promised by Jawaharlal Nehru at Independence. But for now, at least, the "tryst with destiny" that Nehru pledged has turned into a tryst with tragedy manufactured by his self-serving political heirs, starting with Indira Gandhi.

What did Indira Gandhi leave undone? What did Indira Gandhi and her son Rajiv not adequately undertake? An evaluation of the Nehru-Gandhi years would suggest many missed opportunities. These would include:

- *Stimulation of the economy in order to generate more productivity, create more wealth, and better distribute income.* There should have been accelerated dismantling of the bureaucratic License Raj. There could have been greater competition for Indian industry. Opportunities for foreign investment were not widened. In our world of increasing global interdependency, India cannot afford impediments to competition in domestic markets—but Indira did not insist that India's industrialists engage in vigorous domestic competition. This suited the industrialists because they could get away with manufacturing shabby goods which Indians bought anyway because of a lack of choice. As long as Indian industrialists contributed handsomely to the coffers of the Congress Party, Indira let them have their way. Virtually all modern-day economic "miracle" stories from Germany to Singapore have been fashioned from the primacy of exports—but Indira continued her father's emphasis on making India economically self-reliant to the point of neglecting growth in exports. "The basic problem is that our whole industry has built itself on the basis of protection," Rajiv Gandhi admitted. "But if you suddenly remove this protection, then these industries are just not strong enough to face what's coming."[*]

- *The elimination of "socialism" from the national dictionary.* Marxist philosophy, however mildly applied in national economic policy, has proved to be a prescription for disaster all over the Third World. Indira Gandhi often argued that a completely "free" economy would lead to abuses. Yet the situation could hardly worsen beyond the excesses and abuses of statist bureaucracy that Indian-style "socialism" has created. Moreover, the government can always play a better regulatory and monitoring role. But Indira knew that the more controls the government instituted, the more the opportunity for her ruling party to extract tribute from the business community. This was a lesson that her son quickly learned. "We definitely need to remove the controls, the licensing type of controls," Rajiv Gandhi said—a remark that I did not quite believe.[†]

- *Trimming the gargantuan bureaucracy.* In India, "socialism" has too long stood for statism. During Indira Gandhi's tenure as prime minister, the central government's bureaucracy increased from 50,000 to more than a million. The most privileged Indians have been the politicians who proclaimed socialism in the first place, and the upper-echelon bureaucrats who profited by the proliferation of the license system. Bureaucracies breed corruption. Today it is often impossible to even get into a bureaucrat's office without greasing the palm of his peon. But the peon charges you just a handful of rupees; the paper-pushers inside the

[*] Interview with the author and Bernard Kalb, New Delhi, September 1990.
[†] *Ibid.*

comfortably air-conditioned offices in New Delhi secretariats and state capitals demand considerably more—foreign currency payments even. The more Indira Gandhi concentrated on the business of political survival, the less time she had for the business of administration. Not only did the bureaucracy grow in numbers; it grew in clout during Indira's stewardship. Rajiv Gandhi did attempt to tackle the question of trimming India's bureaucracy. "The bureaucracy has to be made to understand that their new role is not to be doing everything themselves—but to create an atmosphere in which every Indian can do his best," Rajiv said. "The bureaucracy's role must be to make India competitive."[*]

- *Encouraging genuinely honest and accountable government.* When Rajiv Gandhi became prime minister, the Indian press instantly gave him a sobriquet: "Mr. Clean." And, indeed, some of Gandhi's early moves were heartening: He got rid of some ministers who were considered corrupt; he drafted a bill that made it virtually impossible for members of Parliament to switch parties for reasons of expediency; he vowed to cut down on election expenses because such costs fuel corruption and enhance the clout of frequently illegal political contributions. But then things settled back into politics as usual. So much so that once-trusted friends and allies such as Arun Singh left government, and Rajiv's circle, in disgust. Rajiv Gandhi, like Indira Gandhi, surrounded himself with men of small moral stature and sycophantic dispositions. Neither Indira nor Rajiv would ever publicly acknowledge the extent to which corruption had eaten into the entrails of Indian life—naturally not, because such acknowledgment would have been an admission of self-guilt. "We were successful in removing some corruption—but, well, many of the charges made by our critics were simply unsubstantiated," Rajiv Gandhi said. "In developing economies, of course, there are shortages by definition. And when there are shortages, and there is a lot of money chasing those shortages, you are going to have problems. So the only real way out of this is fast enough development—so that enough is available, and there are no shortages."[†] It could be argued that many of these shortages are artificial, created by greedy merchants and bureaucrats to jack up consumer prices.
- *Promoting an enhanced secular social agenda.* This means that national leaders must act forcefully to reduce communalism—particularly the increasing religious tensions between Hindus and Muslims. Unfortu-

[*] *Ibid.*
[†] *Ibid.*

nately, the Gandhi administration at times shamelessly pandered to Muslims in order to win votes: It banned Salman Rushdie's novel, *The Satanic Verses*, because some Muslim extremists were offended by the London-based writer's references to the Prophet Mohammed. Earlier, Gandhi bowed to Muslim fundamentalist demands that Muslim women not be subjected to civil laws concerning divorce but to traditional Islamic tenets. Through such compromises, Rajiv Gandhi set into motion a process where secularism will be irreparably eroded. Neither Indira nor Rajiv Gandhi particularly encouraged private voluntary civic organizations that were rapidly sprouting all over the country to tackle the problem of poverty and other social concerns. Many of these groups are stimulating popular awareness of environmental hazards such as acid rain in large cities where industries are concentrated. Private groups are promoting handicrafts and other cottage industries in rural areas, thereby creating badly needed jobs for artisans. Other groups are working vigorously to promote female literacy and employ-ment. Female literacy, in fact, is frequently the key to smaller families, as is female employment. Both Indira and Rajiv said much in their speeches about social causes—but they left specific programs to a moribund bureaucracy that was not as fired with ideas as the Gandhis were.

- *Developing a better working relationship between the central government and India's states.* Gone forever are the days when one party—specifi-cally, the Congress—can control national as well as local administra-tions. As N. T. Rama Rao says, if the limbs are strong, so will the entire body politic. Rajiv Gandhi, unlike his mother, seemed to ap-preciate the thought. His accord in Mizoram State, where an armed rebellion had been waged by local tribes for nearly two decades, was a genuine act of statesmanship. Rajiv Gandhi persuaded the Mizoram rebels to give up their arms in exchange for free elections. Indeed, the local rebel chief, a man named Laldenga, then became the state's chief minister (only to later resign).* Another Gandhi triumph was the Assam Accord, in another eastern border province like Mizoram. Here the tensions were between tribal people from the hill areas and the natives of the plains. Again—as with the Punjab—the prime minister held successful negotiations, which led to elections that a non-Con-gress party won. In 1988, Gandhi secured assurances of cooperation from the virulent Gurkhaland National Liberation Front, which en-joyed the support of more than 600,000 Gurkhas, the fierce warrior

*Laldenga subsequently died.

tribe that fought so valiantly in the British army in several wars and colonial adventures. The Gurkhas were given assurances that they would be allowed to form their own Hill Council to look into local grievances. The common thread in all these developments was Gandhi's willingness to coopt local leaders, not to engage them in confrontation. Rajiv Gandhi was not often given credit for his determination to sculpt better relations with regional opponents. Yet Gandhi was also responsible for the almost universal quick collapse of virtually every one of these promising breakthroughs.

• *Mobilizing young people to participate in the delivery of services to rural regions and urban slums.* More than 50 percent of India's population is under twenty-five years of age. Why not a national program, a sort of domestic "peace corps," under which college or even high school students spend part of their academic year in villages? There are some states that do promote such schemes, but a nationwide program would be highly effective in binding together the nation's different communities. The youths could assist in a variety of projects such as road-building, teaching, and educating rural populations about sanitation and hygiene. In a country where there is little geographical mobility, a national job corps program would also serve to educate youths about life-styles in various states—states that might be as foreign to them as other countries. Indira Gandhi talked a great deal about coopting young Indians into national service—but here again, there was little by way of follow-through. Rajiv Gandhi, aware that the hopes of the post-Independence generation were invested in him, tried to get them involved more in politics by encouraging membership in the Youth Congress, among other things. "But one of the difficulties I found during my period of prime ministership was that the youth of India had gotten too used to being helped by the government," Rajiv said. "Our model of socialism got carried away at the grass-roots level. And it made our people want government to do everything. Initiative has been killed. And that's where I found that when I put challenges to our people, they would sometimes find it difficult to respond to those challenges. Our youth must accept the fact that ultimately they need to take the responsibility to shape their own lives."[*] But how? With an unemployment rate that has hovered around 20 or 30 percent ever since Indira Gandhi took office in 1966, most Indian youths found themselves increasingly mired in frustration. The key to economic growth was a genuinely open market economy—and neither Indira nor Rajiv fully opened the doors to competition and free enterprise.

[*] Interview with the author and Bernard Kalb, New Delhi, September 1990.

• *Fashioning better relations with neighboring nations.* Regional harmony is often the precursor of strengthening international relations. The Sri Lanka Accord of 1987 was meant to resolve the bitter civil war in that island-nation, and Rajiv Gandhi mediated with compassion and with a willingness to use India's clout where appropriate. Sadly, the internal situation deteriorated, making India's original action counterproductive. Indira Gandhi may well have sown the seeds of Sri Lanka's destruction when she tacitly backed the Sri Lankan Tamil guerrillas who operated out of training camps in Tamil Nadu State. Both Indira and Rajiv initially sought the political support of Indian Tamils, and since the overwhelming sentiments of the latter seemed to be with the Sri Lankan guerrillas who fought for a Tamil homeland, Indian policy was weighted in their favor. But Rajiv came to see the folly of such support: After all, India itself had several separatist movements—in Kashmir and the Punjab, for example—that successive Indian governments said were fomented by Pakistan. India could hardly be seen to support a separatist movement in Sri Lanka without there being international charges of double standards. Neither Indira nor Rajiv did much to soften the suspicion of Sri Lankans and other neighbors in South Asia that India sought hegemony in the region. India needed to work out a more amicable relationship with Bangladesh, with whom there had been a long-standing feud over river waters, and with other neighbors—but under Indira and Rajiv, bilateral tensions continued. Tensions also continued unabated with Pakistan, largely over the Kashmir question. Surely Indira and Rajiv could have made imaginative overtures to the Pakistanis to establish a new era of peace?

• *Resolving the China dispute.* In September 1988, Rajiv Gandhi made a dramatic announcement: He would, he said, visit China. Relations between the two countries have been troubled since border clashes broke out in the 1950s. In 1962, India and China went to war, and the Chinese thrashed the Indians, seizing sizable chunks of Indian territory in the process. Moreover, the Chinese have fomented agitation among several tribes in India's border states. The visit by Rajiv Gandhi in December 1988 was the first in twenty-nine years by a leader of either nation; the last high-level visit was made by then—Prime Minister Chou En-lai to New Delhi in 1960. China insists that the McMahon Line was imposed unilaterally. Indeed, Beijing refuses to recognize this border. India, for its part, wants the Chinese to return 14,500 square miles of Ladakh's Aksai Chin region, which they captured during the 1962 war. This dispute has caused much grief over the decades. Perhaps with improved relations, the two countries might even increase their trade, which currently stands at about $145 million annually. Here are two ancient lands both undergoing modernization. Conflict between them involves 40 percent of the world's population. Why not march toward the future in cordiality and cooperation? Indira Gandhi took some tentative steps toward normalizing relations between India and China. But, as was invariably the case with most of her foreign policy initiatives, she did not properly follow up. Politics always got in the way.

To write about India is, finally, to care even more deeply about India. Indians of Indira's generation are the legatees of the extraordinary record of a remarkable political dynasty. Most of us care deeply about India. Some of my acquaintances in India ask me occasionally—and with barely suppressed sneers—how I, an expatriate Indian, could presume to write about a country so large, diverse, and distant from the place where I make my home, New York. I have been privileged to be a journalist for more than two decades, enjoying a front-row seat in the arena of contemporary affairs. Not often does a journalist get personal tutoring on a terribly complicated subject such as poverty and development, and it was my good fortune that I did. The early tutorials came from my parents, who believed deeply in the idea of India as a multicultural and secular state that had the potential to be a great nation.

That is why—despite the daily discouraging headlines—I continue to be hopeful for the India of today and tomorrow. The hopes and dreams of India's founders have only been partially fulfilled over the last four decades. To fully translate those dreams into reality is the task of today's generation. These dreams were foreshadowed by the visions of India's founders. If the ideas of Mahatma Gandhi and Jawaharlal Nehru are not made a reality, India could collapse into a nightmare of a broken country and broken dreams, never to remain in a cohesive form again. If political chaos and economic deterioration accelerate, the centrifugal forces of communalism encouraged by regional rapscallions may prove too powerful for any central authority to withstand. If the fruits of economic progress are not distributed meaningfully and with a driving sense of social justice, no amount of political rhetoric—nor the mythology of the Nehru-Gandhi dynasty—will be enough to hold India together.

But if the political leadership and everyday Indians work at nation-building in a committed, sustained, and energetic way, I really do believe that India can genuinely become a moral, political, and economic giant in the global community. Say this for Indians: They are resilient, and they are resourceful. The national leadership hasn't sufficiently tapped these extraordinary qualities. The leadership does not need to keep redefining India's dreams. The path toward the future was charted with sharp clarity more than four decades ago. It is the navigation that matters, and that is where India has frequently been let down by its helmsmen.

The vision so wonderfully articulated by Jawaharlal Nehru at the time of Independence is still valid. The Asian Century—the Indian Century—beckons this remarkable country. Not long ago, I was talking with Professor Ralph Buultjens, whose personal links with the Nehru family date back to his early youth. He recalled visiting with Nehru many years ago in New Delhi. Nehru, who had a fondness for young people, spoke of the challenges before India, which was then a very young independent nation.

"We are engaged in a desperate race—a race between achieving progress and heading off violent revolution," the prime minister said to Professor Buultjens. "Our people are immensely tolerant, but there are limits to even their patience. If we do not succeed in giving them the basics of life and offering them realistic hope, they will throw us out—and they will be right to do so."

Ralph Buultjens recalls that the conversation took place one cold morning in October many years ago. He can still recall the grave expression on Nehru's handsome face. And he recalls how deeply moved he was as the prime minister spoke to him. Jawaharlal Nehru's caution and challenge to his countrymen still resonate, louder than ever before, and with greater urgency than the much simpler time when he met with an impressionable young man named Ralph Buultjens. But it will be a long time before the race that he spoke about can be won. To translate fully those dreams into reality is the task of today's generation.

"I often wonder what retards India's progress," Professor Buultjens says.

The country has had greater leadership than many other nations. It has an enormous inventory of first-class talent, its natural resources are reasonably plentiful, and modernization is not alien to Indian society. Thinking back, I believe that what Nehru was trying to do became mired in a feckless bureaucracy and a sordid polity. Perhaps Nehru himself is partly to blame. He was a visionary who tried to use the existing mechanisms of administration and politics to achieve his goals. Rarely have national visions been achieved without revolutionary upheaval. Maybe Nehru was too much of a product of the traditional English establishment to engineer such a drastic change. Indira Gandhi seemed to have the right ideas—but was sidetracked whenever crucial moments for action arrived. In the end, she, too, tried to achieve change through the same old structures whose genetic purpose is to resist change. Finally, Rajiv Gandhi did not have either the vision or the capacity to fulfil the breakthroughs that Indians had been expecting for more than four decades. Much has been done—and it is wrong to decry the considerable achievements. But the missed opportunities have postponed India's day of modern greatness for quite some time. To those of us who have grown up with modern India, this is a story tinged with sadness. In so many ways, India is like a beautiful woman dressed in rags. Yet those who know and love India understand that this cannot be a permanent condition. We who are children of postcolonial South Asia see the horizon receding—yet we know the shore is there. I only hope that this promised shore will be reached in our lifetime. *

Although years have passed since the conversation between Jawaharlal Nehru and Ralph Buultjens on that cold October morning, what Jawaharlal said about the tolerance of India's people is even more valid today. Nehru's caution and challenge to his countrymen still resonate, louder than ever before, and with greater urgency than the much simpler time when he fashioned his dreams for a truly great India. Indira Gandhi tried to respond to her father's challenge but in the end it overwhelmed her. Her successors may not fare much better.

Jawaharlal Nehru said in a celebrated speech to the Indian Constituent Assembly minutes before India became independent in August 1947:

"Long years ago we made a tryst with destiny, and now the time comes when we shall redeem our pledge. . . . A moment comes, which comes but rarely in history, when we step out from the old to the new, when an age ends, and when the soul of a nation, long suppressed, finds utterance."

Nehru and his extraordinary daughter are gone now, as is Rajiv Gandhi, the heir to a remarkable political tradition of secularism and national service. Mother India no longer reigns, but her spirit still rules the country that gave her a privileged birth and a tragic death. Maybe the soul of India can one day find utterance in a different type of political leader. Maybe Nehru's political successors will one day redeem his pledge to ensure a decent life for India's masses. His daughter tried to keep his word, but the promise remained largely unfulfilled.

"We can turn our backs to the sun and cast long shadows on the lives of generations to come, or we can let light penetrate, illumine the dark

*Conversation with the author, New York City, July 3, 1991.

patches of the human mind, renew the earth and conserve human and physical resources," Indira Gandhi once said. "The choice is ours."

The choices that Indira Gandhi made during her political lifetime, and the consequences of those choices, will affect India's life for a very long time. It could even be argued that Indira Gandhi's policies restricted the choices of the political generation that has followed her, and perhaps even those of the generation beyond. This is not a legacy that she would have wanted, yet consummate realist that she was, Indira would hardly have been surprised by what India became after the assassination of this extraordinary woman.

Indira Gandhi had a personality replete with contradictions. Greatness and pettiness went hand in hand. Richness of heritage and opportunity were not fully translated into positive action despite numerous opportunities that came her way. Good intentions were often sabotaged by the exigencies of politics. Yet there is a grandeur even in failure. Perhaps the final epitaph for Indira Gandhi is one crafted by British historian Lord Acton. More than a hundred years ago, well before the Nehru-Gandhi dynasty came into being, he suggested that great leaders were not often good individuals. A contemporary political assessment of Indira Gandhi cannot but be harsh. But perhaps history will measure Indira Gandhi by another yardstick: Did India benefit from her stewardship, with all its strengths and flaws? And the answer may well be in the affirmative if Indira's vision of a united and secular India withstands the vicissitudes of today's destructive politics.

Epilogue: The Funeral of Rajiv Gandhi (1944–1991)

Afterward, after the rituals of cremation and mourning, after the lighting of the sandalwood pyre doused with clarified butter in the traditional Hindu style, the dead man's son would be proud that it was a funeral to which the whole world came on that very hot day in New Delhi on May 24, 1991.

The young man's name was Rahul Gandhi, and he had never really imagined that he would be called upon so suddenly and tragically to mourn his father. He had never imagined that he would be standing beside his father's mangled body in order to light the pyre that would consign Rajiv Gandhi to the ages.

Rahul had arrived in New Delhi the previous day from the United States, where he was a sophomore at Harvard University. Just three days earlier, late in the evening of Tuesday, May 21, Rajiv Gandhi had been killed by a suicide bomber during an election trip through the southern state of Tamil Nadu. A Sri Lankan Tamil woman who wore explosives in a belt around her waist triggered a blast as she greeted Rajiv at a campaign rally in the small town of Sriperumbudur, not far from Madras. The assassin was said to be a member of the Liberation Tigers of Tamil Eelam (LTTE), a guerrilla group fighting for a separate Tamil nation to be carved out of the northern and eastern regions of Sri Lanka. Rajiv Gandhi was forty-six years old.

To the world that watched Rajiv Gandhi's funeral on television, the nineteen-year-old Rahul's inner turmoil and pain were not always apparent. He seemed outwardly composed, making the right gestures during the rituals as if the whole thing had been carefully scripted by a director from India's flourishing celluloid industry. Indeed, his late father's friend, the actor Amitabh Bachchan, stood near Rahul Gandhi and occasionally guided him through the complex ceremony of cremation, which began with the lighting of the pyre at 5:25 P.M. Amitabh and Rajiv Gandhi went back a very long way, back to their childhoods in Allahabad where their respective families had lived in the late 1940s. Amitabh, who happened to be visiting the United States when his friend was killed, accompanied Rahul Gandhi on the long and sad plane trip to India. Also with Rahul on the journey home was Rajiv Gandhi's now estranged cousin and political opponent, Arun Nehru. It was Arun Nehru, perhaps more than anybody else, who had ensured that Rajiv became India's prime minister in 1984.

As he circumambulated the funeral pyre of his father, Rahul Gandhi thought about the time less than seven years earlier when he had stood on a similar platform as the body of his grandmother, Prime Minister Indira Gandhi, was cremated. His father, Rajiv, was beside him at the time. Indira, too, had been murdered. Rahul comforted his pretty mother, Sonia, and his older sister, the tall and statuesque Priyanka. He nodded at friends and acquaintances, and he was properly respectful toward the legions of priests and elders who presided over the funeral. There were moments, as he watched his father's body crumble into ashes, when tears welled up in his eyes. But always, the handsome bespectacled face regained control.

The funeral of Rajiv Gandhi was held in traditional Hindu style at Shakti Sthal, near Shantivana, where Indira Gandhi had been cremated. The site was within hailing distance of the Jamuna, the ancient but polluted river that flows sluggishly through Delhi.

Earlier, Rajiv's remains had been kept on view at Teen Murti Bhavan. The bomb blast had torn off his face and much of his torso, so the corpse had been wrapped completely in a shroud. A large photograph of Rajiv dominated the room in which the body was kept. Thousands of mourners trekked through Teen Murti Bhavan to pay their last respects to the young scion of the remarkable Nehru-Gandhi dynasty. Rajiv had been expected by many Indians to lead his Congress Party back to power in the May 1991 election, and there were those among the mourners who had been certain he would become prime minister again.

Janki Ganju was among these mourners. Ganju, a plump and florid man who had long served the Nehrus and Gandhis as their lobbyist in

Washington, had dropped in to meet with Rajiv's staff at Number 10 Janpath—where the Gandhis lived in a government-owned stucco bungalow—on the evening of May 21. At about eleven o'clock, the news came by telephone from Madras that Rajiv had been killed. The local police in Sriperumbudur had fled when the bomb went off in Rajiv's face, and it took a courageous woman named Jayanthi Natarajan, member of the Rajya Sabha, to organize the search for Rajiv's body and then arrange to transport it to the Madras General Hospital. *

"The blood drained from my face," Ganju recalled. "I thought that it was some nightmare, that I would wake up and find that everything was all right. But then it occurred to me that I was already awake, that the sad reality of Rajiv's death was upon all of us. I broke down and wept—wept for Rajiv, wept for his family. I wept for what might have been. I wept for the sheer madness of it all! What had we become in India, what sort of people had we become? I wept, and could not stop. Such a decent young man, and now he was gone."

Janki Ganju visited Teen Murti Bhavan several times over the next several days. Besides ordinary Indians and political luminaries, dozens of foreign dignitaries came to lay wreaths, and offer condolences to the widowed Sonia Gandhi and her two children. Some Congress Party functionaries had already started a campaign to install Sonia as head of the party. Quite shamelessly—and without consulting her—they announced that she would have no choice but to accept such a draft. Sonia, these Congress officials proclaimed, would be able to attract sympathy votes in the election. Wisely, Sonia declined the offer.† She had no time for politics, for she was kept busy receiving mourners.

A conspicuous mourner at Teen Murti Bhavan was Yasser Arafat, chairman of the Palestine Liberation Organization (PLO), whom Rajiv Gandhi—and Indira Gandhi—had long supported. Rajiv, like Indira, had long championed the Palestinian cause, and the PLO enjoyed a prestigious address, presence, and diplomatic status in New Delhi.

"My brother is dead," Arafat said, in Arabic, and then in English.

---

* At least fifteen people were killed along with Rajiv Gandhi in the bomb blast, including the suspected assassin. Indian authorities later said that the LTTE had planned the assassination in late 1990.
† The elections were to be held on May 20, 23, and 26, 1991. The first day of polling was held on schedule. But after Rajiv Gandhi's assassination, the election commissioner postponed the rest of the polls until June 12 and 15. In the event, the Congress Party won 225 seats in Parliament—not a majority, but enough seats to enable it to form a government. The new prime minister was P. V. Narasimha Rao, who had served as a member of cabinets under Indira and Rajiv Gandhi.

"My brother Rajiv Gandhi is gone." Seven years earlier, he had also been in New Delhi, for the funeral of Indira Gandhi.

At the funeral ceremony, Arafat sat in the front row of a section reserved for diplomats and world leaders. In the row behind him was Vice President Dan Quayle of the United States, with his wife, Marilyn, next to him. The Quayles had been on a state visit to Indonesia when Rajiv Gandhi died, and President George Bush asked them to represent him at the funeral. Once or twice Arafat turned around and smiled at the young American couple, and they smiled back.

Another mourner's presence was widely noted. He was Prime Minister Nawaz Sharif of Pakistan. Near him sat his bitterest political foe and predecessor, Benazir Bhutto, whom he had recently defeated in an election. They barely nodded to each other. Near them was Prince Charles, who represented his mother, Queen Elizabeth II. Even though the temperature was above 100 degrees Fahrenheit, Charles wore his full naval uniform—and he did not seem to sweat at all. Prime Minister Begum Khaleda Zia of Bangladesh was present, too, as was President Najibullah of Afghanistan. Foreign Minister Hans Dietrich Genscher of Germany sat stoically in the enclosure. The United Nations was represented by Virendra Dayal, chef de cabinet to Secretary General Javier Perez de Cuellar. They all watched intently as Ganpat Rai Acharya, a Hindu priest from Benaras, conducted the rituals in Sanskrit. The old priest was not unfamiliar with tragedies in the Gandhi family. He had also presided over the funerals of Sanjay Gandhi in 1980 and of Indira Gandhi in 1984.

"Rajiv Gandhi aamar rahe!" crowds kept chanting in the distance. "Long live Rajiv Gandhi!"

The body of Rajiv Gandhi, swathed in flowers, was brought to the funeral platform from the gun carriage of the funeral procession, which had started earlier from Teen Murti Bhavan. The chiefs of the army, navy, and air force had escorted the body to Shakti Sthal. Tens of thousands of people lined the streets of New Delhi as the procession headed toward the funeral site. The body was carried up to the makeshift brick platform by Rahul Gandhi and others, including Rajiv's closest friends, Amitabh Bachchan and editor Suman Dubey. They placed the covered body on a rectangular bed of sandalwood logs and flowers, in the Hindu tradition.

As Janki Ganju watched Rahul Gandhi light the funeral pyre, he wondered about the forces that shaped life and death. Who wrote the master script that determined all our collective destinies? Who willed that Rajiv Gandhi should not live to be fifty, or a hundred? What ancient curse afflicted the Nehrus and Gandhis? What capricious god had authorized the seizing of the lives of Indira and her two sons, Sanjay and Rajiv, when their life's work was not quite fully done? And what would Sonia Gandhi do now, widowed at the age of forty-four? Who would be a surrogate father to Rahul and Priyanka?

The killing of Rajiv Gandhi had been particularly bloody. He had campaigned in several towns in Andhra Pradesh State, and then in Tamil Nadu, that day and was running late. A rally had been scheduled in Sriperumbudur, about twenty-five miles from Madras. Rajiv drove to the rally in an Ambassador car from Madras. He was accompanied by Barbara Crossette of *The New York Times* and Neena Gopal of the Dubai-based *Gulf News*. After he arrived at the rally, Rajiv first garlanded a statue of his mother. Firecrackers were set off by enthusiastic Congress workers in Rajiv's honor. He then walked toward a dais, where he was scheduled to speak. A young woman approached him and bent to touch Rajiv's feet out of deference. She was an assassin. *

Jayanthi Natarajan, the parliamentarian who campaigned with Rajiv Gandhi, later vividly recalled the tragedy: "I must have been about twenty-five feet away. I had my back to him because he told me to go to his car either to check on those two women journalists who were with him, or to bring them to the dais. I hesitated because I couldn't quite understand what exactly he wanted me to do. He said, 'Go,' and so I went." Natarajan was walking toward the Ambassador car when a loud explosion occurred. She thought at first that someone had set off firecrackers again. She stumbled.

"I picked myself up and turned around very slowly, and I couldn't comprehend what had happened," she said. "Where there had been twenty or twenty-five people milling around, now everybody was flat on the ground. . . . I kept walking toward where I thought Rajiv was. Everybody else just ran away. There were legs, hands, bodies, lying around."

Natarajan spotted one of Rajiv's security guards. She held his hand but he was too far gone. "It was then I noticed that on his knee was a head facedown—and I said, 'Oh my God, this looks like Rajiv,' because there was this bald patch and fringe of hair. I kept looking disbelievingly. There-were no clothes—they had been blown off completely. . . . And

---

* The woman has been variously identified as Thanu and Nalayani. These names are most certainly pseudonyms.

then I noticed the shoes—and then I knew for sure because for some strange reason I had looked at the shoes during his press conference at Madras Airport earlier that evening. I knew that this was Rajiv. I tried to turn him over because I couldn't see his face, but I couldn't get a grip. . . ."

With the help of Rajiv's friend Suman Dubey and some Congress workers, Natarajan was able to get the body to the Madras General Hospital in a police van. She saw that policemen were still fleeing the scene. * She sat with Rajiv's body for nearly two hours in a barren hospital room while Suman Dubey called New Delhi and made arrangements to transport the corpse back to the capital. "There was no face at all," Natarajan said. "There were no eyes, no skull, no bone, no nose, nothing. Just the back of the head with the hair. There was no rib cage. There were hollows in the body. It was a truly gruesome sight, it bore no relation to anything human. . . ."

Sonia Gandhi and her daughter, Priyanka, arrived in Madras at about 4:45 A.M. by special plane. Suman Dubey and others helped to load Rajiv's body on the plane for the return flight to New Delhi. At 6:00 A.M., the plane left Madras. It would be Rajiv Gandhi's last journey by air.

On June 20, barely a month after the assassination, Professor Ralph Buultjens visited Sonia Gandhi in New Delhi. She told him that the local authorities in Sriperumbudur and Madras had located the sneakers that Rajiv Gandhi was wearing on the evening he was killed. Sonia said that the shoes had been sent to her. This brought to Ralph Buultjens' mind the thought that they might well become the icons of a specious effort to prolong pseudodynastic pretensions.

The plangent atmosphere around Rajiv's former residence saddened Professor Buultjens as he drove away after his meeting with Rajiv's tearful widow. Reflecting on a lifetime of association with India and its leaders, it occurred to him that a historic period was now concluded. The Nehru-Gandhi family had given so much to the nation and helped shape its destiny in modern times. They were remarkable people who saw themselves as born to leadership and zestfully played the role they created.

It was tragic, Ralph Buultjens felt, that the last standard bearer was perhaps the least distinguished. He had known them all—Jawaharlal in

---

* Barbara Crossette and Neena Gopal later said that Rajiv's driver pushed them into the car and drove off. He apparently feared that they would be attacked. Both women have written moving accounts of the last interview that Rajiv Gandhi gave—to them.

his latter days, Indira in her prime, and Rajiv from his youth. Although the dynasty was latterly showing signs of diminishing quality, it was unique in so many ways—all democratically elected, all leaders of the oldest political organization in the Third World, and all rewarded with the highest prizes that public life had to offer. Yet tragedy stalked all of them, and their moments of genuine happiness seemed to have been limited. All great mountains have their fissures, but when these fissures became larger than the ranges themselves, it was time to restructure the landscape, Professor Buultjens thought.

A melancholy and haunting feeling gripped him as startling images of Jawaharlal and Indira and Rajiv moved through his mind. He knew that he would never see their like again, and yet Ralph Buultjens understood that it was in the karmic nature of things that this order had to change. That, after all, was what India was all about. Hereafter, the Nehrus and Gandhis would move from reality to memory—a transition that all those who knew them well would find difficult to accept. Those who invest so much in friendship often find it hard to live with ghosts.

At his father's funeral, Rahul Gandhi—clad in a flowing white kurta and white pajamas—brought his palms together in a namaskar, a last salute to Rajiv. In Hindu tradition, it is always the men of the family who participate in the final rites at funerals, but Sonia broke this tradition by standing next to her son during the rituals. Rahul Gandhi lit a pair of long sandalwood joss sticks. He then went around his father's body nine times, touching his head with the lighted end each time he passed by. Like the host of other rituals he was required to perform, this act, too, was rooted in thousands of years of Hindu culture and tradition. After completing the ninth round, he thrust the joss stick under the pyre to ignite it, and piled sandalwood logs upon the body. Three volleys of staccato fire from a military honor guard pierced the still air. Buglers sounded the Last Post. Smoke rose from the pyre, as immediate members of Rajiv Gandhi's family, and friends such as Amitabh Bachchan and Suman Dubey, threw fistfuls of samagri, powdered unguents, on the body.

The Hindu priests seated on the ground chanted "*Om shanti, shanti, shanti*"—"Peace be upon you." Their chants provided an eerie soundtrack to the ceremony. A little while later, the priests recited the ancient Vedic incantation that began with the word "Sangachadwam" to liberate the soul and set it on the path to the pitru-lok, toward the heavenly abode of one's ancestors.

Although the cremation rituals were technically completed with those chants, the ceremony continued for more than an hour afterward. This was to allow close colleagues and longtime associates of Rajiv, his friends, officials, and even some diplomats, to come up to the pyre to sprinkle unguents on Rajiv Gandhi's ashes. They walked around the burning pyre, many of them in tears. A couple of days later, Rajiv's ashes would be gathered in brass urns by Sonia, Priyanka, and Rahul. They would board a special train to Allahabad where they would immerse the ashes at the confluence of the Jamuna and the Ganges. The immersion would take place on the thirteenth day after Rajiv's death, as called for by Hindu tradition.

Janki Ganju was mesmerized by the flames that consumed Rajiv Gandhi's body.

"But those flames seemed somehow reluctant to destroy that body," Ganju later recalled. "It was as if the flames were reluctant to put a final seal on what was already a historical fact, the murder of Rajiv Gandhi—and possibly the end of a remarkable political dynasty that began with Motilal Nehru a hundred years ago."

Ganju left New Delhi for Washington a few days later, remembering how blue the sky was on that day of Rajiv Gandhi's funeral, how sad those flames of fire seemed, and how very absurd it was that a young man in his prime had been senselessly killed. He had attended the funerals of Jawaharlal Nehru, Indira Gandhi, and Rajiv Gandhi, and now he was tired and worn out. Ganju was tired of the violence, of the dreams destroyed, of the chaos and confusion and debris and venality of Indian politics.

Janki Ganju had had enough of India for now, enough of pain and tragedy and darkness. He would go home to Washington, where his treasured collection of photographs awaited him. These were pictures of Nehru and Indira and Sanjay and Rajiv—some autographed to him personally. They were happy pictures, pictures of days when India was younger and every soaring dream seemed within reach. His own dreams had been defined to a very large extent by how he had felt about his fellow Kashmiris, these Nehrus and Gandhis—and by how they had responded to his loyalty with attention and affection of their own.

As his plane pulled away from India, Janki Ganju thought about how his heroes were all gone now. He thought about how their dreams for India had gone with them. And then it occurred to him that his own special dreams were gone, too, and possibly the dreams and hopes and expectations of millions of Indians as well. Perhaps one day Sonia Gandhi, or maybe even Rahul or Priyanka, might well decide to plunge into Indian politics in order to continue the tradition of Motilal and

Jawaharlal, and Indira, and Sanjay, and Rajiv. Perhaps, in time, Sanjay and Maneka Gandhi's son, Feroze Varun, would emerge as a political leader. But Janki Ganju knew that even if the political dynasty was resuscitated, things would never again be the same for India, for himself, for the Nehrus and the Gandhis. What was gone was gone forever.

Bibliography

Abbas, K. A. *Indira Gandhi: Return of the Red Rose.* Bombay: Popular Prakashan, 1966.
————*That Woman.* Delhi: Indian Book Company, 1973.
Ahluwalia, B. K., and Shashi Ahluwalia. *Martyrdom of Indira Gandhi.* New Delhi: Manas Publications, 1984.
Akbar, M. J. *India: The Siege Within.* Harmondsworth, U. K.: Penguin Books, 1985.
————. *Nehru: The Making of India.* New York: Viking, 1989.
Alexander, Michael, and Sushila Anand. *Queen Victoria's Maharajah: Duleep Singh, 1838–1893.* London: Weidenfeld & Nicolson, 1980.
Ali, Tariq. *An Indian Dynasty: The Story of the Nehru-Gandhi Family.* New York: G. P. Putnam's Sons, 1985.
Allen, Charles, and Sharada Dwivedi. *Lives of the Indian Princes.* London: Century Publishing, 1984.
Altekar, A. S. *The Position of Women in Hindu Civilization: From Prehistoric Times to the Present Day.* Delhi: Motilal Banarsidass, 1983.
Ambedkar, B. R. *What Congress and Gandhi Have Done to the Untouchables.* Bombay: Thacker & Co. Ltd., 1945.
Asher, Robert E. *Developing Assistance in the Seventies: Alternatives for the United States.* Washington, D.C.: The Brookings Institution, 1970.
Ayres, Robert L. *Banking on the Poor: The World Bank and World Poverty.* Cambridge, Mass.: The MIT Press, 1983.
Azad, Maulana Abdul Kalam. *India Wins Freedom.* New York: Longmans, Green, 1960.
Baig, M. R. A. *Muslim Dilemma in India.* Delhi: Vikas Publishing House, 1974.
Bairoch, Paul. *The Economic Development of the Third World Since 1900.* Berkeley: University of California Press, 1975.
Barnds, William J. *India, Pakistan and the Great Powers.* New York: Praeger, 1972.
Basham, A. L., ed. *A Cultural History of India.* New Delhi: Oxford University Press, 1975.
————. *The Wonder That Was India.* New York: Grove Press, 1959.

571

Bauer, P. T. *Equality, the Third World, and Economic Delusion.* London: Weidenfeld & Nicolson, 1981.

Bence-Jones, Mark. *The Viceroys of India.* London: Constable and Company, 1982.

Bhagwati, Jagdish. *The Economics of Underdeveloped Countries.* New York: World University Library/McGraw-Hill Book Company, 1966.

Bhatia, Krishan. *The Ordeal of Nationhood.* New York: Atheneum, 1971.

———. *Indira.* New York: Praeger, 1974.

Birla, K. K. *Indira Gandhi: Reminiscences.* Delhi: Vikas Publishing House, 1987.

Blaise, Clark, and Bharati Mukherjee. *Days and Nights in Calcutta.* New York: Doubleday, 1977.

Bobb, Dilip, and Asoka Raina. *The Great Betrayal: The Assassination of Indira Gandhi.* Delhi: Vikas Publishing House, 1985.

Bondurant, Joan V. *Regionalism Versus Provincialism: A Study in Problems of Indian National Unity.* Berkeley: University of California Press, 1958.

Bose, Mihir. *The Aga Khans.* London: World's Work, 1984.

———. *A Maidan View: The Magic of Indian Cricket.* London: Allen and Unwin, 1986.

Bowles, Chester. *Ambassador's Report.* New York: Harper & Row, 1954.

———. *Promises to Keep.* New York: Harper & Row, 1972.

Brata, Sasthi. *India: Labyrinths in the Lotus Land.* New York: William Morrow, 1985.

Brecher, Michael. *Nehru: A Political Biography.* London: Oxford University Press, 1959.

Bright, J. S. *Indira Gandhi.* Delhi: New Light Publishers, 1984.

Bumiller, Elizabeth. *May You Be the Mother of a Hundred Sons.* New York: Random House, 1990.

Buruma, Ian. *God's Dust: A Modern Asian Journey.* London: Jonathan Cape, 1989.

Buultjens, Ralph. *Windows on India.* New York: Express Books, 1987.

Cameron, James. *Point of Departure: An Autobiography.* London: Arthur Barker, 1967.

———. *An Indian Summer.* London: Macmillan, 1973.

Campbell-Johnson, Alan. *Mission with Mountbatten.* London: Robert Hale, 1951.

Chaudhuri, Nirad C. *Autobiography of an Unknown Indian.* London: Macmillan, 1951.

———. *The Continent of Circe: Being an Essay on the Peoples of India.* New York: Oxford University Press, 1966.

———. *To Live or Not to Live.* Delhi: Indian Book Company, 1973.

Chopra, V. D., R. K. Mishra, and Nirmal Singh. *Agony of Punjab.* Delhi: Patriot Publishers, 1984.

Clark, William. *From Three Worlds: Memoirs.* London: Sidgwick and Jackson, 1986.

Collier, Richard. *The Great Indian Mutiny: A Dramatic Account of the Sepoy Rebellion.* New York: E. P. Dutton, 1964.

Collins, Larry, and Dominique Lapierre. *Freedom at Midnight.* New York: Simon and Schuster, 1975.

Coolidge, Olivia. *Gandhi.* Boston: Houghton Mifflin, 1971.

Coomaraswamy, Ananda K. *The Dance of Shiva.* New York: H. Wolff, 1957.

Coomaraswamy, Radhika. *Sri Lanka: The Crisis of the Anglo-American Constitutional Traditions in a Developing Society.* Delhi: Vikas Publishing House, 1984.

Correa, Charles. *The New Landscape.* Bombay: The Book Society of India, 1986.

Critchfield, Richard. *Villages.* New York: Doubleday/Anchor, 1983.

Crocker, Walter. *Nehru: A Contemporary's Estimate.* New York: Oxford University Press, 1966.

Dalai Lama. *Freedom in Exile.* New York: HarperCollins, 1990.

Das, Durga. *India: From Curzon to Nehru and After.* London: Collins Publishers, 1969.

572

Bibliography

Das Gupta, Chidananda. *The Cinema of Satyajit Ray.* New Delhi: Vikas Publishing House, 1980.

Davies, Philip. *Splendors of the Raj.* Harmondsworth, U. K.: Penguin Books, 1987.

Desai, Morarji. *The Story of My Life.* Delhi: Macmillan, 1974.

Desai, Padma. *The Bokaro Steel Plant: A Study of Soviet Economic Assistance.* Amsterdam: North-Holland Publishing Company, 1972.

Devi, Gayatri, and Santha Rama Rau. *A Princess Remembers: The Memoirs of the Maharani of Jaipur.* London: Century Publishing, 1984.

Drieberg, Trevor. *Indira Gandhi: A Profile in Courage.* Delhi: Vikas, 1972.

Eck, Diana L. *Benares, City of Light.* New York: Alfred A. Knopf, 1982.

Edwardes, Michael. *The Myth of the Mahatma.* London: Constable Books, 1986.

Elegant, Robert. *Pacific Destiny.* New York: Crown, 1990.

Erikson, Erik H. *Gandhi's Truth: On the Origins of Militant Nonviolence.* New York: W. W. Norton & Company, 1969.

Etienne, Gilbert. *India's Changing Rural Scene 1963–1979.* Delhi: Oxford University Press, 1982.

Fischer, Louis. *The Life of Mahatma Gandhi.* New York: Harper & Row, 1950.

Fishlock, Trevor. *India File.* London: John Murray, 1983.

Forster, E. M. *A Passage to India.* New York: Harcourt Brace Jovanovich, 1965.

Galbraith, John Kenneth. *Ambassador's Journal: A Personal Account of the Kennedy Years.* Boston: Houghton Mifflin, 1969.

———. *John Kenneth Galbraith Introduces India.* London: Andre Deutsch, 1974.

Gandhi, Indira. *My Truth.* Delhi: Vikas, 1981.

———. *On People & Problems.* London: Hodder and Stoughton, 1983.

———. *Letters to a Friend, 1950–1984.* Selected, with commentary, from correspondence with Dorothy Norman. London: Weidenfeld & Nicolson, 1986.

Gandhi, Mohandas K. *The Story of My Experiments with Truth: An Autobiography.* Boston: Beacon Press, 1970.

Gardner, Brian. *The East India Company.* London: Rupert Hart-Davis, 1971.

Garland, Nicholas. *An Indian Journal.* Chicago: Academy Publishers, 1986.

Gascoigne, Bamber. *The Great Moghuls.* New York: Harper & Row, 1971.

Glyn, Anthony. *The British: Portrait of a People.* New York: G. P. Putnam's Sons, 1970.

Greer, Germaine. *Sex and Destiny: The Politics of Human Fertility.* New York: Harper & Row, 1984.

Gross, John. *Rudyard Kipling: The Man, His Work and His World.* London: Weidenfeld & Nicolson, 1972.

Gupte, Pranay. *The Crowded Earth: People and the Politics of Population.* New York: W. W. Norton, 1984.

———. *Vengeance: India After the Assassination of Indira Gandhi.* New York: W. W. Norton, 1985.

———. *India: The Challenge of Change.* London: Mandarin-Methuen, 1989.

———. *The Silent Crisis: Despair, Development and Hope in a World Without Borders.* New Delhi: Vikas Publishing House, 1990.

Guthrie, Anne. *Madame Ambassador: The Life and Times of Vijaya Lakshmi Pandit.* New York: Harcourt, Brace & World Inc., 1961.

Hancock, Graham. *Lords of Poverty.* London: Macmillan, 1989.

Hangen, Welles. *After Nehru, Who?* London: Rupert Hart Davis, 1963.

Hardgrave, Robert L., Jr., and Stanley A. Kochanek. *India: Government and Politics in a Developing Nation.* San Diego: Harcourt Brace, 1986.

Harrison, Paul. *Inside the Third World*. London: Penguin, 1979.

———. *The Third World Tomorrow*. London: Penguin, 1980.

Harrison, Selig S. *India, the Most Dangerous Decades*. Princeton: Princeton University Press, 1960.

Hazarika, Sanjoy. *Bhopal: The Lessons of a Tragedy*. Delhi: Penguin Books, 1987.

Hibbert, Christopher. *The Great Mutiny: India 1857*. New York: Viking Press, 1978.

Hiro, Dilip. *Inside India Today*. London: Routledge and Kegan Paul, 1978.

Hobbs, Lisa. *India, India*. New York: McGraw-Hill, 1967.

Hobson, Sarah. *Family Web: A Story of India*. Chicago: Academy Publishers, 1982.

Hutheesing, K. N. *We Nehrus*. New York: Macmillan, 1965.

———. *Dear to Behold: An Intimate Portrait of Indira Gandhi*. New York: Macmillan, 1969.

Iyer, Pico. *Video Night in Kathmandu and Other Reports from the Not-So-Far-East*. New York: Alfred A. Knopf, 1988.

Jackson, Richard L. *The Non-Aligned, the U.N. and the Superpowers*. New York: Praeger, 1983.

Jain, Devaki, ed. *Indian Women*. New Delhi: Publications Division, Ministry of Information and Broadcasting, 1975.

Jaipal, Rikhi. *Nonalignment: Origins, Growth and Potential for World Peace*. Delhi: Allied Publishers, 1983.

Jaisingh, Hari. *India After Indira*. Delhi: Allied Publishers, 1989.

Jalal, Ayesha. *The Sole Spokesman: Jinnah, the Muslim League and the Demand for Pakistan*. Cambridge: Cambridge University Press, 1985.

Jha, Prem Shankar. *India: A Political Economy of Stagnation*. Bombay: Oxford University Press, 1980.

Jiwa, Salim. *The Death of Air India Flight 182*. London: Star Books, 1986.

Johnson, B. L. C. *Development in South Asia*. New York: Penguin Books, 1983.

Johnson, Paul. *Modern Times: The World from the Twenties to the Eighties*. New York: Harper & Row, 1983.

Joshi, Chand. *Bhindranwale: Myth and Reality*. Delhi: Vikas Publishing, 1984.

Jung, Anees. *Unveiling India: A Woman's Journey*. Delhi: Penguin Books, 1987.

Kalhan, Promilla. *Kamala Nehru: An Intimate Biography*. Delhi: NIB Publishers, 1990.

Kapur, Rajiv A. *Sikh Separatism: The Politics of Faith*. London: Allen & Unwin, 1986.

Karanjia, R. K. *The Mind of Mr. Nehru*. London: Allen & Unwin, 1960.

———. *The Philosophy of Mr. Nehru*. London: Allen & Unwin, 1966.

Kaul, B. M. *The Untold Story*. Bombay: Jaico Press, 1969.

Kaye, M. M. *The Far Pavilions*. New York: St. Martin's Press, 1978.

Keay, John. *Into India*. London: John Murray, 1973.

Kennedy, Paul. *The Rise and Fall of the Great Powers*. New York: Random House, 1988.

Khan, Mohammed Ayub. *Friends, Not Masters: A Political Autobiography*. London: Oxford University Press, 1967.

Khosla, G. D. *Indira Gandhi*. Delhi: Thomson Press, 1974.

Kishwar, Madhu. *Gandhi and Women*. New Delhi: Manushi Prakashan, 1986.

Kothari, Rajni. *Politics in India*. Boston: Little, Brown & Company, 1970.

Lapierre, Dominique. *City of Joy*. New York: Doubleday, 1985.

Lelyveld, Joseph. *Calcutta*. Hong Kong: Perennial Press, 1975.

Lewis, John P. *Quiet Crisis in India: Economic Development and American Policy*. Washington: The Brookings Institution, 1962.

Liddle, Joanna, and Rama Joshi. *Daughters of Independence: Gender, Caste and Class in India*. London: Zed Books Limited, 1986.

Lloyd, Sarah. *An Indian Attachment*. New York: William Morrow, 1984.

Malgonkar, Manohar. *A Bend in the Ganges*. London: Hamish Hamilton, 1964.

————. *The Devil's Wind*. London: Hamish Hamilton, 1972.

————. *The Men Who Killed Gandhi*. Delhi: Macmillan, 1978.

————. *The Garland Keepers*. Delhi: Vision Books, 1986.

Malhotra, Inder. *Indira Gandhi*. London: Hodder & Stoughton, 1989.

Masani, Minoo. *Is J. P. the Answer?* Delhi: Macmillan, 1975.

Masani, Shakuntala. *The Story of Indira*. Delhi: Vikas Publishing House, 1974.

Masani, Zareer. *Indira Gandhi: A Biography*. London: Hamish Hamilton, 1975.

————. *Indian Tales of the Raj*. London: BBC Books, 1987.

Mason, Philip. *The Men Who Ruled India*. London: Jonathan Cape Ltd., 1985.

Maxwell, Neville. *India's China War*. New York: Pantheon Books, 1970.

Mehta, Gita. *Karma Cola: Marketing the Mystic East*. New York: Simon and Schuster, 1979.

————. *Raj*. New York: Simon and Schuster, 1989.

Mehta, Ved. *Portrait of India*. Delhi: Vikas Publications, 1971.

————. *Walking the Indian Streets*. Delhi: Vikas Publications, 1972.

————. *The New India*. New York: Penguin Books, 1978.

————. *Mamaji*. New York: Oxford University Press, 1979.

————. *The Ledge Between the Streams*. New York: W. W. Norton, 1984.

Menon, K. P. S. *The Flying Troika: The Political Diary of India's Ambassador to Russia, 1952–61*. New York: Oxford University Press, 1963.

Menon, V. P. *The Story of the Integration of the Indian States*. Calcutta: Orient Longmans, 1956.

————. *The Transfer of Power in India*. Princeton: Princeton University Press, 1957.

Mishra, P. K. *South Asia in International Politics*. Delhi: UDH Publishers, 1984.

Mohan, Anand. *Indira Gandhi: A Biography*. New York: Hawthorn Books, 1967.

Moorhouse, Geoffrey. *Calcutta*. New York: Harcourt Brace, 1971.

————. *India Britannica*. London: Harvill Press, 1983.

————. *To the Frontier*. London: Hodder and Stoughton, 1984.

Moraes, Dom. *A Matter of People*. New York: Praeger, 1974.

————. *Voices for Life*. New York, Praeger, 1975.

————. *The Great Cities: Bombay*. Amsterdam: Time-Life Books, 1979.

————. *Mrs. Gandhi*. Delhi: Vikas Publishing House, 1980.

Moraes, Frank. *Indira Gandhi*. Delhi: Directorate of Advertising and Visual Publicity, 1966.

Morris, James (Jan). *Pax Britannica*. London: Faber & Faber, 1968.

————. *Heaven's Command*. New York: Harcourt Brace, 1973.

————. *Farewell the Trumpets*. New York: Harcourt Brace, 1978.

————. *Stones of Empire: The Buildings of the Raj*. New York: Oxford University Press, 1983.

Mukerjee, Hiren. *The Gentle Colossus: A Study of Jawaharlal Nehru*. Delhi: Oxford University Press, 1986.

Myrdal, Gunnar. *Asian Drama: An Inquiry into the Poverty of Nations*. New York: Twentieth Century Fund, 1968.

————. *The Challenge of World Poverty*. New York: Pantheon Books, 1970.

Naipaul, Shiva. *Beyond the Dragon's Mouth.* London: Hamish Hamilton, 1984.

———. *An Unfinished Journey.* London: Hamish Hamilton, 1986.

Naipaul, V. S. *An Area of Darkness.* London: Andre Deutsch, 1964.

———. *The Overcrowded Barracoon.* London: Andre Deutsch, 1972.

———. *India: A Wounded Civilization.* New York: Alfred A. Knopf, 1977.

———. *Finding the Centre.* London: Andre Deutsch, 1984.

———. *India: A Million Mutinies Now.* London: William Heinemann, 1990.

Nanda, B. R. *The Nehrus: Motilal and Jawaharlal.* London: George Allen & Unwin, 1962.

———. *Mahatma Gandhi: A Biography.* New York: Baron, 1965.

Narayan, J. P. *Prison Diary.* Bombay: Popular Prakashan, 1977.

Narayan, R. K. *My Days.* Delhi: Orient Paperbacks, 1986.

Nayar, Kuldip. *India: The Critical Years.* Delhi: Vikas Publications, 1971.

———. *The Judgment: The Inside Story of the Emergency in India.* Delhi: Vikas Publishing House, 1977.

———, and Singh, Khushwant. *Tragedy of Punjab: Operation Bluestar and After.* Delhi: Vision Books, 1984.

Nehru, Jawaharlal. *Autobiography.* London: Bodley Head, 1936.

———. *The Discovery of India.* New York: John Day, 1946.

———. *Glimpses of World History.* New York: John Day, 1960.

———. *India's Freedom.* London: Unwin Books, 1965.

Newby, Eric. *Slowly Down the Ganges.* London: Picador Books, 1983.

Norman, Dorothy. *Letters to an American Friend.* New York: Harcourt Brace, 1985.

Nossiter, Bernard. *Soft State.* New York: Harper & Row, 1971.

———. *The Global Struggle for More: Third World Conflicts with Rich Nations.* New York: Harper & Row, 1987.

Pandit, Vijaya Lakshmi. *Prison Days.* Calcutta: Signet Press, 1945.

———. *The Scope of Happiness: A Personal Memoir.* New York: Crown, 1979.

Parasher, S. C., ed. *United Nations and India.* Delhi: Indian Council of World Affairs, 1985.

Paul, Swraj. *Indira Gandhi.* London: Heron Press, 1984.

Piramal, Gita, and Margaret Herdeck. *India's Industrialists.* Washington, D.C.: Three Continents Press, 1986.

Puri, Rajinder. *India: The Wasted Years.* New Delhi: Chetana Publications, 1975.

Raghavan, G. N. S. *Introducing India.* Delhi: Indian Council for Cultural Relations, 1983.

Rajagopalachari, Chakravarti. *The Mahabharata.* Bombay: Bharatiya Vidya Bhavan, 1951.

———. *The Ramayana.* Bombay: Bharatiya Vidya Bhavan, 1951.

Reeves, Richard. *Passage to Peshawar.* New York: Simon and Schuster, 1984.

Rosenblum, Mort. *Coups and Earthquakes.* New York: Harper & Row, 1979.

Rushdie, Salman. *Midnight's Children.* New York: Alfred A. Knopf, 1980.

———. *The Satanic Verses.* New York: Viking, 1988.

Sahgal, Nayantara. *Prison and Chocolate Cake.* New York: Alfred A. Knopf, 1954.

———. *Indira Gandhi: Her Road to Power.* New York: Frederick Ungar Publishing Company, 1982.

Sarkar, Jadunath. *India Through the Ages.* Calcutta: Sangam Books, 1979.

Savarkar, Vinayak Damodar. *The Indian War of Independence: 1857.* Delhi: Rajdhani Granthagar, 1986.

Schlesinger, Arthur M., Jr. *A Thousand Days: John F. Kennedy in the White House.* New York: Greenwich House, 1983.

Scott, Paul. *The Raj Quartet.* New York: William Morrow, 1976.

Sen Gupta, Bhabani. *The Fulcrum of Asia: Relations Among China, India, Pakistan and the U.S.S.R.* New York: Pegasus, 1970.

Seton, Marie. *Portrait of a Director: Satyajit Ray.* London: Denis Dobson, 1971.

Shaplen, Robert. *A Turning Wheel: Thirty Years of the Asian Revolution.* London: Andre Deutsch, 1979.

Sharada Prasad, H. Y. *Indira Gandhi.* New Delhi: Ladybird Books, 1985.

Sheehan, Vincent. *Lead, Kindly Light.* London: Cassell, 1950.

————. *Mahatma Gandhi: A Great Life in Brief.* New York: Alfred A. Knopf, 1970.

Sheth, N. R. *The Social Framework of an Indian Factory.* Manchester: Manchester University Press, 1968.

Shourie, Arun. *Mrs. Gandhi's Second Reign.* Delhi: Vikas Publishing House, 1983.

Singh, Karan. *Contemporary Essays.* Bombay: Bharatiya Vidya Bhavan, 1971.

Singh, Khushwant. *Train to Pakistan.* London: Chatto & Windus, 1956.

————. *A History of the Sikhs.* Princeton: Princeton University Press, 1965.

————. *The Sikhs Today.* Bombay: Orient Longmans, 1967.

————. *India: A Mirror for Its Monsters and Monstrosities.* Bombay: IBH Publishing Company, 1969.

————. *We Indians.* Delhi: Orient Paperbacks, 1982.

————. *Delhi: A Portrait* (with photographs by Raghu Rai). New York: Oxford University Press, 1983.

————. *The Sikhs* (with photographs by Raghu Rai). Delhi: Rupa and Company, 1984.

Singh, Patwant. *The Struggle for Power in Asia.* London: Hutchinson, 1971.

————, and Harji Malik. *Punjab: The Fatal Miscalculation.* Delhi: Published by Patwant Singh, 1985.

Singh, S. Nihal. *My India.* Delhi: Vikas Publishing House, 1982.

Smith, Hedrick. *The Power Game: How Washington Really Works.* New York: Random House, 1988.

Spear, Percival. *A History of India.* London: Penguin Books, 1970.

Szulc, Tad. *Then and Now.* New York: William Morrow, 1990.

Thapar, Raj. *All These Years.* New Delhi: Seminar Publications, 1991.

Thapar, Romila. *A History of India.* London: Penguin Books, 1966.

Tharoor, Shashi. *The Great Indian Novel.* New York: Arcade Books, 1991.

Theroux, Paul. *The Great Railway Bazaar: By Train Through Asia.* Boston: Houghton Mifflin, 1975.

Trevelyan, Raleigh. *The Golden Oriole: Childhood, Family, and Friends in India.* London: Secker & Warburg, 1987.

Tully, Mark, and Satish Jacob. *Amritsar: Mrs. Gandhi's Last Battle.* London: Jonathan Cape, 1985.

Vadgama, Kusoom. *India in Britain.* London: Robert Royce, 1984.

Vasudev, Uma. *Two Faces of Indira Gandhi.* Delhi: Vikas, 1977.

Walvin, James. *Passage to Britain: Immigration in British History and Politics.* London: Penguin, 1984.

Wanniski, Jude. *The Way the World Works.* New York: Touchstone Books, 1983.

Watson, Francis. *A Concise History of India.* London: Thames and Hudson, 1979.

Wiles, John. *Delhi Is Far Away: A Journey Through India.* London: Paul Elek, 1974.

577

Bibliography

Willcoxen, Harriet. *First Lady of India: The Story of Indira Gandhi*. New York: Doubleday, 1969.

Wirsing, Giselher. *The Indian Experiment*. Delhi: Orient Longman, 1972.

Wolpert, Stanley. *Tilak and Gokhale: Revolution and Reform in the Making of Modern India*. Berkeley and Los Angeles: University of California Press, 1961.

————. *A New History of India*. New York: Oxford University Press, 1977.

————. *Jinnah of Pakistan*. New York: Oxford University Press, 1984.

————. *India*. Berkeley and Los Angeles: University of California Press, 1991.

World Commission on Environment and Development. *Our Common Future*. London: Oxford University Press, 1987.

Ziegler, Philip. *Mountbatten: A Biography*. New York: Alfred A. Knopf, 1985.

Index